*f*P

ALSO BY JOHN D'EMILIO

The World Turned: Essays on Gay History, Politics, and Culture

Creating Change: Sexuality, Public Policy, and Civil Rights
(WITH WILLIAM TURNER AND URVASHI VAID)

Intimate Matters: A History of Sexuality in America
(WITH ESTELLE FREEDMAN)

*Sexual Politics, Sexual Communities: The Making of a Homosexual
Minority in the United States, 1940–1970*

Making Trouble: Essays on Gay History, Politics, and the University

LOST PROPHET

THE LIFE AND TIMES OF BAYARD RUSTIN

JOHN D'EMILIO

FREE PRESS

NEW YORK LONDON TORONTO SYDNEY SINGAPORE

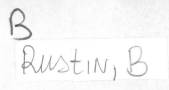

*f*P

FREE PRESS
A Division of Simon & Schuster, Inc.
1230 Avenue of the Americas
New York, NY 10020

For information about special discounts for bulk purchases,
please contact Simon & Schuster Special Sales: 1-800-456-6798
or business@simonandschuster.com

Manufactured in the United States of America

10 9 8 7 6 5 4 3 2 1

Library of Congress Cataloging-in-Publication Data

D'Emilio, John.
    Lost prophet: the life and times of Bayard Rustin / John D'Emilio.
       p. cm.
    Includes bibliographical references and index.
    1. Rustin, Bayard, 1912–1987. 2. African Americans—Biography. 3. Civil
rights workers—United States—Biography. 4. African American pacifists—
Biography. 5. African Americans—Civil rights—History—20th century. 6. Civil
rights movements—United States—History—20th century. 7. Nonviolence—
United States—History—20th century. I. Title.

E185.97.R93D46 2003
323'.092—dc21
[B]
                                                              2003052771

ISBN 0-684-82780-8

CONTENTS

Blessed are those who hunger and thirst for righteousness,
for they shall be satisfied. . . .

Blessed are the peacemakers,
for they shall be called the children of God.

Blessed are those who are persecuted for righteousness' sake,
for theirs is the kingdom of heaven.

MATTHEW 5:6, 9, 10

INTRODUCTION

"Who is Bayard Rustin?"

I have been asked this question enough times to know that "Bayard Rustin" is not a household name in America.

Rustin was not a president, not a four-star general, not a celebrity. He did not die young under tragic circumstances, as did Martin Luther King, Jr., and Malcolm X, two more renowned African Americans whom we do remember. Instead, depending on the circumstances, Rustin was dismissed during his lifetime as a Communist, a draft dodger, or a sexual pervert—and sometimes all three. None are characteristics designed to win a revered place in our nation's history.

Less than two decades after Rustin's death, his enormous contributions to American life—in the struggle for racial equality, a peaceful international order, and a democratic economic system—have been covered over, his name mostly forgotten, his contribution to a world worth living in largely obscured. Except for the briefest walk-on part as the man-behind-the-scenes of the historic 1963 March on Washington, Rustin hardly appears at all in the voluminous literature produced about the 1960s. Instead, he has become a man without a home in history.

This neglect of Rustin is tragic because he is, I believe, a vitally important historical character. He deserves a place in our national memory as one of the key figures of his time. More than anyone else, Rustin brought the message and methods of Gandhi to the United States. He insinuated nonviolence into the heart of the black freedom struggle. He presided over the transformation of direct action tactics from the cherished possession of a few initiates to its embrace by millions of Americans. He resurrected mass peaceful protest from the graveyard in which cold war anticommunism had buried it and made it once again a vibrant expression of citizen rights in a free society.

Rustin was a visionary. He believed that violence could never bring justice and that war could never bring peace. He stood by these convictions during the "good war" against Hitler, during the first decades of the cold war, and during the years of a spiraling nuclear arms race. Rustin was an internationalist long before *globalization* became a catchword in American life. He viewed nationalism as a destructive force in human affairs and conducted himself as if world citizenship already existed. He organized and led protests not only in the United States but across several continents as well.

Rustin was smart. His associates recognized him as a master strategist of social change. He dedicated himself to figuring out how human beings, individually and collectively, could do more than simply go about the business of living. He studied the workings of insurgent movements around the globe so that he might better understand how permanently to alter powerful institutions and longstanding national policies.

Rustin was inspirational to the countless thousands who knew him. He wished more than anything else to remake the world around him. He wanted to shift the balance between white supremacy and racial justice, between violence and cooperation in the conduct of nations, between the wealth and power of the few and the poverty and powerlessness of the many. He believed that the most antagonistic human relationships—between a white sheriff and a black sharecropper, between the European colonizer and the Africans he lorded over, between the filthy rich and the struggling poor—could be transformed. He believed that ordinary individuals could make a vast difference in the world, and he communicated this conviction widely.

Rustin was also wildly controversial in his lifetime. He had been a member of the Young Communist League in the 1930s. He refused the call to defend his country after the United States had been attacked at Pearl Harbor. Segregationists, of whom there were many, and anti-Communists, of whom there were even more, always had ammunition to fire in Rustin's direction. Rustin repeatedly found himself the target of the FBI, local police, conservative journalists, State Department officials, and anyone else beating the drums of patriotic fervor during the cold war decades.

Rustin had ways to counter these vulnerabilities. His Quaker beliefs were a legitimate explanation for his pacifism. He publicly broke with and repeatedly repudiated the Communist Party. His pacifist friends and his associates in the black freedom movement applauded his integrity and courage, and they stood by him when cold warriors and defenders of the racial status quo launched attacks on him.

Not so for his homosexuality. If Rustin has been lost in the shadows of history, it is at least in part because he was a gay man in an era when the stigma attached to this was unrelieved. There were no islands of safety, no oases of acceptance in the decades when Rustin was forging a career as an agitator for justice. In the mid-twentieth century, every state criminalized homosexual behavior. Gay men could be—and commonly were—arrested for touching hands in a bar, for asking another man to spend the night, and for doing in parked cars in secluded places what young heterosexuals did all the time. Rustin's sexual desires brought him trouble repeatedly. Police locked him up. Judges humiliated him in the courtroom. Newspapers exposed him. Worst of all, friends, mentors, and close allies repeatedly abandoned him because how he chose to love and whom he chose to desire put him beyond the pale of what America at that time defined as acceptable.

INITIALLY I CAME to Rustin's life because I wanted to write about the 1960s. At the time, and forever since, the sixties were recognized as a watershed decade in the United States. Look at a photograph of almost anything from 1958 and find a comparable one for 1972. The visual evidence of change will be striking. It was a time of revolutionary upheavals that left almost nothing in America untouched. Americans fought each other in the 1960s, and they have continued to fight about the meaning of the 1960s ever since.

One common plot line of the sixties traces a trajectory that moves from good to bad. The good sixties were composed of heroic student sit-ins and freedom rides, the crusading rhetoric of the New Frontier and the Great Society, the inspiration of an interracial March on Washington and a war against poverty. Trailing right behind were the bad sixties of war in the jungles of Southeast Asia, American cities in flames and occupied by troops, students shot dead on their own campuses by the National Guard and, when it all ended, the stench of Watergate. Why did sweet dreams of hope metastasize into nightmares?

Rustin first commanded my attention because, just as the good sixties were about to turn toward the bad, he authored a bold manifesto titled "From Protest to Politics." More than a generation after its writing, it still reads as a compelling piece of political analysis. Rustin addressed himself to the question of how the growing number of Americans who were protesting racial injustice might move from the margins of the political system to the centers of power. He argued that out of the civil rights movement there could emerge a coalition of conscience capable of becoming a new progressive majority in the United States. His strategy rested on a bedrock optimism that the American political system was flexible and responsive enough to embrace change of revolutionary dimensions. He believed that peaceful democratic means were adequate to the task of remaking relations of power. Rustin also had faith that individual human beings themselves were just as flexible and that, over time, they could be moved to recognize the worth of every one of their fellows and act accordingly.

Rustin's argument was not a mushy utopian exhortation in favor of universal fellowship and peace on earth. It was detailed, thoughtful, logical, and measured in its assessment of the political landscape. Reading it for the first time a quarter-century after it was published, I experienced a thrill of excitement, as if the moment when he wrote was still before me and the opportunities he sketched out still waited to be grasped. Yet the moment was not seized. Militant activists in the civil rights movement and burgeoning New Left scorned Rustin's analysis. They saw it as evidence that this Gandhian organizer of many years' standing, seasoned by decades of campaigns and two dozen arrests, had lost his radical edge. In what may be one of the cruelest ironies of this historical era, conservatives on the right rather than progressives on the left took up elements of Rustin's ideas and ran with them. Conservatives were the ones who used the electoral system to become the governing majority over the next generation.

I knew that Rustin was gay when I began to study his life. It was an important part of what attracted me to his story. I had already written about the history of homosexuality in America, and I knew the intensity of persecution directed not only at Communists and fellow travelers during the McCarthy era but at sexual nonconformists as well. I also knew that Rustin had been convicted for public lewdness in the 1950s and that in the final days before the March on Washington, segregationists exposed the incident. Yet I assumed that "the closet" was so sturdily constructed at this time and that habits of discretion in sexual matters operated so pervasively that Rustin's sexuality would serve at most as an interesting backdrop to the public career. I expected it to be tucked into the corner marked "private life" and imagined that it would only occasionally intervene in the telling of his story.

I now know differently. The boundary between public and private proved very porous in Rustin's life. As I dug through the evidence and interviewed those who knew him, it became abundantly clear that his sexuality—or, more accurately, the stigma that American society attached to his sexual desires—made him forever vulnerable. Again and again, Rustin found his aspirations blocked, his talents contained, and his influence marginalized. Yes, he also found ways to carve out a significant role in the movements he held dear. But he had to find ways to do this so that unpredictable eruptions of homophobia might not harm these causes. It is little wonder that so few Americans today know who he is.

And the disavowal of Rustin continues. As I write this introduction, parents of school-aged children in his hometown of West Chester, Pennsylvania, are rebelling against proposals to rename the local high school after its most accomplished alumnus.

THE BOOK THAT I have written is not what I had originally intended. It still has much to say about the 1960s and the stirring events of that decade. But any thoughts I entertained that Bayard Rustin could be a vehicle for my purposes long ago fell victim to the dramatic nature of his story. *Lost Prophet* is centrally about Rustin—the impact he had on events and the struggles he faced to sustain a role for himself in the most important movements of his times. To take Rustin seriously—

and, trust me, he insists that we do take him seriously—requires paying as much attention to the decades when he toiled in obscurity as to the 1960s, when he had his moment as a national figure.

A biographer could not ask for a more compelling subject than Rustin. His story is heroic and harrowing. It abounds with triumphs and trials. It combines the narrative contours of the saint and the sinner. Rustin displays courage under circumstances that are terrifying to contemplate. His life reminds us that the most important stories from the past are often those that have been forgotten and that from obscure origins can emerge individuals with the power to change the world.

CHAPTER ONE

"Any Road Will Take You There"
1912–1934

THE CHESTER COUNTY Historical Society occupies a prime location in downtown West Chester, Pennsylvania. Its smartly refurbished space testifies to the importance that community leaders attach to history. In its main research room lie stacks of meticulously kept clipping folders. They track the doings of generations of Darlingtons, Butlers, Taylors, and numerous other Quaker families who settled in that part of the state and gave the town its character. Merchants, public officials, poets, farmers, even some stray military officers are among the peace-loving Quakers. The genealogy of these families, minor characters in history to all but themselves, has been carefully maintained.

Not so for the Rustins. Until Bayard began to distinguish himself as an actor on the stage of world history, no one thought to preserve a record of the weddings and deaths, the births and anniversaries, the school graduations and other small triumphs of an industrious black family not far removed from slavery. Except for Bayard's own recollections, recounted through the many interviews he gave later in life, only bits of information survive to reconstruct his origins. Like the shards of a pot scattered across a field, they give hints of the whole even as the missing pieces lend mystery to the circumstances that shaped the man.

BAYARD WAS WELL into boyhood before he learned that his oldest sister, Florence, was actually his mother. While still a teenager, Florence Rustin had taken up with Archie Hopkins, a laborer in town. The

African American community in West Chester was small enough that Bayard came to know his biological father by sight and reputation. He remembered Hopkins as broad-shouldered, muscular, and tall, with deep brown skin and a penchant for trouble. According to Bayard, Hopkins "drank an inordinate amount, gambled an inordinate amount and played around with girls an inordinate amount."[1] No way would Julia and Janifer, Florence's sober, hard-working parents, press Archie to marry their eldest child. Bayard never developed a relationship with Hopkins, nor did he have much of one with Florence, who was gone from the Rustin home long before Bayard started school. No letters, and evidence for only one meeting between them, survive for all the years after he reached maturity. Bayard treated Florence's children by a later marriage not as siblings but as cousins—and distant ones at that.

In every way that mattered, Julia and Janifer Rustin, not Florence and Archie, were his Mamma and Pappa. Julia, a nurse by training, attended the birth on March 17, 1912, and a few days later made the decision with Janifer to raise the newborn as their youngest. Reflecting Julia's long-standing ties to the Quaker culture of the area, they named the boy after West Chester's most illustrious son, Bayard Taylor, a local poet and diplomat. They kept the information of his origins from Bayard until, teased by one of his elementary school classmates about his parentage, he came home one afternoon and asked Julia about it. Standing in the kitchen cooking the evening meal, she said, "Well now I think it's been too long. . . . Florence is your mother, but we're one big family and we are all mothers for everybody." The decision of Julia and Janifer to raise Bayard as their own gave him a secure and loving home. "Never sleep on misery," Janifer once told Bayard, explaining that he and Julia had never gone to bed with bitterness or anger standing between them. Very late in Janifer's life, when a friend of Bayard visited the Rustin home, Janifer whispered in her ear: "I'll be 80, and she is 71—but we're still courting!" Bayard termed their marriage "the perfect union."[2]

The Rustin household was one of the most respected in West Chester's small black community. Janifer had migrated there as a young man sometime in the 1880s. He had been born in 1864, the last year of the Civil War, in Laplata, Maryland, the seat of St. Mary's County in the Chesapeake region of the state. His parents, Janifer and Amelia, were slaves. Because Lincoln's Emancipation Proclamation applied only to the Confederate states, the infant Janifer was legally a slave until the Thirteenth Amendment became part of the Constitution the next year. Why Janifer chose to leave his kin behind remains a mystery, but the timing for a move across the Mason-Dixon line was propitious. By the 1880s, the hopefulness of the post-Emancipation era was fading for the freed men and women of the South, and a new racial caste system was taking shape in the former slave states. West Chester, Pennsylvania, by contrast, was Quaker country. The whole area remained dotted with houses that had once served as stops on the Underground Railroad shepherding slaves to freedom. And West Chester itself had a small community of African Americans, the descendants of free colored people whose presence in town antedated the Civil War.[3]

Among those residents when Janifer arrived was the young Julia Davis. Julia's mother, Elizabeth, had ancestors in Pennsylvania further back than anyone could remember. The Delaware Indians figured in her heritage too, accounting for the high cheekbones that ran in the family. Elizabeth was reared in the household of the Butlers, who produced one member of Congress and, later, a flamboyant army major dubbed the "Fighting Quaker." She spent most of her life working as a domestic in the homes of Mrs. Butler's relatives, who saw to it that Elizabeth's daughter, Julia, received an education in the local Friends School and training as a nurse. Julia was one of the first blacks in the county to have a high school education. Along with her ties to the leading Quaker families, it placed her among what might be considered a local black elite. Though Julia was a member of the African Methodist Episcopal church (AME), she absorbed Quakerism at home and in school, and its influence on her remained powerful.[4]

Janifer and Julia married in 1891, before Julia was out of her teens. The wedding was held at the home of Julia's parents, with the Reverend J. C. Brock, pastor of West Chester's most prestigious black congregation, officiating. Children came often and regularly to the couple. Over the next eighteen years, Julia gave birth to six girls and two boys: Florence, Bessie, Janifer, Jr., Anna, Rhetta, Vella, Ruth, and Earle. Janifer proved a resourceful husband, a proud but reserved man who displayed, in the words of one of Bayard's associates, "a very strong and lovely spirit." Bayard recalled Janifer as having "the most erect carriage of any person you've ever seen." His only vices were a bit of bourbon every night before bed and an occasional cigar. "None of us," Bayard reflected a generation later, after Janifer's death, "can remember a single unkindness in him." For more than three decades, he was employed as the steward of the Elks Lodge in West Chester. The job allowed him to draw on the patronage of affluent white families, one of which rented him a large ten-room home in the east end, where many of the African American families lived. Janifer's work kept the family's kitchen well stocked, as surplus food from lodge parties, including an array of delicacies, often came his way. The long hours of steady laboring made him just prosperous enough so that, with determination, he could maintain in school those of his children whose interests or ambitions tended in that direction. Bessie, for instance, went to the local normal college and trained as a teacher; Ruth became an accountant.[5]

While Janifer earned the family's keep, Julia cared for the family. Just past forty years old at the time Bayard was born, she had her hands more than full with housekeeping and child rearing. Though her oldest children were nearing the point of leaving home, the youngest, Earle, was still a toddler, and two others were not yet in school. Soon after Bayard's second birthday, tragedy confronted the family with the unexpected death of Janifer, Jr., in his sixteenth year. A year later, the grieving family expressed its loss through a poem of remembrance it sent to the local paper:

> *Days of sadness still come o'er us,*
> *Tears of sorrow silent flow,*
> *Memory keeps our loved one near us,*
> *Though he's gone a year ago.*
> *O for a touch of his little hand,*
> *And a sound of his voice that is still.*

In the face of this loss, Julia cherished the young Bayard even more. "I have taken care of Bayard since he was 10 days old," she later wrote in an effort to explain her deep attachment, "so you know how close he is to me."[6]

Without question, Julia was the dominant presence in Bayard's early life, exerting an influence that stayed with him forever. Slender as a young woman, with delicate features and clear brown eyes, she was, according to him, "an extremely dominant personality, but not at all domineering. She towered whenever she walked into a room." The messages he received from her, both by observation and through long hours of sitting with her in the kitchen and listening to her talk as she cooked, were many: to treat everyone with respect, to hear every side of a controversy, to put oneself at the service of others. Most of all, she impressed on him the need to present a calm demeanor to the outside world. "One just doesn't lose one's temper," Bayard heard often, and it became a lesson he later took to heart as he crafted a public role for himself. "She was a remarkable, remarkable woman," he told an interviewer near the end of his life.[7]

Despite heavy responsibilities at home, Julia made time for an active role in the community. Like many other educated women of her generation, she extended her nurturance beyond the immediate family and engaged in a form of "social housekeeping." Melding a Quaker ethic of service with African American traditions of communal solidarity, Julia devoted herself to community affairs. "A dealer in relieving misery" was how Bayard described her. She founded a day nursery for the children of black working mothers, served on the board of a society of visiting black nurses, was a stalwart member of the local Negro woman's club, and organized a summer Bible camp that met in a lot near the railroad tracks. Bayard was there every day, absorbing Old Testament lessons of slavery and freedom that Julia and the other volunteers drilled into their young charges. "My grandmother," he recalled years later, "was thoroughly convinced that when it came to matters of the liberation of black people, we had much more to learn from the Jewish experience than we had to learn out of Matthew, Mark, Luke and John." Those

Bible lessons, he said, "made me extremely militant in terms of achieving things on this earth."[8]

Bayard's childhood coincided with the beginnings of the Great Migration, a massive historic movement of African Americans from Jim Crow in the rural South to the cities of the North. The more economically fortunate migrants boarded trains headed for Chicago, Pittsburgh, Philadelphia, and New York; others had to walk all or part of the way. The Rustin home served as a way station for some of those passing through. Bayard remembered that often he and the other Rustin children "would be hustled out of our beds late at night to make room for a family which didn't have anywhere to go and was passing through town." Julia's perception of injustice did not make her bitter: "I decided long ago that I was not going to let people mistreat me, and in addition give me indigestion," she once told Bayard, but it did nourish a commitment to action. Shortly after the National Association for the Advancement of Colored People (NAACP) was founded in 1909 to protest lynching and other evils of the racial caste system, Julia became one of its first local members. Towering figures of the black freedom struggle such as W. E. B. Du Bois, James Weldon Johnson, and Mary McLeod Bethune stayed with the Rustins when they passed through town.[9]

But the Rustins did not have to look south to find injustice. Like most other Northern cities of the era, West Chester was riven by ethnic and racial divisions. Massive immigration from Southern and Eastern Europe confronted native-born Anglo Americans with customs, languages, religious beliefs, and modes of dress that both seemed alien and stimulated fears of national decline. Nick Bruno, a child of Italian immigrants and a contemporary of Bayard, recalled how "we stayed more or less to ourselves, just like the blacks stayed to theirselves, the Irish stayed to theirselves, the Polaks or whatever. Jewish people stayed to theirselves. We were all in the west end here. And the blacks were in the other section. The east section. Of course, the Quakers, they were all over." In Bruno's experience, assumptions about the criminality of Italians made dating the daughters of the old-line white families impossible. Bayard remembered that when he was a young boy, the Rustins were friendly with a neighboring Italian family, with the

mothers sharing food and the children roaming in and out of one another's home. Yet Bayard had to meet another friend on neutral ground
because of the prejudices of that boy's parents. He also recollected that
the most blatant expressions of hatred he witnessed growing up were
directed against Jews.[10]

Within this patchwork of ethnic tension, the experience of West
Chester's colored citizens remained apart. Despite a history of Quaker
abolitionist activity in and around West Chester, residents of African
heritage, unlike other ethnic groups, faced formal segregation and exclusion. Black children attended the segregated Gay Street Elementary
School in the east end of town; too few in number to sustain a separate
high school, they mixed with other adolescents in the town's only public high school. Institutionalized discrimination came at them in a host
of ways, Bayard recounted: "Sitting on the side of one theater, sitting
upstairs in another, not being able to get food at restaurants, not daring
to go into toilets in the center of town, the feeling you had to go home to
go to the toilet, where the white kids would go into the restaurants to go,
or the shops. . . . we knew we were not welcome." In Bayard's memory
of his childhood, "nobody was complaining about it, except my grandmother."[11]

Discrimination bred communal solidarity. Particularly at the Gay
Street school, Bayard and his peers benefited from a mostly black
teaching staff who, in the words of Mary Frances Thomas, a classmate
of Bayard in the 1920s, "knew what we were going to face, so they had
us very well prepared . . . we were well-fortified." Joseph Fugett, the
principal during Bayard's years at the school and a graduate of Cornell,
built a team of dedicated teachers devoted to their charges and imaginative in their pedagogy. Maria Brock, daughter of the pastor of the
Rustins' church, instructed her students in reading, elocution, and oratory. Under her influence, Bayard began to experiment with the clipped
haughty-sounding diction that set him apart from his peers and led
many acquaintances later in life to believe that he hailed from the Caribbean or had attended elite schools. Warren Burton, who taught seventh
and eighth grades, encouraged his students to think beyond the classroom. With his assistance, Bayard and some of his friends brought black

professionals and skilled artisans to speak at the school. Helena Robinson, who had a degree from Howard University, taught history. "A fantastic lady" in Mary Thomas's memory, she communicated a heritage of resistance and hope, emphasizing the abolitionist movement over slavery, the support of some whites over the depredations of others. "She taught the underground railway in a very creative way," Bayard told an interviewer. Robinson shepherded her classes through old Quaker houses, which still had "the hidden areas and the hidden rooms and the cellars dug out" that had sheltered escaped slaves three generations earlier.[12]

The community watched over its young in a variety of ways. One teacher regularly stopped by the home of a student whose father was alcoholic and whose mother was having "a rough time," and washed the children, dressed them, and brought them to school in the morning. Mary Thomas's mother was raising six children alone. She had much to worry about, Thomas recalled, "but she didn't have to worry about her children, because the neighbors, everybody, kept an eye on everybody else. If we did anything, we knew we dare not because they might give you a spanking and then tell your mother and you'd get another spanking. It was a very secure world for children." On Sundays, everyone got dressed up for church. "You lived in church then. . . . You went in the morning and you went at night. It never stopped. But we enjoyed it because it was a social outing for us," according to Thomas.[13]

The spacious Rustin home was something of a focal point in the life of the black community, at least among the young. Julia's activism made her well known and respected. Her warm spirit and Janifer's generosity beckoned other children into the home. By the time Bayard reached school age, the Rustin brood stretched through several grades, and the house on East Union Street had become a social center for all their friends. "It was a hubbub," according to Bayard. "People were coming and going" all the time. To the youngsters of the east end, Julia and Janifer were simply "Ma and Pa Rustin."[14]

FOR THE GAY STREET pupils who continued their education, high school meant venturing beyond the east end and stepping into an institution dominated by whites. For some, it was a shock. Many black adolescents held down jobs while going to school and were thus cut off from the extracurricular activities that dominated student life. During lunch hour and other open periods when pupils were free to wander from the three-story brick school building, the African American teenagers faced the exclusionary practices of downtown store owners. "We were just a clan, holding on to each other, and surviving this racist atmosphere," Mary Thomas explained.[15]

In Bayard's case, however, all the available evidence indicates that he flourished. He was West Chester's version of a Renaissance man, excelling in everything. And he did a lot. The yearbook for his graduating class shows him with a longer list of activities and honors than any of his peers. As a freshman, he captured West Chester High's prestigious oratory award, "the first colored youth to have won it in 40 years," Julia proudly wrote to the town paper. Two years later, he earned the top honor in a schoolwide essay contest. Bayard won letters in track and football; his poetry often appeared in the school magazine, *Garnet and White;* he played leading roles in dramatic productions, including that of the Roman conspirator Catiline; and he placed into a classical curriculum that emphasized languages, literature, and mathematics. His peers and teachers recognized his abilities, electing him to student government and naming him one of only a handful of commencement speakers.[16]

In interviews two generations later, the recollections of Bayard's schoolmates inevitably reflected the mixture of pride, affection, and awe that his career inspired. They describe him as warm and likeable, with an endearing sense of humor. Mary Thomas remembered him as "fun. Bayard was not a stiff shirt. Not by any means, not with us. Bayard was just part of the gang. We'd tease him and knock him around like we did everybody else, and he did the same. He was just one of us." John Rodgers scrimmaged with him every afternoon during football season and had the job of blocking Rustin. "I always thought he was funny. Very tender," he recounted. "I never blocked him once . . . his bones and his muscles were like steel . . . he was tough. And beautiful with it."

Yet occasionally memories of a sharper edge, of a way Bayard had of creating distance, seep through the pleasantries. Thomas admitted that "sometimes we got very bored with Bayard because he would be in a book, and he never would look up . . . he just blocked everything out." Rodgers too recalled something odd about Bayard's behavior at practice. "He spoke biblical poetry. And Browning. He would tackle you, and then get up and recite a poem." Bayard's antics provoked laughs, yet also seemed to announce that he was different, even superior, to the rest of the team. On a football squad whose members had such light-hearted nicknames as Skatz, Kiggy, and Alky, Bayard was the rare player without one. In his yearbook, the editors wrote a humorous narrative of an imagined future for him that combined in a single paragraph intense giggling, strenuous work habits, and excessive dignity. They were among the few to joke about the armor of protection that he erected around himself. Then and later, Bayard was something of an enigma to his classmates at West Chester High.

Bayard's poems and essays tell something about his character. They are not the product of an emerging literary artist. They are often awkward, trite, and sometimes pretentious. His work suggests a serious, intellectually precocious youth who was wrestling with contending emotions, trying to find his place in the world, and reaching for purpose beyond the confines of a provincial town. In a poem written just before graduation, Bayard rejects the quest for fame. But the tone is wistful and tinged with regret. One can hear in the rhymes a yearning for some kind of legacy, some way to express his passions and ambitions:

> *I ask of you no shining gold;*
> *I seek not epitaph or fame;*
> *No monument of stone for me,*
> *For man need never speak my name.*

> *But when my flesh doth waste away*
> *And seeds from stately trees do blow,*
> *I pray that in my fertile clay*
> *You gently let a small seed grow.*

That seed, I pray, be evergreen
That in my dust may always be
That everlasting life and joy
You manifest in that green tree.

His yearbook editors recognized in Bayard the reach for something great. "Yes," they wrote, "a hero on many a field, rising to the sublime in all because of a determination to be the best and to give the best." Bayard himself acknowledged the intense emotions that at times stirred inside him when he approvingly ended an essay with a quote from Emily Dickinson: "If I read a book and it makes my whole body so cold that no fire can warm me, I know that it is poetry."[17]

By his senior year, Bayard's star was shining brilliantly. While academic success and artistic creativity impressed some, his athletic prowess made him a big man in the high school and in the town. As a junior, Bayard's performance on the football team had merited selection as an all-county lineman. The next spring, he was part of a mile-relay team that won the state championship and set a record time that stood for decades. Charles Porter, a team member, later boasted that they were "the hottest things on the best track team they ever had." With many starting players on the football team returning, Bayard's senior year proved even better. As the autumn progressed and victory followed victory, the town responded with crowds in the thousands. After one contest the local paper reported that "Bayard Rustin played his usual fine game at left tackle, working splendidly with left end, Bruno." Soon, coverage shifted from the sports page to the front page, with a full-width headline announcing the final victory in a perfect season.[18]

It was the stuff of celebration and local myth. The team won both the county and the Philadelphia suburban championships. Sixty years later, no other team from the area had yet matched the unbeaten, untied record. After the players returned home from the game that sealed the championship, boisterous students rode through town on a truck. "They stopped at Bayard's house, Charlie Melton's house. All of them. They gave it a 'one, two, button your shoe' stuff and left," Nick Bruno remembered. "It was pretty good."[19]

But none of these triumphs came without bitterness. The indignities of white intolerance were never far away. In an era when most African Americans still lived in the South and only a few large Northern cities had substantial black populations, athletes like Bayard, Charles Porter, and Charlie Melton were unusual in southeastern Pennsylvania. Their presence sparked reactions from white coaches who refused to field their teams against the integrated West Chester squads. At events requiring overnight stays, securing accommodations sometimes proved thorny. In one case, at a state track contest in Altoona, the black athletes made it clear to their coach, Harold Zimmerman, that they would not participate in the meet unless they could stay in the main hotel with their teammates. Zimmerman ran a tight ship and did not take challenges lightly. "He was the kind of man," one of his athletes recalled, "who would grab a player and throw him against a locker if he didn't perform properly." He fought for their entry, but also later retaliated by denying them the gold running pins that were their due. Even while the local newspaper heralded the performance of outstanding black competitors, those same players and their friends faced restrictions in their home town. If high school athletes wanted to keep playing after the school gymnasium closed for the day, they could continue their practice at the High Street YMCA—except for the African Americans, who were not allowed entry. After a big game at home, students might congregate downtown at the popular Warner Grill—but not the black students.[20]

Friendships created another set of problems. Bayard's best pal in high school was John Cessna. They both ran on the mile-relay team and shared interests in writing, public speaking, and dramatics. As the two male students in their class who excelled across the board, their friendship was to be expected. But Bayard was not allowed in the Cessna household, and in order not to create trouble for John at home, they elected not to meet at the Rustin place either. Besides the gym and the classroom, the only safe neutral territory was the public library, where they spent many hours. The sight of an interracial pair of buddies was so unusual in the social world of West Chester in the early 1930s that their schoolmates referred to them as "whitey" and "blackey."[21]

The most hurtful racial slights could sometimes be the most subtle. For all his academic and athletic success, Bayard's deepest passion was music. As an adolescent, he developed a beautiful tenor voice that captivated audiences. He sang in the choir of his AME congregation and in a gospel quartet that performed in churches throughout the area. Early on, Bayard's interests expanded beyond hymns and spirituals to the Western operatic tradition. At high school assemblies, he displayed his talents, leaving behind indelible memories. A generation later, a classmate, Vera Bostelle, could still recall his rendition of "Una Furtiva Lagrima," an aria from Donizetti's *L'Elisir d'Amore*. "Whenever I hear it sung I can close my eyes and see him standing up there," she remembered in the 1960s. "I will never lose that memory." In the commencement issue of the *Garnet and White*, the editors described Bayard's "Ardent Aspiration" as "to be a Lawrence Tibbett," the celebrated Metropolitan Opera star of the 1920s and 1930s. But as if tacitly recognizing that no black American had ever sung at the Met, they listed his "Anticipated Achievement" as "Cab Calloway's Close Second."[22]

In the interviews that aging West Chester residents gave after Rustin's death, stories of his resistance to discrimination abound. They tell how, denied service one time in a restaurant that he and his teammates had entered, Bayard refused to budge until he was finally ejected. In another incident, he violated custom by sitting in the main section of the downtown Warner Theater. These events and fragments of many others survive as memories reshaped by the knowledge of his later rise to prominence as a civil rights activist. None can be firmly corroborated. But their recurrence, whatever the particulars might actually have been, alludes to a larger truth: even before he finished high school, Bayard had formed a decision, made a moral resolve, not to accept from white America the restrictions it sought to impose. He would go in town where he pleased. He would have anyone he chose as his friend and intimate. He would lay claim to the intellectual heritage of Europe and the culture and creativity of African American traditions. As a teenager, Bayard read Will Durant's *The Story of Philosophy*, which he described as akin to "taking a whiff of something that simply opens your nostrils except that it happened in my brain." For his prize-winning oration in his school's speech contest, he chose "The Creation," one of a series of poems, written in the idiom of the Negro preacher, by James Weldon Johnson, an acclaimed writer and NAACP leader who had once stayed in the Rustin home. Bayard's reach was already large.[23]

The graduation ceremony in spring 1932 was a fitting close to what was, overall, a triumphant time for Bayard. A high school diploma in the early 1930s carried the aura of a special achievement, and the local paper covered the commencement with front-page articles on successive days. The graduating class of 110 was among the largest in the school's history. The girls were all fitted in white evening dresses, "many of them sweeping the floor in the most approved modern style," and each carrying a bouquet of roses. Bayard and the other boys wore white trousers and dark jackets with a pink rose in the lapel. Along with Cessna, Bayard was among the six speakers (the school did not choose a valedictorian or salutatorian) in a program that revolved around the theme of "recreation." Described in the town paper as "the young colored man who has won honors in his class," Bayard spoke on the ability of music "to appeal to the higher emotions in a way that nothing else can and to lift one out of the fatigue and monotony of everyday life." Rustin performed a solo before the assembled graduates and their families, he received special recognition for winning letters in more than one sport, and he scored highest among the graduates in "honor points."[24]

RECREATION WAS AN ODD theme for a graduation in 1932. The nation was approaching the fourth year of the worst economic crisis in its history, and no good news lay on the horizon. Close to a quarter of the workforce was unemployed. States were exhausting their meager welfare funds. Banks had failed by the thousands, closing their doors and wiping out the savings of millions of families. The lines outside soup kitchens were growing longer. In urban parks and on the outskirts of many communities, makeshift shantytowns sheltered the homeless. Violence and disorder spread through cities and the countryside, as unemployed factory workers, angry miners, and displaced farmers expressed their discontent. At the time of Bayard's graduation, veterans from around the country were massed in Washington, D.C., demanding from Congress a special bonus to carry them through the Depression. Before the summer had ended, President Herbert Hoover ordered the army to scatter them and had their campsites burned. In these circumstances, the normally prized high school diploma meant little. Certainly for the few African Americans in the graduating class, prospects must have appeared grim.

Bayard, of course, was no ordinary graduate. But unlike his best friend, Cessna, whom the yearbook recorded as heading toward the University of Pennsylvania, Bayard had no prospects commensurate with his talents. No scholarship offers arrived from colleges, and the Rustin family did not have the means to support him at a school away from home.

At the last minute, an opportunity came to Bayard through the good offices of Dr. R. R. Wright, a wealthy leader of the AME church in nearby Philadelphia. Wright had just accepted the presidency of Wilberforce University, an African American institution in western Ohio with a famed music school and choir. Julia, an active AME member, approached him about her grandson; Wright, who had heard Bayard sing, arranged for him to receive a music scholarship to Wilberforce. And so, in September 1932, "with a pair of chino pants, three shirts and . . . $100" in scholarship money from Wright, Bayard set off by train for college.[25]

Established in 1856 by the Methodist Episcopal Conference of Cincinnati, and named for William Wilberforce, an English statesman and abolitionist, Wilberforce was the first college for Negroes in the United States. Many of its earliest students came from the South, the offspring of male planters and female slaves. When the Civil War cut off this supply of students, the young institution closed temporarily, until officers of the AME church bought the property. Wilberforce thus became the first institution of higher learning in the United States owned and managed by Americans of African descent.[26]

The 500-mile journey to Wilberforce took Bayard farther away from home than he had ever been. Located midway between Columbus and Cincinnati, the campus was a few miles outside the small town of Xenia. The train stopped a short distance away from the school, leaving a twenty-minute trek by foot amid a landscape of gently rolling farm country. The campus consisted largely of two- and three-story brick buildings, including Jones Auditorium, which sat 2,500; Galloway Hall, which housed the theater and music departments; and Beacom Gymnasium. Joining Bayard on campus were students from thirty states, as well as a small contingent from abroad.

Although Wilberforce's offerings included a broad array of liberal arts courses, the school's catalogue betrayed its aspirations. The heaviest concentration of classes could be found in commerce, education, home economics, industrial arts, shopwork, biology, and chemistry. Bayard enrolled in the College of Liberal Arts. During his first year, the school's bulletin listed him with a science concentration; by his second year, he had switched to "classical." Wilberforce was the only black college in the United States with a Reserve Officer Training Corps (ROTC). For male students, course work in the first two years involved mandatory participation in military training. Thus, Bayard, despite his Quaker-influenced background, faced over a hundred hours of drill and command, dozens of hours in rifle marksmanship and musketry, and additional hours in combat principles and military indoctrination.

Despite his success as a high school track and football star, Bayard devoted his extracurricular energies to music, for which Wilberforce was well known. As a member of the chorus and its more exclusive octet, he had an opportunity to shine musically. He became, as he recalled, "more deeply entrenched" in composers like Palestrina, Bach, and Mozart.[27] The octet traveled widely during the school year. The yearbook for 1933 shows a posed picture taken during a midwestern tour; President Wright and Robert Abbott, the editor and publisher of the *Chicago Defender*, are included in the photo. Bayard is seated in the front of the group, on the floor, his long legs bent at the knees, his eyes staring directly at the camera. The dark suit and tie that he sported suggest that he had acquired more clothing since his arrival—or that he exaggerated in later years the poverty of his wardrobe. A newspaper in Jacksonville, Florida, where the Wilberforce Singers performed, described Bayard as "undoubtedly one of the greatest tenors that the race

boasts." His hometown paper also commented on his triumphs, reminding its readers of his earlier accomplishments as a student at West
Chester High School. It mentioned the possibility of a European tour
in 1934, but by then Bayard was no longer a Wilberforce student. "The
school did not stretch me," he reminisced. "I sang in the choir and
quartet [*sic*] and traveled all over the country making money for the
school, but there was really no academic challenge to the place for me."
Accounts of his departure betray inconsistencies, though all suggest
that he had placed himself at odds with the school's authorities. A letter
written only a decade after the events attributed his departure to conflicts stemming from the required participation in ROTC activities and
the consequent loss of his scholarship. In interviews he gave late in his
life, he claimed to have been asked to leave after organizing a student
strike to improve the quality of the food.[28]

The return to West Chester was disheartening. Bayard was twenty-
two. With the Depression still blanketing the country, he had neither
direction nor prospects. "I really didn't know who I was," he reflected
many decades later. "I really was one of those kids who didn't quite
know what he wanted to do." During the summer after his first year at
Wilberforce, he had stayed with Bessie, Julia's eldest daughter, who was
then living in New York, and he went back again after leaving Wilberforce. Harlem was thrilling to him. "A totally exciting experience," he
recalled. "I'll never forget my first walk on 125th Street. . . . I had such
a feeling of exhilaration." But there was no work to be found, and the
city seemed too much to handle. Confused and lonely, he responded to
Julia's entreaties to come home. "You know, Bayard," she told him, "if
you don't know where you're going, any road will take you there."[29]

"A Young Radical"
1934–1941

IN THE FALL of 1934, Bayard enrolled in school once again, this time just a few miles away from home at Cheyney State Teachers College, a Quaker-founded school for black students. Dr. Leslie Pinckney Hill, its Harvard-educated president, was the most eminent African American in the county, respected for both his learning and the uncompromising standards he held out for his students. Impressed as Bishop Wright had been with Bayard's talent and potential, Hill too offered the young man a music scholarship so that, along with his studies, Bayard resumed the local singing he had done in high school. Meanwhile, he also returned to Gay Street Elementary School as a student instructor in the classroom of one of his former teachers, Warren Burton.

In Dr. Hill, Bayard had finally found someone to guide and stretch him intellectually. Hill had studied at Harvard when such major philosophers as William James, George Santayana, and Josiah Royce graced its faculty. Through Hill's tutoring, Rustin wrote to a friend, Santayana became "the first philosopher I read at any length." About this time Santayana's only novel, *The Last Puritan*, was published, and Bayard read it avidly. "I came," he said, "to respect Santayana not only for his prodigious mind and his contributions to thinking but also because he seems to defy being stamped or pigeonholed. He writes with a poetic feeling that is simultaneously lyric and intense." Rustin also absorbed some of the work of William James, particularly a slim volume titled *Talks to Teachers*. One of its chapters, on habit formation, made such an impression that, years later, "in a crisis situation it came back to me almost word for word."[1]

Hill encouraged not only intellectual inquisitiveness in Bayard but a political consciousness as well. By the mid-1930s, world events were impinging ever more insistently on an isolationist United States. Hitler's rise to power and German rearmament, Japanese aggression in East Asia, the Italian invasion of Ethiopia, the eruption of a civil war in Spain that pitted democratic forces against a fascist military: these events portended a slide toward a war as destructive as the Great War two decades earlier. In the years before Pearl Harbor, a vigorous peace movement in the United States resisted the rush toward militarism. Congress enacted a series of neutrality acts to keep the United States out of war. On college campuses, students mobilized in large numbers. Campaigns against compulsory ROTC, peace rallies at scores of schools, and mass declarations of support for the Oxford Oath (a promise not to support any future war) swept the country. In April 1936, while Bayard was at Cheyney State, close to half a million students participated in a simultaneous antiwar strike.[2]

President Hill saw to it that Cheyney State added its voice to the chorus of concern. In 1937, he had the campus play host to the Institute of International Relations sponsored by the American Friends Service Committee (AFSC) and the Emergency Peace Campaign. Bayard was the only Cheyney student to participate, but a hundred others, a majority of them college students drawn from across the country, arrived for the institute. He rubbed shoulders with students from many of the nation's elite colleges and universities. He also had access to a prominent faculty assembled specially for the event. Institute teachers attributed the drift toward war to nationalism, economic imperialism, secret alliances, and the stockpiling of armaments. They urged that class consciousness be substituted for nationalism, and blamed the divisions incited by capitalism for the tensions that led to war.[3]

The heavy antiwar message of the institute must have sat well with Bayard, for just the year before, he had formally decided to declare himself a Quaker. Through Julia, Quaker beliefs had circulated in the Rustin household and informed some of her approach to community

activism and spirituality. In high school, Bayard had come under the influence of the local librarian, a Quaker woman who directed his reading and discussed with him books about war and peace. His experiences
with ROTC at Wilberforce brought the issue of pacifism to the fore-
ground. The Quaker influence at Cheyney, the public debates in the
mid-1930s about war, peace, and economic injustice, and Bayard's
youthful search for a focus to his restless energy and capacious intellect
increased the attractiveness of a socially engaged spirituality. A lecture
by Rufus Jones, a professor of philosophy at nearby Haverford College,
provoked "one of the vital turns" in his spiritual development, and by
the time of the Cheyney Institute, Bayard was, in Quaker fashion, "depend[ing] upon my daily quiet periods for guidance."[4]

SHORTLY AFTER COMPLETING the AFSC-sponsored campus program, Bayard left West Chester for the summer, with $100 voted him
by the college, to participate in a Friends student peace brigade in
Auburn, a small city in the Finger Lake district of upstate New York.
With a few other college students, Bayard joined what was then still
a relatively new experiment among the activist wing of the Quakers:
peace education through immersion in the life of a local community.
After a training seminar in Philadelphia, he and the others settled into
the local YMCA. He worked in a playground as an athletic and craft director, helped with a regular radio broadcast on peace and international
relations, and produced a ballet whose theme was nonviolence. Reflecting back a few years later, Bayard claimed that "I would never have come
to certain social concerns had I missed the experience with the AFSC."[5]

While in Auburn, Bayard also made the acquaintance of Norman
Whitney, a Quaker activist from the area. Whitney was the first of a series of older men to whom Bayard attached himself and who were father
figures to him. Two decades Bayard's senior, the balding, bespectacled,
and somewhat portly Whitney was single and had lived in a household
with his unmarried sister, Mildred, since he started college twenty-five
years earlier. A professor of English at Syracuse University, he had come
under the influence of Frederick Libby, a national peace activist who
was one of Bayard's instructors that summer and "a man of Olympian

proportions" in Whitney's telling. The contact with Libby propelled him to found the Syracuse Peace Council, which he directed for decades. Whitney's pacifism was rooted in a religious sensibility, so much so that he was affectionately known as "the bishop." For Bayard, he became something of a spiritual mentor and confessor.[6]

How much Bayard revealed of himself that first summer of their acquaintanceship is uncertain. But the outgoing Whitney certainly won his trust enough that Bayard later, and perhaps even then, confided in him about the homosexual longings that increasingly preoccupied him. Nothing in their later correspondence suggests even a hint of condemnation on Whitney's part. Whatever misfortunes Bayard later encountered because of his sexuality, Whitney remained steadfastly loyal. In the words of one who knew them both for many years, "Norman was almost a father to Bayard. . . . He loved Bayard like a son and they were very very close." Over the years, the relationship was as important to Whitney as it was to Bayard. "Norman used to say that if he ever doubted the existence of God, he always thought of Bayard because Bayard had come from nowhere, had no opportunity as a young man and he really educated himself. He was so brilliant and so articulate. Norm always said this was beyond human comprehension that anyone could rise to that level."[7]

Bayard's sexuality seems to have played the decisive role in finally propelling him out of West Chester. When he returned home from the summer peace brigade, he was within striking distance of finishing college. With forty-six hours of credit from Wilberforce and sixty-four semester hours from Cheyney State, he needed only one more year of classes to graduate. Yet he finally left West Chester in the fall of 1937 and moved to New York City, where he remained for the rest of his life.

The precise circumstances of his departure remain murky. Bayard was of the generation of gay men for whom homosexuality was something to be lived but not spoken of. Although large cities were already home in the 1930s to elaborate gay social networks and public meeting places, a culture of discretion prevailed. Gay men spoke in coded language in mixed company and sometimes even among themselves. The open acknowledgment of one's homosexuality was likely only to invite difficulty. Over the course of Bayard's adulthood, his sexuality would make him the target of punishment and hostility again and again. It became second nature for him to deflect questions away from personal matters, to construct a life story that gave no notice to the shaping force of gay oppression. Even much later, after a militant gay movement had provoked some welcome changes in the social climate, Bayard continued the habits of a lifetime. When Milton Viorst, a journalist, interviewed him in the 1970s for a major profile of his career, Bayard explained the decision to leave West Chester as if it were an offhanded impulse: "I was making all A's and my sister who was really my aunt, my sister Bessie, was teaching in New York City. She said to come to New York because 'I want you to have an experience where your mind is stretched,' so I came to the city and went to City College." In fact, Bayard did not enroll in City College until three years after moving to New York, and then completed only one course. To August Meier, a historian who interviewed him around the same time as Viorst, Bayard conflated his departure from Cheyney State with the circumstances that made him leave Wilberforce: his role in campus protests. In this telling, "tears came to [Dr. Pinckney's] eyes and he said he wouldn't put anything bad in [his] record."[8]

In the last year of Bayard's life, he gave an interview to Mark Bowman, a gay man active in efforts to make American Protestantism more accepting of homosexuality. Pressed by Bowman, Rustin spoke in great detail about the sexual desires that assumed definable form in late adolescence and early adulthood. He remembered two male high school students who were "fairly outrageous creatures" and whose flamboyance, more than any overt sexuality, made them social outcasts. Bayard, in contrast, was "very much one of the boys, on all the teams, all that sort of thing. Although I felt a certain physical attraction for one or two of the chaps on the team, it never translated itself into any conscious sexual thing." Only when he went to Wilberforce and then, more strongly, when he returned to West Chester did these amorphous desires take shape in his mind as clearly sexual. His family seemed accepting, recognizing a special bond with some of the male friends he brought home, although sex was never the subject of conversation.

Once, he remembered, Julia broached the subject obliquely. "'I want to recommend something to you,'" she told him. "'In selecting your male friends, you should be careful that you associate with people who have as much to lose as you have.'" When Bayard pushed her to explain, she said, "'You have a very good reputation so you should go around with people who have good reputations. . . . People who do not have as much to lose as you have can be very careless.'" Bayard sensed that Julia was telling him something very important.[9]

Julia's advice was not sufficient to protect him from trouble. Davis Platt, a young man who became Bayard's lover in 1943, recalled a story that Bayard told him but never wrote about or spoke of for the record: "There was a family named _____, and there was a son named _____, Jr., I guess who was about Bayard's age, who was white of course, and they were a leading family of the town. And Bayard and he had sex together in a public park, on the edge of a golf course, I'm not exactly sure. And they got caught. I forget what happened to Bayard, but it was very very unpleasant. Nothing happened to the white guy." Platt was not able to pinpoint exactly when this happened, but it most likely occurred while Bayard was a young man attending Cheyney State rather than while he was a high school student. The incident made its way to both Bayard's family and the authorities at the college. Platt remembered Bayard's telling him of his grandmother's acceptance, but it did not sit as well with Dr. Hill. The tears that Bayard recalled from his last meeting with Hill and the reference to preserving his good record suggest his sexuality as the spur to his departure. An episode of this kind would have made Bayard a continuing object of interest to the local police, not an attractive prospect for a young colored man in a city as small as West Chester.[10] If this scenario is correct, Bessie's offer to let him live with her in Harlem promised a welcome rescue.

IN SOME DEEPER SENSE, Bayard's move requires no explanation. Whatever the specific reason for the push out of West Chester, the pull to New York was magnetic. In Harlem, he found the largest, most concentrated black community outside of Africa. Although the Depression had removed some of the luster from life there, in 1937 the neighborhood was still near in time to the glory days of the Harlem Renaissance, when artists, writers, musicians, and singers sustained a flourishing cultural scene. If economic hard times had dimmed that earlier hopefulness, they had replaced it with something equally enticing: a vibrant left-wing politics. Councils of the unemployed, organizations of tenants, consumer cooperatives, boycotts of businesses that refused to employ African Americans—all this and more filled the daily lives of many Harlem residents during the Depression. The Communist Party in particular had established itself as a force on the streets. Its spirited defense of the Scottsboro Boys, a group of young black men convicted of sexually assaulting two white women in Alabama, had won it respect, as had its willingness to fight the eviction of families down on their luck and to organize the jobless.[11]

What was true of Harlem was broadcast on an even grander scale in the city as a whole. New York was awash with political radicalism in the 1930s, with every version of left-wing militancy competing for influence. Manhattan was also the cultural capital of the nation. Besides the creativity to be found in Harlem, Bayard had at his disposal the theaters of Broadway, the cabarets of Greenwich Village, the museums, the bookstores, and the agit-prop dramatics of street corner artists. He also had available a thriving "gay" or "queer" subculture that overlapped spatially with his other worlds. Drag balls, rent parties, and cabarets in Harlem, the street cruising scene along 42nd Street in the theater district, the clubs in Greenwich Village: the neighborhoods and settings that sustained Bayard's racial, political, and cultural identities also enabled his sexual desires to find expression. True, New York City in the mid-1930s was experiencing something of a backlash as law enforcement officials, in reaction against the loose times of Prohibition, cracked down on the most visible manifestations of homosexual life. Yet in comparison to West Chester, New York offered the anonymity— and, hence, safety—that only a large, cosmopolitan city could have provided a full generation before gay liberation.

Arriving in the city, Bayard stayed with his aunt Bessie and her family on St. Nicholas Avenue in Harlem. He was able to find employment through the Works Progress Administration, a New Deal agency that gave jobs to millions. In his first two years in New York, Bayard taught English to the foreign born at Benjamin Franklin High School in East Harlem and then became an assistant recreation director at a youth organization in his neighborhood. By then, he had moved out of Bessie's apartment, to a place farther north on St. Nicholas Avenue, an arrangement that furnished him with more privacy and independence. A later FBI investigation checked the records of the credit bureau for those years and found that he "rented his apartment on a monthly basis and met his bills promptly."[12]

These first years in New York also allowed Bayard to form, for the first time, an extended network of gay friends and acquaintances. In those years, by his recollection, Harlem did not sport separate gay clubs. Instead, there were "hangouts for artistic people" where patrons mingled comfortably and the gay men used "a certain telegraph system among themselves" to identify one another. Soon he found himself invited to private parties where the guests were mainly literati and musicians, some gay, some not. These circles enabled him to have greater personal freedom than was possible in West Chester. Yet there were limits. One could be gay "so long as one did not, as it were, publicize gayness."[13]

The fall of 1939 saw a pleasing turn in his fortunes. He was hired as a member of the chorus in a musical starring Paul Robeson. *John Henry* was to be the vehicle for Robeson's return to Broadway after an eight-year hiatus. During that time, he had established an international reputation as a singer and actor and as something of a political radical. As just one member of a cast of seventy-five, Bayard did not have much intimate contact with Robeson, but he was close enough to make an acquaintance and watch the master at work. He remembered Robeson as "so large, so full of life, so warm, and so totally respectful of everybody."[14] The production tried out in Boston and Philadelphia before opening at the Forty-Fourth Street Theater in January 1940. While the reviewers were generous in their assessment of Robeson, they were unkind to the play. Brooks Atkinson in the *New York Times* called it "an uneven show with music that is also of mixed quality. . . . [The play is] hardly more than a series of miscellaneous pictures in the career of a man of muscle—a desultory narrative, underwritten and put together in a perfunctory fashion."[15] Disappointingly for Bayard, *John Henry* closed after only five performances.

Yet the experience opened other doors. One of the key cast members and the writer of some of the play's music was Josh White, a blues and folk guitarist-singer who later acquired legendary stature in his trade. White had done some recording earlier in the thirties and then disappeared from the music scene. His role in *John Henry* represented his rediscovery, and afterward, Leonard De Paur, who had tracked White down, encouraged him to resume his career. White formed a group, Josh White and the Carolinians, of which Bayard became a member. Several months of rehearsals led in June 1940 to a recording session at Columbia Records and the release of *Chain Gang*, which White's biographer, Dorothy Schainman Siegel, describes as "both a critical and financial success."[16]

Soon the group had secured a regular gig at Cafe Society Downtown. Located just off Sheridan Square in Greenwich Village, it was one of a new breed of cabaret that opened in New York after prohibition. Despite the Cole Porter connotations of the name, its owner was a partisan of Depression-inspired leftist politics and he sought to make his clubs (there was a second Cafe Society uptown in the West 50s) venues where art and politics mingled easily. In comparison to many other places in Manhattan, where de facto segregation still reigned, the patrons and performers were a racially integrated lot. The downtown club also projected a bohemian air, encouraging a crowd that was mixed in other ways as well. Bayard's status as a performer gave him some cachet with the regulars, enabling him to meet like-minded folks, black and white, homosexual and heterosexual, who appreciated both his tenor voice and his striking good looks.

And good looking he was, as the few surviving photographs of this era suggest. A bit over six feet tall, he still had the lean, muscular body of a track star. Depending on his mood or the personality he wished to project, his long, somewhat angular face could appear darkly brooding, or light up the room with a broad smile, or with a turn of his lip suggest the rapier wit that friends and colleagues—and, later, political opponents—remembered so well. Above all there were his eyes—large, dark brown, staring out from his somewhat lighter, caramel-colored complexion. They demanded attention and won Bayard admirers.

By the time he was performing at Café Society, Bayard had groups of friends around the city. Then and later, associates commented on how numerous his circles of acquaintances were and, significantly, how often they remained distinct from one another. Throughout his life, Bayard maintained a catholic set of interests. He refused to honor the lines that marked and separated individuals and that stratified American society. Gay worlds and straight, black worlds and white, spiritual communities and secular political ones, artistic expression and grass-roots activism all appealed to him. Friends who knew him in only one or two of these spheres were surprised to discover the many other milieus in which he moved.

One clique of companions revolved around a cooperative house in Greenwich Village not far from Café Society. Bayard entered the world through Dick Strachan, a young, slender, "soft-looking" man of Scottish descent who was his lover for a time. The dozen or so residents initially formed around a group of New York University students, but its composition had shifted, and what held the group together was an eclectic combination of leftist politics and literary conceit. Charlie Bloomstein, one of the residents who became a lifelong friend of Bayard, remembered it as "a motley group. Most of the guys had leftist roots." The heart of their social life were cheap dinners that often lasted for several hours, with talk ranging from the war in Europe to literature. Bloomstein recalled that Bayard's interests "in the early times were literary. He used to talk about Shakespeare a lot and other books. And he had very good insights and very good literary criticism. He was a master of the language too." The members also shared in the political enthusiasms of the times and expressed them occasionally by participating in the soap-box tradition of street corner speaking that was still very much a part of working-class life in the 1930s. Bayard, Bloomstein claimed, "was a great speaker."[17]

During these first few years in New York, political activism competed with artistic endeavors for primacy in Bayard's life. Decades later, when he had become enough of a public figure so that journalists and historians came to him wishing to record the story of his life, Bayard had a standard version of those years, often repeated, that went something like this:

Living in Harlem, he saw that whenever blacks got into trouble, it was invariably the Communists who were willing to defend them. Other radical groups, like the Socialist Party or assorted Trotskyist organizations, promised gains only after the revolution. So he joined the Young Communist League (YCL), agitated on the City College campus, helped the YCL take over the American Student Union (ASU), the major organization of the national student movement, and soon was traveling all over New York State establishing ASU "cells" on dozens of campuses. Bayard and his young cronies read Marx and Lenin and Bakunin; they volunteered in the district office of Vito Marcantonio, the left-wing member of Congress from East Harlem; and they organized against racial discrimination in the armed forces. When Hitler invaded the Soviet Union in June 1941, the Communist Party dramatically shifted direction and insisted that, in the interest of national unity against fascism, Bayard stop agitating on behalf of racial justice. That became "the straw that broke the camel's back," and Bayard left the YCL rather than comply. For the rest of his life, he remained deeply suspicious of the Communist Party, its autocratic nature, and its subservience to the Soviet Union.[18]

There is no reason to doubt the bare contours of this story—that is, his involvement with the Communist Party through its youth section and his subsequent break with the party in June 1941. During the 1930s, the Communist Party held greater appeal for Americans of conscience than at any time before or since. The magnitude of the Great Depression shook the faith of many Americans in the ability of capitalism to meet even the basic needs of the population; Communists had both an explanation for the crisis and a solution. The Communist Party was also one of the few white-dominated organizations that made the fight against racial injustice a priority. Members agitated not only on the streets of Harlem but in the South too, where support for racial equality carried serious risks. Moreover, as fascism in Europe and Asia

gained strength in the 1930s, Communists were among its most vigorous opponents. American Communists in these years were willing to
tone down sectarian polemics and work with the broadest coalition of
progressive forces, a "Popular Front" that ranged from New Deal liberals to other elements of the left. It meant that a young black man who
bristled at racial discrimination and who was coming to a socialist understanding of class could work with ease in the orbit of a political organization that opposed fascism, racism, and economic inequality. Even
the Hitler-Stalin Pact and the invasion of Poland in September 1939
might not have tarnished the allure of the party for Bayard. Abandoning the Popular Front, the party began in 1939 to work vigorously
against U.S. involvement in the conflict and to sow pacifist sentiments
in the population, including spreading discontent among African
Americans over segregation of the military, positions that Bayard would
have found attractive.

Yet there is also reason to believe that Bayard retrospectively exaggerated his engagement with the YCL. For one, in the thousands of
pages that the FBI accumulated on him in the course of a quarter-century
of recurring surveillance, his membership in the YCL rarely merits
more than a line of mention. Considering the triple jeopardy that Bayard's identity and beliefs created—leftist, black, homosexual—it seems
likely that J. Edgar Hoover's agents would have accumulated more details had his communist involvement been extensive. Moreover, Bayard's interests in this period—especially during the two years when
Hitler and Stalin were putative allies and the U.S. Communist Party
consequently had much to explain to its American supporters—seemed
unusually eclectic for someone deep in the party's culture. He sang in
church choirs in Harlem. He attended Quaker meetings. He maintained his connection with the AFSC and loyalists to it like Norman
Whitney. He sought out a relationship with A. Philip Randolph, the
most prominent black labor leader in the country and a socialist who
was often the target of Communist ire. He was developing ties with
pacifists such as A. J. Muste, whose opposition to fascism was uncompromising and who had no kind words to say about the Communist
Party. In other words, Bayard was an eager young explorer of the Amer-

ican left, broadly defined, in the decade when the left was at its strongest and most varied, in the city where its many varieties were on display. In the words of Carl Rachlin, another young activist similarly exploring progressive politics, Bayard simply "never was a good Communist."[19]

So why might Bayard later have embellished his relationship with American communism? Perhaps because of the aura it would have created in the circles in which he came to travel. Among the Christian pacifists who constituted Bayard's family and community in the 1940s, communism conjured images both alluring and repellent. Communists were deeply committed to fighting against obvious injustice and promoting revolutionary change, yet their moral sensibilities—the ruthless tactics, the sharp polemics, the skeptical, even hostile, attitude toward religion and spirituality—made them seem threatening. To have entered the lair and escaped added a touch of excitement, of daring, to the persona that Bayard soon began to construct for himself.

At the same time, the readiness with which Bayard harkened back to his Communist experience attests to the power and value of it. Even if he was less fully absorbed in the party's work than some of his statements suggest, it nonetheless affected him. As much perhaps as any other radical organization, the Communist Party functioned as a school, teaching its members and supporters valuable lessons. As Bayard described it decades later: "I learned many of the most important things I learned about organization and detail and writing clearly and the like from my experience as a communist. . . . I'm happy I had it. It taught me a great deal, and I presume that if I had to do it over again, I'd do the same thing." They were sentiments echoed by many other young radicals of the 1930s, including those who never joined the party. Dorothy Height, who came to lead the National Council of Negro Women during the glory years of the civil rights movement, recalled the political environment of the Depression decade in ways that resonate with Bayard's assessment: "I learned so much from the Communists. Those were some of the best minds that I ever came upon. And the tactics, the tactics I learned. I think that has something to do with my staying power."[20]

Whatever Bayard's degree of engagement with the Communist Party, he was already moving in another direction when Hitler's invasion of the Soviet Union, on June 22, 1941, led him to drop whatever remaining ties he had. Throughout the winter and spring, Bayard had been devoting some of his time and energy to A. Philip Randolph's March on Washington Movement, an effort by the labor leader to pressure the Roosevelt administration into banning racial discrimination in defense employment. The association with Randolph, which after fits and starts would endure until the older man's death in 1979, could only have exerted a strong pull away from the Communist Party. Randolph had previously tangled openly with the Communists over their role in the National Negro Congress; he distrusted them and harbored no reservations about saying so. Moreover, he could claim the mantle of leader in a way that few Communists could. He had built a successful union in the face of fierce capitalist opposition. Now, in 1941, Randolph was mobilizing the working people of Harlem and other black urban communities to confront the national government.

More significant, by late June Bayard was casting his lot with pacifism, the very part of the American left for which the Communist Party, now eager to have the United States come to the aid of the Soviet Union, had the least tolerance. Through Norman Whitney, his pacifist mentor in Syracuse, he had come to the attention of A. J. Muste, the recently appointed head of the Fellowship of Reconciliation (FOR), a Christian pacifist organization. Muste was aggressively recruiting Bayard to the staff. Meanwhile, Bayard had signed on to another summer project of the AFSC, this time in Puerto Rico, and was already making plans to leave at the time that he quit the YCL.

During his time in Puerto Rico, Bayard performed a mission for Muste and the FOR: an investigation of the conditions faced by conscientious objectors in Puerto Rico and a search for contacts on the island who might help defend them. In San Juan, he met at Muste's suggestion with a minister, the Reverend J. R. LeBron Velasquez. Though they spoke freely about "the New Testament basis of pacifism," Bayard also reported deep distrust of him in San Juan, in part because of youthful radical activities that had once led to rioting and violence. He doubted that LeBron was the best contact for the FOR, but also wrote—in phrases as easily applicable to himself in 1941 as to LeBron—"certainly a man is not to be judged through life on his activities as a young radical."[21]

When Bayard returned to New York on August 28, there was a firm job offer waiting for him. He was to begin working at the FOR as one of its youth secretaries. The position would lead him out of obscurity.

CHAPTER THREE

"A Way of Life"
1941–1943

RUSTIN STARTED WORK at the FOR in September 1941, scarcely a
propitious moment to embark on a pacifist career. To many Americans,
evil itself seemed to be on the march. Hitler's armies blanketed Western Europe and were beginning the work of isolating, identifying, and
exterminating the Continent's Jews. In North Africa, the Germans
were heading toward the Suez Canal; in the east, they were sweeping
across the Soviet Union. The Pacific war was spreading as Japanese military forces moved down the coast of East Asia and its navy extended its
reach in the Pacific. Although the United States remained technically at
peace, President Roosevelt's campaign promise of 1940—to keep American boys out of the fighting—sounded increasingly thin. Congress had
enacted FDR's Lend-Lease program in March 1941, allowing the
United States to provide first the British and then the Russians with
ships and munitions to resist the German onslaught. American and German ships confronted one another in the North Atlantic, while American and Japanese diplomatic exchanges grew sharper. As late as the fall
of 1941, Americans remained divided about the wisdom of entering the
war. But the Japanese attack on Pearl Harbor transformed public sentiment, giving World War II the distinction of being the country's one
"good war." No other American war ever enjoyed such broad support.

Yet even good wars can spur pacifists. The FOR grew during these
years. Its budget expanded an average of 30 percent annually. At the
close of 1943, it had 14,000 members and 450 local chapters. Since

most members were ministers with a wide circle of influence in their congregations and communities, the FOR's reach was potentially larger than the numbers might suggest. But the financial boon simply reflected that the faithful, in a time of adversity, were redoubling their commitment. In fact, the chasm separating pacifists from the rest of America had never been as deep and wide as in the war years.

Paradoxically, many younger pacifists of the era remember it as a thrilling time. The mobilization for war stripped the ranks of the peace movement down to its hard core, leaving only those for whom opposition to violence was like a holy crusade. Homer Jack, a young seminarian from Chicago who would later work with Rustin, described these years as "a pregnant moment in peace history." For Glenn Smiley, a California minister who joined the FOR staff soon after Rustin did, "the whole world opened up . . . I had a gospel at last that meant something." Smiley portrayed these times as "the golden age of the FOR. . . . Not only the staff, but the executive board was composed of giants."[1]

ABRAHAM JOHANNES MUSTE towered over all of them. "AJ," as his friends and associates addressed him, came to the FOR as executive secretary the year before Rustin joined the staff. Even as Rustin arrived, Muste was in the process of transforming American pacifism. For an organization like the FOR, founded in 1915 as part of the revulsion against the Great War, pacifism had been above all about personal moral witness, a refusal to take up the gun and violate principles of universal Christian fellowship. Muste, by contrast, was interested in revolution. "Our only valid objective," he wrote, "is the transformation of society, not the building of a shelter for the saints." He wanted to create a nonviolent mass movement in which resistance to war was one small, almost incidental, aspect. Muste could be blunt about his convictions. "In a world built on violence," he once announced, "one must be a revolutionary before one can be a pacifist . . . a nonrevolutionary pacifist is a contradiction in terms, a monstrosity."[2]

Not many Americans could voice such sentiments and retain their credibility, but Muste's decades of engagement in struggles for social justice gave him a moral authority that few disputed. Born in 1885 in the Netherlands, he migrated as a young child with his family to Grand Rapids, Michigan, where other Dutch had preceded them. Educated in the stern Calvinism of the Dutch Reformed church, he trained for the ministry and quickly displayed a penchant for losing his pastorates. His first position came to an end over his refusal to invoke the literal truth of Scripture. Later, while minister of a liberal Congregational church outside Boston, Muste joined the newly formed Fellowship of Reconciliation as a protest against the war in Europe. Once the United States entered the conflict, members of the congregation with sons fighting abroad expected their minister's support, not his advocacy of peace.

The end of the war brought a period of intense labor agitation and government repression. Muste found himself drawn into local labor disputes, and before long, he had made the cause of the working class his own. He helped found, and then headed, the Amalgamated Textile Workers of America, which espoused a militant industrial unionism. "I do not recall a week when there was not a strike on somewhere in our union," Muste wrote in a memoir. "There was no strike without labor spies; no strike in which we did not encounter arbitrary, and usually violent, conduct on the part of the police."

In 1921, Muste shifted from labor organizer to labor educator. Along with a group of what he called "small s" socialists, he established Brookwood College, a pioneering worker education project set on a rural campus north of New York City. For twelve years, Brookwood gave Muste a base from which he built relationships not only with rank-and-file union activists, but with a broad spectrum of progressive leaders. His position at Brookwood allowed him to agitate within the labor movement. He often found himself the target of vitriolic attack, ranging from right to left. Matthew Woll, an American Federation of Labor (AFL) vice president, called Brookwood "a breeding ground for Communism," while the Communist Party's *Daily Worker* labeled Muste's initiatives "class collaborationist."[3]

A decade's involvement on the front lines of class warfare forced Muste to take a searching look at the religious foundation of his commitments. "I had lost faith in the Church's relevance," he recalled. "The churches were identified with the *status quo*." The hardships of the Great Depression intensified his disillusionment and encouraged a shift toward the left. "When you looked out on the scene of misery and desperation during the depression," he wrote in the late 1950s, "you saw that it was the radicals, the Left-wingers, who were *doing something* about the situation. . . . It was on the Left . . . that one found people who were truly 'religious' in the sense that they were virtually completely committed . . . the Left had the vision, the dream."[4]

Muste immersed himself in left-wing politics. He organized the jobless, participated in unionizing drives in basic industries, and faced police violence and arrest for treason. In 1933, he helped launch his own version of the revolution by founding the American Workers Party. Muste experienced firsthand the vicious sectarian battles within the left. Eventually, he found himself disenchanted not only by the totalitarianism of the Soviet Union but also by the amorality of Communist Party organizers and Trotskyist dissidents in the United States whose ruthlessness was limited, he sometimes felt, only by their lack of power.

In the summer of 1936, after a stretch of particularly ugly factionalism, Muste and his family went to France for a much-needed vacation. Sightseeing in Paris, he walked into one of its many churches. "I sat down on a bench near the front and looked at the cross," he recalled. "Without the slightest premonition of what was going to happen, I was saying to myself: 'This is where you belong.' . . . I felt as if the hand of God had drawn me up . . . and catapulted me back into the Church."[5] Unlike many others who journeyed to the left and back in the thirties, Muste did not turn away from the dream of revolution, but his inspiration now came from the texts of Christianity. He reestablished his ties not simply to Christianity, but to the sector of it committed to pacifist nonviolence. By 1940, his odyssey had carried him into the offices of the FOR, where he assumed the role of leading it through the era of a new world war.

Muste's credibility among his church-oriented constituents came from his passionate appeal to their religious sensibilities. On the eve of the nation's entry into the war, when American pacifists had to look into the face of Nazi malevolence and still say no to violence, Muste told his followers: "To know in one's inmost being the unity of all men in God;

to express love at every moment and in every relationship, to be channels of this quiet, unobtrusive, persistent force which is always there . . .
this is the meaning of pacifism." For Muste, resistance to war was part
of a larger Christian commitment to a life of love and nonviolence tied
to political engagement. "Either we ought to resign from the world . . .
or else we must resolutely carry our political task to its end."[6]

In imagining an effective nonviolence, Muste increasingly drew sus-
tenance from the model of Mohandas Gandhi in India. In Muste's view,
the Gandhian movement combined revolutionary goals with a perspective that was deeply and thoroughly religious. "Pacifism with Gandhi,"
he wrote, "[is] not a tool that you pick up or lay down, use today but not
tomorrow. . . . It was a way of life."[7] To Muste, it was also the key to
building from the ashes of a war-engulfed globe a new world of peace
and justice.

Forceful as his personality and vision were, Muste still had to face the
hard reality of an organization whose ways of approaching its mission
stopped far short of the fiery rhetoric of revolution. John Nevin Sayre,
the FOR's elder statesman, was cut from the mold of the traditional
pacifist. Steeped in social privilege, Sayre came from a wealthy, old-line
New England family. One young staffer described him as "sort of staid,
stolid, solid in that position where he respected government to the
point of almost idolizing it. He didn't do much that was opposed to the
government, except the war. He wouldn't get in there and carry a mus-
ket. . . . He tried to get everybody else not to. . . . But his message
didn't go as far as changing society."[8] Sayre's outlook reflected the state
of the FOR in 1941. While Muste rhapsodized about Gandhi's campaigns of civil disobedience, the majority of the National Council, the
governing body of the FOR, were wary of countenancing direct action
campaigns at home. As one staff member recollected, "On social activism they were conservative. They did agree that they would not participate in war, and that was the only cement. These were people who
lived very comfortable middle-class lives."[9]

To create a counterbalance to this traditional pacifism, Muste quickly
built a staff of radical activists with the same "lean and hungry look"

that he had once seen among labor organizers. Between 1940 and 1942, he fashioned a group of about a dozen, virtually all of them young men, with some working out of the national headquarters in New York City and others located in regional offices around the country. Most were rooted in the Christian social activism of the 1930s. The ranks of student activists in the National Council of Methodist Youth, the most militant Christian youth group of the 1930s, was one fertile source. John Swomley, who became Muste's second in command, had been a national officer of the Methodist group; through him, Muste also came to know Jim Farmer and George Houser. The intellectually precocious Farmer was a Howard University divinity student who was one of thirty youth leaders invited by Eleanor Roosevelt to a White House meeting, which turned messy when Farmer challenged the president's support of British colonialism. Houser, meanwhile, had achieved another kind of notoriety. As one of the "Union Eight," a group of students at the prestigious Union Theological Seminary in New York City, he refused to cooperate with the registration requirement of the military conscription system that Congress enacted in 1940. Their trial, conviction, and sentencing received prominent coverage in the press. Other staff members included Doris Grotewohl, a Berea College graduate who had worked for the YWCA, and Caleb Foote, who in the 1930s had been swept along by the Oxford Pledge campaign and moved on to work with migrant farm laborers on the West Coast. And, finally, there was Rustin.[10]

As one of the FOR's youth secretaries, Rustin's charge was to see that the message of pacifism and nonviolence settled into a generation that had not experienced the horrors of the previous European war. He spent much of his time on the road—rallying the spirits of local FOR groups, lecturing on college campuses and at high schools, running workshops at conferences of church-affiliated youth organizations, or speaking at the Sunday school of churches whose ministers were FOR members. After Pearl Harbor, when the United States formally entered the war, he also began to visit the Civilian Public Service (CPS) camps to which conscientious objectors were assigned and the relocation camps in the West, where the federal government forcibly confined Japanese American citizens.

Initially working mainly in New York State, where he had many campus contacts from his days as an organizer for the American Student Union, Rustin exhibited such an affinity for the work that Muste quickly made wider use of his talents. In a summary of activities that he wrote in September 1942, Rustin reported that, since the spring, he had traveled to twenty states, logged over 10,000 miles, spoken to more than 5,000 people, visited eight CPS camps, attended ten denominational conferences for high school students, lectured on seventeen college campuses, and conducted classes on nonviolence at the summer camps of four historic peace churches. A work log composed three months later showed no sign of a slower pace: 7,000 miles across twenty-four states, including a visit to the Manzanar Japanese concentration camp in the southern California desert and speeches to Rotary and Kiwanis clubs, courtesy of well-placed FOR members. He counseled numerous young men on the decision to become a conscientious objector and especially made contacts "among Negro groups, attempting to create an interest in non-violent direct action."[11]

Though ostensibly preaching the message of pacifism, Rustin inevitably encountered the harsh landscape of the nation's racial mores in his travels. In the South, segregation was maintained with all the force of state power. But in the North and West, too, racial discrimination remained common practice, pernicious in the unpredictability of its appearance. On one swing through the Midwest, Rustin visited the barber shop at the University of Chicago, only to be denied a haircut; meetings with school administrators and the threat of a student boycott soon led to a change in practice. In a small midwestern college town, he sought lunch at a local diner. After the waitress persistently ignored him, Rustin engaged her and the manager in a conversation about the reasons. Having eliminated the plausibility of every argument except the loss of business, he proposed an experiment: serve him at the counter right near the door and see if anyone coming into the restaurant left because of it. When no one did, the manager brought him a fresh hot meal and continued to serve blacks in the future.[12]

Travel in the South posed much greater risk. On a bus trip from Louisville to Nashville in 1942, the price of Gandhian resistance rose dramatically. "I was riding in a bus," he recalled,

> and I was wearing a red necktie—it was hot and I had it open and it was dangling—and as I boarded the bus, a woman was sitting with a child on her lap. And the child, as I was jiggling for my ticket and my tie was flying and my bags were going, the child reached over and grabbed my tie and the mother hit it and said, don't touch a nigger. . . . I had not seen this kind of thing before, so I went in the back and sat down and I began doodling in the back seat by myself, and all of a sudden something began to happen. Next to me was a Negro couple who had a box with chicken in it and having the best time on earth. And I said, how many years are we going to let that child be misled by its mother—that if we sit in the back and are really having fun, then whites in a way have the right to say they like it in the back. . . . I vowed then and there I was never going through the south again without either being arrested or thrown off the bus or protesting.

So Rustin moved to the section reserved for whites, and patiently explained to the driver, who at every stop insisted that he move, that his conscience would not allow him to obey an unjust law. The driver finally called the police, who reached the bus thirteen miles north of Nashville. When Rustin still refused to move, the four officers proceeded to beat him in front of the other passengers. Hustled into the back of the police car, he found himself "shaking with nervous strain" as the police verbally abused him on the way to the station. Once there, the police forced him through a gauntlet. "They tossed me from one to another like a volley-ball," ripping his clothes along the way. Throughout the ordeal, Rustin maintained a Gandhian posture of refusing to fight back physically, attempting to communicate with his assailants, and holding out the religious grounding of his disobedience. Mystified by this strange behavior, the police captain told him, "Nigger, you're supposed to be scared when you come in here!" and left muttering, "I believe the nigger's crazy." In the end, Rustin emerged "considerably rumpled" but with some small victories. A few of the white passengers were moved enough to urge the police to desist from beating him, and one took the trouble of coming to the police station to speak up on his behalf. Meanwhile, Ben West, the assistant district attorney who interviewed Rustin at the station, released him without pressing charges, addressing him as "Mister."[13] Stories such as this, as well as other tales of his exploits, circulated quickly among white pacifists and stirred the imagination of this beleaguered community. "He had almost unbelievable courage," recalled Ernest Bromley, an FOR member in North Carolina.[14]

In the course of his wartime travels, Rustin made an indelible mark virtually everywhere he went. A couple with whom he stayed in Bismarck, North Dakota, wrote to the office that he was "one of the finest spirits it has been our pleasure to know. . . . He made a profound impression." Margaret Rohrer, who met him when he passed through Colorado, recalled that "he had such charisma that you cannot imagine . . . we were enchanted by him." Steve Cary, a lifelong activist with the AFSC, thought he had "an electrifying presence." Ernest Bromley remembered "his way of speaking, his gestures, his tone of voice and inflection, his whole bearing." Caleb Foote was always keen to have Rustin come to California because "he was a huge hit, he was always a huge hit."[15]

Electric. Charismatic. Prophetic. Magnetic. The words occur again and again as his associates recalled those early encounters with him. To Larry Gara, a young pacifist who later did jail time with Rustin, he was "one of the more dynamic pacifist speakers. He was very very charismatic, his personality was just electric." Shizu Asahi, a secretary in the New York office, recalled how, one evening, he "magnetized and charmed" an audience at Union Theological Seminary. Homer Jack, who in the course of a long career met leading Gandhians in Asia, Africa, and Europe, thought Rustin was "a prophetic type, even within the peace movement." Helen Winnemore, a Quaker activist in Columbus, Ohio, saw him as "charismatic . . . a kind of person who was the embodiment of something." Glenn Smiley remembered him as "a sensation. . . . There was a magic about Bayard. . . . He sang like an angel."

Smiley, who later served as a confidant to Martin Luther King, Jr., said of Rustin, "He was my guru and I learned practically everything that I knew at that time of importance about nonviolence from Bayard. . . . I would never have had the courage to have started . . . without the impetus that Bayard gave me."[16]

Vivid in the memory of all who knew the young Gandhian pacifist was Rustin's singing. His musical talents enlivened pacifist conferences. He could take a pliant group of young activists and meld them into a harmonious choir with an afternoon of rehearsals. He often moved gracefully from speech to song and back again, and he used this ability to great effect. Doris Grotewohl described it as "a beautiful singing voice. He could calm an audience. It was a quiet listening when you heard Bayard sing. Just spell-binding." He had at his disposal a raft of Elizabethan ballads, which he performed in more intimate gatherings, but in his lectures and workshops he most often sang Negro spirituals. Emily Morgan came with him to a speaking engagement in Brooklyn one time during the war. "At the end—most memorably!—Bayard sung from the top of the church balcony in his high tenor voice 'Sometimes I Feel Like a Motherless Child.' Hearing that lone voice out of the darkness was so poignant." To stalwarts in the peace movement, it became over time his signature song, provoking those who knew his family history to wonder, as Morgan did, "if Bayard might be as lonely as he sounded."[17]

Rustin also displayed an attachment to principle within the precincts of the peace movement itself. He confronted not only the oppressor on the outside but also the waffler on the inside. When word reached him on the road that his Quaker meeting in Manhattan was considering a proposal to provide hospitality and services to American military personnel, he fired back a firm response: "The primary social function of a religious society is to 'speak the truth to power.' The truth is that war is wrong. It is then our duty to make war impossible first in us and then in society. To cooperate with the government in building morale seems inconsistent with all we profess to believe. . . . The greatest service that we can render the men in the armed forces is to maintain our peace testimony."[18] At other times, Rustin exhibited the ferocity of Jesus driving the money changers from the temple. On the same tour that saw his arrest and beating by Nashville police, he visited conscientious objectors (COs) in a number of CPS camps. The product of a carefully crafted compromise between the federal government, peace movement organizations, and historic peace churches, such as the Mennonites and Quakers, CPS was intended to avoid the disastrous situation of World War I when COs found themselves jailed and physically brutalized. This time, the government allowed religious objectors to be assigned to work camps run by the churches. But as CPS was implemented in 1941 and 1942, its flaws became apparent. To Roy Finch, a college radical of the 1930s who later worked at the War Resisters League, it became a matter of "the iron fist of the selective service in the velvet glove of the Quakers." The work was often meaningless. The men labored without pay and hence had to finance their own stays; the families of COs without financial means were left to fend for themselves; and protests against conditions were suppressed. Listening to the testimony of the men and observing their living and working conditions aroused Rustin's indignation. He reported back to the office the desperate need for a "pacifist emergency fund." COs were in need of clothing, and in one camp the men did not have enough to eat. "How much longer," he demanded to know, "are we going to take care of these needs on a fumbling charity basis?"[19]

When he traveled into the South and realized that the church-run camps were racially segregated, he became enraged. Soon he was counseling men in the camps to follow their moral intuition and refuse to cooperate with the system. He sharply criticized CPS in his talks to Southern FOR chapters. He ruffled the sensibilities of an older generation who, remembering the much worse conditions of the previous war, were loathe to scuttle the fragile new system. While Rustin's stand appealed to many younger pacifists who faced the draft, it left Muste having to compose diplomatic responses to letters of complaint, even as he assured his fiery protégé that FOR policy was one of "intransigent opposition to racial discrimination."[20]

The tensions that sometimes surfaced as a result of Rustin's militancy were not primarily a conflict between one youthful firebrand and the FOR's old-timers. Rustin's views reflected the strategic redirection that

Muste wished to implement and that staff like Houser, Farmer, and Smiley supported. The differences were stark and had major implications for what it would mean to be a pacifist in mid-twentieth-century America. Where pacifism in the FOR had once been a message to preach, Rustin, Muste, and their comrades understood nonviolence as a path toward action. Where the Christian pacifists of the FOR sought to end war, Rustin wished to eliminate injustice. The religious pacifists of the previous generation drew their inspiration from the teachings of a man who lived two millennia earlier, in a world that was long dead. The new breed of pacifist increasingly turned to the example of Gandhi and the anticolonial movement he had spawned. Rustin was in the vanguard of this new confrontational approach that adapted Gandhian nonviolence to attacking racism in the United States.

World War II brought America's racial wrongs into bold relief. Alongside the declarations of the Atlantic Charter and political rhetoric deploring Nazi ideology stood a military whose branches either segregated or barred African Americans, a private sector economy that kept most blacks in menial jobs, and a region where disenfranchisement, segregation, and systemic violence mocked American claims about freedom and democracy. Put these conditions in the face of a young staff at the FOR, and the pull toward racial justice became irresistible.

As the two black field secretaries on staff, Rustin and Jim Farmer were especially attuned to the strategic opportunities at hand. In a memo written near the end of 1942, Rustin reported that "my recent experience indicates that we shall have less and less opportunity to present the direct pacifist message in school, church, and club. However, these institutions are quite open to the presentation of non-violence as a solution to internal and domestic problems." He described meetings in the course of his travels "with local Negro and Jewish leadership, representatives of the AFSC and with FOR people to discuss the use of nonviolence in facing the almost universal rise of racial tension between negro and white, Jew and Gentile." Where peace as a theme went nowhere, racial and religious reconciliation through nonviolence stimulated the formation of action committees almost everywhere he went. Farmer wrote in a similar vein. "By and large," he reported, "the pacifists with whom I have come in contact feel that in the light of present international and domestic circumstances, pacifism can make no greater contribution than that which it can make in the interracial field. They are clamoring for an action program."[21]

In urging a shift toward race relations work, Rustin tried to communicate both urgency and optimism. Detailing several examples of successful, even if modest, nonviolent campaigns, he portrayed a nation facing the emotional stresses of war, of blacks functioning as scapegoats for white grievances, and of an oppressed people deeply disillusioned with national policy, searching for new methods and leaders. "Today," he argued,

> wildcat strikes where white workers resent negroes, violent anti-negro outbursts by southern politicians, an unwise negro press advocating economic and political justice now with or without violence and general economic depression have created fear and increased tension. . . . There is a growing feeling that the negro must solve his own problem. Black nationalism is rampant. . . . Negroes have generally lost faith in the "pink tea social methods" which I have heard described as "well meanin' but gettin' us nowhere." . . . I have heard many say they might as well die right here fighting for their rights as to die abroad for other people's. It is common to hear outright joy expressed at a Japanese military victory. Thousands of negroes look upon successes of any colored people anywhere as their success. As one negro student said, "It is now a question of breaking down white domination over the whole world or nowhere."

Rustin concluded that "only a spark is needed to create a terrible explosion." Yet he coupled this with the more hopeful message that "no situation in America has created so much interest among negroes as the Gandhian proposals for India's freedom."[22]

As Rustin suggested, Gandhi's work was rousing the imagination not only of white pacifists but also of some within the black community.

For more than two decades, the African American press had paid attention to Gandhi. Daring as he did to challenge the world's greatest imperial power, the brown-skinned hero made an appealing subject of study. He had developed his philosophy of *satyagraha* ("holding to the truth") in South Africa, fighting against the treatment of colored people by the white supremacist government. When he returned to India during World War I, he refined both the spiritual basis of his approach and its practical application in a struggle for independence. As early as 1919, W. E. B. Du Bois, who edited the NAACP magazine, *The Crisis*, was directing the attention of his readers toward India, telling them, "We are all one—we the Despised and Oppressed, the 'niggers' of England and America."[23] By the 1930s, as the Indian independence struggle escalated, Gandhi's way was a regular topic of commentary in black newspapers.

More direct connections were established as a small but steady stream of travelers flowed back and forth between the two countries. Some of Gandhi's disciples came to the United States with the explicit purpose of reaching into the black community with the message of *satyagraha*. Some white American missionaries returned to the United States transformed by their encounter with Gandhi and India. They became tireless proponents of Gandhian nonviolence and racial equality. Black leaders also went to India to observe and learn. In 1935, Howard Thurman, the dean of Rankin Chapel at Howard University, and Sue Bailey Thurman, on the national staff of the YWCA, spent several months there. Returning to the United States, they lectured widely on Gandhi's crusade, especially before black colleges, churches, and clubs. As a divinity student at Howard just a few years later, Farmer came under the influence of Thurman.

Gandhi's articulation of *satyagraha* also infiltrated the American pacifist movement, especially the religious wing represented by the FOR. Richard Gregg, an American Quaker who spent several years in India in the 1920s, published *The Power of Nonviolence* in 1935. A detailed exposition not only of how Gandhi employed nonviolence but also of the philosophy behind it, Gregg's book became an essential primer for Rustin and other young religious-minded pacifists. Gregg himself served on the FOR's national council and worked with the AFSC. Another influential book was *War Without Violence: A Study of Gandhi's Method and Its Accomplishments* (1939) by Krishnalal Shridharani, a graduate student at Columbia who had accompanied Gandhi on the March to the Sea in 1930 as a protest against the British salt tax. His presence on the Morningside Heights campus, just a couple of blocks from the FOR's Broadway office, facilitated an active interchange with Rustin, Farmer, and other FOR staff. Finally, J. Holmes Smith, a Methodist missionary who spent nine years in India, returned to the United States in the late 1930s eager to plant *satyagraha* on North American soil. Serving on the FOR's national council, Smith established in 1940 the Harlem Ashram, an experiment in interracial living and a launching pad for nonviolent direct action campaigns. Farmer and other FOR staff lived there for varying periods of time; Rustin visited often. Activities ranged from a largely symbolic interracial trek from New York to Washington, D.C., to efforts to change employment practices at the YMCA, downtown department stores, and Manhattan restaurants.

With Muste's encouragement, FOR staff intentionally injected Gandhian nonviolence into the struggle for racial justice in the United States. In Chicago, George Houser, fresh out of a year in prison for refusing to register for the draft, organized a series of "cells" to address social justice and nonviolence. One, focused on race discrimination, investigated landlords near the University of Chicago as well as businesses such as barber shops, restaurants, skating rinks, and theaters that barred African Americans. As these experiments developed, Farmer, a member of the original cell, sketched out a plan for a national organization to apply Gandhi's method against racial inequality. Rustin, meanwhile, had become FOR's "one-man nonviolent army" through his single-handed exploits around the country.[24]

In April 1942, at a meeting in Columbus, Ohio, FOR's National Council debated the merits of Farmer's "Brotherhood Mobilization." With Rustin, Houser, and Muste adding support, Farmer outlined the need for "a distinctive and radical approach" to American race relations. He called for a creative use of Gandhi's philosophy, tailored to

American conditions. "Pacifists must serve as its nucleus, its moving force," his proposal argued, yet the movement "cannot be limited to pacifists." The goals were big: "Not to make housing in ghettos more tolerable, but to destroy residential segregation; not to make Jim Crow facilities the equal of others, but to abolish Jim Crow; not to make racial discrimination more bearable, but to wipe it out."[25] Though some older FOR members raised objections about the "conflicts" that nonviolent direct action might provoke, the council pledged resources for a racial justice organization.

The launching of the Congress of Racial Equality (CORE), as the organization was called, was historic. Although African Americans had been resisting racial oppression in nonviolent ways for generations, this marked the debut of an organization—indeed, a movement—for whom active nonviolent resistance was not, in Rustin's words, "just a policy," but instead "a way of life."[26] Consciously dressing themselves in the garb of Gandhian philosophy, the young crusaders at the center of CORE made nonviolence a spiritual road to follow. In the years to come, more and more Americans decided to take this road. CORE's founding also marked a formal commitment by FOR to a racial justice mission. The FOR was announcing to its constituents—and to anyone else who would listen—that peace was more than a matter of relations between governments. It also involved fundamentally the social basis of human relationships, the nature of the ties between peoples and communities. The cruelty, exploitation, and indecency inherent in racial caste systems were as much implicated in violence as were declarations of war and the maneuvers of armies. Over the next two decades, the pacifist movement became a key source of personnel and ideas in the black freedom struggle.

In practical terms, the creation of CORE meant that FOR staff—Rustin, Houser, Farmer, Caleb Foote, and others—could dedicate themselves to race relations. It was a thrilling time for all of them, as they engaged in laboratory-like experiments in the efficacy of nonviolence. "We had, really, very little precedent to go on," Houser reminisced. "We felt we were really plowing new ground. If other experiences had taken place, we had heard about them only from a distance. So, when we got together and planned our strategy of sitting in in a particular restaurant, we felt that this was something that we were doing for the first time." Based in Chicago, Houser almost completely centered his work on local experimentation with Gandhi's methods. Foote, the FOR regional secretary in northern California, effectively redefined his job as building CORE in the San Francisco area. "I could do anything I wanted and AJ would support me," he recalled.[27]

Rustin too found ways to parlay his role as an FOR youth secretary into laboring for racial justice. He was already exhibiting the skills of a gifted movement builder. He could move people with his singing, impress them with his analytical powers, awe them with his courage, inspire with his vision—*and* leave a functioning CORE chapter behind. After Rustin made a month-long visit to northern California, Foote wrote that "all around here in San Francisco are the results of what you have done. . . . The CORE group is doing very well." According to Hope Foote, Rustin started them working on restrictive housing covenants, which were commonplace in wartime San Francisco, and on segregated bowling alleys and restaurants. Rustin was "very effective," she recalled. "He had tremendous vitality, and conviction, which was contagious." Little wonder, as Caleb Foote wrote to Rustin a few months later, that he made "converts" among some of the black shipyard workers who had attended his workshops. To one of them, Foote reported, "You are for him what the Bible is for a fundamentalist." Similarly, on a trip to the University of Colorado, Rustin trained students how to conduct nonviolent sit-ins and left behind an animated CORE chapter. One of his pupils, Margaret Rohrer, was so impressed with him that she decided she "wanted to work for the FOR. I met him and had another meeting and that's when I decided to work there."[28]

Rustin neither sugarcoated nor romanticized nonviolence as a means of striking at American racism. "To act with true non-violence in the face of terrific conflict such as race riots demands a great deal of discipline," he told one audience. "Non-violence will be a difficult message to give the Negro people." The required discipline came not by talking about it but "by doing . . . by gradually building it up through the performance of little actions." Nonviolence was not an escape from conflict, he told audiences. He could be witheringly critical of those who embraced it as a passive form of disengaged spirituality. He derided individuals like the philosopher Gerald Heard and the British novelist Aldous Huxley for aiming at "perfection, at perfect love which is a kind of automatic force." Emily Morgan remembered once saying in Rustin's presence, when she was still a "greenhorn" FOR staffer in Chicago, "something about LOVE being the way to go—the key thing in peace making. EEK!! Can't you just *hear* Bayard's fiery explosions?!! He shouted (screamed!) *Love* is *not enough!*" No, argued Rustin. "You *will*," he told one group, "act in certain situations because you are forced to act when confronted with social issues. Furthermore, you must confront others with social issues. . . . Nor must we stop with social issues. We must raise political issues more than we do. In the past nonviolence has been too close to non-resistance with its fear of action."[29]

As Rustin moved about the country, word of this young Negro began to travel beyond the groups he met face to face. In Washington, D.C., Pauli Murray was a student at Howard University in the early 1940s when, she recalled, "nobody had ever really seriously studied non-violent direct action in terms of group participation. But there were people like Bayard Rustin, and James Farmer, who was [*sic*] doing that same thing that I was doing, and I was reading things about Bayard Rustin and he inspired me. . . . And so I began to experiment with nonviolence." With other Howard students, Murray began using the "stool-sitting technique" at restaurants in black neighborhoods that served only whites. Emboldened by some successes, the students then turned their attention to downtown restaurants with the aid of the campus NAACP chapter.[30]

WHILE CORE CHAPTERS were serving as laboratory settings to test Gandhian techniques, an opportunity emerged within the black community to reach a much larger working-class constituency. At the end of 1942, A. Philip Randolph announced that his March on Washington Movement (MOWM) would convene a national conference to explore nonviolent civil disobedience as a means of striking at Jim Crow. As Pauline Myers, one of his deputies, explained, "If the national conference adopts this method the Negro people will be called upon to boycott trains, street cars, buses, restaurants, waiting rooms, rest rooms, hotels, schools and institutions that have jim crow laws. . . . The aim is to harness the flow of rising resentment and indignation on the part of Negro Americans that has become intensified due to the war."[31] Randolph's announcement electrified the Gandhian enthusiasts in the FOR. Muste told the staff it was "as epoch-making as the launching in 1906 of Gandhi's own campaign in South Africa." J. Holmes Smith, who ran the Harlem Ashram, saw it as a "sensational development." It portended, he thought, "thrilling opportunities" to spread Gandhian revolutionary resistance.[32]

The excitement among pacifists was readily understandable, since Randolph enjoyed an eminence that no other black leader could claim. Born in 1889 and raised in Florida, he had come to New York City in 1911 with hope for a career on the stage. But socialism soon claimed him, and he turned his life toward leftist politics. He edited the *Messenger*, a labor magazine; ran for public office; and developed a reputation in Harlem as a great soapbox orator. One who heard him recalled that Randolph "just seemed to carry the young people in his palms." In the mid-1920s, he was invited by some Pullman porters to help them organize a union, and he devoted himself to the task. In 1935, the Brotherhood of Sleeping Car Porters won a federally supervised election to represent the porters, and two years later Randolph successfully negotiated a contract. He remained head of the Brotherhood until his retirement.[33]

Early in 1941, Randolph called for a march on Washington to protest Jim Crow in the military and racial discrimination in defense employment. It was a gutsy move. Not only did it inject racial discord into issues of national defense, but it risked a large public failure since no comparable national mobilization had ever occurred before. Organizations like the NAACP and the Urban League at first distanced themselves from the proposal. Their wariness had little to do with disagreement about goals, since leaders of both organizations were sharply critical of government policy. Instead, they worried about the capacity to control a large crowd, feared the backlash it might provoke, and disapproved of

Randolph's intention to make the march a black-only mobilization. To middle-class organizations committed to interracialism, an all-Negro march of the masses spelled trouble.

Although both organizations eventually lent support, their caution meant that when Randolph's bravado bore fruit, he won the plaudits. The prospect of a march so distressed Franklin Roosevelt that after failing to persuade Randolph to cancel the event, he issued an executive order establishing the Fair Employment Practices Committee and prohibiting job discrimination not only in the federal government but in defense industries as well. Having achieved a significant part of what he sought, Randolph then proved willing to call the march off. While some were displeased—the youth division of the organization, in which Rustin had been active, condemned Randolph's decision—the whole episode made him the man of the hour. The editorial in the *Amsterdam News*, a paper serving New York's African American community, was not unusual. "The rise of A. Philip Randolph to a new and loftier position in the affairs of the race," it commented, "appears to presage the passing of the leadership that has controlled the Negro's destiny for the past 25 years. . . . Randolph, courageous champion of the rights of his people, takes the helm as the nation's No. 1 Negro. . . . Already he is being ranked along with the great Frederick Douglass. His name is rapidly becoming a household word."[34]

Randolph's stature was so confounding to the NAACP and so exhilarating to a Gandhian activist like Rustin because his message was so radical. Whereas the NAACP and the Urban League focused single-mindedly on racial inequality, Randolph wore socialism on his sleeve. His reservations about World War II set race within a context of global imperialism. "Unless this war," he told members of the March on Washington organization, "sounds the death knell to the old Anglo-American empire . . . it will have been fought in vain. . . . This system grew fat and waxed powerful off the flesh, blood, sweat and tears of the tireless toilers of the human race and the sons and daughters of color in the underdeveloped lands of the world. When this war ends, the people want . . . the dispersal of equality and power among the citizen-workers in an economic democracy." At the height of the war, at a concert in his

honor at Carnegie Hall in New York City, he lavished praise on the socialist movement. "Socialism," he said, "armed me with breadth and
depth of understanding. . . . It caused me to look to the economic foundations of the question of race and color." Socialism allowed him "to
spot the multiform, illusive, protective colorations of totalitarian movements. . . . It has helped me to discern and evaluate the political oppor-
tunism of the two major capitalist parties, Republican and Democrat."
For Randolph "only a peace, without imperialism, will be a just peace
that will endure."[35] His sentiments meshed nicely with the views of
anti-Stalinist radicals like Muste and Rustin.

Although Randolph had cancelled the march, he kept a skeletal
MOWM organization in place. In the summer of 1942, he used it to
hold a series of monster-sized rallies in New York, Chicago, and St.
Louis. J. Holmes Smith, who attended the Madison Square Garden
event, reported back that several of the speakers quoted Gandhi as a
champion of racial justice.[36] When Randolph made his announcement
about investigating nonviolent civil disobedience, Muste jumped at the
opportunity and offered to help. Randolph asked for the services of
Rustin and Farmer, and Rustin was eager to comply. In February, he attended a conference in Ohio on black political strategies, at which Randolph was a featured speaker. He excitedly wrote to Muste that "there
was absolute distrust of this war and, indeed, voiced distrust with war as
a means to freedom. . . . Randolph really 'hit the gong.' . . . [He] spoke
in a way that convinced me that he is really concerned to develop an
understanding and use of non-violence by the American Negro. *After
the statements he made here he is committed to follow thru or to face political
suicide.* I feel very much better about the whole situation now. I talked
with him and he is anxious to have us (Jim and me) work with him." At
Muste's behest, the executive committee of the FOR approved release
time for both men. Randolph was pleased. "We are making a great drive
among Negro ministers to win them over to the philosophy of nonviolent solutions," he wrote to Muste. He needed Rustin's and Farmer's
help because "we have quite some opposition from various forces . . .
certain sections of the Negro press, the Negro church, and politicians,
as well as communists."[37]

Rustin was now wearing three hats: FOR staffer, CORE trainer, and organizer for the MOWM. Each role gave him access to a different audience: the middle-class white congregants presided over by ministers affiliated with the FOR, eager young college students invigorated by the action component of CORE, and working-class African American congregations roused by the MOWM. Yet the lines were not always so sharply drawn. White and black ministers would sometimes bring their church members together for joint events, while young turks on the FOR staff, like Foote in San Francisco, could bring a mixed-class, interracial group together through CORE. The work forced Rustin to learn quickly how to communicate to a wide range of Americans and how to fit his message to the audience at hand.

The intensity of it all appealed to Rustin but nothing more so than the opportunities provided by the all-black MOWM. "That work," he reminisced near the end of his life, "was one of the most important things that I ever did." Coming into a new town, learning to use networks of local people, and having to make appeals for money so he could make it to the next town "prepared me for many of the other activities that I was to engage in over the years," he recalled. By the spring, the racial justice work with Randolph was taking so much of his time that Muste was running interference for him, mollifying FOR chapters annoyed that Rustin was canceling speaking commitments he had made earlier. The tension between the demands of a pacifist organization and the appeal of racial justice work would recur many times in the years ahead. [38]

In July 1943, Rustin, Farmer, and Smith attended a giant national convention of the MOWM in Chicago. The theme, "We Are Americans Too," spoke to the resentments and dissatisfactions simmering in the African American community. Smith wrote to Muste a long, animated description of the conference, whose sessions sometimes drew as many as 2,000 and exhibited a strong "proletarian flavor." Randolph, he reported enthusiastically, "sounded the first note for non-violent good will direct action" in his opening speech. The next night, when Rustin had the floor, he "spoke most effectively on it, climaxing with a deep and searching note, asking us to bow our heads and breaking out with

'It's me, O Lord, standin' in the need o' prayer.'" Rustin detailed the range of tactics encompassed by nonviolence, including refusing to obey Jim Crow laws in the South as well as defying the federal government. He provided the audience with concrete examples by using, as Smith reported, "instances from his own experience in the third person, very effectively done." After three days of meeting, the attendees made "the historic decision to adopt NVDA [nonviolent direct action] as a major method and strategy."[39]

Comparing notes at the end, Smith and Rustin were both enthusiastic. About Randolph, Smith waxed eloquent: "I regard him as a very great man, one who compares favorably with any I have met in East or West. . . . One could easily see why he inspires so much love and confidence among his many followers." Smith told Muste that "there was something about the conference all the way through that was spiritually impressive, and the sense of a historic decision in which the Divine Hand was at work."[40] The only sour note involved Farmer's performance. He disappeared for the last two days, just when the debate about adopting a program of civil disobedience took place. "We are not gossiping," Smith told Muste, "but we do feel the need of a very frank and reconciliatory conference about his attitude toward MOWM."[41]

Farmer's behavior affected how FOR's racial justice work, including its relationship to Randolph, developed. In September, at Muste's urging, Swomley presented to the National Council a plan to set up a race relations department in the FOR. Farmer already had the title of racial relations secretary; now, Swomley was proposing that Rustin assume a similar role. That same month, Muste and Rustin—without Farmer—met with Randolph and the executive committee of the MOWM. Randolph, who had watched Rustin's work mature since their first meeting early in 1941, asked for even more extensive use of his services. He particularly wanted help in conceiving and launching an action program against racial discrimination in the armed forces. The difficulties were obvious. Challenging the military in wartime was akin to treason, and it was not typically within the mission of a pacifist group to work for reform of a military organization. Muste agreed to apportion half of Rustin's time to Randolph, while assuring his own organization that it was "necessary to combat the evil of racism wherever it manifests it-self."[42]

As Rustin's stock rose, his relationship with Farmer grew strained. In the course of long careers in the civil rights movement, their paths would cross again and again. To his credit, Farmer often came to Rustin's defense, supporting his leadership in the movement when others thought him too controversial, a danger to the movement's good reputation. But these years at the FOR, when CORE was in its infancy, clearly rankled Farmer, as the account in his memoir makes clear. There, long after the fact, he attributed his difficulties to the different priorities he and Muste had: "Peace was number one for him, whereas for me the top priority was racial equality." He accused Rustin of succumbing to a "divide and conquer" strategy in which Muste played the two black staff members against one another, "with Bayard siding with him on every issue that divides us." Farmer claimed that Muste was intent on clipping his wings.[43]

But there were problems with Farmer's performance. Early on, it had become apparent that, as one report phrased it, "his long suit is not primarily organizational work." Muste saw to it that he was paired with others, typically Houser or Rustin, "who will carry the ball." Houser, who had worked with Farmer in Chicago and continued to have close dealings with him after Farmer moved to New York, was clear about Farmer's limitations. "A great platform speaker," Houser recalled, "a very good front man. Not a good administrator. Not a good organizer. A little sloppy on follow through. . . . He did what he did magnificently. But he was not the organizer." Swomley, who supervised Farmer, remembered that he would often leave on speaking tours and simply not show up at his expected destination, much to the organization's embarrassment. Eventually, his behavior left Muste with little choice but to terminate him.[44]

Yet Farmer intuited correctly something in the dynamic between him and Rustin. As the only two black staff members in an organization whose constituency was historically white, it was inevitable that others would compare them. Half a century later, pacifists who knew them in the 1940s spontaneously linked them without any prompting. Rustin was older and more worldly, "more mysterious," according to Homer Jack. "More flexible," in Swomley's memory. Shizu Asahi remembered Rustin as "much more personal" than Farmer. Rustin "just lit up everything," she recalled, "because he was really charming. . . . You sort of felt a kinship toward him, and you immediately felt close to him, whereas Jim was rather remote." Glenn Smiley volunteered that they "didn't get along. . . . In a sense they were in competitive positions, and the greatest competition was for the affection of AJ." In Smiley's words, "Bayard won."[45]

WINNING THE CONTEST for Muste's affection was a high-stakes game since he dominated the daily life of the FOR. Among the true believers, as most staff and members were, he inspired awe. He was, as Marion Bromley put it, "the figure that just about everybody acknowledged as the leader."[46]

Muste seemed to work constantly. He kept up a prodigious correspondence. He commonly dictated a dozen or more several-page letters a day; when he was on the road, he composed equally long letters in a hurried scrawl. He made his way through a sheaf of newspapers each morning, and clipped articles that he thought would be useful— for his "Nonviolence Wins Again" files, as Rustin jokingly referred to them. On days when he was in the office, he convened the staff at noon for a period of prayer, meditation, and, over brown-bag lunches, freewheeling discussions about the issues in front of them. "It was kind of amusing," Marion Bromley remembered. "AJ would let the discussion go on. And he would be sitting there and not saying anything. Then finally he would come out and he would sum up what one group had said. He would say 'there's this and this and this.' And then he'd say 'And on the other hand' and he would give his own position. . . . It just obliterated the opposition."[47]

Very early on, Rustin and Muste formed a special bond. Everyone noticed it. Some staff explained it through the two men's shared history with the American left. In the genteel world of religious pacifism, the experience of having been a Communist, of whatever sectarian persuasion, set Muste and Rustin apart. Each had encountered the cutthroat factionalism, the dogmatic obsession with the correct path, the secret maneuvering to outflank not the capitalist but one's fellow leftist. More important perhaps, their understandings of politics and economics—of capitalism, class, the role of the state in sustaining inequality, the importance of mass mobilizations to effect change—still came through a Marxist filter.

But there was something more. Houser, who worked alongside them for years thought that "AJ provided a father image for Bayard because he never really had a father. . . . AJ had a special feeling for Bayard." More than with other staff, Muste took Rustin under his wing and mentored him. Toward Muste, Rustin often behaved like a dutiful son, accepting advice and following directions. "They had a good understanding. If AJ didn't want Bayard to do something, I suppose there may have been times when he didn't go along with AJ. But they would have been few and far between." Like a father coaching his son for the big game, AJ was capable of impatient scolding. When Rustin's health remained shaky a few weeks after a tonsillectomy, Muste wrote to him: "Watch your health. That includes your sleep! You are desperately needed, and it is the responsibility of all of us at this critical time to discipline ourselves and to keep 100% fit."[48]

Much of the New York staff found themselves irresistibly drawn to Rustin. Just as he had dazzled pacifists coast to coast in his first two years with the FOR, Rustin made a profound impression on his fellow workers in the office at 2929 Broadway in Manhattan. Doris Grotewohl remembered that "he activated, he energized the office." For Shizu Asahi, Rustin's presence was "a great treat. . . . He was so nice and so loving and had such a nice spirit about him. . . . We were all so nose-to-the-grindstone kind of people and Bayard came and injected a little sense of fun into life." Margie Rohrer recalled the way the staff gathered around him after one of his road trips. "He would be telling the exciting things that had happened. Some of us were even sitting on the floor. And I can see him sitting on the floor. And he'd just kind of, when he finished talking, he would just lean back and sing. In this gorgeous voice." Thinking back upon those days, Dorothy Hassler searched for the right word to capture what Rustin projected: "So much—elan is the only word I can think of."[49]

Rustin seemed especially to bond with the women. In the gendered world of the FOR, with rare exception female staff worked as secretaries or stenographers, while the young wives of male staff volunteered around the office, pitching in as needed. They were at the bottom of the pecking order, their labor keeping the wheels of the FOR turning while they collected none of the glory. Rustin treated them differently. "We lowly secretaries," Asahi commented, "we were nothing. But Bayard never made us feel that way. Everybody was a person of importance."[50]

Each of these comments—and many others like them—depicts Rustin as the man everyone loved to love. The portrait is not concocted. Many of these peace warriors had only sporadic contact with Rustin in the decades after the 1940s; the later encounters were often fraught with tension because of a perceived parting of the ways. Recalling the memory of him fifty years earlier evoked forgotten feelings of affection, respect, even joy. Yet their uncomplicated words of praise smooth the edges of a set of relationships that *had* to have been more jagged.

Now and then, a man more enigmatic in his construction of self, more complex in his bonds to others, emerges. Roy Finch, who first met Rustin in New York during these years, came closest to capturing an unacknowledged dynamic between Rustin and the others. "I found Bayard absolutely fascinating," he reflected. "I thought of him as a four-way outsider. First of all he was black. But, he was a strange black in a way because all of his friends were white and he moved in white circles. And secondly he was a Quaker by birth and a person who had been a pacifist all his life, and that was in his bones. Thirdly he was gay. This was something that got him into a lot of trouble in many ways. Fourthly, he was really an artist. He had a very artistic temperament."[51] There was more that Finch could have added: that Rustin was one of the few pacifists who had once laid claim to a revolutionary Communist identity, that he was the illegitimate child of a working-class teenager, and that his social background and educational attainments diverged markedly from associates who came, many of them, from prosperous families with Ivy League educations and Yankee pedigrees. Rustin, in short, was different, and dramatically so. For the most part, the forms of difference he embodied were markers of inferiority. Race, class, sexual desires, political philosophy—each separated him from a world of status, prestige, power, acceptance. Yet at least in the minds of Gandhian activists, some of these characteristics could be inverted to confer stature.

In ways both innocent and invidious, Rustin's associates exoticized him. But they did it with his cooperation and encouragement. Rustin played on their fascination with his differences. He engaged in an elaborate set of ruses, parlaying their distance from his world of origin into opportunity. He made himself "mysterious," as Homer Jack put it. He passed. Certainly not for white, or even as heterosexual, but nonetheless as someone other than he was. As he did so, he re-created himself as someone new, someone who reached beyond the constraints that society imposed.

Nowhere was this clearer than through the stories that circulated about his origins. The assumption was widespread, even among those who claimed to know him well, that he had antecedents in the West Indies. Grotewohl believed he was born in Barbados; Glenn Smiley thought Julia, his grandmother, hailed from the Caribbean. Certainly Rustin's style of speech contributed to this perception. Clipped and with a hint of the haughty to it, to the untrained ears of white Americans it suggested the British Commonwealth. Since none of these Christian pacifists had much familiarity with Afro-Caribbean culture, it was easy to assume that the speech told something of his origins. Rustin apparently did nothing to disabuse his colleagues of this notion. In fact, John Swomley claimed that Rustin actively fostered the illusion.[52]

Education, too, became an arena in which the truth was bent. Who will ever know whether a newspaper report that had him studying for his master's degree in education represented a journalist's error or his subject's exaggeration? Or what the source was of later stories that he studied at the London School of Economics? What we do know, however, is that Rustin worked among individuals with an elite education.

Houser had gone to Union Theological Seminary and the University of Chicago. Roy Finch and David Dellinger were Yale alumni. Caleb Foote had degrees from Harvard and Columbia. Farmer, whose father was a college professor, had grown up on the campuses of historically black colleges and graduated from Howard. Privilege was in the background of everyone except Rustin who, in working at bare subsistence wages at the FOR, was holding down his first steady job.

As Rustin masqueraded as someone more exotic, more accomplished than he was, he used what he did have, his artistic leanings, to open new worlds for some of these earnest young pacifists. He arranged trips to see Paul Robeson in *Othello* and outings to watch Pearl Primus dance. On many evenings, he traveled by subway with his officemates to Greenwich Village, where they visited clubs and cabarets like Café Society Downtown. Still known by the owner and many of the regulars, Rustin moved with easy assurance in this racially mixed hip milieu, so starkly different from the dourly serious environment of the FOR.

Adding to his allure, magnifying and complicating it, was the sexual energy that Rustin projected and that others projected on to him. He possessed an undeniable youthful handsomeness in these years. Tall, lean, and muscular, with a smooth, brown complexion, he exuded the physical grace of the star athlete he once was. The women on staff noticed it and loved him; many of the men noticed it too, and it made them uncomfortable. In a movement infused with religious principles, inspired by an Indian ascetic who spent half a lifetime stifling his erotic impulses, sexuality was unlikely to be a simple matter of attraction. In Rustin's case, racial difference and gender preferences made the issue especially charged. However sincere their commitment to social justice, the white staff members of the FOR were not immune to three centuries of mythology about the sexual nature of African men. And what were they to do about a man whose interests pointed both across the color line and toward other men?

Rustin's appeal to women was undeniable. Margie Rohrer remembered her first response on meeting him: "He was the most beautiful guy." George Houser chuckled as he recalled how "some women got a real crush on Bayard." Asahi declared outright, "We were all in love with him." Fifty years after her initial encounter with Rustin, Dorothy Hassler's first words of recollection were "handsome, beautifully handsome." Grotewohl said of him: "a good looking man and a good dancer." Half a century and a long marriage later, Grotewohl mused that "I don't know how it happened that I was involved in so many social things with him." But others knew. Davis Platt, who became Rustin's boyfriend in 1943, said "Doris was in love with him. . . . She would have given her life for him." Hassler recalled, almost incredulously in the light of retrospective knowledge, that "they used to date. Literally date. They used to go out. We sort of thought of them as a couple, notwithstanding Bayard's commitments to other things." Asahi also remembered an affair Rustin had with a young dancer from the Martha Graham company. "She was a very beautiful young woman. . . . And it didn't work out. And both of them, or she, decided it was not a good thing for her."[53] Without any surviving commentary from Rustin himself, it is difficult to know whether the sexual energy between him and some of these young women in his work environment was real or imagined, mutual or unrequited.

By contrast, Rustin's attraction to men, particularly young white men entering adulthood, was already pronounced. When and how this initially came to the attention of Muste and other staffers is unclear. Did Rustin drop subtle clues, as some gay men of that generation, seeking to breach the walls of discretion, might have done? Did his close relationship with Muste impel him to go to the older man in search of spiritual guidance? Or did rumors make their way to the office, as they had about heterosexual liaisons, creating around Rustin yet another source of fascination, distance, and attraction? This much is certain: at least by the fall of 1943, two years after he began working at the FOR, Rustin's homosexuality entered the Christian peace movement in the form of Davis Platt, his lover.

Rustin met Platt in June 1943 at a conference at Bryn Mawr College where Rustin was a featured speaker. At the time, Platt was approaching his twentieth birthday, raised in extremely comfortable economic circumstances. He had left high school two years earlier, partly out of boredom, partly to achieve some independence from his family, but had finished his studies at night and was planning to start college in the fall. His family lived in Paoli, Pennsylvania, a few miles from Bryn Mawr and not much farther from Rustin's home town of West Chester.

Living on his own in Philadelphia gave Platt the opportunity to search for what he could find of a gay world. As with other young men of his generation and class, the exploration was not easy. "I was terrified my family would discover this," he recalled. "I was sure they couldn't accept it. I'd never heard a good thing about gay people from anybody. I had haunted the sordid bookstores of central Philadelphia in those days. I got all the books I could that would deal with sexuality. I read Krafft-Ebing. That doesn't help. Not at all. . . . In those days it was very hard to see how you could have integrity and be gay."[54] Platt broke with his family in other ways as well. His paternal grandparents had owned a large rice plantation near Charleston before the Civil War and had relocated to the North afterward. From his father he heard "the aristocratic point of view about 'darkies,' as he called them: they were children, they could be educated up to a point, they were not bad people, but had inferior genetic stock." Before long Platt had hooked up with Quakers in the area, participated in their service projects, and attended local events sponsored by the AFSC.

Although Platt had been having sex with men for years, Rustin was his first serious relationship and the one he still, decades later, most cherished. His memory of their first encounter, at Bryn Mawr College, remained vivid:

The moment our eyes met it was electric. Maybe I fooled myself, but I think he really fell for me. And I certainly fell for him. Just like that. . . . Yes, I remember the room. It was filled with people and Bayard strode in. He made an entrance. And he was so full of life. So full of what I took to be self-confidence, self-love, charm. He was a charmer. . . . In the course of the first afternoon, we took a walk on the campus, and sat under a tree, and talked about God knows what. I think it was perfectly clear to both of us that we were both gay and we were open about it [to each other]. We talked about sex, sexuality, and our attraction to each other. . . .

Bayard visited me that night in my room. He was not afraid to
come. We had sex. It was fabulous.

Completely enamored, Platt approached his godmother, who lived
close to the campus, and asked whether he and a new friend could
spend the night, which they did.

Rustin was immediately on the road again, heading toward Chicago
for Randolph's March on Washington Movement conference. But he
and Platt began exchanging love letters, and the two arranged to meet
a second time. The relationship provoked Platt to make an important
decision. He was just that summer having to pick among Harvard, Yale,
and Columbia; learning that Rustin's office was across the street from
Columbia settled the matter. "It wasn't hard to choose," he recalled. In
September, when it came time to move, Platt's father brought the
whole family to New York for a holiday. Two nights into the trip, Platt
excused himself. Leaving his family at the Vanderbilt Hotel, he rushed
to his lover, who had arranged for them to spend some nights at the
home of Wallace and Franny Lee, close friends of his.

Ensconced on the Columbia campus, the love-besotted Platt popped
into the FOR offices regularly, whenever Rustin was in town. Because
he was young and eager and already leaning toward a Quaker view of
war and social justice, he was made to feel welcome, and soon was
comfortable appearing there regardless of Rustin's presence. He got
to know the FOR staff and socialized with them in the evenings. If
Rustin's inclination toward men was unclear to his workmates before
this, Platt's continuing presence made it plain to many of them. Once,
at an FOR party, after Platt asked Margie Rohrer to dance, Grotewohl
took her aside and told her not to get too involved. The warning was
timely since Rohrer remembered thinking that Platt was "as beautiful
in his blond beauty as Bayard was in his dark."[55]

Accepted as he was by the FOR family, Platt nonetheless recalled
ambivalence from Muste. Muste was kind and generous in his atten-
tions to someone who had attached himself to Rustin. But he also expressed to Platt his reservations about the relationship. "Muste knew
we were lovers," Platt said. "He tried to get me to desist, to leave Ba-

yard and try to get Bayard to give it up. . . . He tried to give me the impression that it was an unsatisfactory lifestyle that wouldn't work. It wasn't that it was wrong or evil, but it was not viable and if Bayard continued this way it could destroy him and hurt the movement." Young and inexperienced, Platt could say little to counter what Muste was telling him. But he did recall that, by contrast, "Bayard never promised [Muste] that he would give up homosexuality, or give me up. He would be careful. That's my recollection." Still coming to terms with a sexuality at odds with social norms, Platt was awed by what he perceived as Rustin's ease with himself: "I never had any sense at all that Bayard felt any shame or guilt about his homosexuality. And that was rare in those days. Rare."

For Rustin, the relationship with Platt came at an exhilarating, exacting, and stressful time. Two years into his tenure at the FOR, he had already made a mark among pacifists. Great things were expected of him, heavy demands placed on him. The work with CORE was expanding, and Muste had recognized his importance as an evangelist of nonviolence in the black community by making him race relations secretary. Randolph had expressed confidence in him and was pressing for more of his time. Opportunities were coming his way, as with a request from the *Baltimore Afro-American* to do trainings on nonviolent direct action in that still largely segregated border city. In his role as mentor, Muste arranged for Rustin to make an extended trip to San Francisco in October and November 1943 in order to have the experience of doing sustained work in a single locale. He pushed Rustin to think more deeply about the race relations work and to map out a bolder strategic plan for insinuating nonviolence into the struggle for racial equality. This Rustin began to do. But even as he plunged ahead with his work and moved steadily into his intimacy with Platt, the war intruded. In mid-November, Rustin received a notice from his draft board to report for his physical.

CHAPTER FOUR

"An Extremely Capable Agitator"
1944

CONSCIENCE, NOT THE LAW, sent Rustin to prison. As a Quaker, he had the option of refusing military service on religious grounds. When Congress passed the Selective Service Act of 1940, it made provision for conscientious objectors. Members of the historic peace churches as well as others who could argue persuasively that spiritual conviction kept them from serving in the military had the alternative of civilian public service (CPS). A product of intense negotiation between pacifists and federal bureaucrats, CPS allowed objectors to work in one of the 150 camps set up by the peace churches after the law was passed.

All the evidence suggests that Rustin initially intended to take this route. In the fall of 1940, he filled in his Selective Service questionnaire and submitted the special form for conscientious objectors. Later, he sent to his draft board in Harlem additional materials intending to buttress his case. He described the influence that the Quakers had on him while growing up in West Chester, his decision in 1936 formally to affiliate with them, his daily periods of spiritual meditation, and the peace activities he had engaged in during his student days at Cheyney State. "I came to the firm and immovable conviction," he wrote, "that war was wrong and opposed directly to the Christian ideal."[1]

By the time Rustin received the order to report for a preinduction physical, he was rethinking this stance. Immersed in the FOR community and under the spell of Muste, he no longer simply harbored a belief in peace. Instead, he saw himself almost as pacifism's chosen messenger.

Also, by 1943, the luster of CPS as a meaningful alternative to military service had dimmed. The camps were rife with discontent; CPS seemed a cruel hoax. Conscientious objectors found themselves sequestered in rural areas, engaged in labor reminiscent of the New Deal's Civilian Conservation Corps and, despite the veneer of church control, ultimately under the authority of the military. The dream that some of the men had, of doing socially meaningful work amid a population that might be influenced by their example, held little relationship to the daily regimen of boring work in isolated circumstances. By 1943, many were going on work strike, walking away from the work camps, or choosing prison instead.

Meanwhile, other pacifist men were taking a stance of noncooperation and choosing jail. One out of six inmates in federal prison during World War II were objectors to war; these prisoners of conscience were turning the institutions upside down. Administrators and guards normally dealt with bank robbers, embezzlers, tax evaders, and Appalachian moonshiners. Now they found themselves faced with a population of highly educated men driven by a philosophy of social activism and a fierce sense of their moral autonomy. "We were a proud, stiff-necked lot," one of them recounted, "who openly boasted we were the most radical men in the country." Muste referred to them as "the shock troops of pacifism."[2]

In the months before Rustin received his induction notice, many incarcerated COs were living up to this description. In Danbury, a minimum-security facility in Connecticut, and Lewisburg, a maximum-security prison in Pennsylvania, the number of politically minded pacifists was large enough to encourage mass action. Racial segregation and the censorship of mail were the issues that provoked them. Inmates went on strike, refusing to leave their cells for work assignment, meals, or recreation. Prison administrators placed the more militant prisoners first in quarantine, and then in the hole, to contain the disruption. When some refused to eat, they were tied down and force-fed with tubes. The strikes lasted for months.

News circulated between pacifists on the inside and those still free. For the jailed COs, letters about the exploits of their comrades outside were a lifeline. A letter to Rustin from Bill Sutherland, one of only a few African American pacifists in prison and the instigator of actions against racial segregation at Lewisburg, gave some indication of the inspiration these reports offered. "Have heard that the March on Washington," he wrote, "has accepted non-violent direct action as the major strategy in the struggle for racial justice. Congratulations!!!! I know that you and Jim Farmer . . . must have worked tirelessly in order to put the move across. When one of the fellows read us the news from his letter, we all cheered spontaneously."[3]

The influence flowed in both directions. Especially that fall, as the strikes at Lewisburg and Danbury dragged on, the outlook of the jailed activists seeped into Rustin's consciousness. John Mecartney, one of the strikers in Danbury, wrote to Rustin that time in prison "has been the greatest and most worthwhile year of my life." Paton Price, a leader of the Lewisburg strikers, composed a series of letters, promptly circulated by his mother, in which he called on pacifists to make greater sacrifices. A week after forced feeding had begun, he wrote a blistering critique of those on the outside who had been less than enthusiastic in their support of the strikers. "I do want to emphasize that 'pacifism as usual' seems a little inadequate and ridiculous in a time such as this," he informed his mother. "What we need is a more revolutionary, dynamic type of non-violent pacifism that initiates attack and does not hurriedly retreat every time a battle is engaged." Sentiments such as these marked the imprisoned COs as torchbearers of the most militant form of nonviolence. For Rustin, the prospect of incarceration offered the opportunity to remain on the front lines of pacifist conviction and to forge an even tougher stance against the coercive power of the war-making state.[4]

Still, *choosing* an extended jail term was no easy decision for a black man. It flew in the face of African American experience. After Emancipation, incarceration became the successor institution to slavery. If the plantation could no longer serve as a prison without walls, the prison could become a forced-labor camp. State legislatures revised their criminal codes to make it easier to lock up black men for petty offenses and then used them on labor gangs. Jails were also places that African Americans sometimes did not leave alive. They were institutions where the full brutality of white racism could be enacted with almost no constraints. And Rustin knew that he would be bringing to jail not only his skin color but also illicit sexual desires and a determination to resist the rules of the institution.

Throughout the fall, he sought information and advice, speaking to as many of those who had been in prison as he could find. "He was perturbed and quite apprehensive about what was going to happen to him in jail," recalled Ernest Bromley, one of those whom Rustin consulted. "He was trying to figure it out. Get some ideas of what he could do in there that would be constructive." Bromley thought that despite the evident trepidation, Rustin was steeling himself for the challenge and settling into a plan of attack. "I remember him saying, 'Well, I'm not going to get into anything that just wants to change the food, or change the diet. I want to do something that's going to mean something. Something that will change society.'"[5]

APPREHENSIVE OR NOT, Rustin had made his decision by the time the letter from his draft board arrived, calling him for a preinduction physical and ordering him to entrain for a CPS camp. On November 16, 1943, he informed the board that he could not "voluntarily submit to an order emanating from the Selective Training and Service Act." He returned his registration and classification cards, and he sent a copy of the letter to the U.S. Attorney's Office in Manhattan. He included with his letter a copy of the *Interracial Primer*, a pamphlet that he had composed for the FOR in which he explained how nonviolent direct action could lead to racial justice, and "The Negro and Non-Violence," the article from *Fellowship* magazine recounting his refusal to conform to segregationist practices in the South.[6]

Events moved steadily forward. Despite a letter from Nevin Sayre, a national FOR leader, requesting that Rustin's work be considered deferrable, his draft board noted in December that he had failed to report for his physical and listed him as delinquent. The federal district court issued an indictment, and, on January 12, Rustin was arrested. The following month, he waived the right to a trial and pled guilty. The judge sentenced him to three years and gave him ten days to settle his affairs.

On the last day of February, Rustin reported to the federal detention facility in Lower Manhattan, where he waited assignment to one of the
system's prisons.

From friends and associates came letters bidding him farewell.
Robert Vogel, Norman Whitney's assistant at the Syracuse Peace Center, wrote that "you will be dreadfully missed. . . . The days ahead will
be difficult for you. . . . You will be constantly in my prayers." Randolph applauded him for his convictions. "Your action will give heart
and spirit even to those who may disagree with your philosophy," he
told Rustin. "Be assured that the fight for racial equality and social justice will be carried on to the extent that my frail powers and abilities
will enable me." George Houser, who had already served time for refusing to register, expressed regrets that Rustin would not be free much
longer. "There have been lots of ideas developing recently in my mind
in regard to the pacifist movement," he wrote to his comrade in struggle. "I wish we might have a chance to talk about them, [but] it appears
we will have to wait for a few years." Perhaps the most comforting message came from John Dixon, who had just finished a sixty-three-day
hunger strike at Lewisburg: "Remember, wherever you go, you will
have friends."[7]

While expressions of support came from every quarter of the peace
movement, Rustin's decision was hard on his family. He had written
about it to his hometown newspaper, which reported that "he has declined to accept a call to the colors." Handling the news as thoughtfully
as it could, the paper recited Rustin's accomplishments in high school
and identified him as a follower of Gandhi's methods, as if to soften the
reaction of local residents whose sons were fighting and dying overseas.
Most members of the family, Rustin thought, "were somewhat humiliated by it." His grandmother, however, "understood it very well." Julia
wrote to the paper that she and Janifer "feel greatly the fact of our son
Bayard's imprisonment, but feel that he must follow the dictates of his
conscience."[8]

Still, Rustin knew that his decision to go to jail was cause for Julia to
worry. He communicated his concerns about her to those with whom

he worked, and just after he surrendered himself to federal authorities, Sayre penned a sweetly caring letter to Julia. He assured her of the respect and affection that he and others had for Bayard. He told of their travels together and spoke feelingly of her grandson's talents and prospects: "Every time Bayard made a deep impression on the audience. He has a combination of gifts in singing voice, dramatic recital of experiences, and personality inspired by loving nonviolence. I believe these gifts will take him very far . . . if he can maintain his inner sweetness and humility of spirit on the one hand, in the face of the bitter sufferings of the Negro race . . . and on the other hand against the adulation which will come his way because of his talents." Sayre judged that "the ordeal of prison will be a hard one." But, "like all suffering, the effect is to make a man either better or worse. In Bayard's case, I believe it will be better."[9]

Rustin spent ten days in the West Street jail. He quickly made his presence felt. Two days after his arrival, according to the meticulous files that prison administrators kept on him, he was "proving to be very troublesome. Came to the business office without authorization. Later, became obstinate when ordered to go to his cell." Soon Rustin was in solitary, having refused to accept segregated tables in the dining hall.[10]

Troublesome was hardly the word to describe the relationship between Rustin and the Bureau of Prisons. The bureau classified him as one of the system's "notorious offenders," a designation he shared with Al Capone, the Chicago mobster serving time in Alcatraz. From the beginning, he alarmed administrators, including James Bennett, the director of the bureau in Washington, who found himself having to pay inordinate attention to this obdurate inmate who willfully ignored prison rules, followed the dictates of his own conscience, and dared guards to tame him. Throughout Rustin's twenty-eight-month imprisonment, Bennett was plagued by letters from subordinates who pleaded for advice on what to do about Rustin and from Rustin's supporters on the outside who kept an eye on his treatment. That the director of the entire federal prison system should have to devote so much time to a single inmate, whose arrest and conviction had commanded no headlines, speaks both to Rustin's determination to leave his mark on the system and the strains that two long years of dealing with war resisters had placed on the bureau.

First on the agenda was the matter of where to assign him. An early report noted that "he is very intelligent and in conversation seems to be a reasonable person. On the other hand he has a reputation of being vehement on matters affecting the race question." Bennett initially decided to send Rustin to Mill Point, a federal prison camp in West Virginia where security was minimal and the routine liberal, and where very few conscientious objectors had been placed. The few black prisoners in Mill Point were "not of the type who would be easily incited into trouble," if Rustin served his time there. By contrast, sending him to Danbury or Lewisburg, where COs were wreaking havoc on daily routines, simply invited unrest.[11]

The experience at West Street quickly scotched those plans. "Reliable sources" informed bureau officials that Rustin was openly boasting he would walk away from any facility that did not keep him forcibly confined—and take other COs with him! Bennett ordered an interview, and the transcript did little to allay his fears. Again and again, Joseph Rosenberg, the parole officer conducting the interrogation, pressed Rustin for a direct answer to a simple question: Would he take "French leave" if sent to a prison farm? But he could not pin Rustin down. Depending on the circumstances—the treatment of Negro prisoners, the openness of the warden to negotiate changes in conditions—he might, or might not, walk. After playing cat and mouse for several minutes, Rosenberg terminated the session in exasperation, noting at the end of the transcript: "The subject then went into a dissertation on philosophical concepts pertaining to mind, matter, theories, etc. The question was completely evaded."[12]

After reading the report, Frank Loveland, who apportioned new inmates among the federal institutions, informed the superintendent at Mill Point not to expect Rustin after all. "We feared," he wrote, "that it would be only a matter of weeks before he found some reason to 'take a stand' on some issue, real or fancied, and cause you no end of trouble.

We fully expect to have plenty of trouble with him anyway, but would prefer that it start at Ashland." To Robert Hagerman, the warden at Ashland, Loveland sent the post-sentence report and what almost amounted to a letter of apology for "the type of burden you are to be saddled with."[13]

THE FEDERAL PRISON at Ashland was located in rural northeastern Kentucky, along the banks of the Ohio River, where Kentucky, Ohio, and West Virginia meet. Many of its inmates were white men from the Appalachian South, with little formal education, jailed for failing to pay federal taxes on the liquor they distilled at home and sold in their environs. Robert Hagerman, the warden at Ashland, was a medical doctor who had chosen prison work out of a wish to be of service; among senior administrators in the system, he had a reputation as a liberal, enlightened man. Many of the conscientious objectors under his watch had kind words to say of him, though they were less generous in assessing some of his subordinates.

Rustin arrived there on March 9. The authorities fingerprinted him, took mug shots, and gave him standard-issue prison clothing. In order to obtain permission to send and receive letters, Rustin signed a disposition form that allowed prison officials to inspect his mail, and he submitted for approval a list of correspondents. He then went into quarantine, the customary practice with new inmates. Over the next weeks, investigators sought background information about everyone on the list. A social worker visited the aging Julia and Janifer in their home, while local police responded to queries about whether the women on Rustin's list were "single or divorced" and whether any had reputations as "seditious." Prison officials also did a thorough check on Rustin: his education and work record, his West Chester years and his time in New York.[14]

On March 17, a week after arriving, Bayard celebrated his thirty-second birthday quietly. No greetings arrived from the outside, since none of his correspondents had yet been cleared, but he and Julia had arranged beforehand to each read Psalm 56 at one o'clock that afternoon:[15]

Be gracious to me, O God, for men trample upon me;
all day long foemen oppress me;
my enemies trample upon me all day long,
for many fight against me proudly . . .
All day long they seek to injure my cause;
all their thoughts are against me for evil.
They band themselves together, they lurk,
they watch my steps. . . .
in God I trust without a fear. What can man do to me?
My vows to thee I must perform, O God . . .

The trouble everyone was anticipating began soon enough. Besides a large number of Jehovah's Witnesses, Ashland housed perhaps three dozen conscientious objectors out of a population of almost 450 inmates. With one of their members assigned to work in the mailroom, the COs had access even to information that censors tried to intercept; they also created their own oral "newsletter" with rotating editors who passed information along during recreation in the yard and, for inmates in quarantine, through the ventilating system. On Friday evening, March 25, some of the COs in cell block C raised "holy hell" for several minutes. One of them communicated to Rustin in quarantine, and an officer overheard Rustin providing advice on how to build "a concerted campaign" against a particularly disliked guard and how to press for the freedom of a CO in isolation. Rustin then began singing, through the pipe space in the ventilator, "Strange Fruit," Billie Holliday's signature song about lynching in the South. "This was loudly applauded by the colored boys," according to one of the white guards.[16]

A few days later, while still in quarantine, Rustin sent Hagerman a several-page memo on racial segregation in the prison and how to end it. He proposed a small experiment of placing some "well-trained Negroes" in roles that would provide "a tacit challenge to creative thinking" about race relations. Specifically, Rustin suggested that he be allowed to teach in the prison's education department a course on American history to white and black inmates alike. He wrapped this modest recommendation in a lengthy disquisition on the principles and practice of nonviolence. As if instructing a deficient student, Rustin walked Hagerman through the range of possible responses to injustice, from violence, acceptance, and avoidance, to nonviolent resistance. To the warden of a prison in which the lines of power and authority were supposed to be unambiguous, Rustin's memo could only have appeared as a threat.[17]

The disturbance in cell block C and Rustin's memo on nonviolent resistance provoked Hagerman to begin what proved to be a steady correspondence with Bennett in Washington. "Everything seemed to be going along very well here until Bayard Rustin arrived about three weeks ago," he informed his superior. "Our radical group of conscientious objectors have accepted Rustin as their leader and they apparently seek to prove to him that they are not 'going to let their brothers in other institutions down.' I am sure that Rustin has taken every advantage of this attitude." Under Rustin's prodding, the COs were "seeking the help of the colored inmates" at Ashland, some of whom had participated in the Friday evening disturbance.[18]

Hagerman described Rustin as "an extremely capable agitator whose ultimate objective is to discredit the Bureau of Prisons. His motives are well camouflaged with many references to his desire to bring about desirable changes in racial relations through patient understanding. He is plausible, smooth, and ingratiating and . . . possesses in abundance the rare quality of leadership." The warden emphasized that the COs had already coalesced around him and that Rustin was now recruiting support among the general black inmate population. Hagerman asked that Rustin be transferred promptly. "The institution had been running along quite smoothly with no upheavals . . . until Rustin arrived," he reiterated. "This man will be a constant trouble maker." To drive the point home, he wrote to Bennett again, a few days later, this time including two letters Rustin had written to Doris Grotewohl. In them, Rustin criticized the segregationist practices of the institution and asked Grotewohl to publicize them.[19]

Bennett convened a special meeting of his advisers in Washington to evaluate the request but rejected transferring Rustin. Instead, he counseled Hagerman to confront his irksome charge with the inconsistency between his memo about patience and his encouragement of unrest among inmates. "He will have to earn back [our] respect and faith in him by accepting any routine assignment given him and showing that he can get along." Perhaps because Bennett knew Rustin had friends on the outside who were monitoring events, he urged Hagerman to exercise restraint: Rustin "should receive this in the nature of a warning rather than as a definite disciplinary action and understand that he is being treated with unusual consideration." But Bennett also promised relief in the future: "If he then proves to be an agitator who is out to stir up trouble, I think you would be justified in recommending his transfer."[20]

Bennett's advice reflected his belief in the tenets of what, in the mid-twentieth century, was considered enlightened penology. He believed incarceration was meant to rehabilitate and that most inmates, if offered the right combination of discipline and incentive, could be fitted for law-abiding lives. Yet in Rustin's case (and in those of many other COs in the system), Bennett was facing something new in his career. Rustin approached incarceration from a stance of moral righteousness. He saw his agitation not as troublemaking, but as ennobling. It threatened disorder, but in the pursuit of justice. Efforts to discipline him became proof of the effectiveness of his campaign; attempts at reason only opened the door for Rustin to articulate his cause. To Rustin's mind, the prison, not the pacifist, needed fixing.

Over the next few months, a stalemate developed. Captive and captors engaged in a series of advances and retreats as the former challenged the social order of the institution and the latter tried to maintain it. Occasionally the prison authorities would give ever so slightly, but always carefully documenting Rustin's infractions, building a dossier of misbehavior for a time when it might be needed.

Early in April, at the weekly movie showing, Rustin refused to sit in the section designated for colored inmates. Two days later, he and Charles Butcher, a white CO, demanded that Rustin be allowed to visit the upper floor of cell block E, which housed some white pacifists. The next day, a guard wrote him up for blocking a doorway and refusing to move when ordered. When Rustin discovered that some of the guards were grilling other black inmates about him and warning them that Rustin "would get them in trouble," he wrote a condescending letter to the associate warden and took him to task for sowing dissension: "When in the future you wish to know my attitude or my plans, feel free to call upon me directly. I shall be happy both to analyze any existing problems and to outline a corrective synthesis." As if in response, prison officials let him know that some of his outgoing letters had been seized since he was using his mail privileges to release inflammatory public statements. According to R. M. Larkin, Hagerman's assistant, Rustin appeared unfazed by the information and vowed to "resort to surreptitious, sneaking or underhanded means" to get his messages out.[21]

Even as this drama of resistance and discipline unfolded, Hagerman proved willing to bend. The warden approved Rustin's request to teach a history course to white inmates. Rustin was ecstatic. "At last I have been given my class," he wrote to Platt. "Finally I am a full teacher with about 15 students. They are all typical of the poorer white people of Kentucky and Tennessee hill country." The course gave some focus to his restless energy as he busied himself preparing sessions, writing away for teaching materials, and grading exams and assignments. But mostly he was pleased because of the possibilities it opened. "Being taught by a Negro is for them a revolutionary situation," he reported to Platt. Reading more into the experience than was warranted, he took it as evidence that "white southerners may be ready for some real progressive changes," and assumed that the success of the class would be ammunition in his campaign for further desegregation of the prison.[22]

Hagerman had also decided to acquiesce, at least obliquely, to the request for free movement between white and black sections in Rustin's cell block. Although he issued no directive announcing a change, he instructed the guards to leave unlocked the gate dividing the races. No black inmate took advantage of the option except Rustin, who joined his friends on Sundays to listen to symphony broadcasts on the radio. But his violation of the color line infuriated a white inmate. "Judge" Huddleston had served in statewide office in Kentucky before being convicted on charges of fraud. Like most other Southern politicians of the era, he had built his career on the unshakable assumption of white supremacy. Rustin's confident disregard of segregationist practice was more than he could swallow. One Sunday, when Rustin had joined a few of his friends in the common area for whites, Huddleston stormed out. He returned a few minutes later with a stick the size of a mop handle and immediately began beating Rustin. As blows landed on Rustin, the other COs rushed to restrain Huddleston. But Rustin ordered them to desist and, true to his Gandhian beliefs, simply covered his head as he absorbed the blows, telling Huddleston all the while, "You can't hurt me." Meanwhile, the attacker was striking out wildly, hitting the other pacifists who by then were following Rustin's example. "The club splintered and broke but was still large enough to use but Huddleston stopped," one CO reported. "It was a perfect example of what Richard Gregg described in his *Power of Nonviolence*. Huddleston was completely defeated and unnerved by the display of nonviolence and began shaking all over and sat down." Guards soon arrived at the behest of some black inmates who had heard the commotion. X-rays revealed that Rustin had suffered a broken wrist, and the white COs came away with some bumps and bruises. The warden disciplined only Rustin and some of the other COs and took no action against Huddleston.[23]

The injuries and disciplining notwithstanding, Rustin and his comrades emerged from the fracas with their stature significantly enhanced. The story quickly entered the peace movement's lore about Rustin's courage. On hearing about it, Muste waxed ecstatic. Through Grotewohl, he communicated a message to all the COs involved: "It is difficult to put into words the joy I feel over the fact that their spirits under severe testing remained pure and true. If they were the sons of my flesh, I could not feel more closely bound to these young men than I do. . . . They incarnate the force and they are learning to use the method which can break the barriers of race and caste." Inside Ashland, too, the results were beneficial. Among the black inmates, one pacifist reported, "The prestige of the COs who were involved has gone way up. The fact of a white man actually taking the side of a Negro in a crisis was a fact they could not believe until it happened." For his part, Hagerman backtracked from his original response. He apologized to Rustin for initially blaming him for the disorder and thanked him and the other COs for their restraint under pressure.

All in all, this latest trial by fire pleased Rustin. Not only did he and the other pacifists hold to their principles, but they also emerged with substantial moral capital. Huddleston's attack "placed us in a position," he informed Grotewohl, "where we could ask the administration to maintain a firm and progressive position" on racial policy within the prison.[24]

In one sense, Rustin came to prison prepared for its challenges. He had, after all, braved racial violence alone in the South. In federal prison, there were other foot soldiers of pacifism nearby, and the bureau's administrators knew that Rustin had allies beyond the walls, ready to spring to his defense. He and the other COs also understood the distinction between their situation and that of the general inmate population. "We used to say the difference between us and other prisoners is the difference between fasting and starvation," he recalled. The former was voluntarily chosen, the latter imposed. Still, nothing in his past matched the ordeal of a lengthy incarceration. Decades later, Rustin described his time in federal prison as "the most profound and important experience I've ever had."[25]

The lessons were not uplifting. "I learned that prisons are designed to brutalize persons and not to help them," he went on. "I've seen strong men of great character come to the prison and in a few weeks, they are less than babies, totally dominated by other people, who take all their cigarettes, take all their money, and will do anything they tell them to do." For Rustin, the crime of incarceration lay in its attempt to obliterate moral autonomy. "The real brutalization is that in prison you can make absolutely no decisions for yourself, and that therefore you cannot be a human being. . . . A bell rings and you are permitted to take a shower. A bell rings and you must stop. A bell rings and you can go to eat. A bell rings and you must leave the dining room. . . . What makes prison so horrible is the inability ever to make a decision of your own."[26]

Rustin's capacity to resist this dehumanization came in part from his

ties to the outside world. Once the bureau approved his list of correspondents, a steady stream of mail arrived. The vagaries of time—and of
prison record keeping—have left only a partial glimpse of this correspondence. Virtually no letters to or from his grandmother have survived.
Davis Platt carefully saved all of the mail he received, but none of his
letters to Rustin were preserved. By contrast, those that Rustin penned
to Doris Grotewohl have mostly perished, while hers to him remain.

Grotewohl filled her letters with news of the pacifist movement,
keeping Rustin informed about what others were doing in his absence—and keeping prison officials aware of the wide circle of activists
watching out for this cantankerous inmate. In one early letter, she relayed "scads of messages for you" from pacifists across the country. In
another, she related doings within New York's radical world: the activities of the War Resisters League and the latest conflict between Randolph and the Communist Party.[27] Grotewohl fed Rustin a diet of
reminders of the influence his life continued to exert on the quest for
racial justice and a nonviolent world. She passed on a report from Caleb
Foote about the "CORE group in San Francisco that resulted from
Rusty's visit which continues to meet weekly and is doing a pretty good
job." Later in the spring, after Randolph visited San Francisco, Grotewohl shared with Rustin the excitement there about the "real job of
conversion" that he had accomplished. "In his mass meeting a week ago
he spent much of his speech insisting that Negroes use non-violence
[and] discussed Rustin and CORE in detail." From Pauli Murray at
Howard University, she forwarded a long description about nonviolent
sit-ins at downtown restaurants in Washington. At one, the demonstrating students, carrying signs that read "Are You for Hitler's Way
(Racial Supremacy) or the American Way (Racial Equality)" and "We
Die Together. Why Can't We Eat Together," won the support of some
black soldiers in uniform who joined them. Within hours, the management capitulated.[28]

Not all of Grotewohl's scribblings came weighted with political import. While traveling with Muste in North Carolina early in April, she
cheered her jailed friend with visions of spring: "Redbud trees and
plum trees in blossom. . . . Jasmine and wisteria are all over the place.

What delights me is the way cherry blossoms or any sort of flowering tree reach way across sidewalks." The next month, spring had traveled north. "Some of us nibbled lunch in Riverside Park. The miniature magnolia trees in the parkway here on Broadway are in bloom and trees are losing that undressed look." She also told him of concerts at Lewisohn Stadium, of singing hymns with Platt and of visiting mutual friends. Always she communicated her affection and concern: "And to you, my sparrow, my love—don't break any wings!"[29]

Rustin's letters to Platt give some sense of his thoughts and feelings during his incarceration. He learned quickly, of course, that nothing left Ashland without passing through the warden's office. He consequently curbed any excesses of intimacy, but was surprisingly frank in describing prison life as well as his political convictions. Since Rustin was not given to self-revelatory writing, these letters offer a rare glimpse inside the man.

Early on, he disclosed to Platt some of the hardships of imprisonment. "The difference between life and slow death here," he wrote, "may revolve about a candy bar or a package of cigarettes. Little things—a cigarette butt, a scrap of colored paper, a smile, or the snatch of a song—many, many little things, which on the outside are lost or wasted, take on real significance here." The daily contact in his segregated cell block with other black inmates, whose tales of misfortune stunned him, made him reflect on his own good fortune. "There is such suffering in this world. . . . Not one penny should be misplaced or one moment wasted by men of social concern. . . . Pleasures pale into the distance as one is brought face to face with suffering of the intensity revealed in lives here."[30]

News from the outside provoked inner musings. A few nights after the D-Day landing in Normandy, inmates heard President Roosevelt on the radio. Listening to him close the broadcast with a prayer, Rustin informed Platt, "I wept inwardly—somehow the more for God who must have been bewildered by it, by so many millions of his children asking for victory, . . . yet all of them meaning something different." Rustin prayed, too, "more these days and constantly." He wished that "some new and creative forces can be brought into the stream of history."

Incarcerated and with so much time on his hands, the "man of action," as he styled himself, meditated on what was to come when the global bloodletting ended. "I certainly am convinced that there is need of a spiritual revolution," he told his lover. "I am equally certain that some totally dedicated and spiritually radical group, giving itself constantly and wholly to a life of the spirit, will (by its witness) usher in the forces that will make genuine change possible. Whether I am to be of that group I doubt. . . . I know that at present I must work in the field of action. However, I believe that certain men are doing a great deal thru their lives of prayer. . . . Political, social and economic changes, no matter how radical, will not bring bread, beauty, and brotherhood to men. A radical spiritual 'revolution of our total culture' is needed."[31] On other occasions, fury replaced quiet reflection. Conflicts with prison officials over mail censorship made him rue the signature he had provided them upon arrival—"giving away a birth-right," he wrote, "for a few boneless letters." Aware that a bureau employee was reading every word, he told Platt that "tyranny is no harsh term for deeds practiced here. . . . We are held slaves to a state which 'grinds the faces of the unfortunate in the dust.' One ought to resist the entire system! . . . Perhaps the time rapidly approaches where such behavior will be the only honorable thing for several of us."[32]

Prison left Rustin with plenty of time for study. He wrote to Platt about his reading, which, despite the power of the warden's office to regulate the material available to inmates, included such books as Trotsky's history of the Russian Revolution and Lillian Smith's recently published novel, *Strange Fruit*, a tale of interracial love in the South and the violence that attends it. Smith's book enjoyed immense popularity among the inmates, with Rustin's copy having circulated to more than thirty. "It is amazing that certain people should request it," he wrote, "but they do." He also pointed Platt to a new biographical study of Walt Whitman by Henry Seidel Canby. "Best analysis of Walt I have seen," he noted. "Good job in Chapter XIX," he concluded, referring to the chapter that addressed Whitman's homosexuality.[33]

Rustin refrained from using any endearments in his letters to Platt—"your friend and brother" is how he often closed them—but he jumped at the suggestion of a visit. "I am so anxious for you to come as soon as possible," he wrote. He sent careful instructions about how to request permission, since generally only family members could come, and he urged Platt to write in a hurry. "You should have asked for a two-hour visit," he brusquely informed his lover in a later letter, after learning that Platt had requested only an hour. Meanwhile, he also tried to negotiate permission from his end, arguing to R. M. Larkin, Hagerman's assistant, that he had not had any visitors at all in his three months at Ashland.[34]

When Platt arrived on June 28, he brought not only himself but also a mandolin. Rustin had gingerly requested it, starved as he was for access to music and with the time now to teach himself how to play. Given the distance Platt had traveled, the warden allowed him two blocks of time, an hour in the morning and a somewhat longer stretch in the middle of the afternoon. Other inmates, both the black ones in his cell block and the Southern whites in his class, wanted to know the identity of the tall, handsome, young white man who had traveled so far to see him. How much he revealed to the general inmate population is unknown, but some of the COs, Charles Butcher among them, knew that Platt was Rustin's lover.

Afterward, Rustin was happy. "Your visit was a real success," he wrote. He thanked him again for the mandolin, "a beauty . . . with a wonderfully clear tone," and he described lessons he was already receiving from an imprisoned CO who was a violinist by profession. "Someday I shall reward you by doing some 16th century ballads on it for you." The musical prospects sent Rustin on flights of fantasy, as he began planning for the choir he had formed—"interracial, interfaith, including 'whiskey men'"—to learn some Bach and Palestrina. But he returned to earth soon enough, complaining to Platt that "the fellows lean toward the most weak and sentimental lyrics with the most sickly melodies."[35]

BY EARLY SUMMER, Rustin was ready to press ahead toward the goal of fully integrating Ashland. On July 13, he wrote to Hagerman and detailed the segregation he confronted in the dining hall, the sleeping quarters, and the theater. "Rather than stand on naked conviction and resist immediately when faced with these conditions," he wrote the warden, "I have tried to give consideration to existing circumstances and to the problems involved in racial change." Rustin enumerated the reasons for believing that integration now could proceed. The athletics program mixed black and white together; the kitchen staff had begun eating together in view of the inmates; Southern whites had accepted him as a teacher. The time had come to push further. He proposed that the next step be the provision of integrated tables in the dining hall. "Certainly," he argued to Hagerman, "a northern Negro in Kentucky teaching white students who have been conditioned in Virginia and Tennessee is far more revolutionary an affair than Negroes and whites voluntarily sitting together at meals." He closed with a veiled warning: "I am faced with an almost impossible situation at each meal time. Lately I have had to mobilize my mental and emotional forces to be able to enter the dining hall. . . . Rapidly I am moving to a position where it is close to impossible for me to eat in an area where absolute separation exists."[36]

The following day, Rustin secured a meeting with Hagerman. He offered the warden a carefully detailed plan for moving toward racially integrated facilities. Gradualism and voluntarism were at the heart of his proposal. Make E cell block, where he and some other COs lived, "a model" of integrated living; extend the integration of the sleeping quarters to the dining room for E cell block inmates; let other inmates who wished to eat at those tables do so.[37] Their dialogue encouraged him. He wrote Platt that "things are going very well and at this point I have every reason to believe that progress will be made." Meanwhile, Muste had received permission to visit, and the two discussed the negotiations to desegregate Ashland. The meeting left Rustin "wiser and happier," he told Platt.[38]

Muste also met with Hagerman. Later, he sent the warden a lengthy letter in which he argued the case for integration and addressed issues Hagerman had raised about Rustin's role in fomenting inmate discontent. "I am pretty confident," Muste attested, "that he has himself well in hand and that personal inconvenience or humiliation do not count

for more than they should in the situation." Muste tried to shift the focus away from Rustin. He knew many of the incarcerated COs "pretty
intimately," he wrote Hagerman, "and I am sure they are just as deeply
concerned. . . . I think therefore that even if he were not there the issue
would have arisen in some form or other." Unknown to the warden,
Muste also began an effort to build support on the outside. He sent to
both Roy Wilkins of the NAACP and Randolph a lengthy memorandum on segregation at Ashland and Rustin's efforts to challenge it.[39]

Through August and early September, Rustin pushed forward. He
reached beyond the core group of conscientious objectors to the generally acquiescent population of Jehovah's Witnesses, who were imprisoned not because of their opposition to war but because Selective
Service refused to recognize each of them as a minister and hence deferrable. Rustin wrote to Carl Johnson, their leader, of the plans he was
initiating. "May I ask you and your brothers in the faith prayerfully to
consider giving a complete and mighty witness when the opportunity
comes," he inquired. "They did agree to go along with Bayard," Larry
Gara recollected. "That scared the hell out of the prison authorities."
The COs also constituted a committee to represent them so that Rustin
did not have to carry on the negotiations alone.[40]

Rustin kept a detailed log of their efforts. Early in August, he informed Platt that the administration was permitting interracial seating
in church. Later that month, Bennett made an appearance at Ashland
and met with Rustin's committee. "He was urbane," Rustin noted, "but
the general impression . . . was that he did not intend to move fast or
far if at all." A few days later, the prison doctor surprised Rustin with a
query as to whether he would consider a transfer to another institution.
Taken aback by the request, which he construed as a ploy to disrupt the
desegregation campaign, Rustin replied that he "would resist transfer
to the point of refusing to wear clothes, insist upon being carried, etc.
etc." The white COs, meanwhile, decided to each write to Hagerman,
apprising him of their support for integrated facilities and their upset at
the proposal to transfer Rustin. When Hagerman interpreted the batch
of letters as pressure, they hurriedly met to regroup.[41]

In the wake of Bennett's visit, however, Hagerman indicated that he was prepared to move slowly forward. On September 2, the warden provided for an interracial section in the theater, but in Rustin's words, the plan was a "complete flop" since no black inmate other than himself crossed the color line. Then word came that some tables in the dining hall would carry signs announcing "interracial." Rustin and the others thought this would only inflame some inmates, and they refused to sit there. Finally, the signs came down. On September 7, Bayard noted, "Plan ran well. No problems," and the next day, "plan still going well." That evening, he penned a letter to inmates in cell block D in an effort to draw others into the experiment. "We have reason to rejoice," he wrote exuberantly.[42]

Rustin spoke too quickly. Only a few days later, prison officials confronted him with sexual misconduct charges.

CHAPTER FIVE

"Hard and Bitter Experience"
1944–1946

EVEN UNDER THE BEST of circumstances, incarceration tested the beliefs and character of the pacifists who chose prison. Men for whom moral autonomy was their most prized possession ("independent souls and lovers of liberty," Rustin called them) found themselves subject to a system that regimented every aspect of daily life. When Platt wrote to Rustin that he was considering refusal to cooperate with conscription, his jailed lover hastily wrote back a warning: "The pressure of prison is sufficient to cause well-grounded men to change radically."[1]

Rustin's sexuality brought an added liability. Throughout the federal government, the war years heightened concerns about homosexual behavior. In the State Department, pressure built to have Roosevelt dismiss Sumner Welles, a trusted adviser, because of evidence of his sexual encounters with men. The military was tightening its system of regulation to keep gay men and lesbians out of the armed forces while punishing those it caught inside. In the federal prison system, the reforming spirit of James Bennett did not encompass tolerance of sexual infractions. In fact, Bennett saw homosexuality as the primary source of "fights, stabbings, and unrest."

As a sexually active man in his early thirties, Rustin suddenly found himself living under intense surveillance, in close quarters, in an all-male environment. In the confined atmosphere of federal prison, the boundary between public role and private desire collapsed; the window of tolerance for his sexuality that Rustin had found outside vanished.

Little wonder that, as he approached the first anniversary of his incarceration, he commented, "There is terrific pressure both in physical and psychological restraint."[2]

Warning flags about Rustin's sexuality preceded his arrival at Ashland. In collecting background information to determine where to assign him, a bureau official noted that "a statement was made that he has homosexual inclinations, although we have no factual basis for such a statement." The postsentence report recorded that he "attends theatres, concerts, visits art galleries, models clay," activities that, in the medical theorizing of the era, were signs of gender inversion and hence indicators of homosexuality.[3]

At Ashland, suspicions quickly began to swirl around Rustin. Amid the circles of dancers, musicians, bohemian students, and Christian pacifists in which he had moved, Rustin's presentation of self passed muster. It remained within the boundaries of acceptable masculinity. Gestures, the pitch of his voice, his accent, physical grace, a sardonic wit, his cultivated tastes: each could be variously interpreted as forms of theatricality, sophistication, sensitivity. They might be expected of a young man of artistic sensibilities and strong spiritual convictions. In prison, the boundaries and norms shifted dramatically, and Rustin persistently chose to flout them.

Shortly after his arrival at Ashland, a group of pacifist inmates prepared a set of skits for an evening entertainment. With Rustin's reputation as a singer preceding him, some of his friends convinced him to perform. As Donald Wetzel, one of the pacifists, described it, Rustin "sat informally at the edge of the stage in the prison auditorium and sang Negro folk songs, a cappella, in a high, thin, sweet falsetto." Listening to him sing in a woman's voice, Wetzel thought, "You fucking idiots. . . . It did not seem to me the smartest way for a man to be introduced to his fellow prisoners." Another inmate agreed. "It's all right that he's smart, and if he wants to talk like an Englishman, but he should know better than to sing like that. . . . They'll kill his ass."[4]

Just as he defied prison regulations around race, Rustin continually violated unwritten prohibitions about physical closeness among inmates. Sitting in a meeting soon after his release from quarantine,

Rustin bent forward and gave Charlie Butcher an affectionate kiss on the neck. As the weather warmed and inmates had more time in the yard, Rustin startled everyone with his displays of affection. One officer observed him "sitting with different other inmates, his arms around them, rubbing their legs and other parts of their bodies, while rubbing his cheek against theirs." Another guard, perched atop an observation tower, watched him "walking around the yard with his arm around several different inmates, in a very loving and personal manner."[5]

By August, Hagerman was receiving reports from officers about a "peculiar relationship" that had developed between Rustin and one particular inmate. The two men regularly strolled the yard together, arms around each other's waists, Rustin occasionally leaning his head on his companion's shoulder. Sometimes they sat on the concrete abutments near the dormitories, the one man's head "resting in Rustin's lap while Rustin would be stroking _____'s face with his hands or running his hands through _____'s hair." Guards observed them in the machine shop. "When it came time to part," an officer wrote, "they would hold each other's hands for long moments. This ardent performance on their part naturally gave the casual observer the impression that he was viewing two lovers who were loathe to part company." Another officer informed Hagerman that "neither of them shows the slightest interest in any activities that may be going on at any time. They seem absolutely engrossed in each other's company." Soon inmates were complaining to the guards, asking why they had to eat and socialize with "such known characters." To these queries, the guards could only reply, "No proof."[6]

Although none of Rustin's affectionate behavior broke any formal regulations, it did train the gaze of prison officials more keenly in his direction. Why would he do this? Why, especially, when he was assuming leadership of a campaign to challenge racial hierarchies in the prison system? Rustin has left no commentary, but it is hard not to speculate on the motives behind behavior that proved so reckless.

Shortly before he began to draw the attention of guards, he had finished reading Canby's study of Walt Whitman. The scholar's analysis of Whitman's sexuality, as Rustin wrote Platt, made a deep impression on him. Today, more than half a century after its publication, the book appears as nothing more than a bowdlerized version of a gay life in which the biographer invented heterosexual attractions and engaged in intellectual contortions to deny the contrary evidence. But in the early 1940s, when any discussion of homosexuality that neither condemned nor ridiculed was unusual, Canby's handling of Whitman's sexuality might have struck a different chord in a gay reader. Describing the sexual energy that suffused Whitman's work and life, Canby invested it with almost transcendent meaning. Without a Whitmanesque passion for men, he wrote, "there can be no comradeship strong enough to hold together an ideal democracy." The "passionate, physical love" of Whitman for men was, in Canby's reckoning, "very common, especially among strong creative intellects, whose imaginative sympathies penetrate beyond sexual differences."[7]

Was Rustin's behavior simply one more form of resistance to the authority of his captors? Was it, like his speech, another affectation of difference intended to connote superiority? Was he attempting to suggest something more, perhaps asserting a claim to the creative powers that Canby attributed to Whitman? Just as he presented himself around issues of war and racial injustice as someone with a heightened moral sensibility, did his conspicuous demonstrations of affection mean to communicate an arrogant disregard for the sexual restrictions that prison imposed?

As Rustin's campaign against segregated dining moved into higher gear, the prison administration began gathering statements implicating him in sexual activity. On August 18, two inmates described to Captain Huntington, one of Hagerman's senior officers, an incident from earlier in the summer. They came upon Rustin performing oral sex on an inmate, Whitlock, behind a curtain on the stage of the prison auditorium. A few days after they saw him, Rustin approached each of the two and asked them to keep their observations quiet. "He said he knowed he couldn't quit that," one of the witnesses told Huntington, "but he was going to stop it while he was in here because he knowed people was talking about it. He said he didn't want people to know what he was doing. He said he was through with that while he was in here." Neither witness put much stock in the promise. "They are always looking at each other when they are playing music like they wanted to kiss each other," one observed. The other told Huntington that "I have seen them kissing out on the yard and all of that kind of stuff. You can catch them out on the yard loving around most any time. They go in the trucks like they was studying the bible or something and naturally the officer can't see them." A third inmate told Huntington that he had seen Rustin perform oral sex in the machine shop.[8]

Placed alongside the reports filed by guards about Rustin's displays of affection, the testimony of inmates provided a compelling case against Rustin. Hagerman next sought to pry information from those who had been the target of Rustin's desires. Whitlock, who had been discovered with Rustin in the auditorium, agreed to testify against him in a disciplinary hearing and accuse Rustin face to face. Another, "a physically well developed youth, rosy cheeked, who presents a thoroughly masculine appearance," reported sexual approaches made toward him by two inmates, one of whom was Rustin. He described their coming separately into his cell at night, sitting on his bed, and turning the conversation toward sex between men. He rejected both advances but felt himself the object of stares and grins, shared looks and knowing conversation between his two admirers. A third swore to an encounter in which Rustin offered "to take care of you," which the inmate understood to mean "he would suck my prick." When he laughed the proposition off, Rustin repeated the offer, throwing at him a Mae West line, "Come up and see me some time." Afterward, the inmate repeated the story to several other prisoners and, in turn, was told by Whitlock of his own sexual episode in the auditorium with Rustin.[9]

On September 13, a disciplinary board of several officers convened to hear the case. They brought in Whitlock, "a colored inmate" according to the record of the proceedings, who proceeded to describe, under questioning, what had happened in the auditorium. Whitlock sounded very much like a reluctant witness, saying as little as possible, avoiding embellishment, and eschewing any gratuitous attacks on Rustin. When asked by Dr. Janney, a member of the hearing board, whether he was mad at Rustin, Whitlock replied, "No sir. I ain't mad at him. He never done nothing to me."[10]

The disciplinary board then brought Rustin in and immediately put the charge to him: "This boy has just told us that while he was in quarantine he made a trip up to the education department and you arranged to take him back in the auditorium and suck his penis." When Rustin vehemently denied the charge, the officers made Whitlock repeat the story. Rustin denied it again with more force. Visibly shaken, he accused Whitlock of lying and pressed him as to why he would wait four months to make this accusation. "I would if anybody had asked me about it," Whitlock replied. "I did tell some inmates about it. It had just now been throwed up on me." Rustin seized upon the statement. "What do you mean 'throwed up on you'? Who told you to tell that?" According to the transcript of the hearing, the two were by then becoming more and more agitated. "If you ever told the truth in your life, for God's sake tell it now," Rustin demanded, "because this is important, very important." Whitlock did not back down.

The board called in a second accuser, the "rosy cheeked youth" who repeated his story of sexual approaches, spurned by him, from Rustin and another. Rustin kept denying everything. "You fabricate and forget," he shot at his accuser. "What makes you think I winked my eyes? . . . Did I ever say anything to you about sucking pricks?"

After dismissing the witnesses, the board gave Rustin a chance to make a final statement. "I have a lot I would like to say," he told them. "First of all, I claim that the first report was an absolute lie. A complete and absolute lie in every sense of the word. I don't understand how a man could tell a lie like that. I have no fears of it because I know it is a lie. The second report is also false." Rustin made one last futile attempt to evade the accusations. He offered an elaborate story, blatantly concocted, of inmates telling him of rumors that were circulating about him, of his efforts to track down the source of the stories, and of trying to have the perpetrator desist.

Watson, the associate warden who was supervising the hearing, informed Rustin that they were placing him in administrative segregation. When Watson called in some guards to escort him away, Rustin raised his voice in protest and resisted. He wrapped his legs around the base of the swivel chair, grasped the seat with one hand, and used the other to break the grip of one of the guards. They carried him from the room by his arms and legs. Because of his resistance, Rustin was put in isolation.[11]

Among the conscientious objectors, many immediately rose to Rustin's defense. The timing of the punishment—the day before another action to push racial integration further—aroused their suspicions. Larry Gara, who by his own recollection was "real real confrontational" (even Rustin cautioned him once that "if you don't bend, you're gonna break"), decided to find out. "I didn't believe it," he reminisced. "I just couldn't believe that before [our planned action]—this isn't Bayard! So how do we know? Well, here's the hole. Downstairs. I decided to find out. Now, there's a guard at the head of the stairs. . . . I ran past the guard. He didn't know what was going on. I asked Bayard, 'Was it true that you were involved in a homosexual act as they said just now.' And he said, 'No.' And I ran up and I said it's false. So half a dozen of us said, 'Well, we can't trust the administration any longer, we're going on strike.'" Several of the COs were placed in administrative segregation as punishment for their actions in defense of Rustin.[12]

THE STEPS TAKEN by the administration against Rustin effectively disrupted the campaign against racial segregation. The revelation of his sexual activity—and the lies that Rustin told to both prison administrators and his comrades—precipitated a series of crises in his relationships with Muste, Platt, and the community of imprisoned pacifists. It piled another layer of rancorous antagonism on his relationship with his jailers. Now that he had been labeled a sexual deviate, prison officials from Bennett in Washington down to the most junior guard had one more compelling reason to monitor and control his every move.

As mentor to many of the incarcerated pacifists, Muste had been kept closely informed about the progress of the campaign against racial segregation. Word of Rustin's punishment quickly reached him in New York. He called Hagerman and Bennett, from whom he received the painful details. Their advice as well as his own inclination led him to schedule an emergency visit to Ashland for late in September. On September 19, six days after the disciplinary hearing, Grotewohl wrote to

Rustin that Muste was coming. "We have been able to get a fairly complete picture of the story. Know that no matter how deep the tribulation our support is undiminished. . . . On the personal problems and other concerns that are involved," she added, "you and he might counsel together when he sees you." Grotewohl meant her words to reassure. But to Rustin, still denying any sexual activity and claiming that he had been framed, the knowledge that Bennett and Muste were conferring must have been less than comforting.[13]

On September 22, Donald Clemmer, a psychiatrist employed by the Bureau of Prisons, arrived at Ashland to conduct an investigation for Bennett. He interviewed all of the parties—Rustin, his accusers among the inmates, several of the conscientious objectors, and prison staff—and forwarded a lengthy report to Bennett. About Rustin, Clemmer had nothing favorable to say. "Rustin presents," he wrote, "a classical picture of a constitutional homo—the invert type, the high voice, the extravagant mannerisms, the tremendous conceit, the general unmanliness of the inmate frame a picture, together with the historical record, that it does not take a Freud to diagnose." He described Rustin as superficially cordial but intent on verbal dueling. Rustin admitted that a " 'situation existed' " but denied all the charges against him.[14]

Determined to push past Rustin's denial, Clemmer asked what he thought ought to happen in the face of the "situation." Rustin insisted he should be returned to his regular duties, housed among the general population, and allowed to continue teaching. Rather than accept restrictions that implied guilt, he insisted that, if necessary, he would stay in isolation for the rest of his term. Should they attempt to transfer him to another facility, he "would have to be carried from the institution." Clemmer's final evaluation of Rustin was unsparing: "This man impresses me as a confirmed homosexual whose conceit is so extreme and whose homo traits are so deep in the personality, that combining these two features he could not refrain from further homosexual acts, both because of his instinctive need and because of his personal dynamics to outwit any supervising authorities in order to maintain his conceited personality organization."

Though he shrewdly assessed aspects of Rustin's character, Clemmer's evaluation also evinced his own hostility to homosexuality. He viewed Rustin through a system of belief, now thoroughly discredited, that viewed men who desired sexual intimacy with men as mentally ill and emotionally crippled. He identified signs of homosexuality in a broad range of behavior and appearance. When he interviewed Rustin's "followers," Clemmer discounted their belief in his innocence by imputing sexual deviance to them. About Francis Hall, whom everyone in the peace movement described as a saint with habits bordering on monkish asceticism, Clemmer wrote: "[Hall] himself, though he has no reputation of homosexuality, is an even-featured, silken-haired, soft-skinned beardless boy. It would not take much imagination to indicate that he has more than his fair share of latent homosexuality." Of another pacifist who professed belief in Rustin's innocence, he said: "Like many of the rest of them he is a weak-voiced, smooth-skinned, silken-haired young man. . . . He admitted that he knew Rustin on the outside."

Muste arrived on September 27, after Rustin had been in isolation for two weeks. He met with Rustin and many of the other protesting COs. The day after his departure, he telegraphed words of support: "You are in my thoughts and prayers. My admiration for your courage and estimate of your possibilities never greater. God is our refuge and strength." But he could not have been encouraged by the meeting. Though Rustin was willing to acknowledge "a certain carelessness . . . about gestures in themselves innocent," he remained steadfast in the claim that the administration had framed him.[15]

Spending long days alone in a cell, Rustin had plenty of time to reflect on his situation. As a leader in a movement grounded in moral rectitude, he had demonstrated an alarming lapse of integrity and judgment. In choosing quick physical pleasure, he had traded his hope of bearing witness against injustice for the withering censure of a system—and a society—that had little tolerance for his brand of sexual desire. And he compounded one mistake with another when he lied to protect himself from disgrace.

On October 2, after a month-long silence, Rustin wrote Platt a letter apologizing for the lack of communication and obliquely mentioning "a decided turn for the worse" in his situation. The letter offers the first suggestion that he was looking at his circumstances with a measure of realism. He described a scene from a biography of Francis of Assisi, the only book he had read in solitary. As a doctor prepared to cauterize one side of the ailing saint's face with a hot iron, Francis simply said, " 'Deal courteously with me, Brother Fire, for I have always loved thee.' " Rustin concluded his letter with these words: "When I am free some day I shall explain to you in full the period through which I am going. Until then, as you think of me—think of St. Francis. Think of his words, for I too, say 'Deal Courteously.' "[16]

Muste returned on October 21 for a second long visit. This time, Rustin admitted at least some of the sexual episodes but continued to blame the prison administrators and accuse them of "sinister designs" against him. This proved too much for Muste, who until then had approached Rustin tenderly. Now he demanded that Rustin face squarely the depth of his betrayal of his cause. The next day the older pacifist wrote Rustin a blistering letter:

> You have been guilty of gross misconduct, specially reprehensible in a person making the claims to leadership and—in a sense— moral superiority which you were making. . . . You had deceived everybody, including your own comrades and most devoted friends. . . . You were capable of making the "mistake" of thinking that you could be the leader in a revolution of the most basic and intricate kind at the same time that you were a weakling in an extreme degree and engaged in practices for which there was no justification, which a person with a tenth of your brains must have known would defeat your objective. . . . You are still far from facing reality in yourself. In the self that has been and still is you, there is nothing to respect, and you must ruthlessly cast out *everything* in you which prevents you from facing that. Only so can your true self come to birth—through fire, anguish, complete and child-like humility.

Muste told Rustin that if he ever expected to win prison officials to his beliefs in racial equality, he had to earn their respect first; his behavior had made them justifiably skeptical of everything he stood for. He closed by quoting Psalm 51: "'Have mercy upon me, O God, according to thy loving kindness—wash me thoroughly from mine iniquities and cleanse me from my sin . . . Create in me a clean heart, O God, and renew a right spirit within me. . . . Then will I teach transgressors thy ways.'"[17]

Two days after Muste's visit but before his letter arrived, Dr. Janney, Ashland's chief medical officer, interviewed Rustin at great length. After an hour of what Janney called "harangue and counter-harangue," Rustin offered the outlines of a personal history: the illegitimate child of a mother who had four other children by four male partners, including two very light-skinned offspring; a visit to his mother at Christmas at age fourteen during which he shared a bed with an adult male who provided him with his first sexual experience; his association during his college days with a group of wealthy young whites with interests in art and culture, among whom homosexual behavior was common and who took Rustin into their crowd as an expression of their liberalism. According to Janney, "Rustin wept freely" and acknowledged for the first time having sex with two inmates. He told Janney that he had abstained since June. He promised not only to continue to exercise restraint but also to demonstrate his good intentions by doing whatever menial work the prison staff might assign to him. Janney thought the work proposal made sense and that Rustin could begin to have some contact with other inmates, but he also informed Rustin that his "arrogance, insolence and open contempt" for institutional rules had to be eradicated. "This," Janney wrote in closing to Hagerman, "he tearfully promised to do."[18] The Rustin who emerges in this recounting—the free expression of emotion, the recitation of a sexual history, the promise of submission to authority—is so out of character that it dramatizes how dire his emotional condition was. Six weeks in isolation, the visits from Muste, the time to reflect alone on the gravity of his situation: all combined to provoke the upheaval portrayed in Janney's report.

A few days later, Rustin penned to his mentor a lengthy missive overflowing with contrition. "I want you to know that I love you," he wrote. "I wanted to unburden myself. You will never know the relief and joy which has followed." He went on to retrace his reaction to the disciplinary hearing, his inner turmoil, and the merciless self-scrutiny to which he had recently subjected himself. "I feared facing the reality of the ugly facts," he told Muste.

> I feared the humiliation and dishonor. In my frustration I blamed the administration. . . . I did not simply face the fact that . . . it was my own weakness and stupidity that defeated the immediate campaign and jeopardized immeasurably the causes for which I believe I would be willing to die. You have helped me to come closer to the truth, to see my own guilt clearly. . . . When success was imminent in our racial campaign my behavior stopped progress. . . . I have misused the confidence the negroes here had in my leadership; I have caused them to question the moral basis of nonviolence; I have hurt and let down my friends over the country and caused people like you and Doris to grieve.

Rustin recounted his reading, after Muste's visit, of the parable of the prodigal son in the New Testament. The decision to return home and face the father, he explained, came not because the son blamed others for his plight, but because "he said simply, 'I will arise. I will have done with my past ways which have ended in animal behavior. I will be a man.'" As if emulating the character in Luke's Gospel story, Rustin continued:

> I am thus asking you and the FOR and all others to forgive me for the damage I have done. I have asked the C.O.s here to do so. . . . I am a traitor (by our means of struggle) just as surely as an army captain who willfully exposed military positions during a battle. . . . I have thought I was dedicated to "race and non-violence," but I now see that the mistakes I made have come because I have really been dedicated to "ego." I have thought in terms of my power, my time, my energy and of giving them to a great struggle.

I have thought in terms of my voice, my ability, my willingness to
go into the non-violent vanguard. I have not humbly accepted
God's gifts to me. . . . [This] has led, I now see, first to arrogance
and pride and then to weakness, to artificiality, and to failure.

Having laid out this rare self-assessment of his character, Rustin described a spiritual discipline for himself. He also promised humility
toward the authorities in order to earn back their respect and redeem
himself in his own eyes and those of his comrades.[19]

Rustin's letter brought "great relief to my spirit," Muste hurriedly
wrote back. "I experienced much anguish knowing the hard and bitter
experience through which you were passing," he acknowledged. "Your
letters are greatly reassuring. You are on the right path. Look humbly
to God for grace to persevere in it." Muste and Grotewohl also brought
Platt into the circle of communication by finally divulging to him the
content of Rustin's troubles. Platt's letter to Rustin has not survived.
But from Rustin's response, it seems that his young lover insisted that
he pledge to remain celibate in prison and faithful not only to Platt but
also to the high moral standards he claimed for himself. "Your letter,"
Rustin responded, "humbles me. . . . I have betrayed you and the things
for which we stand. I offer no defense. I accept you and A.J.'s alternative as the only one. . . . I failed, Davis, more miserably than you can
imagine."[20]

RUSTIN'S RESOLVE TO deal humbly with authority proved difficult
to implement. From November into the following spring, reports filed
by prison officers reveal a pattern of oscillation between rebellion and
docility, resistance and compliance. By this time, the prison staff was
unwilling to cut Rustin any slack; their accounts must be read as the
worst possible interpretation of his actions. Two weeks out of isolation,
several guards wrote him up for resisting orders. Each described a
physical confrontation in which he had to be dragged into his cell by
several of them. Later, when ordered back into isolation because of the
disruption, he refused to budge from his cell, gripping the bars until
guards pried his fingers loose. They characterized Rustin as insolent,

threatening, and imperious. "His struggling had been as violent as that of any mental patient," according to one officer. "He acted as one completely mad."[21]

Hagerman particularly had lost all tolerance for Rustin. Through late fall and winter, he kept up a flow of letters to Bennett in which he asked for relief from the burden of Rustin. Two days after the struggle between Rustin and the group of guards, Hagerman described him as a "true psycopath [*sic*]" and begged to have him transferred. For a while, Hagerman and Bennett debated sending Rustin to a federal medical facility where inmates labeled psychopathic were confined, a move that would have branded him a homosexual. Early in January, after a lull in the correspondence, Bennett penned a short note to Hagerman. "I hope no news is good news," he wrote. But Ashland officials were preparing their pre-parole report on Rustin, describing him as "a homosexual, an obstructionist, and a rabble-rouser." Hagerman never revised these views. A few months later, he curtly described Rustin as "this colored homosexual."[22]

Rustin presented an unsolvable puzzle to prison administrators. The gulf in understanding was too wide to bridge. Unregenerate as he appeared to his captors, in some respects he did modify his behavior after his release from isolation. When called to task for rude or insolent remarks to staff, Rustin often apologized. His letters suggest a persistent struggle to contain what he himself called a tendency toward "selfishness and strong spitefulness."[23] He knew that at times, he lashed out in ways that were not merely unwarranted and unwise, but un-Christian as well. He seemed powerless to restrain himself. The arrogant edge that allowed him to adhere to unpopular beliefs also made it difficult to bend even when circumstances counseled that he try. Despite his disgrace—or perhaps because of it—he felt all the more the need to make a stand within the enclosed world of the federal prison system. When prison officials denied Larry Gara the "good time" that would have made early release possible, Rustin joined other COs in a work strike. Although his credibility with the inmate population had been compromised, he continued to lodge individual protests against the segregated seating in the dining facilities. Each week, it often seemed, brought another situation that called forth his resistance. The experience of incarceration by a government engaged in war hardened his convictions. "I am ever more conscious of the evils of regimentation in any form," he wrote Platt. "I am even more convinced that conscription is to be fought in the most complete sense." Although he had promised Muste to behave respectfully toward his jailers, "I never indicated that I was willing to accept conscription or a new philosophy of Government."[24]

As he looked beyond prison toward a world at war, he saw only more evidence of the need to resist violence and coercion. Rustin was never fool enough to believe that the goodwill of pacifists alone could stop the plunders of a Hitler. Still, he grasped the danger that victory through the power of arms inevitably carried. "Having established the principles of violence," he wrote to Platt, "the users will not be able to rise above it and eradicate it. . . . The criminal demand for unconditional surrender, the British policy of intervention in Greece, the American race superiority in the Orient, the essentially violent nature of Dumbarton Oaks . . . all are disturbing witnesses to the correctness of pacifist analyses and project a gloomy picture for future world violence." Assaying the role of pacifists like himself, he told Platt, "the vicious circle must be broken now and witness given to another way of life."[25]

RUSTIN USED HIS DAYS in prison to reflect on more than issues of war and peace, nonviolence and racial justice. The crisis provoked by his sexual behavior prompted a season of intense spiritual struggle. During this time, he revisited the decision that he had made earlier in his life to pursue rather than repress his sexual attraction toward men. He debated with himself, as well as with Muste and Platt, the ethics of sexual relationships. He contemplated the possibility of becoming, through an exercise of will, heterosexual and even speculated about his capacity for celibacy. Only fragments of the correspondence have survived. But they provide a tantalizing and, for the era, an unusual glimpse into the thinking of one gay man wrestling with his sexual desires. They also tell us something of the views of Christian radicals toward sex, love, and intimacy.

Information about the evolution of Rustin's sexual identity is meager. Some of the silence can be attributed to the man. However introspective he might have been, Rustin saved his most creative writing for the issues that his generation of radicals considered political: racial equality, economic justice, war and peace. He never kept a journal or diary, and his letters tended to be about his work. The few exceptions are those he wrote while incarcerated, and they had to be phrased carefully because of prison surveillance. Thus, even when he did move from the public to the personal, Rustin wrote in ways that were stilted and detached. But much of the silence can be attributed to the times. It was an era in which homosexual and heterosexual cooperated in an elaborately choreographed dance of discretion.

The reasons were complex. There was fear of sanctions in a society that proscribed homosexual behavior by law. The revelation of one's sexual desires might lead to loss of employment, the rupture of relationships, and violence. There was the sense of shame that many gay men internalized when there was little in the broader culture that affirmed their inclinations. There were the social inhibitions that heterosexuals and homosexuals of that generation would have experienced over bringing such matters into a conversation. Even between gay men, much was conveyed obliquely, assumed rather than stated. Groups of friends might socialize for years without ever alluding to the identity that brought them together. Between heterosexual and homosexual, the clues, hints, and suggestions might grow so complex that one could never be sure who knew what. In other words, while silence did not imply ignorance, it nonetheless bred uncertainty and confusion. Individuals might know, but couldn't say; they might assume knowledge on someone else's part, but wrongly. Of the pacifists interviewed who worked with Rustin in the 1940s and 1950s, every one of them said that they knew he was gay, even while saying that, at the time, no one spoke about it. Hence, they could not remember specific conversations, or any coming-out moment. But then how did they know? What did they know? And when did they know it? Answers to these questions would reveal much about how Rustin integrated his sexual identity into his world of work and political activism and the degree of acceptance he found. But such answers are elusive.

One example is telling. In September 1943, Davis Platt left his family at the Vanderbilt Hotel to spend a few nights with Rustin at the home of Wallace and Franny Lee, a Quaker couple with whom Rustin was close. For the twenty-year-old Platt—crossing a racial divide in his intimacy with Rustin, embarking on his first serious gay relationship, entering the social milieu of a man older and more worldly than he— the ability to make love in the home of a heterosexual couple signified the psychological distance between him and the man he loved. Whereas Platt had been struggling mightily with his sexual attraction to men, Rustin appeared confident, assured, and free of guilt. His homosexuality was an integral part of him, openly accepted by the heterosexuals in his life. Yet the interactions that Platt construed as signs of honesty Franny Lee interpreted differently. Over Thanksgiving weekend, 1944, a month after Rustin's epistle of contrition to Muste, she penned a letter of exquisite tenderness and caring. Muste had communicated to her what had happened, and she had already sent Rustin a quick note expressing love. Now she communicated her thoughts about Bayard's situation. But she prefaced her ruminations with this surprising comment: "I have never minded the physical angle, and I've *always* known of it— The only thing that bothered me . . . is that you tried to hide it from me, and therefore it made any close relationship slightly unreal because of that pretense always between us."[26] Rustin had slept in her home with a young man thoroughly infatuated with him, yet Lee saw secrecy as the defining element of their relationship.

Lee segued smoothly from the matter of duplicity to issues of love, intimacy, and promiscuity, matters that weighed heavily in the moral calculations of these Christian radicals. Her letter captures the flavor of the debate that raged within Rustin and between him and Muste:

> I would still be not at all concerned at [the physical] side of things
> if I felt a sense of real love for another person—For it is in the to-
> tality of your relationships with other people that I think the diffi-

culty lies—You know how it has been—Relationships have been
intense perhaps, but basically very casual for you. . . . It dulls
everything into intense momentary pleasures, with no regard for
the whole personality of the other human being involved—When
these pleasures become so important, then everything else becomes less so and it is easy to lie and pretend always more. . . . [I]
do not begrudge anyone *any* sort of relationship if it is the basis of
a really creative and constructive life. . . . However, now I wonder
somehow, for you, if it ever *can* lead to stable or secure relationships, or whether it *can* be satisfying in the long run—I wonder if
it isn't ultimately only frustrating and therefore a natural header
into promiscuity . . . it is not the physical side, but the promiscuity
and carelessness which bothers me—They lead absolutely nowhere,
and I am so concerned that you find a way that is absolutely right
for you—you have so much to give to others, and are inherently
such a creative and forceful person that it would be so wrong for
you not to find it.

Lee went on to speculate about whether Rustin needed to renounce homosexual expression or whether he should only refrain from sexual engagement with someone "until you were very clear about the totality of
any relationship."[27]

Rustin took to heart the words of his friend. Through the fall and
winter, he struggled to tame the powerful yearnings that drove him to
the sexual relationships that Lee described. To Platt, he made a pledge
to remain celibate in prison. In coded letters in which Rustin referred
to Platt as "Marie" or "M" he described the impact: "Between me and
M there has been since October a series of experiences that represent
less fear, less deceit, and more understanding than between me and any
other human with whom there has been any love. . . . It came about
gradually in letters, little acts of thoughtfulness, real criticism she made
that I knew hurt her to make and [showed] her loyalty at a time when
most people suffering as she suffered would have run wildly in another
direction for self protection."[28]

Soon, Platt's generosity of spirit began to pierce Rustin's emotional armor. "I began to write 'real' letters," he recalled the next spring. "I had not really had exchanges of the little things that make life grow. Unable to send all the words, clippings, etc. that I wished, I got a folder, marked it M., and each day I spent time with her in the folder—reading little lists I know she would want to hear, copying little poems I write that she would laugh with me over, collecting material on race that she would find interesting, making notes of what to say in the next letter." For Rustin, these awkward acts of caring were the bricks and mortar of a new intimacy that he worked to construct. "I know that I need to give myself," he wrote, "to build (as you have analyzed) a beautiful and sincere relationship—to overcome that disbalance between adventure and emotional security you so excellently and accurately described. To find beauty and peace with another for only in this way can love flow back toward humanity." Meanwhile, his pledge to Platt stood "not only as a barrier to any promiscuity but as a bond of real and spiritual love that can cut off any tendencies to feel lost or cut off from someone who cares."

IN THE MIDST OF his emotional turmoil, an urgent message arrived at the prison from Julia. "Father Janifer Rustin critically ill asking for Bayard," she cabled the warden. "End expected soon." Hagerman extended permission for an emergency bedside visit and, accompanied by Carter, one of the senior guards who had often disciplined him, Rustin left Ashland on March 28 for the overnight journey by train.[29]

Platt learned of the trip and quickly arranged to visit family in nearby Paoli. Astoundingly, Carter allowed his charge, as Platt recalled it, "to be in my custody for an entire afternoon. And my uncle, who lived across the street from where I lived, from where my parents lived, agreed to vacate his house so that I was able to make lunch for Bayard, and make love to Bayard, and be alone with him for about three hours." Their lovemaking and the words of commitment they exchanged seemed to rescue Rustin from what he called his "dark night of struggle." As he wrote to Platt the next week, "few times in my life have I been so happy."[30]

On the return trip to Ashland, Rustin and Carter changed trains in

Columbus, Ohio. Helen Winnemore, a Quaker activist there, was waiting to meet them. A decade older than Rustin, Winnemore had often
hosted him in the home she shared with her mother and sister when his
travels brought him to Columbus. Their connection was close enough
that Rustin placed Winnemore on his correspondence list. Throughout
his first year in prison, Winnemore had repeatedly written to bureau
officials for permission to visit. In explaining the relationship, she described it as "a friendship more than personal. . . . Bayard is not my
friend in at all a casual sense." Hagerman, who read her correspondence
to Rustin, interpreted Winnemore's interest as "romantic," which he
found "hard to understand . . . with [Rustin's] known depravity."[31]

Carter allowed Rustin and Winnemore to speak privately. In a letter
to Platt, Rustin recounted the gist of what she said: "I believe your
greatest immediate need is real love, real understanding and confidence. . . . I tell you without shame of the love I have for you, of my desire to be with you thru light and darkness, to give all that I possess that
the goodness within you shall live and flower." Her words shocked
them both into a period of silence. For Rustin, her declaration was an
invitation to reconsider his whole sexual history, to question his commitment to Platt and his assumption that he was irrevocably homosexual. Winnemore had "pushed open a door long closed . . . she led me to
tell her all (the very worst and much I had never had the courage to discuss with a woman)." Rustin found himself confessing "every emotional
impulse I have had. . . . I told her 'Helen, there are times when I feel
that I can't go on trying any longer.' . . . Still she said she believed in
me." The experience took on the quality of a religious epiphany. "Never
had I heard such unselfish love speak in a woman. Never had I sensed a
more simple and complete offering. . . . I felt that she had been sent by
God as messengers from Him are recorded appearing to mortals in the
Old Testament." Three weeks later, the recollection still evoked the
language of a religious conversion: "a joy that is almost beyond understanding—a flash of light in the right direction—a new hope . . . a sudden reevaluation . . . a light on the road I know I should travel."

Rustin's anguished soul searching is evident in the many pages he
wrote to Platt. The hardships of a year in prison, the shame and humil-

iation that his deceitfulness brought down on him, the long weeks of sober reflection that solitary imposed, the fear that his chosen vocation might slip away because of sexual desires out of his control—together these had left Rustin emotionally lacerated and desperate to explore anything that promised some peace of mind. "I must now carry on toward the goal until every stone is turned," he wrote Platt. "I must pray, trust, experience, dream, hope and all else possible until I know clearly in my own mind and spirit that I have failed, if I must fail, not because of a faint heart, or for lack of confidence in my true self, or for pride, or for emotional instability or for moral lethargy or any other character fault, but rather because I come to see after the most complete searching that the best for me lies elsewhere." Doubts plagued him. "How does one come to a decision," he wrote.

> Is one inwardly ready to decide? Can a decision have meaning that does not grow into being? Are there times when one must simply cut oneself off? . . . I see the power M. has exerted in helping me in holding the line [against sex in prison]. Is not this valuable, I say? But then I wonder, am I rationalizing? Is such dependence on a love object necessary? Can more prayer replace this apparent need? Can one strongly driven exist without a harness? . . . Is celibacy the answer? . . . I have a real desire for following another way but I have never had a desire to completely remove sex from my mind. What can celibacy become without such an inner desire? Does not holding M. before me as an object toward whom I project these terrific impulses stifle the beam of light I saw when I spoke with H?

The questions seemed endless and, Rustin knew, not resolvable amid the sexual tensions of prison. "It is not easy to remain here in a mono-sexual world and make progress. So much of one's energies is taken in building up resistance for keeping the simple pledge of abstainence [*sic*]," he wrote. "As Alice said to the Queen in observing Wonderland, it takes a great deal of running to stand still." Rustin, in other words, was deciding not to decide. He was putting aside the question of what kind of life he would have on the outside, while keeping his pledge to refrain from sex in jail.

Rustin instructed Platt to share these letters with Muste and Grote-wohl, which suggests that he conceived his struggle not as a solitary one, or even a private reckoning between two lovers, but as part of the business of a Gandhian movement in America. Indeed, Muste was considering whether Rustin's behavior could be reconciled with a revolutionary movement planted in religious soil. Muste was disturbed by Rustin's indecision. The relationship with Platt, he feared, "would inhibit . . . attempts to take up H's way." In long conversations with Platt, he encouraged the young man to consider intimacy with women, which, he suggested, "could in time probably reach a real and even more perfect union."[32] To Rustin, he penned a quick but brief note. "You have had word from Davis which has given you an insight into the general trend of my thinking," he wrote. "My mind and heart are a good deal disturbed."[33]

Muste, an inveterate correspondent, waited an uncharacteristically long two months before writing again to Rustin in any great detail. In a letter dated June 18, Muste laid out a moral philosophy of love, which he called "the essence and supreme value in life." It combined mystery and rationality, spontaneity and restraint. This was the paradox embedded in the pursuit of ethical relationships: "How utterly barren and horrible when not spontaneous; how utterly horrible and cheap where there is no discipline, no *form* in the relationship." Just as the "artist with the freest vision, the most powerful creative urge . . . submits to the severest discipline," so too must the lover tame spontaneity in order to reach "the discipline, the control, the effort to understand the other." Promiscuity failed the standard he had set for love. "Where *that* happens it seems to me we come close to the travesty and denial of love, for if love means depth, means understanding above the ordinary . . . means *exchange* of spiritual life-blood, how can that happen among an indefinite number of people? *Physical* relationship, yes . . . but this is not love. Since it involves an essential *indifference* toward the person . . . an unconscious impulse to use and exploit rather than to understand and nourish, it is the opposite of love." Applying these standards, Muste advised Rustin to abandon altogether the pursuit of sexual intimacy with men.[34]

Two weeks later, Muste wrote again. He reiterated his belief that the only choice for Rustin was a life of promiscuous homosexuality or the rejection of sex with men. He urged the latter because of what homosexuality had meant for Rustin "in the concrete instance, not in the theoretical." "We don't have a problem of whether it's a good idea in general to cut off people's right hands. The problem is: 'If thy right hand offends *thee*, cut it off.'" In Rustin's case, the preponderance of evidence seemed clear: "How utterly undisciplined and deceitful your past course has been . . . how ruinous and searing your conduct has been."

Muste made the implications for Rustin's future unambiguous. "There cannot be the slightest question as to what this means for your participation in the pacifist or any other social movement which has any ethical implications," he wrote. "I have a responsibility to discharge in that respect and I need not say to you that I would not hesitate to discharge it . . . unless of course you make a decision which makes this possible." He also tried to impress on Rustin that the stakes were "a lot deeper than any question about your *role* in *any* movement."

> It has to do with *you* as a person. Don't you see that with your undiscipline, deceit practiced on your dearest comrades, superficiality, jumping about, arrogance, you are—in one sense—running away from your self and—in another—destroying yourself? How often have you denounced luke-warm pacifists and workers against Jim Crow—people who wouldn't do and sacrifice for the cause—oh, Bayard, Bayard. No one, *no one*, has any business being self-righteous—but to *ourselves* we do apply standards and there are *some limits* to self-indulgence, to lying, to being the play-boy, for those who undertake to arouse their fellows to moral issues.

Muste pleaded with his protégé to come to his senses. "I know there is that in you which shrinks from a decision here because you want *personal* security, love, warmth, being wanted. We all do and, God, what we don't do to get these things. But you are not getting them. . . . This failure to *fix* upon an object—to dig down to where there are so many ties that you *are* secure—is evidence of that. . . . I don't know—no one can be sure in advance—what *expression* true love will find . . . but in you there are depths and gifts which will bring you security, warmth, exhilaration, ecstatic joy, if only you give up what amounts to a death-wish."[35] Tough words, written with the passion of a moralist arguing his case who, finally, could not imagine homosexual love.

Rustin resisted Muste's logic. Perhaps he sensed how impossible it would be to withstand the longings that drove him toward men. Perhaps he disagreed with Muste's assessment of his options. Knowing the effort he had made since November with Platt to, in Muste's words, "dig down to where there are so many ties that you *are* secure," perhaps he believed he could experience a lasting relationship with a man. In any case, some sparring continued through the mails, with Muste urging "a decisive parting of the ways" and Rustin just as resolutely refusing. "I did not feel prolonged discussion by mail to be of much value," he finally wrote Platt. "There is nothing more I can say."[36] With that, the correspondence ended.

AND STILL HE WAS in prison. In May 1945, Ashland received a new infusion of radical conscientious objectors, men from the CPS camp in Germfask, Michigan, who had collectively refused to cooperate any longer. The arrival of these militants emboldened Rustin to launch a new round of protests against racial segregation. When Hagerman refused even to discuss his demands, Rustin led many of the COs in a hunger strike. He also wrote to the inmate population an appeal for support with a noticeably harder edge than in his writings of the previous year. "We are tired of talking about segregation. We have acted," he announced. "We know we ain't dealin' with our grandmothers. But we are not slaves either. We will not accept a slave's mind. We are willing to pay a price for our freedom. We will have a degree of freedom no matter what happens—for we will feel we are men for having protested."[37]

This new protest was too much for Bennett. "I am a little weary of Rustin," he wrote to Hagerman. "We have done everything in the world we can to help him and to protect him from the social disgrace which I should think he would feel if he were transferred to Springfield because of his homosexual tendencies." Hagerman set in motion the steps to justify a different transfer. Staff composed disciplinary reports in which they let all their impatience show. "He is known to be a schemer, an organizer, and a crusader for race issues," said one. "Rustin's arrogant manner and picayunish attitudes combined with a deep urge for attention and a basic dishonesty have contrived to irritate and rasp many employees as well as inmates," wrote another. Recognizing that Rustin's "case is hot" because of the support he had on the outside, Hagerman proposed that several prisoners be transferred simultaneously "so as to appear not too conspicuous or pointed toward the particular case of Rustin." Bennett agreed, and on August 3, the transfer was effected. With his mandolin, six music books, two prayer books, some pictures, and miscellaneous letters, Rustin was sent to the penitentiary in Lewisburg, Pennsylvania.[38]

The mug shot that Lewisburg officials snapped upon his arrival reveals the toll of his seventeen months in prison. Rustin appears thinner than a year earlier. Instead of the detached, almost serene look that characterized his Ashland photograph, the newer one shows him glaring at the camera, angry, embittered, morose. And with good reason. Not only had he suffered through a harrowing year, but the point of his trials was rapidly fading. The war was ending. Within days of his arrival at Lewisburg, American forces dropped atom bombs on Hiroshima and Nagasaki, ushering in a new era in human history. American troops in Europe and Asia were being demobilized, yet conscripts of conscience like Rustin continued to languish in jail.

Lewisburg was also a different institution from Ashland. As Ralph DiGia, a member of the War Resisters League, remembered it: "Lewisburg has a wall with guards and guns on the top. And the people! . . . In prison, the persons with the longest sentence were top gun. You get to Lewisburg, you know, [our] three years is nothing. 15 years, 10 years, 25 years . . . bank robbers. It was a rough place."[39] W. H. Hiatt, the warden at Lewisburg, managed his institution accordingly. His approach to the conscientious objectors sent to him was both tough and pragmatic. He had dealt with their protests over censorship

and racial segregation, with hunger strikes and work stoppages. By the
time Rustin arrived, Hiatt had settled on a simple solution: he set up a
makeshift dormitory in the prison library, segregated all the troublesome conscientious objectors there, and let them stew in each other's
company.

"It was the simplest way," Larry Gara recalled. "Get them out of the
way. Out of sight. Let them have their own [space] and drive each other
nuts. And we did. . . . It was a real circus there. . . . Meals were taken to
us. . . . We never left that room. Never left that room." As Gara, who
had been sent to Lewisburg for violating his parole, remembered those
months: "We talked about all kinds of things. We talked about taking
over one of the Western states where the population is [small]—not
taking over, but moving in in a pacifist way. We feared that militarization would be very prominent and would continue. Some of us thought
we might be in prison all our lives. We talked about the race situation.
I read Myrdal's book in there. Bayard was very impressed with that. *An
American Dilemma.*"[40]

The confinement in Lewisburg was immensely dispiriting to Rustin.
For one, the stigma of his sexuality followed him there, if only in an at-
tenuated way. "Bob Brooks evidently knew what the rest of us didn't
know much about," Lawrence Templin, another imprisoned CO, recalled. "Or some did and some didn't, I don't know who knew what.
About his being gay. And it was for him, for Bob Brooks, it was an awful thing that someone high up in the pacifist movement would be gay.
And he made some remonstrance, I don't remember what it was, about
Bayard being in our midst."[41]

Even more disheartening was the pointlessness of his continuing incarceration, the inability to make it count for anything. Whatever he
possessed of the spirit of Gandhi deserted him at Lewisburg. Making
little effort to win over his opponents, he directed sharp, abusive language at the prison personnel. He engaged in protests—against the use
of registration numbers as identifying marks when asking for medical
supplies, for instance—that represented resistance for its own sake.
When Julia, his grandmother, visited in November, she seemed "rather

put out" by his petty rebelliousness and "warned him on this point." Fiercely loyal to her beloved grandson, she nonetheless contacted the warden and implored him to allow a visit from Muste. "I really think if Mr. Muste was permitted to visit Bayard he would have great influence in getting Bayard to do the things we all wish him to do," she wrote to Hiatt.[42]

Rustin's recalcitrance meant that he was unable to accumulate "good time" for early release. His adamant refusal to cooperate might have kept him incarcerated until March 1947. To his colleagues on the outside, his behavior seemed to have passed beyond reason, and they tried to entice him into cooperation. Even before he had left Ashland, Grotewohl wrote to him about CORE in New York. "Some of us here are searching for new nonviolent direct action techniques to be used in CORE action projects. The old tricks seem to us to be just about worn out. . . . Bayard, believe me, those who are working on the race situation need you." George Houser wrote as well, telling him of conversations he was having with Randolph, Roy Wilkins of the NAACP, Roger Baldwin of the ACLU, and George Schuyler, a columnist for the *Pittsburgh Courier*, about plans for an interracial mass movement. "I think that [you and I] might be able to work well together," he told Rustin, and he encouraged his jailed comrade to think about the future and "come out prepared to do the things that you can do."[43]

With the number of COs at Lewisburg dwindling to little more than a handful, Rustin made one last futile stand against segregation in prison. On February 28, he commenced another hunger strike. Within days, he was being tube-fed in the prison hospital. The action galvanized Muste, who finally persuaded Hiatt to let him visit. Muste reasoned with Rustin as best he could. The atom bomb, the escalating tensions with the Soviet Union, and the prospect for breakthroughs in race relations all demanded that Rustin be out of jail, where his talents would count for something. But that would mean, Muste said, abandoning his protests, abiding by the institution's rules, and doing whatever it took to secure an early release. At last Rustin complied. "My final decision after considerable thought and prayer," he wrote to Bennett in Washington, "is to dedicate my energies solely to release, and upon release to the problems [Muste] so clearly helped me understand to be the problems of our age."[44]

Events moved quickly after that. Hiatt assigned him to the minimum-security prison farm, where Rustin cooperated with the daily routine. In May, Hiatt informed Bennett that Rustin was "doing a good job as a teacher and clerk and his influence as an agitator has been excised from the institution." One more small flap occurred when Rustin, yielding to a last imperious impulse, expressed displeasure at the clothes the prison was providing for his return to civilian life. But a release date of June 11, 1946, was set and adhered to. He exited the front gate at 11:20 in the morning, wearing a two-piece blue suit, with thirty dollars in his pocket, and took the train to Penn Station in Manhattan where an over-joyed Julia waited to greet him.[45]

CHAPTER SIX

"The Gadfly Which Has Stirred Men into Action"

1946–1947

RUSTIN'S FIRST DAYS of freedom brought reunions with old friends and comrades. Almost immediately he went to the annual conference of the War Resisters League (WRL), a pacifist organization on whose board he served, and entranced those attending with the "plaintive, moving lyricism" of his singing. A few days later, he attended the yearly gathering of Friends in Cape May, New Jersey. There he created, as one of the participants remembered, "a great stir" when he went to one of the evening dances at a local hotel and, ignoring the color line of the still-segregated vacation resort, spun around the floor with a white female partner.

Rustin was no more willing to accommodate the continuing demands of the federal prison system than he was the social mores of southern New Jersey. Muste quickly put him on the lecture circuit, sending him to colleges, churches, and organizational conferences to address issues of pacifism, nonviolence, and racial justice. This placed Rustin in conflict with the conditions of his parole, which required that he request permission any time he expected to leave New York City. Rustin let Maurice Sanders, his parole officer, know that he was prepared to inform Sanders of his plans. But "if permission is not granted," he would violate his parole "by making the trip without permission." Soon he was telling Sanders that any request for information from him "is pointless since he is going to carry on his work and travel as necessary whether we grant permission or not." At one point, a frustrated

Sanders asked for a warrant for Rustin's arrest, but the Board of Parole thought twice about serving it. "Nothing would be gained by requiring him to serve the remainder of the federal sentence," it decided; the warrant was dropped and the case closed. Defiant and headstrong to the end, Rustin had the last word in the long battle with his jailers when he authored an article for the Pennsylvania Prison Society, "Imprisonment from the Inside." Prisons, he wrote, "are schools for crime and immorality." It roiled James Bennett when he read it, but all Bennett could do was protest privately.[1]

TWENTY-SEVEN MONTHS IS not a long time in the life of an individual, even less in the history of a nation. Yet Rustin—and the United States—had changed profoundly over the course of his prison term.

At the time he went to jail, Rustin was still testing his wings as a pacifist and advocate of Gandhi's way. There was certainly enough in his background—the Quaker influence, Julia Rustin's community activism, his personal stands against race discrimination while still a youth—to make this a plausible path for his life. His first two and a half years at the FOR, in which he experienced the heady sense of developing new approaches to the struggle for racial equality, demonstrated that he brought passion, skill, and charisma to the work. But many are the young men and women who make their way to the doors of a movement for revolutionary change, enter for a time, and then leave. Rustin might easily have become one of those who lend their labor for a while and then move on to a life dominated by private concerns.

Incarceration closed that exit. The bone-chilling terror of losing his freedom so completely, the shame and humiliation his sexual transgressions inflicted upon him, the weeks in solitary, and the even longer time in which he and other COs hashed through ideas about the new world of peace and fellowship they hoped to create—after all this, Rustin emerged from Lewisburg with a steely commitment to redeem himself and to prove that his sacrifice mattered. To use the language of prison, he was now "a lifer."

But the America to which he returned had changed too. In March 1944, when he entered Ashland, the nation was at war. Now the Axis powers were utterly vanquished. Hitler was dead, German cities were in ruins, the horrifying reality of the concentration camps was fully exposed. Hiroshima and Nagasaki had experienced the terrible power of the atom bomb. As the sole possessor of the most destructive weapon ever made, the United States emerged from the global conflict with its power dramatically enhanced.

The war brought substantial material benefits to most Americans. Their nation was the only major combatant to escape its ravages at home. The casualties, though too high for the families, friends, and communities who lost loved ones, were low in comparison to what the Soviet Union, Germany, Japan, China, France, Poland, and Britain endured. The war also closed the door on a decade-long economic depression. It put Americans to work and filled their pockets, their purses, and their savings accounts. It opened opportunities for millions of GIs who took advantage of federally subsidized housing loans and educational benefits.

But war does not make for a simple calculus of gains and losses, as Gandhian pacifists like Rustin knew. The GIs who survived combat with their bodies intact had lived through wrenching violence. The families and communities to which they returned had suffered the agony of anticipated loss. In one sense, it mattered little that the deaths were fewer than those of other nations or that the homes of Americans were still standing. The feeling of sacrifice was just as deep, the resolve to preserve the fruits of victory hard and sure.

The collective psychology that pacifists posited as the reason that war can never create peace—violence unleashing more violence, hatred spawning hatred, the demonization of an enemy generating more enemies to demonize—was much in evidence in postwar America. By the time of Rustin's release, the country seemed headed toward a new international crisis. Early in 1946, Winston Churchill, the British leader who had shepherded his nation through the war, gave his "Iron Curtain" speech to an American audience. He warned that a totalitarianism every bit as malevolent as Nazism was spreading westward from Russia and blanketing Eastern Europe under a new tyranny. In the United Nations, U.S. and Soviet representatives sparred over the issue of atomic weapons and rival plans to prevent their spread and use. Harry Truman, who unexpectedly became president in 1945, embraced a rhetoric of toughness in his dealings with the Russians.

These early signs of an emerging cold war took on a sharper hue in the succeeding years. Early in 1947, the president enunciated what came to be called the Truman Doctrine when he asked Congress to approve economic and military aid to Greece and Turkey. In apocalyptic language, he portrayed a world divided between good and evil, a global struggle between freedom and tyranny. The United States, he vowed, must be the front-line defender of democracy. Soon, headline-making international events became common fare: the Soviet blockade of Berlin and the dramatic U.S. airlift; the creation of the North Atlantic Treaty Organization, the first peacetime alliance in America's history; the Soviet explosion of an atom bomb; the Communist victory in China. At home, Congress enacted peacetime conscription, and Truman approved plans to develop an even more destructive hydrogen bomb. A country whose military establishment in 1938 had been smaller than Belgium's was moving toward permanent militarization. As it did so, it grew suspicious of dissent and nonconformity of every kind and searched for enemies in its midst.

These events were still to come when Rustin left Lewisburg. They suggest, however, that a wide gulf separated the future that he longed for from the expectations of policymakers in Washington and most other Americans too. Like Rustin and other imprisoned COs, the non-pacifist majority had sacrificed, suffered, and steeled their will to resist forces that seemed unmistakably wicked. But the conclusions that Rustin drew from his wartime suffering about how to build a world of peace and justice were dramatically different from the lessons learned by a nation on the edge of the cold war.

ON A MUCH SMALLER scale, the FOR had also changed while Rustin was away. Concerns from the 1930s, such as industrial conflict, had faded. The move to apply nonviolent resistance to America's simmering racial cauldron had gathered strength during the war. And the dangers posed by the atomic bomb loomed large in the minds of pacifists.

Some of the faces were different as well. Doris Grotewohl and Shizu Asahi, with whom Rustin had bonded so easily, were gone. So was Jim Farmer. To fill his place, George Houser, a CORE founder from Chicago, had moved to the national office in New York. Many of the male staff had spent time in jail. The experience bred a tougher resolve on their part that often kept them several paces ahead of a less committed membership. It also kept them frustrated when the members of the Fellowship never seemed to catch up.

Even before the war ended, Muste was turning his attention to what would follow, calling on his comrades to consider "how pacifism could be made into an effective revolutionary force" in the postwar world. American pacifism's elder statesman had little faith in either the good intentions of Allied leaders—Roosevelt, Churchill, and Stalin—or their ability to construct a postwar order tending toward peace. Muste regularly referred to the Dumbarton Oaks conference, at which the first sketch of a United Nations was laid out, as "Dumbarton Hoax." The coupling of an international organization with Allied war aims of unconditional surrender struck him as akin to linking the League of Nations to the war guilt clause of the Versailles Treaty a generation earlier.[2]

The destruction of Hiroshima and Nagasaki added an element of apocalyptic urgency to Muste's ruminations about the future. In a memo written two months after Japan's surrender, he predicted "an armaments race of fantastic proportions" unless the atom bomb came under international control. "If the war against the atomic bomb is lost, there is an end in our day and for generations to come of any progressive social program. If it is won, the solution of other major issues in the realm of economics, government, race, etc. will be greatly simplified."[3] The succeeding generation of American politics would prove Muste remarkably prescient. Dreams of racial justice, of ending poverty, of creating, in Lyndon Johnson's later phrase, a "Great Society," would falter when cold war assumptions led the nation into war in Southeast Asia.

Muste's views on the need to make effective witness against the atom bomb had persuaded Rustin to drop his stance of noncooperation in prison so that he could lend his voice to the struggle for peace. "Our program is to make pacifists of people," Rustin once explained, and in

the months after his release from Lewisburg, he toured the country trying to do just that. A traveling evangelist for a world without war and
weaponry, he was an especially popular speaker at youth camps run by
the AFSC and at denominational colleges operated by the historic
peace churches.[4] In his lectures and seminars, he held out a moral challenge to his listeners as well as a contagious optimism about the future.
Notes taken by a member of the audience at a conference in Ohio reveal Rustin's telling the crowd that advances in human affairs "don't just
happen. They are the result of a determined and persistent courageous
insistence that a vision of a better world shall be to some extent realized." The rewards, he promised, would be great. "There are forces for
good in the world," he told them, "which cannot be stayed nor long denied."[5]

As he had before his prison term, Rustin left his mark on many of
those who encountered him. Dave McReynolds was a college student at
UCLA when he first heard Rustin speak in the late 1940s. "I was transformed listening to him," McReynolds said. "I was absolutely hypno-
tized. . . . He left such an impact on me that I spoke like him and used
his gestures for a week or two afterwards." George Houser, who saw
Rustin in action time and again, marveled at the response he elicited.
"You would see people with tears coming out of their eyes. He could respond to a group or get in touch with them because he was a likable creative personality."[6]

But Rustin's pacifist work in these years was generally more dispiriting than satisfying. The revulsion against militarism that developed after World War I never materialized in the 1940s. The moral rationale
for fighting the war struck most Americans as too clear to provoke retrospective regrets; even the horrific destruction of Hiroshima and Nagasaki seemed justified. Americans wanted peace, but not pacifism, and
in the postwar world, peace increasingly came to be linked with military
preparedness. Rustin found himself preaching mostly to the choir. The
frustrations played themselves out in staff meetings, board gatherings,
and organizational retreats, since the FOR in these years was a house
divided. It included men like the venerable Nevin Sayre, who announced to one national meeting that "the problem of prayer must

have much of our attention . . . the tapping of sources of energy, wisdom, and light," and Milton Mayer, a faculty member at the University of Chicago, who announced at the 1946 FOR national conference that "pacifism is not enough. . . . The only true pacifist is a fighting pacifist; the only person who is against war is the person who is fighting against injustice wherever injustice is."[7]

In these debates, Rustin embraced the most militant uncompromising positions, so much so that his stance sometimes led to sharp words and hard feelings. For instance, ever since the closing stages of the war, the FOR had watched closely the debates in Washington over universal military training. From 1945 on, it took the lead in forging an anticonscription coalition in Washington with mainstream organizations ranging from the American Civil Liberties Union to the American Federation of Labor. The work occupied much of the staff time of John Swomley. Rustin was openly contemptuous of initiatives that emphasized lobbying and the legislative process. He expressed himself so unsparingly that even the normally placid minutes of FOR meetings sometimes could not mask the internal conflicts. Rustin criticized Swomley and the campaign for relying on arguments from expedience—that there was no external threat sufficient to justify conscription; that the cost would be onerous; that there were other ways to meet the nation's military requirements. Only a deep transformation in attitudes would bring peace, and that required a clear, uncompromising message. "If we really believed our pacifist arguments," he said, "we would use them."[8] The FOR, he told its governing board, had to be "willing to take an all-out position." He wanted the organization to move in the direction of open resistance to a war-mongering state. "If the Germans had begun to break laws when Hitler came to power they would not have ended up by putting Jews into furnaces." Rustin took his own advice. While Swomley crafted a coalition to lobby Congress, Rustin led meetings in New York City where he asked young men to burn their Selective Service registration cards.[9]

Sentiments like these did not endear Rustin to Swomley or the more cautious majority in the organization, but they did speak to a small constituency in the FOR and other groups where male pacifists predominated. After the war, some radicalized COs, fresh from prison or CPS camp, were experimenting with more militant organizational forms. Convening in Chicago early in 1946, several score of them formed the Committee for Nonviolent Revolution. In New York, it attracted pacifists like Ralph DiGia, Roy Finch, Igal Roodenko, and Dave Dellinger, who also was publishing a magazine, *Direct Action.* Like many other small radical groups, it was strong on fiery rhetoric, weak on concrete achievements.[10]

Rustin kept appraised of what other young turks in the peace movement were doing. When the committee faltered, he and Muste, along with Dellinger, Houser, and Dwight Macdonald, the publisher of the radical journal *Politics*, issued a call for another Chicago conference. Assembling under the shadow of a Communist coup in Czechoslovakia, 200 men and women gathered in April 1948 to plan "more revolutionary and disciplined pacifist activity." Peacemakers, the group that formed out of the conference, appealed to Americans to "JOIN US in building this new world community. JOIN US in trying to live by its principles now. JOIN US in seeking this transformation now." Writing afterward to Selma Platt, a Kansas pacifist who had also been there, Rustin effused that the meeting was "a wonderful experience."[11]

Peacemakers came together just as Congress entered the last stages of debate over a conscription bill. Consistent with Rustin's dictum that pacifists "have to begin breaking laws," its first campaign sought to stimulate resistance to the draft. It urged young men to refuse to register and to make that refusal public. In a few cities, Peacemaker chapters convened public meetings for that purpose, but the campaign was an inglorious flop overall. Indeed, though Peacemakers hung on for several years, it never became more than the reflection of the utopian wishes of a few absolutist pacifists. While Rustin hoped that it would grow into an organization with the discipline of the Communist Party, Peacemakers remained mired in individual perfectionism. "You, one man, can begin to live non-violently," its founding manifesto declared. "You can begin the inner transformation. . . . You can build the World Community."[12] It championed tax refusal as a way of opposing the warmaking state, a course of action that few Americans were willing to espouse. Foreshadowing the 1960s, many adopted back-to-the-land subsistence lifestyles to escape federal withholding taxes. In doing so, they set themselves even further apart from their fellow citizens.[13]

Although not averse to taking absolutist stands himself, Rustin did not want to live the pure life. He wanted to win converts who were eager to be mobilized. He took extreme stands to prick the conscience of others. Corresponding with Selma Platt, who shared his enthusiasm for "an all out position," Rustin tried to articulate something of a theory of social change. "You and I believe," he wrote to her, that the key agent of radical change is[14]

> the group which insists that change for the better must take place immediately and far-reachingly [and] which because of its insistence activates at less direct levels many other more conservative people who would not become activated unless we were insisting upon change coming immediately. In a sense, the radical who insists upon far-reaching and immediate change has throughout history been proved the gadfly which has stirred men into action. . . . We must be prepared to be looked upon as queer and although I would not compare ourselves with such men as Socrates, Luther, Lincoln, Thoreau, these men played very much the same function and were looked upon by their contemporaries as foolish, unrealistic, idealistic, premature, and doing more harm than good.

Rustin saw extremism as a prelude to engagement. He was drawn to it, as were all the other members of Peacemakers and other small militant groups, but he also wanted results. He wanted a radicalism that provoked action. As the cold war heated up, it was not likely that the cause of peace would find many takers.

RACIAL ISSUES WERE another matter. Rustin pressed for these to become FOR's focus. He viewed apostles of nonviolence as roving champions of change, always searching for the places of friction in society where their message might have the most compelling appeal, the most immediate applicability. "Now the area of conflict [in American life] is in the racial field," he informed FOR's leadership. "Our program must follow." Information from members like Selma Platt, who advised Rustin that her Kansas chapter "does not show much life except in the area of racial problems," only confirmed his inclinations.[15]

Rustin spoke with good reason, for the war years had unsettled the racial status quo. The insatiable demand for labor had opened better economic prospects for black Americans, and many of them voted with their feet. The migration out of the South accelerated in the 1940s, bringing African Americans to large cities in the North, Midwest, and California. They still confronted patterns of segregation, job discrimination, and hate-motivated violence, but they also had more freedom to maneuver in daily life and could exercise the right to vote. Even in the South, the war brought a population shift from the countryside, with its grinding poverty and relative isolation, to towns and cities. Wartime mobilization affected racial consciousness as well. The contradiction between fighting against Aryan supremacists in Germany while maintaining Jim Crow at home was lost on neither African Americans nor many white Americans. Although the military remained segregated, the Negro soldier became a symbol of rights both denied and deserved. Returning home at war's end, black service members expected to be treated differently than they were before the war; they carried those expectations into the routines of daily living.

Change especially showed in the political organization of the black community. From its beginnings in the early twentieth century, the NAACP had always found its greatest support in the cities. As the urban population grew and the war years highlighted issues of job discrimination and military segregation, the NAACP experienced a period of explosive growth. The number of chapters tripled to almost a thousand, and the number of members multiplied nearly tenfold, approaching half a million. Randolph's March on Washington Movement, with its success in forcing concessions from President Roosevelt, had also contributed to a heady sense that here was a moment in which victories could be won and gains consolidated.

Rustin was at least as aware of the dangers of the moment as he was of the opportunities for dismantling America's race-based caste system.

During the war, tensions and discontent had exploded in serious riots in Detroit and in Harlem, and the months after demobilization had witnessed a major escalation of violence against blacks, particularly in the South and particularly directed at former service members. The violence, which included six lynchings in 1946, was acute enough for Walter White, the head of the NAACP, to press for a meeting with President Truman. Though unwilling to have the federal government intervene directly, Truman did appoint a presidential commission on civil rights to investigate and make recommendations.

The FOR had continued its work for racial justice while Rustin was in prison. Until the summer of 1945, when he was finally released, Farmer had lectured widely on the link between nonviolence and racial justice. Muste maintained ties with black civil rights leaders, particularly Randolph, but also with figures like Roy Wilkins and Thurgood Marshall of the NAACP and the columnist George Schuyler. First in Chicago and then in Cleveland, George Houser continued to treat CORE as a laboratory for learning. Not only in midwestern cities but on the West Coast as well, Houser instigated action campaigns that cracked a discriminatory color line in hotels, roller skating rinks, department stores, YMCAs, and restaurants.

For Houser, the work with CORE was life changing. Although he had first come into the limelight for his refusal, as part of the Union Eight, to register for the draft in 1940, Houser's passion had become not what he called "straight pacifist work" but an attack on racism. By the end of 1945, Houser and other CORE stalwarts were seriously debating whether the ferment unleashed by the war made it possible to launch an interracial movement pledged to direct action. He wrote to Rustin at Lewisburg to share his thinking about a new mass organization and inquire about Rustin's own plans. "I am tremendously interested in seeing something like this started," he wrote. "If it should be impossible to get a new mass group started now, then it seems to me that the FOR can do some valuable softening up work through workshops, institutes, and summer projects. . . . I wanted to write to you to find out if you were contemplating going back with the FOR. . . . I think that we might be able to work well together."[16] Restrictions on

Rustin's correspondence privileges kept him from responding, but Houser decided anyway that staying at the FOR would move these larger goals forward. He relocated to New York and took a position as race relations secretary.

Muste made sure that Rustin, too, would be working not just on pacifist concerns but on racial justice issues as well. As he wrote to Sayre shortly after Rustin returned to the staff, it was important not to withdraw Rustin from projects against racism since it "would certainly not give Bayard the feeling that he had an opportunity to express some of his profoundest concerns." Muste thought a Rustin-Houser partnership would enhance the organization. "George and Bayard together," he wrote, "would do a much better job than Jim Farmer did."[17]

Muste's prediction proved to be an understatement. Over the next six years, Rustin developed an effective working partnership with Houser. As an interracial team, they made for an interesting contrast—in appearance, style, and experience. Houser was short, Rustin tall. Houser displayed the reserve and understatement common to his midwestern roots; Rustin could often be the picture of flamboyance and extravagance, a paragon of the sophisticated metropolis that had become his adopted home. Houser prepared meticulously for a workshop or public action and tried to anticipate any eventuality; Rustin liked to seize control of the unexpected and turn it to advantage. Houser came to public life through the observation of oppression from a position of privilege. The son of missionaries, he had seen the poverty of the Philippines under American imperial rule, the chaos of China in the 1930s, and the suffering of Americans during the Depression. Through the Methodist youth movement of the 1930s, he turned these formative experiences into a foundation for decades of social activism. Rustin too had strong religious values that impelled him toward his public commitments, but he also had known injustice directly. Yet despite—or perhaps because of—these differences, together they managed to do more than any others in these years to seed the emerging civil rights movement with the philosophy of Gandhi and the method of nonviolent direct action.[18]

Rustin's and Houser's situation was less than ideal. It depended on having Muste as their constant advocate within the FOR so that the organization's resources might be bent toward racial justice. But as long as Muste remained committed to the work and held the traditional pacifists at bay, the FOR supported their lecturing and training on Gandhian nonviolence, and they were able to use their staff time to build CORE.

THE SAME MONTH AS Rustin's release from Lewisburg, the Supreme Court handed him and Houser an opportunity. For years, individual blacks had defied Jim Crow seating arrangements on buses and trains, as Rustin himself had done on his travels south in the early 1940s. The arrest of one of them, Irene Morgan, opened the way to a constitutional challenge. In June 1946, in *Morgan v. Virginia*, the Supreme Court announced that segregation in interstate transportation was unconstitutional. For bus companies like Greyhound and Trailways, the decision seemed nightmarish, as it would force them to distinguish between passengers with tickets for travel across state lines and those traveling within a single state and hence still subject to Jim Crow laws. Early signs indicated the carriers were loathe to implement the decision unless directly pressured. In fact, the experience of an FOR member on a Greyhound bus in the Southeast that summer suggested that the company planned "to ignore and frustrate the Court's decision."[19] Here was a chance to apply direct action to an issue that had national visibility. In mid-September, Rustin and Houser traveled to Cleveland for a meeting of the national executive committee of CORE. The group discussed the *Morgan* decision at great length and decided to make a test tour, sponsored by CORE, extending from Baltimore to New Orleans.

Rustin convened a working group in New York to plan the action. It included Bill Sutherland, whose refusal to accept Jim Crow arrangements in Lewisburg Penitentiary had launched CO protests there in 1943; Ella Baker, who had just finished a several-year stint as a field secretary for the NAACP and had contacts throughout the South; Pauli Murray, who had earlier initiated sit-ins at Washington cafeterias; and Bill Worthy, a journalist working for the New York Council for a Permanent Fair Employment Practices Commission. In the course of the fall, the group made a number of decisions, one of which did not sit well with the few women who participated in the discussions. The action would be confined to the Upper South, since serious violence was almost certain to come in the Deep South, and contacts there, among both white liberals and black activists, were few. The team would be interracial, consistent with the orientation of CORE and the FOR. Finally, only men would make the trip, in order to sidestep the inflammatory issue of interracial sex that a gender-mixed group would provoke.

Throughout the winter, Rustin and Houser consulted with leading figures in the black civil rights struggle: Randolph, Wilkins, Walter White, Thurgood Marshall, and a number of journalists whom they wanted to cover the event, now being dubbed the Journey of Reconciliation. Most were dubious. "Every Negro leader I talked to except for Randolph and Wilkins," Rustin recalled, "thought we were absolutely insane. Thurgood said, 'you know, Rustin, you are insane to try this, just dumb.'" Houser confirmed Rustin's recollection. "Thurgood Marshall was not hot on this project," he remembered. "He was fairly conservative in his outlook . . . and took a dim view of it. He was not a direct actionist. He believed in legal action." Roy Wilkins, by contrast, had "a fairly positive response." In later years, after he became head of the NAACP, Wilkins shied away from militant action projects and jealously protected his organization's preeminence, but at this point CORE was too small, too inconsequential, to pose any kind of competitive threat. Instead, Wilkins appreciated how a project like the Journey, with "some guts behind it," might invigorate NAACP branches in the South that found ways to participate.[20] Through him, the NAACP provided critical help. "They gave us their whole list of branches in the states and cities we were touching and their list of lawyers," according to Houser. "We got in touch with some of the top branches, and presidents of branches, and lawyers all the way along. We made contact with them wherever we went."[21]

In December, Rustin traveled to Washington, the Journey's embarkation point, to firm up contacts. In January, armed with names supplied by the NAACP, FOR, and others, he and Houser scoped out a potential route, riding as an interracial pair on buses in Virginia and North Carolina, before Houser went on alone to Tennessee and Kentucky. They met with local people and arranged public receptions to generate advance excitement. In the towns where they expected the riders to stop, the two conferred with key activists, including lawyers, whose help they would need if trouble erupted. "We were enthused by the support," Houser said.[22]

Meanwhile, Rustin recruited volunteers for the Journey. Virtually all of them were peace movement workers or civil rights activists affiliated with CORE. Participants included James Peck and Igal Roodenko, both members of the WRL and veterans of CO prison strikes during the war; Ernest Bromley, who had worked in FOR's national office and was now a Methodist minister in North Carolina; Joe Felmet, a North Carolinian who had spent time in Ashland prison and worked for the Socialist Party's Workers Defense League; Conrad Lynn, a civil rights attorney in New York, and Bill Worthy, who had helped plan the Journey; a coterie of activists from Cincinnati CORE, including Wally Nelson, Andrew Johnson, Nathan Wright, and Worth Randle; Dennis Banks, a Chicago musician; Homer Jack, who had helped found CORE; and Eugene Stanley, a faculty member at North Carolina A&T in Greensboro. Two journalists, Lem Graves of the *Pittsburgh Courier* and Ollie Stewart of the *Baltimore Afro-American*, also agreed to go.[23]

On April 7, 1947, two days before boarding buses for the first leg of the Journey, the group convened in Washington for some training and intense discussion. "Nobody knew what was going to happen," Bromley recalled. "Everybody on this thing went into it with apprehension because they knew what could occur and what had occurred. . . . I wouldn't say we were terror-stricken, but everybody was frightened." The project was fraught with dangers greater than what CORE had confronted in its work in Northern cities. "There were a lot of unknowns," Houser reflected. Though they were traveling from city to city, much of the route would be along isolated country roads. "You have to figure the word's going to get around about it, and maybe at some point they can get ready for you. . . . You're mostly in rural areas. You're in small towns. And if somebody wants to foment mob action, it's pretty easy to do. You can come on and pull somebody off the bus and hang him or beat him up."[24]

Dividing themselves between Greyhound and Trailways, the group left for Richmond on Wednesday, April 9. They established a routine for each bus. In the front area customarily reserved for whites, an interracial pair sat; on segments of the trip where their numbers were large enough, an interracial pair also sat together in the back. Meanwhile, at least one of the white participants sat alone in the front and one of the black activists in the back, each prepared to act as disinterested observers listening to what passengers were saying, trying to lower tensions in case of any incidents, and educating riders along the way about the *Morgan* decision.

On both buses, the ride to Richmond occurred without incident. "No one seemed especially concerned," Wally Nelson recorded in his log of the trip, and, indeed, a number of other passengers ignored the color line. The trip to nearby Petersburg likewise went smoothly, and the Journey was in danger of becoming one large disappointment. The group soon learned, through the investigative work of Lem Graves of the *Courier,* that state officials in Virginia had "passed the word down that it does not want any cases involving the application of the Irene Morgan decision brought to trial." But one black passenger counseled Houser and Roodenko not to let down their guard. "Some bus drivers are crazy," he told them, "and the farther South you go, the crazier they get."[25]

As the Greyhound contingent headed toward Durham, North Carolina, the anxiety level began to rise. At one point, Rustin caught a glimpse of Felmet's face through the rearview mirror of the bus. "He said I looked really agitated," Felmet recalled, "and I can believe that I did. Because we didn't know what was going to happen." And then they began to encounter opposition. The Greyhound driver told Rustin to move and threatened to eject him at Blackstone, a small hamlet about thirty miles southwest of Petersburg, but backed down when several passengers, black and white, expressed support for Rustin. In Oxford, North Carolina, Rustin faced another threat of arrest, but once again the driver desisted. The Trailways crew was not as fortunate. On the stretch from Petersburg to Raleigh, Conrad Lynn was arrested for sitting in the front of the bus. The driver, Houser reported, was "courteous but insistent," and even apologized. But, as he told them, he "was in the employ of the bus company, not the Supreme Court. . . . I don't care where you sit, but I have my orders." Lynn's arrest delayed the arrival of the riders in Raleigh. Somehow word reached their hosts; by the time they finally appeared at the community meeting that evening, they were greeted by the largest throng of supporters yet.[26]

Strained encounters continued in North Carolina. By the third day, Ollie Stewart noticed that everyone was "tight-lipped and grim."[27] The Trailways group traveling from Raleigh faced a surly bus driver who informed Lynn and Nelson that they wouldn't reach their destination. When the bus made its scheduled stop in Durham en route to Chapel Hill, the interracial party noticed that among the Greyhound buses, Rustin, Peck, and Andrew Johnson were being packed into a squad car. So it was with some relief that, later on Saturday, the dozen or so Gandhian demonstrators finally converged on the university town of Chapel Hill. There, Charles Jones, a white Presbyterian minister who served on the national board of FOR, and Nelle Morton, of the Fellowship of Southern Churchmen, were waiting for their arrival.

Chapel Hill had a reputation as an enlightened oasis in the middle of the segregated South. The University of North Carolina laid claim to being the premier public institution of higher education in the region. Frank Porter Graham, its president of many years, was known as a liberal on racial issues; a few months earlier, he had been appointed to Truman's national Commission on Civil Rights. Still, anyone in a state-funded position had little room to maneuver institutionally, and the university in this era was a segregated institution. Just a few weeks before Rustin and the other riders came to Chapel Hill, Graham had created an uproar in state political circles by opening the campus auditorium for a concert by Dorothy Maynor, a celebrated black soprano. The event sparked ample debate among the white student body about segregation, and the arrival in town of an interracial team challenging Jim Crow on the region's buses added momentum to the conversations. On Saturday, the riders participated in two interracial discussions about race relations and nonviolent activism. Lem Graves waxed eloquent in his report to the *Courier:* "an atmosphere as relaxed and natural as it could have been in Boston or New York . . . gave this observer a feeling that, if there remained in the South any hope for racial progress, the fountain head of that hope was Chapel Hill."[28]

But as Gandhian activists claimed, progress, however slight, often raised hatred closer to the surface. On Sunday, the riders planned to depart in two different parties for Greensboro. While Houser and a few others remained at Jones's house, Rustin led a group to the bus station. As they boarded, Felmet and Johnson sat as an interracial pair in the front, Rustin and Roodenko near each other in the back, and Peck and Stanley alone as individuals in the white and black sections of the bus, respectively. When the driver entered, he immediately spotted Felmet and Johnson together and ordered Johnson to move. Citing the *Morgan* decision, the two disputed the order, but the driver was having none of it and went to the police station across from the bus terminal for assistance. The police arrested the pair. Felmet, who hesitated when ordered to disembark, was lifted bodily from his seat and shoved into the street.

In the meantime, conversation had spontaneously erupted among passengers, both white and black, about what was going on. Without any prompting, passengers objected to the driver's decision, and many refused to fill out the complaint cards that the driver distributed to serve as evidence in any court proceedings. Sensing a groundswell of support, Rustin and Roodenko decided on the spot to make a second challenge. Acting as if they were strangers to each other but outraged by what had happened, they moved to the front of the bus, occupied the vacated seats, and announced that they too were prepared to face arrest. The driver cooperated by summoning the police yet again. Soon Rustin and Roodenko were being hauled to the station where Peck had gone to keep track of Felmet and Johnson.

The bus terminal was also the site of a taxi stand, and as the delay of the bus extended into its second hour, the white drivers who were lounging about became increasingly agitated. When Peck emerged from the police station and returned to the bus, one driver accosted him, accused him of "coming down here to stir up the niggers," and struck him hard on the head. Eugene Stanley attempted to intervene but was curtly told, "You keep out of this."[29] Tensions were now on the edge of escalating out of control. Someone in the group, perhaps Stanley, had earlier made a call to the home of Charlie Jones, where the others were still waiting, so that Houser might come down to provide bail money. Now they contacted Jones again, and he rushed to the station. He packed the riders into his car and made what he thought was a quick and safe escape back to his house. But the minister was well known around town, and the drivers, along with cronies who were hanging about the station, were bent on extracting satisfaction. A few minutes later, their "mud-splattered automobiles—country, rickety old things—encircled the house," and the passengers emerged armed with makeshift clubs. As Rustin described the scene that then unfolded, "The telephone began to ring. [Jones's] wife began answering the telephone and there were threatening calls coming in saying they were going to lynch us, that she had better get her two children and her husband out of the house because they were going to burn it down. Sooner than we had thought, stones began to come in the windows from the back, from the side, from the front—a beautiful old colonial house he lived in." Time seemed to slow as the riders waited inside, eerily enthralled by the drama which they had provoked. "Bayard and I were standing together," Houser recalled. "And Bayard grabbed me and said 'George, just look at this, huh?' Like, it's fascinating to see these people."[30]

While Jones called the police, his wife left with the children and drove to the campus, where her husband had a following among students. She managed to rally a group of them, who raced to the house to protect those trapped inside. When the police finally arrived, they were more than willing to defuse a situation just a hair's breadth away from tragedy. As police held the taxi drivers in check, Jones organized a caravan of cars that took the entire team to Greensboro. There, relieved to have escaped, they held "a very spirited meeting," in Houser's recollection. "Bayard was the person who handled it. He was uniquely good at doing that sort of thing, dramatizing what had happened . . . drawing other people in. He was a master."[31]

Although nothing else approached the intensity of the scene in Chapel Hill, the remainder of the trip was hardly uneventful. Altogether, members of the Journey conducted more than two dozen tests of the *Morgan* decision and suffered twelve arrests. They dealt with drivers and police across four states; they engaged thousands of Southerners, black and white, in dialogue about Jim Crow. Their evening meetings also instigated intense discussion about how to provoke change in the South, and particularly about how active nonviolent resistance might serve as a lever of progress. In his last report to the *Baltimore Afro-American*, Stewart claimed the Journey had "knocked several props from beneath the already tottering Jim Crow structure.... White and colored persons, when the whole thing was explained to them as they sat in their seats on several occasions, will never forget what they heard (or saw)."[32]

The Journey certainly achieved a high profile in the black press, insinuating the model of nonviolent direct action further into the consciousness of its African American readership. It received prominent coverage in papers like the *Raleigh News and Observer*, whose reports hinted that the Journey created quite a stir in the state. Indeed, the Chapel Hill incident stimulated mass assemblies on campus, and a few weeks later Rustin returned for more meetings and trainings. The Journey had communicated to a wide audience that segregation had its challengers, including some who were ready to engage in determined action to hasten its demise.

As both Rustin and Houser, the chief instigators, retrospectively recognized, the Journey functioned as prelude rather than catalyst to the mass movement they yearned to induce. The infrastructure of organizations and activist relationships across the South was not strong enough to have the Journey launch a sustained regionwide assault on Jim Crow. Unlike the sit-in at a lunch counter in Greensboro thirteen years later, the Journey of Reconciliation was ahead of its time. It was one short scene in a drama whose main acts were yet to come. Still, as Houser summed it up a generation later, it was "a hell of an experience."[33] It certainly sustained Rustin in his belief that Gandhian approaches to racial injustice had the capacity to work.

CHAPTER SEVEN

"Mad Enough to Do Something Desperate"
1947–1948

ALTHOUGH THE JOURNEY was Rustin's most ambitious direct action project in these years, it was by no means the only occasion for tense confrontations. As Rustin moved about the country doing work for the FOR and CORE, he refused to brook any infringements on his own civil rights. In Reading, Pennsylvania, he extracted an apology from a hotel manager after a clerk denied him a room he had reserved in advance. A similar incident in Buffalo provoked a complaint to the city's community relations board. In St. Paul, Rustin conducted his own "sit down and wait" protest over the denial of a room. During the night, members of the local FOR chapter and NAACP branch joined him in the lobby until, the following morning, the hotel finally yielded. It gave Rustin vibrant new material for his talks in the Twin Cities.[1]

Another time, traveling from Washington to Louisville on the Southern Railway, Rustin balked at sitting behind the Jim Crow curtain in the dining car. Seating himself at a table in the middle of the eating area, he remained there for several hours, from breakfast through lunch, waiting for service. Rustin had made contact with some of the waiters before he took his action, prepped them on his plans, and supplied them with phone numbers to call for legal assistance in case of arrest. "The open moral support I received from all the waiters," he wrote, "acted as a brake on the trainmen, who at one point were about to eject me bodily. . . . The nervous steward, I believe, feared a general walkout by the waiters if I had been removed." As often happened during these acts of resistance in the South, Rustin succeeded in eliciting the support of some white patrons.[2]

But Rustin was aiming for more than individual resistance. He wanted to stimulate a *movement*. With Houser as a dependable partner, he worked to train leaders, spread the word, and seed projects that he hoped would become larger, more powerful, and permanently effective over time. Much of his activity in the late 1940s was in the Northeast and the Midwest, though he also made extended trips to the West Coast and some forays into the South. He lectured before NAACP and FOR chapters, at universities or to church congregants, always hoping for a few folks to separate themselves from the crowd and become the kernel of a new direct action group. Often his travels entailed closer work, sustained over several days, with members of CORE and FOR chapters wanting to develop local drives against racial discrimination. In Chicago, for instance, CORE conducted a successful boycott against the Wonder Bread Company, which led to the hiring of several black drivers. For activists in Kansas, Rustin sketched plans for an effort to desegregate restaurants in several communities.

The heart of Rustin's work in these years were race relations institutes that he and Houser offered in communities across the country. Sometimes as short as a weekend and occasionally as long as a month, the institutes were designed to promote action. Participants received some basic information about the economic and legal status of black Americans, the forms discrimination took, and the theory and practice of nonviolence. Then they divided into interracial teams, fanning out across the city to test the practices of shops, restaurants, and other businesses. The groups reported back, analyzed what they had learned, and, in the best cases, mapped plans for further action. Sometimes the institutes included appearances of public officials, who occasionally got quite an earful, depending on what the forays into the community had uncovered. Now and then, "real life" cooperated. At a week-long institute in Toledo, held in February 1947 at the downtown YWCA, Rustin and Houser went out to dinner before an evening session. "To our amazement," Houser recalled, "they weren't going to serve us because Bayard was black. We'd been through this kind of thing many times, but we just hadn't expected it." Telling the waitress they intended to wait, the two agreed to let the workshop know where they were and what was happening. "Everybody came over," Houser continued. "The management then called the police and a big crowd started gathering. And newspaper people began coming. . . . And we got served."[3]

By far the most ambitious of these ventures was a month-long interracial workshop in the nation's capital during July 1947. Washington had grown rapidly in the course of the Depression and World War II as the size of the federal bureaucracy expanded enormously. After the war, it also became the nerve center of global politics, with embassies representing countries from all over the world and an international press corps. But Washington was also a rigidly segregated town, consistent with its location between two former slave states and with the power that white Southern politicians exerted in Congress. It was thus uniquely suited for a Gandhian incursion.

The workshop attracted about three dozen participants, recruited from eleven states and including several Southerners. The group targeted a number of coffee shops and restaurants in the heart of the city, particularly those connected to religious institutions or to the federal government. After being refused service at the terrace café of the National Zoo, one delegation headed to the congressional subcommittee charged with approving funds for the zoo. Some targets, like the cafeteria in the Methodist Building near the Supreme Court, fell after a couple of tests and some leafleting. Others displayed more resistance, such as the coffee shop at the YMCA downtown. There the Gandhian trainees experienced two "drama-packed" days, as the manager tried to incite patrons against them by posting signs that read, "What Are the Communists Up to Now?" When negotiations failed, twenty-two members of the workshop occupied tables, while the manager poured ammonia into the air-conditioning in order to drive them out. By week's end, the recalcitrant management had at least agreed to negotiate. "In a Hollywood atmosphere of clicking cameras, press statements and curious crowds," according to the report composed afterward, the YMCA announced the formation of an interracial committee composed of board members and District citizens to work out a change in policy.[4]

When it was all over, the workshop could point to a few places in town that had desegregated and about thirty columns of newspaper coverage. Rustin and Houser left behind "the Interracial Workshop," a new organization dedicated to continuing what the summer group had started, and an enthusiastic leader of the NAACP youth branch in Washington, D.C., who was impressed by what he had experienced. Similar outcomes happened in other places, where institute or workshop participants, rather than affiliate with CORE or the FOR, simply formed a freestanding local group to carry on the struggle.

Evaluating his and Rustin's work retrospectively, Houser was typically modest in his appraisal. "We knew that we had something that worked to a certain extent on the local level," he told an interviewer in 1967. "From a nonviolent point of view, we felt that that tactic was being vindicated in that period in history by the victories that one could list of all kinds of places that had changed policies as a result of projects we had carried on. We spent some time thinking about 'Are we creating a mass movement?' We never in that point in history got to the place where we felt that the national movement was all set to be launched." Rustin gave their work more credit. These years, he reflected long afterward, were "perhaps one of the most useful periods in the life of what Mr. Randolph and A.J. Muste and some of us were doing. . . . That period of eight years [from 1946 to 1954] of continuously doing this," he continued, "prepared for the 1960s revolution, prepared for the 1954 Supreme Court decision." Without the constant experimentation, "I . . . do not believe Montgomery would have been possible nor successful except for . . . the long experience people had about reading about sitting in buses and getting arrested, so that people had become used to hearing this."[5]

FOR AWHILE, IT SEEMED that the campaign against segregation in the armed forces might be the vehicle to spark a mass nonviolent crusade. Throughout World War II, the military's racial policies were an open wound on the body of the African American community. Black men and women served with distinction across the globe, but quotas restricted their numbers, the roles open to them were severely limited, and, above all, their service was confined to segregated units. Roy Wilkins introduced an NAACP report on their treatment with the comment that "this memorandum would be 40,000 words in length if I were to attempt to set down a mere illustrated outline of what Negro soldiers and sailors suffered in World War II."

> They were separated at draft induction centers. They rode Jim Crow trains to training camps. Their barracks were in "Negro" locations when they trained with white troops. They had to buy at the "Negro" PX only. They were segregated in the "roost" in post theatres. At one camp in Tennessee, Negro commissioned officers with rank as high as major were ordered out of a post theatre at the point of sub-machine guns because they sat in the section for officers instead of the section for "Negroes." They were beaten, shot and killed by white civilian bus drivers, country constables and city police—and not a civilian was ever punished. . . . Negro doctors and dentists were turned down on the old saw that they treat only Negroes, when every well-informed person knows that Negro doctors and dentists even in the Deep South have white patients. Negroes with Ph.D. degrees and masters in business and other subjects served in labor battalions . . . while white boys with half the education and experience were working in the finance office.

In his travels after the war, Wilkins said, he "found Negroes cynical and hard-bitten. . . . Negro veterans are mad about this. Their wives, sweethearts, mothers, fathers, and other relatives are mad. There is no use pretending they are not mad. They are mad enough to do something desperate if they have to go under the same system again."[6]

By 1947, it appeared as if they might have to. All that year, a Republican-controlled Congress wrestled with Truman's request for a universal military training bill to replace the wartime conscription system that had expired. The bill that came out of the House Armed Services Committee mandated racial segregation of trainees.[7] Bill Worthy, who had participated in the Journey of Reconciliation, passed this information on to Randolph. "A fight against peacetime conscription,"

Worthy wrote, "might be a popular and dramatic issue." Maybe, he suggested, "you would be willing to call a meeting . . . to plan action in a crisis equally as grave as the 1941 job crisis." Randolph replied the next day and expressed serious interest. Worthy then contacted Rustin, and late in August, the three men met in Philadelphia.[8]

For years, Randolph had exerted an influence on Rustin as powerful as Muste's, though for different reasons. Muste tapped the spiritual sources of Rustin's motivation, something that the secular, almost anti-clerical, Randolph could not touch. But Randolph's ability to inspire black working people—the people from whom Rustin had come—drew him irresistibly. True, Randolph's March on Washington Movement had not become a permanent mass organization. But Randolph had come closer to succeeding than anyone else of his generation. And Randolph's socialist views and union constituency kept him rooted in collective approaches to political struggle that relied on working-class support. All this made Rustin willing to throw his energies into the campaign against a Jim Crow army. Never mind the troubling contradiction of a pacifist advocating that the armed forces should make it *easier* for some young men and women to serve. The prospect of a national mobilization was so exhilarating that it quelled any doubts.

In September, Rustin and Worthy traveled to Cleveland to bring the issue to CORE's national meeting. While CORE agreed to endorse, it declined to throw significant resources into the project because Randolph's campaigns lacked the explicit interracialism that was CORE's hallmark. The decision forced Worthy, who was already too invested to back away, to leave his job with CORE in order to continue working with Randolph. Muste, however, agreed to let Rustin devote staff time to inaugurate the military desegregation campaign. Late in September, Rustin met with Randolph again, and the elder leader decided to call a formal meeting to plan "militant action" against a Jim Crow military. Many organizations responded, but the NAACP, skeptical of Randolph's penchant for mass mobilizations, pointedly did not. To give the new organization, the Committee to End Jim Crow in the Military, broader credibility, Randolph recruited Grant Reynolds to serve as co-chair. An army chaplain during World War II who had risen to the rank of captain, Reynolds was active in the Republican Party and served as New York State commissioner of corrections. His public profile was about as different from the socialist union leader as was possible.

Throughout the fall, Rustin worked hard on the preliminary stages of the campaign, in anticipation of the opening of the new session of Congress in 1948. He worked his contacts in the black press—like Lem Graves of the *Courier* and Jimmy Hicks of the National Negro Press Association—prepping them on Randolph's plans and securing information from them about the political scene in Washington. In November, he wrote to Randolph that a coterie of reporters in Washington, D.C., was "cooperating with us in every way" and urged Randolph to hold a large press conference for as big a launching as possible. On November 22, when Randolph finally went public with his intentions, the Committee to End Jim Crow in the Military had secured endorsements from over a hundred prominent African Americans.[9]

In some ways, the timing of the campaign seemed perfect. The month before, Truman's Commission on Civil Rights had issued a stunning report that described in chilling detail the violence against Southern blacks and the pervasive denial of basic civil rights. Randolph tried repeatedly through the winter to secure a meeting with Truman about the military issue. But the president conspicuously avoided responding, and the best that Randolph could secure was an offer, which he rejected, of a meeting with White House aides. Key congressional leaders were no more forthcoming. Walter Andrews, a New York Republican who chaired the House Armed Services Committee, stonewalled requests from black organizations and veterans to testify on the conscription bill.

All this was a kind of politicking beyond Rustin's reach and, in these years, his interest. Instead, he searched for ways to inject militant tactics and nonviolent resistance into Randolph's calculations. Just before Christmas, he reported to FOR staff about tentative plans to have significant numbers of black veterans converge on Washington and confront members of Congress with stories of the indignities of life in a segregated military. With Worthy, Rustin seized every opportunity to bend Randolph's ear about "new racial techniques," as Worthy put it in a letter, by which he meant the methods of Gandhi. "You owe it to the

Negro and white public to begin disseminating these ideas in a constant and regular fashion," Worthy wrote to Randolph.[10]

Rustin kept Houser apprised about the debates within the Committee to End Jim Crow and encouraged him, as a national officer of CORE, to approach Randolph about a direct action component for the campaign. In mid-February 1948, Houser sent Randolph the rough outline of a proposal for civil disobedience. He described a campaign to secure, from several thousand men in the military, pledges to refuse to cooperate with Jim Crow and to activate those pledges if the government failed to dismantle segregation. From Rustin, Houser knew that such an idea was, at least, "in the back of [Randolph's] mind," but committing it to print was a big step since soldiers risked court-martial for the kind of action Houser suggested.[11] That same month, Randolph and Reynolds held a press conference in Washington. Surrounded by other black leaders, they went public with their criticism of Truman and Congress and linked the supporters of a segregated military to opposition to both antilynching bills and efforts to outlaw the poll tax.

By this time, complex political calculations had entered into how Democrats and Republicans viewed the military issue. Republicans had captured control of both houses of Congress in 1946 and were using their power to stymie any efforts to extend New Deal legislation. Many were also proving recalcitrant as Truman tried to craft an internationalist foreign policy. With good reason, Republicans saw the coming national elections as an opportunity not only to maintain a congressional majority, but also to reclaim the White House after sixteen years of a Democratic presidency. Truman was an extremely vulnerable candidate. Having become president only because Roosevelt died in office, he governed at a time of enormous difficulties. The transition from war to peace was fraught with anxieties, and at home and abroad, challenges arose at a galloping pace: the collapse of the wartime alliance with the Soviet Union; the spread of communism in Eastern Europe; record levels of strike activity by workers in basic industries; an upsurge in racially motivated violence in the South; fears of runaway inflation or of a recurrence of the mass unemployment of the 1930s. Truman lacked the charisma of his predecessor, and frustrated New Dealers were displeased with how their dreams of new reforms were unraveling under Truman's watch.

As the year began, each party considered how it might work various issues to advantage. At certain points in history, the Republicans had embraced the mantle of reform. But in the wake of the Depression and the party's repudiation by a huge majority of Americans, it had hunkered down, hardening into a role as the party of business, small government, and conservatism. By the late 1930s, many of its members in Congress were making common cause with conservative Southern Democrats; together, they successfully stalled the reforming zeal of Northern urban liberals. For generations, black Americans had been a secure Republican constituency, associating the party with Lincoln and Emancipation. But the New Deal had begun to pry some of them away. Should the Republicans try to win them back and hold on to those still loyal to them? Or might they play on the simmering dissatisfaction of white Southern Democrats who perceived their own party as abandoning its support of white supremacy?

Truman too had to craft a campaign strategy. For much of his presidency, he had been on the defensive, reacting to the initiatives of others—whether of Stalin in foreign affairs, or labor unions whose strikes paralyzed the economy, or Republicans trying to undo Roosevelt's legacy. As the year began, he particularly worried about the threat from the left wing of the Democratic Party. Would Henry Wallace, the man he replaced as Roosevelt's running mate in 1944, steal away the most militant New Dealers through his campaign as a candidate of the Progressive Party? The combative president, at last ready to seize the initiative, decided to position himself as the inheritor of Roosevelt's mantle. In his State of the Union message to Congress in January 1948, he rolled out a wide-ranging package of reforms that he called a "Fair Deal" for America. In February, he delivered a strong civil rights message as well, including in it many of the recommendations of his civil rights commission. The message angered Southerners in Congress who were committed to holding fast against any blurring of the color line.

Thus, among both Democrats and Republicans were elements inclined to resist and support desegregation of the military. Unlike Rustin, who was looking ahead to a long resistance, Randolph wanted to navigate these crosscurrents in order to bring more immediate successes. It was a new moment in twentieth-century national politics: African Americans, though still outsiders to the world of Washington decision making, had some leverage.

LATE IN MARCH, RANDOLPH finally got his meeting with the president when Truman invited a group of black leaders to the White House. Randolph told him that an antisegregation provision in the conscription bill before Congress was not negotiable and that a segregated military would meet black resistance. Randolph repeated his views publicly on March 31, in testimony before the Senate Armed Services Committee. He described the "bitter, angry mood of the Negro" and told senators that "Negroes are in no mood to shoulder a gun for democracy abroad so long as they are denied democracy here at home." Sounding like one of Rustin's converts, he predicted that a Jim Crow draft would spark a civil disobedience movement comparable to what Gandhi had launched against the British. "Negroes will be serving a higher law than any passed by a national legislature," he testified. "I personally will advise Negroes," he added, "to refuse to fight as slaves for a democracy they cannot possess and cannot enjoy. . . . I personally pledge myself to openly counsel, aid and abet youth, both white and Negro, to *quarantine* any jim crow conscription system. . . . I shall call upon all Negro veterans to join this civil disobedience movement and to recruit their younger brothers in an organized refusal to register and be drafted." Randolph closed with a stirring personal stand. "I feel morally obligated," he concluded, "to disturb and keep disturbed the conscience of Jim Crow America. In resisting the insult of Jim Crowism to the soul of black America, we are helping to save the soul of America."[12]

Randolph's testimony set off a firestorm. Senator Wayne Morse, a Republican liberal who sat on the board of the NAACP, responded viscerally. To Morse, Randolph's statement skirted the edge of treason. Privately, he tried to extract from Walter White, the head of the NAACP, a disavowal of Randolph. But Morse also went public with his objections in a speech to the Senate. To Grant Reynolds, Randolph's cochair and a Republican, Morse's behavior was reprehensible. "I would expect this type of continued campaign by Morse from Senator East- land [of Mississippi], but not from a so-called liberal."[13]

If Morse and other national political figures thought they could iso- late Randolph, they miscalculated. The reverse occurred. Randolph's stand had raised the ante for the nation's black leadership. Responding to Morse, White iterated that the NAACP "neither advocates nor be- lieves in civil disobedience," but he also told the senator that "the Ne- gro is totally fed up with segregation in the armed services." To Randolph, White wrote that he would fight for "your right to say what I know you honestly believe." White was soon pledging that the NAACP would provide legal aid to those who resisted conscription.[14] Three weeks after Randolph's Senate testimony, Secretary of Defense James Forrestal invited a group of black civil rights leaders, from which Randolph was conspicuously excluded, to a meeting about the Negro's role in national defense. The unyielding commitment of his army sec- retary, Kenneth Royall, to the status quo so angered the participants that they staged an angry walkout.[15]

Rustin found these developments thrilling since they portended a more militant approach. By mid-April, he was reporting to the FOR staff that "a national war resistance movement may result" and that the FOR had, at all costs, to be identified with it. In the meantime, he was doing everything in his power to encourage such a movement. On April 11, he and Houser dressed for a banquet at the Waldorf-Astoria, where the two received, for their leadership of the Journey of Reconciliation, the Thomas Jefferson Award from the Council Against Intolerance in America. Seizing the opportunity of an event well covered by the press, Rustin promised in his speech a national campaign of civil disobedi- ence. "Segregation in any part of the body politic is an act of slavery and an act of war," he told the applauding audience. "Civil disobedience against caste is not merely a right but a profound duty . . . it will prick the conscience of America as Gandhi's campaigns stirred the hearts of men the world over. . . . If the Government continues to consider such action treason, let them recall the advice that Justice Jackson gave the German people at the opening of the Nuremberg trials: Men, he said, are individually responsible for their acts, and are not to be excused for following the unjust demands made upon them by Government." Rustin's speech received favorable notice in liberal white papers like the *New York Post* and *PM* and from black journalists who knew his work.[16]

Soon Rustin was spending virtually all his time on the campaign. At the inaugural conference of Peacemakers in April, Rustin extracted commitments from many there to serve as the activist nucleus in the fight against Jim Crow. Building on the favorable image of the Journey of Reconciliation, he organized the riders and other wartime COs into a tax refusal movement in support of desegregation. With Bill Sutherland, he visited colleges to promote resistance to conscription. Administrators at Howard University, nervous about antagonizing Congress, from which they received their operating funds, denied the two permission to speak, but a crowd of enthusiastic students followed them off campus to an alternative meeting place. From around the country, Rustin reported, pledges of resistance were coming to Randolph's headquarters, while letters to the editor in both black and white papers were running heavily in favor of refusing to cooperate with segregation. Early in May, he joined Randolph and others in a picket line outside the White House. One placard read: "If we must die for our country let us die as free men—not as Jim Crow slaves." The action provoked Richard Russell, the leader of the white Southern Democrats in the Senate, to introduce segregationist amendments to the conscription bill. Rustin delighted at the campaign's ability to force racist sentiment to the surface.[17]

As Congress debated conscription, opposition to Jim Crow remained in the public eye. In May, in a speech in Boston, Randolph took a step that shocked even many of his supporters. Likening a Jim Crow military to a fascist organization committed to "a pure Aryan race," he called upon "Negro and freedom-loving whites in the armed services both here and in occupied countries to consider laying down their guns in protest" if Congress perpetuated segregation. A poll of black college students on twenty-six campuses revealed that 71 percent endorsed Randolph's call for resistance; three-quarters of those polled had served during World War II. Yet despite the signs of discontent, when Congress passed a peacetime conscription bill in June 1948, it failed to mandate integration and ban discrimination. Randolph called on Truman to issue an executive order abolishing Jim Crow, but the president simply signed the bill into law and offered no signs of encouragement to a frustrated, dejected Randolph.[18]

To Rustin, the new law was an opportunity rather than a defeat. It meant that a civil disobedience campaign was next on the agenda. In the spring, he had developed an action component for Randolph's Committee to End Jim Crow. Now Muste proposed that, with conscription in place and registration day approaching in August, talk of resistance needed to shift from theory to practice. With the agreement of Randolph and Reynolds, Rustin and Houser launched an independent League for Nonviolent Civil Disobedience, with Bill Sutherland as the main field worker.

Rustin threw himself into his new role. Scheduled to go to India that summer to meet with leaders of the Indian independence struggle, he postponed the trip indefinitely. To the FOR board, he predicted that the civil disobedience campaign might occupy his time for years to come. "Many more people of all groups are signing up than we had believed would be willing or able to," Rustin and his coworkers wrote. "Young men of draft age in and out of college are signing [our pledge] daily."[19] The stakes seemed very high. "The army is now America's largest and most influential business concern," one of the bulletins prepared by Rustin asserted. "It touches almost every other economic, social, and political institution. If the millions of Negroes and white people in the Army are in mixed units they will eat, travel and sleep together. They will have recreation together, work together, and travel on boats about the world together. In the South they will live, sleep, and work together in and beyond army camps. What could be a more revolutionary blow to the caste system? How under these circumstances could jim crow survive?"[20] Letters from around the country indicated that "many thousands of people . . . individually and organizationally support us." Several NAACP chapters "stand 100% behind us" even though the national organization did not. Rustin recruited volunteers in Philadelphia, Buffalo, Dayton, Chicago, St. Louis, Minneapolis, San

Francisco, and Los Angeles. In Harlem, a group of ministers were canvassing their peers around the country to sign a call for civil disobedience. Rustin knew that not everyone would "draw the same line when it comes to the place where they will resist." But he believed the ranks of resisters would grow steadily.[21]

The Democratic Party convened in Philadelphia on Monday, July 12. At an outdoor rally the evening before, Randolph called for "the most drastic demonstration of opposition" to Jim Crow. He renewed his call for civil disobedience, announced the appointment of a dozen field directors to organize the movement across the United States, and promised that he was ready to be the first one arrested for abetting resistance to conscription.[22] The next morning, outside the convention hall, Rustin organized a picket line of several dozen supporters of the League for Nonviolent Civil Disobedience. After he, Randolph, and others had marched for several hours, Rustin recalled, "finally a white man comes out and joins us, and none of us know who he is." He introduced himself as Hubert Humphrey, the mayor of Minneapolis who was running for the U.S. Senate. Randolph encouraged Humphrey, one of a new generation of cold war liberals, to "take the platform tonight or tomorrow and tell the world about civil rights." Two days later Humphrey made an impassioned—and successful—appeal to the Democratic delegates to endorse a civil rights plank much stronger than what party leaders had proposed. "The time has arrived," he told the convention, "for the Democratic Party to get out of the shadow of states' rights and walk forthrightly into the bright sunshine of human rights."[23] The success of Northern liberals in incorporating civil rights into the platform led many white Southerners to withdraw from the convention and run their own candidate, Strom Thurmond of South Carolina, for president.

Still, the issue of segregation in the military remained unresolved. On Saturday evening, July 17, Rustin's League sponsored a street rally in the heart of Harlem. To the *Pittsburgh Courier* reporter watching in the twilight, it brought back memories of the previous decade when Harlem was in ferment. "There was in it," he wrote, "more than a little of the half-forgotten do-or-die, hell-and-brimstone, the-opposition-be-damned fighting spirit that characterized the mid-depression Harlem struggle for better housing, increased political representation and the right to work where one spends one's money. . . . It was a gathering militantly in the tradition of the past decade's street corner harangues— those shoulder-rubbing, perspiring, down-to-earth, deadly-in-earnest attacks on the evils of racial injustice." These were the kind of scenes Rustin had first encountered when he moved to Harlem a decade earlier. As he worked the crowd, engaging young men in conversation about the draft, he could hear Randolph address the throng. "There comes a time in the life of a people," the labor leader intoned, "when they must stand up and dare to win their rights, regardless of the cost, without consideration for the sacrifice. . . . I will oppose this segregated army even if it costs me my freedom and I rot in jail." By evening's end, Rustin and his fellows had exhausted the buttons and pledge cards they had brought with them.[24]

By this time, Rustin had at least half a dozen full-time staff devoted to the league's campaign. When Truman, as part of his electioneering strategy, hastily called Congress back for a special session, Rustin set them to work planning demonstrations in Washington "to dramatize and advertize our cause": a poster walk with civil disobedience outside the Republican and Democratic national committee headquarters when Congress reconvened on July 26; a "revival meeting" on civil disobedience led by clergy at a site like the Lincoln Memorial; and, at the end of August, when registration became mandatory, picketing the White House and draft centers in major cities, urging young men not to register.[25]

Trouble was brewing in the campaign. Ever since the league had been created as an entity separate from the more broadly based Committee to End Jim Crow, Worthy had nursed a building anger toward Rustin. The reasons cut across personal rivalry and political differences. Worthy had been the chief staff person for the committee and had shaped its day-to-day operations more than anyone else. Now he watched as Rustin built an independent platform from which to launch more militant attention-grabbing activities. Worthy also distrusted the influence that FOR pacifists, almost all white, seemed to exert through

Rustin on an issue central to the fight for racial equality. He sensed that Rustin's and their purpose in all this was not primarily a desegregated military, but a Gandhian movement against war and violence. Since the lines between the two organizations were porous and both worked out of the FOR offices, Worthy had daily contact with Rustin and the FOR staff. At meetings, Worthy increasingly became a silent onlooker rather than an animated participant. Afterward, he would take his grievances to Reynolds, who then relayed the complaints to Randolph and Muste.

Soon a contentious correspondence was flying back and forth. Reynolds informed Randolph of "a squeeze play by Bayard" to remove Worthy. He was "completely fed up with the way Bayard operates," he wrote to Randolph. "Some pretty crude politicking and jockeying for position under the cover of charm and verbiage seems to be going on." Reynolds warned that "our movement is being taken over by the FOR."[26] Muste responded as sharply. He described to Randolph behavior on Worthy's part that he thought bordered on financial malfeasance. He criticized Worthy's obstructionist behavior. Muste acknowledged that he was "not suggesting that Bayard is free from all shortcomings," but, he added, "on the basis of seven years continuous association, I have great confidence in him."[27]

In order to finesse the antagonism between Rustin and Worthy, Reynolds and Muste decided to make the formal distinction between the Committee to End Jim Crow and the League for Nonviolent Civil Disobedience a hard-and-fast division. The two stopped sharing office space, finances were separated, and Rustin ran the league while Worthy kept the committee operating. An arrangement originally intended to magnify the strength of the movement against Jim Crow by expanding the range of available tactics had degenerated into a hostile sundering of the two approaches.[28]

Even as tensions simmered, the campaign was about to achieve a signal victory. On July 26, as Congress reconvened in special session, the president issued an executive order addressing racial discrimination by the military. "It is hereby declared," the order read, "that there shall be equality of treatment and opportunity for all persons in the armed services without regard to race, color, religion, or national origin. This policy shall be put into effect as rapidly as possible, having due regard to the time required to effectuate any necessary changes without impairing efficiency or morale."[29] Simultaneously, Truman issued another order instituting fair employment practices throughout the federal civil service. Reporting on the orders, the *New York Times* predicted they would have "a thunderbolt effect on the already highly charged political situation in the Deep South." Implicitly crediting Randolph for provoking the action, the paper depicted Truman as "caught between two fires on the civil rights issue": the most extreme Southern Democrats on one side and militants like Randolph on the other.[30]

But at the time, the executive order was ambiguous. In 1948, the separate-but-equal doctrine enunciated by the Supreme Court half a century earlier still held sway. Thus, as a matter of law and public policy, "equality of treatment and opportunity" was perfectly consistent with a commitment to segregation. Fears that such was the case, that Truman's order was devoid of content, received reinforcement when General Omar Bradley, head of the Joint Chiefs of Staff, told a reporter the next day that the army was not a laboratory for social reform and that segregation would remain in force as long as it was common practice in the United States.

Randolph had said all along that he would drop his call for civil disobedience if Congress or the president prohibited Jim Crow. Initially, his public statements expressed skepticism toward the presidential order, but he was willing to reserve judgment and give Truman time to clarify. Truman sent one of his political lieutenants, Senator J. Howard McGrath, to meet with Randolph in order to win him over.

Remembering that, seven years earlier, Randolph had canceled the March on Washington, Rustin worried that Truman's action might mean an end to the resistance campaign. As Randolph and Reynolds continued discussions with McGrath, Rustin tried unilaterally to forestall a compromise by issuing a press release for the league, under Randolph's name, that dismissed the executive order. Truman's action, it declared, "appears merely to continue the destructive 'separate but equal' pattern which has kept the American Negro in semi-slavery since the Civil War." In the release, Rustin had Randolph saying, "I call upon all youth of draft age, Negro and white, to refuse to register or refuse to serve on August 30th unless segregation has been abolished." The league, Rustin wrote, "shall relentlessly continue its struggle."[31] The peremptory action especially infuriated Reynolds. The press release "upset me no little," he wrote to Randolph, and he insisted that Rustin be relieved of the right to issue any public statements without sign off from both Randolph and himself. To Reynolds, it was further evidence that "there were those now using the movement for purposes other than the elimination of Army Jim Crow."[32]

At a private meeting on August 16, Randolph and Reynolds decided to call off the resistance campaign since the executive order, they believed, was "a step in the right direction upon which it is possible to build for the future." The next day, the two made their decision public. As Randolph wrote to a friend a few days later, "My position is that no order or law made by man is perfect. . . . Although I do not consider the order and its clarification by the President wholly satisfactory, I believe that it is a definite gain and a victory." To another he explained, "I felt I was morally bound to call off the civil disobedience."[33]

Rustin was not in a conciliatory mood. With the support of an interracial group of militants—Muste, Conrad Lynn, St. Clair Drake, Homer Jack, and Bill Sutherland—he pressed forward. He held a press conference of his own to announce that the resistance campaign would continue. His public statement was hard-hitting and hostile to Randolph. He described the executive order as a "weasel worded, mealy mouthed sham which has accomplished nothing but confusion," and castigated leaders who "fail to follow through." Rustin promised that supporters of civil disobedience would make the ten days that remained until the new draft law went into effect "'the ten days that shook the world.'"[34]

On the first day for complying with the conscription law, Rustin and several placard-carrying pickets congregated outside a Harlem registration center shouting for men not to register. Similar picket lines formed in Philadelphia, Boston, and a number of other cities. Rustin wrote to Selma Platt in Kansas about "the terrific responses we got all over the East," with coverage by lots of radio stations and the daily press, and he was pleased that so far there was no evidence that the government was going to "crack down."[35] But if federal district attorneys were laying low, New York City police were not. Rustin was arrested for disorderly conduct and spent fifteen days in jail. By the time he was released in late September, it was hard for him to deny the obvious: the combination of Truman's executive order and Randolph's public acceptance of it had taken out of Rustin's resistance movement whatever small head of steam it had.

If the resistance movement was in reality dead, the harsh feelings were very much alive. In mid-October, perturbed over some of the comments that Rustin and others had made about them, Randolph and Reynolds issued a stinging rebuttal accusing Rustin and Muste of using the military campaign as a "front for ulterior purposes" and engaging in "unethical tactics." Rustin, they implied, was trying to snatch a defeat from victory. The support for resistance was so weak, they claimed, that continuing the civil disobedience campaign would only have discredited the method. "Gandhi in India and South Africa never engaged in mock heroics," they said.[36] Over the next several months, Muste, Houser, and Swomley wrote back and forth with Randolph, trying to repair relationships and clarify their respective positions. But there was no doubt that for a time, the ties between Randolph's civil rights camp and the Gandhian pacifists around the FOR were badly frayed.

As for Rustin, afterward he felt miserable about how he had behaved in the waning stages of the campaign. "It was two years before I dared see Mr. Randolph again, after having done such a terrible thing," he recalled. When he did finally visit Randolph to repair the breach, "I was so nervous I was shaking, waiting for his wrath to descend upon me." But Randolph had by then put the conflict behind him and was happy to have their working relationship restored.[37]

Whatever the personal feelings it aroused, the campaign to desegregate the military raised a host of issues about strategy, tactics, and goals. When was compromise a choice with integrity, and when did it represent a betrayal of principle? When did one seize the victory at hand, and when did one opt to keep the troops roused for victories not yet imminent? How did two sets of activists and two social movements with overlapping but distinct goals work together with integrity in a coalition? Which was more important: an institutional change that led to equal treatment of black and white or building a movement that placed peace and nonviolence above all other goals? Was the objective to create widening circles of resistance or to achieve a concrete reform that pointed in the direction of justice? The tensions embedded in these questions would confront Rustin and other American radicals with painful dilemmas again and again in the next two decades.

CHAPTER EIGHT

"An Iron Lung of Militarism"
1948–1952

ON OCTOBER 1, 1948, just days after the end of his jail sentence for anticonscription protests, Rustin boarded the *Queen Mary* for a voyage to Southampton, England, the initial leg of a five-month journey. He was to meet with pacifists and lecture to audiences in several European nations and then depart for a newly independent India to attend a world pacifist meeting. Though the trip had been months in the planning, Rustin's exit from New York bore the marks of a great escape. It provided a welcome physical distance from Randolph and allowed him for awhile to push the conflict out of mind.

The trip was a splendid opportunity. India served as a lodestar for believers in nonviolence. Around the globe, the country carried special meaning for peoples of color inspired by this first major success in shaking the foundations of European imperialism. In the United States, the black press had not only watched the independence struggle closely but also used the Gandhian movement as a measuring rod for assessing race relations at home. When the Indian parliament abolished untouchability in 1947, the *Pittsburgh Courier* declared that it "makes Lincoln's proclamation pale in significance by comparison. . . . [India] has moved far out in front of the United States."[1] Repeatedly in the campaign against military segregation, Randolph had held up Gandhi and India as models to emulate. Now Rustin was to have a firsthand view of the Mahatma's legacy and bring the lessons back to the United States.

In the year before his death, Gandhi initiated plans for a world gathering of proponents of nonviolence. After his assassination in January 1948, his followers determined to move ahead with the conference anyway. They planned to hold it near Calcutta, at Santiniketan, where Rabindranath Tagore, the nationalist poet, had established a school devoted to the study of social change and political reform.

Leaders in the American Friends Service Committee pushed for Rustin to be among the four Americans invited to participate and volunteered the bulk of the funds for the trip. Ray Newton of the AFSC told Muste that he felt it essential for "Bayard to spend some time now close to the leaders of non-violence in India. . . . I know of no one in this country who . . . is more apt to use it effectively than is Bayard."[2] The original plan called for Rustin to depart in July for an eight-month stay, but the campaign against the military made him hesitate. Newton pushed Rustin to take the longer view. "The experience in India would," Newton wrote, "mean much to you as you look forward to the next five or ten years. . . . you will probably have a place of great leadership in developing some of the non-violent and non-cooperative efforts in this country, and a couple months in India would seem to me to be most useful."[3] John Haynes Holmes, the pastor at the politically radical Community Church in New York, pushed Rustin too. Holmes had done much to introduce Gandhi's work to American audiences in the 1920s and was enthusiastic about Rustin's trip. "I know of no one who can more truly and devotedly represent this cause than yourself," he wrote. "I think of what the conference which you are attending and all the accompanying journeys will mean to you. The whole thing is just perfect."[4]

Rustin and Sayre, who accompanied him on the *Queen Mary*, arrived in Britain on October 7. During his first days abroad, Rustin spent much time walking the streets of London, marveling at the architecture and the layers of history that the neighborhoods of the city offered. He also saw close up the devastation of war. Doris Lessing, another first-time visitor to London in these years, has left a description of the post-war city: "It was unpainted, buildings were stained and cracked and dull and grey; it was war-damaged, some areas all ruins, and under them holes full of dirty water, once cellars. . . . The war still lingered, not only in the bombed places but in people's minds and behaviour. Any conversation tended to drift towards the war, like an animal licking a sore place." Still, the spirit of the city seemed generally to agree with him; London became his favorite destination abroad, and he returned many times over the next decades. Rustin began on this trip the practice of scouring the establishments of art and antique dealers, where he sought out bargains that he peddled to their counterparts in New York.

By mid-October, Sayre was putting Rustin to work. The peace movement in Britain had crumbled during the war, and pacifists there were hungry for signs advocating that nonviolence mattered. They were especially interested in how Rustin had applied nonviolent methods to issues of racial conflict. With Indian independence achieved, they knew it was only a matter of time before agitation to end colonialism swept irresistibly across Asia and Africa. How had American Negroes used nonviolence, they wanted to know, and how might the race relations institutes that Rustin had created be adapted for use between the colonizer and the colonized? Between late October and the end of November, Rustin also made two speaking tours on the Continent, first to France and the Netherlands and then to Germany.

An emotional high point of his travels in Europe was the visit to the village of Le Chambon sur Lignon, located in the rugged plateau of southeastern France. There, he was the guest of André Trocme, a Protestant minister in the town, and his wife, Magda. The Trocmes were pacifists of long standing who in the 1930s had established an international pacifist school in the village. In the postwar years, they achieved among religious opponents of war near legendary status for the work they had done to save Jews from extermination. Enlisting the support of the entire village, they supervised the sheltering and transport of several thousand children across the border into Switzerland. The pastor, his wife, and their congregants kept the operation going for four years under the nose of the Vichy authorities and, near the end of the war, with Gestapo agents everywhere. For Rustin and other American pacifists of his generation, the example of Le Chambon sustained their faith in nonviolence. They needed to know that in the face of an evil as great as the Holocaust, pacifism was not moral cowardice. It meant all the more to

Rustin, then, that in the eyes of these villagers, his was a message that moved them. He came at a time when a wave of strikes was sweeping across that part of France, and his lectures, according to Magda Trocme, "made [the villagers] think over the whole question of non-violence once more, and this in a particular and critical situation." Rustin had done "very good work indeed," she wrote to Sayre. The Trocmes were so impressed that they invited him back to tour the region's churches after his return from India.[5]

For a time, the Indian leg of the journey was in doubt. Sayre learned in London that the world meeting of pacifists had been postponed. Should Rustin go anyway? Muriel Lester, a cochair of the international FOR and a devotee of Gandhi, and Devadas Gandhi, the Mahatma's youngest son, begged Sayre to send Rustin anyway. "The pacifism of a good many people in India is in a somewhat critical state," they wrote; pacifist leaders there would employ Rustin "in a very useful way." Sayre persuaded Muste and the AFSC that it would help Indian pacifists a good deal "if they could meet Bayard and hear his testimony as an American Negro. . . . Bayard with his personality and background would strike a different note and may ring a different bell." Rustin and Lester left London together on November 25 for the long passage through the Suez Canal to the subcontinent. Sayre's parting advice was "to give a lot and to get a lot."[6]

Traveling with Lester proved a wise decision. The older woman, who had spent many years in India and had a close relationship with Gandhi, regaled Rustin with stories about the charismatic leader. Rustin's association with Lester also guaranteed him access to highly placed individuals. After docking at Bombay, they made their way to New Delhi, where Devadas Gandhi took them under his wing. They were "being taken care of beautifully," Rustin reported, "and I am seeing everyone and everything I desire."[7] Devadas had the pair installed at Government House as guests of the governor general. Soon Rustin was being interviewed, like a visiting dignitary, by a string of Indian journalists.

As was true for most other Westerners journeying to India for the first time, the sights, customs, crowds, and poverty overwhelmed Rustin.

He learned quickly that to "touch a woman in public is considered the highest form of vulgarity." Soon he was substituting for the Western handshake a slight bow, palms together and fingers pointed to the sky, and the greeting "Na-mas-te." After a few days of eating while sitting on the ground, with "my legs doubled up under me," he lost his stiffness and effected the posture gracefully. He also abandoned his Western clothes. "I wore plain white Gandhi cloth and was very comfortable. In the evening I wore Gandhi cloth and carried a Gandhi shawl" to compensate for the cooling temperatures. He exchanged shoes and socks for sandals, washing his feet frequently because of the dust he kicked up on most roads. As he moved about the country, he stayed in accommodations where "men, women, children, dogs, cats, and cows" slept together in the same room. "The Indians," he marveled, "are able to dress and undress, bathe, and change clothes in public without bearing [sic] flesh."

During his seven weeks in India, Rustin traveled a good bit—south from Bombay to the province of Mysore, where he visited villages of untouchables in the area; north to Delhi and to Jaipur, to attend a major gathering of the Indian National Congress Party; a trip to Lahore in neighboring Pakistan; and, always, many stops along the way. Train travel was often stressful. The cars were so densely packed with India's poor that "I got a very bad skin rash from close contact with unfortunate people who had not been able to take care of themselves properly, and it took me several weeks of careful medication to get rid of it." Food and drink also had their treacheries. Rustin found himself laid low for several days with dysentery. To a friend planning a trip to India, he warned against drinking any unboiled water and eating any fruit that did not have a thick covering. "This may seem too cautious," he wrote, "but believe me it is not." Still, the time there was exhilarating. Wherever he traveled, people of color predominated. Dorothy Height, an acquaintance of Rustin who visited India about this time, commented on what it was like. "A unique experience," according to Height. "It was just unbelievable. They were all colors, very black Indians, different shades, mulatto types and so on, but I had never seen that many colored people. . . . I just had never seen it."[8]

Rustin lectured almost continuously on pacifism and nonviolence. He told audiences about the hardships faced by COs in the United States—the jail terms and the prison strikes by incarcerated pacifists during the war. Rustin quickly learned that "the people in India actually do not have respect for Western pacifists," as he reported to Muste, "because they believe we are not people who have in any way made a sacrifice. . . . They are amazed to learn of the things that we have endured." Commenting on the inspirational impact Rustin had on his listeners, one Indian pacifist wrote to Sayre: "How we need a man like him in our colleges just now!"[9]

The heart of Rustin's lectures and interviews was the application of Gandhian methods to America's racial caste system. He explained the work of CORE in cities around the country, and particularly described the Journey of Reconciliation. Coming from a man of color, his talk of resistance to racism had a special resonance for Indians who had just thrown off white European rule. Lester marveled at the effect. "He can do, and does at once, 3 times as much as a white pacifist," she wrote Muste. "His quiet ways, his commanding stature (he really looks a mighty man of valour in his Indian style homespun), his irresistible friendliness and his savoir faire endear him to all." American press reports on his tour commented on his "warm reception and stirring speeches." Coverage in the Indian press was extensive enough to prompt cables to Washington from the American consul in Bombay and the embassy in New Delhi. Rustin, the consul's office noted, "spoke very unfavorably and in an inflammatory manner regarding racial conditions in the United States." In the cold war battle for the loyalty of the world's nations, the barest allusion to racial inequality was perceived by State Department officials as dangerous and, in the words of the consul, "anti-American."[10]

Exciting as his sojourn was, Rustin also found it sobering. Attending the several-day session of the National Congress Party, Rustin not only listened to debates and talked with delegates, but also engaged in extended discussions with Pandit Nehru, Gandhi's close associate and India's first prime minister. Nehru talked to Rustin about his intention to keep India out of the grip of the cold war. "India can save world peace," he thought, "by helping in the construction of a third entity" that sided with neither East nor West. The prime minister reminisced how Gandhi "refused to show up at the celebration of independence because he was heart broken by so much violence." But Nehru also told Rustin that "the tap root of Gandhi's motivation was nationalism" and that, since independence, the centrality of nationalism in the struggle to remove the British had become clear.[11] Rustin's own observations about Indian politics echoed Nehru but went further. Without underestimating Gandhi's achievement, Rustin emphasized that nationalism had corrupted the movement from the beginning and, without the continuing influence of Gandhi, the nonviolent movement in India was in deep trouble. Military spending consumed half the national budget, and the government was debating proposals for compulsory military training. "We should reevaluate the Gandhian movement," he told his associates. "We have overlooked its negative aspects. It was non-violent in its means, but essentially violent in its ends, which was nationalism." Nonviolence in India was a matter of "expediency . . . embraced because they had no guns."[12]

Lester shared Rustin's disappointment, but she also believed pacifists were anxious to regroup and exert, as they had during the independence struggle, a more formidable influence on events. Impressed with the impact Rustin was having, she and some of her associates attempted to persuade Muste and Sayre to allow him to stay for a year. "He can do a job here that no white Westerner can do," one of them wrote. "Do try to give him this year with us in India. It is strategic." Lester told Muste that Rustin was "getting into the very centre of power here and perhaps no one else could work so effectively with Nehru against militarism." Wherever he had gone in the country, "things started happening about pacifism," she reported. "Now is the moment in India," she concluded, and Rustin's continuing presence was *utterly necessary.*"[13]

Muste was not persuaded. "There is a good deal to be said for the proposition that the most critical field for pacifism is in the United States," he countered, and Rustin "is needed here right now." Muste questioned whether a long Indian interlude was in the best interest of Rustin's development. "Bayard's qualities are such," he wrote, that "he will practically never be in any country without the demand developing that he stay. . . . We might easily slip into a situation where to all intents and purposes he was a roving ambassador. . . . Unless a person has proved over a considerable period of time, in a situation where he has to assume continuous responsibility, that he is equipped, his work elsewhere is bound to be shallow. . . . [Bayard] ought to dig in in the American situation at least for several years before coming to be regarded as a person who can be called out of that situation for extended periods." Muste asked Lester to take his sentiments into account and see whether she still felt it a priority to keep Rustin in India.[14]

The debate did not last very long. At home, the effort to overturn Rustin's conviction, stemming from the incident in Chapel Hill during the Journey of Reconciliation, had exhausted every legal avenue. "You must feel somewhat like Gandhi when he returned to India from the Round Table Conference," one of his comrades from Ashland penitentiary wrote. "The British put him in jail."[15] At the end of January, Rustin began the long trip back to the United States, knowing he would have to spend time in a Southern state prison.

DESPITE THE WILLINGNESS to endure jail as the price of civil disobedience, Rustin never expected to serve his sentence. The Supreme Court ruling in the *Morgan* case placed the law on his side, and the arrests were opportunities to gain publicity, test the effectiveness of nonviolence, and aid in the shift toward integrated seating. Except for the Chapel Hill incident, all of the charges against the riders were dropped before trial or thrown out by judges. But Orange County prosecutors seemed intent on pushing forward, and the judges who presided at trial and on appeal were especially tough. Joseph Felmet, one of those arrested, remembered the trial judge being so incensed at a white Southerner's challenging segregation that he "tried to give me six months instead of the maximum thirty days." Igal Roodenko, as a New York Jew making trouble in the South, also raised the judge's ire. The case ought to have been won on appeal, but the outcome rested on the ability to prove that the riders were traveling on interstate tickets. Roy Wilkins of the NAACP, whose local attorneys were handling the case, shamefacedly let the men know they would have to serve time, since the

Durham attorney had lost the tickets. Felmet called the attorney "frankly incompetent," and Rustin and Houser wondered if white authorities had brought pressure to bear on the lawyer.[16]

On March 21, Rustin surrendered at the courthouse in Hillsboro, North Carolina. The next day, he was driven through the rain in a "dog car"—a small, enclosed truck where he was locked in the back with two others—to the prison camp at Roxboro, a penal institution for blacks. Conditions were awful. Mud tracked in by the prisoners, who spent each day working in gangs maintaining state roads, caked the floors, and roaches scurried everywhere. Despite the heavy physical labor, inmates received only one set of clean clothes each week; by Tuesday, the stench in the dormitories was "thick enough to cut." In three weeks at Roxboro, Rustin got but a single towel. Sleeping quarters were so crowded that prisoners had to walk sideways to maneuver between the double-decker beds. Lights shone brightly all through the night, and the rule requiring inmates to call out for permission to urinate meant that sleep was regularly interrupted.

Although incarceration was not a new experience for Rustin, never before had he confronted so directly the raw power of the state to brutalize the bodies of its captives. In North Carolina prisons in the 1940s, physical abuse was endemic and uncontrolled. Sadistic guards kept the men in a constant state of fear. Early on, Rustin's "walking boss," the man who supervised his ten-hour-a-day work crew, let him know that "you ain't in Yankeeland now. We don't like no Yankee ways." Crews had armed guards watching them; Rustin's made prisoners dance for him under threat of gunfire. "Shoot straight for his feet. Cripple 'em up," the captain shouted at one guard who was taking aim at a complaining prisoner. Guards kicked, punched, and clubbed inmates for minor infractions, and they also liberally employed a leather strap. The worst punishment of all, in Rustin's estimation, was hanging on the bars. "When a man is hung on the bars," Rustin reported, "he is stood facing his cell, with his arms chained to the vertical bars, and there he must stand until he is released." After a few hours in this position, the feet and groin started to swell; one inmate remained hanging for seventy-two hours.[17]

Released for good behavior after twenty-two days, Rustin immedi-

ately went to Chapel Hill, where friends had arranged for him to lecture. His presentation was so graphic that faculty at the university formed
an ad hoc group to press the governor for reforms. Rustin promised to
produce a report for them to use in their campaign, and with the memory still fresh, he dashed it off in a couple of weeks. One reporter to
whom Rustin sent it thought it had the power of a novel. An editorial
writer at the *Baltimore Sun* raced through it "without being able to put
it down. . . . When nonprofessional writers produce a manuscript as
vivid as yours, I feel like throwing away my typewriter and going back
to plumbing."[18] Both the *New York Post* and *Baltimore Afro-American* se-
rialized the report. The committee in Chapel Hill put the report in the
hands of Governor Kerr Scott. As Scott deliberated over a suitable
course of action, a scandal broke over the very practice of hanging from
the bars that Rustin had documented. In Rockingham, where Felmet
had been subjected to the punishment, a guard was indicted and convicted for inflicting bodily harm on an inmate. The incident pushed the
governor to overhaul disciplinary procedures and appoint a watchdog
committee.[19]

The outcome pleased Rustin. When Connie Muste, who edited
FOR's magazine, queried him on how much credit the organization
could take for what happened—or whether, even, the reforms were
worth claiming—Rustin responded in a way that exposed his thinking
about the relationship of direct action protest to social change. "The
idea," he wrote, "was to show our membership that the general effect of
our Journey was not merely protest but the development of a report
that did get published in the north, that was read in the south, that the
governor did read, that a southern committee did use behind closed
doors . . . to show our membership that we work not only as a protest
to injustice but as a part of the constructive efforts to bring gradual and
basic reform. . . . This kind of material can do a great deal to educate
our membership, or at least that segment which looks upon *direct* action
as trouble making—period."[20]

ONE ASPECT OF Rustin's report that received no comment in his correspondence or in the press was his discussion of homosexuality. In

broaching the topic, he was hardly breaking new ground. Among crim-
inologists, there was a long tradition of writing about sex in prison. In
the 1930s and 1940s, journalists took up the issue of sex crimes, a cate-
gory that included all homosexual acts. Most notably, Alfred Kinsey
had published his landmark study, *Sexual Behavior in the Human Male*,
in 1948. The press and the public seized upon his work. Not only did it
become a best-seller, but it also spawned endless debate in magazines
and newspapers, as well as a spate of books capitalizing on its notoriety.
Central to much of the attention that Kinsey's study received was his
finding that male homosexual behavior was widespread. Rustin did not
treat the subject as boldly as Kinsey, who saw homosexual expression as
a natural capacity that society should refrain from stigmatizing, but neither was he condemnatory. He exposed the severity of North Carolina's
criminal code (sentences as long as sixty years for conviction of a "crime
against nature"), questioned the absurdity of the expectation that men
confined in a single-sex environment could refrain from homosexual
acts, and proposed instead hospitalization for men who might be cured
of it. In the 1940s, this was considered an enlightened liberal approach.

More significant than the content was Rustin's willingness to discuss
the matter at all. In the three years since his release from federal prison,
the issue of his own sexuality had continued to bedevil him. He and
Muste wrangled over it, and incidents kept occurring that threatened to
sabotage his public role as a Gandhian revolutionary. In these circumstances, Rustin's inclusion of the topic in his report might be considered a small act of defiance, an effort to resist the wish of all those
around him to keep homosexuality secret and taboo.

Sometime after Rustin left Lewisburg penitentiary in 1946, he and
Muste seemed to reach a tacit accommodation about sexual matters.
Rustin had made it plain that he was not prepared to renounce gay relationships, but the letters he had written to Davis Platt and to Muste
also made clear his inner struggle over his promiscuity. From inside the
prison walls, he tried to cultivate his attachment to Platt, to deepen the
connection so that it was good not only in its own right but as a barrier
against sexual adventuring.

In preparation for Rustin's release from prison, Platt secured a spacious two-bedroom apartment on 124th Street, just north of the Columbia campus where he was a student and a dozen blocks from the FOR office on Broadway where Rustin worked. The two set up house, the first time Rustin had done so with a lover, and began to build a common life. "I had a very romantic notion of love. I'd never loved anybody like this before," Platt reminisced. "When we were living together, after he got out of prison, the people who had been his friends in prison visited us. And many of the other friends from before visited us there. And we visited outside somewhat, but our lives were very much ourselves. We cooked our own meals typically. . . . We went out to theaters, we went out to cafes, and concerts. . . . [Bayard] was never at a loss for words, and he was never without humor, never without wit. He was fun to be with." Recalling the best of those times, he said: "We had very few disagreements, spats."

Except for one. Contrary to Platt's expectations, Rustin continued having sex with others. "It was quite a while in my friendship with Bayard before I realized that he was sleeping with lots of people," Platt recalled. "Traveling all over the country for the FOR, he met people all the time. He seduced people right and left." Had the escapades occurred only away from home, Platt might never have been the wiser, but "coming home one day and finding him in bed with somebody else was not my idea of fun." For a time, he tried to adapt. He too began having sex outside the relationship, and the two occasionally shared casual partners. But the arrangement proved untenable. "I couldn't stand his need to be with other people. I couldn't take that," Platt recollected. "It wasn't just an occasional trick, but anybody who appealed to him." In May 1947, just shy of a year of living together and four years after meeting, Platt "threw him out. . . . I don't remember how I put it—'I can't live with you anymore'—and asked him to leave. We never had sex again. I wanted him [but] for many months we were distant."[21]

Rustin's sexual activities were noticed not only by his lover. His frequent trips away from home were occasions for advances toward men he encountered in the course of his work. About this time, Robert Vogel, an AFSC staffer who had met Rustin in Syracuse when Vogel worked with Norman Whitney, was approached by Rustin during an

AFSC institute on international relations. "As I recall, it was quite casual and happened in the men's room. There was no conversation; I simply said that I was happily married and not seeking sexual relations with men." Not everyone responded so evenly. Another male pacifist, who later married Rustin's secretary at the FOR's national office, was so put off by a solicitation that he refused his fiancée's wish to have Rustin sing at their wedding. Even in New York City, where the anonymity of the metropolis ought to have provided cover, Rustin's behavior drew notice. "I ran into Bayard once down on Times Square when he was out with some sailor," Houser recalled. "It was obvious that this was not somebody that he really knew and it was a pickup of some sort. I just didn't go for that very much. . . . I thought it was kind of cheap."[22]

Adding to the clash of moral sensibilities that Rustin's behavior provoked was the danger of public disgrace. As Houser's recollection of Times Square suggests, Rustin was searching for sexual partners in urban spaces, among men he did not know. The practice was common among gay men of this era. Public cruising was central to the development of social ties ranging from casual sexual experience, to lasting romantic relationships, to broad friendship networks of long duration. But it also carried with it, always, the threat of arrest. A tall, striking, and often elegantly dressed black man, Rustin was especially likely to draw the unwelcome attention of white police officers on patrol or plainclothesmen in search of gay men to entrap.

In October 1946, only four months after his release from Lewisburg and while he was still living with Platt, a police officer arrested Rustin at the edge of Morningside Park, just a block from home, for solicitation to commit a lewd act. Around the same time, police carted Rustin off to jail for his soapbox oratory on Broadway. Reading Rustin's arrest record before imposing a sentence, the judge suddenly "exploded with rage," according to an eyewitness. "The sheet of paper in his hand shook as he shouted again and again the word 'degenerate.'" The following September, an officer arrested him along Riverside Drive for being in the park after midnight. According to Glenn Smiley's recollection, another incident occurred during a trip to the Deep South, perhaps in 1949. "He had just gotten out of jail in Louisiana," Smiley said.

"He had been terribly beaten, not over his pacifism but over his homosexuality, by the police. They stood on him in the backseat of the car, knocked his teeth out. . . . A.J. called me and said 'Bayard is ill. He's having a rough time. Can he come and recuperate at your house?' We said yes, of course. So he came out and lived with us about three months." There were enough incidents during these years to create around Rustin the whiff of expectant scandal.[23]

On more than one occasion, Muste confronted him directly. John Swomley, Muste's second-in-command, participated in some of these discussions. The gist was simple: they could not tolerate something happening again, and they wanted "absolute rock-bound" assurances that nothing would. "It was a very tense and dramatic session," Swomley claimed. "Bayard cried. He didn't want to leave, but he didn't want to promise this." Muste arranged for Rustin to see a psychiatrist in the hope that "with competent psychiatric help he could change." But, Swomley recalled, eventually "it was discontinued."[24] Rustin was left tensely poised between desires that threatened to sabotage his vocation and demands to exercise a control that eluded him. In his work, the willingness to take risks and put himself in the path of danger made him heroic in the eyes of his comrades. The same characteristic in pursuit of sex brought him trouble and endless conflict. Dave McReynolds, who met Rustin during this period and was also struggling with how to be gay, remembered him as troubled. "The homosexual community was so profoundly underground and so profoundly illegal and lived a life so difficult to comprehend looking back from here. . . . Bayard was leading a divided life."[25]

Divided, yes, but not always fraught with danger and disquiet. In between the long hours of work and the many weeks of travel, Rustin carved out for himself an independent life in the city. After Platt asked him to leave their Morningside Heights apartment, Rustin moved into a tenement flat on Mott Street, on New York's Lower East Side. The building, which had housed immigrants and their children since the turn of the century, was dark and old, only recently electrified, with bathtubs in the kitchen. It offered cheap living in the midst of the postwar housing shortage. And, since many neighborhoods outside Harlem would not rent to Negroes, Rustin was happy to have it.

The building and neighborhood offered him a community. Igal Roodenko lived in an apartment on the floor above. On Mott Street, and on neighboring Mulberry and Kenmare streets, young adults of radical and dissenting dispositions were gathering, trying to make their way in a society that had survived depression and war. Rustin and Roodenko, along with a set of young married couples with ties to the left, spent evenings together eating cheaply, attending concerts, and talking about the political causes that consumed them.

For Rustin, the location was ideal. Not only did it take him away from the neighborhood in which he worked and had lived, but it brought him closer to second-hand furniture merchants and art dealers whom he was coming to know well. He began collecting old musical instruments—lutes and mandolins—to repair. Some he kept; others he sold. He scoured the streets for discarded furniture as second-generation ethnics left the neighborhood of their parents for the outer boroughs and the suburbs. Rustin learned how to refinish the pieces meticulously. By the early 1950s, his ramshackle dwelling, a "slum hostel" in many ways, had the contrasting elegance that "quite beautiful furniture" gave it, according to one visitor.[26]

THE POLITICAL CLIMATE in these years made the small community of like-minded folks on Mott Street especially important for Rustin. As the decade turned, the cold war shaped not only foreign affairs but domestic policies too. Anything that smacked of dissent, anyone who questioned the order of things, attracted suspicion. The anti-Communist hysteria that seized the country shrank considerably the political ground on which radical pacifists like Rustin could move, making them aliens in their own land.

In the months that elapsed between the campaign against a segregated military and Rustin's return from India, the change was palpable. In 1948, Henry Wallace, who had served as vice president during Roosevelt's third term, ran as an independent candidate for president. He challenged Truman's hard line toward the Soviet Union, promised to restore the spirit of the wartime alliance, and sought to rally New Dealers around a renewed reform crusade. But his campaign foundered disastrously, as Truman painted Wallace and his Progressive Party as being under the spell of Communists. Wallace's failure removed the last obstacle to a cold war foreign policy. It also proved the effectiveness of attaching the Communist label to an opponent. The search for Communists at home became a way of life in these years. The House Un-American Activities Committee (HUAC) conducted investigations into Communist influence in Hollywood. Emboldened by the attention the hearings elicited, HUAC rolled out comparable investigations of broadcasting, labor unions, universities, and public schools. In 1947, Truman initiated a loyalty security program that empowered the FBI to delve into the backgrounds of government workers, question them about their organizational affiliations, and pass judgment on an American's loyalty without due process. Many states established their own investigating bodies, searching for Communists and fellow travelers in every cranny of American life.

The pivot around which much of the anti-Communist hysteria spun was the case of Alger Hiss, a second-tier government official in Washington during the New Deal and World War II. First through HUAC hearings, and then in two perjury trials, Americans were audience to eighteen months of sensational revelations worthy of the best spy novel. Whitaker Chambers, a former member of the Communist Party, claimed that Hiss had been his contact in Washington and had supplied documents that he then relayed to the Soviet Union. Chambers matched every denial by Hiss with new accusations and evidence, from the Hiss-owned typewriter that had produced copies of the documents to a hollowed pumpkin on a Virginia farm where Chambers had hidden reels of microfilm. Richard Nixon, a young member of Congress, rode the hearings to political fame, while the conviction of Hiss on perjury charges seemed to confirm the truth of the accusations. Americans were given reason to believe that a fifth column was operating at home and threatening national security.

The Hiss case and the Wallace campaign together propelled the political spectrum to the right. They created strains between liberals and the left, fracturing the loose coalition that had mobilized in the 1930s. From social security and unemployment benefits to the unionization of industrial workers, liberals and leftists had overcome enough mutual suspicion and mistrust to move a political agenda forward. Now they were splitting sharply, with Democratic Party liberals lining up behind Truman's cold war policies and abetting anticommunism at home. Meanwhile the left, in both its Communist and anti-Stalinist varieties, found itself increasingly marginalized.

These events impinged on Rustin's work directly. He and his associates often had the Communist label thrown at them. The specter of Stalinist totalitarianism and the claims of a Communist menace at home left the rank and file of the FOR confused and demoralized. Rustin's base of support thus grew less secure. And much to Rustin's frustration, the sense of an approaching Armageddon that the nuclear arms race stimulated impelled Muste to shift him away from work on racial justice toward peace education and international relations.

Time and again Rustin and his coworkers found themselves accused of communism. A restaurant manager in Washington used the claim to foment anger among his customers when Rustin and Houser organized a sit-in on the premises. During the summer "peace caravans" that the FOR sponsored, where a small group of pacifists moved into a community for a few weeks and attempted dialogue about peace and disarmament, antagonisms flared more easily than before. In 1950, caravaners in East Harlem in Manhattan met active hostility on the street, and the police arrested several for disorderly conduct. In Lancaster, Pennsylvania, Rustin encountered hostile editorials and a statement by the mayor and the lieutenant governor about the dangers of peace movements. A local veterans' group organized a communitywide rally to counter the band of five pacifists whose speaking engagements were almost all canceled. The following summer, at a retreat Rustin was leading in upstate New York for young pacifists, FBI agents arrived unannounced and arrested a participant. That same month, Rustin, Dave Dellinger, and a small contingent of demonstrators in midtown Manhattan faced physical assault from an onlooker incensed at their call for peace.[27] The most ordinary work now came with danger. After Rustin and some caravaners distributed leaflets in Philadelphia, a television broadcaster used his airtime to call the material "blatant Red propaganda." He attacked the FOR as a "communist front." About pacifists he told his viewers: "They are aiding directly in the Communist conspiracy against the United States. They should be dealt with accordingly. In our anxiety to avoid hunting witches, let's not forget we're still tracking down a bear."[28]

The Communist label proved particularly nettlesome for Rustin and the FOR. Christian pacifism and Gandhian nonviolence certainly fell within the orbit of the left, broadly conceived, and almost all of Rustin's close associates would have identified themselves as some brand of socialist. What they stood for, how they expressed themselves, and the work they did for social change bore many resemblances to the program of the Communist Party. Neither Rustin nor Muste nor any of his other comrades wanted to feed the right-wing hysteria of these years. They recognized it for what it was: a convenient device for discrediting any work that challenged the status quo. And yet Rustin, Muste, and other stalwarts of the peace movement were themselves firmly anti-Communist. Philosophically, they could not accept the willingness of Communists to countenance violence as a tactic; they rejected the language of class warfare, even as they were staunchly anticapitalist; they were dismayed by what they viewed as communism's godless materialism; and they recoiled from the murderous violence of Stalinist rule. Rustin's experience with the Communist Party added another layer of suspicion. He had seen the ease with which it could switch political direction, and it left him with a permanent perception of party members as opportunists who betrayed the fight for racial equality when it no longer fit their strategic plan. As he wrote to one FOR member in the South, "It is absolutely impossible to depend on them in the showdown."[29]

Rustin and the organizations in which he worked simultaneously refused to tone down their own message, condemned the assault on civil liberties that right-wing anticommunism inspired, and at the same time distanced themselves from the Communist Party. CORE issued a "Statement on the Communist Issue" in the summer of 1948. It began with a strong declaration against the red scare and then asserted its own disapproval of the "undemocratic tactics which Communist and Communist-front groups use." Yet the CORE leadership also made clear that "we are fundamentally opposed to imperialism and to acts and policies of injustice, whether initiated by the Russians or by the government of the United States." Just after the start of the Korean War, FOR issued a similar statement. It placed itself against both the war-making policies of the U.S. government and the totalitarianism of the Soviet Union. It also stood fast in its defense of civil liberties for all.[30]

Rustin's work often put him in situations where he had to make decisions about his relationship to Communist Party members or party-dominated organizations. He stayed away from any involvement with the Civil Rights Congress, a left-wing organization active on racial justice issues since the 1930s, because its policies mimicked the line of the Communist Party. In 1948, when he and Randolph were picketing outside the Democratic National Convention, he chased away a group of Wallace supporters who wanted to join them. On another occasion, a North Carolina pacifist asked his advice about whether to invite Paul Robeson, the celebrated singer and actor, to give a concert in Chapel Hill. Robeson in these years was very closely identified with the party. "My feeling is that it would be a very terrific mistake to have Paul Robeson come," he wrote back. "He follows completely the line of the Communists and as far as I can see he has done a very damaging job in the field of race relations in the past two years." Rustin warned that Robeson was unlikely simply to offer a recital. "Unless you are willing," he continued, "to advertise that people are coming both to a concert and to hear a lecture advocating whatever at the moment Stalin is in favor of, I would propose that you not have Robeson."[31]

But Communist influence was not at the top of Rustin's concerns in these years. Far worse was the toll that strident anticommunism was exacting on the already small world of Christian pacifists. Rustin watched in dismay as FOR's membership dwindled, and the support of those who remained became threadbare. The number of chapters shrank from 400 during World War II to fewer than half that number during the Korean War. Minutes of meetings from the early 1950s commented

on the "defeatism" prevalent among FOR members, the "lack of vitality" among local groups, and the "deplorable" condition of the peace
movement generally. Approval among members for the staff's direct action projects evaporated. A pervading sense of drift, crisis, and help-
lessness deepened. Even efforts to counter this mood exposed how
deeply it had set in. "No time is hopeless," the FOR's National Council
declared in 1950. "Today's world is not lost." Could there be a clearer
indication of how bleak the era must have seemed?[32]

Rustin absorbed the gloom of these times even as he rebelled against
it. After an extended road trip late in 1950, he composed a long memo
to Muste and the rest of the staff. "The members of the Fellowship of
Reconciliation have never, according to my view, been more confused
than they are at present," he wrote. "I find any number of liberals in the
FOR . . . who are going along with the present action in Korea." Rustin
detected a spreading "lack of faith in a pacifist way." During another
trip, he found "church and labor people little prepared to question the
H-bomb. The feeling is: 'But if we don't make it the Russians will.'"
People were "in so fearful and demoralized a position that they are prepared to give in on *anything* to stop the Russians that the government
calls for." Rustin predicted that "we shall be facing more and more difficult times . . . for we are living in 'an iron lung of militarism.'"[33]

The capitulation of these erstwhile pacifists drove Rustin to distraction. It made him contemplate the dramatic gesture, the extreme action
that would, by its very extremism, force his fellow citizens to wake up
and notice the madness of a global arms race and a cold war that kept
turning hot. He urged consideration of a program of "direct action by
men who are prepared to *make terrible sacrifices now, to look mad now, to
give up all now if necessary.*" It was imperative, Rustin wrote to Muste,
"to do something *rash* now. . . . We must find some way to let people
know that *now* we are prepared to go to jail or even to give up all—to
get shot down if necessary—but to cry out. . . . Only such extreme behavior can reach to the real conscience through the veneer of fear, cynicism, and frustration today. . . . If not now, when do men of concern
act with their whole body? . . . Let us resist with our whole beings!" If
they did not, he concluded, "the stones themselves will cry out."[34]

No action as dramatic as what Rustin was proposing materialized, but he and other pacifists did put themselves in the path of arrest again and again. During this era, it was not uncommon for police to jail on disorderly conduct charges citizens who formed even peaceful picket lines. For several years, Rustin and others had lined the route of New York City's annual Easter parade and held aloft posters calling for disarmament. They risked arrest outside the French consulate in New York and the French embassy in Washington over the jailing of Garry Davis, an expatriate American pacifist, and the failure of the French government to recognize conscientious objection to war. In the spring of 1950, Rustin and other members of Peacemakers conducted a nine-day "Fast for Peace" in Washington; it included vigils outside the Pentagon and the Soviet embassy, as well as other public actions. Several times Rustin led peace caravans in the Northeast, placing himself in harm's way as he and his younger followers held open-air meetings in town squares and distributed leaflets along streets lined with shoppers.

Rustin unquestionably touched the hearts of many who heard him speak. He shaped the outlook of the young pacifists-in-training with whom he worked intensely. Yet whereas he could point to successes in the work for racial justice, it would be hard to claim that his activities in these years shifted by even a degree the trajectory of the cold war. Certainly that was how Roy Finch, a veteran of CPS camp during World War II and part of the inner circle at the War Resisters League, saw it. "What we thought was going to happen," he reminisced, "was that there would be an inevitable swing toward peace after the war. The fact is that the war never ended, and we never expected that. . . . I think people just had the feeling that all you could do was sort of symbolic things. . . . The peace movement was helpless. Absolutely helpless. I don't think it did a thing."[35]

But something did come out of this work for Rustin. In ways hard to calculate, it was a learning time. Through his contact with a broad range of audiences, through the efforts to train others in nonviolence, through the trial and error of actions in cities and towns across the country, Rustin was taking the measure of the hybrid of Gandhian philosophy and Christian spirituality to which he had committed himself.

Some of what he learned was about himself and what it would take to realize his goals. He had watched the turbulent decade of the 1930s fade into history. He had left behind the intense existence of the incarcerated war resister, when every moment brought struggle. Now he was living through a grim era of warmongering rhetoric and frenzied searches for enemies, even as most Americans went about their daily business as if nothing untoward was happening. It impressed on Rustin that it would be "a long pull" indeed before the world of his dreams materialized. "This requires," he wrote to a local activist in Chicago, "a patience and a forgiveness and a long term view which I must admit I am not always capable of."[36] He came to see the risks that the espousal of nonviolence carried. Employing nonviolence to resist evil, Rustin knew, inevitably "brought already existing violence to the surface." The pacifist had to accept this. "Basic social change," he wrote to a student who had heard him speak, "involves a vast deal of physical violence. The pacifist is not a man who is afraid of violence nor in a sense opposed to it because often social change cannot be made except under situations where violence is to a degree inevitable. The pacifist is opposed to *using* violence, but he must be prepared to accept it as a part of social change." As Jesus did, the pacifist had to "take it unto himself" and recognize that "you cannot take a stand for truth and justice without . . . causing some suffering."[37]

For Rustin, the willingness to absorb the violence that his stands were sure to provoke had little to do with Christian beliefs in the redemptive power of suffering. Instead, it came from his moral sense of the nature of evil and his belief that it could only be combatted by good, never by tools or methods that were in themselves evil. "Separation, it seems to me, is the chief sin," he wrote at this time, "precisely because violence is automatically the result of separation and ostracism between individuals or groups or nations." From his direct encounters with Southern racists and rabid anti-Communists, Rustin saw that "if I had struck them they would have been on familiar ground and able to defend themselves and to strike me back."[38] For Rustin, the belief in nonviolence blended a moral imperative with a long view of how permanent change would come. Defensive violence might provide immediate satisfactions and even temporary gains; it might block for a moment an evil that needed to be stopped. But it would also lock the antagonists in a continuing cycle of retaliation and response in which the evil to be overcome—the rupture in the human community—remained as alive as ever before.

IN THE MIDDLE of the Korean War, an opportunity arose to escape the deadeningly conservative atmosphere of the McCarthy era. For more than a year, Rustin had been planning a trip to Oxford in the summer of 1952 as a delegate to the World Conference of Friends. As the time for his departure approached, Rustin's attention, as well as that of Houser, Bill Sutherland, and other close associates, turned toward events in Africa. In South Africa, the African National Congress had launched a series of demonstrations against apartheid. Manilal, one of Gandhi's sons, informed Muste that the campaign bore all the markings of a nonviolent resistance movement. "Father's spirit seems to be watching over and guiding them," he wrote with pleasure.[39] In West Africa, resistance to colonialism was gathering. Especially in Nigeria and the Gold Coast, political movements led by Nnamdi Azikiwe and Kwame Nkrumah seemed to be developing along lines pioneered by Gandhi's fight against British imperial rule.

Rustin and Houser began hatching a plan that melded their commitments to peace, racial justice, and nonviolence. What if they reoriented their work toward support for African decolonization? How could Americans, themselves a product of a revolutionary war against an empire, not respond with empathy? Might opposition to Western colonialism be a way to preach nonviolence, win support for campaigns against racial injustice, and avoid being tarred with the brush of cold war anticommunism? And so Rustin's trip to Oxford became instead part of a larger expedition to Africa to meet independence leaders and see how American pacifists might support the freedom struggles there.

CHAPTER NINE

"Bayard's Trouble"
1952–1953

"THE SMELL OF THE earth in Africa is heady to a black person,"
Maya Angelou has written. So it was for Rustin. The lectures on
African history and politics that he composed soon afterward offer tantalizing glimpses of why, as he wrote in one of them, "traveling in Africa
has meant much to me." His weeks in the Gold Coast and Nigeria, his
meetings with Kwame Nkrumah and Nnamdi Azikiwe who were leading
their countries' independence movements, his contacts with Africans
on the streets of Lagos and Accra—together they touched something
deep. The six weeks in Africa unlocked passions both political and
personal.[1]

Initially Rustin had expected to tour extensively in North and West
Africa. He planned to visit both French and British colonies, but was
unable to obtain a visa from the French, who knew of him through his
protests at the embassy in Washington. When he finally gave up trying,
he decided to restrict his time to the Gold Coast and Nigeria, the two
British colonies in West Africa with the most developed freedom
movements. He made contacts in the African political community in
London and, armed with introductions, set out in the last half of August 1952.

Much of the excitement of his travels stemmed from politics. "Africa
is afire," he wrote to colleagues at home. "From the Mediterranean to
the Cape of Good Hope, every imaginable form of resistance is being
used to break 300 years of . . . European domination. Everywhere

African nationalism is rising."[2] The Gandhian in him thrilled to the commitment to nonviolence that he found among some of the independence leaders, but he also saw that its roots were not deep. Hatred of the colonizer was rife, and in Rustin's view, it boded poorly for the future. Without a liberation strategy anchored in the goodwill of nonviolence, "Africa may reach independence but miss freedom. A change of exploiting leadership from white men to black men is not worth the struggle," he wrote. "But just such a limited change is highly possible unless a revolutionary method is used that can recognize evil everywhere it exists—even in the African community—and accepts good everywhere it exists—even from the European settlers." Looking at African politics through the eyes of a Gandhian apostle, Rustin saw nonviolence as "perhaps the only method that can keep Africa from turning further toward communism and black nationalism. . . . It is the only power method ultimately capable of drawing a clear line between progressives and reactionary elements."[3]

Rustin spent a good deal of time with Azikiwe at his home outside Lagos and with Nkrumah at the headquarters of the Convention People's Party in Accra. He bonded well with each of them. Both leaders had studied at Lincoln University in southeastern Pennsylvania during the years when Rustin was a young man living nearby in West Chester. With Azikiwe, he engaged in animated conversations about Jerry Hannon, captain of the Lincoln football team in the 1930s, and the heated competition between the Lincoln and Howard University squads. Azikiwe was an eager student of Gandhi's campaigns, and so Rustin described his encounters with Nehru a few years earlier. Ruminating on his meetings afterward, Rustin observed that "I have never met two men more alike than Zik and Nehru. Each is fiery and sensitive. Each has a world view. Each has the love of his people. Each is willing to expend all for the people." Most of all, Rustin reflected poignantly, "each respects the ideals of Gandhi and each is inwardly sorry he cannot see clearly to follow him all the way." Nkrumah also made a powerful impression. Rustin was struck by "his organizational genius, his animal magnetism, his honesty and his judgment of the temper of the people." Rustin rated him "not just a nationalist. He has a burning revolutionary spirit. . . . He is an internationalist." Attuned to the power of music, Rustin noticed that wherever he went in the Gold Coast, he heard improvised tunes about Nkrumah.

Rustin's African travels meant more to him than the excitement of encounters with revolutionary leaders. Each day he saw evidence of ordinary folks acting with dignity and courage, "a new spirit" overtaking them. In a bank in Lagos, a diminutive African woman, balancing on her head a box that weighed a hundred pounds, chided a British colonel who had walked to the head of the line. "'I wait a long time. You no see people here?'" she scolded him. At public gatherings, when the first chords of the customary "God Save the Queen" were played at the close, Africans in attendance would exit en masse. "'We do not recognize the British Queen as our ruler,'" one teenager told him. "'We must be free to make our own choices.'" Rustin characterized his tour of a new school in Nigeria as "the most encouraging sign" of the trip. Describing it as a combination of Tuskegee Institute and Antioch College, he saw it as a creative departure from the elite colonial British system of education. Wandering the slums of Accra with Roy Ankara, who had recently won the featherweight championship of the British Empire, he never escaped the sickening stench of open sewers. "But I never had a better time," he wrote afterward. Africans would gather around the American visitor and pepper him with questions, while the sounds of Cab Calloway's records hung in the air.

Africa tapped old resentments even as it shaped a new sense of pride in his ancestry. "I discovered that my education kept me ignorant of Africa," he wrote in a speech aimed at African American audiences. "Our history books did not mention it except for slavery." His own reading over the years had given him some facts, but not enough to shake off the limitations of his early schooling. Firsthand experience opened his eyes: "I have visited a black king whose forefathers were using iron and making magnificent jewelry of gold, when the British were in the stone age. I have seen women with simple sticks and a frame, making cloth that Hattie Carnegie would give her eye teeth to acquire. I have seen a system of decentralized democracy in which the degree of individual freedom is like unto nothing the west has yet devised. I have seen ancient cities with drainage, roads, and sewage-disposal systems that rival anything the Romans did. I have seen sculpture in wood and stone, done by men with unbelievably simple tools, that makes the realistic classical works of Greece and Rome seem cold and photographic."

The last week in September, Rustin returned to London. He conferred with Fenner Brockway and Reginald Sorensen, left-wing pacifist members of Parliament who were outspoken foes of British colonialism, and with Michael Scott, an English clergyman who was campaigning against South African apartheid. Rustin also strengthened his contacts with London-based organizations working for African independence. Before he returned home, he wrote to Carl Murphy, publisher of the *Baltimore Afro-American*, to see whether he could spark Murphy's interest in covering an emerging Gandhian resistance in West Africa.[4]

RUSTIN REPORTED ON his African trip to the executive committee of the FOR at its October meeting. He was not yet prepared to make a substantive proposal to reorient the FOR's work toward African affairs, but he knew that this was the audience who would eventually decide its merits. His presentation was designed to impress. He emphasized the discussions with Nkrumah and Azikiwe about the relevance of nonviolence to their independence struggle. Rustin attempted to convey something of "the feeling and temper" of contemporary West Africa, particularly his observation that the British resistance to independence threatened to push Africans toward terrorism and Communist-inspired freedom strategies. He also shrewdly mentioned his meetings in London with Scott, Sorensen, and Brockway, knowing that their names would carry weight.[5] The next day, Rustin wrote to Jim Bristol of the AFSC, which was sponsoring a fall speaking tour for him. The titles he proposed for his various lectures suggest the direction of his thinking: "Africa Aflame"; "Africa—A New Chapter in Non-Violence"; "Africa and the World Struggle"; "America and the African Struggle for Freedom." He spent the rest of the month drafting his talks. Fluent as he was as a platform speaker, the unusual care Rustin lavished on these essays testifies to his sense of urgency.[6]

Late in October, Rustin left for six intense weeks of travel, lectures, workshops, and meetings. His stops included six days in Boston, followed by six in Columbus, five in Richmond, Indiana, five in Chicago, and a final six-day stay in Wichita. Each city served as a base from which he made side trips to places like Milwaukee, Louisville, and Lexington, Massachusetts. He spoke before Quaker meetings, liberal church congregations, black organizations, college groups, and businessmen's lunches. Black audiences particularly seemed to warm to his message, and displayed a hunger for information about African freedom struggles. A talk before the Urban League in Milwaukee, according to one of those in attendance, was "received by all present as the most informative and dynamic presentation Milwaukee has had to date." At a Friends Meeting in Indiana, "the Negro visitors that evening . . . left enthusiastic."[7] The trip exhausted Rustin. To Glenn Smiley and Robert Vogel, who were arranging a winter tour on the West Coast, he wrote that he was "worn out," and begged them to exercise care in mapping his schedule.[8]

In the weeks between his fall tour and the winter trip, Rustin worked to build support within the FOR for an African venture. His proposal was as much directed toward American domestic politics as it was toward African independence. Based on the response of audiences during the fall, Rustin believed that decolonization pointed a way out of the cul-de-sac in which the cold war had trapped pacifists. "People can readily see," he wrote Muste, that "if money is to be available to deal with problems in Africa, we must disarm. I am amazed in question periods on this trip how readily they see the connection. . . . The presentation of a specific need to disarm is more convincing than a general moral plea. This aspect could be hammered away at—thus bringing people closer to our basic position." Because of the rising concern among some American blacks about apartheid in South Africa, Rustin thought that "Negroes in America can be more readily brought to an interest in pacifism through an interest in Africa than in any other way."

Among white church women and college students, he detected an eagerness for information and a desire for action that circumvented cold war constraints on political mobilization. And, he noted, "The fact is that subconsciously white people have a deep guilt feeling about the injustice to Africa coupled with a great fear of black men using violence. . . . We can reveal the relation of our basic position to the need for real change in foreign policy if we are not to have more trouble in Africa."[9]

But the African proposal was about more than political strategies. Rustin requested a year's trial assignment in West Africa to set up a center devoted to nonviolence and to create a "servants of Africa" program for young African men and women hungry for effective methods of fighting for freedom. To Muste, he explained that "it is not merely my desire to work on the African problem but, I believe, a clear calling to do so—a calling that I cannot easily ignore." He asked Muste to communicate these sentiments to members of the organization's governing board, and he let Muste know that should his proposals be rejected, he would ask for a leave of absence to pursue the work independently. Azikiwe had offered him a job in Nigeria and, if the FOR was too cautious to move ahead, Rustin was prepared to accept it.[10]

Early in January, Muste submitted to the executive committee the staff's work proposal for the year. Central to it was the reorientation toward Africa. Rustin would spend the winter and spring on speaking tours, designed to build awareness of the independence movements, and then go to Nigeria to set up a training center and work camps for young men and women. Muste emphasized the "real tie-in between our work among Negroes and inter-racial work generally in the United States and the African situation."[11] He and the staff faced tough questioning. Lyle Tatum thought the proposal would eviscerate efforts to promote pacifism at home, while Sayre argued that a focus on Africa would strip to the bone the work among college students and the help to local chapters. He wondered why the staff needed to travel several thousand miles on behalf of racial justice when there was plenty to do at home. Charles Lawrence pointed to the extensive missionary efforts of the AFSC in Africa. Why did the FOR need to duplicate these efforts?[12] Rustin argued that the rise of black nationalism in Africa and the severity of the independence struggle required someone to take sides against imperialism rather than follow the Friends' philosophy of negotiation and compromise. He also pointedly said that "a Negro with a reputation in the field of non-violent work—certainly not a white person—is needed for success." The fact that he was willing to wield his racial identity as an argument in the debate, an unusual tactic for him, attested to how strongly he felt about the plan.[13]

A vote was taken and the plan was approved, although not unanimously. One executive committee member left feeling that he had been "railroaded." Sayre continued to "oppose the thing for all I was worth" and, as he later wrote to a friend, "I had some brief words with A.J. and John Swomley in the office. . . . I confess that I lost my temper with A.J."[14] The outcome was a triumph for Rustin. He would be going back to Africa to engage in the freedom struggle of a continent.

But first there was more travel and lecturing. In the middle of January 1953, he left by train for the West Coast, on another tour sponsored by the AFSC, with week-long engagements in and around Los Angeles, San Francisco, Portland, and Seattle. By now, he had both sharpened and refined his message. In a radio interview in Los Angeles on Wednesday, January 21, he offered listeners an analysis of international affairs. In exchange for European contributions to NATO, he argued, the United States was backing away from opposition to colonialism. In the United Nations, the American delegation was turning a deaf ear on African petitions for independence. Thus had the cold war crusade against communism turned the United States away from its own historic ideals. "How do you stop Communism and encourage revolution which is non-communistic?" he asked. "How can we help the African in his desire for self-determination when our own foreign policy makes that almost impossible?" Before denouncing Mau Mau uprisings in Kenya, he warned, Americans should "change attitudes in our own country and solve our own racial problems." Indignation about violent revolution abroad was hypocrisy for Americans who "do not allow Negro membership in their own church."[15]

In the evening Rustin spoke at an event sponsored by the American

Association of University Women at the Pasadena Athletic Club. According to one of the local papers that covered the event, his "sparkling lecture on world peace charmed" the audience.[16] As always when Rustin spoke, many in the crowd lingered afterward, eager to have a bit more of his time and to draw from him a few last words of inspiration. Rustin passed up the offer of a ride and, when everyone had finally dispersed, began walking alone back to his hotel.

He never arrived. A few hours later, carrying the $600 in cash and checks that he had collected from his lecture, he was still wandering the deserted streets of downtown Pasadena. Just before 3:00 A.M., a car with two young white men cruised by slowly, and Rustin waved. After the driver pulled over, Rustin approached the car. "He asked us if we wanted a good time," one of them said later. "We asked him what he meant, he replied that he couldn't offer us much, but he could blow us." The two still had with them the box of unused condoms they were carrying that evening from their unsuccessful search for female companionship, and they accepted Rustin's offer. Rustin was in the back seat performing oral sex when two county police officers approached the car. The police promptly arrested the three of them on charges of lewd vagrancy, and Rustin's world began to unravel.[17]

Taken in for booking, Rustin managed to reach an AFSC staffer who had arranged his speaking tour. A group of Friends came to the police station, bailed him out pending a hearing later in the day, and quickly found a lawyer to represent him. They also telephoned Muste in New York and Glenn Smiley locally, who immediately rushed to the jail. A remorseful Rustin told Smiley to call Muste and extend to his mentor deep regrets for what he had done. He also asked Smiley to let Muste know that, under the circumstances, he would resign from the FOR. In court that afternoon, the judge rejected an appeal to free Rustin on the condition that he leave the state immediately. Instead, he sentenced all three defendants to sixty days.[18]

In New York, Muste spent Thursday and Friday informing staff and hurriedly conferring with members of the FOR executive committee. Any inclinations he might have had toward forgiveness were overwhelmed by a sense of betrayal. Smiley, whose communication with

Muste was by phone, recalled a restrained reaction on Muste's part. "He didn't break out sobbing or anything else of the sort," Smiley recollected. "He said we have a real problem here because this has happened so frequently that I have given Bayard an ultimatum that if it happened again he would have to resign." But Houser, who received the information directly from Muste and observed the many calls and meetings of the next few days, saw beneath the surface reserve: "It was devastating for AJ. AJ was not a person to talk about himself very much. You couldn't tell—he wasn't one who was saying I feel so and so. He wasn't built that way. So, whatever self examination he did he would have done within himself and nobody would know about it. Objectively speaking, he felt he'd been betrayed because they had spent time talking about this and Bayard had made certain agreements that he understood, that AJ understood. And he felt that he'd been violated by what had happened." By Monday, when John Swomley returned to the office from a trip to Texas and received the news, the emotional toll on Muste was visible. In a letter to Rustin the next day, Swomley wrote, "I don't think I have seen him looking so haggard."[19]

The executive committee convened on Monday, and Muste told them what he knew of the arrest and conviction, including the publicity it had received in West Coast papers, where Rustin was identified as a "nationally known Negro lecturer." On Wednesday, the FOR released a lengthy statement. "To our great sorrow," it began, "Bayard Rustin was convicted on a 'morals charge' (homosexual) and sentenced to 60 days in the Los Angeles County Jail on January 23, 1953. As of that date, and at his own suggestion, his service as an FOR staff member terminated." The statement then summarized the FOR's history with Rustin's "problem": how it did not become known until he had been on the staff for some time; how it was seriously aggravated by his wartime incarceration; how the FOR had sought to provide him with counsel so his "exceptional gifts" might be used in the cause of peace and racial justice; and how it was always made clear to him that he would have to exercise "rigorous discipline" if he expected to stay on staff. "Until the unhappy recent event," it continued, "the situation seemed to be moving along these lines. . . . Bayard was growing spiritually as

well as intellectually and proving a powerful exponent of non-violence."
When rumors arose, "as happened from time to time," the staff investigated and found that the story arose from an earlier period. "We are
grateful to Bayard," the statement concluded, "for the many services he
has rendered, and sorrow with him over the fact that he is not able to
continue as an FOR member."[20]

The FOR distributed the statement widely among pacifists. In doing
so, it ensured that a story buried deep within the local southern California press became common knowledge among the circles of people
who mattered most to Rustin. Thus ended his dozen years of service to
a Christian organization dedicated to peace and social justice.

THE PASADENA ARREST proved to be a pivotal event in Rustin's life.
The man whom many considered an exemplary prophet of nonviolence
had been branded a sex offender and cast adrift from the cause to which
he had devoted himself, the people with whom he shared a vision of justice, and the organization that had provided him with his only secure
employment. The arrest trailed Rustin for many years afterward. It severely restricted the public roles he was allowed to assume. Though he
fought his way back from the sidelines, he did so at a price. As both the
peace and civil rights movements grew dramatically over the next
decade, as a philosophy of nonviolence became familiar to millions of
Americans, Rustin's influence was everywhere. Yet he remained always
in the background, his figure shadowy and blurred, his importance
masked. At any moment, his sexual history might erupt into consciousness. Sometimes it happened through the design of enemies to the
causes for which he fought, sometimes through the machinations of
personal rivals, sometimes through the nervous anxieties of movement
comrades. But underneath it all was the unexamined, because as yet unnamed, homophobia that permeated midcentury American society.

In one sense, the Pasadena incident was an event waiting to happen;
it was emblematic of gay life in this era. Men were regularly arrested on
charges of lewd behavior for dancing with one another in a gay bar or
on charges of disorderly conduct simply for patronizing the bar. They
were arrested for solicitation when they asked another man to go home

with them; they were arrested for loitering when they stood too long on a city street known to be a cruising strip. The police arrested gay men who had sex in secluded public places like the back seat of cars or urban parks at night. Arrests of gay men were common rather than exceptional, with hundreds occurring each day in the United States. One study done in the 1950s estimated that fully one out of five homosexual men had encountered trouble at the hands of the police.[21]

The mass persecution of gay men by law enforcement officials in a democratic society occasioned little protestation. It rested on historical traditions of long duration and contemporary social strains that scapegoated homosexuals. At least since the Middle Ages, Christian teaching had condemned sodomy, buggery, and other "crimes against nature." In Reformation England, these religious injunctions became embedded in the secular criminal law, were then incorporated into the statutes of the North American colonies, and in the twentieth century were still part of the penal code in every state. Moreover, as the medical profession in the nineteenth century began to claim authority as experts about sex, another layer of cultural condemnation, this time under the rubric of disease, came to rest on the heads of gay men.

Powerful as these ways of thinking were, in practice they had often faded into the background of American life, exerting little impact on the day-to-day lives of men who chose to pursue sexual intimacies with other men. But in the decades of Rustin's adulthood, antihomosexual prejudice in the United States assumed a hostile, aggressive edge. In large American cities, gay subcultures were coalescing in the twentieth century, and, at least in New York, Rustin's home since 1937, the gay world was becoming assertively visible. In the post-Prohibition era, the city's police targeted homosexuality and, with some ebb and flow to its activity, continued to harass gay men with impunity until well into the 1960s.[22]

But the forces at work in these decades were more than local in nature, and they served to make gay men the scapegoat for a broad range of anxieties. The Depression had placed tremendous strains on American families, particularly disrupting the ability of men to fulfill their breadwinner role. The specter of homeless males—vagabonds and hoboes—riding the rails, camping out on the edge of town, or wandering city streets fed concerns about disorder that, in the strange way that social fears transmute, erupted into a panic about sex crimes, about men preying on helpless women and children. In the postwar years, worries about the adjustment of returning veterans, trained to kill and now let loose on a civilian world, added another layer of alarm to the sex hysteria. The image of the crazed psychopath, the uncontrollable sex fiend, filled the newspapers. It received endorsement from J. Edgar Hoover, the director of the FBI. It elicited commentary from figures such as Adam Clayton Powell, Jr., a clergyman and congressman from Harlem who, in 1951, warned against "an alarming growth of sex degeneracy" even within the churches of the black community. In the minds of many, the degenerate and the homosexual ("the boys with the swish and the girls with the swagger," in Powell's phrasing) were scarcely distinguishable.[23]

To the perception of homosexuals as dangerous sex criminals was added the image of them as a threat to the nation's safety. During World War II, the armed forces engaged in a spirited debate about policy toward homosexual members. Even as manpower needs encouraged the pragmatic inclination to look the other way, the system of regulation became more expansive. In the course of the 1940s and 1950s, military policy incorporated medical definitions of homosexuals as unfit and shifted from a simple prohibition against homosexual behavior to a more comprehensive ban against "tendencies." As a large military became a permanent feature of American society in the cold war decades, its active homophobia, displayed through recurring witch-hunts, carried more and more social weight.[24]

The cold war also fed obsessive concerns about national security. While much of this centered on the dangers of Communist infiltration, it also triggered delusional fears about the homosexual civil servant who sapped the nation's moral fiber and betrayed its secrets to the foreign agent. Running through the political rhetoric and popular culture of the 1950s was an image of the homosexual as a menace. It was expressed in congressional hearings, magazine articles, speeches by public officials, and Hollywood films. Indeed, at the moment of Rustin's arrest, the new Eisenhower administration was preparing an executive order to ban homosexuals from all federal employment.[25]

Under these circumstances, how did gay men manage to build lives filled with the intimacies, pleasures, and ordinary satisfactions that love and sexual passion might be expected to produce? Sometimes not at all, to be sure; often with great difficulty; but also in a surprising variety of ways. As Alfred Kinsey discovered in the research he conducted in the 1940s into male sexual behavior, men in rural areas still commonly had sex with men without the sense of being different, or queer, that was characteristic of urban society. In small towns, two men might share a home, remain an integral part of their family networks, and find acceptance by locals, who saw them simply as two of their own, familiar rather than threatening. Others chose to leave their communities of origin, as Rustin did, migrating in search of the freedom, anonymity, and opportunities that a large city might offer to the sexually different.

In midcentury New York, men whose sexual and emotional yearnings pulled them toward other men might respond to those longings in any number of ways. At one end of the spectrum were those who, either because of their own inner conflicts or out of fear of the potential consequences of discovery, kept their sexual desires buried. They might marry, or they might not. Their homosexual experiences were sporadic and fleeting, the unplanned response to needs they could no longer contain. Most often finding sex by soliciting strangers in places like parks or public lavatories, they were also very susceptible to entrapment and arrest. Closer to the other end of the spectrum were the growing number of men who accepted their affectional preferences and, while still observing the era's norms of discretion, immersed themselves in a gay world. At work and with family, they might appear straight, but at night and on weekends, they moved in an elaborate social milieu. They drank together in bars, sunned themselves in sections of city beaches, strolled and conversed in parks, congregated on stoops in gay-identified neighborhoods, partied in each other's apartments, and met at the theater or the ballet or the opera. All the while, they were expanding their network of friends, acquaintances, and familiar faces, any one of whom might become the object of sexual or romantic interest. These men, too, might encounter trouble with the police. But when it happened, they possessed a community of sorts that offered comfort, affirmation, and support.

Rustin's life fit neither of these patterns. When measured against the norms of the era, he appeared rather comfortable with his sexuality and unusually open about it. But his chosen profession left little room for constructing a gay-centered personal life. His work was a calling, not a job. His arduous travel schedule, his frequent stays at the homes of FOR members when he was on the road, the workshops and conferences and summer camps that consumed his weekends: all this gave him precious little time to build the social networks capable of relieving the aching loneliness that, in moments of vulnerability, he acknowledged. In other words, it was ironically Rustin's devotion to the cause of revolutionary nonviolence that in some measure made him prone to engage in random pickups, casual cruising, and public sex.

This his comrades in the Christian peace movement were unable to see. Then, and later, many of them insisted, as Dorothy Hassler put it, that what made the FOR release him was "not the fact that he was gay, but that he was sort of promiscuously gay." Glenn Smiley remembers Muste telling him that "we can not condone [Bayard's behavior] any more than we would heterosexual irregularities."[26] But the claim erases some critical differences. In practice, homosexuality and promiscuity were closely linked, not through any inherent connection between them but because condemnatory laws, cultural biases, hostile social attitudes, and restrictive institutional practices—not nature—encouraged the very forms of homosexual expression society then censured gay men for exhibiting. For instance, in ways never remarked on in the historical sources on the peace movement or the recollections of participants, an organization like the FOR served as a marriage market for young heterosexuals. The staff, the volunteers, the student enthusiasts who attended workshops and conferences, met, dated, fell in love, and wed in the course of their pacifist activities. The presumption of heterosexuality made every member of the opposite sex a potential mate. Once married, the couples at the heart of the New York FOR went home at night to communities rooted in patterns of heterosexual family life.

For Rustin and other gay men, the opprobrium that rained down on homosexuality precluded such easy sociability. The overwhelming majority of urban gay men in this era kept their identity hidden when not in an explicitly gay environment. At best they might drop subtle verbal cues in mixed company, designed to escape the notice of the uninitiated, but meaningful to someone who was gay; at worst they might misjudge another's interest and make a pass at someone who would take extreme offense. Or, traveling, they might find themselves in a parked car in the middle of the night, as happened to Rustin in Pasadena in 1953.

At the time of Rustin's arrest, no readily accessible language of gay pride and affirmation was available through which either he or his fellow pacifists might interpret the experience. True, in 1951, a pseudonymous Donald Webster Cory had published *The Homosexual in America*, a book that, considering the era, stood as a ringing defense of the rights of homosexuals and a plea for acceptance. Simultaneously, in southern California, a group of left-leaning gay men had formed the Mattachine Society, thereby giving birth to the modern American gay rights movement. A few months before the Pasadena incident, Dale Jennings, one of the Mattachine's founders, had been the victim of police entrapment in Los Angeles, and the organization had rallied to his defense. Ironically, word of the Jennings case had traveled quickly enough through male homosexual networks so that Gerard Brissette, a gay FOR member in Berkeley, wrote to the Mattachine when he heard of Rustin's arrest. The group could do nothing for Rustin, but Brissette went on to establish a chapter in the East Bay. Thus, Rustin's misfortune had the unintended consequence of fostering the growth of this infant gay movement, even as the movement exerted no impact on him or on those who were deciding his fate.[27]

From within the FOR, no evidence survives of any appreciable dissent from Muste's conviction that Rustin had to go. Dorothy Hassler retrospectively claimed that her husband, Al, opposed it, but mostly the record is silent, reflecting the discomfort of an organization with an issue that it obliquely referred to as Rustin's "problem" and "the recent unhappy event." Houser recalled that he left the matter to Muste and the executive council and chose to stay out of the discussions entirely, a strange reaction from someone who had been Rustin's closest work partner for more than six years and had faced down segregationist mobs with him. In reminiscences, staff members such as Swomley and Smiley seemed to take it as a given that Rustin's resignation would be accepted. He had been warned too many times, the agreement with Muste too clear, for there to be any doubt as to the organization's intentions and Rustin's culpability. To everyone in the FOR, his careless promiscuity made it an open and shut case.

Occasionally some contrary evidence slips through. Comments from Dorothy Hassler, who was trying to reconstruct the thinking of an earlier generation, revealed the way different concerns bled into one another until simply being gay became the problem:

> As long as it didn't become a point of contention on a public scale, nobody thought anything about it. It was the publicity that A.J. was worried about, I guess. And the moral factor. At that point one didn't think of homosexuality as being innate, one thought of it as being psychologically imposed by the society or the background. And therefore, if Bayard was in touch with a lot of young men whom he would lure into being gay, he was considered a kind of threat, especially visiting colleges all the time and working with young people. I think it was more like that.

The general uneasiness about homosexuality came through in the actions of Margie Rohrer, an FOR secretary who later married Swomley. To her fell the job of sorting through Rustin's office files in the wake of his resignation. "I can distinctly remember some of his letters that I saw as damaging the reputation of the FOR," she told me. "A staff member writing letters of encouragement to homosexuals whom he had some contact with, to tell them artistic people were very often this way. So I can remember some of those letters, and those were destroyed."[28]

Because the AFSC had sponsored Rustin's speaking tour, it too had to grapple with his arrest. A lively debate momentarily opened in which Rustin had his defenders and detractors. Steve Cary, an AFSC staffer who had known Rustin for years, was unabashed in the belief that the

Friends should continue to use Rustin's services. "I have felt confident that the Committee was not exposing any of its young people to risk. I still believe this to be the case," he wrote to one of Rustin's critics. Jeannette Jamison wrote to Lewis Hoskins, the executive secretary of the AFSC, "to beg you" to retain Rustin. "He has so much more of value to give than 99% of the human race that he should not be cast out. . . . Many highly respected white men have the same fault that is now casting its deep shadows over Bayard's life. Don't give him up."[29]

But the AFSC proved no more understanding than did the FOR. Internally, it faced intense pressure from some who were outraged that despite knowing about Rustin's homosexuality, it had used him for years as a speaker and workshop leader. Eleanor Clarke wrote that "to have used a man with this particular history in the public way we did was, it seems to me, a constant threat (more emotional, undoubtedly, than physical) to the young people to whom we sent him, and could not have done other in the long run than hurt the causes of peace and race relations." Thomas Jones, president of Earlham College, reminded Hoskins of the trouble that the State Department was confronting for employing persons "known to have this weakness," a strange rationale for a peace-loving Quaker to use. Hoskins himself had no doubts about the imperative of distancing the AFSC from Rustin. "Thee is right that a great setback to our work in peace and race relations has occurred," he wrote back to Clarke. "We were wrong in taking these risks."[30]

WHILE ASSORTED PACIFISTS did what they thought necessary to protect their organizations from the taint of sexual impropriety, Rustin languished in jail. Letters came from friends and comrades expressing support and caring, but many of them must have sounded hollow to Rustin, coming as they did from men who were ready to cut him loose from his livelihood and his calling and who had added to his humiliation by publicizing his arrest. He had occasional visitors during his two months in jail—Glenn Smiley; Dave McReynolds, a twenty-three-year-old socialist living in Los Angeles who saw Rustin as his political mentor; Jim Bristol of the AFSC—but mostly he had time to himself—time to reflect on the mess he was in.

Rustin described these weeks as a journey "through hell." When McReynolds visited him halfway through his sentence, Rustin "looked terrible . . . he looked thin and depressed and haunted. . . . He was in jail for a reason that was stupid. Not one that he could defend morally. . . . He had lost everything that he had." In a letter to Sayre, Rustin described "a long and frequently barren struggle" as he prayed and waited for insight to come. To Swomley, he wrote of "God's way of turning ugliness and personal defeat to triumph." Rustin had gone "deeper in the past six weeks than ever before and feel that I have at last seen my real problem." As if to make clear that he did not view things exactly as those who had decided his fate, he told Swomley that sex "has never been my basic problem. I know now," he acknowledged, "that for me sex must be sublimated if I am to live with myself and in this world longer." Rather the core issue was an arrogance deep in his personality. "In most of the dramatic ways, the so called big ways, I was prepared to give all. I would, I believe, have died rather than join the army. But in the small and really primary ways I was as selfish as a child. I am sure that in a way I must have *known* this. Now I *feel* it and know that pride must be overcome. . . . I have pledged before God that I will live more non-violently in the small ways that support the big ones if they are to be real."[31]

McReynolds, who himself was gay and, at least in these years, in difficult personal struggle over it, had invited Rustin to visit before he headed home to New York. "Ocean Park has more of Greenwich Village and less of 21 Audubon Avenue [the address of the FOR office] than any place else in L.A.," he wrote Rustin in jail. As they talked over dinner, McReynolds recalled, Rustin said "something about loneliness, and how terribly lonely his life was. That seemed to be very much on his mind. He was feeling lonely. He wasn't making a pass. He was just saying 'you have no idea how lonely—loneliness is so terrible.'"[32]

As if to fortify himself for the ordeal of returning home in disgrace, Rustin stopped in Syracuse and visited with Norman Whitney and his sister, Mildred, for a few days. He had known Whitney since 1937, stayed with him and Mildred whenever his travels took him to upstate New York, and had confided in him early on about his homosexuality.

Rustin described the two as "like family" to him, and Norman in particular as "my spiritual guide, and thus my father." Of all the letters he
received while in jail, Whitney's was the most unqualified in its love and
support. Free from any hint of censure, it was filled with the spiritual
sentiments that Rustin, at that moment, most needed. "I hope that my
faith and trust may surround you. If you think of me, be sure that these
are real and unshaken," Whitney wrote. "You and I have together seen
that this might happen. . . . I know nothing of the particular circumstances; I think I know something of the agony of your body and
soul. . . . You are called upon to minister to your fellow men and to
your time uniquely. You are, therefore, called upon to bear the burden
of the world's suffering uniquely—even this. I am confident that out of
this experience you will come still further refined and enriched to be
the instrument of God's way of love, his will of peace, his witness to
truth. . . . In fellowship and in humility, I love you and need you."
Decades later, Rustin feelingly recalled Whitney's kindness: "Norman
Whitney stood with me firmly. . . . I just cannot overemphasize what
it was like at the point where one feels deserted by one's closest
friends. . . . When I got out of prison, he invited me to come and spend
the week. And I think that saved me from myself because I was so despairing. . . . If it had not been for [his] support at that period, I would
never have had the courage to pick myself up and go on."[33]

Through a referral that came from a pastoral psychiatrist at Union
Theological Seminary, Rustin began therapy as soon as he returned to
New York. Dr. Robert Ascher was just starting private practice when
Rustin came to him. His parents were politically progressive. They
were close friends of Roger Baldwin, a founder of the American Civil
Liberties Union, and his mother had worked for the organization in
Chicago. They were also "quite violently pacifist," he reminisced, until
his father decided that Hitler had to be countered with more force than
pacifists would ever muster. Ascher brought an understanding ear to
the values and outlook of his patient whose principles, he thought,
"were absolutely right."[34]

Ascher's goal was to see that Rustin "got on his feet and could make
it on his own again. . . . It wasn't a deep therapy." In those early sessions

Rustin appeared "down-and-out. He was crushed. . . . He was very depressed. He was tearful. And he felt very alone." Listening to Rustin talk about the past and the present, Ascher saw a man who, beneath the guilt and the depression deriving from his current circumstances, was seething with anger. He was angry at his mother for the circumstances of his birth; angry at his grandmother for approving everything he did; angry at whites for the constraints they placed on his life from an early age. "It's interesting that this boy with all this rage later becomes a pacifist," Ascher noted at the time.

Ascher affirmed for Rustin that "his childhood rage was quite justified," and prodded him to see the connection with his pacifism, how "he was trying to master something in himself." The doctor pushed him to recognize how this unsubdued fury was expressing itself through his homosexual behavior, which had become "a way of hitting back." Sex, Ascher believed, was "always a combination of aggression and libido." The therapeutic goal was not to have Rustin renounce his sexual desires, as Muste had tried to have him do, but to make sure that he wasn't destroyed by them. "My agenda," Ascher recalled forty years later, as he paged through his notes from the therapy, "was to equip him to do his thing and not get into trouble. So, yeah, I was trying to tame him. That all his principles were absolutely right but that he was trying to work in a world that was not ready to deal with [his homosexuality] and wouldn't he be better off if he didn't get himself arrested, get himself stoned—for that!—since that wasn't his program." Ascher counseled Rustin to keep his sexual behavior private and refrain from the activities that had gotten him in trouble again and again. "I advised him a lot that we have a choice about what we say and do. . . . If you're going in there to do a certain job, park sex outside the door. Get in there and do the job."

While Ascher was helping Rustin emotionally, practical issues about his future still loomed. There was clearly no place for him at the FOR. When he returned to New York, barely two months had elapsed since his arrest. But at least as far as the FOR was concerned, it was as if the earth had opened, swallowed him whole, and closed again without a trace. Early in April, the minutes of the executive council meeting, in which Rustin had often sat as a staff member, sparingly recorded that "Bayard Rustin has returned to New York, has been put in touch with a psychiatrist, and is looking for a job."[35] Relationships of long duration and deep meaning atrophied. Three years passed before Rustin crossed paths again with Glenn Smiley, despite the fact that Smiley credited Rustin with converting him to pacifism and nonviolence. In the future, Rustin would again work very closely with Muste. Rustin learned to put aside his sense of abandonment, but never again would he see Muste as mentor or guide.

Rustin's misfortune served as opportunity for others. Sayre wrote to FOR leaders in the United States and abroad of "Bayard's trouble" and how the FOR "cannot now go ahead with the African program" that Sayre opposed. But the African plan took on a life of its own. Houser used it as the occasion to leave the FOR. He created a new organization, the American Committee on Africa, which became his life's work. In Rustin's place, New York pacifists proposed sending Bill Sutherland, another black American pacifist, to West Africa in order to seed Gandhian nonviolence there; Sutherland sank permanent roots in Africa, where he married, raised a family, and worked for various African governments. Closer to home, Rustin's departure from the staff led to Smiley's shift from California to the national office, from which he became FOR's traveling emissary to the South and its emerging civil rights movement.[36]

In contrast, Rustin was close to desperate. The FOR had kept him on salary while he was in jail, so several hundred dollars awaited him when he returned to New York. But the subsistence pay he earned hardly constituted a nest egg. And what was he to do about work? He was black, which, as no one needed to remind him, meant seriously restricted job opportunities under even the best of circumstances. His were not the best. It was the height of the McCarthy era, and the Korean War was raging. Rustin had been a draft resister during World War II, a former member of the Young Communist League, a radical with a long arrest record for protests of one sort or another, and a convicted sex offender. Most of his work history was with an organization that now would have none of him.

Rustin scrambled to make do. He tried unsuccessfully for a job in publicity with Harper & Row. He made contact, to no avail, with labor unions to try to get work as an organizer. He had a short stint with the Rosenberg Defense Committee in the weeks before the couple was executed. Strong and fit, for a while he moved furniture but, as he reported to a social worker to whom Ascher had referred him, his education made it difficult to get laboring jobs. "Wherever he goes to get this type of work," the social worker noted, "the employers feel that he is too good for the job." On her part, the social worker was unable to see beyond the color of Rustin's skin. She "suggested that hospitals always need personnel for cleaning jobs, etc., and suggested also the possibility of his getting a job as a domestic, that is, as a butler."[37] Such was the plight of the man whom, a few months earlier, many were calling an American Gandhi.

CHAPTER TEN

"I Can Again Be Useful"
1953–1955

MANY TIMES IN Rustin's life, the door to the future seemed to close: when he left Wilberforce in the depths of the Depression and returned to West Chester with no prospects before him; when his sexual activity in prison during World War II aborted his campaign against segregation and the disgrace rippled through the world of conscientious objectors; when his arrest in Pasadena pushed him outside the circle of Christian pacifists. There would be other such moments in the years ahead. Yet always he found a way forward.

In the early fall of 1953, six months after his return from California, opportunity came to him from friends in the War Resisters League. Like the FOR, the WRL was a product of the revulsion against militarism that World War I provoked. Founded in the early 1920s by Jesse Wallace Hughan, a socialist schoolteacher in New York, it saw itself as a secular companion of the FOR. Also like the FOR, it was connected to an international federation of like-minded organizations around the world. But whereas the largest portion of the FOR's membership were ministers with congregations to mobilize, the WRL's members came as independent radicals, bringing to the organization only their dues and their enthusiasm.

After the war, the WRL had experienced its own internal nonviolent revolution. Like Rustin, the insurgents all had histories of resistance during World War II. David Dellinger, a student activist at Yale in the 1930s, was one of the Union Eight, the seminarians who were the first to resist the new Selective Service system in 1940. Jailed a second time in the middle of the war, he proved to be a militant leader of COs at Lewisburg Penitentiary, rivaling Rustin in the degree to which he tangled with prison administrators. Roy Finch, who knew Dellinger at Yale and covered his 1940 trial as a reporter for the *New York Herald Tribune*, spent much of the war in a CPS camp. So did Igal Roodenko, a working-class Jew from New York who was trained as a printer. Other young militants included Ralph DiGia, the son of an Italian anarchist who had immigrated to New York in the early part of the century, and Jim Peck, who grew up on Park Avenue and was the scion of a department store magnate. Both DiGia and Peck had served time as noncooperators and had been active in prison strikes against censorship and segregation. Bound together by an experience in World War II that only young men could have, the rebels seized control of the organization from an older mixed-sex generation of leaders who had shepherded it through the heady years of the 1930s peace movement.

Finch, Dellinger, DiGia, and others like them came out of the war wanting action. "We wanted demonstrations and actions in the street, more a street thing rather than just plain education," DiGia reminisced. Roy Finch, too, recalled that this new group of militant pacifists "were not socialists any more. We were direct action, sort of anarchists." By the late 1940s, when he and his comrades had taken control of the WRL, it was filled with "chain-yourself-to-the-lamppost characters," Finch said. "Very much the individual. You know the type. These people were WRL's soul. We always felt very close to anybody who was an individualist who was doing outrageous things like that." As if to emphasize the point, he added, "This was not the FOR's style. The FOR wanted to be very accepted. You know—by rich churches."[1]

In a number of ways, Rustin and the WRL were a good match. Many of the men at the heart of it in New York had known Rustin for years and were close working comrades of his. Roodenko and Peck had accompanied him on the Journey of Reconciliation and were arrested with him in Chapel Hill. Peck also worked closely with Rustin and Houser in CORE after the war. Roodenko lived in the same tenement on Mott Street as Rustin did and was also gay. To these secular pacifists with the independent temperament of the anarchist, Rustin was a skilled organizer, a courageous fighter for justice, an individualist of the first order—not the tarnished soul banished by the ministers of the FOR or, in DiGia's words, the "smiling Quakers" of the AFSC who thought "if you smile at people everything will be alright."[2]

The first signs that the league might approach Rustin's troubles differently came in April. Rustin, who served on the organization's governing board, had submitted his resignation, but the executive committee turned it down. Instead, it passed a resolution saying that it "looks forward eagerly to working with him in our common cause of war resistance." In August, the league hired him on a temporary basis to plan its upcoming annual conference for which, Finch reported, Rustin was able to "generate new enthusiasm" and "has gotten remarkable results." So when the league's executive secretary announced his intention to resign, Rustin was on the mind of many executive committee members as they debated how to reconstitute their staff.[3]

Still, hiring Rustin was not an automatic sell. Muste and Houser were both members of the WRL's executive committee, and Muste quickly let it be known that he considered the idea "a serious mistake."[4] Because the pacifist world was such a small one, bringing Rustin on to the staff meant that he would inevitably be working with his former colleagues at the FOR and the AFSC, whose feelings were still raw after Pasadena. Nor was everyone else in the WRL leadership immune to reservations about having a known homosexual on the staff, especially in the midst of the McCarthy era, when pacifists already felt themselves under siege. Why, in such difficult times, should the organization take on another burden?

Finch, who chaired the WRL's governing board, was Rustin's strongest supporter, and he conducted a shrewd campaign to hire him. He did not bring the subject up before the executive committee until Muste was out of town. Given approval to explore the proposal, he began polling members of the national advisory council one by one and tailored his arguments to the individual.[5] He received strong backing from Dellinger, whose fierce resistance as an imprisoned CO gave him a great deal of moral credibility in the deliberations. Dellinger penned a very strong defense of Rustin. "I see no sense," he argued, "in trying to force on Bayard a Puritanical abstinence from the form of sex which apparently is natural to him, however unnatural it may be to some of the others who will be concerned with Bayard's position in the League. . . . If a strong stream is flowing through a channel that it has cut out for it-self over a number of years, you dam it only at the risk that it will break out, as it did in California, in another more harmful place. I always felt that the FOR insistence on rigid abstinence led to an impossible situation which was dangerously close to encouraging hypocrisy (on the part of both Bayard and the FOR), guilt feelings, and an explosion." Dellinger unreservedly endorsed the hire. "I can't think of anyone else who can approach Bayard," he wrote. "I know of no one who is a more inspirational speaker. . . . Bayard is available for long-term service, with his exceptional talents and dedication. Further, the League has gone further down hill, to the point that unless it steps up its program and has an infusion of new life and imagination (such as I am confident Bayard can bring), it will not be a vital force in the world."[6]

Finch secured the desired result. The vote in the advisory council was fifteen to five in favor. On the executive council, where Muste sat and could argue his case, the vote was much closer—six to four, with Houser abstaining. Muste "did not have sufficient confidence," the report on the discussion noted, "to feel that Bayard could now handle a WRL job without future embarrassment to the League and himself and possible risk to young people." Muste did not lose gracefully; he resigned from the executive committee soon afterward. But Finch was unapologetic about the outcome: "It was unmistakably the majority opinion that the best interests of the WRL would be served through Bayard's employment."[7]

To Finch, hiring Rustin was a real coup. "In a way WRL had nothing much to lose. We didn't have the reputation," he recalled.[8] But there was much to gain. Rustin had wide contacts among African American activists. He had long-standing ties with pacifists across the country. He was well connected to the non-Stalinist democratic left in New York. Rustin brought skills accumulated through years of organizing people in nonviolent direct action. And there was something else, too.

Rustin "brought style," as Finch described it. "He was not your typical New York radical. Your typical New York radical is a rather scruffy character. . . . Bayard had a certain elegance. He liked to dress in a kind of elegant way. He had a presence. He had a manner. Even his voice. . . . The WRL really needed this." In a sense, Finch was saying that the very aspects of Rustin's self that were acceptably coded "gay" in American culture—style, elegance, cultivation in a man—made him desirable to the WRL, even as the sexual behavior connected to it made him undesirable in the eyes of others.[9]

RUSTIN STAYED AT the WRL for a dozen years. He began as program director in the fall of 1953, but became executive secretary a year later and in that capacity shaped the direction of the organization. Di-Gia, who worked with him through most of those years, said that the staff "almost ran the organization. Bayard had all the ideas."[10] Under his leadership, the WRL experienced growth and achieved a greater visibility than it had ever before enjoyed. As the country crept out from under the pall cast by McCarthyism and as dissent from cold war militarism emerged, Rustin positioned the WRL as a serious player in a reviving peace movement.

But those years were still to come. In the meantime, Rustin found himself working in an organization that, for all its good intentions and militant sentiments, perfectly exemplified the marginality and insignificance of both the left and the pacifist movement in the early 1950s. The WRL had always been small, and the fear of political radicalism that overtook the country in these years made it shrink even more. When Rustin started, its annual budget barely exceeded $10,000. His weekly salary was $75. It had a staff of two and no regional offices. It had fewer than a thousand members and a mailing list just more than double that. It was a testament to how compelling Rustin felt the message of Gandhian nonviolence to be—Gandhi's way "satisfied an inner need in me," he reminisced later—that, even putting aside his admittedly difficult circumstances, he saw the job as an opportunity.[11]

Rustin's first years at the WRL were not a time for bold initiatives, dynamic mobilizations, or impressive campaigns by American disciples of Gandhi. At the end of 1953, Senator Joseph McCarthy was enjoying the power that Republican control of the Senate invested in him. He was preparing hearings on alleged Communist influence in the army and using the new medium of television to publicize his investigations. Although the Korean War had ended, another crisis was emerging in the French colonies in Southeast Asia. Meanwhile, the death of Stalin had not brought any respite in cold war tensions. Under Eisenhower and John Foster Dulles, his secretary of state, the doctrine of massive nuclear retaliation became central to America's military strategy. Dulles's famed brinkmanship—his willingness to engage in rhetorical saber rattling at the slightest provocation—injected a discomforting sense of danger into everyday life.

Along with others among the pacifist faithful, Rustin worked as best he could in this deeply discouraging environment. Much of his work at first consisted of initiatives designed to attract attention to the organization and to find an audience for its message so that the League might rebuild. He redesigned the *WRL News* so that it was less of an organizational newsletter and more like a magazine, with provocative opinion pieces meant to incite debate. Using his contacts from long years in the peace movement, he arranged speaking tours for himself in the Northeast. Despite the whispered concerns about the dangers his sexuality posed, Rustin pushed the WRL in the direction of work with youth out of the recognition that a revived peace movement depended on stoking enthusiasm in the next generation. When the New York Friends hired Robert Gilmore to run the Friends' Center in Manhattan, Rustin, who attended the same Quaker meeting as Gilmore, established a close working and personal relationship with him. Soon the two were planning joint seminars on peace and international relations for high school and college students in the New York area.[12]

Rustin put the stamp of his own personality on the everyday routines of the WRL. DiGia and Finch both remembered his humor, dry and precisely targeted—the kind that took its audience by surprise. DiGia, who functioned as bookkeeper, office manager, and general clerical assistant, was Rustin's polar opposite, and the two joked endlessly as they picked at each other's foibles. "He used to be the aristocrat and I was the peasant," he recalled. "We had that kind of thing going. I was the anarchist and he was the socialist. I used to have fun with him." DiGia teased Rustin about his inability to type, while Rustin enjoyed immensely the irony of having Jim Peck, a perennial volunteer and the heir to a fortune, taking dictation from him. His hours on the phone were spent with a cigarette dangling precariously from his lips. During particularly long conversations or at lengthy meetings to plot strategy, Rustin occupied himself by sketching "fantastic doodles," according to Finch. "Everybody would be talking . . . but everybody was watching while he was drawing. . . . These doodles were incredible." And always there was his thinking, the sharpness of his intelligence applied to the issues at hand. "He did have the most dynamic ideas," DiGia said flatly.[13]

Rustin's skills, however, did not extend to the miraculous. No amount of energy, initiative, or intelligence was going to transform the WRL in those years into a powerhouse for world peace and social justice. But the core group of pacifists who presided over the organization were pleased with his performance. Just a year after he became executive secretary, the minutes of the executive committee meetings recorded that his initiatives had "increased the number of new members and tripled the prospects and potential contributors." And a few months later, the minutes reported that the organization's financial position was "greatly improved." Looking out beyond the confines of the organization, Rustin himself commented on the "improved campus situation," at least in comparison to the Korean War.[14]

EVEN IN THE WORST of times—and so the first half of the 1950s seemed—the call to bear witness remained powerful. The radicals in Rustin's world acted and improvised and tried things out because they had to; an inner compulsion to set things right in the world drove many of them. In decades like the 1930s and the 1960s, when masses of Americans were motivated to join their fellow citizens in political activism of one sort or another, almost any decision seemed a good one, because there was always an audience eager to respond. But in the mid-1950s, as the country slowly emerged from the worst of a decade-long red scare, the audience was sparse. Radicals embarked on a variety of initiatives never knowing which choices, which undertakings, would cut a pathway to the future, and which would lead to yet one more political dead end.

In retrospect, just two of the many ventures of New York City's pacifist community in these years carried the promise of a reawakened movement. Rustin was deeply involved in both. In the summer of 1955, leaders of several organizations staged a public protest against the government's civil defense program. Over the course of the same year, a small group of radicals laid plans for *Liberation*, a new magazine of the independent left.

As the nation's nuclear arsenal grew in the 1950s and anti-Communist rhetoric made a Russian attack seem plausible, planning for the worst took ever more bizarre twists. Civil defense drills became part of American life; states and municipalities enacted laws requiring that citizens "take cover" during them. In 1955, the federal Civilian Defense Agency announced plans for Operation Alert. Scheduled for midday on June 15, it was designed to test whether Americans could take cover efficiently in the event of a nuclear attack. As President Eisenhower and several thousand government officials headed to secret locations, school children crouched under their desks and bus passengers fled to the nearest building.

To Dorothy Day, the revered founder of the pacifist Catholic Worker Movement, this was beyond insane. She drew in stalwarts from the WRL, the Women's International League for Peace and Freedom, and the FOR, and together they planned their public witness against the arms race. They contacted the media, the mayor's office, and federal officials to let everyone know that they would not be heeding the call of the sirens. On the morning of Operation Alert, twenty-nine pacifists, including the WRL's staff of Rustin, DiGia, and Peck, made their way to City Hall Park in Manhattan. As New Yorkers all around them scurried to hide at the stroke of noon, they waited outside for the inevitable arrest. They were brought before Louis Kaplan, a judge who seemed to have forgotten that Operation Alert was a mock emergency. Calling them "murderers," he set a surprisingly high bail and sent them to jail while supporters collected the funds to get them out.[15]

Once released, the arrested pacifists set up a Provisional Defense Committee to coordinate an approach to their trial and extract the most publicity from it. Rustin offered space at the WRL offices, so much of the post-arrest activity flowed around and through him. As the case dragged on, it provided continuing opportunities to search out more support and, over time, the PDC won some favorable notice. *Commonweal*, a liberal Catholic weekly, editorialized strongly in its favor. "A society without its radicals is a dead society," it declared, as it compared them to historical figures like Joan of Arc and Henry David Thoreau. Most of the coverage of the case focused less on the issue of militarism and more on the threat to basic liberties. "One would expect at most a mock arrest in a mock air raid," the *Pittsburgh Post-Gazette* commented. "If we must take cover, let it be the cover of our constitutional rights."[16]

At the time, the resistance to Operation Alert hardly registered in the consciousness of either cold war analysts or ordinary citizens. Yet it proved to be the opening rehearsal for a long-running production with a large cast and ever-larger audience. One can trace a direct line of descent from the collective act of disobedience at the edge of New York's financial district to even more dramatic confrontations at missile bases in the American West, at atomic testing sites in the Pacific and the Sahara Desert, and on the streets of cities in the United States and Europe as protest against the dangers of nuclear weaponry escalated in the coming years.

In a similar way, the effort to establish a new magazine of radical politics seemed a shot in the dark. But it managed to light a way toward the activism of the New Left. Muste was the instigator. Retired from his position at the FOR, he was still searching for a way "to begin the building of a *movement* in the United States for radical social change . . . to reconstitute a non-totalitarian movement of the left."[17] Working through the WRL, which, under Rustin's leadership, agreed to support the project, the team of Muste, Rustin, Finch, and Dellinger early in 1955 began meeting to launch the magazine.

The prospectus they produced laid out a vision of a refashioned American radicalism that would echo through more famous manifestos of the 1960s like the Port Huron Statement. It lamented the "decline of independent radicalism and the gradual falling into silence of prophetic and rebellious voices." It deplored the way national leaders "everywhere openly or secretly idolized" power and called for "changes in our deepest modes of thought." The editors of *Liberation* cast a skeptical eye on both classical liberalism and Marxism, the two great traditions of nineteenth-century Western political philosophy. Rather, the politics of the future—and the perspective of the magazine they were founding—required "a creative synthesis of the individual ethical insights of the great religious leaders and the collective social concern of the great revolutionists." Instead of "seizing state power," as the Communist left conceptualized it, they saw the growth of the militarized, centralized, and bureaucratized state as part of the problem. They sought a redefinition and restructuring of power, a transformation of society by human decision and action. Nonviolence, democratic participation, and human control of decentralized institutions described both where they wanted to go and how they proposed to get there. They applauded the utopian impulse in human affairs, which they celebrated as "the growing edge of society and the creative imagination of a culture."[18]

Liberation premiered in April 1956, thanks in good part to substantial financial backing from the WRL. During the 1950s, its subscription list hovered under 2,000, though the distribution of issues at major events, like civil rights rallies at Madison Square Garden, meant that it circulated more widely. But even at this level, the magazine exerted an enormous influence on the new generation of radicals that emerged in the early 1960s. The heavy blows that the left suffered during the cold war's red scare had threatened to rupture the continuity of a vital historical tradition of indigenous American radicalism. *Liberation* acted as something of a transmission belt of perspectives and experience across three generations. Its early issues provided a forum where crusaders born at the end of the nineteenth century—people like Dorothy Day, Lillian Smith and, of course, Muste—might address a contemporary audience. It also provided a platform for those who came of age at midcentury. Social critics like Michael Harrington, Paul Goodman, and William Appleman Williams, whose writings in the 1960s reached a mass audience, used *Liberation* as a medium to debate ideas and provoke discussion within the independent left. As the protest movements of the 1960s emerged, some of its leaders, like Tom Hayden and Staughton Lynd, used the magazine as well. The magazine covered the antinuclear movement that spread in the latter part of the 1950s, the burgeoning civil rights movement in the South, and the revolutionary struggles developing throughout the Third World. A faith in nonviolence as means and ends suffused it, and *Liberation* floated many of the ideas, like participatory democracy, that became hallmarks of the 1960s.

For Rustin, *Liberation* was a major commitment of time and energy. He raised money for the magazine, wrote for it frequently, and shaped the content and perspective. Every Wednesday for years, he, Muste, Dellinger, and Finch met in the basement office on Christopher Street in Greenwich Village, occasionally joined by a small number of others. There they brainstormed, debated, and thrashed through political disagreements—with Rustin, as was his custom, doodling his way through a pad of paper as afternoon turned into evening. Dave McReynolds, who had moved to New York from Los Angeles and for a long time was the magazine's only paid staff person, remembered the sessions vividly. "Those were wonderful, wonderful meetings," he recalled. "There was wonderful discussion and tension, like an incredible seminar. Can you imagine the debate about whether you should send troops into Little Rock [to desegregate the schools], whether that was a nonviolent position?" Often the debates pitted Rustin and Muste, the socialists, on one side of an argument, with Finch and Dellinger, the anarchists, on the other. "All I can tell you," McReynolds concluded, "is that it really was a give and take. It was a slugging match of the four of them."[19]

DURING THESE YEARS, through all his various activist endeavors, Rustin felt himself on probation. In part, it was self-imposed, as he wrestled with the seeming conflict between his sexual behavior and a moral system, held very dear by him, that placed spiritual connection, mutual respect, and community above all other values. Some of it came from his comrades and colleagues, whom he knew harbored profound reservations about his suitability as a spokesperson for pacifist nonvio-

lence. And much of it stemmed from a sober assessment of the place occupied by homosexuals in America. With their public vilification as a
menace to the nation and its moral welfare, it hardly made sense to have
a convicted sex offender leading a movement that itself was suspect in
cold war America.

The anxieties surfaced constantly. Rustin's participation in the civil
defense protest would have been unremarkable before Pasadena, as he
was many times arrested for acts of civil disobedience. But once the decision was made to go to trial rather than plead guilty, and with the
prospect of the extended scrutiny of an appeal, Rustin began to get nervous. "He was worried that it would come out somehow or other that
he was homosexual. And he really worried about the other people," Di-
Gia remembered. "He wanted to get out of the case . . . he thought he
might ruin the whole thing. He went through a lot of pain in that
period."[20]

Then there was the relationship with Muste, a constant reminder of
what had transpired. When the WRL hired Rustin, Muste resigned
from the executive committee in protest, an action that seemed gratu-
itously cruel. But after his retirement from the FOR in 1954, he came
back to the league. Muste was chosen for its governing body the same
month that Rustin was promoted to executive secretary. Thus, Rustin
and Muste saw each other frequently, and the planning of *Liberation* intensified the relationship.

Somehow the two men put Pasadena and the years of struggle that
preceded it behind them, and they worked in partnership for many
more years. DiGia knew that Rustin was hurt by Muste's stance and
thought that Muste apologized soon after coming back to the WRL.
Though Muste was certainly capable of owning up to his errors, no evidence suggests that he retracted his position. McReynolds offered a
more complex—and plausible—explanation of their continuing relationship. "Those two men needed each other very badly," McReynolds
declared. "Bayard had a genuine ability to understand tactics that
Muste never grasped. AJ had a very profound sense of the moral center
of things. Often in meetings Bayard would say 'we should do such and
such' and AJ would say 'but that wouldn't be right' and Bayard would

say 'you're right.' Or, AJ would say 'well, we could do this and this' and Bayard would say 'Oh, AJ, that will never work' and AJ would say 'you're right.'" But more than mutual need was at play. McReynolds vividly recalled a conversation with Rustin from this period. In reflecting with the younger McReynolds about the experience of a life devoted to revolutionary change, Rustin spoke of how he and Muste shared something profound. Each had been "broken," Rustin said. "'AJ was broken by the Trotskyist movement. He was disillusioned. And I've been broken partly by the physical beatings, but just by events,'" Rustin's way of alluding to the sex issue. Working almost daily with the two of them for a decade, McReynolds implied that this was the source of a bond, an understanding, that allowed them to transcend, even while not forgetting, what each saw as betrayal by the other. "I think the broken part was a very important thing," McReynolds insisted. "Both Bayard and AJ were broken and healed. They'd been recovered."[21]

One part of "reknitting himself into a person who was going to survive," as McReynolds put it, was the accommodation Rustin reached, with himself and the world around him, about sexual matters. One night in 1953, just after he had started working for the WRL, Rustin treated McReynolds to dinner. The younger man, still painfully in struggle over "my queerness" as he wrote to a friend, "had a long talk with Bayard about the problem of homosexuality. . . . [Bayard] pointed out that sexual expression between any two people is possible—that is, that their sex isn't the determining factor. That, unless we are going to limit sex to procreation, sex for enjoyment alone with a woman is no different from the same with a man. At the same time he pointed out that promiscuity is an impossible situation since no element of personality [*sic*] respect enters in." Rustin seemed to have adopted Ascher's dictum to avoid pronouncements of his identity in a society that made no place for it. He cautioned McReynolds to avoid "public declarations." In other words, Rustin was telling McReynolds to remain in the closet. "[I] can follow Bayard's advice about keeping my sex attitude to myself—a number of folks would never guess it if I didn't tell them,"

McReynolds wrote his friend. "Maybe I have overcome the need for 'revealing statements.'"[22]

What a later gay community might reproach as the duplicity of the closet, someone like Rustin, "outed" four decades before the word was coined, saw as a prudent form of discretion. Rustin did not pretend to be heterosexual. He did not lie about his intimacies. He simply chose not to tell. But in the 1950s, that still left ample room to be, paradoxically, publicly gay. Here is Roy Finch, in 1993, struggling to explain the situation across a generational gap in experience and attitude:[23] "He didn't flaunt his gayness in an offensive way. I think that's the wrong way to put it. Now what do I mean? I mean, I guess people see things and it means different things to different people. So that if Bayard was always with a young man—he wasn't, but he had companions—that wouldn't register on a lot of people. . . . But there might be some people who would say 'that's his paramour.' . . . This is the way it is, isn't it? People don't see things." Like many other gay men in the generations before a substantial public discourse affirming gay love was there to absorb, Rustin had crafted his own form of self-acceptance. He adapted to the constraints that a deeply homophobic society imposed while also carving out a space for love and pleasure.

MANY OF THE THEMES of this period of Rustin's life—the choices available to radicals in a bleak political era; the moral basis of his motivation and how it suffused both his political vision and his personal struggles; the ways his private life impinged on his public role—converged in a Quaker-sponsored project from these years. In 1954, the AFSC convened a working group to produce a passionate, though reasoned, statement of dissent from American foreign policy. Steve Cary, who had known Rustin for years and was one of his staunchest defenders after the Pasadena arrest, chaired the group. Other members were Norman Whitney, Rustin's spiritual mentor; activist Quakers such as Jim Bristol, whom Rustin knew well; Bob Gilmore, the new AFSC secretary in New York City; and Muste. Rustin too was included in the group.

Speak Truth to Power, the manifesto they produced, drew its title from a charge given to eighteenth-century Friends. Although the final document was certainly a collaborative effort, Rustin's mark was everywhere. As Cary wrote to a Quaker activist in California, "Those of us on the working party . . . know the tremendous contribution which Bayard has made to the whole study. I think it is safe to say that there is no one in the group who played such a major role in so many areas." When it came time to compose the final version, Rustin joined Cary and Whitney, his closest friends in the group, in fashioning the disparate drafts into a seamless whole.[24]

Speak Truth to Power reads in some ways like a work of prophecy. It describes the corrosive effects that the creation of a massive permanent military, rooted in fears about national security, was to have on American institutions and character—the ways it would compromise an allegiance to democratic values and civil liberties; the power that would accrue to the national government at the expense of individual freedom; the corrupting impact such power would have on those who wielded it; the psychology of hatred that a preoccupation with enemies would engender in soldier and civilian alike. It pointed to one of the great paradoxes of the cold war: "While the most powerful *feeling* in the United States is hatred of the Russian totalitarian system, the most powerful *process* in the United States is its imitation."[25] The forms of democracy remained, but the requirements of a global struggle eviscerated their substance.

Chapter 4 of *Speak Truth to Power* outlined a nonviolent approach to international politics and social change. It presented nonviolence as moral philosophy, political strategy, and psychological theory. The phrasing reads like a collection of snippets from Rustin's lecture notes and presentations and, indeed, one AFSC activist identified the chapter as heavily bearing "Bayard's imprint." It is worth quoting for the window it offers into Rustin's ethical framework:

At its heart, [the nonviolent method] is the effort to maintain unity among men. It seeks to knit the break in the sense of community whose fracture is both a cause and a result of human conflict. It relies upon love rather than hate, and though it involves a willingness to accept rather than inflict suffering, it is neither passive nor cowardly. It offers a way of meeting evil without relying on the ability to cause pain to the human being through whom evil is expressed. It seeks to change the attitude of the opponent rather than to force his submission through violence. It is, in short, the practical effort to overcome evil with good.[26]

Yet even as Rustin worked closely with his Quaker associates to draft the manifesto, the Pasadena arrest hovered over them. From the AFSC office in southern California came a letter to Cary reminding him of "the vulnerability that Bayard Rustin's name still holds in this region." Rustin himself urged the working group *not* to include his name on the report, much to the dismay of Cary, Whitney, and others who knew how central his role had been. Arguments to the contrary left him unmoved. "I have given considerable thought to the question of my name appearing," he wrote to the group. "I am convinced that it should not be listed. My reasons for this are largely personal. . . . My being listed might very well lead to some new attack which might gravely delay the time when I can again be useful. . . . If we delay a while yet before my name appears publicly, sufficient time will have passed for making a clear stand. Although I personally, inwardly, feel prepared to make that stand at present, I am aware that there has not been enough time for people with questions in their minds to be convinced." He ended the letter bluntly: "This is my final and considered judgement in the matter."[27]

Rustin's name did not appear in *Speak Truth to Power* when it was released in 1955, but the discussion about it led him, Cary, Bristol, and Whitney to plot his return to AFSC programs. Understanding the Quaker need for consensus, they did not move too quickly. With Rustin's approval, Bristol wrote to Ascher in the fall of 1955 and asked for his medical judgment. Rustin, who had not seen Ascher in two years, arranged to go back for an appointment. Ascher told Bristol that "from a psychiatric point of view I could see no reason why the Committee could not safely employ Mr. Rustin in any capacity. The basis for that statement is that he has apparently learned to keep his sexual activity private and is no longer acting it out in the community at large."[28]

By the close of 1955, Rustin once again seemed to have carved out a place for himself in the American peace movement. He had a secure, if small, organizational base from which to work. He had formed a new set of day-to-day work relationships and was restoring some of the older ones that had frayed after Pasadena. And he had devoted a great deal of reflection to the moral foundations of both his personal life and his public role. For the next decade, the WRL would be the home from which he ventured out with the gospel of nonviolence, eager to refine it as a "practical effort" to overcome evil.

CHAPTER ELEVEN

"No Force on Earth Can Stop This Movement"

1955–1957

Since the campaign to integrate the military, Rustin had only glancingly worked on issues of racial justice. There were the race relations institutes he did with Houser and his brief African interlude. There were many speeches on Gandhian nonviolence in which the content of the lesson was almost always his experience resisting segregation. But for the most part, Rustin spent the first half of the 1950s focused on the cold war, the arms race, and the militarism that seemed to be engulfing the world.

Yet these very years were decisive ones for the black freedom struggle. In the South particularly, acts of resistance were multiplying, and protest was becoming a collective, rather than an individual, enterprise. A bus boycott in Baton Rouge, an economic boycott of white businesses by blacks in Orangeburg, South Carolina, voter registration campaigns in cities of the Upper South—all testified to a deepening discontent and a determination to force change.

Above all, the Supreme Court's historic ruling in *Brown v. Board of Education* in May 1954 signaled a new era of upheaval in American race relations. The case itself was evidence of the growing resources and confidence of the civil rights movement. NAACP lawyers had developed the legal strategy that brought the suit to the Supreme Court's door; they, in turn, depended on black parents willing to brave white reprisals to challenge Jim Crow in education. The unanimous opinion of the Court's nine justices that separate was inherently unequal and, hence, unconstitutional threw open the possibility of a revolution in the South's, and the nation's, racial hierarchy.

In the wake of the *Brown* decision, communities throughout the South saw blacks and whites locked in a pattern of action and response. Across the region, black parents petitioned school boards to have their children enrolled in previously all-white schools. As panic appeared to grip white Southerners, a "Citizens' Council" movement—"the KKK in gray flannel suits" Rustin called them—spread outward from Mississippi.[1] The Councils attracted prosperous whites of the business and professional classes. Black Southerners found themselves forced off the land they rented, denied credit for their businesses, or fired from their jobs. The Council movement also fostered a climate of violence. In the Deep South especially, activists might be driven from their homes, beaten, and killed. By early 1956, the white political leadership in the South was openly urging massive resistance to the Supreme Court's decision.

Rustin naturally was drawn to developments in the South. Late in 1955, he joined with an eclectic group of New York leftists to provide assistance to Southern black activists targeted by white supremacists. Ella Baker, whose work as an NAACP field secretary in the 1940s gave her a broad network of contacts in the South, was a key figure in the effort. So, too, was Stanley Levison, a political acquaintance of both Baker and Rustin, who was active in the American Jewish Congress. A lawyer who had prospered through real estate dealings, Levison had been for a number of years a secret operative of the American Communist Party. With the support of Randolph, the three approached unions, civil rights groups, and liberal religious leaders about forming a support organization to raise funds and win publicity for the Southern struggle. They secured commitments from, among others, Jerry Wurf of the State, County, and Municipal Workers Union; Cleveland Robinson of District 65, the socialist-oriented Jewish Labor Committee and Workers Defense League; and the American Jewish Congress.

To avoid conflict with the turf-conscious NAACP, which was handling the legal aspects of the integration struggle, "In Friendship," as the new group called itself, provided economic aid "to race terror victims." It raised money for farmers whose credit had been cut off because of their activity for school desegregation; it provided emergency funds to buy food and clothing for families evicted from their tenancies. With Randolph as the titular chair, In Friendship pressed the socially conscious wing of the labor movement to contribute financially to the battle for racial equality in the South. Already by March 1956, just two months after its launching, Norman Thomas, the long-time head of the Socialist Party and a respected figure in New York radical circles, was complimenting Randolph on its "pretty promising beginning."[2]

Just as In Friendship was taking shape, word reached New York of a new manifestation of black discontent. In Montgomery, Alabama, a boycott of city buses had begun. As in many other Southern communities, African Americans had been pushing against the limits set by Jim Crow laws for some time. There had been voter registration drives after World War II. Early in the 1950s, a Women's Political Council had formed, and it had made segregated seating on the buses as well as the offensive and sometimes violent behavior of the drivers and the police, a major focus of its work. In 1955, several incidents occurred in which black riders refused to vacate seats for white passengers and were arrested. The event that finally precipitated community action was the arrest, on December 1, of Rosa Parks.

A seamstress who was well known in the black community through her involvement in the local NAACP, Parks quickly became the rallying point for resistance. E. D. Nixon, a Pullman porter who had presided over the state NAACP, pressed some of the city's black ministers to call a one-day boycott of the buses. The one-day event became a sustained community-wide mobilization. To coordinate the boycott, the leadership formed a permanent organization, the Montgomery Improvement Association, and selected a recent arrival in town, the Reverend Martin Luther King, Jr., to serve as its spokesman. By the time of In Friendship's inaugural conference in early January, the boycott had lasted a month. It enjoyed virtually unanimous support in the African American community, which had succeeded in patching together an extensive car pool to provide an alternative to public transportation. The boycott also took strength from the central involvement of the city's

black ministers. A continuing series of remarkable mass meetings ro-
tated through the community's churches and gave the protest the aura
of a religious crusade.

The In Friendship group quickly grasped the potential of Montgomery. Until then, recalled Levison, "a handful of very brave people
were ready to take their lives in their hands and go out into the street in
small demonstrations. But the mass of people were not involved."
Rustin was entranced by the evidence of religious leadership. Unlike
his own experience as a Quaker, where there was a heavy emphasis on
social change in this world, the Baptist tradition of many Southern
black ministers was essentially about "soul saving" and "come to Jesus."
Montgomery might portend, he thought, "a revolution in the Negro
church," with enormous consequences for the future of the black freedom struggle.[3]

Then, at the end of January, came news that the home of the main
spokesperson for the Montgomery protesters, Martin Luther King, Jr.,
had been bombed. "It could have been a riot, a very bloody riot,"
Coretta Scott King recalled afterward.[4] Two nights later, a second
bomb exploded in the yard of Nixon, the principal instigator of the
boycott. The eruption of white supremacist violence made Rustin and
other New York pacifists worry that the black community might respond in kind and unleash a race war that the oppressed were sure to
lose. The FOR resolved to send Glenn Smiley, who had trained Southerners in nonviolence, on a trip to Alabama. Within the WRL, discussions about Montgomery also began, provoked by Rustin's eagerness to
be in the thick of events that bore the spirit, if not the name, of Gandhi.

RUSTIN'S INVOLVEMENT WITH King and the Montgomery bus
boycott was as critical to the course of his career as was his arrest in
Pasadena. The relationship with King placed him in the midst of the
most important events of the era. In King, Rustin found the person
who might take his own deepest aspirations and broadcast them to the
nation and the world. But Rustin came to King as damaged goods, as
someone with a history that threatened as much as it promised.

Surprisingly, Rustin's memory of the circumstances that led him to

Montgomery was strikingly inaccurate. According to his recollection, Rustin went to Montgomery through the efforts of Lillian Smith, a white Southern writer who had served on the national advisory board of CORE and thus knew of Rustin's nonviolent labors. Smith wrote to King and recommended Rustin to him and also telegraphed Rustin encouraging him to offer his services to King. As Rustin remembered it, he arrived before Christmas, when the boycott was barely three weeks old.[5] But in fact Smith did not write to King until after Rustin had come and gone from Montgomery and, though she wrote favorably of Rustin ("a fine man," she informed King), she did so in the context of warning King against accepting the advice of Northerners. Nor was Rustin likely to have arrived so early in the boycott, when it had still barely registered in the consciousness of Northern activists. Rustin did not travel South until the last week in February, after the bombing of the homes of King and Nixon had escalated tensions and just as the Alabama courts were preparing indictments against the boycott leaders.[6]

The most plausible account of the genesis of Rustin's mission to Montgomery comes from James Farmer, who remembered a discussion that Randolph held at his office for a small group of activists. Besides himself and Randolph, Farmer attested to the presence of Rustin, Bill Worthy, who was freelancing as a journalist for the black press, and Jerry Wurf, a union head, which suggests that the meeting evolved out of the In Friendship network. "We decided that somebody should be sent by this group down to Montgomery," Farmer recalled. "Somebody who had had more experience with nonviolent technique. We decided by consensus that Bayard should be sent." One of the WRL's wealthy contributors donated money for the trip. Rustin left with the intention of setting up workshops on the theory and practice of nonviolence. By the time he departed, his mission carried an added sense of urgency since Rustin had learned from Ben McLaurin, one of Randolph's trusted lieutenants, of an "arsenal in Mont[gomery] smuggled by ministers and porters."[7]

It made sense that Rustin would be eager to go and that the others would settle upon him as the logical emissary. He was as accomplished a proponent of Gandhian nonviolence as anyone in the United States.

His long arrest record testified to his commitment; his willingness to employ it in the South was evidence of his courage. And because, unlike most other Gandhian activists in America, he was black rather than white, Rustin would be able to move within the African American community of Montgomery without having to cross a racial divide that the boycott had only sharpened.

Rustin arrived on Tuesday, February 21, the day that a grand jury delivered indictments against more than a hundred leaders of the protest, charging them with violating the state's law against boycotts. The indictments were meant to disrupt the boycott by stoking fear into the hearts of leaders and participants alike and by consuming the community's scarce resources of time and money. Any encounter with the white South's criminal justice system was a fearful prospect for a black man or woman; it was especially so in the heated atmosphere of the boycott. Just a few days earlier, thousands of whites had attended a mass public rally sponsored by the Citizens' Council. A leaflet distributed to the crowd was overt in its incitement to violence: "We hold these truths to be self evident that all whites are created equal with certain rights, among these are life, liberty and the pursuit of dead niggers."[8]

Rustin's ties to Randolph made it easy for him to establish contact with the bus boycott's leadership. The day Rustin arrived, King was in Nashville, so that afternoon he met instead with both Nixon and Ralph Abernathy, another of the local ministers who had already become King's closest confidante. In the wake of the bombings, guards patrolled Abernathy's home round the clock. "This is like war," Rustin was told. In the evening, he attended a meeting of the Montgomery Improvement Association (MIA), the organization formed to coordinate the boycott and negotiate with the bus company and the city government. Later, he walked through the Negro section of town. Volunteers were stationed around King's house, and lights had been strung around it to expose would-be attackers. Rustin was advised that if he went out at night alone, he should "leave in the hotel everything that identifies you as an outsider."[9]

Rustin immediately threw himself into the work. To the tune of a familiar country revival hymn, he composed a set of lyrics meant to capture the spirit of the boycott. He drafted speeches for the leadership on the theme of nonviolent resistance. And he turned his attention to the daunting challenge of the indictments. Rustin proposed a classic Gandhian tactic. Rather than wait at home for the sheriff to arrive and be taken like common criminals, all of the indicted should don their Sunday best and present themselves in groups to the authorities. There was no reason to cower, Rustin told them. They should wear the indictment with pride.

Rustin was at the courthouse early the next morning. It was a remarkable scene. As he had suggested, many of those indicted arrived in groups, dressed in their finest clothes, with large numbers of Montgomery's black citizens gathered outside to applaud. The initiative had, in Rustin's view, "a startling effect. . . . White community leaders, politicians, and police were flabbergasted. Negroes were thrilled to see their leaders surrender without being hunted down." Watching how Abernathy handled himself and the assembled crowd, Rustin saw the minister as "a real Gandhian in spirit." Afterward, he attended a mass prayer meeting where they sang the stanzas that Rustin had composed the night before to the tune of "Give Me That Old Time Religion" and closed with the chorus: "We shall all stand together / We shall all stand together / We shall all stand together / Till everyone is free."[10]

By his second day in Montgomery, Rustin was rethinking his original plan to offer formal training on Gandhian nonviolence. Opportunities to teach were occurring organically, as each new situation unfolded. "Perhaps—I don't know yet," he wrote to Arthur Brown, his roommate in New York, "it will be better to deal with each matter functionally and realistically in terms of nonviolence as they arise. Already much discussion of philosophy has been brought about in this way."[11] On Thursday, Rustin attended a meeting of the steering committee of the MIA and met King for the first time. Friday was designated a day of "prayer and pilgrimage" in the wake of the indictments. The black citizens of Montgomery chose to walk that day rather than ride in cars or taxis, and all the African American churches convened mass prayer meetings. Rustin's attendance at these, and at the MIA meeting where many members were pastors, provoked excited musings. To Brown and to Di-

Gia at the WRL he wrote: "I am convinced that perhaps one of the really major results of Montgomery will be a revolution in the Negro church. The 'come to Jesus' approach that has almost degraded the Negro church since 1910 is now being replaced by a *social action* phase. This means more than appears on the surface. For one thing the NAACP's character may be changed for the better by this—they may have to take on widescale CORE activity or be lost in a few years."[12] Only a few days into his trip, and already there danced before Rustin's eyes a vision of a mass insurgency. "No force on earth can stop this movement," he observed.[13]

Over the next few days, Rustin and King conferred several times, initiating a long and complex relationship that would last until King's assassination. Rustin became teacher to a pupil whose fame would soon outstrip his mentor's. "We hit it off immediately," Rustin recalled, "particularly in terms of the whole concept of nonviolence." Through his theological education, King had a passing acquaintance with the philosophy and career of Gandhi, but it was hardly a resource to draw on in the midst of the pressures of the boycott. Rustin initiated the process that transformed King into the most illustrious American proponent of nonviolence in the twentieth century. "The fact of the matter is," Rustin recalled, "when I got to Montgomery, Dr. King had very limited notions about how a nonviolent protest should be carried out." There were guns lying all about King's house, and Rustin often recounted a humorous incident with himself and Bill Worthy. As Worthy, who had followed Rustin to Montgomery by a couple of days, prepared to sit on one of the chairs in King's living room, Rustin called out to him, "Bill, wait, wait. Couple of guns in that chair. You don't want to shoot yourself."[14]

To Rustin, efforts either by King's followers or by historians to present King as a fully developed Gandhian at the start of the boycott were a disservice to the man. "He had not been prepared for [the job] either tactically, strategically, or in his understanding of nonviolence," Rustin emphatically told an interviewer. "The glorious thing is that he came to a profoundly deep understanding of nonviolence through the struggle itself, and through reading and discussions which he had in the process of carrying on the protest, not that, in some way, college professors who had read Gandhi had prepared him in advance. This is just a hoax." Arriving in Montgomery a week after Rustin, Glenn Smiley confirmed Rustin's evaluation. About Gandhian nonviolence, Smiley insisted, King "knew nothing."[15]

Rustin's Gandhian credentials were impeccable. He had what King most immediately needed: extensive experience in nonviolent protest. But Rustin also had something more—years of serious meditation about how the philosophy, strategy, and tactics of nonviolence were of a piece and how together they might fashion a transformative revolutionary movement. Rustin particularly remembered one long discussion that he characterized as "very important" in which he shared with King his reflections on the Indian independence movement. His trip to India, he told the young Montgomery leader, taught him that the mass of Indians who followed Gandhi were not philosophically wedded to nonviolence. But they were willing to take it up as a tactic because they believed it would be the most effective way to end British rule. That made it all the more critical, Rustin impressed upon King, for the leadership to "be dedicated to it in principle, to keep those who believe in it as a tactic operating correctly. . . . If, in the flow and heat of battle," he told King, "a leader's house is bombed, and he shoots back, that is an encouragement to his followers to pick up guns. If, on the other hand, he has no guns around him, and they all know it, they will rise to the nonviolent occasion of a situation." From the start, Rustin communicated to King not only the efficacy and moral value of nonviolence, but the special responsibility of leaders to model it fully.[16]

By the time of his first weekend in Montgomery, Rustin's presence was sounding alarms. Nattily dressed, possessed of a strange, foreign-sounding accent, he was soon attracting attention from the police and the local press. His appearance at the county courthouse, the many conversations he provoked among the black onlookers, and his prominence in an Associated Press photograph of King and Abernathy all combined to provoke the *Montgomery Advertiser* to track down the identity of this mysterious stranger.[17] Rustin's association with Worthy made matters worse, as a black reporter from Birmingham who knew of

Worthy's left-leaning writings threatened to expose them both as Communist sympathizers. To his New York colleagues, Rustin wrote that "there must be no talk of my being here. . . . Already they are watching me closely and I am sure they report telephone conversations. . . . I have been followed by police cars and never go out after dark alone." One white female journalist who had come from the North to cover the boycott told him "to be careful, [that] every move I made was being watched, that I should be prepared to leave town by car at a moment's notice, that the rumour was being spread by a reporter on the local paper that I was a communist NAACP organizer . . . planning a violent uprising." For protection, he had extra bolts placed on the windows of his hotel room. "How complicated things become in the heat of a struggle," was his terse response.[18]

To Rustin's own misgivings about whether he should stay were soon added the panicked reactions of his associates in New York. In a cloak-and-dagger scenario whose details defy easy summary, pacifists and civil rights leaders in New York met, telephoned, and dispatched letters with dizzying speed. Rustin, they argued, was a danger to the movement. It was not only, or even primarily, that he was a New Yorker with a Communist past. Rather, his arrest in Pasadena would compromise his effectiveness and subject the Montgomery movement to serious peril.

John Swomley, who had replaced Muste as executive secretary of the FOR, and Charles Lawrence, who was national chairman of the organization and remembered the shock of the Pasadena arrest, had harbored reservations about Rustin's going to Montgomery in the first place. Lawrence worried that "it would be easy for the police to frame him with his record in L.A. and New York." Swomley, who had often tangled with Rustin at the FOR, thought "there could be an actual incident." Always uncomfortable with Rustin, he told an associate that Rustin might easily stage a "dramatic effort in which he becomes the focal point," and he claimed, on no grounds whatsoever, that Rustin wanted to "try to organize an independent show."[19]

After Nixon called Randolph to sort through the rumors about Rustin, Randolph hastily convened a meeting in New York to reconsider the wisdom of Rustin's journey south. According to various recollections, as many as twenty folks gathered at Randolph's office on Tuesday, February 27. Farmer and Norman Thomas were there, along with Swomley, Lawrence, Ben McLaurin, Bob Gilmore of the AFSC, and Arthur Brown, Rustin's roommate who had received two long written reports from him. The framework for the discussion was Randolph's view that "the Montgomery leaders had managed . . . far more successfully than any of 'our so-called northern experts' a mass resistance campaign," and it was arrogant to believe they needed outside direction. "We should learn from them rather than assume that we knew it all," Swomley reported Randolph as saying. Yet it was not outsiders in general but Rustin in particular who animated their concerns. Except for Brown, all agreed that Rustin should leave town immediately rather than subject King and the boycott to the burden of his past. According to Swomley, "there are some here who feel the local leaders ought to know about Bayard's personal problem but dare not mention it over the phone. They ought to know the risks that are being taken." Norman Thomas briefed Homer Jack, another Northern activist who traveled to Montgomery, about the meeting, telling him that Rustin was "entirely too vulnerable on his record—and I do not mean his record as a c.o." Any association with him would "greatly handicap Southern Negroes."[20]

Swomley's concerns bordered on hysteria. In the space of two days, he wrote Smiley four letters, reiterating the need to give Rustin a wide berth. "You should be wary of him," he first wrote. "He is apparently also to some degree persona non grata with some of the Negro leaders in Montgomery or they would not have started the ball rolling with Philip Randolph to have him called back." When Swomley learned that Smiley had been in touch with Rustin, he wrote scoldingly: "I am wondering why you felt you should do this. . . . It would seem off-hand that your job there would be more difficult if you establish any relationship with Bayard." To Charles Walker, a black FOR staffer who was urging consultation with Rustin, Swomley was unbending. "Whether rightly or wrongly you have created the impression that you are eager to collaborate with Bayard. . . . We are clear nationally . . . that we must not be involved with Bayard on any such project because of the potential dangers."[21]

Smiley, who had arrived in Montgomery the day before the meeting in Randolph's office, offered quite a different view. From what he gathered through his talks with King and others, he disputed the claim that outsiders had nothing to offer. "Randolph is wrong in several respects," he wrote to Swomley. "Montgomery leaders have managed a mass resistance campaign, but it was petering out until 1. the indictments and arrests, 2. King suddenly remembered Gandhi." Smiley admitted that "we can learn from their courage and plain earthy devices for building morale, etc." But, he added, "they can learn more from us, for being so new at this. King runs out of ideas quickly and does the old things again and again." Against Randolph and Thomas's position that the boycotters were doing fine on their own, Smiley countered: "He wants help, and we can give it to him without attempting to run the movement or pretend we know it all."[22]

Smiley had little patience for Swomley's allegations about Rustin and the orders to stay away from him. "I don't forbid well," he reminisced years later with a glint of mischief in his eye. Smiley humored Swomley by telling him that the contact was unintentional and just in passing, but in fact, Rustin had provided him with the much-needed introduction to King, filled him in on what he had learned, and gave King assurances that Smiley, a white Southerner whom King had never met, could be trusted. "I continually depended on Bayard," he generously acknowledged. "Bayard was my guru all this time." Under pressure from Swomley, he was content merely with trying to correct some of the charges against Rustin that his New York associates were making from afar. "Bayard has had a very good influence on King, wrote the much quoted speech of last week, and was in on all the strategy," he informed Swomley. Though he understood the reasons for wanting Rustin to depart, he saw the call for his exit as "really unfortunate. . . . Wish we had Bayard of the old days in this," he continued in his letter. "He really could make a mark here. Smiley is a pore, pore [sic] substitute."[23]

Meanwhile, Rustin did not need to be told to leave. He understood full well the dangers that were lurking, as his letter to Brown and Di-Gia, written three days before the meeting at Randolph's office, attested. He and Worthy left town on Wednesday, February 29, and spent the next week in Birmingham, where he conferred at the behest of Randolph with black trade unionists to see what kind of material help they might offer the boycotters. He also attended the hearing in federal court about Autherine Lucy's attempt to be the first African American to attend the University of Alabama. Earlier in February, the prospect of her imminent appearance on the Tuscaloosa campus stimulated a riot among students, and the trustees expelled her before she was even able to register. Rustin was also biding his time in Birmingham, awaiting the arrival of King, who wanted to confer about building Northern support for the Montgomery movement.

The alarm that his New York colleagues displayed from afar revealed more about *their* perceptions of Rustin than about the situation in Alabama. They seriously misjudged Rustin. He had faced danger enough times to know how to appraise an incendiary situation, and he had worked with local community leaders frequently enough to have honed the ability to offer advice without seizing control. Of course, he longed to be "in the heat of the struggle," as he described Montgomery, but his purpose was not self-aggrandizement. To his colleagues, however, Rustin's grand manner signaled overbearance, while his sexual history generated panicked conclusions that were rarely subjected to rational scrutiny. Ironically, it was Worthy's public record as a journalist who had questioned cold war orthodoxy that first roused ire among some of the black Alabamans. But it was upon Rustin that the anxieties of Northern activists settled.

RUSTIN AND KING made for an interesting contrast. In appearance, the former was tall, thin, elegant in bearing, and sometimes haughty; the latter was short and squat, with a developing tendency toward overweight and a soothing manner meant to put his congregants at ease. Rustin was born to simple circumstances, but had absorbed the cosmopolitan outlook of a great metropolis and had traveled across four continents; King came from the relative privilege of a successful minister's family and had made forays north for his education, but he lived very much within the social world of the segregated South. Rustin was a Quaker and King a black Baptist. At least on the surface, a huge gulf in experience, culture, and outlook seemed to separate them.

And yet the close connection that developed between them was, in the shrewd observation of Dave McReynolds, "the least mysterious subject. . . . The better question," McReynolds went on, "would be 'how would it have been possible for King not to have become a protege of Bayard?' Not how did he, but how could he not have been? . . . Bayard's charismatic, he's basically pretty decent, he's funny, and he's very very helpful. There's no mystery at all."[24] Rustin held out to King an abundance of offerings. He had a wealth of specific skills developed through years of applying Gandhian methods to the fight for racial justice. He had a vast network of contacts outside the South, among pacifists, union leaders, the democratic left, civil libertarians, journalists, and politically engaged entertainers. Rustin also had cultivated the habit of thinking strategically, of scrutinizing a situation with an eye toward what doors it might open for future campaigns. Though their spiritual traditions were different, they shared a moral impulse to bear witness against evil. Rustin had been acting publicly on that impulse for two decades. King was taking his first steps.

But there was something more, something that made Rustin the perfect mentor for King at this stage in the young minister's career. Rustin had melded Quaker, Gandhian, and Marxist persuasions in ways that were unusual, if not unique. His Christian faith, which ran deep, kept his moral outlook clear and in focus; the Quaker inflection to his faith, with its pacifist tradition and nonconforming stance, made social activism his gospel. In Gandhi's biography, Rustin had found a practice that breathed life into his values, promising their realization in this world, not just in the next. And from Marxism, Rustin drew the conviction that the pursuit of peace and racial justice was inextricably bound to a quest for economic justice. Putting these influences together made Rustin a radical strategist able to combine vision, values, and program.

Students of King's place in history have debated at length whether the nonviolence he adopted arrived through the importation of a foreign influence—Gandhi—into the Southern freedom struggle or whether

King's activist philosophy sprouted naturally from the roots of his black Baptist culture. But unraveling the origins of King's adherence to non-violence may be less important than understanding how he came, in the course of a tragically short public career, to espouse so grand a vision of social change, how he moved beyond the simple embrace of passive resistance to a bold, revolutionary outlook. Rustin's life suggests some answers. As we will see, in the ensuing months and years, Rustin left a profound mark—on the unfolding of the Montgomery boycott as a national story, on the evolution of King's role as a national leader, on the particular association of nonviolence with Montgomery and King. Rustin was as responsible as anyone else for the insinuation of nonviolence into the very heart of what became the most powerful social movement in twentieth-century America.

Finding Rustin's imprint is not easy, however. Though in private he might display arrogance with his activist colleagues, in public he strove to render himself unseen. Some of this invisibility was attributable to a leadership style he had long cultivated, a Quaker and Gandhian modesty that rarely drew public attention to himself. But more often, in these post-Pasadena years, working in the shadows was forced on him. His skill at concealment was a concession to the dangers to which his sexuality exposed both him and the movements he cared about. Rustin affected a pose, his own version of the mask that gay men of this era wore. In this effort to hide the traces of his influence, he enjoyed the collusion of his associates who, for motives of their own, were happy to cooperate. In King's subsequent account of the Montgomery boycott, for instance, Rustin received not a mention; other memoirs of this period barely give him a walk-on role.[25] Rustin's dissembling, if it can be called that, fooled not only contemporary observers but some historians as well, who have tended to understate his role in events.

Contrary to appearances, and despite the alarm signals emanating from many quarters, King came to rely on Rustin early—and Rustin knew it. Although Rustin tended, even late in life, to deflect credit away from himself when asked about his role, he was uncharacteristically direct in assessing his relationship with King. "I think I would say without any modesty," he professed to an interviewer in the mid-1980s, "that my presence there was incommensurate and stimulating to Martin. I think he needed someone to talk to. I think he totally depended on me, not that I was always right, but I would tell him the truth." Trying to identify the form of his influence, Rustin pointed to the implications for political engagement of their contrasting religious traditions. Quakerism, he claimed, "gave me a concept of the responsibility of religion not to save souls, as was the tradition in the Baptist church, but to save souls in this life by making it simpler for people to be good. Therefore, I think King had come out of a background which was essentially soul-saving, and that while he had been exposed to some degree of social change, I don't think he had any of what I would call a socialist education." Occasionally someone else also perceived Rustin beyond the prejudices that attached to him and assessed with generosity his impact. Homer Jack, who had known Rustin since the early days of CORE, crossed paths a couple of times with him in Montgomery. "I saw very quickly that he was on very good terms with the Kings," he reminisced. "Early on he was strategizing with them." To his contacts in the North, Jack wrote after his first trip to Montgomery: "Bayard seemed especially effective in counseling with the leaders of the protest during the crucial 2 weeks after the mass arrests for the boycott. His contribution to interpreting the Gandhian approach to the leadership cannot be overestimated."[26] But Jack's praise was sadly exceptional. His was about the only voice, save Smiley's, to ascribe to Rustin a favorable influence.

EARLY IN MARCH, while Rustin was still in Alabama, he and King met secretly in Birmingham to discuss what assistance the boycott required and what support could be mobilized in the North. Both men understood how white Southerners would use the cry of "outsider" to disrupt the protest, and so they planned accordingly. Always, Rustin wrote in the memo detailing their conversation, the Montgomery Improvement Association "must give the appearance of developing all of the ideas and strategies used in the struggle." But King, he went on, "is very happy to receive outside help." King, Rustin reported, needed suggestions and plans for education in nonviolence, techniques to keep the

protest vibrant, and assistance in spreading widely the idea of nonviolent resistance. The boycott could use infusions of cash, people with
specific skills to do training, and public demonstrations elsewhere in
the country to win attention and sympathy. King himself needed a
ghostwriter, since the pressures on his time were too great for him to be
able to tell in print the Montgomery story.

Immediately upon arriving home, Rustin set to work fulfilling King's
wish list. The day after his return, he mailed to King the draft of an article he had begun while still in Alabama. He highlighted the messages
that he believed had the most strategic value: that the boycott signaled
the birth of a "new Negro" and a "revolutionary change in the Negro's
evaluation of himself"; that "economics is part of our struggle"; that
the boycotters had discovered "a new and powerful weapon—non-violent resistance"; and that the leadership demonstrated that "our church
is becoming militant." Telling King that he deliberately emphasized the
"moral aspects" of the story, Rustin asked permission to publish it under King's name in the April issue of *Liberation*. It was King's first venture into print. It points to the trust that already existed between the
two and suggests Rustin's capacity early on to ascribe to King's work a
meaning that the novice activist felt able to embrace.[27]

The threads of Rustin's influence extended far and wide. He labored
steadily to inject into Northern peace networks a consciousness of the
developing freedom movement. By the end of March, the WRL had
published a pamphlet he wrote on the boycott that circulated widely
among pacifists. Rustin quickly sparked the formation of a Committee
for Nonviolent Integration to give substance to support efforts in the
North. Muste and Farmer were among its lead sponsors, and it drew
organizational backing from the AFSC, the Women's International
League for Peace and Freedom, and other peace groups. During King's
first trip to New York in April, Rustin brokered the meeting that put
King directly in touch with Randolph, Muste, and Farmer. The relationship that developed between King and Randolph, in which Rustin
functioned as intermediary, became especially critical in the ensuing
months and years. When Randolph proposed a Madison Square Garden rally to draw attention to Montgomery, the WRL gave Rustin a

two-month leave to work on it full time. Rustin, Baker, and Levison, along with staff from Randolph's union, pulled together a massive display of support for the Southern freedom struggle—the largest since the rallies of the March on Washington Movement during World War II. Though King could not appear, Nixon, Autherine Lucy, and other Southern activists were there and received standing ovations. Liberal dignitaries like Eleanor Roosevelt, rising political figures like Jacob Javits, then the attorney general in New York, and Broadway stars like Tallulah Bankhead filled the evening program, which extended past midnight. Except for a tangle that Rustin had with Adam Clayton Powell, the limelight-stealing congressman from Harlem, the evening went off smoothly. It successfully raised money for Montgomery and other Southern battlefields and served as a mass distribution point for copies of the Montgomery issue of *Liberation*. Even Roy Wilkins, who had recently become head of the NAACP and was suspicious of rallies and demonstrations, described it as "an overwhelming success."[28]

Support for the Southern freedom struggle consumed Rustin for the rest of the year. In May, he forwarded to King a $5,000 check he had secured from an anonymous donor. He toured campuses in the North, interpreting the significance of Montgomery to students who were being characterized as "silent" by the press but who would soon be roused to activism. Rustin made more forays into the South. He met with beleaguered black activists in communities where the threat of white violence was so high that no one was willing to be seen with him during the day. In one Mississippi town, the handful of members from a once-thriving NAACP chapter operated, according to Rustin, "as the underground did in Nazi Germany." One of its leaders had been chased from the county; the body of another had been found floating in a creek. None of these communities received the press attention that Montgomery did.[29] There were other conferences with King, in New York and in the South, where the men talked nonviolence and bent their heads toward strategy. The two telephoned and wrote. King felt the freedom to be frank with Rustin. "The pressure of the situation has not yet been relieved," he informed him in one letter. "I hardly have time to breathe." In Rustin's letters, there was often the sign of the teacher who formulates pointed questions for his pupil to consider as a way of crystallizing key issues.[30] In the fall, the In Friendship team began organizing a fund-raising concert in New York, at which King's wife, Coretta, would sing. Rustin was also putting together a special issue of *Liberation* commemorating the anniversary of the boycott; Eleanor Roosevelt, Ralph Bunche, Harry Emerson Fosdick, and Randolph were among the contributors.

THE MONTGOMERY BOYCOTT and the encounters with King thrust Rustin into the thick of things and sparked in him excited speculation. He placed the stirrings in the South in a global context and extracted from them meaning that reached deep into the history of the United States. He ruminated about how the Montgomery protest might portend change in the United States far beyond the matter of seating patterns on city buses. To Rustin, the expanding protest movement in the South held revolutionary implications.

Rustin did not interpret international politics in the terms set by cold war ideologues. He saw the conflicts erupting around the world not as a fight between communism and capitalism but as variations of anticolonial revolutions. Just as Hungarians were rising against Soviet hegemony in 1956, just as Egypt was challenging the dominion of Britain and France over the Suez Canal, just as Asia and Africa were throwing off colonial rule, American blacks were chafing against subjugation. "What is happening in race relations in the United States," he told an audience in Cambridge, "is the same thing which is happening all over the world. The dominant factor of our time is the struggle for freedom of groups of people, a movement which is essentially anticolonial. . . . In our own country there is something going on which is quite as profound as what is happening in Hungary, which is quite as profound as what is happening in Egypt, and that is a part of . . . the worldwide revolutionary movement." America, he wrote, "which brought her colonial subjects home from Africa, cannot escape this conflict."[31] Freedom for Southern blacks promised to make the nation whole for the first time in its history. To Rustin, the claims of the American Revolution, confounded first by slavery and then by segregation, might finally be realized.

Rustin viewed the white supremacist South as the obstacle in the way of a broad social justice agenda. "The one-party system in the South," he explained, "is so frustrating to every social development which comes before the national Congress. . . . [It] makes it so difficult to get social insurance for our grandmothers, to get free education for our children, to get free medical care, and so on. . . . This fact has thrown up a political structure in which there are limited choices for all of us."[32] The solid South, as it was then dubbed, gave its segregationist leaders a stranglehold on Congress. Kept in office term after term by a closed political system that stifled dissent in the name of racial solidarity, Southern Democrats controlled the key committees of both houses of Congress. Any legislative agenda that, directly or indirectly, promised blacks autonomy from white control withered under their scrutiny.

Rustin saw the freedom struggle in the South emerging from larger economic and social forces that the diehard segregationist leadership of the region could not contain. The agrarian South was fading into history. For almost two generations, blacks and whites alike had been leaving the countryside and making their way into an urban industrial economy. The flight to the city was, for Rustin, implicitly a move toward freedom. African Americans in cities were less under the eye of the landlord and more easily able to engage in collective action. The Citizens' Councils might try to maintain the same level of control that their terrorist predecessors exerted, but they were doomed to failure.[33]

Ever the Marxist, Rustin predicted that these changes in economic life would inevitably recast politics in the South. As a white middle class tied to urban commerce and industry grew, so too would the attractiveness of the Republican Party, despite memories of Lincoln and "the war between the states." The national Democratic Party, meanwhile, would have a harder and harder time accommodating its Southern conservative wing. It would have to "remake itself radically or fall apart." Out of this might emerge a two-party system in the South. For Rustin, these developments offered no sure outcomes, just a set of contingencies that left room for popular movements and their leaders to influence in one direction or another. Would racial loyalties remain the defining characteristic of party fealty in the South, or would the two parties be more sharply distinguished by class? Might the restructuring of politics in the South open the possibility of a new party altogether, like the populists of the late nineteenth century? Would labor become a major force in American politics, as it was in much of Western Europe, and campaign for broad economic and social reforms?

Rustin trained his thinking on the new stage of the African American freedom struggle that Montgomery represented. Rustin hoped that Southern blacks who could vote would make their ballots "instrumental in the disruption of the 'solid South.'" But the prospect hardly excited him. "There is something fantastically unreal and at the same time tragic," he wrote, "about fighting desperately at the risk of one's livelihood or even life itself to gain admission to a polling booth in a typical Southern state, and then having to use this hard won achievement to indicate a choice between the present Democratic and the present Republican party." That very summer, in 1956, civil rights forces had experienced bitter disappointments. At their national conventions, neither Democrats nor Republicans had taken decisive stands for racial equality.

Instead, Rustin turned his hopes toward nonviolent collective protest. "It is difficult to assess the importance of a one-shot performance at the polls in November," he argued. "But the tremendous effects of day-to-day nonviolent protest go on through the year. . . . The more widespread it becomes, the greater will be its effectiveness as real political action." Nonviolence would build support outside the South. It would also over time cripple the capacity of white supremacists to maintain their rule. In the short run, nonviolent protest would drive the leadership of the Citizens' Council into more extreme measures, in the hope of provoking black violence. But if, "despite this provocation, the Negro holds fast to the spirit of Montgomery, he will be able to work with white workers and farmers to create a new political force for social progress. . . . Nothing can so thoroughly disarm their terror as the determined adherence to nonviolence."

*   *   *

MEANWHILE, IN MONTGOMERY, the white power structure used every tool available to break the boycott. Car pool drivers were arrested for minor traffic violations; road accidents kept occurring that seemed engineered by the police; insurance companies cancelled the policies of vehicles used to transport black workers to and from their jobs. Fred Gray, the chief lawyer for the MIA, found himself stripped of his draft deferment and confronted with disbarment procedures. The Alabama attorney general brought an injunction against the NAACP to force it to cease operations in the state, while Montgomery's city commissioners sought one against the car pool. Acts of violence continued to erupt. But these were, in the words of King, "death groans from a dying system." Early in June, a federal district court ruled that segregation on intrastate buses was unconstitutional. Though the state and the city appealed to the Supreme Court, it seemed inconceivable that the justices, two years after the *Brown* decision, would support segregation in public transportation.[34]

In November, Rustin traveled to Montgomery to help plan what would happen when the boycott ended. While he was there, the Supreme Court sustained the lower court ruling and in effect declared all bus segregation statutes unconstitutional. The front-page story in the *New York Times* said the court had "placed a headstone at the grave of Plessy v. Ferguson," the decision that, sixty years earlier, had ushered in the separate-but-equal era.[35] Amid the jubilation, it was clear to Rustin, King, and the other boycott leaders that the transition to integrated buses had to be handled thoughtfully to avoid outbursts of violence. They discussed the content of a week-long institute on nonviolence, scheduled for early December and intended to draw activists from across the South. Rustin agreed not to attend. He did not want to make his influence obvious at an event bound to draw attention from the press and the Alabama authorities. For the same reason, he decided not to return to Montgomery later in December, after all the court orders had been delivered and the time for integration had arrived.

But if Rustin missed the drama of the boycott's successful conclusion, he was more than occupied hatching plans for the future. In the course of the year-long struggle, protests had emerged elsewhere in the South. In Tallahassee, another bus boycott was underway. Glenn Smiley, who was on the road almost constantly during 1956, reported that "incidents multiply much more rapidly than we have been able to service them . . . the good that we have been able to do has been of a limited nature." At the same time, Smiley found enthusiasm for nonviolence high: "Not since the first days of World War II have I participated in such eager discussions of pacifism."[36] To Rustin, observations such as these confirmed his intuition that the model of Montgomery and the qualities of King as a leader begged to be institutionalized. Spontaneous protest was fine; all signs indicated that it would happen in place after place. But without an organization, without conscious planning and direction, the optimism, creativity, and effectiveness would drain away.

Throughout the year, Rustin, Baker, and Levison had speculated among themselves about the possibilities that Montgomery opened. Rustin and Baker were an especially suited pair for this moment in history. Through her years on staff at the NAACP, Baker had seen at close range its top-down culture and unshakable allegiance to legal strategies. Rustin's devotion to nonviolent direct action also put him at odds with the giant dominating the civil rights arena. Both were looking for ways to rouse whole communities to action, to help ordinary people make history. "We began to talk," Baker recalled, "about the need for developing in the South a mass force that would somewhat become a counterbalance, let's call it, to the NAACP." In Baker's view, there was no doubt that what became the Southern Christian Leadership Conference emerged from those conversations, not from initiatives in Montgomery.[37]

Almost from his first meeting with King, Rustin had raised the issue of a permanent organization. Hardly a conversation occurred between the two in which the topic did not surface. Over time, King too came to understand the wisdom of Rustin's insistence. In December, the institute for nonviolence elicited so much enthusiasm (attendance reached 3,000) that any hesitation on King's side evaporated. To the ministers from elsewhere in the South who were pressing for change in their communities and who attended the institute, King issued a call for another smaller gathering, to convene in Atlanta in January at his father's church.

King leaned heavily on Rustin for the planning of the Atlanta meeting, and Rustin set to work. Just before Christmas, he sent to King
some short papers he and Levison had prepared. Rustin offered King a
broad historical view of the black freedom struggle—the phases it had
moved through since slavery, the various strategies that had been tried,
the key leaders who had made a difference in the past. It was a generous
assessment, finding value even in the approaches of men like Booker T.
Washington and Marcus Garvey with whom Rustin, committed to interracialism and mass protest, might have been expected to disagree.

Rustin's memos treated Montgomery as the event toward which history had been inexorably moving: "the first mass protest that was completely Negro and completely nonviolent." He wanted to impress on
King what made it unique. Unlike the school desegregation battles,
which left the fight to "heroic but isolated individuals," the bus boycott
drew in "all social strata of the community" and "did not rely exclu-
sively on a handful of leaders." The unity it engendered evoked among
the people a "quality not to be lost." Rustin reached back to the nation's
founding in describing it. "The fellowship, the ideals, the joy of sacrifice for others," he wrote, "have given people something to belong to
which had the inspiring power of the Minute Men, the Sons of Liberty,
and other organized forms which were products of an earlier American
era of fundamental change." Rustin saw Montgomery as akin to the
opening salvos of the first American Revolution. He wanted to be mid-
wife to the next.[38]

Rustin also laid out the tasks ahead. The movement had to extend its
reach into the political system. It had to encourage local organization
and bring local leaders together into a bigger federation. There needed
to be a vehicle for developing national strategy so that spontaneous
outbursts of discontent could be guided into a broader, deeper channel
of organized activity. Rustin urged King to look to the experience of
others who had built broad-based movements; significantly, all the examples he chose were of labor leaders. And he put justice in a larger
frame: "The fight of the Negro for integration and equality is a vital
component in the fight of the common man, Negro and white, to real-
ize higher living standards, higher education and culture, and a deeper

commitment to moral and ethical principles. It is contributing to the movement of America to achieve a nation capable of utilizing its vastly impressive industrial might for the benefit of all."[39]

A few days after Christmas, Rustin drove to Baltimore with Levison. Through Rustin, Levison was meeting King for the first time. Along with Harris and Clare Wofford, two American disciples of Gandhi, they conferred with the Kings, who had flown up from Montgomery. They talked with the couple about funding for a proposed trip to Africa and India and, with the Atlanta meeting just two weeks away, engaged in conversations about strategy in the aftermath of the boycott. Rustin received the go-ahead from King to develop the ideas contained in his earlier memos into a series of working papers to guide the Atlanta meeting. Rustin would be writing for an audience of Southern black ministers, few of whom knew him.[40]

For most of the next two weeks, he busied himself with the task. He sketched out a historical and economic context for the current period of ferment. He addressed the issue of state power, and when it might be relied on and when not. He discussed the ways that the political and economic elites in the South might be divided and how the black community might play off one against the other. He talked about the need eventually to broaden the movement from one of protest to one of political engagement, and what would be required to move from bus boycotts to voter registration and political campaigns.

Most of all, Rustin hammered away at the importance of building a mass movement across the South. He outlined the key qualities required for a mass movement to succeed, using Montgomery as the concrete instance. He raised the issue of whether isolated protest campaigns could succeed unless other areas of protest sprang up, and left little doubt as to what he thought the answer was. He insisted that the group create "the machinery for stimulating new protests and coordinating the bus protests into a single movement." Rustin called their attention to the need for leadership and for disciplined groups prepared to act as "nonviolent shock troops." He impressed on attendees that the movement for racial equality was at a turning point. "Historically, the major emphasis in our struggle to obtain civil rights has been legal and legislative," he wrote. Now a new stage had been reached. *"The center of gravity has shifted from the courts to community action.* It is on the community level that court decisions must be implemented. . . . Law will be very important in this process, *but something new must be added.* . . . We must recognize in this new period that *direct action is our most potent political weapon."* Rustin laid out the implications of such a position—the fact that, at some point, extralegal action would be required and mass arrests might result—and asked them to consider its feasibility. "We must not be afraid to explore new ways," the last of his seven papers exhorted. "We must not be timid, and must be prepared to pay the price involved."[41]

With drafts in hand, Rustin traveled to Atlanta with Baker. They met with King and Abernathy to plan the two-day event. Just before the conference began, the two ministers had to return to Montgomery because of new segregationist violence. But the meeting went ahead anyway, as sixty leaders from twenty-nine communities in ten Southern states plotted strategy. The conferees approved a "Statement to the South and Nation" that bore all the hallmarks of Rustin's thinking: placing the black struggle in a global context; assessing the broad political and social impact on the nation of white supremacy in the South; issuing a bold call for all blacks to resist segregation with the weapon of nonviolent protest. Couched in the language of Christian love, the statement made a moral appeal to white Southerners and a political appeal to the president, the vice president, and the attorney general, to take concrete actions to bring the white South into compliance with the Supreme Court.[42]

The ministers in Atlanta also agreed to meet again in New Orleans a few weeks later. It would still be several months before their association adopted the name and shape of the Southern Christian Leadership Conference. But Rustin left Atlanta secure in the knowledge that he had moved the struggle for racial justice a huge step forward.

Janifer Rustin [1], Bayard's maternal grandfather, moved to West Chester, Pennsylvania, from Maryland as a young man in the 1880s. He and his wife, Julia [2], raised Bayard as their youngest son, naming him after Bayard Taylor, a local poet and diplomat.

An adolescent of many talents, Rustin was a member of his high school's championship track [3] and football teams [4; Rustin is third from right, front row]. Later, as a student at Wilberforce University, Rustin [second from left, front row on floor], toured the United States as part of the school's well-regarded octet [5].

6

7

8

In the 1940s, Rustin achieved renown among American pacifists. A.J. Muste [6; Muste is on the left] was his mentor at the Fellowship of Reconciliation; Rustin is shown here with Evan Thomas at a War Resisters League retreat in 1942 [7]; picketing the French Embassy in the late 1940s to protest France's mistreatment of conscientious objectors [8].

9

Rustin spent twenty-seven months in prison for refusing induction during World War II. These two mug shots, one taken in March 1944 when he entered prison [9], and the other taken in August 1945 [10], suggest the emotional and physical toll.

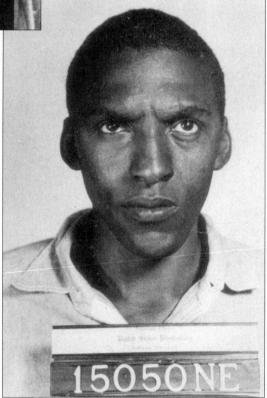

10

11

During his time in prison, he struggled over his sexuality, a struggle symbolized by the two who loved him deeply, Davis Platt [11] and Helen Winnemore [12].

12

13

14

15

Rustin pioneered the use of nonviolent direct action to protest racial injustice. He and George Houser [14], another FOR staff member, worked together as a team in the 1940s. In 1947, they led an interracial group [13] into the South to protest segregation on interstate buses. In 1948 Rustin and Houser, shown here with cartoonist Bill Mauldin [15], received the Jefferson Award from the Council Against Intolerance in America for their efforts.

16

17

Rustin traveled the globe in the two decades after World War II as an advocate of nonviolent solutions to international conflict. Here he is wearing homespun on a lecture tour of India in 1949 [16]; meeting with Kwame Nkrumah, a leader of Ghana's independence movement, in 1952 [17].

18

19

Rustin and his team preparing to journey into the Sahara in 1959 to protest French nuclear testing [18]; and addressing a rally in Tanganyika (today's Tanzania) in 1962 in support of Zambian independence [19].

20

21

22

The Montgomery bus boycott raised Rustin's hope for a nonviolent mass movement to end segregation in the South. Rustin met Martin Luther King, Jr., in February 1956 in Montgomery [20] and soon became King's mentor and adviser. Shown here in the background on 125th Street in Harlem [21], Rustin organized support in the North for the boycott and spoke about the Southern freedom struggle on many campuses [22].

23

24

He also made contact with local activists elsewhere, including Mississippi [23]. Rustin defended nonviolence as a strategy in public debates, as in this one with Malcolm X at Howard University [24].

25

26

Rustin was the key organizer behind the historic 1963 March on Washington for Jobs and Freedom, which put him in the national spotlight for the first time. Here he is shown in the March's office with A. Philip Randolph [25], who first proposed a national march in 1941, and on the podium in front of the Lincoln Memorial, addressing the crowd at the end of the day [26].

27

28

As the civil rights movement crested in the mid-1960s, Rustin threw himself into the politics of racial justice and worked especially closely with King in 1964 and 1965. Here he is out on the streets of Harlem during the riots there in the summer of 1964 [27]; and with King and other key national leaders planning strategy [28].

29

30

Rustin riding in a motorcade with King to rally voters during the 1964 election [29]; as part of the entourage to Oslo when King received the Nobel Peace Prize [30].

31

32

Outside the Alabama state capitol, Rustin took part in a rally in support of voting rights [31]. By 1968, after King's assassination, Rustin's support of Hubert Humphrey's presidential campaign [32] placed him at odds with a new militancy in black communities and among white antiwar activists.

33

34

35

Late in life, Rustin returned to his interest in world affairs, which he expressed through support for human rights campaigns. He met with Lech Walesa, a leader of the Solidarity Movement in Poland [33]; campaigned with Liv Ullmann, a Swedish actress, on behalf of refugees [34]; and visited refugee camps in Southeast Asia [35] several times.

36

37

Rustin made his final trip to India in the early 1980s [36]. For the last decade of his life, he lived in an intimate union with Walter Naegle [37], who encouraged him to speak out on behalf of gay rights.

CHAPTER TWELVE

"More Going On Than Most People Would Gather"

1957–1959

CHANGE IS CONTAGIOUS. Especially in the twentieth century, when modern technologies seemed to shrink the size of the planet, the stirrings of the human spirit for dignity in one corner of the globe might reverberate anywhere. The work of a self-effacing physically frail man in India echoed in the mind of an artistic young Quaker living in Harlem, who then infused an eloquent preacher in Alabama with the conviction that the aspirations of his local community might seize the stage of world history.

As Rustin worked to create an organization that built on the bus boycott, he sensed that something was reviving not only in the United States but around the rest of the world too. The previous year had witnessed any number of dramatic developments. In the Soviet Union, Nikita Khrushchev, first secretary of the Communist Party, denounced the "cult of personality," a coded attack on Stalin and his terrorist rule. In North Africa, Gamal Abdel Nasser, the president of Egypt, seized the Suez Canal in the face of French and British opposition and survived a joint French, British, and Israeli attack intended to restore Western control. Ghana was poised to become the first nation in sub-Saharan Africa to achieve independence from European rule, signaling the beginning of the final stages of Western colonialism. In Hungary, a revolt against Soviet domination erupted, and although Russian military power brutally suppressed it, the images of Hungarian freedom fighters lingered. Everywhere, it seemed, events were shaking cold war certainties. Military power neither demonstrated invincible might nor permanently suppressed the aspirations of people for freedom and justice.

These were headline events. They rolled through Rustin's world, setting off initiatives that made the grim days of the early fifties recede quickly.

EVER SINCE HE BROKE with the Communist Party in 1941, Rustin not only had maintained a distance from it but also had avoided affiliation with any element of the organized left. Still, the political circles in which he traveled and to which he felt akin were populated by those who viewed politics through the lens of Marxian socialism. Norman Thomas and Dave McReynolds represented two generations of the Socialist Party. Muste maintained connections with many of his old Trotskyist comrades from the 1930s. Levison and Ella Baker had friends and associates whose beliefs marked them as travelers in the world of organized communism. Through them and his own friends, Rustin moved in a New York crowded with leftists of various stripes. Like Muste, he functioned as a bridge connecting an anti-Stalinist left to radical pacifists who drew their inspiration not from Marx but from religious faith and the example of Gandhi.

Now the left was in flux. At least since the mid-1930s, the Communist Party of the United States of America (CPUSA) had been the dominant presence, dwarfing its competitors in size and influence. But the party had suffered a series of body blows over the years. Revelations about the Stalinist show trials and purges in the 1930s had weakened its credibility among progressive intellectuals. The advent of the cold war, which had sharpened the identification of communism with subversion and disloyalty, made more Americans of liberal persuasion wary of the party. Within the labor movement, where the CPUSA had especially tried to sink roots, many unions purged Communists from leadership. The relentless persecution of the McCarthy era had taken its toll as well. Congressional hearings, the indictments and trials of key members, FBI harassment, state investigations, the constant projection of the image of the Communist as menace—all these together had shrunk the party's reach. Membership declined, key loyalists went underground, and much of the wider circle of sympathizers simply evaporated.

Khrushchev's denunciation of Stalin was another jolt. Within the party, it opened a short period of vibrant debate. Long-suppressed doubts surfaced, and open exploration of political alternatives was temporarily possible. Within the non-Stalinist left, it raised the promise of a reconfigured socialist politics. Disaffected Communists, independent leftists, and small sectarian groupings might join together to give birth to a new democratic left. In New York, with its unusually large concentration of radicals, the politically engaged were abuzz with expectation. Through much of 1956, while Rustin occupied himself with Montgomery, Muste was attentive to the turmoil on the left. The two were in frequent contact—at weekly meetings of *Liberation*, as key members of the WRL, and through other peace initiatives—and so Rustin was privy to much of what Muste was concocting. In June, shortly after the Madison Square Garden rally in support of the Southern freedom struggle, Muste instigated a public forum on the future of American radicalism at Carnegie Hall. Two thousand came, far more than for any other such event in years. In December, as the bus boycott was ending, Rustin attended a two-day closed meeting in New York that Muste planned. "It is difficult to think of a time," Muste expounded, "when patterns that seemed fixed . . . began dissolving as extensively and rapidly as is the case now. Everywhere there is ferment and motion." Muste posed for independent leftists the stark choice between "a new beginning or increasing sterility."[1]

In February 1957, Rustin was invited to the national congress of the CPUSA. It was the first time in memory that the party allowed outsiders to observe its deliberations, a sign of the upheaval in the organization. His participation brought him to the attention of the FBI. In the succeeding decade, memo after memo about him referred to his presence there as the self-evident reason to amass information and maintain surveillance of his activities. Rustin also signed on to a new experiment of Muste's, the American Forum for Socialist Education, a loose association of individuals designed to stimulate debate within the left and smooth the path toward a new socialist organization. But Muste's willingness to open it to disaffected Communist Party members sparked vitriolic anti-Communist attacks, and Rustin quickly reconsidered his sponsorship. In his letter of resignation, he deplored the misrepresentation of the project: "The press created the distortion that the Forum's purpose was to provide a new political action group for the Communist Party. In the present climate of fear and political conformity, this distortion has done grave injury to work I am doing in another area. . . . I must reluctantly withdraw completely. . . . I take this step solely to refrain from compromising in the eyes of a confused public those with whom I am currently associated in other very important endeavors." Rustin sent a copy to King, signaling that his concerns were primarily about burdening King and his organization with the taint of Communist affiliation. He remained aloof from further attempts by New York radicals to create a political vehicle designed to launch a post-Stalinist left.[2]

Although Rustin remained organizationally unaffiliated, his influence reached far into these worlds. His connection to King and the emerging Southern freedom movement rooted him in contemporary mass struggles in ways that most white leftists in New York were not. Rustin transmitted the Montgomery story and other instances of black community mobilization into New York's left. For the denizens of this sectarian world, he opened a window onto vibrant efforts to change American society. Through Rustin, the crowd around Irving Howe, who had just founded *Dissent*, an independent leftist journal, and around Michael Harrington, a former member of the Catholic Worker Movement who had gravitated toward the socialist orbit of Max Shachtman, another fixture of the New York left, trained some of their attention on the South. In long evenings of drinking and sociability at Greenwich Village bars like the White Horse Tavern and the Paddock, Rustin drew from the civil rights struggle broader analytic conclusions about popular mobilizations, the state of American politics, and the prospects for revolutionary upheavals. He spun out half-formed conjectures about what he called "social dislocation," how protests could raise the cost of maintaining the status quo so high that those in power would have to act. Since, as Michael Harrington described these years, the left in New York was "so short on practice we had nothing else to do but become long on theory," Rustin at least gave them something concrete to speculate about. In these circles, he appeared akin to what the Italian Communist writer, Antonio Gramsci, described as an "organic intellectual." He had accumulated two decades of resistance to racial injustice and was shaping these experiences into new understandings of how to build effective radical movements.[3]

THE INSPIRATION THAT Montgomery offered not only percolated among American leftists but also infected the nearly moribund domestic peace movement. Although the imminence of world war appeared to have receded with the end of the conflict in Korea, fears of an atomic holocaust remained close to the surface of popular consciousness in the mid-1950s. Hollywood released a parade of B-grade science-fiction movies that played to the subliminal anxieties of Americans. Apart from the civil defense protest in New York in 1955, American pacifists had hardly stirred since the start of the Korean War. But in the spring of 1957, peace organizations seemed to awaken as if from a stupor. Suddenly there was movement again where for years there had been none.

Rustin played a unique role in the pacifist revival. As head of the WRL, he was part of the ongoing conversation within peace circles about issues, strategies, and tactics. His opinion carried weight, partly because of the personal sacrifice that his pacifism had demanded during World War II, but also because of his front-line experimentation with active nonviolence as a route to racial justice. Rustin stood at the juncture linking various political tendencies within American pacifism. He had ties to the religiously motivated and to those coming from the left; he had made his own moral witness and had embraced the call to action as well. Most of all, Rustin transmitted the experience of the black freedom struggle to peace activists. Throughout 1956, he traveled, lectured, and wrote, communicating vividly and passionately the power of nonviolence as it made its strength felt on the sidewalks of Montgomery. He tried to explain how the movement for racial justice might transform American politics, creating a space for the message of peace to be broadcast loudly once again. In the pages of *Liberation*, Rustin made every effort to trumpet the good news. As the boycott ended and Rustin met with Southern clergy to lay plans for the future, *Liberation*'s opening editorial of 1957 proclaimed "the rebirth of nonviolence. . . . Not since the death of Gandhi has there been so much discussion of nonviolence as there is today."[4]

In this context, representatives from most of the peace organizations that had survived the McCarthy era assembled in Philadelphia in April 1957. Rustin was there, as were Muste, Robert Gilmore of the AFSC, and Norman Thomas. The key item on the agenda was a campaign against nuclear weapons testing. Because the participants embraced a range of perspectives on pacifism and social change, they could not settle on a unified plan of action, so they decided to pursue two different approaches and hope they would work to the advantage of each. One group opted for mainstream advocacy dedicated to publicizing the dangers of the arms race and nuclear testing. Over the next months, the pacifists who took this approach formed the Committee for a Sane Nuclear Policy. SANE, as it came to be called, made a big splash in the fall, when it placed an ad in the *New York Times* calling for an end to nuclear testing. The outpouring of support led to rapid growth, and chapters formed around the country.[5]

The other group, of which Rustin was part, resolved to apply direct action methods to the nuclear weapons issue. Rustin and the WRL joined with representatives from the Catholic Worker, the Women's International League for Peace and Freedom, the FOR, and the AFSC to create a loose, ad hoc committee to coordinate a series of actions. Eventually naming themselves the Committee for Nonviolent Action (CNVA), they chose Lawrence Scott, who had long worked within the orbit of Rustin's influence, to direct the project. Rustin served on the executive committee and, with Bob Gilmore, was responsible for raising money.[6]

In mid-June, Rustin left for a six-week trip to Britain. The main order of business was the War Resisters International triennial gathering that brought together pacifists from twenty-one nations. Rustin pushed "to get a project started among all the WRI sections for the purpose of banning H-bomb tests." He also delivered word of what had happened in Montgomery, which he called "a post-Gandhian contribution to the practice of non-violence."[7]

Rustin returned to New York on August 6, the twelfth anniversary of the bombing of Hiroshima, just as activists in CNVA were completing their first major protest on the nuclear testing issue. Almost fifty pacifists from around the country, half of them members of the WRL, had assembled in Las Vegas late in July and converged on the desert site of the next above-ground nuclear explosion. Eleven of them, including Jim Peck from the WRL staff, passed through the gate at Camp Mercury and were immediately arrested. Although the test took place the next day ("a nightmare come true," in Peck's words), journalists reporting on the test publicized the protest in newspapers around the country, including the *New York Times*.[8]

Excited by the visibility of this first action, the sponsoring organizations of CNVA reconvened in late August. As Rustin reported, they decided to set up "a national long-term action project to continue the protest against testing nuclear weapons," seeing the work "as the first step toward disarmament."[9] Intent on embracing high-profile actions, Rustin and the core group in CNVA settled on two main projects for the following spring. They decided to sail into the South Pacific, where the Eisenhower administration planned another round of atomic tests, as a way of dramatizing their opposition. Simultaneously, a delegation of pacifists intended to visit major European cities, with Moscow as their final destination. Wanting to make clear to a nation obsessed by communism that they were not part of a Kremlin conspiracy, they planned on engaging Soviet citizens in public debate and meeting with government representatives.

Rustin arranged to have both events publicized and coordinated from his office, and he was soon caught up in the swirl of activity surrounding them. He had been chosen as one of the members of the "Mission to Moscow," as the trip was jokingly called, while Jim Peck, another WRL staffer, had volunteered to be on the crew of the *Golden Rule*, the ketch that would sail to the South Pacific. Each week that winter, Rustin and Gilmore traveled to Philadelphia, where they put in two days of work in the CNVA office. Just before departing for Europe, Rustin helped launch a peace walk to New York, with several hundred pacifists converging on the United Nations from Philadelphia and New Haven.

In April 1958, Rustin participated in what became the signature event of the British antinuclear movement: the first Easter weekend march from London to Aldermaston, the site of a nuclear weapons facility. At the kick-off rally in Trafalgar Square, he was a featured speaker, an emissary from the American peace movement. "There is a great deal more going on than most people would gather from what the press reports in Britain," Rustin explained to the crowd. He told them about the *Golden Rule*, which at that moment was sailing to Hawaii. "Come what may, even if they are burnt to death they are going to sail into the test area," he dramatically expounded. Rustin stressed the need to stop the headlong rush toward destruction. He tied the rally to Gandhi's work in India and antiapartheid campaigns in South Africa. He urged them to think beyond nationhood and see themselves as part of a common humanity. Describing how blacks in Montgomery had put themselves on the line for freedom, Rustin exhorted them all to "use our bodies in direct action, non-cooperation, whatever is required to bring our government to its senses."[10]

Rustin's remarks received mention in the press in Britain and at home, which drew the attention of the FBI. J. Edgar Hoover asked his subordinates for information "as to identity of Negro allegedly leading demonstrations in London" and "whether or not he had been called to Director's attention in connection with his present activities and if not, why not." The responding memo reported that "this Negro had been a problem in the past. . . . Rustin is ardent pacifist and is considered to be foremost Negro exponent in U.S. of doctrine of 'passive resistance.'" The State Department, it concluded, "is well aware of his background, having been furnished investigative reports" from the FBI in the past.[11]

Still accustomed to American peace protests that were attracting at best a few hundred people, Rustin was thrilled by the crowd that marched to Aldermaston. "It was a moving experience," he later wrote in *Liberation*, "to be part of the ten thousand who left London on the fifty-mile hike. For a good part of the way, we had to contend with a slow English drizzle, which dampened everything but our spirits." He took heart from the presence of "hundreds upon hundreds of young people." Linking them to the "beat generation" at home, Rustin saw in miniature the awakening of the next generation to peace and justice issues.[12]

A few days after the march, the other members of the delegation to Moscow joined Rustin. Except for Lawrence Scott, they were not strongly identified as peace activists but were deliberately chosen to represent a concerned American citizenry. In London, they delivered a letter at 10 Downing Street. They reached Paris just as the French government was overthrown and the Fourth Republic was collapsing. Among everyone, Rustin found, "all political discussion led to Algeria," where the French were struggling against a fiercely determined independence movement. The right, the center, and even elements of the left believed France had to develop a nuclear arsenal to be considered a major power; it needed the Sahara to test the weapons. "This means that Algeria must be held at all costs," Rustin wrote. The connection between the arms race and colonialism had never seemed clearer. In Germany, they made stops in Cologne, Bonn, Berlin, and Hamburg. The visit to Hamburg coincided with the largest antibomb rally on the Continent so far—"tens of thousands," according to his WRL report."[13]

Rustin and the tiny peace delegation arrived in Helsinki on April 28. The Soviet embassy in Washington had promised to have visas waiting for them, and Rustin carried a letter to that effect. For the next two weeks, they made daily inquiries at the consulate. A Finnish travel agency that worked with Soviet Intourist made calls for them to Moscow. Rustin and his traveling partners wrote to the Soviet ambassador in Helsinki and to Andrei Gromyko, the Russian foreign secretary, to no avail. A Soviet functionary let them know that they should not expect the visas. When Rustin asked for notification in writing, he was told that none would be forthcoming. The Soviet government did not want to put in print its denial of visas to a group of Americans whose outlook confounded the polarized politics of the cold war. As their final effort, they sent a letter directly to Khrushchev explaining their mission, and another letter to 150 nongovernmental Russian leaders—scientists, writers, educational administrators, artists. After sixteen days of waiting, Rustin and the others had no choice but to return home.[14]

Although Soviet intransigence left the five deflated, the trip provided Rustin with grist for political speculation. On a positive note, he reported that the team received "excellent press" in England, France, and Germany. "The group was a great inspiration to the European movement." Their travels had opened "unusual opportunities . . . to talk with scientists, educators, and political leaders," he told the WRL. "The most significant aspect of the trip was the exchange on techniques and program and discussions with the key pacifist leaders in Europe."[15]

But Rustin also had a more sobering analysis of what he had seen. He shared his reflections with the pacifist and socialist readers of *Liberation.* "The problem in Europe—as in the United States—is the absence of a vital socialist movement," he wrote. Everywhere he went, he had seen evidence of a rising opposition but one that lacked a political home. The parties of the democratic left—Labour in Britain, the Socialists in France, the Social Democrats in West Germany—were too deeply implicated in cold war politics to be able to rally discontent over the nuclear arms race. To his comrades in the reviving peace movement at home, Rustin directed a pointed message: "The central problem facing the peace movement is that of creating a political form through which it can express itself on both domestic and foreign policy. If no such political form is created, the peace walks and demonstrations will have had no practical meaning, but will prove to have been only a futile protest, a kind of broken, faltering voice raised against the ominous thunder of rockets and H-bombs."[16] Unspoken but implied was a nagging dissatisfaction with the peace movement. Would it ever break through its isolation? Would Rustin continue to organize events that offered emotional satisfaction to participants but left cold war rivalries and the arms race as entrenched as before?

Rustin's musings seem especially prescient because the peace movement at home was about to confront bitterly divisive issues of strategy and tactics. It was hovering between the solitary acts of witness that

Rustin knew well and actions that might pierce public consciousness. The *Golden Rule* project was the precipitating agent.

Albert Bigelow, the captain of the *Golden Rule*, was not a typical pacifist. A New England blue blood and U.S. Navy commander with distinguished service during World War II, he had been deeply shaken by the bombing of Hiroshima and increasingly disaffected from the military. During the Korean War, he resigned his commission in the naval reserves. He became a Quaker, encountered activist pacifists like Rustin, and soon found himself working to build bridges between Americans and the Japanese survivors of the atomic blast.

Bigelow and his crew first departed from California in February. After a series of mishaps, they finally arrived in Honolulu, only to be served with a court injunction. This they repeatedly defied as they tried to reach the testing site. Finally jailed by a judge who had lost all patience with them, Bigelow and the others spent much of the summer incarcerated. As the crew of the *Golden Rule* languished behind bars, Earle and Barbara Lewis, along with their two teenaged children, were heading straight toward the testing area. The Lewis family had been on vacation in Hawaii as the pacifist drama unfolded, and it moved them enough that they resolved to take up the call. Acting spontaneously, they evaded the coast guard and made it into the test zone before being stopped.[17]

The saga of the *Golden Rule* surpassed the best expectations of the pacifists in CNVA. The press ate the story up. Each phase allowed the peace movement to plan other activities—a vigil outside the White House, picket lines in front of federal buildings in cities around the country, a sit-in at the headquarters of the Atomic Energy Commission—that raised the profile of the antitesting campaign considerably. "This was propaganda of the deed, one's physical body thrown into a void," one supporter noted.[18] It was an approach to change that Rustin had advocated when he spoke in Trafalgar Square.

Later that summer, this "propaganda of the deed" escalated. Some members of CNVA initiated an action without the approval of the coalition. Converging on Cheyenne, Wyoming, near the construction site of the first intercontinental ballistic missile (ICBM) base in the

United States, several dozen pacifists attempted to win over the construction workers to their view. When days of leafleting and talk led to nothing but hostility from the local people, the protesters shifted toward obstructionist tactics. Attempts to prevent trucks from entering the construction site brought arrests and jail terms; it also led to the serious injury of a protester who was run over by a vehicle. The Cheyenne action precipitated a debate among pacifists that lasted the better part of a year. Issues surfaced not only about tactics and strategy but also about the moral basis for political action. In many ways, the discussions foreshadowed conflicts that erupted during the next decade—in the black freedom movement, New Left, and antiwar movement.

Lawrence Scott had been deeply upset both by the choice of the construction site as the next target of protest and the deployment of obstructionist tactics. To Scott, the Cheyenne action violated everything that had made CNVA work well until then. It was planned by a few over the reservations of many. The tactics broke with the spiritual foundation of Gandhian militancy. The protesters had thrown "the whole burden of the inherited and current complex of evil that center in an ICBM Base upon an uninitiated truck driver." Scott pleaded that "we not corrupt the means which we use or destroy the little soul-force we may possess by coercion and obstruction." Extremist actions around a goal for which little education had been done, would let the government label them as "a crack-pot nuisance" and lose them the goodwill they had previously generated through the press.[19] Scott insisted on patience as well as passion, restraint as well as initiative. He asked that the activist always be strategist, even if it meant disciplining one's moral outrage. But the moral fervor that pacifism unleashed in many of its partisans made rational calculation difficult. Weighed against the adrenaline that direct action released, a call such as Scott's fell on deaf ears.

Brad Lyttle, Scott's chief opponent in these debates, perfectly illustrated the contrary position. Considerably younger than Rustin, he grew up in a pacifist household and refused conscription into the military during the Korean War. Lyttle had participated in the Cheyenne actions, which he likened to "spiritual explosions." In response to Scott, he wrote that pacifists "had a moral imperative for obstructing work [on the missile site] by every moral, non-violent means available. The action was a religious witness and act of conscience that made real to the construction workers the moral issue of murder."[20]

When it became clear that a large number of CNVA activists, Muste among them, shared Lyttle's view, Scott resigned from the organization, as did Bigelow and some others. In the spring of 1959, CNVA went ahead with plans for an action similar to that at Cheyenne, this time at an ICBM base just outside Omaha. There were vigils, public meetings, leafleting, and, finally, civil disobedience. Muste, well into his seventies, attempted to scale a fence to get inside the military installation. The actions antagonized many in the broader pacifist community. The press was almost entirely negative, and pacifists made few happy contacts with local people. But for those with "philosophical anarchist leanings" and those with a penchant for "absolute witness," as Scott described them, the action was a great success.[21]

Rustin was present throughout these debates. He was on the executive committee of CNVA and was an editor of *Liberation,* in whose pages these debates were played out. Jim Peck, a WRL staff member, very much supported obstructionist tactics. Yet Rustin's views are uncharacteristically absent from the written record, and one can only speculate as to the reason for the silence. Rustin had certainly been on the militant side of such debates before. He had often taken what he once called "the all-out position." In the early 1950s, when the cold war had shifted into the hot war in Korea and pacifist prospects were at low ebb, he urged his comrades in the FOR to put their bodies on the line for their beliefs. At the WRL, he led a constituency that tended to be on the militant edge of the peace movement. So one might reasonably believe he welcomed this militant turn.

But perhaps not. Perhaps the silence indicated reservations, not agreement. Rustin had been mulling over the long-range strategic tasks of the peace movement, the need for it to break through its isolation and create, as he had put it, "a political form" to carry through its agenda for domestic and international politics. To the degree that Cheyenne,

Omaha, and similar actions fractionalized the peace movement and isolated it from mainstream Americans, it would have triggered doubts in
Rustin, reminding him of the "futile protest" and "broken, faltering
voice" about which he had recently written.

IF RUSTIN DID HARBOR reservations about the tack that militant
pacifists were taking, they came from his deepening involvement with
the black freedom struggle in the South. There, Rustin had before him
the model of a successfully expanding movement. Even as he attended
to the business of the WRL and the new peace activism, he pushed to
free up time to work with King and build Northern support for the
Southern struggle. In partnership with Levison, Baker, and others, he
debated strategy and tactics for black freedom in the wake of the *Brown*
decision and the Montgomery boycott. During these years, the two
causes, peace and racial justice, pulled at him insistently; the experience
he had in one informed how he looked at the other.

In February 1957, a few weeks after the Atlanta conference that
launched the Southern Christian Leadership Conference (SCLC),
Rustin traveled to New Orleans for a second gathering with King and
the ministers allied with him. To the surprise of no one, President Eisenhower had rejected the appeal of the Atlanta meeting that he address
the issue of compliance with *Brown* and so, in New Orleans, Rustin
helped draft a rejoinder. The telegram spoke of "an organized campaign
of violence and terror" to deter school integration, "a breakdown of
law, order, and morality," and "a threat to government by law." It again
urged Eisenhower to use "the moral weight at his command" to avert
tragedy. In the absence of presidential action, the ministers told Eisenhower that "we shall have no moral choice but to lead a pilgrimage."[22]

Charged with moving the "Prayer Pilgrimage" along, Rustin returned to New York. Easily securing Randolph's endorsement, he had
Baker and Levison help him flesh out plans for the event. They framed
the proposal in ways designed to appease the NAACP's wariness about
populist mobilizations.[23] In March, King and Randolph conferred with
Wilkins, who found it difficult to remain aloof from an event that was
already being talked about. The three agreed to hold it in May, on the

third anniversary of the *Brown* decision, the NAACP's great triumph. The rally would not be directed against Eisenhower, an overwhelmingly popular figure, but instead would aim its message at Congress, where civil rights legislation was on the table. Early in April, Randolph, King, and Wilkins met again, this time in Washington with sixty black ministers and community leaders, and they announced the pilgrimage at a press conference.[24]

Responsibility for organizing the event fell to Rustin. The WRL released him from his duties while he worked on it. He pulled on his peace networks to ensure that pacifist contingents would be there. Through Randolph, he worked the union leadership in New York to secure endorsements and financial backing. Thomas Kilgore, the activist pastor of Harlem's Friendship Baptist Church, went on the road to win over ministers outside the South. Now that Wilkins had committed to the event, he issued orders to chapter presidents to mobilize their troops for the occasion. Baker reached out to her In Friendship contacts, and Levison helped with the finances. As word of the event circulated, volunteers poured into the NAACP office in Manhattan, where Rustin had set up shop. Nothing like this had happened in recent memory, and Rustin's personality and energy inspired them to work harder. Excitement percolated through the office whenever news arrived about the contingents that were coming: a freedom train from Boston, a caravan of buses from Los Angeles, a large group from the United Auto Workers in Detroit.[25]

The rally at the Lincoln Memorial proved a great success, a first rehearsal for the more famous March on Washington a few years away. Rustin constructed a program that moved back and forth between prayer, song, and political remarks. Soloists and choruses performed the National Anthem, "My Country 'Tis of Thee," "Lift Ev'ry Voice and Sing," and a number of spirituals. Ministers read from Scripture. James and Theresa Gordon, two youngsters who had braved abuse to integrate schools in Clay, Kentucky, placed a wreath at the foot of the Lincoln statue. Activist ministers like C. K. Steele of Tallahassee and Fred Shuttlesworth of Birmingham reported from the front lines of the Southern struggle. Several members of Congress—Adam Clayton

Powell, Charles Diggs, Paul Douglas, and Jacob Javits—spoke about pending civil rights legislation. Randolph, Wilkins, and Mordecai Johnson, president of Howard University, made remarks. King, the last speaker, linked events in the United States to freedom struggles in Africa. Delivering a Gandhian message, he shaped this first national oration around the refrain, "Give Us the Ballot." Throughout the program, the crowd was reminded that this was a religious assemblage and was asked not to applaud. The silence added a solemnity to the whole affair that magnified its power for participants. Septima Clark, a respected Southern activist based at the Highlander School in Tennessee, wrote immediately afterward of how she "wept tears of joy" to see those people massed at the Lincoln Memorial. "I'll never forget that day," she told Randolph. Estimates of attendance ranged from 15,000 to 25,000, large enough to please all the planners. [26]

Two weeks later, the glow cooled when an editorial in the *Amsterdam News*, New York's chief African American newspaper, heaped praise on King and called Wilkins to task. "Dr. Martin Luther King, the 28-year-old minister from Montgomery, has emerged from the Prayer Pilgrimage to Washington as the number one leader of sixteen million Negroes in the United States," the piece opened. "In calling the Pilgrimage and getting out in front of it, King gambled his entire future as a leader—and won. . . . The big question now is—whither now, Rev. King? . . . the people will follow him anywhere." James Hicks, the writer, went on to criticize Wilkins for not throwing "the full weight" of the NAACP behind the pilgrimage. Hicks said King could snatch Wilkins's job from him "thumbs down" if he wanted it. He painted Wilkins and others as discredited figures "standing on the sidelines wondering how to get back as the head of their flock."[27]

Wilkins responded furiously. Extremely protective of the NAACP, he sent a thirty-point letter to the paper enumerating in precise detail every contribution it had made to the event. Wilkins also dashed off a letter to King, calling the article "a crude attempt to stir jealousy and rivalry." Adding to Wilkins's frustration, NAACP chapters around the country were trying to snag King as a speaker, thus magnifying his stature. Wilkins himself had announced, just before the article appeared, that the NAACP was bestowing on King its prestigious Spingarn Award.[28]

As if to confirm what Hicks had to say, King was back in Washington in June conferring with Vice President Richard Nixon. The meeting materialized out of an unplanned encounter, when the two men chatted at the independence celebrations in Ghana. Nixon casually invited him to continue their conversations in Washington, and King pursued the offer. Since Eisenhower had avoided meetings with civil rights leaders, King's visit with Nixon was an important opening to the administration. Rustin told King that the meeting was "already regarded among Negro forces and the Negro press as an event of singular importance— indeed, as a 'summit conference.' " He and Levison prepped King about what to ask for and what to avoid.[29] The Nixon meeting was particularly galling to Wilkins, since the NAACP maintained a continuing presence in Washington while King was essentially still a local leader.

Rustin was hardly displeased at the public criticisms of Wilkins and the NAACP or by the attention King was receiving. King's rise to prominence struck Rustin as just what the civil rights movement needed. With Baker and Levison, Rustin spent long hours in these years speculating about how to dislodge the NAACP from its pride of place as the preeminent voice in the civil rights field. Baker recalled that the three of them "used to sit up until two and three o'clock in the morning" debating what could be done to inject "some degree of mass orientation" to the freedom struggle. The NAACP had the membership and the organizational infrastructure, but "its philosophy had not been expressed in the direction of real confrontation or using mass action." Levison, too, remembered the private discussions of these years. He described the late 1950s as "a period of a little-observed internal struggle between two tendencies. One was that of the NAACP and Roy Wilkins. . . . They felt that mass action—and Roy Wilkins stated this very frankly— only had the value of letting blacks blow off steam. . . . He simply didn't believe in it." Rachelle Horowitz, a young associate of Rustin, remembered that "he was always outflanking the NAACP." Randolph, who was privy to many of these discussions, allowed himself to be used as "a cover . . . a cloak for Bayard." As Rustin pushed for mass action, he could present himself as acting on Randolph's behalf. "Mr. Randolph asked me to, Mr. Randolph wanted me to" were refrains he used often.[30]

Certainly by the time of the Prayer Pilgrimage, Rustin had decided that King offered the greatest hope of a counterbalance to the NAACP, one that might provoke popular mobilizations for racial justice. Although King's understanding of politics and social change was still limited, Rustin recognized his advocacy of nonviolent resistance and his charismatic qualities as essential resources for transforming the black struggle. Already, by the spring of 1957, Rustin detected new stirrings. In Friendship had awakened the interest of organizations like the AFSC in events in the South, while CORE chapters, quiescent for a number of years, were experiencing an infusion of energy. Rustin believed that King had the capacity to accelerate these incipient trends. As he wrote to King a week before the pilgrimage, "Actually, Martin, the question of where you move next is more important than any other question Negroes face today."[31]

For the rest of the decade, Rustin applied himself to King's emergence as a national leader. He made himself useful in all sorts of ways. He introduced King to labor leaders, like Ralph Helstein of the Packinghouse Workers, who then became financial supporters of the SCLC. He drafted speeches and articles for King and provided line editing for King's own writing. Rustin helped prepare *Stride Toward Freedom*, King's account of the Montgomery bus boycott, offering comments on chapters and working with King's agent and publisher to help with the book's promotion. When King had important meetings, such as the conference with Nixon, Rustin advised him about how to proceed. Rustin pushed the inexperienced young minister always to see the broader context for the fight against Jim Crow. He argued with King that "the uplift of all poor people is part of the struggle of Negroes for justice." He drew connections between the freedom movement in the South and those for independence in Africa, at times inserting into King's talks material he had used in his own lectures on Africa. Rustin linked King with social justice organizations like CORE and the AFSC. He put his own contacts at King's disposal. Before the trip to Ghana in 1957, Rustin asked Bill Sutherland to help shape an itinerary so that the trip might be most useful for King. When Tom Mboya, a Kenyan labor leader, came to the United States, Rustin arranged for Mboya and King to meet.[32]

Rustin communicated with King by frequent telephone calls rather than through lengthy letters. Unlike in later years, when FBI taps of both King's and Rustin's phones offer a rich source for reconstructing the texture of their working relationship, the evidence is often less direct for these years. Occasionally there is a letter from King, imploring Rustin to "let me hear from you immediately concerning this please." More often, one can glimpse through Levison's letters to King the indispensable role that Rustin was playing. Levison and Rustin lived a block away from each other. They visited sometimes daily and often ate dinner together; their topic of conversation was frequently King. Like Rustin, Levison was trying to make himself useful to King, though he had much less to offer. Levison's letters almost always mentioned Rustin. "Bayard and I" was a common refrain. "Bayard and I labored long into the night," Levison wrote at one point. Or "Bayard did express himself." Or "these are some of my thoughts, which Bayard shares." At times it seemed as if Levison was using Rustin, referring to him not simply because they did talk frequently but as a source of legitimacy.[33]

Rustin was doing so much work for King that he was put on the payroll of the cash-strapped SCLC. His involvement inevitably meant that he was less available to serve the pacifist goals of his own organization. Yet at least in these years, the WRL seemed comfortable with Rustin's commitment. "It was an exciting time," Ralph DiGia said of the period after Montgomery. "We were glad. We wanted [Bayard] to go. It was very important to the peace movement, this man. I think that Martin Luther King put nonviolence on the map. I mean, before people would speak about Gandhi. But the civil rights movement put it on the map. People started to talk about it."[34] With the United States barely removed from the worst days of the McCarthy period, nonviolent protest on one issue contributed to a climate that made dissent on other issues easier as well. King's commitment to nonviolence and direct action, thanks in no small part to Rustin's influence, was a boon to the mission of the WRL, and Rustin's association with King gave the organization more credibility than it had ever had. Rustin's base in the WRL made it

easier for him to navigate around the discomfort of some of the ministers in SCLC about his politics and sexuality. His location in New York
gave him just the degree of separation he needed to be able to keep
working with King and not set off too many warning bells.

But striking a balance between the needs of organizations, individuals, and movements was not always easy to achieve, and when Rustin
had to choose, he chose King. A trip to India in 1959 was a case in
point. From the time King's work in Montgomery became an international story, a chorus of voices pressed King to travel to Gandhi's homeland. Certainly Rustin encouraged the idea, as did many others in the
American pacifist community. Unlike in 1949, when Rustin's presence
in India provoked concerned cables from American diplomats, by the
late 1950s, King's stature in the movement for racial equality made him
an ideal American emissary to an Asian nation unaligned in the cold
war. Chester Bowles, a former American ambassador to India, wrote to
King excitedly about the prospect of a visit. "Nothing would spread
more goodwill for America than a visit here by someone who has tried
to apply Gandhi's principles in the United States," Bowles wrote King.
"As you know, there is nothing that hurts our relations with Asians
more, or undermines America's prestige more than our lingering racial
discrimination."[35]

The AFSC contributed much of the financing for King's 1959 visit,
planned an itinerary to coincide with King's wishes, and provided King
and his wife, Coretta, with a guide. It saw the trip as an opportunity to
deepen King's connection to an international community dedicated
to nonviolence. Yet the venture proved disappointing and frustrating to
the AFSC. Jim Bristol, the staffer in India who devoted weeks of time
to it, was disturbed because "this whole trip is being thought of in terms
of the *return* to U.S.A. and what will make an impact and produce an effect there." He described the Kings as "going through India wearing
BLINDERS." By the time they left, all Bristol could say was that "the
whole experience has been a nightmare." Within the AFSC, much of
the blame was directed at Rustin. "There certainly was insufficient communication between the Kings and AFSC," the staff person in the Phila-

delphia office complained. "As you know, Bayard Rustin was acting as intermediary." Rustin had filtered the requests the AFSC was making of King in ways that shaped the trip toward King's wishes, not those of the AFSC. "We will never get ourselves in such a situation again."[36]

Besides the day-to-day assistance Rustin offered, he also attempted to chart a direction for King's new organization. Initially, SCLC was simply a collection of Southern black ministers who gathered around King. The Prayer Pilgrimage launched the group. The crowds graphically displayed for the attending ministers the potential national power that might accrue to their efforts. Still, they lacked a program to move the South away from Jim Crow and toward a dream of racial justice.

Rustin saw the civil rights legislation that Congress was debating in 1957 as an opportunity to construct such a program. By early August, Congress was nearing the final stage of its deliberations. Though amendments in the Senate considerably diluted the strength of the original bill, it was still the first such national legislation since Reconstruction. The 1957 law established a federal civil rights commission and authorized creation of a civil rights division in the Justice Department with the power to investigate voting rights violations. Even as conflict continued to rage in the South about Jim Crow school systems, the new legislation offered civil rights activists a promising second front in their struggle and new weapons for fighting. Rustin explained to King the bill's potential. In a memo he drafted while the Senate was still debating amendments, he pointed out that "history sometimes has demonstrated that inadequate legislation supported by mass action can accomplish more than adequate legislation which remains unenforced for the absence of a determined mass movement. . . . The full effect will depend in large degree upon the program of a sustained mass movement." He argued for seeing the right to vote as "not alone a political necessity. It is a moral imperative."[37]

At a meeting of the SCLC in August 1957, the group endorsed a proposal from King to launch a "Crusade for Citizenship" that winter, a regionwide voter registration campaign among blacks in the South. Rustin worked during the fall on plans for the crusade, which involved simultaneous kickoff meetings in a score of cities. Using the model of the race relations institutes that he and Houser had implemented a decade earlier, he outlined the contents of a training workshop. Participants would learn about the provisions of the new federal law, hear from community leaders about the history of local efforts to register, and then fan out across town to conduct fact-finding interviews with public officials and black residents about voter registration. Rustin wanted the ministers of SCLC to use their pulpits to deliver sermons on the franchise and make their churches sites for citizenship education. He envisioned the crusade as the basis for a "grass-roots movement" rising out of Southern black communities and reaching for national influence. The effects could be dramatic. By election time in 1958, Rustin thought it might be possible to mobilize communities around nonviolent action if the South remained obstructionist and the federal government lackadaisical in its response. "If people use legislation, often they achieve . . . more than the law ever intended," Rustin explained.[38]

For a time, it seemed that Rustin himself might go South to see these plans through to fruition. Neither King nor his associates in the SCLC knew how to implement a community organizing plan of such broad scope. Without an experienced hand to guide it, the crusade faced a premature death. But Rustin's sexuality and radical politics made him an unpalatable choice to many of the ministers. In circumspect fashion, Ella Baker later told an interviewer that "there are a number of things that are said as to why [Bayard] didn't go, but from this end, he said he was too busy." Baker's formulation suggests that objections within the SCLC nixed Rustin as the choice to head the project. The uneasiness of King's associates with Rustin meant that, with the expected launch only a few weeks away, no one was shepherding the project along. After a meeting with King at La Guardia airport in January, Rustin and Levison got together with Baker and, in essence, told her that "they had promised [King] that I would come to Atlanta almost immediately. . . . I suppose this is one of the few times in my life that I accepted being used by other people . . . there was the need to start this thing right away. . . . We sat up and talked all night." Soon she was heading to Georgia, working there without an office as she tried to plan inaugural meetings in twenty cities scheduled for Lincoln's birthday.[39]

Baker was a seasoned organizer and well known in the South. Under her guidance, the Crusade for Citizenship had a respectable debut. By April, there was much encouraging news about registration drives in, among other places, New Orleans, Shreveport, Mobile, Houston, Memphis, Durham, and Tallahassee. Baker's reports offered "a fine tonic," Levison wrote to Randolph. They offered relief from the silence of a Northern press that seemed to cover only major crises from the land of Jim Crow.[40] Baker's prognoses, however, did not remain hopeful for long. By midsummer, she was writing to Rustin and Levison, sounding desperate for "a session with you two now. . . . It is obvious that more spirit needs to be injected in the civil rights struggle in the South." She was disturbed by the tendency to freeze Rustin out of work that would bring him into contact with the ministerial base of the SCLC, even when his experience would be critical. "How can Bayard not be included in the leadership of discussions on non-violence?" she asked. Her patience with the ministers was wearing thin. Many of them did not take kindly to a woman in authority, and she was despairing of their self-absorption. SCLC, she later reflected, "never really developed an organizing technique." All that the ministers seemed inclined toward was "just big meetings . . . and other big meetings" where they could hear themselves declaim. To King she sent an impatient memo that summer telling him forthrightly that "we are loosing [*sic*] the initiative in the Civil Rights struggle in the South." SCLC needed to offer something "to inspire thousands of people to act with some of the dramatic force of the Montgomery 'Walk for Freedom.'" The Crusade for Citizenship was not doing this. With only lukewarm follow-through from the ministers, the campaign was kindling little popular enthusiasm.[41]

SCLC's failure around the voting rights issue propelled Rustin to look for another way to build a mass insurgency. More than anything else, school integration remained a burning issue in the South, rousing black families to acts of courage and the white power structure to demagoguery and resistance. Throughout the previous year, Little Rock, Arkansas, had been the scene of a continuing drama. Orval Faubus, the governor, mobilized the National Guard to prevent the integration of Central High. When a federal court injunction ordered the removal of the troops so that integration could begin, mobs of jeering parents greeted the arrival of a group of black students, and white students rampaged through the building. The violence forced Eisenhower to have the National Guard carry out the court's wishes, the first time since Reconstruction that federal troops were dispatched to the South to protect the rights of African Americans. Troops patrolled the corridors of Central High for the remainder of the school year. As the 1958 fall term approached, Faubus threatened to shut the school rather than integrate. State legislatures across the region passed laws designed to obstruct compliance with the *Brown* decision, and school districts besides Little Rock preferred to close their schools rather than compromise on apartheid in public education.

Rustin saw in Faubus and the spreading white resistance an opportunity to mobilize support in the North for the school desegregation effort. He proposed to Randolph a youth march for integrated schools to bring thousands of high school and college students to Washington to press for enforcement of *Brown*. With Randolph's approval, he drafted a telegram that the older leader sent to activists in New York City, calling them to a meeting in early September. "Crisis is at hand for civil rights," the message declared. "Bitter segregationist taking offensive in effort to destroy constitutional government and courts. To support and encourage embattled forces and noble children . . . imperative that forthright active steps be taken."[42] Rustin secured an agreement from King to speak at the rally, which guaranteed attention from the press, and so the group that met with Randolph on September 5 endorsed a call for a youth march five weeks later. Once again, the WRL let Rustin work on the project, and he set himself up in the offices of the Brotherhood of Sleeping Car Porters. Rustin scheduled a "kickoff" rally at the Hotel Theresa in Harlem for September 19, where Randolph announced the march to the press and tied the mobilization to the saga in Little Rock.

The next day, as Rustin was working in the office, he received the alarming news that King, in the midst of a book-signing event just down the street, had been stabbed and seriously wounded. The news sent shock waves through civil rights circles, and for a few days work on the youth march virtually stopped until King's survival seemed assured. Randolph announced that the march would be delayed until October 25.

A month was very little time to pull together a major rally in Washington, and a mass demonstration of adolescents carried its own particular set of challenges. Rustin used the NAACP youth affiliates as one source for recruiting participants and tapped the contacts he had from his college tours under the auspices of the WRL and AFSC. The Young People's Socialist League (YPSL) also took the march on as a project, using their campus chapters to enlist students to attend. Through the canvassing of Maida Springer, a labor activist close to Randolph, unions coughed up much of the funds needed to plan the event.

The day went off without a hitch, with beautiful fall weather smiling on the more than 10,000 young people who came to Washington that day. Rustin got Jackie Robinson, a national hero as the first black baseball player in the major leagues, and Harry Belafonte, a singer and actor whose star was rising very rapidly in the late 1950s, to lead the marchers along Constitution Avenue to the Lincoln Memorial. They provided an air of excitement for their legion of young admirers. Coretta King delivered her husband's speech. Playing on the theme of marching for freedom, it called up images of Moses leading his people out of Egypt, slaves making the long trek north before the Civil War, Gandhi and his followers striding to the sea and, of course, the people of Montgomery crushing bus segregation under tens of thousands of walking feet. "You are proving," Coretta told the young crowd, "the so-called 'silent generation' is not so silent. And the so-called 'beat generation' . . . is definitely not 'beat.'" Afterward, presidential aides received a delegation at the White House.[43]

Almost everyone involved in planning the march came away thrilled by the outcome. Levison shared with King his view that "it definitely triggered a student movement for civil rights on major campuses." He called it "a development of incalculable value." Rustin prepared a post-march report for supporters in which he described the event as "the largest youth demonstration ever held in Washington." In his estimation, "students and young people in general were awakened and mobilized to *active* participation in the movement for racial equality." From his vantage point as chief organizer, he was most impressed by how "a remarkably broad [coalition] . . . worked together in closest harmony to make the March the tremendous success it was." So high was the enthusiasm that when Rustin proposed a second mobilization for the spring, no one but the NAACP dissented. Wilkins grumbled that "mass lobbying is looked upon with horror" by professionals in Washington, but the swell of support was so spontaneous that he had to acquiesce.[44]

Randolph asked the WRL to release Rustin for six more months to work on the march, but Rustin already had a speaking tour planned early in the year so his board balked, approving instead a much shorter leave. Still, building on the success of the first one, he was able to extend the reach of his organizing. As part of the plan, he conceived a petition campaign so that young people in their high schools, colleges, neighborhoods, and churches could collect signatures from the many youth who would not be able to march. He had Randolph approach Daisy Bates, the charismatic leader of the Little Rock integration effort, and invite her to speak because he knew her presence "would electrify everyone." He convened a meeting of major labor leaders in New York, like Mike Quill of the Transport Workers Union and Harry Van Arsdale of the Central Labor Council, to secure not only their endorsement but the money to support a national campaign. He successfully lobbied the National Student Association, which represented student governments on more than 400 campuses, and won its agreement to circulate the petition among all its member groups. Sam Rayburn, the Texas representative who was Speaker of the House, promised to receive a student delegation with the petitions. Ten days before the march, Randolph sent Wilkins an excited letter informing him that "an impressive success is certain." He was especially pleased that, through Rustin's efforts, the campaign was "awakening new support in many uncultivated areas." Rustin reported that contingents were coming from

Chicago, the Deep South, Los Angeles, the San Francisco area, and the Pacific Northwest. Reasonable estimates of the crowd that assembled in Washington on April 18 placed the numbers at 25,000, and the student activists brought with them petitions carrying ten times that number in signatures.[45] To someone of Rustin's generation, the outpouring of young people augured good things about the future.

The march was so successful that it pushed Wilkins to squelch any talk of a continuing mobilization. The next month, he wrote to Randolph reminding him of the understanding that both the first and second marches were the product of a temporary coalition of organizations. "We did not intend either last year or this year to finance the setting up of a continuing permanent or semipermanent organization," he informed Randolph. "We have our own permanent and continuing NAACP youth group. Likewise, we have no intention of financing the setting up of a Youth Lobby or any other lobby in Washington." Randolph was quick to reassure Wilkins that the "ad hoc project . . . is to be terminated," but he also sparred with the NAACP leader over the importance of mass mobilizations. The march, he replied, "exceeded the expectations of all of us from the point of view of its dimensions and significance. . . . It is my feeling that there may be numerous other projects for the advancement of civil rights that need dramatization through mass demonstrations."[46]

Although Wilkins was able to forestall the creation of a new organization, he could not stop Rustin from devising yet more schemes to keep the emphasis on popular mobilizations and direct action. Hardly had the coalition that planned the youth marches disbanded when Rustin, Levison, and Randolph began formulating a new project to usher in the 1960s. During the summer, they started discussions about a "convention project" to inject the issue of civil rights into the presidential campaigns of 1960. Rustin had worked on a somewhat analogous plan in 1956 during the Montgomery bus boycott; then, he and Randolph had proposed a civil rights march on Washington in October, a few weeks before the election. But Adam Clayton Powell, Harlem's representative to Congress, and Wilkins had scotched the proposal.

Now Rustin envisioned something larger and more strategic—massive demonstrations outside both conventions coupled with testimony inside. The demonstrations would either force a strong statement on civil rights into the national platforms of the major parties or provoke civil rights proponents into further actions during the election season.

THE WASHINGTON RALLIES THAT Rustin organized in these years had a continuing impact. The Prayer Pilgrimage and youth marches served as training grounds for students and young adults yearning to express idealistic impulses in a decade when anti-Communist fervor squelched most forms of progressive activism. Rustin in particular became something of a magnet, attracting those disaffected by the mainstream. Figures like Stokely Carmichael, Bob Moses, Eleanor Holmes, Tom Kahn, Norman Hill, and many others who became fixtures in the world of civil rights in the next decade spread their activist wings through the connection with Rustin.

By all accounts, he was a thrilling figure to be around. Rachelle Horowitz, a Brooklyn teenager whose life was irrevocably changed by her association with Rustin, said of the environment he created that "it was like being in the presence of history." Rustin not only assigned tasks and provided instruction but was able to regale his young recruits with dramatic stories of activism from the previous two decades and explain to them how the present struggles and opportunities came out of work done in the past. Gerda Lerner, an adult volunteer for the Prayer Pilgrimage, still remembered decades later Rustin's "ability to connect with people and to handle stressful problems with seeming ease. He was witty, and in that dingy office with its poor lighting, worn desks and hard chairs he seemed to be having a good time." Rustin's manner "lent style to whatever he was doing." Like many other young folks who first encountered Rustin, Stokely Carmichael, a Trinidad-born teenager attending high school in New York City, was awestruck by him. "The first time I saw Bayard Rustin," he told an interviewer many years later, "I said 'that's what I want to be.' . . . When I saw him I said, 'that's it, a black man who's a socialist, that's the real answer.' . . . He was like superman. . . . At that moment in time, in my life, he appeared to be the revolution, the most revolutionary man."[47]

While Wilkins worked to abort any new national mobilizations, Rustin directed the energy of these young recruits to a host of local opportunities. He pointed them in the direction of CORE chapters, YPSL campus groups, and AFSC projects. He drew them into citywide campaigns in which he had some involvement, like building support for a fair housing measure in New York City or aiding the efforts of parent organizations to improve the quality of education for black children in the public schools. Just a few weeks after the second Youth March, Local 1199 called a strike among nonprofessional hospital workers in the city. Laboring long hours in laundries and kitchens at barely subsistence wages, many of the workers were black or Puerto Rican. Rustin activated his network of young radicals to help, thus directing someone like Carmichael toward a multiracial labor conflict. "It was through your efforts," Leon Davis, the president of 1199, wrote to Rustin afterward, "that so much public support was mobilized for the strikers."[48]

Of the many youth who passed under Rustin's influence in these years, two came to figure centrally in his political world and personal life. Still teenagers when they met Rustin in 1956, Tom Kahn and Rachelle Horowitz were already budding political activists. They were members of the youth group of the International Socialist League, one of the small Trotskyist organizations comprising the anti-Stalinist left in the 1950s. Its founder, Max Shachtman, had been a fixture in the New York left since the 1920s; he and Muste had ties going back to the Depression decade. Michael Harrington, who had connections to the religious pacifist community and was a drinking buddy of Rustin, was a leader of the group, and he first directed the two Brooklynites to Rustin during the Montgomery bus boycott. Completely enamored of this seasoned organizer, Kahn and Horowitz drank up every bit of political lore Rustin shared and took on any tasks he offered them, no matter how menial and trivial. Attaching themselves closely to Rustin, they worked on all of the mobilizations of the late 1950s.

Along with Harrington, Kahn and Horowitz pressed Rustin to leave the WRL, which they considered an organization of little relevance to the socialist movement they hoped to build. Why, they asked him, was he "hiding my candle under this little tiny pacifist bushel?" though the Socialist Party of the 1950s and the International Socialist League were hardly paths to fame and influence. They also pushed Shachtman to meet Rustin. "Bayard was in the real world," Horowitz recalled. "Bayard was Max's connection to what was really going on in the world." From Rustin, Shachtman absorbed an appreciation of the dynamism of the black freedom struggle, the depth of the discontent and the potential for mobilization in Southern communities, and the implications it might have for a revolutionary politics in the United States.[49]

In the case of Kahn, the attraction that developed was more than political. The culture of the young Trotskyist left in the 1950s bore little resemblance to the asceticism often associated with communist movements. Horowitz described the milieu as "bohemian" and characterized herself and Kahn in those years as "bohemian nut cases," inclined toward sexual freedom and experimentation. Kahn "was gay," Horowitz said, "but wanted to be straight. . . . It was such a different era then." Meeting Rustin changed all that. "Once he met Bayard, then Kahn knew he was gay and had this long-time relationship with Bayard which went through many different stages." Though Kahn was a quarter-century younger than Rustin, he was intellectually precocious, well read, a good writer, and, already as a teenager, thoroughly engrossed by progressive politics and social movements. He could more than hold his own in conversation. Even while Rustin was mentoring Kahn politically, the relationship had a quality of peerness that had been missing in Rustin's romantic life before. The fact that Kahn was also, in the memory of Dave McReynolds, "very good looking . . . a very attractive guy," made the budding relationship all the more appealing. It was all "love and romance" in Horowitz's observation. Before long, Kahn was spending many of his evenings at Rustin's apartment and, in the observation of friends, had practically moved in. As the decade drew to a close, Rustin seemed to have found not only thrilling political engagement but also an intimacy with someone who shared his public commitments.[50]

CHAPTER THIRTEEN

"An Employee of Others"
1959–1960

BEFORE RUSTIN COULD move very far with the 1960 convention project, he was drawn away by a peace movement initiative as audacious as any yet proposed. Late in 1958, France had disclosed that it was developing nuclear weapons. The following year, Charles de Gaulle, the French president, confirmed that France was building a test site at Reggan, deep in the Algerian Sahara. Throughout Africa, de Gaulle's announcement provoked expressions of outrage that a Western colonial power would explode a nuclear weapon on African soil. At a conference of European pacifists early in 1959, April Carter and Michael Randle, two young radicals in the direct action wing of the British antinuclear movement, suggested that an international brigade converge on the test site. The idea met with a chilly response from French pacifists, but Carter and Randle would not let go of it. Carter wrote to George Willoughby, the new director of the CNVA, explaining the concept and asking for support.[1]

The Sahara plan seemed farfetched even by the standards of American direct action pacifists who had sailed into the Pacific and were scaling fences at isolated missile sites. The test site was hundreds of miles from the nearest border. If the team approached from Morocco, they would face electrified barbed wire fences, French ground and air forces, and the prospect of being shot on sight. If they came through Ghana and French West Africa, they would have to travel for days through the most forbidding sections of the Sahara. The American response was decidedly negative. Willoughby thought the chance of eluding the French military across hundreds of miles of barren desert was at best "slim" and described the project as "in the dream stage." Al Hassler at the FOR thought it "completely unrealistic and fanciful" and advised against "wasting any time" discussing it.[2]

But the British pacifists were not to be deterred. Carter and Randle approached Bill Sutherland, who was still working as an assistant to the finance minister in Ghana. His involvement promised contact points for collaboration across the imperialist divide. Carter and Randle also won over the Reverend Michael Scott, a British Gandhian and anti-apartheid activist with high credibility among African leaders and Western pacifists. In London, Carter opened discussions with the expatriate African community, whose members "enthusiastically" embraced the idea. Late in August, British pacifists and Africans together sponsored picketing outside the French embassy and a march from Marble Arch to Trafalgar Square, where they rallied against the proposed tests. They immediately began soliciting African volunteers for the project.[3]

Flying to New York in late September to extract American support, Sutherland met with Rustin. What intrigued Rustin was the "very direct link between the campaign against nuclear weapons and the struggle of the African peoples for freedom."[4] Early in October, he and Michael Scott addressed CNVA's executive committee. They must have been persuasive because Rustin, Muste, and the rest decided to reverse a decision they had made just three weeks earlier and throw CNVA's resources into the project. Sutherland particularly stressed the importance of Rustin's participation in the project. Not only did he have more experience organizing complex direct action projects than did any of the British pacifists, but the fact that he was black and so deeply involved in the Southern freedom struggle would bring credibility among Africans. The WRL voted to send Rustin to Britain and Africa for up to eight weeks in order to supervise planning for the Saharan adventure.

When Rustin arrived in London on October 14, a mess awaited him. His first report, written four days after his arrival, "made everyone groan" in the WRL office. The project, he told them, was "pretty disorganized and confused." The cost was likely to be twice what the

British had estimated; so far they had raised less than £200 of the £6,000 pounds they needed. The project had deepened already existing divisions within the British antinuclear movement. A more moderate faction, led by Canon Collins of the Campaign for Nuclear Disarmament, was actively working to undermine it, as Collins spread the view that the direct action folks were "irresponsible and crack-pot." Ties with the African community in London had also frayed, and negotiations over African participation had broken off.[5]

Rustin revived the contacts with London's Africans. He secured a statement of support from their leaders, which he knew would be helpful once he got to Africa. He met officials at the Moroccan embassy, who offered secretly to finance the cash-starved scheme. The Moroccans urged that the project set off from their own territory, only 300 miles from the site. Rustin sensed that underneath the support was a political minefield. The Moroccan diplomats viewed the project through the lens of Algerian independence. They saw it as an opportunity to embarrass the French and create an international incident that might further erode colonial rule. Although Rustin was sympathetic, he knew he could not confuse the message of the project. He and other radical pacifists were anticolonialist, to be sure. But they were marching into the Sahara in opposition to the nuclear arms race and would have done that no matter which nation exploded an atom bomb. Willoughby and the others back home agreed and insisted he reject any money not offered above board and without strings.[6]

Rustin's arrival in Ghana proved something of a triumphal return. He had met Nkrumah, the prime minister, and Gbedemah, the finance minister, on his first trip to Africa in 1952, when the two were leading the independence movement. Now they governed the first nation in sub-Saharan Africa to break free of colonial rule, and they embraced the antinuclear project. Rustin traveled around Accra in chauffered limousines provided by the government. He spoke at assemblies of several thousand, attended the opening conference of the All African Trade Union Congress, and addressed open-air rallies in Accra and Kumasi. As women's groups paraded on the streets, Rustin and the others delivered to the embassies of the nuclear powers letters of protest against atmospheric testing. Because of the government's backing, the Sahara project was in the newspaper and on the radio almost daily. Rustin received expressions of interest from Nigeria, Guinea, Nyasaland, Basutoland, and Cameroon.

Randle has left a vivid picture of Rustin during these weeks. "He clearly found it immensely exhilarating," Randle wrote. "He delighted in this living proof of an African civilisation stretching back over the centuries—the works of art, the drumming and dancing, even the system of tribal chiefs." On a trip to Kumasi, in the rich cocoa-producing lands of the interior, Rustin "took great pride in being introduced to the traditional chiefs, including the Asantehene (the chief of the warrior Asante tribe) before whom he bowed low on being introduced. . . . I remember he passed some remark to me when we were introduced to the Asantehene about how much he would like some of the people back in the States to witness the scene."[7]

The weeks in Ghana were demanding. For one thing, the climate was enervating in the extreme. The weather, Rustin wrote to Jim Peck, "requires the healthiest of people to rest two or three hours in the heat of the afternoon. . . . An eight-hour day out here leaves one flat on his back." Soon he was referring to "Accra-Amnesia. . . . One will be in the midst of a sentence and completely forget how to go on."[8] Climate, however, was the least of it. "The political and psychological job here has been very difficult," Rustin noted. The situation called for his best organizing and negotiating skills. Dealing with the team's hosts fell on him, since Randle, as a white Englishman, was "open to suspicion." Rustin soon discovered that the support of Ghana's government was a mixed blessing. True, it opened the door to financing, media coverage, recruits, and mass public enthusiasm. But it also created difficulties. The hostility between France and Ghana was extreme, as Ghana was taking the lead in the United Nations in rousing anticolonialist sentiment. "We are caught in the spying that is going on between French and Ghana governments," Rustin wrote. "We have had a time making certain that we are not, from the French view, Ghana agents." The backing of Gbedemah, for whom Sutherland worked, also meant that at any moment, the project might fall victim to the power struggle under-way between him and Nkrumah.[9]

Even with these challenges, after just a few days in Ghana, Rustin was expressing unbridled excitement. "This is one of the most poten-tially important projects that the pacifist movement has been associated with," he wrote to several New York colleagues. "Millions of Africans oppose further testing, but throughout Africa, including Ghana, there has developed no incident or occasion or project around which this sen-timent could crystalize."[10] As the days passed, it became clearer that his role in the project was essential. "Bear in mind," he wrote in one of his reports, "that my experience with African leaders, my being a Negro and my not being as Bill [Sutherland] is, involved in Ghana politics, has been very valuable." Both Gbedemah and aides to Nkrumah communi-cated that his participation was "absolutely necessary." Rustin began to contemplate a longer stay that would allow him to participate in the journey into the Sahara. Since the team assumed that they would all be arrested and might receive up to three years in jail, his return to the United States might be delayed indefinitely.[11]

Rustin's announcement set off alarms among his associates at home. Kahn, who missed the intimacy of their relationship, wrote about the "heightened political activity in many spheres" and told him pointedly: "Your absence is conspicuous and keenly felt." King wrote to Levison about Rustin that "we are in desperate need of his services." The for-tunes of the SCLC were at low ebb that fall, and King was considering drastic action. He had decided to move from Montgomery to Atlanta and was urging his supporters to "practice open civil disobedience. We must be willing to go to jail en masse." Under the circumstances, King was eager not only for Rustin's advice but also his services. Levison re-ported that the SCLC leadership had decided to offer Rustin a staff po-sition. "The conclusion was unanimous that you be sought," he wrote. King, he continued, "is deeply dependent on your guidance and imagi-nation." Even the "possible public relations problem" did not seem to daunt him or the other ministers.[12]

Of most importance to Rustin were the worries of Randolph. Rustin consulted Randolph before going abroad. He wanted to make sure that his absence would not adversely affect their plans to protest at the national political conventions in 1960. Randolph seemed to bless his participation in the African venture, but now that he was talking about staying into the new year, he began to hear differently. Levison offered another take on Randolph's feelings. "The concern you expressed when you left that Phil showed no disturbance when you told him you had to go was a misreading," Levison wrote. "The very first thing he said to me when I called him [about your plans] was, 'Stanley, I was shocked when Bayard said he had to leave. Where are we now? Will this do us serious damage?'" Kahn communicated similar sentiments to his absent lover.[13]

The news about Randolph rattled Rustin. To Willoughby, Muste, and Levison, he fired off a several-page memo outlining his concerns. Knowing that Levison and Kahn were more than mildly contemptuous of his pacifist ventures and not above manipulating him into returning, he was not sure he could trust their descriptions of Randolph's views. But he also knew that, for different reasons, Randolph and other black activists harbored suspicions about the peace movement and its commitment to racial justice. Rustin was not willing to leave matters to chance. "It is imperative that Stanley, A.J. and Randolph get together with Finch and Willoughby to evaluate the situation in the U.S. so that there can be some collective advice on what my course of action should be," he admonished them. He insisted that "others in the Negro community" be included in the decision making. "This is sound," he lectured them, "not only for me, but for the pacifist organizations and the role that we can play in the Civil Rights Movement. I am deeply, very deeply concerned that I not be placed in a position where I can be accused of irresponsibility or shirking in duty in the Civil Rights struggle. I feel that any such inference will play directly into the hands of those who basically disagree with our nonviolent and mass approach to the civil rights struggle. . . . We need to be extremely sensitive that we are acting out as clearly as possible the role which the pacifist movement can play in developing a truly non-violent movement at home." At a distance of so many thousand miles, Rustin did not feel himself in a position to make a decision unilaterally. "I am prepared to trust your collective judgment."[14]

If Rustin had hoped for a unanimous opinion, he was disappointed. Meeting in Randolph's Harlem office on November 13, the two groups of activists reached no consensus. Instead, as Peck wrote to Rustin, the "main theme music throughout the meeting was your indispensability for ALL non-violent action projects." Peck saw it as a "merited and genuine tribute" to Rustin, but also as a "sad situation" that the ranks of nonviolent leadership, particularly in the civil rights movement, were so thin. The cable that Levison and Muste sent the next day presented the conflict starkly: "Conferees unable agree single view. Randolph expressed firm view civil rights struggle paramount and decisively important to African colonial struggle as well as peace fight. Your indispensable role in domestic actions requires return. . . . Muste holds that Africa project potentially more important, capable of major contribution to civil rights struggle here as well as struggle against new nuclear colonialism."[15] The next day, Muste sent off a letter of his own. "Hope to God this reaches you before final decisions taken!" he began, before launching into one of his hectoring disquisitions. "There are times when a strike or other struggle is at such a stage, and one's relationship to it of such a character, that one has to see it through. . . . Failure to do so means letting people down, raising doubts as to whether one can in future ever be trusted . . . Such intangibles may be the decisive element in one's career in determining whether one is a leader or an adventurer or perhaps simply an employee of others."[16]

Rustin summarized the communications as "next move up to you, Rustin." And move he did, in ways that suggested where his deepest loyalties resided. He began to lay the groundwork for a return by year's end in order to resume his work with Randolph and King. He first tested the waters with Gbedemah and Nkrumah, both of whom proved sympathetic as long as he left the Sahara project in good hands. Playing on Muste's vanity, Rustin telephoned him from Africa. The Sahara protest group and even Nkrumah, Rustin told him "off the record," wanted him there to provide counsel because the project was taking on "big proportions." Rustin knew his former mentor well enough to real-ize that Muste would never consider himself inadequate to a situation. Muste took the bait. Before the end of November, he had flown to Ghana, giving Rustin the leeway to plan a departure.[17]

But not immediately. Over the preceding weeks, Rustin had in fact become central to the Sahara project. Within a few days of arrival, even Muste was singing Rustin's praises. *"Bayard is magnificent,"* he wrote to Willoughby. "Don't see how project could possibly have got off ground without him." Rustin had raised more than $25,000, and the publicity in Africa exceeded anything pacifists had achieved in the States. "An immense propaganda job for the idea of nonviolence has been done among the masses," Muste observed. Rustin had also succeeded in giv-ing the project as much of an African focus as a pacifist one. Rustin was simply too invested to think about leaving without participating in this wild desert adventure.[18]

By early December, plans were set. The route would take the team of nineteen, a majority of them African, first into Upper Volta and then French West Africa, before they reached Algeria—a journey of 2,100 miles. On Sunday morning, December 6, Rustin and his traveling mates rose before dawn for a farewell rally at the Accra arena. More than a thousand were on hand as Gbedemah praised the team's com-mitment and harshly criticized the French for planning tests on African soil. To the Westerners in the group he said, "You are now a part of Africa. . . . You are forever enshrined in the hearts of Africans." People lined the streets as the cavalcade rode through the city—two Land Rovers to carry the team, a truck filled with supplies, and a third jeep in case of emergency.[19]

Seven hours later, they had arrived in Kumasi, Ghana's second largest city, where another mass meeting was held. In Tamale, on Mon-day, team members were guests of honor at a rousing rally; they had to fend off requests from young men eager to join the expedition. In town after town, people filled the streets—to stare, to cheer, to welcome this strange international assemblage. In Navrango, a border village, Rustin and Sutherland conferred with Amadu Sedou, the district commis-sioner for the region. He passed on the information his scouts had discovered about French patrols on the Upper Volta side of the border. Taking his advice, they decided to make the crossing near Bawku on Wednesday.

With his love for a good story, Rustin in later years spun out a wonderful tale of this stage of the adventure: "We had thought—and nobody was there who had lived in the Sahara—that the Sahara was going to be warm, hot, which of course it is—by day. But by night it is absolutely *freezing*. We were not prepared for this, so we had to camp and send a group back to pick up additional material and bring it up." The border territory was "such wild country that even the Ghanaians didn't know where their country left off and Upper Volta began. I guess about the fourth morning after we had hit the wilderness we got to a small town. All over West Africa they make something that is similar to a donut, except it doesn't have a hole in the middle of it and it isn't so sweet as a donut and they fry them in oil. This morning when we got up and hit this little town, and went out to buy some of these donuts, they were light as feathers. One of the young men with us, who was French, said, 'Uh huh, we are now in French territory.'" Despite the humor, the days in the desert were fraught with anxiety. Especially to the Africans, the French were "the arch-devils." In Guinea the year before, after a vote for independence, de Gaulle had stripped the transitional government of everything—desks, typewriters, even light bulbs. Everyone was aware, as Muste wrote home ominously, "what French paratroopers do to Algerians." Entering French territory meant "taking your life in your hands."[20]

But the project had attained enough visibility—in the African press, in the United States and Britain, among diplomats at the United Nations—that the participants had created a wall of protection around themselves. When they encountered the first control post in Upper Volta, a French military patrol detained them. For the next several days, military officers and antinuclear protesters engaged in a game of cat and mouse. The French tried to seize the keys of the vehicles, but the team succeeded in hiding them. The protesters attempted to distribute flyers among the villagers of Bittou, but the Legionnaires confiscated them. Rustin, Sutherland, and the others debated whether to put on their knapsacks and attempt to bypass the control post, but the French stationed military all around them, making it difficult for them to move beyond their campsite.

The following Sunday, the team decided to return to Ghana and re-group. They reached the border under close guard. They decided to make a second entry, at a different location, with a much smaller team. Sutherland and Michael Scott led the party of seven, with Rustin re-maining at the border to receive communications and serve as contact person. This time they made it only eleven miles into French territory before being apprehended and escorted back.

The project continued into the new year, with another effort—not much more successful—to penetrate deep into French territory. But the intent, as Rustin had argued, was to draw as much attention to French nuclear policy as possible, not reach the test site. Protests con-tinued through February: tens of thousands rallying in Casablanca, more demonstrations in Accra, a resolution from the labor federation representing French teachers that condemned the government's plans, a speech to the Nigerian parliament by Harold Macmillan, the British prime minister, announcing his opposition to atmospheric testing. The actions did not stop the tests; the French exploded their first nuclear bomb in mid-February and a second in early April. Yet the project had served as a building block in a growing international effort to end above-ground testing. When Rustin returned to New York in early January, he knew he had done well by the project.[21]

DURING RUSTIN'S ABSENCE, Levison had been acting almost as if he were Rustin's agent, promoting both the man and his projects. As Rustin already knew, King wanted him on the SCLC staff so that he might have ready access to Rustin's advice and talents. Levison had also filled Rustin's usual role of catalyst and schemer and had pushed the convention project forward. In the fall, he brought Randolph, King, and Wilkins together to discuss it. Wilkins, Levison recounted in a letter to Rustin in Africa, "had clearly put on his militant suit for that day. . . . Roy refrained from throwing up objections in his cynical style with us and Phil because he does not want to reveal this side of himself to Martin."

Just as King and the SCLC were in a state of drift that fall, the NAACP was slowly depleting the political capital of earlier victories. Wilkins needed something to mobilize its supporters and bring the organization public attention. Thus, instead of the usual criticisms that Wilkins raised to mass action, Levison reported that "to my utter astonishment, Roy said it was a good idea." Levison felt that the meeting had effectively eliminated "the spectre which always haunts us at the beginning of our projects: is NAACP with it, opposing it, faking cooperation, etc."[22]

Rustin thus found himself in an unusual and exhilarating position. King had overcome the reservations other SCLC members had about Rustin and was ready to invite him to join the staff. A civil rights project had been launched that brought key leaders and organizations together not for a symbolic rally, but to pressure the major political parties through mass demonstrations. Randolph was endorsing him as central to the plan's success. "I don't believe he has ever before taken so strong a stand on *you*," Kahn told Rustin after sitting in on a meeting. Levison was positively enthusiastic about the prospects. "Two of the projects we sought most eagerly are *now in our laps!*" he wrote Rustin. The King alliance and the convention activities promised "a new image for you as a public figure, blotting out some of the past shadows."[23]

The next step was to get the approval of the WRL. With Rustin just back from three months in Africa, the board wanted its executive secretary attending to the organization's needs. In January, Muste reported to the WRL's executive committee that Randolph and King were seeking Rustin's services for up to a year. Muste and Ed Gottlieb, the board's chair, met with Randolph and Levison to discuss the request. They were persuaded to recommend Rustin's release, but "under some controlled conditions." Rustin had to attend executive committee meetings to stay abreast of developments in the organization and the peace movement. He had to remain part of the editorial board that produced *Liberation*. And his pacifist colleagues reserved the right to reconsider their approval. They intended to review periodically the progress of his civil rights work "to make certain that it is really and continuously making a contribution to the development of a sound, non-violent philosophy and action in American race relations."[24]

Rustin immediately began assembling a team for the convention project. He drew in Thomas Kilgore and George Lawrence, both respected black ministers in New York, and Maida Springer, a labor movement organizer. From his leftist friends, he recruited Michael Harrington, Rachelle Horowitz, and Kahn, who began working as Rustin's secretary. Bob Moses, a philosophy graduate student from Harvard, also volunteered to help out in the New York office, and Norman Hill, a member of the Socialist Party in Chicago, agreed to coordinate in that city, where the Republican convention would meet.

Before planning proceeded very far, events with far-reaching consequences for the black freedom struggle erupted unexpectedly. Across the South, a sit-in movement exploded, with college students challenging Jim Crow practices at lunch counters and other public facilities. The sit-ins began when four male undergraduates from North Carolina A&T entered a Woolworth store in downtown Greensboro, sat at its lunch counter, and, in defiance of almost a century of segregated practice, requested service. When they were refused, they stayed until closing time, quietly reading at the counter. They returned the next day with reinforcements, and with even more recruits the day after that. As newspapers began reporting the startling event, black students at other colleges in the state picked up the tactic. By mid-February, sit-ins had spread beyond North Carolina. By early March, like an unstoppable contagion, protests were occurring in every Southern state except Mississippi. Arrests numbered in the thousands.

To outside observers, the wave of protest seemed like an act of nature, unpredictable and unplanned. But the sit-ins grew from solid roots. Organizations like the NAACP had a network of youth chapters throughout the Upper South. The bus boycotts in Montgomery and elsewhere had offered a model of resistance to segregation. Organizations like the FOR, CORE, and SCLC had been evangelizing for non-violence for years. In 1958 and 1959, a first round of sit-ins in border state cities of Kansas, Oklahoma, and Missouri had met with a fair amount of success. In Nashville, where protesting students went on to play major leadership roles throughout the decade, James Lawson of the FOR had been conducting workshops in nonviolence for months.

The sit-in movement changed everything. William Chafe, who has studied the Greensboro movement exhaustively, called the events nothing less than "a watershed in the history of America." The sit-ins grabbed the attention of every civil rights organization in the country. Almost immediately, the NAACP began mobilizing its chapters, North and South, and implemented what it called "a racial self-defense policy on an expanded scale." A report from the National Urban League, an organization devoted to social welfare rather than to politics, concluded that "these demonstrations have done more than any single development in the last one hundred years to destroy the myth of the contented southern Negro." The Southern Regional Council, a voice for white liberal activists, echoed these sentiments. Surveying the breadth and depth of the protest movement, it commented that the sit-ins "have spread with such contagion as to make brightly clear that the South is in a time of change, the terms of which cannot be dictated by white Southerners."[25]

Perhaps so. Yet in the short run, white resistance was fierce. In many cities, gangs of young men harassed and assaulted the peaceful protesters. In Orangeburg, police used tear gas to disperse demonstrators. In Marshall, Texas, they used fire hoses. In Nashville, a white supremacist bombed the home of the one black member of the city council.

Meanwhile, in Alabama, state officials chose to indict King, who had recently moved to Atlanta, on charges that he lied on his state tax returns. By framing the offense as perjury, the state threatened King with a felony for which he could serve ten years. Although Alabama had harassed King steadily over the years, the timing of the indictment—a day after King delivered a major speech extolling the student sit-ins—conveyed an especially ominous message. Serious as the indictment was, Rustin saw it as an opportunity to position King and the SCLC at the center of the new militancy. He quickly moved into high gear. "I am working full time here," he wrote to Maude Ballou, King's secretary in Atlanta, two weeks after the indictment.[26] He had already formed the Committee to Defend Martin Luther King. Rustin drew on many of the usual suspects in his network of New York civil rights activists, but he was also looking for novel ways to seize public attention. He per-

suaded Harry Belafonte to form a cultural committee to mobilize celebrities in the entertainment industry on King's behalf.

Rustin intended the Defense Committee to raise money not only for
the trial but, "equally important, for the work of the SCLC." He drafted
a telegram for King to send to all of the organizations that King had
helped in the preceding years by lending his name to fund-raising appeals or by endorsing publications. The telegram requested access to
their mailing lists and identified Rustin as the man in charge of the operation. Meanwhile, Belafonte's committee planned several events, including a concert in Boston, a major affair in Harlem, and celebrity
fund-raisers in Los Angeles, where the Democratic National Convention was to be held. "I cannot overemphasize the importance of Harry's
assistance," Rustin reported to King.[27]

The centerpiece of Rustin's campaign was a full-page appeal in the
New York Times. As a fund-raising device, it was rhetorically shrewd. It
linked King and the inspirational actions of black students so tightly
that they became virtually indistinguishable; it made a check to King's
defense committee the cutting edge of support for the freedom struggle. "Heed Their Rising Voices," the headline ran.

> Thousands of Southern Negro students are engaged in wide-
> spread non-violent demonstrations in positive affirmation of the
> right to live in human dignity . . . they are being met by an un-
> precedented wave of terror. . . . Small wonder that the Southern
> violators of the Constitution fear this new, non-violent brand of
> freedom fighter. . . . Small wonder that they are determined to de-
> stroy the one man who, more than any other, symbolizes the new
> spirit now sweeping the South. . . . The defense of Martin Luther
> King, spiritual leader of the student sit-in movement, clearly,
> therefore, is an integral part of the total struggle for freedom in
> the South.

Signatories included white actors with roots in the New York theater—
Marlon Brando, Shelley Winters, Stella Adler, John Raitt—and a
"who's who" among African American entertainers and writers: Bela-

fonte, Nat King Cole, Dorothy Dandridge, Sammy Davis, Jr., Lorraine Hansberry, Langston Hughes, Mahalia Jackson, Eartha Kitt, Sidney Poitier, Jackie Robinson.[28]

Through the late winter and into the spring, Rustin and Levison had almost daily contact. They plotted strategy for the interlocking King defense effort and the convention project. They chewed over the implications of the protest movement sweeping the South, wishing that King and the SCLC had spawned it. Early in May, when King came to New York to have Rustin and Levison take stock of Wyatt Walker, his candidate for executive director of SCLC, the two men impressed on King the significance of the moment. "This is a new stage in the struggle," Rustin and Levison emphasized. "It begins at the higher point where Montgomery left off. The students are taking on the strongest state power. . . . The country is stirred by them."[29]

Rustin especially saw the sit-ins as the occasion finally to break the grip of the national NAACP in setting the direction for the civil rights movement. As Levison summarized the discussion, the NAACP "wanted to give a tranquilizer or pacifier to the whole movement. . . . More and more they are revealing themselves as gradualists in reality while they pretend to be uncompromising and firm." The goodwill they had accumulated from a string of court victories and their work on school desegregation was dwindling. "Sooner or later their policy will have to change or their influence will sharply diminish and the true forces of struggle will move into effective leadership." Rustin wanted to position King and his commitment to mass action to fill the vacuum. "We need you more now than ever," he wrote to King.[30]

Rustin's jockeying was dangerous. The upheaval within the civil rights movement did not sit well with Roy Wilkins. Wilkins was an NAACP "lifer." He had joined the organization as a teenager and was working in its national office before he was thirty. When he became executive secretary in 1955, the NAACP was still riding the crest of the historic *Brown* decision. Its name had become synonymous with the civil rights movement. It shaped the movement's strategy and priorities. King had not yet appeared as a rival center of influence, and only a few starry-eyed radicals advocated nonviolent direct action. Like many other career activists in dominant organizations, Wilkins combined an unshakable loyalty to the NAACP with the conviction that what was best for the organization was best for the movement and the black community.

Though undeniably exciting, the student movement rattled Wilkins and other NAACP careerists. Even while the protests in the South were still exploding, Gloster Current, the NAACP's director of branches, was framing the sit-ins in competitive terms. "NAACP units," he wrote in a memo, "should be urged to sponsor their own mass meetings, demonstrations, picket lines, petition campaigns, etc. and insist that NAACP literature, signs, and materials be used at all times. NAACP leaders should also be encouraged to become more aggressive in their actions, rather than participating in programs which are directed and coordinated by other groups." Current told Wilkins of criticisms that some CORE members were making of the NAACP. "I don't see how we can further permit cooperation with this group," he concluded.[31]

In April, under Ella Baker's instigation, King and the SCLC sponsored a conference of Southern student activists. The gathering at Shaw University in Raleigh brought together for the first time many of the sit-in leaders. James Lawson was a keynote speaker. His visionary address about the power of nonviolence and the need to develop leadership among masses of people took the NAACP to task for its conservative emphasis on "fundraising and court action."[32] Lawson set a tone of militancy, while Baker did everything she could to make sure that adult caution did not constrain the young. Out of the conference came not a youth division of the SCLC, but a new organization, the Student Nonviolent Coordinating Committee. SNCC ("Snick," as it was called) quickly became the leading edge of Southern black militancy.

Lawson's remarks articulated perfectly the spirit of these new activists. SNCC never took kindly to the methods and outlook of the NAACP. Later that spring, Baker brought a delegation of Southern student leaders to meet key staffers in the NAACP's office, including Thurgood Marshall. Marshall, the chief architect of the strategy that led to *Brown*, dressed the students down for their willingness to choose jail. "Thurgood told them," one staff member wrote Wilkins, "that it is an insult to any lawyer for a client to insist on remaining in jail. . . . If a defendant told him in advance that he did not wish to accept bail and would stay in jail, he personally probably would not accept the case." The meeting so soured the students that Baker had to spend the rest of the trip "mend[ing] fences, to nip in the bud any misconceptions about the NAACP."[33]

Incidents such as these did not bode well for the NAACP. Sensing that its leadership position might slip away, Wilkins sent King an agitated letter. He was "puzzled and greatly distressed" at the public criticisms of the NAACP. "We feel deeply aggrieved over this unwarranted attack." Wilkins described to King all that the NAACP had done to support the sit-ins in the South, and reminded him that no group—not CORE, not the SCLC—had the right to claim full credit for the new movement. Wilkins also hinted ominously at "disturbing elements in the picture which I would not care to go into here, but which you and I should discuss privately." King, who had considered hiring Lawson, backed away from the plan in order to avoid a breach with Wilkins.[34]

Rustin posed a problem of a different order. He joined together a whole slew of challenges to the NAACP's preeminence. Rustin was able to construct competing strategies and possessed a different long-range vision of social change. He believed in mass mobilization and direct action; he saw race relations as linked to other social ills. He had the trust of both Randolph and King and, as the convention project demonstrated, could link the stature of the two men together in a plan for political mobilization.

Over the course of the spring, Rustin's work on the King Defense Committee increasingly irked Wilkins. The outpouring of celebrity support threatened NAACP fund-raising. The claims that the committee made about the work of the SCLC seemed to him outrageous. Soon he was hearing unsettling reports about discussions to set up a rival organization. One informant told him that at a meeting at Belafonte's home, "Harry recommended that a national membership organization be organized, stating that there was a need for such organization because the NAACP is not doing the job that needed to be done. A Committee was appointed to work out ways and means . . . [including] Bayard Rustin and the same gang."[35]

As the summer approached, the convention project became the target of Wilkins's ire. All of the strands of his discontent seemed to gather around it. Rustin was preparing for King a set of platform demands to present to Chester Bowles, the chair of the Democratic Party's platform committee, and Thurston Morton, head of the Republican National Committee. He was also helping student leaders in SNCC map their own plans for the summer conventions. In early June, Rustin organized a press conference in New York in which Randolph and King formally announced a nonviolent "March on the Convention Movement for Freedom Now." Randolph told reporters that they were planning on having thousands of demonstrators converge on both convention sites, with masses of picketers stationed there for the duration. He also claimed the full involvement of the NAACP. To Wilkins, who often acted as if the national political scene was the private domain of the NAACP, the convention project was trespassing on his territory.

Rustin miscalculated in planning the press conference. Thinking that the NAACP was too far in to back out, he told Wilkins of the event just a few hours before it happened. Wilkins seized the opportunity to claim that Rustin had excluded the NAACP from consultation. Ignoring Rustin, he fired off to Randolph an indignant, near-hysterical letter. "We have never agreed specifically to a 'march' on any convention," he declared. "We submit that [your] statement misleads the public as to the role of the NAACP in this project. . . . We have never agreed to recruit or join in recruiting '5,000 pickets.' . . . The NAACP cannot permit its name to be used as a sponsor of mass picketing around each convention." Wilkins framed the political differences with Rustin and Randolph starkly: "We do not believe a mass picket line which will clog entrances, irritate delegates and officials and possibly erupt into name-calling or disorder will advance the cause." And he added the red herring standard in cold war America: "irresponsible and politically undesirable persons with ulterior motives can and will enlist."[36]

Accustomed to receiving letters like this from Wilkins, Randolph waited a full eight days to respond. By then, events were spinning out of control. Wilkins shrewdly took his grievances to Adam Clayton Powell. A man with a huge ego and a flair for controversy, Powell expected activists to work through him if they wanted access to the Democratic Party. He and Rustin had a history of run-ins, most notably in 1956 when Powell used the Madison Square Garden rally as a place to grandstand. Powell, who was quite the womanizing minister, had also used his pulpit to denounce homosexuals. There was little love lost between him and Rustin. Since Powell could be something of a loose cannon, Wilkins knew what he was doing in going to him with a story about Rustin.

On June 19, Powell addressed the delegates to the National Sunday School Congress, who were meeting in Buffalo, New York. He used the speech to launch a strike upon his, and Wilkins's, rivals for influence. As the *Courier*, the Pittsburgh-based African American newspaper, reported it, "Powell asserted that certain Negro leaders were 'captives' of behind-the-scenes interests. . . . Powell contends that Rev. King has been under undue influences ever since Bayard Rustin of the Fellowship for Reconciliation [*sic*] went to Alabama to help in the bus boycott. He insists that Randolph is the captive of socialist interests and that he is guided principally by one Stanley Levinson [*sic*]." Powell framed his attack as an appeal for unity. He criticized King and Randolph for not consulting Wilkins. He feigned admiration for "'the good intentions'" of Randolph and King, but pointedly said, "'This is not unity. . . . This is one reason we must be on guard against our best leaders being captured by anyone.'"[37]

Rustin ignored the broadside. "Adam was always maneuvering," he recalled later, and this was just his latest move to generate controversy and put the spotlight on himself. Randolph too shrugged off the reports. The idea that he was the captive of Stanley Levison—and that anyone might believe this—was too ludicrous for words. But King was worried about the taint to his reputation and called Powell to challenge the claims in the *Courier* article. Powell denied the comments outright and maintained that he had been misquoted. "I made no such statements while in Buffalo to anyone at any time," Powell told King. He had only made public what Wilkins had reported to him—that the NAACP had not been consulted. Giving King some public satisfaction, Powell issued a press release to that effect.[38]

Thinking the matter resolved, King left for Brazil for a meeting of the Baptist World Alliance. But Powell was not about to bend to the wishes of a minister twenty years his junior. Word reached King in Brazil that unless he dropped the convention project, Powell was prepared to make far more serious charges. In a panic, King called Rustin. He was "very very agitated indeed," Rustin remembered, "and said that on second thought maybe we ought not to proceed with marches. . . . He wants out. He doesn't want to make any trouble. . . . And I said 'Martin, why do you want to get out.' And he said, 'I don't want to talk about it on the phone. I'm being threatened and it's going to be embarrassing and I want out.'" A puzzled Rustin reported the conversation to Randolph, who called King and pressed him for details. Powell had let it be known that he would charge that King and Rustin were having a sexual affair.[39]

Rustin was furious. "[Powell] couldn't possibly have that kind of information," Rustin told an interviewer years later. "Martin knew goddamn well he couldn't have that kind of information. You can't sleep with a guy without his knowing it." Randolph cautioned King not to cave in to this kind of threat, and said that he, Randolph, was proceeding with the convention project in any case. Rustin and Randolph waited for King to make up his mind, but King continued to hesitate. "Martin had one very major defect," Rustin later said. "He did not like contention with people who were supposed to be friends. . . . He sort of folded on in-fighting." Rustin offered to resign in the hope that this would force the issue. Much to his chagrin, King did not reject the offer. At the time, King was also involved in a major challenge to the conservative leadership of the National Baptist Convention, and one of his ministerial lieutenants in the fight was also gay. "Basically he said I can't take on two queers at one time," one of Rustin's associates recollected later. And so Rustin took matters into his own hands. He publicly resigned as an assistant to King. Referring directly to Powell's charges in the *Courier*, he accused the congressman of seeking "to weaken, if not destroy, the march on the conventions for his own obvious political reasons." Since Powell had claimed that Rustin's association with King was causing division in the civil rights movement, "I cannot permit a situation to endure in which my relationship to Dr. King and the Southern Christian Leadership Conference is used to confuse and becloud the basic issues confronting the Negro people. . . . In such a situation I am no longer able to be of effective service. . . . Congressman Powell has suggested that I am an obstacle to his giving full enthusiastic support to Dr. King. I want now to remove that obstacle. I have resigned as Dr. King's special assistant and severed relations with the Southern Christian Leadership Conference."[40]

The convention project went ahead without Rustin. There were pickets outside the conventions, and the demonstrations did get some media attention, but the impact was nothing approaching what he had hoped for. The disruption that the public controversy had caused and the absence of Rustin's guiding hand in the final weeks of organizing no doubt had an effect. But the responsibility lay even more directly at the door of Wilkins and the NAACP. In the weeks before the convention, the national office made it abundantly clear to its branches, especially in Los Angeles and Chicago, that the organization was having no part in public protests outside the convention halls.[41] Even in the wake of the student sit-ins, mass mobilizations in support of civil rights in this period still needed the cooperation of the NAACP to succeed—and the NAACP still hesitated to provide it.

FOR RUSTIN, THE POWELL-KING imbroglio was devastating. Dave McReynolds, who worked with him at the WRL during this period, recalled that afterward, "Bayard spent the most miserable time I have ever seen during those months. He was completely demoralized. He and Tom Kahn had worked on the plans. And it came to nothing. . . . They had some little march. But they had planned a major thing and Bayard was helpless and was in New York and was deeply depressed. . . . Absolutely broken by this. I hadn't seen Bayard except in the jail period so destroyed." Rustin had fought his way back from pariah status after his arrest in Pasadena. He had shaped and nurtured and devoted himself to King's career. He had drawn up the plans for what became the SCLC. He had been the invisible hand behind many civil rights initiatives for years. And yet, again, he was being discarded, this time for something that had never happened and that went publicly unnamed. Because the sexual slander behind the resignation remained hidden, the events appeared puzzling and hazy, and they generated little press commentary. One exception was Nat Hentoff, who penned an eloquent defense of Rustin. "He has worked for years as the most brilliant tactician in the civil rights field," Hentoff wrote in the *Village Voice*. "Powell's flamboyance on a platform . . . is a poor substitute for Rustin's integrity and skill in the wings." Months later, in *Harper's*, James Baldwin criticized King's behavior but phrased his comments with the utmost discretion. For the most part, silence reigned. No allusion was ever made to the role played by Wilkins and the NAACP, which stayed below everyone's radar screen.[42]

The incident essentially dissolved Rustin's relationship with King and the SCLC for years to come. Not only did Rustin no longer have a formal role as King's assistant in New York, but King stopped seeking Rustin's advice, and Rustin no longer offered it. They occasionally corresponded, but the content suggested how distant they had become. "Hope all goes well with you and the hard job you have to do," Rustin wrote in one letter the following winter. "I hope things are going well with you," King replied a month later. Closer to home, Levison dropped Rustin precipitously. Since the mid-1950s, Levison had been "following around after Bayard," Rachelle Horowitz recalled. "Bayard was his access into the black movement." Their almost daily routine of talking and dining together stopped abruptly. In the wake of Rustin's resignation, "Stanley said goodbye, ended the relationship, and didn't talk to him again until after the March on Washington."[43]

Randolph tried to find something that would keep Rustin engaged in the black freedom struggle. It disturbed Randolph that every time Rustin seemed to "stick his head up . . . somebody would chop it off so easily, especially if he was in a position of prominence and visibility." Randolph discussed "the tragedy of Bayard" with James Farmer. "Something should be done to change this," Farmer remembered the older man saying. Randolph was just launching a new project, the Negro American Labor Council, and he proposed that Rustin come work for him and perhaps even head the venture. But Rustin decided against it.[44]

For a brief time, Rustin thought he might be able to play a role in the Southern freedom struggle through his relationship to the students in SNCC. In July, Marion Barry, who became SNCC's first chairman and who, with Rustin's help, spoke before the Democratic Party's platform committee, wrote to Jane Stembridge, another SNCC activist, that "it is regrettable that Bayard had to resign." As SNCC members laid plans for a major conference in October on the philosophy and strategy of nonviolence, they turned to Rustin often. Stembridge acknowledged his "concrete, penetrating suggestions" and wrote to a friend in August that he was "continuing to be of inestimable help to us." Rustin expected to play a prominent role in the conference and was listed on the program. But the ripples from the clash with Powell continued to spread. Ella Baker reported that the executive council of the AFL-CIO, which was funding the conference, had raised objections to Rustin's participation. Barry wrote to George Meany, president of the labor federation, confirming "a change in our programing." Rustin, he told Meany, "is not now and will not be connected with our movement in the future." Although Rustin had drafted key recommendations that were presented at the conference ("which fact must never be known by our conference or SNCC or anybody," Stembridge wrote a friend), he was not there to watch SNCC's transformation into a permanent organization.[45]

Two decades of devotion to the goal of racial justice. Two dozen arrests as evidence of his commitment. Rustin had traveled far from his origins and far from the disgrace of Pasadena. He had come so close to power and influence. Now he was on the margins again.

CHAPTER FOURTEEN

"Ours Is Not a World-Shaking Project"
1960–1962

DEVASTATING AS THE BREAK with King was, Rustin's situation was very different from what he had confronted after Pasadena. This time he had a place to which he could return. To the WRL, Rustin was a treasure. Ed Gottlieb, the chair of its executive committee, told Randolph that whenever it released Rustin to work in the civil rights movement, "his absence is a real loss." McReynolds agreed: "He was very important to us. We reaped a lot of benefits from Bayard."[1]

Still, the return was very much a letdown. For all the respect that Rustin's leadership brought to the WRL, the organization remained very small. Its annual budget in 1960 was just under $20,000. Many days the work seemed like little more than menial labor. "Bayard was right in there with me and Jim [Peck]," DiGia recalled, "stuffing envelopes and sealing them, and then we had to go up to the damn post office, two blocks away. He would say something like this: 'Thirty years in the movement. And what am I doing? I'm carting these envelopes to the post office.' He would joke about it, but it was true."[2]

Nor did pacifism tug at Rustin's heart or provoke his strategic imagination in the way it once had. His commitment to nonviolence remained as strong as ever. Indeed, the experience of the sit-ins confirmed it for him as the leading edge of a new social order. When he paused to assess the prospects of the Southern civil rights movement, the aspirations of his people for freedom were beginning to seem reachable. But a world without war and violence had the appearance of a utopian dream.

At the start of the 1960s, as Rustin rejoined his pacifist comrades, the peace movement in the United States faced a curious mix of opportunities and obstacles. No one questioned that the movement was experiencing a revival, that the repressive years of the early cold war were over. Though they were still the work of a few, the nonviolent direct action campaigns of the late 1950s had been dramatic and visible. On Northern campuses, young activists had formed the Student Peace Union. SANE had grown by leaps and bounds since its founding in 1957. In May 1960, it had packed Madison Square Garden with over 20,000 supporters of a nuclear test ban. Yet peace campaigners remained vulnerable. Shortly after SANE's Madison Square Garden rally, the organization faced an attack by Thomas Dodd, an anti-Communist senator from Connecticut. Dodd claimed that Communists had infiltrated SANE and demanded that it purge itself of subversives. A panicked leadership attempted to comply, but then SANE found itself torn by bitter internal conflicts and never regained momentum. The rhetoric of the cold war still exerted enormous power.

Nor did the election of a Democrat to the White House portend better days. In the closing weeks of the 1960 campaign, Rustin had described himself and other New York pacifists as "deeply troubled to find both Nixon and Kennedy avoiding a serious debate on foreign policy."[3] The first months of John F. Kennedy's presidency confirmed that he and his inner circle were every bit the cold warriors that Eisenhower and Dulles had been. The new president's rhetoric gave an idealistic tone to the role of nuclear superpower. His inaugural address was a virtual call to arms. "Let every nation know," he declaimed, "that we shall pay any price, bear any burden, meet any hardship, support any friend, oppose any foe to assure the survival and the success of liberty." Addressing a joint session of Congress a few days later, Kennedy darkly announced that "each day we draw nearer the hour of maximum danger."[4] Crisis after crisis seemed to erupt. He dispatched military advisers to Laos. Hostility toward the Cuban revolution escalated into the disastrous Bay of Pigs invasion. In Vienna, a summit meeting with Nikita Khrushchev, the Soviet premier, collapsed amid angry recriminations. At home, Kennedy expanded the nuclear arsenal and pushed a civil defense program involving massive construction of bomb shelters. For American pacifists like Rustin, the challenges were huge, their resources extremely limited.

As PART OF HIS DUTIES at the WRL, Rustin resumed attending the meetings of the Committee for Nonviolent Action. That summer and fall, CNVA sponsored protest actions against the nuclear submarines that docked off the coast of Connecticut near the naval base in New London. Members were also debating a proposal, put forward by Brad Lyttle, to sponsor an intercontinental peace walk, from San Francisco to Moscow. Rustin very much opposed the plan. His trips abroad in the previous few years had given him a firsthand sense of the political complexities of pacifism in Western Europe. He knew how difficult it would be to shape both a message and a style of protest that appealed across national boundaries. There was also the considerable challenge of winning entry into Eastern Europe and the Soviet Union. Rustin had spent weeks in Helsinki in 1958, futilely trying to negotiate visas for a small group of Americans who had not planned any public displays against militarism. Why would Communist authorities welcome an even larger team of Americans leafleting the people of Eastern Europe and the Soviet Union and encouraging them to refuse to pay taxes and reject conscription? But his argument left the rest of the CNVA members unpersuaded.[5]

As 1960 ended, Rustin prepared for a trip to India. The War Resisters International was holding its tenth triennial conference there, the first time it would meet outside Britain. The American delegation was small. Besides Rustin, it included Willoughby, the head of CNVA, and Jeannette Rankin, the first woman to serve in the U.S. Congress and the only American elected official to have voted against participation in both world wars. Friends like Bill Sutherland and Michael Scott attended; altogether, sixty-four countries were represented.

The choice of India was both symbolic and strategic. Traveling to the country that had been home to Gandhi honored the memory of a man who was a heroic figure to everyone in attendance. The Indian locale also implicitly challenged the stance of many Western pacifists. The

War Resisters had formed in Britain in the wake of World War I as an uncompromising voice against the staggering carnage of the conflict. Over the years, its members had tended overwhelmingly to emphasize a pure and simple opposition to warfare. But Gandhi used nonviolence differently. He directed it against colonialism. His target was injustice—the injustice of one nation exploiting and impoverishing another and robbing it of dignity and autonomy. In 1960, the continuing struggle to end European imperial rule preoccupied the delegates from Asia and Africa. It was at least as vital as opposition to nuclear weaponry, which absorbed Western pacifists. Moreover, the site of the conference was at Gandhigram, a training center and retreat founded by G. Ramachandran, a disciple of Gandhi. Gandhigram served as a base for the chief manifestation of nonviolence since independence—the reconstruction of village life along egalitarian economic and social lines.

Some of the exchanges that occurred at the conference were particularly vigorous. To the Indians, for instance, the single-minded focus on war made no sense. It avoided responsibility for the ugly heritage of colonialism and allowed Europeans to ignore the inequities of their liberal democracies. Ramachandran laid out his disagreement in a welcoming address to the delegates. "How we pursue our economic life together is part of peace making," he told them. "You can't have an exploiting society talking of peace. You cannot evade the issue of injustice and then talk of peace. I think peace without justice will be a complete fraud."[6]

But the Westerners also laid out a challenge to their hosts. At the time of the conference, India was moving in the direction of militarization. Border skirmishes with Pakistan over Kashmir, tensions with the Chinese over Tibet, and the continuing irritation of Portugal's presence in Goa had led Nehru to turn toward armed strength in response. Nehru had been Gandhi's closest partner in the struggle for independence. Since then, he had retained the admiration of peace activists because of his leadership of a neutral bloc of nations who refused entanglement in the cold war. But now he was leading India in another direction. His government's latest proposal called for mandatory military training in India's colleges and universities. To the pacifists from Western Europe and North America, these actions demanded a response. But the Gandhian movement in India had demurred, claiming that in a democracy where citizens could express their will through electoral channels, direct action campaigns were coercive. Instead, they argued, all their efforts should go toward building a "Gandhian society" that would willingly reject armed violence. But, Rustin reported, "before long it became apparent that many Indians feel that use of direct action 'embarrasses Pandit Nehru, our old friend and leader.'"[7]

Rustin played a critical part in these debates. More than anyone else there, he bridged the clashing positions of Western pacifists and anti-colonial activists. As a citizen of the world's largest military power, capable of annihilating much of life on the planet, Rustin took up the banner of Western opposition to militarism. But as a member of a subordinated racial group, a colonized people within a liberal democracy, he also embraced the call for social justice. Rustin spoke with passion about the black freedom struggle at home. He placed it squarely within the tradition of Gandhi, and he used it to speak to the issues dividing the conferees. Rustin talked feelingly not only of the physical violence but also of the economic coercion faced by Southern blacks who resisted segregation. The protests waged by young blacks, he acknowledged, were coercive. But, he said, "it is greater coercion to turn one's eyes from injustice, from the problem of poor people who must do without land. . . . We must not disregard social injustice. As I understand Gandhi, we must act, act now, even though we do not always see the future clearly."[8]

Rustin spoke about his concept of social dislocation, of the need for pacifists to create what he called "nonviolent confusion" in society. He urged upon his listeners the broadest possible conception of their mission. "I have learnt in my work the greatest lesson of all," he told them. "Whether the problems be that of colour or caste, man can be unjust to man, American to American, Indian to Indian. The problem is rooted in man's ability to be unjust; and therefore, can only be approached basically if we are opposed to all injustice." By the time the conference ended, his words had carried the day as conference participants endorsed—for the first time in the WRI's history—the use of nonviolence "to achieve social justice as well as peace."[9]

When the conference ended, Rustin and Willoughby stayed in India for several more days. They traveled together to Calcutta to meet Vinoba Bhave, the inheritor of Gandhi's mantle and the instigator of the campaigns to redistribute land voluntarily in India's rural villages. For several days, the two Americans traveled with Bhave through the countryside, trekking from village to village. At one point, the two men made an excursion to an ancient Buddhist center. "It was in ruins," Willoughby recalled. "We went out there very late at night or early in the morning, bright moonlight. Here's this vast pile of ruins. And you know Bayard was a collector. 'Look at these things!' Bayard was just wild to see this whole field. There were hundreds of feet of ruins of these old Buddhist temples. You could just push around in them."[10]

ON THE WAY HOME, Rustin stopped in London to confer with April Carter, Michael Randle, and other British pacifists about the San Francisco–to–Moscow peace walk. CNVA leaders needed a European to handle the logistics of the European half of the journey, and they wanted Carter to do it. Carter agreed since CNVA was "our sister organization. They asked for our support and we gave it." But she and the others insisted that someone with closer ties to CNVA also be involved. The memo they sent to Muste, Gilmore, and others in New York made their wishes clear: "Someone representing CNVA . . . should be in Europe for a protracted period to work with April Carter. . . . The group meeting in London strongly recommended that Bayard Rustin be assigned to this task." And so Rustin, a dissenting voice, was now charged with seeing to the success of the walk in Europe.[11]

Early in March, Rustin settled into London for a three-month stay. As he had predicted, planning the peace walk was complicated to the point of being nightmarish. Beyond the not small issue of logistics, Rustin had to make sure that across the boundaries of politics and culture, the meaning of the intercontinental walk remained clear. American pacifists were stressing a message of personal moral responsibility:

each individual had to take a stand against the threat of nuclear holocaust. The walkers were calling for unilateral disarmament. They insisted that opposition to war transcended ideology. So it was especially
important that their message remain uncontaminated by the cold war
rhetoric of either side.

Since the Campaign for Nuclear Disarmament (CND) was the dominant player in British peace politics, Rustin had to win it over to the
peace walk. Its leader, Canon John Collins of St. Paul's Cathedral, was
a wily character who hid his maneuvering behind the mild demeanor of
an Anglican cleric. Collins was actively hostile to direct actionists and
sought as much as possible to distance CND from civil disobedience.
Rustin set up a meeting with Collins as quickly as was feasible and received the canon's account of "the relationships and problems that exist" between CND and other peace groups. Collins made it clear that
because the walk endorsed unilateral disarmament and civil disobedience, CND could not "sponsor" it. But he agreed to "welcome the
American team" by staging a massive rally at Trafalgar Square to kick
off the team's trek to Southampton. Unable to fathom the difference
between a welcome and a sponsorship, Rustin wrote to Muste that "the
Canon, like his boss, 'works in strange ways his wonders to perform.'"
But he left the meeting satisfied that Collins "will be of great help."[12]

Negotiating with British pacifists was easy compared with the trials
posed by the various national and peace issues on the Continent. Rustin
faced difficult decisions about which route the walk should take across
Europe. He had to extract from European pacifists commitments to
generate publicity, bring out their supporters along the route, and stage
demonstrations in their countries. He wanted them to provide additional participants to make the walk increasingly multinational as it
passed from country to country. He also hoped that pacifists in those
countries the walk bypassed would organize tributary marches that
eventually all converged.

In mid-March, Rustin traveled with Carter to Gröningen, in the
north of the Netherlands, for a weekend meeting with European pacifists. "The problems that arise multiply," Rustin wrote back in a memo.
Pacifists from across the Continent wanted the walk to pass through

their territory, but each country posed a different set of difficulties. The Finns and the Austrians, both from nations that maintained neutrality in the cold war, were aghast at the prospect of civil disobedience occurring along their borders, should the walkers be refused entry into the East. French pacifists were completely preoccupied, as was their whole nation, with the escalating violence of the Algerian independence movement and the political crisis it was engendering at home. Among German peace advocates, the walk provoked both excitement and resentment. Many were eager for the walkers to attempt a crossing into East Germany and tried to calculate its impact on the labyrinthine politics of German reunification. They were also irritated by the American presumption of initiating the walk without prior consultation. Since Germany was emerging as the most likely route from West to East, Rustin had to secure the cooperation of German pacifists. But, as he reported to associates in New York, "peace leaders are scarcely on speaking terms" with one another, and "it appears that no leader of an established organization can call a meeting without others staying away." Rustin begged Muste to use his influence to surmount the factionalism so that a support team could finally be constructed in Germany.[13]

To his dismay, Rustin learned in Gröningen that a Swedish pacifist by the name of Oscarsson had launched an effort to organize a competing cross-continental peace march that summer. The idea of two such projects was absurd, and many pacifists at Gröningen thought they should simply be combined. But Rustin had heard rumors that Oscarsson had contacted peace councils in Eastern Europe whose sponsorship would, in American eyes, damn any project as Communist inspired. Rustin persuaded the Swede to abandon his march and help make the CNVA walk a success. Writing to everyone back home, Rustin described Oscarsson as "a political idiot and very naive. . . . He has felt that love requires working with everyone." But the meetings with the Swede also convinced Rustin that "he is a sincere pacifist . . . he is not a fellow traveller."[14]

By early April, key decisions had been made so that Rustin, Carter, and the rest of the London group could devote themselves to the logistics of the walk. They selected a route through France, Belgium, the two Germanies, Poland, and the Soviet Union. Rustin boiled the message down to a few simple slogans. Taking into account the laws of various countries and different national cultures of dissent, Rustin and Carter decided to restrict protests to military headquarters in national capitals, but to veto acts of civil disobedience at military bases, as CNVA had sponsored in the United States.

As recruitment for European walkers continued, Rustin supervised their training. Volunteers discussed the tactics and philosophy of nonviolence. He planned sociodramas to simulate the kind of confrontations they might encounter. He especially insisted that they acclimate themselves to the discipline required for an action like the walk. "The group should discuss until they understand," he wrote, "the need to accept democratically agreed upon leadership in a project where decisions must often be made quickly. . . . There will be many occasions [on the walk] when full discussion is not possible."[15]

All this time the walkers were crossing the United States, on foot near population centers but transporting themselves in vans through long, unpopulated stretches of the American West, which they traversed in winter. Nothing ominous had happened to them, but neither had their actions captured the American imagination. In some places, the local press had covered the event when these peace emissaries arrived in town, but the walk never became a national story. As they came closer to Washington, participants requested an interview with President Kennedy. But the president was too busy and instead assigned the meeting to Arthur Schlesinger, Jr., a special assistant very low in the pecking order.

The American team was scheduled to land in Britain on June 1. Having surmounted a host of potential complications in Europe, Rustin was not prepared for the obstacles thrown in his way by the walkers and the CNVA office. For weeks he had been writing home, reporting on his negotiations with European pacifists, alerting the CNVA leadership to assistance that he needed, and requesting advice on decisions he was making. He received little in return. Rustin had carefully worked out the content of placards with his colleagues on the Continent; to the Americans, he had explained in detail why certain choices had been made.

Yet just days before the arrival of the Americans, Rustin learned that Brad Lyttle, the leader of the walk, wanted to use the signs that were carried on the American walk: "Refuse to Serve in Armed Forces" . . . "Refuse to Work in Military Industries" . . . "Refuse to Pay Taxes for War." "We are puzzled," Rustin and Carter fired back, "that Brad should urge these signs be carried in Europe. . . . We will alienate all European contacts and will be refused entry into almost all, if not all, European countries if we try to carry such signs. . . . The slogans we have adopted can NOT be changed."[16]

Rustin's ire continued to grow. When he heard that Lyttle was insisting that, to save money in Europe, the whole team stay in whatever accommodations were most affordable and that the use of cars for transport be eliminated, he expressed his impatience with "Brad's . . . insensitivity to other people." Muste was accompanying the walkers from London to Moscow, and Rustin knew the journey would be arduous for the old man. He wrote to Muste privately: "I *forbid* you to stay [in youth hostels]," or to "camp in barns or fields. . . . At your age and the amount of work you have to do *before*, *during*, and *after* the march, it would be childish and silly for you not to insist on what your age and future usefulness rightly require." Meanwhile, repeated requests that the New York office send publicity materials had yielded nothing except a thick package of unedited logs from the journey in the United States. Rustin made no attempt to disguise his impatience: "We are spending thousands of other people's money on a project that has untold complications (a fact that I foresaw long ago when I advised against the walk) and which we have slaved in London to bring off against great odds. We are almost at the point of having a great possibility of success and I have been writing for over *one month*, trying to get a *press rundown* and *human interest document* on the march to hand over to experienced people here. . . . Why can't it be done?" Rustin returned the package of material. "If it is necessary to go over the log to get what I want, then have it gone over. . . . We want what we ask for and not a pile of junk we don't have time to go through."[17]

The difficulties with Lyttle and the CNVA brought into the open something that Carter had detected in Rustin as they worked together each day. Rustin, she recalled, "was a bit removed from the more purely pacifist movement." He was "quite caustic . . . almost contemptuous" toward Lyttle and the other marchers, whom he characterized irascibly as "these anarchistic people who won't do what they're told!" He thought they were, ironically, profoundly "apolitical," often quite unconscious about the political environment in which they were moving and the ramifications of their actions. Carter remembered the enthusiasm that Rustin had displayed two years earlier over the Sahara project. He thought it was "enormously worthwhile precisely because it wasn't just a kind of pacifist bearing witness [but] linked up with a major anti-colonial movement." With the peace walk, she recalled, "my sense really was that he was doing his duty . . . that he was rather impatient with the march but because it was his role he would do his best for it."[18] In their many hours together, Rustin expressed much more enthusiasm about civil rights activity in the United States, where dramatic Freedom Rides that spring had become an international news story, than about anything related to the peace walk.

Though Rustin could not put his heart into the work, he did enjoy the months abroad. He stayed at William Penn House, a Quaker lodging in Bloomsbury, although he did not seem to share the ascetic style of those around him. Carter, who sometimes visited, remembered him smuggling bottles of whiskey to his room, contrary to the rules of the residence. Rustin, she said, "was very open" about his homosexuality and "very obviously had contacts in the gay scene" in London. Whenever he could, he scoured the many flea markets in the city, where he picked up beautifully tailored suits for a fraction of their worth. The sight of a tall, elegantly appointed black man haunting the antique shops and outdoor stalls along Portobello Road and in other neighborhoods was unusual, and Rustin became a familiar figure to many dealers. With his well-developed eye, he acquired wonderful furniture and pieces of art that he shipped home. He extended his explorations to the Continent as well. On a trip to Paris, Rustin dragged Carter along on one of his jaunts to translate for him. "He was obviously very knowledgeable," she realized, "and the woman who ran the shop obviously recognized that he was knowledgeable."[19]

Throughout his stay, visa problems plagued Rustin. The British government, like that of the United States during the cold war, was not eager to facilitate the work of dissidents. Rustin received permission to stay month by month. The last extension expired in June, and there was no last-minute reprieve. And so Muste, rather than Rustin, accompanied the team across Europe. Rustin did at least get to participate in the almost festive mood that surrounded the Americans throughout their time in Britain. The depth of organizing there against nuclear weapons was obvious in the crowds that greeted them. Over 10,000 turned out for the welcome rally in Trafalgar Square; 5,000 marchers escorted the team out of London on the road to Southampton; and villagers lined the streets along the way to offer a show of support.

Although the peace walk did eventually make it all the way to Moscow, the few days in England proved to be the most gripping part of the journey. Throughout the nine-month-long trek, the walkers repeatedly found themselves upstaged by the very sort of events they were marching to oppose. In mid-April, as they approached the east coast, the Bay of Pigs invasion dominated the news. In June, as they enjoyed the crowds of enthusiasts in England, the collapse of the Vienna summit meeting between Kennedy and Khrushchev drew the world's attention. On the Continent, France was in such a state of crisis over Algeria that authorities would not even let the team enter the country. "France is in a near state of war," Muste wrote to the CNVA office. The crises continued until the very end. The team arrived in Germany just as the East German government constructed the Berlin Wall and provoked the most serious crisis in Europe since the Berlin airlift a dozen years earlier. During the trek across Poland and Russia, the Soviet government resumed atmospheric testing, and the United States announced it would follow suit. "Ours is not a world-shaking project," Muste said, surely as understated a form of self-criticism as one could imagine.[20]

The transcontinental walk may have been a dud, but the time in England set Rustin to thinking. He had dealt closely with peace activists from across Western Europe and had observed at close range the antinuclear movement in Britain. It took little perspicacity to see that on the Continent, as in the United States, pacifists were utterly marginal to the politics of war and peace. International tensions were spiraling in 1961—between the superpowers, on the African continent, in the Caribbean, and across South Asia—but most Western pacifists had little more than symbolic forms of protest to offer. In Britain, Rustin noticed something different. The issue of nuclear disarmament had captured the popular imagination there in a way that it had not elsewhere. The Campaign for Nuclear Disarmament was a mass organization, with chapters throughout the United Kingdom. It had achieved a fair degree of-legitimacy. It drew the media's interest. Many members were deeply involved in local branches of the Labour Party. Labour was out of power for much of the 1950s, but it would, someday, receive a popular mandate to form a government. Antinuclear activists might then be in a position to shape the policy of a nation that possessed nuclear weapons and was a key player in global politics. At the same time, radical activists like Carter and Randle were able to pull off bold actions that dramatized the dangers of nuclear war and lent urgency to the issue. Rustin was especially taken with the ability of the British movement to mobilize large numbers for public rallies and marches. Randle recalled that Rustin was present at one of the big sit-downs in central London that winter. "He was impressed," Randle recalled, "that we could get so many people out on the streets and remarked to me that a mass demonstration of this kind had real political clout. 'It's something,' he said to me, 'I can never get the pacifists in the U.S. to appreciate.' "[21]

DURING THE MONTHS in London, Rustin also devoted himself to another pacifist project just then taking shape. In 1948, immediately after Indian independence, Gandhi had proposed the creation of a people's nonviolent army, recruited from all over the world, to intervene in places where war threatened. Gandhi's assassination had forestalled any efforts at implementation, but the idea continued to circulate through pacifist networks. At the Gandhigram conference, Ramachandran had broached the concept in his welcoming address. "Nationalism and what are called national states have become largely menaces to the human spirit and to human society," he told the international assemblage. He challenged them to "go beyond patriotism and nationalism. We must declare that we can accept no frontiers of any national state. . . . Humanity is one and we are citizens of one world." Jayaprakash Narayan, another Indian delegate, followed with a specific call for a "World Peace Brigade." Rustin drew warm applause when he called for the use of direct action as "an integral part of any such international brigade."[22]

The idea of a peace brigade, in the words of the final report, "caught the imagination of the Conference." Scott was put in charge of a working group to develop the idea further. Rustin, who was listed as one of the sponsors, was skeptical. As he wrote to WRL members at home: "If the Michael Scott committee can, with the help of world pacifist leaders, develop a real World Peace Brigade which can do constructive work all over the globe and which can be sent into areas of potential tension prior to an explosion—the WRI conference will have achieved a miracle." Over the years, Rustin had been privy to many visionary pacifist schemes that turned out to be little more than pipe dreams, and he was impatient. "Discussion of a World Peace Brigade has plagued us since World War II, and the idea should either be implemented or forgotten," he told his fellow pacifists.[23]

Despite his brusque tone, Rustin wanted it to work. Its boldness appealed to him. More than the moral witness of a transcontinental walk, it promised direct intervention to forestall mass violence. It called for the kind of courage that Rustin had displayed in his younger days, when he had first attached himself to a peace movement. And it expressed faith in the revolutionary potential of nonviolence to remake social relations. He was particularly intrigued by the role a peace brigade might play in Africa. Events in 1960 had shown how easily violence could erupt in the continuing battle against European rule and white-settler hegemony. In Sharpeville, a black township in South Africa, white police had fired into a large, peaceful crowd of unarmed blacks who were protesting the government's pass laws, killing several dozen. Although the massacre elicited international outrage, it only confirmed the white supremacist government in its hard-line suppression of any opposition. In the Congo, a bloody civil war had erupted immediately after independence. In Northern Rhodesia, the resistance of the white settler population to black majority rule was rising.

The several months he spent in England in 1961 gave Rustin the opportunity to work more closely with Michael Scott on the peace brigade. He often shunted the daily work of the San Francisco–to–Moscow walk over to April Carter as he investigated the possibility of pacifist intervention in Africa. London was populated with an African nationalist community, and Rustin had contacts there from his previous trips. He formed an especially strong connection with Kenneth Kaunda, the head of the militant independence party in Northern Rhodesia, or Zambia as it was called after independence. Kaunda had been to India and had studied the independence struggle there. His political rhetoric commonly featured references to nonviolence. Among African leaders, probably no one was closer ideologically to pacifism than Kaunda.

Through the fall of 1961, pacifists in Europe, Asia, Africa, and North America engaged in a spirited, often contentious, debate about just what this peace brigade should do. At first, the division seemed stark and simple. Some proposed raising a massive army of volunteers to be dispatched around the globe for conciliatory projects of relief and technical assistance. To the more militant activists like Rustin, Carter, Sutherland, and some of the Indians, this threatened to make the brigade into little more than a "replica of the International Red Cross." Instead, they wanted "the sharp clean emphasis on action in emergency situations" to remain front and center.[24]

But those who favored nonviolent direct action were not of one mind. Rustin, Scott, and Sutherland thought in terms of colonialism, while Brad Lyttle was pressing to expand protests against nuclear testing. He wanted the brigade to acquire an ocean vessel "large enough that it could not be readily blocked" and have it make its way to testing sites in the Pacific. He also suggested a squadron of long-range aircraft to fly into nuclear testing areas. "The planes themselves," he wrote, "would be expendable." Crews would "circle ground zero until their fuel was exhausted," and then parachute to earth.[25] Proposals like Lyttle's drove Rustin to distraction.

Right after Christmas, Rustin, Muste, and Bob Gilmore traveled to

Lebanon for a conference to launch the brigade. Held at a Quaker high school in a suburb of Beirut, the meeting had impressive sponsorship: independence leaders like Julius Nyerere of Tanganyika and Kaunda of Zambia; philosophers like Martin Buber of Israel and Bertrand Russell of Britain; Martin Niemoller of Germany, a theologian whom the Nazis had imprisoned for seven years; Danilo Dolci, the Italian radical often described as "the Gandhi of Sicily." Assembling in the unheated school, which was closed for the holidays, and suffering through unusually cold weather, the delegates from thirteen countries endorsed recruitment of a multinational nonviolent army. "Nothing could be more fantastic," remarked Gilmore, as he contemplated what it meant to take on the power of imperial interests and cold war alliances.[26] Specifically, the conference decided to approve a plan to assist African independence movements.

After Beirut, Rustin stopped in London to work out with Scott and Randle a concrete African proposal. Despite the conference's endorsement, Rustin knew that decolonization was not central to the thinking of Western pacifists. Yet success depended on the resources that only Westerners could mobilize. The document he prepared pointed to the "deep crisis in the whole of Central and Southern Africa. The white extremists are attempting to consolidate their position and to 'seal off' the area of African liberation." Rustin argued that "there was a very close connection between the anti-war movement in the West and the African and Asian uncommitted nations who stood for neutralism and independence in the Cold War." With the endorsement of Nyerere, who had just become prime minister of Tanganyika, Rustin outlined a plan to establish a nonviolent training center in Dar es Salaam. "The first function," he wrote, would be "giving the opportunity to men and women from Central and Southern Africa to study positive action and to develop a more effective strategy, and to return home to lead this struggle." The center would organize actions as well. Rustin suggested "international direct action" to focus world attention on the plans for white minority rule in Northern Rhodesia.[27]

Rustin returned to New York to secure permission from the WRL for his African venture. By early February, he was on his way to a rendezvous with Scott and Sutherland in Addis Ababa, where they attended the conference of the Pan African Freedom Movement for East and Central Africa. The talk among many was of the need for violent uprisings, and Rustin learned of plans to train refugees in sabotage and guerrilla warfare. But there was also interest in nonviolence. Kaunda particularly spoke against the sentiment to take up arms. As Rustin reported, when delegates challenged Kaunda's pacifism, the Zambian leader replied that "Africa must not add to the violence of the West which already threatens the existence of mankind. . . . We must find another way or perish." In meetings with Kaunda and Nyerere, the three pacifists confirmed the understanding that Nyerere would support their effort to open a training center in Tanganyika, and that they would put the center's resources at Kaunda's disposal. Rustin left Addis Ababa feeling that "the fate of nonviolence in Southern Africa depends on the success of this project."[28]

Kaunda wasted no time in taking advantage of the offer, even if the training center was, at this point, nothing but a good intention. In Northern Rhodesia, the British had scheduled an election for later in the spring, with rules that guaranteed that the white minority would capture most seats. Soon after the Addis Ababa conference, Kaunda addressed a rally in Lusaka. He called for a general strike to demonstrate opposition to the rigged election. He promised that on the day of the strike, "thousands of volunteers from the World Peace Brigade would peacefully invade the country from Tanganyika." The marchers, he said, "will not come equipped with guns. . . . If arrested they will sit down."[29] The threat seemed credible enough that the colonialist government rushed troops to the border.

Rustin and the others were welcomed in Dar es Salaam. They received lodging in the former home of Tanganyika's vice president and used the residence as the initial headquarters for the training of volunteers. Blessing their efforts, Nyerere told Rustin and his associates that they "have already done a great service to Zambia's independence." In March, they called a press conference, partly to worry the British about the planned march to the border and partly for visibility to recruit volunteers. Scott made the opening statement but, as one paper reported, he very quickly was "completely overshadowed by American Bayard Rustin, who answered most of the questions and generally took control of the assembly." As Rustin explained to his audience, "We will start to march when Mr. Kaunda gives us the call. . . . We are prepared to face arrest, imprisonment or being shot at." Rustin likened the planned march to the Freedom Rides in the United States the previous year, which had captured headlines around the globe. His remarks seemed incendiary enough that a State Department officer in Dar es Salaam wired a request to the FBI asking for information on Rustin.[30]

In April, Rustin returned home to attend to WRL business. Kaunda also came to New York that month and testified before the UN Committee on Colonialism. While he was in the city, he also spoke at the WRL's annual dinner, quite a coup for a small, radical organization. But his address was also strategic, since Rustin wanted the league to release him for further work in Africa. After hearing Kaunda's inspirational speech about the Zambian freedom struggle and getting a report from Rustin on the trainings under way, the executive committee let Rustin rejoin Scott and Sutherland in Dar es Salaam.

Events unfolded rapidly. The African boycott of the election in Northern Rhodesia was almost complete and shook British hopes that the white settler government could make legitimate claims to rule. Rustin arrived in Tanganyika in time for a rally of 10,000 in the town of Mbeya, just seventy-five miles from the border with Northern Rhodesia. Rustin spoke and was well received. Kaunda praised the efforts of the Brigade and urged that preparations for the march continue.[31] But the combination of pressures led the British government to formulate a new proposal for elections, one that Kaunda found encouraging. He told Rustin, Scott, and Sutherland that, for now at least, plans for a march across the border should be put on hold. Though the march never materialized, for a few months Rustin had found himself in the midst of a heady freedom struggle.

TRAVELING ABROAD IN these years somewhat assuaged the frustration Rustin felt being at arm's length from the civil rights movement. It also eased the transition that had occurred in his relationship with Tom Kahn. Living together had not been easy on Rustin. Their styles were dramatically different and, ultimately, incompatible as partners in the daily routines of life. Rustin was fastidious in his personal habits, a model of order and neatness. Indeed, his apartment, which housed his growing art collection, was coming to have the appearance of a museum exhibit. Kahn was, at best, careless, leaving socks and clothes scattered about. He was also, in these years, ahead of the curve of the student culture of the 1960s in that he was already smoking marijuana. Rustin enjoyed belting down a few drinks at the end of the day, but the illegality of drugs disturbed him, especially in these years before the buying, selling, and consumption of marijuana became a mass phenomenon among youth. When Kahn decided to enroll at Howard University in Washington, Rustin was both sad and relieved. The two remained close, personally and politically, but their romantic entanglement ebbed.

Between his international adventures, Rustin continued to direct the WRL. The organization always seemed financially strapped, and Rustin's time abroad made the cash shortage especially difficult. In the midst of his London stay to plan the peace walk, he wrote to Muste that "WRL is sure hard hit now, and so is *Liberation*. I hope both can pull through."[32] In the fall of 1961, in between his work in London and Africa, Rustin toured college campuses in the Northeast and Midwest. His reputation and his flair on the podium made him a sought-after speaker on the college circuit. His appearances also brought income to the WRL.

Campus visits allowed Rustin to stay in touch with the shifting mood among the new student generation. Building on the excitement generated by the sit-ins, the Freedom Rides through the Deep South in 1961 had ignited even more interest in nonviolent action among college students. Chapters of the Student Peace Union (SPU) were forming on campus after campus. By spring 1962, it had more than a hundred local groups; by the following year, over two hundred. Rustin could be counted on to help the SPU raise money as he put them in touch with an older generation of financially secure Quakers. When the WRL moved into larger space in 1962, it was no coincidence that the SPU decided to put its national office there. During these years, Rustin held tremendous cachet among an emerging activist generation looking for role models and a sense of history.

In 1961, Rustin also participated in a new initiative among American pacifists. When he came back from Britain that summer, he discovered that his political network in New York shared his concern about spiraling international crises. Norman Thomas, the Socialist Party's venerable head, spent the summer polling many of his associates. "Pessimism is unnatural to me," he wrote to many of them, "but I have shared with you this summer a despair and foreboding I find hard to voice." To Thomas, the Kennedy administration seemed to be a "captive of the right," particularly of the Pentagon. It was lurching from one war-inducing event to another. "There must be a left in this country in the field of foreign policy," Thomas wrote, or else the drift to war would be unstoppable. In September, Rustin joined Thomas and a group of twenty others to plot strategy.[33]

Rustin quickly found himself on the steering committee of what came to be called Turn Toward Peace (TTP). Unlike SANE, it was not a new organization but a coalition. It brought together not only radical pacifists but representatives of progressive trade unions and liberal organizations like Americans for Democratic Action. Also unlike SANE, it moved beyond a focus on nuclear weapons to broader questions of war and international conflict. TTP saw its mission as building "enthusiastic public attitudes" for peace among a large segment of the American public, and it generated high hopes when it started. Robert Pickus, an AFSC stalwart for a generation, told Thomas he thought it was "our best chance" since the end of World War II "to put the peace movement together." Rustin, who had just witnessed the broad-based British disarmament movement at close range, was eager for the kind of coalition effort that TTP promised. For the next several years, he attended strategy sessions of the steering committee.

But the work of CNVA continued to occupy more of Rustin's energies. In the fall of 1961, radical pacifists received a large, and unexpected, boost, with the debut of Women's Strike for Peace (WSP). Presenting themselves as ordinary middle-class housewives whose civic concerns flowed from their maternal impulses, they added a new voice to the direct-action wing of the peace movement. Although WSP tried to avoid being tagged as extremist or radical, its willingness to engage in public protest and its appeal to ordinary Americans made it a promising addition to the ranks of peace activism. With the involvement of WSP, the protests that WRL and CNVA sponsored began to grow. In March 1962, 3,000 opponents of nuclear testing gathered in New York's Times Square, and after the rally, some of them engaged in an impromptu sit-down. The next month, over 5,000 participated in the annual Easter Peace Walk, which Rustin addressed outside the United Nations. In October, in the midst of the Cuban missile crisis, Rustin coordinated a quickly planned demonstration in front of the UN. The rally brought together more than 10,000 marchers, the largest peace demonstration in New York since the cold war began.

Even with these larger numbers, Rustin was not optimistic about the capacity of the movement to make a difference at home. Early in 1962, he told his fellow activists in CNVA that "Kennedy cannot be influenced." After the missile crisis, and despite the large rally at the UN, he declared again at a meeting that "there is no possibility" of influencing the government. Drawing on the excitement he had experienced in Africa and in observing the dynamism of the British peace movement, he speculated that perhaps American activists needed to keep their attention outward, toward the rest of the world, and look for ways "to help develop a radical pacifist movement in other countries." Early in 1963, in a wide-ranging discussion of the peace movement's prospects, Rustin drew an interesting analogy. "CNVA at the present time," he said, "is no more relevant than was CORE in the 1940s." Two decades earlier, the young organization supported people who were "on fire with an idea." Perhaps the main function of CNVA was "to keep the ideas embodied in our major concerns alive until the situation is ripe for their acceptance by a large and really effective movement."[34]

AS THE ANALOGY WITH CORE suggests, the civil rights movement was very much on Rustin's mind, even while he worked as a roving pacifist organizer. The civil rights movement grew by leaps and bounds in these years. Organizing campaigns and direct action protests were reaching across the South, extending even into the Deep South. In the North, support activities were spreading, especially among college youth, and local movements to attack de facto segregation in schooling and housing were popping up in city after city. There was more than a bit of frustration in Rustin's enforced inactivity because, even as the civil rights struggle was growing, it confronted entrenched resistance. In Mississippi, SNCC had established community organizing projects to stimulate voter registration among blacks. The harassment and violence were horrific. In 1962, Martin Luther King lent his effort to an ongoing desegregation campaign in Albany, Georgia. The local police chief made so many arrests that the jails of neighboring counties had to house the demonstrators. The tempo of civil rights activities was certainly rising, but there were few institutional gains to show for it. The movement seemed up against immovable obstacles.

One of the largest obstacles was the Kennedy administration itself. For all the idealistic rhetoric that emanated from the White House, President Kennedy and his brother Robert, the attorney general, were reluctant to act on behalf of racial justice. Civil rights leaders were highly critical. Jim Farmer, who was the head of CORE during these years, said of Kennedy that "he did not know much about Negroes or their struggle." King described the president's approach as "a sort of crystallized tokenism." Even Lee White, a loyal presidential assistant who handled much of the civil rights business, acknowledged that Kennedy's approach was that "there was going to be plenty of time to fight the battle of civil rights legislation." Meanwhile, "his desire to do first things first" meant that racial justice remained relatively low on his list of priorities.[35]

For Rustin there was something achingly bittersweet about the way the civil rights movement was unfolding without him. In the spring of 1961, while Rustin was in London planning the peace walk, CORE launched dramatic "Freedom Rides." Integrated teams of civil rights activists rode buses into the Deep South and attempted to desegregate bus terminals. News headlines and television cameras captured the violence that the riders encountered, and the event drew international attention. It was the first major civil rights crisis that the Kennedy administration confronted. Rustin had been a CORE stalwart throughout the 1940s. He had planned and executed the first interracial bus rides in the South in 1947. He had spent time on a North Carolina chain gang because of these efforts. Rustin and Farmer had worked together in CORE in the early days, but Farmer had little to do with the organization after its first couple of years. Now Rustin was reading about Farmer, the new executive director of CORE whose role in the Freedom Rides catapulted him into the ranks of national civil rights leadership. Rustin was not ordinarily given to envy, yet he must have experienced twinges of it as he contemplated his distance from the center of the action.

Rustin kept as best he could some connection to the fight for racial justice. A mesmerizing speaker, he was a great crowd pleaser and remained much in demand. During 1961 and 1962, he engaged in a series of public debates—in New York, Chicago, and Washington, D.C.—with Malcolm X, a charismatic leader in the Nation of Islam with an especially strong following in Harlem. The events drew large audiences eager to hear their verbal dueling. The Nation of Islam, or Black Muslims as they were popularly called, espoused racial separatism and advocated armed self-defense. Rustin easily held his own in these encounters. His advocacy of mass action and strategic nonviolence when sit-ins and freedom rides were capturing the public's imagination more than matched the rhetorical militancy of Malcolm X. And Rustin could taunt his opponent on the weakness of the Nation's political strategy. "The Black Muslims have put forth, as you ought to know, no concrete program except speaking on 125th Street," he said during one of their debates.[36]

Most of all, Rustin tried to maintain ties to the emerging generation of black student activists. He considered those working in the South "the most advanced group of American youth today." Through his work with Randolph and King in the 1950s, he already had contacts with key individuals like Bob Moses and Stokely Carmichael, another

SNCC activist now at Howard University.[37] Rustin found ways to deepen and extend these relationships. With Kahn attending Howard University, Rustin was able to develop a good connection with the SNCC affiliate there. Ed Brown, one of its members, recalled that "Bayard . . . had a very, very decisive influence on me and I think the rest of us for a long while."[38] When SNCC opened a Northern office in New York City, it was housed at the same address as the WRL headquarters. Rustin had regular contact with SNCC members who worked there or who passed through.

Still, Rustin always had to act with caution because the stigma of his sexuality might, at any moment, rise to curtail his influence. Richard Momeyer heard Rustin speak in the fall of 1961 at Allegheny College in Pennsylvania, where Momeyer was a sophomore. He remembered Rustin as "an especially intense, even charismatic individual who was singularly articulate and powerfully persuasive." Rustin challenged the audience to desegregate their own institution, and Momeyer and a few other students responded enthusiastically. One day, the campus chaplain took him aside. "He wanted to caution me," Momeyer recalled, "that we should not identify our efforts too closely with Bayard Rustin. . . . Rustin, he said, could be a problematic connection, because he had a 'morals record.'"[39] So Rustin continued to operate on the sidelines, an observer as the struggle for racial justice built toward a crescendo.

CHAPTER FIFTEEN

"One of the Great Days in American History"

1963

THROUGH HIS PERIOD of exile from the civil rights movement, Rustin had remained close to Randolph. The trust and affection between them ran deep. It was fed by dreams and goals they held in common. It rested on the bonds that develop when two comrades in struggle face bitter disagreements and then repair the damage. Their respective life histories bore an uncanny resemblance. Each had been a star athlete in high school. Each affected a cultured style of speech that bred misapprehensions about their backgrounds. Each had made the pilgrimage to New York City as a young adult, hoping to succeed on the stage or in the concert hall. Instead, they both found their way to radical politics and chose to become agitators for justice.

Randolph had already savored his finest moments as a public figure. He had tasted the satisfaction of knowing that presidents had worried about his intentions, segregationist senators and army generals had fulminated against him, and middle-class Negro leaders feared his stealing a march on their constituents. Now he watched with a tinge of concern as a new generation mounted assaults on the citadels of intolerance. Missing from the impending civil rights revolution, at least as far as Randolph could see, was the passion for economic justice that had shaped his own career. Rustin, younger than Randolph by more than two decades, had recently turned fifty. He was still waiting for his day in the limelight, though likely believing it would never come. Prejudice of another sort, still not named as such in midcentury America, had curtailed his opportunities and limited his effectiveness.

Neither of them quite remembered, and none of their associates knew, which one first suggested a mass mobilization in Washington, but it surprised no one that the idea had emerged in a conversation between them. Near the end of December 1962, Rustin had made one of his periodic visits to Randolph, whose office was in Harlem. Their conversations often ranged widely over politics and history, and this time they were reflecting on the imminent centennial of the Emancipation Proclamation. Both viewed the Reconstruction era as a failure, a time when the full promise of Emancipation, the economic independence of "forty acres and a mule," was never realized. Perhaps Randolph began to reminisce about the march that never happened on the eve of World War II, when he threatened to bring the black masses to Washington to demand jobs. Perhaps Rustin himself raised the idea of a march, aware of what it meant to the older man. In either case, Rustin knew in a flash that he would devote himself to the project. From the start, he reminisced, "[I was] deeply involved emotionally. . . . I knew [Randolph] always had a hankering for a march and my emotional commitment was . . . to bring about what had always been one of his dreams."[1] Not incidentally, the march also held out to Rustin the promise of a road back to the burgeoning civil rights movement.

OVER THE HOLIDAYS, Rustin traveled with Muste to England to attend an international conference of the non-Stalinist left. As soon as he returned, he brought together Tom Kahn and Norman Hill to help him draft a proposal. Kahn was home for a few weeks, between semesters at Howard. Hill now was based in New York, on CORE's national staff. The three of them, Hill recalled, "sat down to try and put together a preliminary memo which would outline in kind of rough form what the plans were to be for such a march."[2] For all of them, issues of class inflected their understanding of racism, and they brought this perspective to their deliberations.

Rustin's original prospectus put economics front and center. "The one hundred years since the signing of the Emancipation Proclamation," he began, "have witnessed no fundamental government action to terminate the economic subordination of the American Negro." The glaring issue before the nation, he wrote, was "the unresolved crisis of the national economy." Automation was creating an expanding class of displaced unskilled workers. These trends hit black workers especially hard, as the growing racial gap in unemployment rates demonstrated. Current civil rights strategies were insufficient. "Integration in the fields of education, housing, transportation and public accommodations will be of limited extent and duration as long as fundamental economic inequality along racial lines persists. . . . When a racial disparity in unemployment has been firmly established in the course of a century, the change-over to 'equal opportunities' . . . does not wipe out the cumulative handicaps of the Negro worker." The purpose of the mobilization was "the creation of more jobs for all Americans." Rustin called for "a massive effort . . . by all progressive sectors," yet he also placed black America at the center of the action. "The dynamic that has motivated Negroes to withstand with courage and dignity the intimidation and violence they have endured in their own struggle against racism," he wrote, "may now be the catalyst which mobilizes all workers behind demands for a broad and fundamental program of economic justice."

Rustin envisioned action in Washington on a much grander scale than the rallies he had organized in the late 1950s. He proposed two days of activities that would have protesters spend the night in the nation's capital. On the first day, "a mass descent" on the Capitol would "so flood all congressmen with a staggering series of labor, church, civil rights delegations from their own states that they would be unable to conduct business on the floor of the Congress." The next day, a "mass protest rally . . . [would] project our concrete 'Emancipation Proclamation' to the nation." The rally would hold political leaders accountable by "reporting to the assemblage the response of the President and Congress to the action of the previous day."[3]

Randolph liked Rustin's proposal, and the two thrashed out how best to proceed. "There was one nagging question," Rustin recalled. "Before we went finally to Wilkins and King we needed an agency which says we are calling for the march and we will do it if we have to do it alone." Three years earlier, Randolph had founded the Negro American Labor Council (NALC) to press against the discriminatory practices of the labor movement. Rustin suggested that Randolph go to the NALC board and get its agreement to sponsor the mobilization. Other civil rights groups, but Wilkins and the NAACP especially, would then face the stark choice of coming on board or being left out of a potentially dramatic national event.[4]

Rustin spent much of February in Dar es Salaam, working on the World Peace Brigade. As always, trips to Africa nourished him. "The white people may talk of the backwardness of Negroes," he wrote in a group letter to Randolph and others. "But the rate of progress being made here is wonderful. The spirit is high and every person seems to be working for a common end." To friends back home he said, "It makes me feel good to be black." But his specific mission was discouraging. Bill Sutherland lacked the organizing skills to sustain the training center Rustin had set up the previous year, and he had alienated his African hosts. Assessing the situation, Rustin found "a larger mess than I had thought. . . . The government does not want us here any longer and does not want Bill to stay around." Any indications of sympathy from Nyerere or Kaunda toward nonviolent strategies brought sniping from opponents, particularly Communist activists. "The available evidence points toward a period of eclipse for non-violence" in Southern and Central Africa, Rustin reported. He saw no option but to close the center immediately and thus bring to an abrupt end yet another pacifist project that had once kindled his hopes.[5]

By the time he returned, Rustin was ready to push ahead with the proposed march, which Randolph had scheduled for mid-June. Early in March, Rustin traveled to Georgia, where he, Muste, and Glenn Smiley led an institute on nonviolence for about fifty key leaders in SNCC, CORE, and SCLC. Rustin talked up the idea of a Washington mobilization and lobbied members of each of the groups to endorse it. By the end of the month, Julian Bond, the communications director of SNCC, had written to say that the march had "the fullest support and backing" of the organization. Jim Farmer brought CORE on board and agreed to forward some money, though he warned that CORE's finances were shaky. When no word came from SCLC, Rustin lobbied Fred Shuttlesworth, one of its more fiery activists, to intervene with King. Not until early May did Clarence Jones, an associate of King, finally tell Randolph to include King as a sponsor.[6]

Meanwhile, Randolph approached Whitney Young, the new director of the National Urban League, and Wilkins of the NAACP. Young expressed concern. The Urban League, he told Randolph, had found "through some rather bitter experience that unless we participate at the level of planning and policy making . . . unfortunate misunderstandings can occur." Randolph was happy to open up the decision-making process if it meant capturing the league's support. He even told the NALC board that they should postpone the mobilization until October to allow time to bring others on board. But his willingness to bend was to no avail. After much dickering on the phone and in person, Young finally informed Randolph that his board was declining. "The real impact and significance of the March would be to pressure for immediate legislative action," Young wrote, and the league's tax-exempt status prevented it from lobbying. He told Randolph that he feared compromising "our present active working relationship" with many officials in Washington. "These would be quick to point out that their doors are completely open to us, and they would look with some suspicion, if not confusion, on our participation in the March."[7] Randolph fared no better in his dealings with Wilkins. "I am writing you first," Randolph informed him, because "the movement needs the great moral weight and influence of the Association." But he secured neither a firm yes nor a clear no and so, late in May, when Randolph finally announced an October "Emancipation March on Washington for Jobs," the NAACP was noticeably absent from the list of sponsoring organizations.[8]

However much he wished to realize Randolph's dream, Rustin could see that prospects for a march were dimming. The unwillingness of the NAACP and the Urban League to come on board did not bode well, since they alone had the resources to make it a success. King and the SCLC were deeply engaged in massive protests in Birmingham. Community organizing and voter registration in Mississippi absorbed the energies of SNCC. CORE chapters were pulling in too many different directions, and Farmer did not have the ability to direct their energy toward a single national campaign. Randolph's NALC, the chief mover, was a shadow organization, designed primarily to give him a bully pulpit for battling the AFL-CIO.

Even if the march did happen, it looked as if Rustin's own involvement was likely to be peripheral. Early in April, Muste informed Randolph that the board of the WRL was turning down the request to have it release Rustin to plan the march. "This is not the first time," he wrote, that Rustin's services were wanted. "The War Resisters League cannot be expected to release Bayard Rustin at this time." The league, he continued, "desperately needs the full time of its staff, in which Bayard is such a key figure, for work on the international front." Muste condescendingly informed Randolph that "we all recognize that the causes involved in this discussion—civil rights, economic issues, including abolition of unemployment, and peace—are one cause. . . . We are confident that your and your colleague's concern about the cause of people in the nuclear age will offset your disappointment." Randolph's response was short and curt: "I can understand that Bayard is practically indispensable to the League through this period of storm and stress throughout the world." So Rustin watched as others made decisions for him, until Birmingham changed everything.[9]

FOR THREE YEARS, protests had wracked the South. Lunch counter sit-ins had occurred in scores of cities. The Freedom Rides had traced a route across a wide swath of the region. African Americans waded in at public pools, picketed theaters that confined them to balconies, entered white-only restrooms and dressing rooms in department stores, pushed their way into public libraries that prohibited their entry, and blocked the entrance to motels that refused to register them. Black parents brought their children to all-white schools, and lawyers filed suit after suit in court forcing cities and counties and states to respond. Sometimes these actions were scattered events of short duration; sometimes they were sustained campaigns that shook a community for months. Some protests remained local events only, escaping anyone's notice beyond the immediate area. Others, like the Freedom Rides, caught the attention of the world.

The Birmingham protests were the work of King and the SCLC. As 1962 ended, King and his circle knew that SCLC was in trouble. Its work that year in Albany, Georgia, met shrewd resistance from the local sheriff, and its desegregation campaign stalled. Elsewhere, SCLC could boast of no recent major victories and no dramatic scenes that might rally the troops, rouse a complacent national public, or goad the Kennedy administration into action. King's image was fading from view, his stature shaken. So King and his associates decided that in the spring, they would come to Birmingham and spearhead an assault on this bastion of segregation. Birmingham offered clear attractions. It boasted Shuttlesworth, an outspoken activist minister who had been with SCLC since its founding. Shuttlesworth had often crossed swords with the city's NAACP leadership and had formed his own organization as a militant alternative. He was ready to take on the white establishment in town. Birmingham also had a reputation, even in the Deep South, as a hard city—"the toughest town in the South," Andrew Young called it[10]—a place where racist brutality respected few limits. It was rigidly segregated, and Bull Connor, its police chief, was known for his meanness. The arrival of King and the launching of a drive against segregated businesses downtown were bound to rile him, it was hoped, in ways that redounded to the benefit of the civil rights movement.

Demonstrations began in early April during Easter Week. Through three weeks of demonstrations, Connor kept his police under tight control and arrested protesters in orderly fashion. He avoided acting in ways that might generate the sensationalistic media attention King wanted. By the last weekend in April, the black community in Birmingham had sustained twenty-five consecutive nights of mass meetings and was losing steam. "We've got to get something going. The press is leaving, we've got to get going," one of King's assistants remembers him saying. "We had run out of troops," according to Wyatt Tee Walker, the staff director of SCLC.[11] So King elected to cross a line that had remained inviolate in his previous campaigns. SCLC decided to risk the safety of Birmingham's black youth by mobilizing high school children to demonstrate. Word spread through the city's black schools and, on May 1, the first contingents marched downtown. In just two days, police arrested more than 500 students.

Connor's restraint snapped. As masses of teenagers converged on the city's center, Connor unleashed snarling police dogs to drive them back and ordered high-powered fire hoses turned on the demonstrators. News photographers and television cameras captured images of dogs biting the legs of young girls, teenagers slammed against walls by the force of the hoses, and helmeted police beating terrified youth. The police kept at it, arresting and detaining more than 2,500 demonstrators in the course of a week. The Ku Klux Klan, not always distinct from the Birmingham police, also moved into action; bombs exploded outside the home of King's younger brother and at the motel where King himself had been staying.

The chaos in Birmingham shocked the Kennedy administration out of its torpor. In February, the president had delivered a civil rights message to Congress, but had offered proposals that even one of his most loyal assistants called "a fairly puny package."[12] In the early stages of the Birmingham crisis, he and his brother, Attorney General Robert Kennedy, stuck to the position they had held all along toward events in the South: they did not want to antagonize segregationist Democrats in Congress and did not want to expand the federal role in racial matters. To civil rights forces, the Kennedy White House counseled patience. It contemplated federal intervention only after chaos threatened.

In the Justice Department, Burke Marshall kept abreast of the situation in Birmingham and passed on to Robert Kennedy frequent summaries of developments. Early on in the SCLC campaign, Shuttlesworth flew to Washington to argue for federal assistance, but Marshall simply repeated the administration's rationale that it had no legislative authority to take action. Late in April, Marshall reported that "there has been no break in the situation" and that it continued to be "dangerous," though his worries seemed to focus not on police behavior, which he praised for its restraint, but on reports that "a good number of Negroes carry weapons of some sort." Fears of black violence leaked out even when responding to something as outrageous as the Klan bombings. A

White House press release condemned the lawlessness of "extremists on either side," as if the deeds of the Klan and the SCLC were morally equivalent.[13]

All this changed with the police violence and mass arrests of early May. Flying to Birmingham to negotiate a settlement, Marshall saw at close range the bedlam. "It was a very unpleasant week for the president," he recalled. "There were every day hundreds, thousands, of Negroes demonstrating in the streets of Birmingham . . . there were hundreds of arrests made . . . the pictures of the police dogs and fire hoses going throughout the country stirred the feelings of every Negro in the country, most whites in the country, and I suppose particularly the colored persons throughout the world. And all of that emotion was directed at President Kennedy." By the time he returned to Washington, Marshall detected a shift in everyone's thinking. "The President wanted to know what he should do—not to deal with Birmingham but to deal with what was clearly an explosion in the racial problem that would not go away, that he had not only to face up to himself, but somehow bring the country to face up to and resolve."[14]

The next few weeks were "pretty frantic" ones as the administration finally moved into a state of frenzied activity. Exhibiting the authority that a summons from the White House implied, the administration convened a series of large meetings in June and brought to Washington almost two thousand leaders from many walks of life. It assembled most of the nation's governors. It brought figures from business, labor, education, religion, women's groups, and the legal profession. It impressed on them the urgency of the situation. The sense of crisis was so palpable that at times, even the attorney general seemed to be endorsing demonstrations. Through these gatherings, the Kennedys hoped to stimulate voluntary action to speed desegregation. According to Marshall, the meetings had "immense repercussions," as reports flowed in of theaters, restaurants, and hotels integrating in scores of Southern cities.[15]

But Kennedy and his advisers also knew that the days of voluntarism were over. The widespread outrage over Birmingham had given the administration the political courage to ask Congress for civil rights legislation. Early in June, before the U.S. Conference of Mayors, the president made civil rights the focus of his speech. "I am here to discuss with you a problem which is not local, but national," Kennedy told them. "Not Northern or Southern, Eastern or Western, but a national problem . . . the time for token moves and talk is past." Two days later, George Wallace, the new governor of Alabama, fulfilled his pledge to "stand in the schoolhouse door" and blocked two black students from registering at the University of Alabama, before stepping aside for federal marshals. Kennedy used Wallace's defiance as the opportunity for a televised address to the nation. He spoke of the "moral crisis as a country and a people" that America faced. "The heart of the question is whether all Americans are to be afforded equal rights and equal opportunities, whether we are going to treat our fellow Americans as we want to be treated. . . . We cannot say to 10 percent of the population that you can't have that right; that your children can't have the chance to develop whatever talents they have; that the only way that they are going to get their rights is to go into the streets and demonstrate. I think we owe them and we owe ourselves a better country than that." He announced that he would send to Congress a comprehensive civil rights bill, and a week later he fulfilled his pledge.[16]

The Birmingham events and Kennedy's initiatives changed the outlook for a march on Washington. King, who had not shown much interest in the earlier overtures from Rustin and Randolph, suddenly began to talk excitedly about a nationwide mobilization, as if the idea were brand new. In early June, he told Stanley Levison and Clarence Jones, another adviser, that "we are on the threshold of a significant breakthrough and the greatest weapon is mass demonstration." He proposed a mass march—or at least the impression of one—with "literally thousands and thousands of people . . . going to be organized on Washington." King seemed almost ready to go public with the idea when Jones, who was in contact with Randolph, suggested that they consult Randolph first. Andrew Young, one of the ministers on SCLC's staff, invited Rustin to come to Birmingham to advocate with the staff for the proposed march.[17]

The trip south gave Rustin the chance to do more than plead the case for the march. It allowed him to observe at close range the depth and breadth of the community's involvement in the events of the preceding two months. He could feel the intense excitement and anger that were bubbling everywhere and believed that Birmingham signaled a seismic shift in the racial landscape. "The events in Birmingham," Rustin recalled years later, "were more important for organizing [the March on Washington] than . . . me or anything else." His nod toward Birmingham wasn't just a show of modesty, an attempt to downplay his own centrality to what became a historic event. Nor was it the wisdom of hindsight. At the time itself, Rustin invested the Birmingham protests with great meaning. "For the black people of this nation," he wrote right after his return, "Birmingham became the moment of truth." Birmingham meant that "tokenism is finished." Instead, "the package deal is the new demand." Trying to absorb the impact of Birmingham while events there were still unfolding, Rustin argued that "the civil rights movement has reached yet a new stage in its development. For the first time a thoroughgoing revolution is occurring in the South. . . . It is a movement that consciously intends to transform the white power structure in this country. . . . The Negro community is now fighting for total freedom. . . . The Negro masses are no longer prepared to wait for anybody. . . . They are going to move. Nothing can stop them." Wave after wave of black bodies challenging white authority directly in Birmingham created, in Rustin's estimation, "such social dislocation" that power structures were shaking. The use of mass action, "nonviolent disobedience and nonviolent noncooperation," was to become the rule rather than the exception. Realizing that the images from Birmingham had reached into black communities everywhere, Rustin felt that "the lid can blow off this summer." With an eye toward the Washington mobilization whose prospects were brightening by the day, he wrote: "What is needed is an ongoing massive assault on racist political power and institutions."[18]

Kennedy's call for civil rights legislation added political immediacy to the idea of a march, something lacking when Rustin drew up the first plans. Although the NAACP was always loath to support mass mobilizations, Wilkins's typical arguments against mass action suddenly lacked plausibility. Historic legislation was now on the table, and

Southern senators were threatening a filibuster. African Americans everywhere were roused and in motion. Holding back had become too costly an approach. Birmingham set the bar for retaining credibility so high that even Wilkins got himself arrested, in a demonstration in Jackson, Mississippi, during the brutal days of mass protest there in June.

Rustin's argument that mass nonviolent action was now the main weapon in the arsenal of the movement so persuaded his colleagues at the WRL that the board reversed its earlier decision and told him to devote himself to the march. As Randolph tried to convene an emergency meeting of organizational leaders, Rustin recast the proposal to keep it in tune with events. The new plan now specified two goals, jobs and freedom, to take into account Kennedy's pending civil rights legislation. He reduced the event from two days to one but still included a demonstration at the White House, another at the Capitol, and a mass march to the Lincoln Memorial. Rustin also kept his plan to have marchers lobby in Congress, with delegates "free to sit in" the office of members who refused to meet with them.[19]

Rustin gave close attention to a structure for planning. He knew he needed to allay the fears of Wilkins and Whitney Young about decisions over which they had no voice. Yet he also recognized that the actual work had to be in the hands of those who could pull off the massive organizing in very little time. Birmingham had given King and the SCLC sudden credibility, and Rustin was as worried by the prospect of King's team running the show as he was that Wilkins might find ways to sabotage it. For all King's virtues, of which there were many, Rustin understood that organizing was not one of them. "All King needed around him were people who had hard asses and perseverance," Rustin told one interviewer. "They didn't have to have a pea in their head as long as they would sit down and be arrested and sit down on their hard behinds and persevere again. I know Martin very well . . . he did not have the ability to organize vampires to go to a bloodbath. The organization was done by Southern brutality." And so Rustin offered a plan that kept the setting of broad policy in the hands of the "Big Six"— Randolph, Wilkins, Young, Farmer, King, and John Lewis, SNCC's chair—but placed the daily work in the hands of a director, a role he expected to fill. An administrative committee of representatives from the Big Six organizations would supervise the director.[20]

Even before Randolph convened the leadership, word of the march began to circulate in Washington. "Everyone started getting panicky," Burke Marshall recalled. "People down on the Hill particularly thought it was going to be terrible." Charles Diggs, a black member of Congress from Detroit, expressed to King his "increasing concern" about the proposed march and urged him to scotch the proposal. "I am sure that a graceful withdrawal could be conceived," Diggs wrote. On Saturday, June 22, Kennedy held a morning meeting with a large number of civil rights leaders, including all of the Big Six. According to Lee White, Kennedy's assistant on civil rights issues, the president's goal was to stop the march. "He believed that not only was there an inherent danger in it, but that it just couldn't possibly succeed." Lewis remembered that Kennedy "started saying that this march would hurt his proposed legislation. . . . He was so afraid that there was going to be disorder and all types of trouble was going to take place in the capital and that there would be no way to get any type of legislation passed." But Randolph had faced down presidents before and, in his calmly authoritative way, told Kennedy that the march was going forward. Now no one among the civil rights leadership could afford to break ranks.[21]

On Tuesday, July 2, civil rights leaders finally assembled at the Roosevelt Hotel in Manhattan to make key decisions. Rustin came with Randolph. Norman Hill, who had participated in the planning from the start, accompanied Farmer. Ralph Abernathy was there with King. So were representatives from other organizations, including Cleveland Robinson whose union, District 65, had bankrolled the planning. The meeting did not begin auspiciously. Lewis remembered a lot of "petty politics. . . . There was a big argument at the beginning. . . . Wilkins wanted to know what [all the others] were doing here, why SCLC has so many representatives. They had to formally leave the meeting." After Wilkins had cleared the room of everyone but the six organizational heads, he got to the point: Rustin could not be the director. "He's got too many scars," Wilkins said. Randolph asked him to explain, and Wilkins trotted out the whole list of handicaps—the jail sentence during World War II, his association with communism during the 1930s, and, above all, the arrest in Pasadena. "This march is of such importance that we must not put a person of his liabilities as the head," Wilkins told him. Randolph polled the others. Farmer defended Rustin's abilities. Never able to face down Wilkins, King hemmed and hawed. Finally, Randolph seemed to acquiesce and said that he would assume the role of director but, naturally, would choose his own assistants. Wilkins knew Randolph had outmaneuvered him. "You've got it, Roy," is the way Rustin recounted the story later, though it is hard to imagine the dignified Randolph using that phrasing. "That means I want Bayard to be my deputy."[22]

A GENERATION LATER, marches on Washington have become ritualized dramas, carefully scripted and with few surprises. By the end of the 1960s, they were commonplace, as opponents of the Vietnam War made the White House and Congress the targets of their discontent. In the decades since, virtually every cause, every constituency, every identity group has descended on the nation's capital, paraded through its streets, and assembled on the vast Mall to hear an array of speakers and entertainers. Increasingly these marches are professionally produced. By the 1990s, the fax machine, the laptop computer, e-mail, the World Wide Web, and the mobile phone had dramatically simplified the tasks of communicating and organizing, yet the fact that dates of marches are typically chosen more than a year in advance suggests that they are detached from immediate events, timely goals, or explosive political situations. Marches are often set for weekends, slow days for the national media when Congress is not in session and many members are home in their districts. Marching on Washington has evolved into public spectacle, weekend entertainment posing as politics.

This was not the case in 1963. Then the idea was bold, fresh, and untried. No one had ever witnessed a mass descent on the nation's capital, unless one counts the Bonus Expeditionary March of veterans at the height of the Great Depression, an undertaking disastrous in every way. Now the civil rights leadership was proclaiming its intention to bring 100,000 protesters to Washington. At their July 2 meeting, they set

Wednesday, August 28, as the date, giving them less than two months to make it happen.

Those eight weeks were the busiest of Rustin's life. He had to build an organization out of nothing. He had to assemble a staff and shape them into a team able to perform under intense pressure. He had to craft a coalition that would hang together despite organizational competition, personal animosities, and often antagonistic politics. He had to maneuver through the mine field of an opposition that ranged from liberals who were counseling moderation to segregationists out to sabotage the event. And he had to do all this while staying enough out of the public eye so that the liabilities he carried would not undermine his work.

For staff, Rustin turned to many of the young men and women whom he had mentored. Tom Kahn served as his personal assistant, making his phone calls, setting up meetings, drafting his correspondence, and reminding him each day of the details that needed attention. Rustin assigned Rachelle Horowitz, whose reliability he could depend on, to the job of transportation coordinator, a task that mushroomed as the numbers expected in Washington grew and grew. He made Norman Hill, whose services CORE lent to the venture, the director of the field staff. Hill traveled the country, drumming up support in city after city, firing up the local organizers. Each of the Big Six organizations provided a staff member or paid for one. Rustin also prevailed on the FOR, the Workers Defense League, and Students for a Democratic Society to lend staff. Courtland Cox, Eleanor Holmes Norton, Ernest Green, Joyce Ladner, and other activists lived and breathed the March on Washington that summer. The mostly young group felt a deep loyalty to Rustin. One visitor to the office was taken with "his dedication and his capacity to communicate vision . . . his raw energy for long hours of hard work" that his staff willingly emulated.[23]

The offices, located in Harlem on West 130th Street, were donated by Thomas Kilgore, the activist pastor of Friendship Baptist Church who had often worked with Rustin on joint projects. Now the church building was active as a beehive, with phones ringing, constant traffic in and out, and several animated conversations taking place at any given moment. The operation lacked an intercom system, so staff were constantly racing up and down flights of steps or shouting messages up the stairwells. Many ate their meals in the office; some slept there too, as they tried to stay ahead of the work. Through it all, Rustin presided over everything. He chain-smoked his way through meetings and telephone conversations, simultaneously passing notes to staff, answering the questions that interrupted almost everything he did and, to calm himself, drawing elaborate doodles on stray pieces of paper. Taking in the chaotic scene on one of his visits to the office, John Lewis said "This was Bayard at his best."[24]

Rustin left nothing to chance. "We planned out precisely the number of toilets that would be needed for a quarter of a million people," he recalled, "how many blankets we would need for the people who were coming in early . . . how many doctors, how many first aid stations, what people should bring with them to eat in their lunches. Plan it so that everybody would come in to Washington after dark the night before, and everybody would be out of Washington by sundown on the day of the march. We had, of course, to have fantastic planning of all the parking lots for the thousands of buses and automobiles." Dreading chaos in the Northeast Corridor where the bus traffic was certain to be heavy, Rustin had Horowitz contact New Jersey Turnpike officials to arrange stopover points for the buses and make sure that maps were available showing the location of rest areas. No detail was too small for the staff. "We anticipated all problems," Rustin said afterward, with the confidence of the master planner.[25]

Holding together the organizations sponsoring the march was far more challenging. As the civil rights movement had grown, so too had rivalries, resentments, and conflicts. Differences in approach—litigation or demonstrations; professional lobbying or mass action; community organizing or civil disobedience—were becoming deep philosophical divides. Competition for funds from foundations, wealthy benefactors, and membership fees made organizations jealous of the press coverage that other groups received. Most of these clashes remained hidden from view as the civil rights leadership preserved a unified public face. But in private conversations or closed meetings, tensions surfaced and generated ill will that made working partnerships difficult to maintain.

Rustin had to manage those conflicts so that they did not disrupt march planning. At the very least, day to day, he needed to have his administrative committee, composed of representatives of each of the major organizations, not be paralyzed by disagreements. "As a Quaker," he recalled, "I started out by saying that I thought we had to make all decisions by consensus. Consensus does not mean that everybody agrees. It means that the person who disagrees must disagree so vigorously . . . that he is prepared to fight with everybody else."[26] Rustin sensed that no one wanted to be labeled as the obstructionist.

Harder still was making each of these overstretched, underfinanced organizations take the march seriously as a priority. Each day of effort lost could never be recovered. Norman Hill had pushed hard for CORE to back the march from the start, and CORE's national convention had agreed that "all CORE chapters give this project priority." SNCC too worked to make it successful. But the Urban League was far more cautious. Fears about mayhem in Washington were so great in Urban League circles that the organization seemed reluctant to be drawn too closely to the event. As the group waffled over its commitment, several league officials wrote urgently to Whitney Young. "This is a most important and significant expression of concern on the part of the entire Negro population," one of them argued. "To fail to identify ourselves at this critical point, we believe, will seriously damage our image and influence for a considerable time to come." Neither was SCLC quick to mobilize. In mid-July, Rustin told Clarence Jones that SCLC still had not appointed someone to the administrative committee; even into August, Kahn was having to send King reminders to pay SCLC's share of staff salaries. Rustin later commented on the irony of its threadbare contribution since, in memory, the march came to be so closely associated with King's "I Have a Dream" oration.[27]

Surprisingly to some, the NAACP worked hard and steadily to rally its membership. Whatever his reservations about Rustin or mass demonstrations, Wilkins knew that the credibility of the movement was now riding on the success of the march. He wrote to every local branch, youth council, and state conference of the NAACP and ordered them to activate the membership. The event had to bring "no less than 100,000" to

Washington, he told them. As Hill traveled from city to city during July and August, he found community leaders very receptive to his efforts to set up local March committees since letters from the NAACP national office had preceded his visit. Its vast infrastructure made it indispensable.

Rustin had conceived the Washington event as a militant one, with activities ranging from lobbying and rallies to marches and sit-ins. He and Randolph had also seen the march as a vehicle to raise demands for economic justice. Building a coalition meant that, slowly, the purpose shifted and the scope shrank. At first the voices of moderation were confined to the NAACP and the Urban League. Wilkins was putting so many resources into the march that his views, never favorable to demonstrations, carried weight. Urban League staff strategized about how to "keep [the March] adequately 'near' to the League." Tom Hanlon warned Whitney Young that "those who have a 'radical' vision of the total reformation of the American society see in the March great opportunity." Additional moderating pressures came when the Big Six expanded to become a Big Ten, as the civil rights organizations broadened the coalition to include Walter Reuther of the United Auto Workers as well as prominent religious leaders: Matthew Ahmann, a Catholic; Eugene Carson Blake, a Protestant; and Joachim Prinz, a Jew. Accordingly, Rustin had to submit to the March leadership a "revision of the *call* [and] a revision of *why we march*." Congressional consideration of Kennedy's civil rights proposals pushed the call for jobs and economic reconstruction further down on the list of demands. By early August, when Rustin printed a second manual to guide organizers, there were no plans to lobby, no demonstrations other than one large march and rally, and no calls for civil disobedience. Only the Big Ten would meet with members of Congress before the march and with President Kennedy afterward.[28]

To some on Rustin's staff, each of these constraints provoked great lament. Horowitz remembered wails of dismay whenever Rustin reported a new concession. Others viewed these developments with equanimity. Hill reflected that the moderating winds were "kind of inevitable" given the need to build a broad coalition. "If you refer to militancy as the idea of having sit-ins in congressional offices, I think clearly bringing the NAACP in and later on expanding the Big Six to the Big Ten ensured that this kind of tactic would not be a part of the March." SNCC's representative argued that "just the fact of 200,000 people being in the capital . . . would be demonstration enough." Rustin, whose whole history was one of civil disobedience and active nonviolence, agreed. The march would still, he assured his staff, be an event of historic significance with immensely positive consequences for the black freedom struggle. And, besides, his role as chief organizer was giving him a platform for his own ideas about social change, and these were anything but moderate. In one radio broadcast, Rustin talked of the need to "create greater counter pressures." Success, he said, "depends on people going into the streets. . . . I see mass demonstrations continuing in this country for the next five years, covering wider and wider areas, and becoming more intense."[29]

Even as Rustin handled tensions inside the March organization, he kept an eye on the storm outside. The Kennedy administration had no choice but to acquiesce to the decision of the civil rights leadership to go forward, but it was not happy. Throughout the summer, Robert Kennedy received a flow of reports tracking the mushrooming number of public disturbances. In neighboring Maryland, the city of Cambridge was living under martial law; in Savannah, demonstrations continued for weeks without a break. The black press carried headlines like "The 'Revolution' Spreads." Between May 20 and August 10, the Justice Department compiled reports of over 1,100 demonstrations in 36 states and 220 cities. To Robert Kennedy, the March was a disaster in the making, larger than any other protest and right there at the seat of government. "It was very, very badly organized," he thought, with "many groups of Communists . . . trying to get in."[30]

Rustin took the issue of violence seriously. He thought continuously about how to combine militancy with discipline and order. "My theory of maintaining order," he wrote afterward, "is not to have somebody who is strong to take care of a situation which becomes confrontation. My theory was, you deal with avoiding confrontation." With images of white police officers beating black demonstrators fresh in everyone's mind, Rustin "did not want any possibility of any racial friction, where a white person was arresting a black person." A key part of his plan was to make sure that "there should not be a single Washington policeman policing the line of march." Instead, he recruited a force of his own, consisting of out-of-uniform black officers from cities up and down the East Coast. Throughout the summer, Rustin led training sessions in nonviolence for the hundreds who volunteered their services.[31]

Rustin brought these concerns with him to a meeting in mid-July, where he faced the skepticism of District police, the National Park Service, and the Justice Department. One of the deputies frankly told Rustin that he could expect to see "a lot of policemen around" on the day of the March to see "that your people don't violate the law." Rustin gave no ground. He told them of his plan to recruit his own force of police officers and labeled their expectations of violence as one more form of racism. "Historically, groups of Negroes have no history of creating violence in their demonstrations," he told the group. "Violence usually has been created by agents outside the Negro protest and very often in the South by police." Trying to turn the tables, he asked how the Department of Justice planned to protect Southern bus riders traveling to the march if they were attacked on the highway by white supremacists. The Justice Department official told him point-blank that it would take no preventive action to protect the travelers.[32]

A stealthier opposition was also brewing that summer, and it was scheming to sabotage the March. J. Edgar Hoover, the director of the FBI, was overt in his distaste for the black freedom struggle. Hoover's agents tracked civil rights activity closely. Bureau officers exchanged information about African American protest with local police in the South. The practice sustained an atmosphere in which Southern sheriffs who suppressed demonstrations knew they had friends in the Bureau, while FBI agents saw the protection of civil rights activists as outside their mission. Hoover saw in each act of civil disobedience a breeding ground for communism. "The Negro situation," he told one congressional committee in 1958, "is being exploited fully and continuously by Communists on a national scale." Hoover's views saturated the culture of the FBI. In 1963, as civil rights demonstrations spread, the FBI worked overtime to keep abreast of the racial upheaval sweeping America. "We are right now in this Nation involved in a form of racial revolution," one of Hoover's close aides wrote as the March on Washington approached. "The time has never been so right for exploitation of the Negroes by communist propagandists."[33]

Once the Birmingham protests exploded, much of Hoover's animus focused on King, who now had a national spotlight trained on him. Hoover particularly scrutinized King's ties to Stanley Levison, whom Rustin had introduced to King and who remained one of King's closest confidants. Hoover had amassed huge files on Levison, who had been one of the highest-ranking Communist operatives in the United States. He passed this information on to the Kennedys, who expressed their concern directly to King and urged him to sever his connection with Levison. For a time, King communicated with Levison, only through emissaries, but his loyalty to Levison remained deep, and the FBI, which was tapping Levison's phones, knew it.

Although information about Rustin had circulated within the FBI for more than two decades, he had never attracted sustained interest until 1963. The March on Washington changed all that, as events in August demonstrated. Early that month, Strom Thurmond, a South Carolina senator who had led a Southern break from the Democratic Party in 1948 and run for president as a Dixiecrat, launched a new assault on the civil rights movement. The FBI, according to one officials, considered Thurmond "one of our strongest bulwarks in the Congress," and he was a favored recipient of Bureau information. Southern journalists regularly received tips from Thurmond suggesting Communist influence on the demonstrations sweeping the region. But their articles remained regional stories only, and so on August 2, Thurmond asked permission to place into the *Congressional Record* "considerable materials showing Communist connections." Prominent among them were articles charging "definite leftwing links among some leaders of the planned August 28 march" and detailing Rustin's long history of radicalism. Five days later, Thurmond inserted additional materials.[34]

Thurmond's actions set off warning bells. King sought information from Ted Brown, a Washington-based labor activist, about the prospects of new efforts to discredit Rustin. Brown passed along the rumor that Southerners in Congress intended to ask Hoover to release the Bureau's file on Rustin. "They are going to make a hell of a mess out of it," Brown told King. Southern politicians were "getting ready to unload" their heavy fire in Rustin's direction. In New York, Randolph and Wilkins sent telegrams to the whole Big Ten leadership, announcing an emergency meeting at the Urban League offices on Friday, August 9. Kahn began drafting statements for Randolph to use if confronted by reporters. Scenting blood, the press descended on the Harlem headquarters to grill Rustin about the charges and whether he intended to resign. Rustin was pleased to talk with journalists about the March, but brushed aside questions about himself and passed the reporters on to Randolph. To a group of correspondents hounding him about whether he intended to remove Rustin, Randolph rolled his eyes, as if he had faced this once too often, and simply responded "No, Rustin is Mr. March-on-Washington himself."[35]

On Sunday, August 11, the *Washington Post* carried a major feature on the upcoming event that placed Rustin directly in the sight lines of Hoover. It presented the March glowingly and put Rustin front and center in its account. "Organizer of District of Columbia March Is Devoted to Nonviolence," the article began. "Friendliness, Not a Gun, Is the Proper Weapon, Veteran of Past Protests Here Believes." Susanna McBee, the author, took much of the information Thurmond had inserted into the *Congressional Record* and gave it a positive spin. She emphasized Rustin's decisive break with communism and detailed his long record of arrests on behalf of peace and racial justice. Rustin emerged articulate and heroic, a man praised by both King and Randolph.[36] The next morning, Fred Baumgardner, one of Hoover's chief aides, telephoned the Bureau's New York office. He ordered agents there to "expeditiously prepare a current investigative report" on Rustin. "Allegations have been made concerning former communist activities of this individual, together with allegations concerning morals charges," Baumgardner told them. "Our reports should be comprehensive." Although the information in the *Post* about Rustin's political history was already in the Bureau's possession, its public display as news in an article favorable to Rustin triggered more intense scrutiny of him.[37]

The *Post* article enraged Thurmond. Two days later, he made it the centerpiece of another diatribe in the Senate. He criticized it as "a classic example of news reporting because the reporter took a series of ludicrous [*sic*] facts and directed them so that they literally came out smelling like a rose and looking like a gilded lily." Thurmond lashed into Rustin. He put into the *Record* articles from the *Los Angeles Times* from 1953 that reported Rustin's conviction on sex charges. He included the police booking slip from the incident, not an easily obtainable document. The police record he placed before Congress consisted of a long, detailed "criminal check" issued on June 2, 1959. It contained a history of Rustin's arrests and convictions on a variety of charges. For those with eyes to see, it was obvious that Thurmond's source was the FBI itself, which had given him access to privileged information to discredit Rustin, the March, and, by extension, the entire civil rights struggle. Yet none of the accounts of Thurmond's charges that appeared in the press commented on this peculiar aspect of his actions. In 1963, the reputation of Hoover and the FBI was so lustrous and cold war assumptions about the Communist menace so ingrained that Thurmond neither saw the need, nor took the trouble, to disguise the material he presented in the Senate.[38]

For Rustin, despite years of attacks on his homosexuality, Thurmond's diatribe represented something new. In 1953, a few pacifists were made privy to Rustin's arrest in Pasadena, but the event was a throwaway item in local papers. In 1960, the conflict with Adam Clayton Powell rippled through the nation's press, but the substance remained unnamed. Thurmond made the labeling process clear and ubiquitous. He named Rustin a sexual pervert in the *Congressional Record*, and newspapers across the country gave the story play. Not of his own choosing, Rustin had become perhaps the most visible homosexual in America at a time when few gay men or lesbians aspired to any public attention.

The outcome was also unique. Rarely in American public life had anyone been so overtly labeled a homosexual and survived the attack. Because the accusation was so public, because it was leveled by a white supremacist, and because it came just two weeks before an event on which the movement was banking so much, civil rights leaders had to rally to Rustin's defense. When Thurmond made his attack, Randolph was at an executive council meeting of the AFL-CIO, trying—unsuccessfully—to persuade the giant labor federation to endorse the March. As soon as he returned to New York, key civil rights leaders assembled at a press conference. "I speak for the combined Negro leadership," he told reporters, "in voicing my complete confidence in Bayard Rustin's character. . . . I am dismayed that there are in this country men who, wrapping themselves in the mantle of Christian morality, would mutilate the most elementary conceptions of human decency, privacy and humility in order to persecute other men." With the dignified Randolph as spokesman, journalists did not ask probing questions about sexual perversions.[39]

For Rustin and those close to him, Thurmond's attack and the public defense that followed it seemed a turning point. Rustin later called it "the best thing [Thurmond] could have done for me." He was particularly affected by the backing of Wilkins. "Any number of people's attitude would have been, 'I told you so!'" he reminisced. "Roy's attitude was, 'We're not going to let him get away with this kind of attack.'" To Gloster Current at the NAACP, Rustin wrote, "It's a long, hard pull. . . . It's nice to know that one has friends who will stand up and be counted when the time comes." Kahn, exceedingly circumspect about his own sexual identity, recalled being "tremendously moved by a press conference that Randolph called . . . he did not let Bayard speak. He argued that he would not let Bayard be put in a position where he had to defend himself, that he would defend him. He simply reiterated that he had great confidence in Bayard's moral integrity. And that was that. . . . It was like a boil being lanced." To Jane Stembridge, working for SNCC in the South, Kahn wrote that Thurmond's provocation "seems to have done us more good than harm. All kinds of people who formerly were a little shaky have rallied to Bayard's defense." Responding to Stembridge's worries, Kahn concluded "things are going very, very well indeed. See you in Washington."[40]

KAHN'S ASSESSMENT REFLECTED the general state of mind among March organizers. In the last weeks before the event, the staff knew they had rounded a corner. Caution turned to excitement, worry to anticipation, as evidence accumulated that the size of the march was likely to surpass anyone's wildest dreams.

Everything fell into place. Catholic activists began to mobilize in earnest toward the end of July. John Sisson, the head of the National Catholic Conference for Interracial Justice, called the March "the most significant civil rights demonstration since Gandhi led the Indians to freedom." He told all his chapter presidents to mobilize for "a great moral crusade." Labor unions were lining up their members, renting buses all through the Northeast and Midwest. Although George Meany had nixed an endorsement by the AFL-CIO, individual unions were free to participate. Among the giant unions, the UAW and the Steelworkers lent their assistance, as did the Ladies' Garment Workers, the Packinghouse Workers, and the Electrical Workers. In a number of cities, central labor councils endorsed the March and contributed funds. In Hollywood and New York, celebrities declared their intention to attend and, in some cases, to perform on the Mall. Harry Belafonte coordinated the celebrity mobilization. Burt Lancaster, Sidney Poitier, Charlton Heston, Sammy Davis, Lena Horne, Marlon Brando, Paul Newman, Joanne Woodward, Eartha Kitt, and Joan Baez were among those who promised to be there.[41]

From Washington, too, Rustin saw indications of success. Early in the summer, Rustin had written to every member of Congress and invited them to attend the rally at the Lincoln Memorial. Most sent back excuses. Then, in August, the House of Representatives began work on Kennedy's civil rights legislation. The congressional activity focused attention on the Washington March and dramatized the need for a massive turnout. "As we got closer," Rustin recalled, and members of Congress "saw it was going to be bigger and more important, the relatives became less important, the trips home became less important, the

going to Europe became less important." Rustin's own moment of revelation came when Adam Clayton Powell, who had caused Rustin so
much anguish, began pressing for inclusion in the program. "Nobody
can smell success like Adam," Rustin snickered.[42]

As July turned into August, local groups firmed up their travel plans.
Marchers from Los Angeles, Chicago, and Minneapolis hired planes.
In Florida and Georgia, prospective marchers reserved dozens of railroad coaches. Buses were coming from everywhere. Rachelle Horowitz,
the transportation coordinator, was keeping meticulous records. At one
point in August, she told Rustin she was sure that at least 89,000 people
were coming. When Rustin brought the number to a meeting of the
top leadership, Wilkins laughed and said, "We're home free." Horowitz's
figures did not take into account all those coming from the Washington
metropolitan area or those buying tickets from commercial carriers like
Greyhound. As the March drew closer, the press predicted huge numbers. In New York, the *Amsterdam News* wrote of 250,000 participants;
the *Herald Tribune* speculated that up to 200,000 might arrive.[43]

As Rustin readied the program for printing, one last internal conflict
surfaced. Anna Arnold Hedgeman, who served on the administrative
committee, dashed off a memo to Randolph about the exclusion of any
female civil rights workers as speakers. "In light of the role of Negro
women in the struggle for freedom and especially in light of the extra
burdens they have carried," she wrote, "it is incredible that no woman
should appear as a speaker." Hedgeman reminded Randolph that she
had earlier counseled that the leaders of black women's organizations
be included in an expanded Big Six, a suggestion that, if accepted,
would have rendered this omission impossible. Knowing that time was
short, she proposed that Myrlie Evers, the widow of the recently slain
Mississippi activist, Medgar Evers, be invited to make remarks and introduce a few other distinguished women activists. Though Randolph
hurriedly agreed to Hedgeman's proposal, he did not put to rest concerns about gender that soon would be exploding in every corner of
America. When it came to light that Randolph intended to address the
National Press Club the week of the March, a group of women in jour-
nalism protested his planned appearance since the club excluded women

from membership. In this case, Randolph was unresponsive, provoking a bitter letter from Pauli Murray. "Human rights and human dignity are indivisible," she told the venerated labor leader. "In 1963 discrimination solely because of sex is just as morally indefensible as discrimination because of race. . . . 'Tokenism' is just as offensive when applied to women as when applied to 'Negroes.' "[44]

The Saturday before the March, Rustin and his staff kicked back and enjoyed a midnight bash that Belafonte had put together at the Apollo Theater in Harlem. Headliners included Quincy Jones, Thelonius Monk, Tony Bennett, Herbie Mann, Carmen McRae, and Billy Eckstine, and they packed the house. The festivities continued almost until dawn. The benefit raised over $30,000 and created a celebratory air that fed into the final days. Later that morning, Rustin and most of the Big Ten leadership made their way to Washington. Before departing, they issued a final statement about the upcoming event: "It will be orderly, but not subservient. It will be proud, but not arrogant. It will be nonviolent, but not timid. It will be unified in purposes and behavior, not splintered into groups and individual competitors."[45] In Washington, the group set up unofficial headquarters at the Statler Hilton. They spent the next two days in press interviews with the army of journalists who were pouring into the District and in strategy sessions to plan their meetings with congressional leaders and the president. Randolph set a tone that carried through most of the coverage of the March: "No force under the sun can block or stem the civil rights revolution that is on the way."[46]

Meanwhile, Rustin made his way around Washington, checking in with local March organizers, meeting with the National Park Service and District police, and touring the Mall where the crowds would assemble and the rally be held. Despite his endless iterations of a commitment to nonviolence, he could tell that everyone was jittery. The police commissioner had allocated two-thirds of the District's force to cover the march. Another 5,000 reservists, National Guard, firefighters, and Park Service police had assignments to assist in keeping the peace, and the military had deployed several thousand soldiers and marines at nearby bases in case of trouble. The District's liquor authority had banned the sale of all alcoholic beverages from midnight Wednesday until Thursday morning. The Washington Senators cancelled two major league baseball games. Hundreds of businesses planned to close, and many federal employees were taking the day off in order to avoid the District altogether.

Nervousness extended even to those close to and supportive of the March. The day before, an unexpected glitch occurred that threatened the unity Rustin had so carefully nurtured. Each of the Big Ten leadership had prepared a speech for the rally at the Lincoln Memorial, and by Monday night, copies of some speeches were circulating. John Lewis had put together a fiery oration befitting the mood of the young SNCC activists who were putting their bodies on the line in the Deep South. The speech attacked Kennedy's civil rights bill as "too little and too late" and announced SNCC's intention of opposing the bill. It spoke over and over of "revolution." Lewis criticized the political system for blocking change and called on his listeners to "take matters into our own hands and create a source of power, outside of any national structure, that could and would assure us a victory." With the editorial help of Kahn, Lewis concluded the speech with a historical image that captured the militancy of the movement's front-line fighters: "The time will come when we will not confine our marching in Washington. We will march through the South, through the Heart of Dixie, the way Sherman did. We shall pursue our own 'scorched earth' policy and burn Jim Crow to the ground—nonviolently. We shall fragment the South into a thousand pieces and put them back together in the image of democracy."[47]

A copy of the speech made its way to Patrick O'Boyle, the Roman Catholic archbishop who was to deliver an opening prayer at the rally. The harshness of its tone offended O'Boyle. He sent word of it to friends in the Kennedy administration and let it be known that he would not appear at the rally unless Lewis revised it. On Tuesday night, Rustin hastily convened a small group to negotiate the issue with Lewis and other SNCC members, who were outraged at the intrusion. For the next eighteen hours, almost until the moment when Lewis strode to the microphone to speak, the arguments continued. Rustin thought,

"Here's a nonviolent movement talking about marching through Georgia as Sherman did. You can't have it." In the end, the seventy-four-year-old Randolph made a plea that Lewis could not refuse. "I've waited all my *life* for this opportunity," he told Lewis. "Please don't ruin it."[48]

On the morning of the March, Rustin was up by dawn and, with Hill, Horowitz, and some others, walked to the Mall. The city was eerily quiet, as if it were a Sunday rather than a bustling workday. Around the Washington Monument were green and white striped tents, billowing in the morning breeze. The first arrivals, a group of teenagers from Albany, Georgia, and a busload from Des Moines, were hanging about, outnumbered by security personnel and journalists. Norman Hill, who had wandered away from Rustin but was still in earshot, saw a knot of reporters approach him and watched as a "uniquely Bayard" scene unfolded. "He carried in those days a pocket watch, a round pocket watch in his pants. And I remember him pulling out the watch, looking at the watch, and then pulling a piece of paper out of the side pocket of his jacket. And he looked at the watch, looked at the piece of paper, and then turned to the reporters. He took on a scholarly British accent, and said 'everything was right on schedule.' What the reporters didn't know was that the piece of paper was blank."[49]

Rustin left his staff on the Mall and returned to the hotel so that he could shepherd the Big Ten group through a series of meetings on Capitol Hill. They conferred with Mike Mansfield, the Senate majority leader, and with Everett Dirksen, the Senate minority leader who controlled the votes necessary for breaking a Southern filibuster; with John McCormack, the Speaker of the House; Carl Albert, the House majority leader; and Charles Halleck, the House minority leader. Meanwhile, the throng at the mall began to grow. By 9:30, it had reached 40,000. By 11:00, police estimated the numbers at 90,000, and still folks continued to pour into the area from every direction until the final count reached a quarter-million. Many of the Hollywood celebrities who were scheduled to perform in the morning were delayed at the airport, but the good-natured crowd improvised, as several choruses spontaneously formed to sing spirituals and other anthems of the freedom movement.

Rustin had planned to have two lines of march form at the Washington Monument at 11:30, and then have the crowd file toward the Lincoln Memorial along both Constitution and Independence Avenues. But with the sun now high in the sky and the day warming up, some just poured into the street and headed toward the rally site. Thousands of others quickly followed. "My God," Rustin called out, "they're going," and he scrambled to pull the Big Ten together, inserting them in a break in the line of march. The irony of the leaders following the masses was not lost on this seasoned radical.[50] As the marchers, mostly silent, approached the Memorial, they heard the voices of singers from the makeshift platform on the steps. Peter, Paul and Mary, the popular folk trio, performed, as did Odetta and Joan Baez. Josh White, with whom Rustin had sung more than two decades earlier, took a turn on the stage: "Ain't nobody gonna stop me, nobody gonna keep me, from marchin' down freedom's road."[51]

The entertainment was prelude to the heart of the program, the speeches of each of the ten chairmen. Randolph, whose idea it was, had pride of place, and spoke first. "We are the advance guard of a massive moral revolution for jobs and freedom," he proclaimed. Drawing on the long history of slavery, during which "our ancestors were transformed from human personalities into private property," he called for a radically different future where "the sanctity of private property takes second place to the sanctity of the human personality." Roy Wilkins surprised many by his criticisms of Kennedy. "The President's proposal," he told the crowd, "represents so moderate an approach that if it is weakened or eliminated the remainder will be little more than sugar water." John Lewis gave a speech that one reporter described as "tindery." Even with all the last-minute revisions, his speech packed more outrage than all the others together. The references to Sherman were gone, but the calls for revolution poured from his mouth as he cried to the throngs to "get in and stay in the streets of every city, every village and hamlet of this nation until true freedom comes, until the revolution of 1776 is complete." The controversy over the speech redounded to the benefit of Lewis and SNCC, as many press accounts reported the incident and quoted the offending excised passages.[52]

Rustin had allotted each speaker four minutes on the platform, but most went on for much longer. They tested the patience of the crowd, lots of whom had been on the road since the night before and had already spent hours on the Mall. Lewis's oratory revived them; his speech elicited roars of approval. But many were starting to drift away until the magnetic voice of Mahalia Jackson drew them back. "She moved her huge audience to tears," according to one observer. "But in the very next breath, she would break into an expression of expectant happiness. . . . People who had been sobbing a second before began laughing, sharing in her expectancy." Jackson served as warm-up for the final speaker. Rustin had deliberately put King last in the program, because the other speakers had begged not to be placed after him. King's speech was instantly recognized as historic. Writing in the *New York Times*, James Reston put King in a long line of Americans stretching back to Roger Williams and linked to the present through such figures as William Lloyd Garrison, Henry David Thoreau, and Eugene Debs. King began with a rhetorical device that he had used before. He spoke of America having defaulted on its promissory note to its black citizens, instead presenting them "a bad check." He spoke of the "sweltering summer of the Negro's legitimate discontent." He talked of the militancy sweeping the South, the pain and the suffering, the trials and tribulations. He called on everyone "not to wallow in the valley of despair." He built toward a peroration that swept the crowd with him, declaiming about his dream, "a dream deeply rooted in the American dream . . . a dream that one day this nation will rise up and live out the true meaning of its creed." And he closed with the image of Americans of all colors and creeds joining hands together, singing the words of an old spiritual: "Free at last! Free at last! Thank God Almighty, we are free at last!"[53]

After the roar had died down, Rustin introduced Randolph again, and the elder statesman of the black freedom struggle enumerated the demands of the marchers. Rustin then led the crowd in a recitation of a pledge to continue the struggle: "I affirm my complete personal commitment for the struggle for jobs and freedom. . . . I pledge that I will not relax until victory is won. . . . I pledge to carry the message of the March to my friends and neighbors back home and to arouse them to an equal commitment. . . . I will pledge my heart and my mind and my body unequivocally and without regard to personal sacrifice, to the achievement of social peace through social justice."[54] The Big Ten left for the White House, where they met with President Kennedy, who congratulated them on the success of the event. As the crowds evaporated quickly, a crew of volunteers swept through the Mall and left it as clean as it had been at dawn.

Rustin lingered behind, marveling at what had just happened. Not too many years before, he had been arrested simply for holding aloft a placard along the route of New York's Easter Parade. Even in the wake of Birmingham, with protests erupting everywhere, demonstrations still seemed radical to most Americans, beyond the norms of civic culture. Now, he reflected, the March had brought moral power to mass protest. Disciplined and orderly, it had "planted a seed deep in the American conscience whose fruit," he hoped, "may someday astonish us."[55]

For those closest to the planning, it had been an exhausting yet exhilarating day. Norman Hill left with "a feeling that something special had happened." Rachelle Horowitz basked in "this incredibly sweet mood" that radiated from everyone. Rustin remembered "electricity in the air. Everyone who was there knew that the event was a landmark." It had lived up to his expectations as "one of the great days in American history" and, he might have added, perhaps the greatest of his life.[56]

CHAPTER SIXTEEN

"On the Threshold of a New Political Movement"
1963–1964

FOR WEEKS AFTERWARD, the congratulations kept arriving. Edith Jackson, Rustin's fourth-grade teacher, said she was "proud" to have taught him. Mary Frances Thomas, a high school friend, conveyed the feelings of many of the "ole gang" from West Chester when she wrote, "We always knew you were born to lead." Dorothy Knoke, who had picketed segregated restaurants with Rustin in Ohio in the 1940s, took pleasure in telling him, "How we have rejoiced in saying 'we knew him when!'" Alluding to the hard times he had seen, Franny Lee, one of Rustin's closest friends in New York a generation earlier, wrote: "The joyous thing for me about you . . . is that the setbacks have never set the direction. You still see the road ahead."[1]

Rustin had always operated from the margins, distant from power and influence. The political views he espoused, the issues he picked to champion, and the organizations he worked for all conspired to strengthen an outsider's stance. Standing alone along the edges suited the personality that he sometimes showed—the air of arrogance that he projected, the armor of superiority that he wore. Still, he had always tried to reach beyond this. Especially in the post-Montgomery years when the cause of racial justice was at last poised to receive its due, Rustin labored to make his efforts count for something. Yet so often his effort to grasp something more, to step beyond his place, came crashing against the stigma of his sexuality.

The success of the March on Washington changed all that. Overnight, it seemed, he had acquired the mantle of civil rights leader. Suddenly he enjoyed a media profile and public recognition; his comments, his opinions, and his actions were all newsworthy. He received a steady stream of interviews, invitations to lecture, and opportunities to participate in national conferences. The March revived his relationship with Martin Luther King, Jr., who once again sought Rustin's advice and drew him into the affairs of the SCLC. *Life*, the weekly photo magazine that was sold everywhere in this era, put him on its cover. *Newsweek* placed him at the center of its story on the March, captioning its photo of him "out of the shadows." The phrase was a common trope of gay life in this era. Its use by *Newsweek* was recognition that the perversion card, played so often in Rustin's career, had finally been trumped. Or, so at least it seemed.

IN THE DAYS and weeks after the March, Rustin obsessed about its meaning. He calculated the balance of opportunities and dangers that it had thrown up. The task before him and others was to prove that "the unity and strength displayed on the 28th of August is not ephemeral, but will be carried forth into future activities of even more meaningful kinds." In Rustin's estimation, the March held immense promise for the future, but its value could be multiplied or squandered depending on how the civil rights establishment responded.[2]

Above all for Rustin, the March conferred legitimacy on mass action and public protest. Just two months before, the White House and congressional leaders openly questioned the wisdom of protest. Editorial opinion was skeptical of its value. Religious leaders cautioned patience. Even the labor movement had grown estranged from the time in its own history when sitdown strikes built industrial unions. Nor did the largest organizations within the civil rights movement applaud direct action. All of these reservations found expression when the idea for a march first surfaced. But its triumphal success turned opinion around. Protest had become American.

Rustin also marveled at the solidarity that the March engendered within the civil rights movement. "This was a time and one of those few moments in American history when there was an almost absolute unity

within the black community," he recalled. The moderates and the radicals, the lobbyists and the street agitators, spoke with a single voice on
a national platform. Moreover, the expansion of the March organization to become a Big Ten created an unprecedented coalition for racial
justice. "Only the unity of the civil rights organizations and their white
allies could have produced that spectacular success," Rustin wrote to
the March leadership in September. "No one organization or narrow
coalition of organizations could have done the job." The result was
something new. "The moral impact of the March has given an unfore-
seeable weight to a new entity commonly called the 'big ten,'" Rustin
reasoned. "When they speak as a group today they represent not
merely this or that organization but, in the broadest sense, the vast majority of decent Americans."[3] This was coin not to be spent carelessly.

Finally, there was the matter of numbers. One out of a hundred
African Americans had come to Washington that day. For the rest of
the year, pledge cards signed by marchers arrived at the New York office. Women and men were taking seriously the words they had recited
at the end of that day. Behind the mass of cards, Rustin saw Americans
"prepared to move as never before." This was the raw material for a
movement to transform America. It was rich beyond anything he had
encountered since the Depression years in New York.[4]

Yet Rustin found much to worry about as well. Despite years of
protest, there had been no decisive breakthrough. "In whatever field
one may name, progress, if measured against the goal to be reached, has
been minimal," he wrote to King. Racial segregation still ruled in the
public schools. Law enforcement in the South sustained white supremacy, and blacks remained disenfranchised in much of the region.
Congress was a long way from passing tough civil rights legislation.
Meanwhile, the opposition to racial justice was growing rather than di-
minishing. In the Deep South especially, white supremacists were conducting a "reign of terror" that could portend "ultimate failure . . .
[unless] met with a more militant as well as astute counter-strategy."[5]

As if to confirm Rustin's musings, tragedy struck even before the
warm glow from the March had faded. On September 15, a bomb exploded in a black church in Birmingham and killed four young girls.

The moment he heard the news, Rustin was on the phone urging "swift and vigorous action" by local committees of the March organization. In New York, he hastily convened a press conference and lashed into the Kennedy administration for not being able to "protect children in Sunday School." He persuaded the Big Ten leaders to declare the following Sunday a national day of mourning. Communities everywhere quickly pulled together marches, vigils, and memorial services. Rustin spoke at one event after another. Outside the federal courthouse in Lower Manhattan, he told a crowd of 10,000 that Americans of conscience ought to invade Department of Justice offices throughout the country, sit down in the elevators and offices and lobbies, and stay there until "we make it so difficult to operate they'll have to listen to us." With Farmer and others, he addressed a mass meeting at Town Hall in midtown Manhattan. Later, with James Baldwin, he spoke at the Community Church on the East Side to a crowd of more than a thousand. Calling on the audience to escalate its commitment to militant nonviolence, he sensed the "palpable undercurrent of anger and frustration" in the cavernous auditorium. In the words of one observer, Rustin "suddenly pointed a long finger at the audience and shouted, 'If there is anyone here who advocates violence as a solution, *let him stand up!* . . . Let him stand up and I will show you someone who proposes to do *nothing!*'"[6]

The Birmingham bombing drove Rustin to press even more fervently to preserve the March organization. The need was "compelling," he wrote. "The dissolution of the movement can injure the morale at a critical stage in the civil rights revolution. . . . Continuation of the movement can provide us with the moral and material strength to meet the current counter offensive." He spun out the ambitious plans a permanent coalition might initiate. He urged that fact-finding commissions travel south, take testimony, and expose the daily violence that the press and the federal government ignored. He proposed collaboration with trade unions to launch mass action for full employment. He outlined a "March on Washington Congress—Let Democracy Work" scheme to spur passage of a civil rights act. The movement would convene its own mock congress. It would bring a thousand citizens a day to Washington for as long as a Senate filibuster against

Kennedy's legislation might last, to hold its own shadow hearings and town meetings. He asked the Big Ten to issue a call for action in communities everywhere as a way to fulfill the pledge that participants had made at the March.[7]

In late September, Rustin argued passionately for his position at a meeting of Big Ten representatives. He addressed openly the fear that extending the life of the coalition might "disrupt or impede . . . the established organizations." The coalition, he said, would be the mouthpiece of the Big Ten, its actions "the consensus of those organizations."[8] But as Betti Whaley, who sat in for the Urban League, reported to Whitney Young, "It seemed apparent the greatest force behind continuation . . . was Mr. Rustin." Rustin's ambitions crashed against the rivalries and distrust that circulated within the civil rights establishment. Inside the NAACP, resentment simmered over the way press reporting had ignored its part in the March. "We were victimized by gross omission," wrote Henry Moon, its director of public relations. "It could not have been accidental." Farmer, too, was leery. He saw the Big Ten as "a device for throttling CORE." He feared that "Bayard would take over CORE" if given the chance, and he did not want to give Rustin a platform.[9]

The "showdown meeting" about keeping the March office open happened in late November. Wilkins was adamantly against it, and Farmer agreed. In the face of Wilkins's obduracy, Rustin knew that Randolph, his most loyal backer, was "not prepared to put up a fight about it." He told King, who himself was not inclined to take on Wilkins, that "it's a fight nobody could win when the other boys were just going to let Roy have his way." So the decision was made that the office in Harlem would finally close in January. In Tom Kahn's words, Wilkins just "murdered" the March on Washington organization.[10]

Blocked from the role he wanted, Rustin used whatever platform he could find. He was thinking outside old grooves, anticipating what might be called a "post–civil rights" orientation. Just as in the 1950s he had ruminated over what held the antinuclear movement back, he now reflected on what it would take to achieve the breakthroughs that still eluded the freedom movement. He began to argue that, strategically, civil rights and progressive politics were inextricably entwined. He saw the fight for racial equality as "the spearhead of a broad movement for political and social reforms in this country." At the same time, he thought the civil rights revolution would emerge victorious "to the extent that we succeed in moving this country to the left." The movement needed, he announced in one forum, not just a campaign to achieve legal equality, but "a plan to get jobs for everyone." Rustin saw a certain tactical "crackpotishness" slipping in. "That which is unusual is considered militant," he told one audience. Demonstrations often had "no relation to the fundamental question of how to get rid of discrimination." They were becoming "gimmicks," and direct action was seen "as an end in itself." Addressing a CORE chapter in Syracuse, he pressed its members to go beyond "dramatic action." The movement needed not just more militancy but "more cooperation, more allies, more thought."[11]

At the end of November, Rustin traveled to Washington to address a SNCC conference. He had good relations with many in SNCC, and it was an ideal audience for testing out his thinking. Rustin said that the civil rights movement was losing ground. It had reached an impasse and in some cities was retreating. Rustin told SNCC activists that the movement "had gone as far as it could with the original approach" and that they had to "broaden their objectives to include all depressed and underprivileged minority groups if their own movement is to make another leap forward." Speaking to perhaps the most courageous group of activists in the country, Rustin challenged them to think beyond the next target of protest and not get lost in the mystique of movement heroics. "The ability to go to jail should not be substituted for an overall social reform program. We need a political and social reform program that will not only help the Negroes but one that will help all Americans. Only then can we win."[12]

Rustin's message did not go over well. His performance in front of SNCC foreshadowed the resistance his ideas would generate in the coming years. Norman Hill remembered that Jim Foreman, SNCC's outspoken executive secretary, "took the position that SNCC had to work on discrimination and not worry about the broader economic issues." Rustin himself was taken aback by the intensity of the response to his suggestions. A few days later, he wrote to a friend, "I think we are in for some very difficult days ahead."[13]

SINCE THE PREVIOUS JUNE, Rustin had barely attended to the business of the WRL. Now, as he turned over to Horowitz and Kahn the demoralizing task of shutting down the March office, the WRL offered him a distraction. Early in January, Rustin embarked on a ten-day trip to Britain and Sweden to attend peace movement conferences.

Pacifists in London loved Rustin, and in his few days there, they feted him, picked his brain, and implored him for help. Rustin met with the leadership of the Campaign for Nuclear Disarmament and learned about its spring mobilization plans. Peggy Duff, the staff person at CND, asked him to return in late winter to coordinate their efforts. His assistance would be "not only tremendously helpful but enormously important," she told him. "The key to a successful Easter March may well be [you] and the link with the Washington March." Rustin encouraged the plan and, when the WRL board later approved it, Duff was ecstatic. "The bells are ringing all over Britain since we heard that you would be here for Easter."[14]

From London, Rustin made his way to Tyringe, a small resort town in the south of Sweden. There, pacifists from across the Continent gathered in yet another effort to launch a confederation of antinuclear organizations. As always at these meetings, Rustin was a magnetic presence. "You left a strong and unforgettable memory behind you," a Swedish university student wrote afterward. Rustin's talk about the power of nonviolence excited them; he communicated some of the magic of the civil rights movement by leading the group in song. "It had a physical effect on me," one delegate wrote. "I have sensations of life being very near to me." Another thanked him for "the night in the basement when we were singing our heads off under your guidance. I can now understand the spirit of the rallies, creating an atmosphere of dedication and a feeling of being invincible. We shall overcome."[15]

The trip to Europe gave Rustin a brief respite from the issue of his future, which was still very much in the air. On his return, he told William Kunstler, a New York radical lawyer who did civil rights work, that Wilkins had offered him a job at the NAACP. But he planned to turn the offer down since "this is just an effort to control [me]." On January 20, Rustin flew to Asheville, North Carolina, to attend a three-day retreat at Black Mountain College for the staff of SCLC. Since the March, King had begun turning once again to Rustin for advice. He had invited Rustin to address the SCLC's national conference the previous September and had asked him to draft a long memo on strategy, which Rustin did. Their telephone conversations resumed. Now, at Black Mountain, Rustin was among King's inner group as it looked long and hard at the state of the organization and the larger movement. King had been worrying since the fall about a lull in the tempo of civil rights activism. He thought the country needed "another dramatic push." He and his staff also pondered issues of economic justice. Whether Rustin's analysis had seeped into King's thinking, or whether the two had come independently to the same outlook, the compatibility was evident enough that Rustin came home with the offer of a job.[16]

The prospect was attractive to Rustin, and he told a friend that he planned to accept. Rustin did not carry political grudges. He saw SCLC as a key center of the civil rights struggle and King as a key leader. Rustin had much to offer King. For all the headlines it got, SCLC was almost broke that winter, and its New York office, according to Stanley Levison, was in "bad shape." Rustin could make a critical difference. His understanding from the Black Mountain discussions was that he would start before spring. He "would have an office in New York and . . . serve as liaison with labor and white church groups and would be in charge of direct action."[17]

In the meantime, Rustin had received an urgent request to help organize a boycott of New York City's public schools. Although national attention in the past decade had focused on school integration in the South, black students in Northern cities suffered from a de facto racial separation that grew out of residential segregation and school board policies. In New York, spending on black and Puerto Rican students averaged one-seventh of that on whites. Fewer than 3 percent of the system's teachers were black, and many of them were locked into substitute teaching positions. Problems intensified in the early 1960s as a substantial migration of Southern blacks and Puerto Ricans to New York raised the population of students of color above 40 percent. Parent activists pressed school officials to ameliorate the situation, but the Board of Education remained unresponsive. School segregation increased during these years.[18]

In the fall of 1963, civil rights organizations formed the Citywide Committee for Integrated Schools to coordinate a strategy. Independent grass-roots groups, like the Harlem Parents' Committee and the Brooklyn Parents Workshop for Equality, were central to the effort. Several NAACP and CORE chapters signed on; the Urban League, always reluctant to be caught demonstrating, participated as an observer. It was a fragile coalition, since the militant rhetoric of some community leaders, like the Reverend Milton Galamison in Brooklyn, rubbed Wilkins and Whitney Young the wrong way. Yet the coalition moved forward. By the end of the year, it was leaning toward a one-day boycott to dramatize grievances and bring pressure for change.

Returning from Europe, Rustin had a call from Galamison, who asked him to coordinate the boycott. Worried about the minister's reputation for unilateral action, he checked in at the NAACP and CORE before committing himself. John Morsell, an aide to Wilkins, bent Rustin's ear. It was an "uneasy alliance," he said. But he urged Rustin to take the job. The coalition, Morsell said, "need[s] him to whip it into shape."[19]

The boycott was scheduled for February 3, giving Rustin two weeks to exercise his talents. He set up shop at Galamison's Siloam Presbyterian Church in Brooklyn and virtually lived there while he coordinated the citywide action. Boycott leaders wanted to march to Board of Education headquarters in downtown Brooklyn, hold a rally outside City Hall, and picket Governor Nelson Rockefeller's office in Manhattan. In every neighborhood with a substantial black and Puerto Rican population, they planned to open an alternative "freedom school" for the day. To reduce the chance of violence, Rustin met with police officials and extracted from them a pledge not to interfere with peaceful picketing, rallies, or the distribution of flyers near public schools. The Friday before the boycott, he was predicting success. "When a huge stone is rolling down a hill, you cannot stop it," Rustin told a reporter. "There are no means by which this boycott could be stopped."[20]

On Sunday evening, Rustin and Galamison spoke at Concord Baptist Church in Brooklyn at a lively rally that brought a "Deep South flavor" to the city. Over a thousand attended, and the crowd roused themselves with freedom songs. Rustin put the biggest possible interpretation on the next day's protest. "This is the black capital of the western world," he declared. "Whatever we do will be felt in every hamlet." From there he went to the headquarters at Siloam and spent the night answering calls from reporters and fretting over last-minute details. One reporter who camped out at the church spied the fifty-one-year-old Rustin, at 4:00 A.M., jumping from his seat for an impromptu song and dance:

> *A-men, A-a-men,*
> *Fifty thousand in the streets,*
> *A-a-men, A-a-men.*

He then went back to the business of dispatching volunteers before dawn to lead the picketing at schools around the city.[21]

Despite subfreezing temperatures, the boycott exceeded expectations. Rustin had anticipated the involvement of perhaps 200,000 students and parents, but attendance figures revealed that more than 460,000 pupils—almost 45 percent of school enrollment—stayed home, making the boycott the largest civil rights protest in the nation's history. Puerto Rican participation was substantial too; it was the first major mobilization in the city that brought African Americans and Puerto Ricans together. There were no reports of violence. A midday march of several thousand children to Board of Education offices created a festive atmosphere in downtown Brooklyn, as workers on lunch break lined the streets to watch. Pickets were set up at more than 300 city schools. Boycott supporters ran almost 500 freedom schools for the day, with 100,000 children attending. James Donovan, the president of the Board of Education, tried to dismiss the day's events by claiming that students stayed away from school because of "intimidation." He called the boycott "mostly a fizzle" and described its impact on the board as "none whatever." Donovan so angered Rustin that he called for the man's dismissal on the grounds that the school chief lacked "the insight for the job."[22]

The boycott put Rustin on the front page of the city's papers and gave him a platform from which to interpret current affairs for a broad audience. The New York action was not an isolated event. Cincinnati, Chicago, and Boston also experienced massive school protests that winter, as did a number of smaller communities. Rustin saw these mobilizations of Northern black communities as "fair warnings that the civil rights revolution has reached out of the South and is now knocking at our own doors." He predicted that, at least in New York, "we are on the threshold of a new political movement—and I do not mean it in the party sense—that is going to change the face of New York." He warned that "winds of discontent are about to sweep over our city" and advised those "who stand aloof from the frustrations and deprivations of the ghetto" to prepare themselves for more upheavals.[23]

Exhausted from nights without sleep, Rustin cancelled plans to travel to Syracuse University for a speaking engagement the evening after the boycott. Instead, he accompanied Muste to the Soviet mission to the United Nations, where they met with members of a citizens peace delegation from Eastern Europe. News reporters and photographers were waiting, and they photographed and interviewed Rustin, who told them about the work of CNVA, which he was representing. The next morning, Rustin was on the cover of the *Daily News*, New York's largest-circulation tabloid, under a headline "Boycott Chief Soviets' Guest." That afternoon, the *Journal-American*, the Hearst newspaper, carried a similar headline, "Just a Red Guest, Says Boycott Chief." The story described Rustin with his "Russian-type fur hat" enjoying the hospitality of the Soviets "only slightly more than 24 hours after masterminding the school protest." A *Daily News* editorial lashed into Rustin for "consorting with the Soviets." Other city papers were less inflammatory, but they all covered Rustin's visit.[24]

THE PRESENCE OF PHOTOGRAPHERS and reporters outside the Soviet consulate was not fortuitous. The FBI orchestrated it by using information gathered from its wiretap on Rustin's phone. In the wake of the previous summer's protests, Hoover had ordered intensified surveillance of civil rights activities. Just before the March, his lieutenants had reported to him that there was little evidence of Communist influence on the movement, but Hoover dismissed their conclusions as flawed and told them to look harder. The Bureau created a new subject heading in its voluminous security files, "Negro Question, Communist Influence Racial Matters." Rustin was one of those caught in the FBI's secret surveillance.

Cold war logic allowed the FBI to justify not only tapping Rustin's phone but also using the information to "neutralize and frustrate the party's endeavors."[25] Once the Bureau added Rustin to its "Security Index," a classification for individuals deemed dangerous enough to be jailed during a national emergency, it could justify disrupting Rustin's work and damaging his reputation. Well over a thousand civil rights activists fell within the Bureau's loose definition of security threat. The information the FBI gathered allowed it to shape the course of the nation's history. With the knowledge it secretly acquired, it could disrupt events, sow dissension in organizations, ruin relationships, and destroy the credibility of individuals.

Hoover had secured the approval of Attorney General Robert Kennedy to tap Rustin's home phone, and on November 15, 1963, agents placed a bugging device at Rustin's residence on West 28th Street. The first day, the agent in charge of protecting the nation from Bayard Rustin picked up the following: "Engaged in a conversation with an unknown male. This conversation was replete with obscenities, and propositions of a homosexual nature were made." Two weeks later, an agent reported that "Rustin said the civil rights revolution will succeed to the extent 'that we succeed in moving this country to the left.'" Everyday conversations about sex and race were seen by the FBI as proof of the danger he posed and served to justify its spying on him.[26]

On February 4, the day after the boycott, the agent listening on Rustin's line recorded a call from Muste asking if Rustin was going to the Soviet consulate that afternoon. When Rustin said yes, the agent immediately reported the information to Donald Roney, head of the

New York office, who contacted national headquarters. By midafternoon, the FBI's assistant director was able to let the New York office know that he had "just given this information to Mr. _____ of the New York Journal American newspaper, who said he would have a photographer and reporter at the scene to get a picture of Rustin entering the Soviet UN Mission and would give the matter good publicity." To make sure there were no mistakes, Roney dispatched an agent to the scene to identify Rustin for the reporter and photographer. Cooperation between the FBI and the press was commonplace during the cold war. The FBI fed reporters information it collected in the name of national security. Reporters then wrote stories confirming that threats were everywhere and thus provided the FBI with more proof of the need to spy on Americans.[27]

For the rest of the month, FBI agents wrote about the embarrassment they had caused Rustin and looked for ways to compound the damage. The New York office asked permission to call Roy Wilkins anonymously and relay stories about Rustin's contacts with alleged Communists during the time he was organizing the school boycott. When *Time* magazine picked up the Soviet consulate episode, the New York office reported to Hoover that "the doubt about Rustin's loyalty persists due to the publicity given to his attending the USSR affair. . . . Rustin now is at the very least a controversial figure and this doubt about him will follow him in all his future activities." Agents commented about "the widespread ramifications extending into the Puerto Rican community . . . which is upset about Rustin link with reds." Six weeks later, memos about the impact on Rustin's place in the civil rights movement still passed back and forth. From the FBI's Atlanta office, Hoover learned of the "considerable potential" for developing "certain animosities" between Rustin and King's circle.[28]

The agents working on Rustin's case had every reason to be confident of their assessment since their access to his private conversations as well as those of King opened to full view the inner workings of the civil rights movement. The weeks after the exposé were difficult ones for Rustin. Publicly, he called the accusation of communism "ridiculous" and dismissed the uproar as a "red smear" of the school boycott by the conservative newspapers. Privately, he admitted to a friend that the visit to the Soviet consulate had been "a mistake." Once again he had put the civil rights leadership in the position of having to defend him. In television appearances that week, both Farmer and King fielded questions about Rustin. Randolph too spoke out on his behalf. Then, in late February, it came to light that Rustin had promised to speak at an event sponsored by a group providing disaster relief to Cuba. The matter so unsettled New York's civil rights establishment that Wilkins convened a special meeting to dress Rustin down. According to the FBI log, Wilkins "called him in with all of the heads of the civil rights groups. . . . Wilkins said that 'they' had already defended him three times. . . . Wilkins stated that he knew Rustin was not a Communist but asked him not to appear at this meeting." About the whole episode, Rustin told Muste, "It is pretty awful."[29]

The flap that the FBI caused upset the delicate negotiations that were leading Rustin back into King's inner circle. On the eve of the boycott, King discussed with Clarence Jones the possibility of a staff position for Rustin and spoke of his desire to have "a close association."[30] Now, with Rustin the object of unfavorable publicity, King and his New York advisers reopened the discussion among themselves. Levison reported that King was receiving a lot of mail warning him away from Rustin. Jones thought "assets have to outweigh liabilities" in order to hire Rustin, and he wasn't sure that they did. Cleveland Robinson said he "would not recommend Rustin for dog catcher." King debated whether to give Rustin some warning that the matter of his working for the SCLC was being "reconsidered." But, in the end, he did not have to. Rustin picked up the signals all too clearly. Protecting himself from the humiliation of another rejection, he put out the word that he was not interested in working permanently for any of the existing organizations. Instead, he was in search of a "free-lance arrangement" while he and Randolph worked to create something new for him.[31]

King's decision to back away yet again from Rustin was more complicated than it seemed. Behind the deliberations provoked by a momentary flap over an innocent visit to the Soviet consulate lay a much more tangled skein of discomfort. Even as King, Levison, Jones, and others were drawn to Rustin for his mixture of skill, intelligence, and boldness—his "moxie," as Levison once put it—their feelings about his sexuality remained unresolved. As King and his circle privately discussed Rustin, they rewrote their own histories with him. They explained prior actions and attitudes in ways that deflected attention away from themselves and scapegoated Rustin for their own failures.

The FBI transcripts of telephone conversations allow a glimpse, decades later, into the hidden homophobia in Rustin's world. Shortly after the March on Washington, King and Jones had a conversation about Rustin. Jones asked why Rustin had been let go in the first place. King attributed it to complaints that Rustin's homosexuality had generated from students in the sit-in movement. "He controls himself pretty well until he gets to drinking and he would approach these students and they started talking with people about it and there was something of a reflection on me so that was really the main problem." King made no mention of how Adam Clayton Powell had manipulated King's fears and how King had caved before Powell's threats.[32]

King told Jones to go to Levison, who "knows the problem very well." But it is doubtful whether Jones received much enlightenment from Levison, since Levison's view of Rustin was neither detached nor objective. Levison had cut Rustin out of his life after the Powell incident in 1960. Just a few weeks after the triumph of the March on Washington, Levison criticized Rustin harshly in a conversation with a business associate, describing him as "a shrieker." To his brother, Levison offered the opinion that Rustin and James Baldwin, with whom Rustin had appeared at rallies, "were better qualified to lead a homosexual movement than a civil rights movement." In the twenty-first century, such a statement might seem astute; in the vastly different setting of 1963, it expressed ridicule and contempt. Levison explained Rustin's dismissal years before in terms that seamlessly blended politics and sexuality. "Tom Kahn," he said, "is the Lenin of the Socialist Party . . . and Bayard is absolutely manipulated by him. This was Bayard's downfall years ago. That's why he was really gotten rid of— because [of] his . . . unhealthy relationship with Tom."[33] Just as the image of the homosexual and the Communist bled into one another in the political culture of the cold war, so too did the boundaries dissolve, in his associates' minds, between Rustin's sexuality and his politics.

There is something ironic—and unseemly—about the way King, Levison, and others debated Rustin's fate. They reveal King's decrying Rustin's sexual behavior because of how it might damage his own reputation, while FBI phone taps were picking up information about King's extramarital affairs and circulating it among the Washington political establishment. King worried about the charges concerning Rustin's past political associations, yet King's continuing ties to Levison made him—and the broader civil rights movement—the target of massive government surveillance. The taps show Levison, best described as an armchair radical with deep pockets, ridiculing Rustin's political savvy just weeks after Rustin pulled off perhaps the greatest protest demonstration of the century. Levison had a secret political past that made him expert in the art of political deception, but he claimed that Rustin was the victim of manipulation by a twenty-two year old whose political affiliations were open and above board.

The outcome? It forced Rustin, as shrewd a strategist as anyone in the civil rights movement, into the role of minister without portfolio, a roving ambassador without a base of his own. True, his free-floating status gave him the independence to speak his own mind free of institutional constraints. But this also made it easier for others to dismiss his ideas. It made him still vulnerable to marginalization, as had so often been true in his past.

FOUR YEARS EARLIER, when the conflict with Adam Clayton Powell had erupted, Randolph had proposed that Rustin come work for him. Now, distressed at this latest turn in Rustin's life, he suggested something else: that Rustin use Randolph's name to raise money to create an organization for himself. Randolph, Rustin recalled, "always felt that my strength was with new ideas." The elder labor leader was "against my getting tied in with an institution with an already established concrete program. He felt that over the years we had started things that other people would not have started, but went along with." The proposed "A. Philip Randolph Institute" promised a solution to Rustin's organizational homelessness.[34]

At first, Rustin thought of the new venture as "an action as well as a study institute." But competition among the established civil rights groups made any effort to start something new potentially treacherous. He fast backed away from any organizing component and started describing it as "a service agency" for civil rights groups.[35] In April he started soliciting money from wealthy individuals whom he knew. The association with Randolph gradually opened doors to the labor movement as well.

Meanwhile, Rustin may have lacked portfolio, but he seemed to be everywhere that winter and spring, always in the papers, always in motion. Reporters sought his views on any and all civil rights matters. The *Herald Tribune* featured him in its Sunday magazine in an article titled "Socrates of the Civil Rights Movement."[36] Between interviews, he worked on one "freelance" project after another. A coalition of New York civil rights groups and labor unions hired him to plan a statewide march on Albany. In April, he participated in another high-profile event, this one sponsored by national CORE, at the opening of the New York World's Fair. Rustin started the day on a picket line outside the Louisiana exhibit and later sat in at the New York City building until police arrested him and scores of others. Rustin also came to the aid of the Northern Student Movement, a network of mostly white college activists who supported the civil rights movement. Bill Strickland, one of its key organizers, praised him for sensing "exactly what's been on our minds."[37] Even King wanted Rustin's insight. Though unwilling to put Rustin on staff, he did invite Rustin to be part of a small New York "research committee" that he consulted frequently.

Rustin found himself especially drawn into the work of CORE. Norman Hill, the national program director, leaned on Rustin a lot during these months. From Hill, he heard stories of CORE chapters taken over by militants who talked a strong line but left chaos and disorganization in their wake. They "sow confusion and compound frustration,"

Rustin told an associate, "while offering the Negro masses no concrete alternative." Hill saw to it that Rustin regularly appeared before regional conferences and local chapters, producing what Farmer sarcastically described as "a traveling road show" with Rustin as the main act. Farmer's resentment grew so intense that he began to imagine that Hill was plotting to oust him and make Rustin the next head of CORE.[38]

The school issue also continued to pull at Rustin's attention during these months and contributed mightily to his sense of a looming crisis in the civil rights movement. The same week as the boycott, dissatisfaction over Galamison's shoot-from-the-hip style had erupted within the city's NAACP chapters. "Roy [Wilkins] is out to kill me, man, and do the whole movement in," the Brooklyn minister had told Rustin over the phone.[39] When Galamison announced on his own a second boycott for mid-March, the NAACP, CORE, and the Urban League broke with him publicly. Participation dropped by almost 200,000 students. It was a disheartening setback and exposed deep rifts in the movement in New York.[40] Meanwhile, Parents and Taxpayers, a group of whites opposed to any transfer of students out of neighborhood schools, staged a noisy demonstration of 15,000 in City Hall Park. The city's civil rights establishment felt compelled to respond and asked Rustin to organize a counter rally. The event barely drew 4,000 to City Hall. "I will not play the numbers game," Rustin lamely told a reporter.[41]

Rustin was so frenetically busy in these months that he cancelled the trip to England to coordinate its spring antinuclear mobilization. Peggy Duff called his decision "devastating news." Muste tried to smooth things over with British pacifists. "Things continue to boil furiously," he explained. "Bayard has come to be a very central figure in the civil rights movement. . . . [He] can contribute a drive and militancy to the nonviolent movement as no one else can." Rustin mended fences as best he could. "Please tell Peggy for me how sorry I am not to come," he wrote to a mutual friend in London. "But we are really in a crisis situation here." Rustin pushed himself so hard in this period that he landed in the hospital for several days, near exhaustion and with fears that he might be suffering a heart attack.[42]

*   *   *

EXCEPT FOR THE New Deal years of Franklin Roosevelt, Rustin had experienced the American presidency as a force for reaction. Truman, Eisenhower, and Kennedy had each primarily devoted themselves to building an American arsenal that allowed the United States to police the world. Government grew, but mostly in the service of national security and military power. The militarism of the cold war sustained inequality at home. Fear of communism inhibited the impulse toward social and economic justice since egalitarian proposals smacked too much of the leveling impulses of revolutionaries. Rustin consequently had put little energy into national politics. Presidential elections barely registered for him except as something around which to organize protests. The leadership of both parties served mostly as an obstacle toward his goals. Instead, he had looked for ways to develop insurgencies from below. Now, in 1964, Rustin saw something else at play. Lyndon Johnson was emerging as an instigator of progressive change. He had embraced the core goals of the civil rights movement and was championing a domestic war against poverty.

Like the bombing of Pearl Harbor or the terrorist attack on the World Trade Center, the assassination of John F. Kennedy in November 1963 stunned the nation. Johnson stepped into the presidency with a healing sensitivity. He seized the moment and transformed tragedy into a mandate for action. Johnson made passage of Kennedy's civil rights bill his highest priority. "No memorial oration or eulogy," he told Congress, "could more eloquently honor President Kennedy's memory than the earliest possible passage of the civil rights bill. . . . We have talked for one hundred years or more. It is time now to write the next chapter."[43]

Johnson's commitment proved more than rhetorical. He invited to the White House a parade of civil rights leaders and promised them the bill would become law. Following the legislative proceedings closely, he shaped strategy and plotted tactics. As the debate on the bill dragged on—736 hours in the Senate from mid-March until mid-June—Johnson pressed his former colleagues from the South to "soften the quality of the debate and the kind of opposition which they'd give."[44] Eventually seventy-one senators voted to break the Southern filibuster, and in June, Congress passed a bill much stronger than the one Kennedy had first proposed. Its core provisions outlawed discrimination in public accommodations and facilities as well as in employment; gave the attorney general the right to initiate court action in cases where he found a pattern of infringement on the right to vote; and empowered the federal government to withhold funds from state and local agencies that practiced discrimination. The Civil Rights Act was a milestone in the history of race relations. Rustin called its passage the moment when the legal foundations of racism were destroyed.[45]

Rustin found even more to admire in Johnson's leadership. For Rustin, jobs and a decent standard of living for everyone were essential planks in an agenda for racial justice. Now Johnson was making an attack on poverty a linchpin of his presidency. In his first State of the Union message, in January 1964, Johnson announced that "this administration, today, here and now, declares unconditional war on poverty in America."[46] In March, he sent to Congress a proposal for an Economic Opportunity Act that would create a Jobs Corps program to train unemployed youth and a Community Action program to spark local antipoverty efforts. Later in the spring, delivering a commencement address at the University of Michigan, Johnson placed both his poverty and civil rights initiatives in a grander context. "We have the opportunity," he told the graduates and their families, "to move not only toward the rich society and the powerful society, but upward to the Great Society." Johnson described his vision of the Great Society as resting on "abundance and liberty for all. It demands an end to poverty and racial injustice, to which we are totally committed in our time. But this is just the beginning," he informed them. His Great Society was "not a safe harbor, a resting place, a final objective, a finished work. It is a challenge constantly renewed."[47]

Johnson's vision was not the only one circulating in national politics in 1964. Rustin's encounter with Parents and Taxpayers in New York was symptomatic of a much larger political reaction captured by the phrase *white backlash*. The emergence outside the South of a vigorous opposition to the civil rights movement shocked Rustin; it threatened to abort the civil rights revolution just as it was achieving some signal victories. During the spring George Wallace, the white supremacist governor of Alabama, took his political message north. He entered the Democratic primaries in a number of states and did surprisingly well.

The Republicans were also experiencing massive upheaval as right-wing forces hostile to civil rights and social welfare took control of the party. Throughout the primary season, Barry Goldwater, a staunchly conservative senator from Arizona, was rousing enthusiasm and placing moderate Republicans on the defensive. In the 1950s, under Eisenhower's leadership, the Republicans seemed to have made their peace with Roosevelt's New Deal. The party remained under the control of its moderate wing. On civil rights issues, it retained traces of its founding principles as an antislavery party. In the debate over the Civil Rights Act, a greater proportion of Republicans than Democrats supported the measure. But Goldwater was not of this tradition. He opposed government involvement in matters of social and economic welfare, expressed reservations about social security, pressed for lower taxes, and wanted most functions of government, beyond national defense, to rest with the states. Just two weeks after Johnson signed the Civil Rights Act, Republicans chose Goldwater as their candidate. His selection marked a turning point for the party.

For Rustin and other civil rights proponents, the Republican National Convention was nightmarish. There were only fourteen black delegates out of a total of over 2,600. From the South where, for a century, African Americans had faithfully supported the party, many states sent all-white delegations. Goldwater's acceptance speech was chilling to black activists. In its most striking passage, it declared that "extremism in defense of liberty is no vice . . . moderation in pursuit of justice is no virtue."[48] Stripped of its context, the statement might easily have been one that Rustin could have made. But no one could have mistaken what Goldwater meant. Delegates calling for a federal role in civil rights policy were booed and hooted. Goldwater was on record saying that civil rights should be left to the states, a position dear to the heart of every segregationist. Soon after the convention, Goldwater persuaded Wallace, who was threatening to run as a third-party candidate, to drop out of the race. Meanwhile, Ku Klux Klan leaders in the South urged members to support Goldwater. The presidential campaign was shaping up as the most starkly polarized choice since the contests of the Depression, and race was at the center of it all.

RUSTIN HAD BEEN ARGUING since the previous fall that the civil rights movement needed to think beyond demonstrations that created drama but little else. In Mississippi in 1964, activists were doing just that. As Johnson mobilized the party's liberals to support racial equality and fight poverty, civil rights forces were mounting a sustained challenge to the segregated structure of political power in the Deep South.

Since 1961, under Bob Moses, one contingent of SNCC workers had eschewed direct action and instead settled in rural Mississippi communities in an attempt to register local blacks to vote. In the state as a whole, less than 6 percent of adult African Americans in 1960 were registered; in rural areas like the delta, the figures were lower. SNCC confronted intransigent county registrars, brutal sheriffs, Klan violence, and a Justice Department unwilling to use federal power to protect civil rights workers. Despite all the attention the civil rights movement had captured, the everyday lives of blacks in Mississippi attracted little notice.

Late in 1963, Moses and others hatched an imaginative scheme to change all that. Working under the Council of Federated Organizations (COFO), an umbrella group for Mississippi activists, they decided on a two-pronged approach to the 1964 elections. At every level of Democratic Party organization, they went through the paces of trying to register, attend precinct and county meetings, and participate in the selection of delegates to the national convention in Atlantic City. Blocked at each step, they created a parallel structure, the Mississippi Freedom Democratic Party (MFDP), which held its own precinct, county, and statewide gatherings. Choosing a slate of "freedom" delegates, activists expected to send them to Atlantic City to challenge the segregationist regulars. To make sure their efforts drew attention, SNCC recruited a thousand college students from the North to volunteer for Freedom

Summer. The decision was a calculation born of sad experience. The lives of blacks deep in the rural South were not deemed as newsworthy as those of privileged white students from elite universities.

"Freedom Summer" had implications far beyond Mississippi. The project struck directly at the centrality of racism to the American political system. Ever since Reconstruction, a segregated Democratic Party had monopolized Southern officeholding. The Democratic majorities that had dominated national politics since the 1930s depended on the party of white power in the South. The region's senators and representatives often remained in Congress for decades, accumulating seniority that allowed them to wield enormous power. They shaped the national legislative agenda by voting with their Northern colleagues when they saw fit but joining conservative Republicans when it suited their racial interests. In contesting the right of segregationists to represent Mississippi, civil rights workers were challenging the substance of political power in America. A victory would have implications for the whole Democratic Party. Its ripples would extend to who controlled federal patronage in the South, who chaired key congressional committees, and what domestic legislation emerged from Congress. The MFDP might easily become, as one early memo speculated, "the big story" of the election year.[49]

Rustin was "all in and out of here during that time," recalled Aaron Henry, a Mississippi activist. As early as March, when plans were still evolving, he was in frequent contact with civil rights workers on the scene. James Lawson, who was traveling around the state, reported that activists were "under siege" and urged him to lend his skills as a teacher of nonviolence. Rustin and Moses conferred regularly, and Moses asked him to spend time there so that he could "interpret his findings" to people in the North. Rustin used his contacts in New York to draw attention to the Mississippi movement. *The New Yorker* covered an early MFDP fund-raiser, and Rustin was the main speaker at a benefit for the project, which also featured Theodore Bikel, a Broadway luminary, and Tom Paxton, a popular folk singer. Rustin introduced Mississippi workers to potential financial contributors in New York.[50]

In June, Rustin traveled to Oxford, Ohio, and the campus of the

Western College for Women, where several hundred Northern student volunteers were receiving training. His task was to speak to the group about the power of nonviolence, not an easy mission under the circumstances. By the time Rustin arrived, the mood had grown somber. News had reached Oxford that three civil rights activists had disappeared in Neshoba County and were presumed dead. SNCC insisted that summer workers, like its own staff, not carry weapons, although guns were everywhere in the state. Now, in the face of these deaths, it seemed as if the students "were being sent as sacrificial victims," as one trainee put it. Coming into this environment, Rustin drew on decades of commitment to militant nonviolence as he described to these college youth the motive that needed to animate their work. "All mankind is my community," he told them. "When I say I love [Mississippi's Senator] Eastland, it sounds preposterous—a man who brutalizes people. But *you* love him or you wouldn't be here. You're going to Mississippi to create social change—and you love Eastland in your desire to create conditions which will redeem his children. Loving your enemy is manifest in putting your arms not around the man but around the social situation, to take power from those who misuse it—at which point they can become human too." Rustin "had the crowd's respect before he began," said Sally Belfrage, one of the volunteers, "not only for his organization of the March on Washington, but for his principled nonviolence based on a pacifism tested in many jails."[51]

Rustin's credibility among SNCC organizers was high enough that they offered him a formal role in the project. They needed someone outside the state to lay the groundwork for the confrontation in Atlantic City, someone who could win allies among party liberals, draw reporters to the story, and stay on top of the maneuvering sure to occur as the convention approached. The COFO leadership tried to persuade him to do it. He proposed that the work outside Mississippi be centralized in a single office under his authority. But the Mississippi movement was an exercise in populist empowerment. Moses and other key workers were intent on keeping local people at the center of decision making. "We didn't want to give all of it over to Bayard," Ed King, an MFDP leader, recalled. "Not because anybody was against Bayard, but because this removed it too far from Mississippi. . . . Bayard [was] feeling that he couldn't do it, that it was too loose. Our feeling was that if it didn't stay loose, the Mississippi people wouldn't have anything to do." The discussions, which stretched over several weeks, eventually collapsed. But they were serious enough that Rustin cancelled yet another trip to Europe in the event that he was called on to run the operation.[52]

As ACTIVISTS PRESSED AHEAD with Freedom Summer and while the Republicans were still meeting in San Francisco, an incident occurred in New York that augured years of disorder ahead. On Thursday, July 16, Thomas Gilligan, an off-duty policeman, shot and killed James Powell, a fifteen-year-old black adolescent. Powell and some friends were attending summer school at a junior high on Manhattan's predominantly white Upper East Side. When a building superintendent on the block sprayed the boys with his water hose, an angry exchange ensued, and Gilligan, who was nearby, intervened. Two shots from the police lieutenant, and Powell was on the ground bleeding to death.

Rustin had been saying for months that it would take very little to create an explosion in the urban ghettoes of the North. The shooting of Powell, who was armed with nothing but a boy's standard pocket knife, ignited one in New York. On Saturday night, the crowd at a CORE rally on 125th Street in Harlem decided to march to a nearby police precinct and demand Gilligan's arrest for murder. When it tried to push into the station house, a shoving and shouting match began. "We had to get a little tough," said one officer on the scene.[53] Over the next several hours, thousands rioted in the surrounding blocks—banging on cars, throwing bottles, smashing windows. The police pursued with revolvers drawn and fired so many shots into the air that new supplies of ammunition had to be rushed to Harlem from around the city. Rioting continued for three more nights and spread to Brooklyn. The toll was 1 dead, over 500 arrested, 100 civilians and 50 police injured, and damage to hundreds of businesses.

Rustin learned of the disturbances on Sunday morning and soon was out on the streets doing what he could to restore calm. On Sunday evening, he spoke at a massive rally at a Harlem church. Rustin could hardly believe it when Jesse Grey, a community activist, asked for a hundred black revolutionaries ready to die. "He literally called on people directly and indirectly to use violence," Rustin informed a friend. "Nobody in his right mind would have called for that kind of a demonstration at the height of this conflict."[54] But Grey had more accurately read the crowd's emotions than Rustin. When Rustin spoke against the use of guns and urged nonviolent patrols to ease tensions on the street, loud booing erupted. Later that night Rustin, Jim Farmer, and Joe Overton, one of Randolph's union aides, linked arms together and tried to lead a peaceful march. Rustin found himself "spat upon and insulted" by angry Harlemites who had no use just then for preachments on nonviolence. All in all, Rustin accomplished little. "I have spent the last four evenings in Harlem trying to calm things and get people to their homes," he wrote to Whitney Young. "I am, frankly, terribly depressed."[55]

Robert Wagner, the city's mayor, was in Spain when the riots erupted and refused to cut short his trip. When he did return, he asked Martin Luther King to help restore peace. In a television interview, Rustin had called Wagner derelict in the performance of his duties. Now Rustin tried to steer King safely through New York's racial politics. When King arrived on July 27, Rustin met him at the airport and accompanied him in two days of meetings with the mayor. He advised King to retain the right to criticize Wagner's performance. He pressed King to deliver a message that "law and order do not exist in a vacuum; to the degree that you have justice—to that degree can law and order be maintained."[56] Rustin urged him to link the riots to the crisis in schools, jobs, and housing that New York's black population faced and to insist on creation of a civilian review board to investigate police brutality. He prepared for King a statement to read to the press.

Following so closely on the heels of Goldwater's nomination, the Harlem riots so shook Rustin that he wondered if, for a time, it would not be best for the civil rights movement to pull back from demonstrations. All around him, Rustin was noticing signs that the allegiance to nonviolence was fraying. He could see it in the rhetoric of local activists like Jesse Grey and in the increasingly disruptive tactics of some CORE chapters. It was obvious too in the growing cachet of Malcolm X. In March, Malcolm had announced his break with the Nation of Islam and his intention to create an organization of his own. He was promising a program. He was making approaches to members of SNCC, particularly the group based at Howard University, where nationalist sentiment was percolating. Malcolm had given a fiery speech in Harlem, which he repeated in many locations, saying the stark choices were "the ballot or the bullet." He declared "the day of turning the other cheek to those brute beasts is over." Malcolm's initiatives troubled Rustin enough that he began to refuse to debate him. "For just so long as he advocates rifle clubs and a mau-mau type movement," he responded to one such offer, "he falls outside the civil rights movement as far as I am concerned." Even in SNCC, Rustin noticed, some were "rejecting the concept of nonviolence . . . [and] are advocating quite openly limited forms of violence."[57]

Rustin discussed with Randolph the idea of a moratorium on demonstrations until after the elections. Randolph, who had seen the riots firsthand and was himself worried by the Goldwater candidacy, told him to get Wilkins to sign on first. Accustomed to having Rustin maneuver him into support of one demonstration after another, Wilkins was surprised by Rustin's proposal but was happy to endorse it. Together, they drafted a telegram that Wilkins sent to the rest of the Big Six leadership group. "The events of the past 72 hours . . . the tragic violence in Harlem . . . the end of the Wallace candidacy . . . the Goldwater nomination are all linked together in ways that may produce the sternest challenge we have yet seen," the telegram read. "The Civil Rights Act of 1964 could well be diminished or nullified and a decade of increasingly violent and futile disorder ushered in if we do not play our hand coolly and intelligently." The message raised the specter of a Goldwater victory in November. "[He] can win and he can be helped to win if enough wrong moves are made," Wilkins warned.[58]

Wilkins, Randolph, King, Young, Farmer, and Lewis met in New York on July 29. Unlike in the past, this time Wilkins had no reason to exclude Rustin, who took the lead in arguing for a moratorium. Demonstrations, he said, were a matter of tactics not principles, and tactics had to be chosen intelligently. A few days before the rioting broke out in Harlem, he wrote to a friend that "Negroes have been put in a desperate situation and yet everyone—myself included—must urge them to behave not with desperation but politically and rationally." Now the rational thing to do was to hold back from actions that played into the hands of white reactionary forces. Rustin argued the case vigorously enough that the group agreed on a joint press release.[59]

The statement of the Big Six was so remarkable that it became front-page news. Farmer and Lewis did not formally sign on, since they felt they needed to bring it back to CORE and SNCC for approval. But at the press conference, they made their individual agreement clear. The statement described the Goldwater nomination and the Republican platform as a threat to liberal democracy. "We believe racism has been injected into the campaign," the civil rights leaders declared. The danger was so palpable that it demanded "a voluntary, temporary alteration in strategy . . . a temporary change of emphasis." Addressing a movement that had made headlines by defying government authority, they called on their organizations "voluntarily to observe a broad curtailment, if not total moratorium, of all mass marches, mass picketing and mass demonstrations until after Election Day." They proposed that the focus be "political action," by which they meant voter registration and get-out-the-vote campaigns.[60]

In some ways, the call for a moratorium was a smart tactical stroke. In parts of the South, the Civil Rights Act was quickly yielding results, and the need for demonstrations was not quite as pressing. In the North, attention was shifting spontaneously to the political rallies associated with a national election. The civil rights leadership had the opportunity to score points with Johnson without really putting the brakes on its constituency. But cool calculation was not necessarily the order of the day. The call for a moratorium provoked turmoil. Many in SCLC grumbled since some of its staff had just come off weeks of protests in St. Augustine, Florida, where mobs daily attacked civil rights marchers. The moratorium caused an uproar in CORE. Despite his later protestations to the contrary, Farmer had supported it. On August 4, he called Jack Valenti, an aide to Johnson, to assure him that the Syracuse CORE chapter would observe the moratorium when the president came to town that week. But when CORE's National Council met a few days later, sentiment to repudiate it was too strong for Farmer to resist. Farmer's about-face so disgusted Norman Hill that he resigned from the staff.[61]

Despite his own advocacy of the moratorium, Rustin was not rigidly wedded to it. Just a few days after the statement was issued, he spoke on WLIB, a New York radio station with a large black audience. Commenting on Mayor Wagner's rejection of demands for a civilian police review board, Rustin said that demonstrations "cannot be curtailed in a vacuum." Because of Wagner's intransigence, Rustin said he would not urge anyone in New York to comply with the moratorium. Still, the general call for it was not an easy position for Rustin to take because of his own history and the mood in activist circles. "I got in trouble with the black community when I convinced Mr. Randolph that there should be a moratorium," he recalled. The moratorium came to be viewed as an opening salvo in a new battle between moderates and militants in the civil rights movement. For the first time in his life, but not the last, Rustin found himself tarred with the moderate label.[62]

ALL OF THESE CONCERNS figured into Rustin's stance toward the Mississippi project in the month before the Atlantic City convention. He remained supportive, even excited, about it because of its potential to remake political power in the South. In mid-July, he wrote to a friend that he hoped "a significant fight within the Credentials Committee and on the floor of the convention will be made." Early in August, he was in Washington at the MFDP office, meeting with Ella Baker and the other staff, discussing strategy and identifying sources of political support for the challenge. But he also harbored reservations. He worried about whether SNCC was up to the task. SNCC's emphasis on local leadership was all fine and good, but he wondered whether it could pull off a campaign of this magnitude without accepting the resources—and hence the constraints—that working cooperatively with the larger movement and with national Democratic Party allies demanded. A trip to Mississippi in late July to confer with Moses and other key staff did little to allay his concerns. Just a month before the convention was set to open, Moses was telling SNCC workers that the MFPD challenge was "in very bad shape all around the state." Rustin came back from the visit convinced that trouble was brewing. The pressure SNCC workers lived under was likely to lead them to act rashly. "They are going to try and accuse everybody of selling them out," he predicted to King. Their actions were bound to look like "an assault on our friends."[63]

Whatever difficulties Mississippi organizers faced, they had succeeded in at least one important way by the end of July. The looming battle over which delegation to seat had captured the attention of Johnson and his key aides. They were taking the challenge extremely seriously. Lee White, who monitored civil rights activity for Johnson, told Rustin he thought the whole situation had "explosive potential." Goldwater's nomination had made the South a battleground in the election, despite the fact that an incumbent Southerner would be the Democratic nominee. The Goldwater candidacy helped make the Mississippi Freedom Democrats a national news story weeks before delegates arrived in Atlantic City. Immediately after the Republican convention closed, the *New York Times* put the MFDP on its front page.[64]

In the weeks before the convention, civil rights leaders tried to persuade Johnson to recognize the MFDP. John Lewis wrote an impassioned letter detailing the violence in Mississippi. "Since June 21, when the Mississippi Summer Project began," he informed Johnson, "there have been at least 60 beatings, 8 unsolved killings, 17 church burnings, 13 bombings, 23 shootings, and innumerable other acts of intimidation." In the name of justice, he implored Johnson to seat the MFDP. Joseph Rauh, who was acting as legal counsel to the MFDP, told Lee White that seating them would eliminate "the central reason for demonstrations at Atlantic City." Robert Spike of the National Council of Churches cautioned the White House that "the chances of serious violence are high" unless the national party was responsive to the MFDP.[65]

Rustin too tried to influence the administration. Throughout these weeks, he had frequent contact with King about how to push Johnson on the Mississippi issue. He suggested playing the moratorium card—telling the president it would be impossible to contain demonstrations if the convention did not seat the MFDP. Serving as King's emissary, Rustin called White to arrange a private conference between King and the president. Rustin thought King could then parlay the meeting into press interviews and thus take the MFDP case to the nation. Whether this might have worked was moot. Since the FBI was tapping Rustin's phone, the White House knew of Rustin's intentions and refused to meet alone with King.[66]

As the convention approached, the MFDP challenge threatened to steal the spotlight from Johnson. The Thursday before, the press covered a meeting at the White House between the president and several civil rights leaders. Although Johnson kept the conversation away from the Mississippi events, the *Washington Post* headlined the story, "LBJ Gets Negro Warning on All-White Party." It quoted a telegram that Rustin had helped prepare in which King announced his support of the MFDP and warned of the political dangers if the convention did not recognize the challengers. An editorial in the *New York Times* spoke in favor of the Freedom Democrats. "Who still believes the nation can placidly accept what Mississippi calls normal?" it asked.[67]

The MFDP delegates arrived in Atlantic City on Friday, August 21, for hearings of the Credentials Committee. If enough members of the committee supported a petition to seat the Freedom Democrats, they could file a minority report that would bring the issue to the whole convention. On Saturday, the committee heard the case. The high point of the hearings came when Fannie Lou Hamer, a Mississippi sharecropper, testified. In spellbinding cadences, she recounted the price of daring to insist on her right to vote. She and her family were ejected from the plantation where they had worked for years; she was beaten, bruised, and bloodied for her activism. "All of this is on account of we want to register and vote," she exclaimed. "If the Freedom Party is not seated now, I question America."[68] Network television carried Hamer's testimony live. It was so compelling that Johnson, watching from the White House, called an immediate press conference as a ruse to get the cameras away from her.

Rustin arrived in Atlantic City early in the week and, on Tuesday, persuaded a group of MFDP leaders to meet with him, Hubert Humphrey, Walter Reuther, and some of the national civil rights leadership to consider possible solutions. The Freedom Democrats were prepared to make concessions. For instance, Congresswoman Edith Green had suggested seating whichever members of the two delegations were willing to support the national ticket in November. Another proposal called for seating every member of the two delegations, with each one receiving half a vote. But party leaders offered much less. They promised to overhaul the rules so that no segregated delegation would ever receive recognition in the future, a change that, in itself, promised a new Democratic Party in the South. But for the present, they offered only two at-large seats, and they handpicked the two delegates acceptable to them, Aaron Henry and Ed King. As the group sat in a hotel room discussing the proposal, Moses heard an announcement on the television that the MFDP had accepted it. Angered by the duplicity of the Johnson people, he "stalked out, violently angry."[69] Discussions never resumed.

Over the next two days, Mississippi activists debated what to do. To the local church that served as their headquarters came a parade of civil rights figures, Rustin prominent among them, to argue that they put aside their absolutist position and accept the compromise. Wilkins antagonized the entire delegation with his condescension. In more measured tones, King, Farmer, Rauh, and others all urged them to accept the offer, imperfect as it was. Rustin spoke especially strongly in favor of acceptance. In the words of one delegate, he gave "a brilliant talk on politics and the meaning of compromise." By choosing to move beyond demonstrations and participate in mainstream politics, he argued, they were entering a world where the give-and-take of negotiation was the way an agenda moved forward. Johnson's offer might not in some abstract sense be just, but it recognized the rightness of the MFDP's cause by promising to change forever the rules of the party. He applauded their courage and everything they had done thus far, an achievement that he thought was monumental. In fact, he told them, contrary to what it seemed at the moment, they had actually won their case. But,

Rustin said, by standing firm now, they were "trying to pluck defeat out of the jaws of victory."[70] His arguments were of no avail; the Freedom Democrats remained unyielding.

Then and later, many of the key young activists in the civil rights and student movements saw the Atlantic City convention as a great divide. John Lewis called it "the turning point for the country, for the civil rights movement and certainly for SNCC." Todd Gitlin, a campus activist who later wrote a major history of the 1960s, called the convention a "watershed" for both radicals and liberals. It was, he said, a "Moment of Truth. The very name became synonymous with liberal betrayal." Ed Brown, a SNCC activist, believed the events "challenged the whole concept of the use of coalition politics for social change. . . . Where was the coalition?" Staughton Lynd, who coordinated the Freedom Schools in Mississippi that summer, described the experience as "traumatic. . . . Bitterness at those national civil rights personalities who urged acceptance of the compromise on grounds of political expediency—Martin Luther King, Bayard Rustin, Joseph Rauh, as well as Walter Reuther and other erstwhile allies—was indescribable." Bob Moses said afterward that SNCC was going to "pursue our own goals, and let the chips fall where they may."[71]

This view of Atlantic City circulated widely among activists and quickly assumed gospel status. Their brief moment approaching the sanctums of power revealed to these young radicals something incontrovertibly ugly about American politics. These accounts display a conviction of inevitability that makes the rest of the sixties seem like classic Greek tragedy, unfolding to a denouement that no one wants but that everyone foresees and is helpless to prevent. The "good sixties" of heroic sit-ins, daring Freedom Rides, a peaceful march on Washington and the stirring rhetoric of Kennedy and King was about to slide into the "bad sixties" of angry militants, urban rebellions, campus disorders, and wanton violence in Southeast Asia. Hope, optimism, and a creative idealism suffused the good sixties; cynicism, destructiveness, and a despairing pessimism filled the bad. Atlantic City was the moment when all stood poised at a crossroads. Liberal leadership was found wanting, and two political roads diverged.

But perhaps the accounts themselves are the tragedy and their interpretation of these events suspect. At the time, there were other points
of view, other ways of looking at the story, and other courses of action
that plausibly suggested themselves to participants. For instance, Lyndon Johnson was so driven to distraction by the power of the MFDP
challenge that he thought it might cost him the election. He briefly
even toyed with abandoning his candidacy. Johnson was completely
baffled by the upset among Mississippi activists. "They don't know the
victory they got," he told Walter Reuther. "Next time no one can dis-
criminate against Negroes." Across the country, the press looked at the
events in Atlantic City and, almost with a single voice, pronounced the
convention a triumph for the movement. The *Washington Post* called
the outcome "a spectacular victory" for the MFDP. The *New York Times*
described it as "a remarkable victory." No previous convention, it said,
would have taken their claims seriously. The fact that they were heard,
that the convention promised a change of rules, and that any seats were
offered a group that had operated in only a fraction of the state's counties made the compromise "a triumph for moral force." The *Denver
Post* observed that the MFDP had "succeeded in penetrating to the heart
of the Democratic party." Instead of always protesting from the outside,
this time the civil rights movement had pushed its way to the center of
American politics.[72]

Ironically, local activists in Mississippi, to whom SNCC claimed loyalty, drew lessons from Atlantic City vastly different from those of the
young militants who organized them. Rather than come away devastated, many saw the confrontation as "another beautiful thing, especially where we were able to hold out against those two seats."
Returning home, they actively worked for the national Democratic
ticket, put forward a slate of their own for Congress, and planned to
travel to Washington in January to challenge the seating of Mississippi's
all-white delegation to Congress. For them, Atlantic City was neither
an ending nor a turning point, but one more step in a long struggle.[73]

Rustin grasped the moment with all its complexity and contradiction. In his own musings about strategy, he believed the MFDP "played
a revolutionary role both within the Civil Rights Movement and within

the Democratic Party." He thought the challenge "demonstrated beyond a doubt that politics and protest could be combined intelligently." He also understood the way that, for SNCC, raw feeling infused their political thinking and led to conclusions that brought disastrous consequences. "Those kids, who had been shot at, beaten up, brutalized, seen their buddies murdered, could scarcely have been prepared to accept compromise," he reflected. "To a certain extent I would have been very disappointed in them if they had." Rustin had cast himself in the role of absolutist before—in his fight with Randolph over resistance to military segregation, for example. "I understood them perfectly," he said, "but to understand is not to say they are right." As with other activist generations, "history begins with their discovery of themselves," he told an interviewer a decade later.

In this case, the price of generational conflict was high. In 1948, Rustin's intransigence had done nothing but lead to a temporary estrangement from his mentor. Atlantic City, by contrast, was "a very vast turning point." The political system was opening the door to Southern blacks. "All right, you've won; come on in" is how Rustin interpreted what happened, yet SNCC activists could not emotionally abandon the role of the aggrieved protester who shouted at those inside but refused to enter when the door was ajar. Atlantic City was, Rustin reflected, "the beginning of the end of SNCC. . . . Their usefulness was practically over."[74] What he did not say, perhaps because he did not see it, was that the events of the summer also opened a breach between him and militants in the movement that only widened as the decade wore on.

CHAPTER SEVENTEEN

"From Protest to Politics"
1964–1965

WHILE MANY IN SNCC left Atlantic City "bitter, frustrated, torn apart, battle fatigued and everything else," in the words of John Lewis, Rustin came home with his sights on the election.[1] His schedule that fall was especially hectic. He traveled the country speaking to civil rights groups, labor union conventions, and conferences of student activists. Although his emphasis varied depending on the audience, the elements were always the same. The civil rights movement had created a political opening that made progressive reforms possible. Labor, civil rights, and other liberal groupings had to work together. The Goldwater candidacy was menacing. Rustin infused his political analysis with passion and conviction. After addressing the Teamsters annual convention, one union official wrote back that his talk was "the most significant of the Conference. Some of our tougher, more pragmatic Teamsters are telling me that it was the most meaningful thing they have heard on the subject of Civil Rights." After his talk to the Cleveland City Club was broadcast on radio, the station was "deluged with requests" for copies. A club officer told him that "rarely have we had such an eloquent address as yours. . . . Coming from one who hears thirty to forty speeches a year, perhaps you can appreciate my compliment."[2]

To some who were accustomed to the Rustin of radical pacifist days, his new message was disquieting, and he often had to defend his position. After a campus lecture at Penn State in October, Rustin replied to a critic who had taken him to task for his support of Johnson. "I am going to vote for Johnson," he explained, "not because he is perfect, but because he is for civil rights, medicare and the poverty program, and because he is for progress. Barry Goldwater is a reactionary and a danger to world peace. I secondly want Johnson to know that the Negroes, liberals, intellectuals, students, and the labor movement are giving him his majority—for I want him to be more dependent on us. I don't believe that Johnson is anything more than a shrewd politician—but that is a far cry from his opponent who is a war-happy reactionary who aids and abets racism." Rustin took issue with peace activists who were putting forward third-party candidates for Congress. "I don't believe an independent political campaign is the means we should use," he wrote one of them. "Our main political job this year is to continue the work begun by the Mississippi Freedom Democratic Party . . . to kick the Dixiecrats out . . . and to build a new Democratic party." He urged pacifists to conduct "massive voter registration campaigns" and to "push Johnson to the left" by making clear that his base of support was coming from liberals and progressives.[3]

Rustin's ties within the civil rights movement were undergoing a reconfiguration that fall. After Atlantic City, many in SNCC were "very much down on me," Rustin recalled. He also found himself estranged from CORE. Farmer, who was facing challenges to his leadership within the organization, was increasingly hostile toward him, and Norman Hill had resigned from the national staff. Hill's letter of resignation bore the marks of Rustin's political analysis. He criticized CORE for "a calcification of tactical imagination" and "the glorification of demonstrations as ends in themselves." Hill urged a reorientation away from protests and toward political mobilization. "The growth of [Goldwater's] right wing menace is the most significant development on the American political scene in decades," he wrote. "We can no longer stand on the outside crying 'a pox on both your houses.'"[4]

Rustin's relationship with King deepened during these months and began to approach, politically if not emotionally, the closeness of their tie in the 1950s. The regular meetings of King's research committee, the guidance Rustin had provided after the Harlem riots, and the frequent consultations over the MFDP had kept the two men in steady contact. Rustin continued to view King's charisma as one of the movement's greatest assets and saw his unwavering commitment to nonviolence as especially critical for preserving the moral basis of the struggle. Signs of Rustin's influence on King and of King's willingness to lean on Rustin were abundant during these months. When SCLC convened late in September for its annual convention, Rustin's language appeared all through King's address. "Citizens do not have the moral or political right to dream up or to engage in fantastic gimmicks to arouse public attention," King told the organization's supporters. "Demonstrations are tactics, not principles." King declared that they had to look beyond public accommodations to jobs, housing, and quality education. "These areas require political action," he said. "Negro people do not themselves possess the political power to create full employment alone. We must add our political power to that of other groups." Rustin wrote the economic resolutions that the convention approved. His planks included not only fair employment practices but also a call for massive public works, universal health coverage, a higher minimum wage, and a vastly enlarged war on poverty.[5]

Rustin encouraged King to translate these sentiments into actions, particularly through involvement in the elections. King did not explicitly endorse Johnson, but he traveled to a long list of cities with large black communities and spoke at huge get-out-the-vote rallies whose leanings were clear. Rustin coordinated public relations for the tour and appeared with King at a number of events. On election evening, once it became apparent that Johnson and the congressional Democrats had won an enormous victory, Rustin spoke to King by phone. They needed quickly, he said, to have discussions on "how to 'cash in' on the election results . . . and how to put pressure" on Johnson.[6]

Before these conversations proceeded very far, another item of King's business diverted Rustin. In October, King learned that the Nobel Committee had awarded him its Peace Prize. It was an extraordinary honor, raising King's stature enormously and focusing international attention on the use of nonviolence in the struggle against racism. King asked Rustin to arrange a European tour. Rustin flew to London in mid-November, where he met with Peggy Duff, Canon Collins, April

Carter, and other peace activists. They planned a London visit for King that included preaching in St. Paul's Cathedral, an address before a mass peace rally, and a reception with members of Parliament and the cabinet. British pacifists were especially eager that King link the civil rights movement to the fight against colonialism and apartheid, and Rustin included major remarks about Africa in the drafts he prepared for King.[7]

Rustin's work on the Nobel journey wore him out. The scope of the assignment kept growing. When King first asked his help, the two had imagined a traveling group of perhaps six. By the time they left for Europe in early December, the number had swollen to over forty as family members, friends, advisers, and SCLC staff importuned King to be included. In London, Rustin kept track of the entire itinerary and advised pacifist leaders there. By the time the party arrived in Oslo, where Norwegian royalty feted the group, Rustin was exhausted. He appeared drunk at one of the receptions and engaged in "erratic, utterly cynical" conversation, according to one observer.[8]

The cynical comments may have had something to do with one of the situations Rustin had to handle in Oslo. In the early hours one morning, an anxious call from King's secretary awakened Rustin. Apparently, as he later told a friend, "members of King's entourage had naked girls running up and down the corridors of a hotel where they stayed and were bringing white prostitutes to their rooms." Police had intervened and threatened to detain the women. King's brother was implicated, and Rustin could smell the trouble that would erupt if the women went to the press. He persuaded the police to release them and let them keep the money and valuables in their possession. The irony of the situation was not lost on him. Here he was, a man so frequently targeted because of his sexuality, now having to preserve the reputations of a group of heterosexual men among whom ministers predominated.[9]

RUSTIN RETURNED FROM EUROPE poised for a major transition in his career. In January 1965, he tendered his resignation as executive secretary of the WRL, ending two dozen years of employment in the peace movement. Later that winter, at a press conference in Harlem with Randolph by his side, he announced the launching of the A. Philip Randolph Institute (APRI).

Through the previous fall, in between his electioneering and the work for King, Rustin had embarked on steady fundraising for the institute. He had amassed almost $40,000 in pledges from wealthy individuals and, with that in hand, began to canvass unions, using Randolph's name to open doors. Ralph Helstein, the head of the Packinghouse Workers and one of the most left-leaning labor leaders in the country, was a member of King's research committee; he readily promised a grant from his union. After leaving CORE, Norman Hill had moved to the Industrial Union Department of the AFL-CIO. Created when the AFL and CIO merged in the 1950s, it was largely controlled by Walter Reuther and the UAW, and it retained a vision of the labor movement as a force for progressive change. Hill lobbied hard for it to seed Rustin's project, and Reuther came through with a $25,000 contribution. The largest source of support came from George Meany and the AFL-CIO Executive Council. Donald Slaiman, who traveled in the Socialist Party circles to which Rustin was close, had just become head of the federation's civil rights division. Aware that Meany "knew he had made a mistake" in not endorsing the March on Washington, he saw the Randolph Institute as a way for the labor leader to make amends.[10]

The prospectus that Rustin prepared as he attempted to sell his idea reflected the economic bent to his thinking ever since the March on Washington. "The primary purpose of the A. Philip Randolph Institute," he explained, "is to strengthen [the] broad coalition of forces in the struggle for racial equality." APRI would conduct research. It would build connections between labor unions and civil rights organizations. It would press for inclusion of economic issues in the civil rights agenda and argue for the importance of civil rights to the health of the labor movement. APRI would allow Rustin to advise civil rights groups and develop specific campaigns. Rustin invited on to the board of directors the heads of the major civil rights organizations, high-ranking labor officials, and individuals from the progressive wing of American liberalism.[11]

Just as he was launching the institute, Rustin published a political manifesto that became his signature statement of strategy in the 1960s. The dramatic election results in 1964 drove him to write it. Rustin saw the election as a harbinger of major change. Lyndon Johnson had won a landslide victory, comparable to the victory of Franklin Roosevelt in 1936; Democrats had better than two-to-one majorities in both the Senate and the House. The national electorate had decisively rejected the views of Barry Goldwater, and the way seemed clear for a season of liberal reform. Four years earlier, 60 percent of black voters had cast ballots for Richard Nixon, the Republican candidate; now 90 percent of them had voted for Johnson. There was reason to expect that their support would count for something in the coming four years.

Yet the course of national politics was more fluid and open than the vote totals suggested. The Democratic victory came at the same time as a massive defection of white Southerners. Goldwater carried six Southern states. Could a permanent Democratic majority be configured without the Dixiecrats? Might black voters become the core of a future regional majority? Would the new national party move to the left and revive the crusading spirit of the New Deal? Or would it remain a party of the center, as it had since Truman? Would Dixiecrats join Republicans to build a new conservative majority? All of these questions mattered to Rustin. On the answers depended, as far as he could see, the future of the struggle for racial and economic justice in the United States. The right intervention now could have immense consequences on the shape of things to come.

In February 1965, Rustin published "From Protest to Politics: The Future of the Civil Rights Movement," in *Commentary* magazine.[12] Until then, Rustin had always written for journals and magazines of the peace movement or the left. *Commentary* in the 1960s was a liberal magazine. In choosing it, Rustin was reaching for a new audience, a readership of influential white liberals whom he hoped to sway. His writing was spare, pointed, unsentimental, and without the polemical excess that often characterized writing by the left. He tried to open a window for white liberals into the minds and hearts of civil rights activists and the broader black community. Yet he also seemed careful in what he chose to tell. He communicated urgency but not pessimism and acknowledged dangers while holding out a sense of opportunities too. A generation later, his manifesto still reads well.

Rustin's argument went like this: The ten years from the *Brown* decision to the Civil Rights Act were likely to be remembered as the decade when the legal foundations of racism "virtually collapsed." Important as the victories were, the changes came in institutions—theaters, restaurants, libraries, bus terminals—that were peripheral to power. In other words, the civil rights movement hit racism where it was anachronistic and dispensable. The college students, ministers, and other middle-class participants in the movement successfully targeted an "imposing but hollow" structure. Rustin termed this decade the "classical" phase of the civil rights movement.

Yet in Birmingham, the black community moved beyond public accommodations to matters of jobs and housing, "the package deal." In many communities, the movement had expanded to include working-class constituents and the poor. Northern black communities were mobilizing too. Through Bob Moses and the Freedom Democrats, the movement was making "a conscious bid for *political power*. . . . Direct action techniques are being subordinated to a strategy calling for the building of community institutions or power bases."

Alongside the gains, Rustin found disturbing trends. School segregation was spreading, not declining, and had become a national problem. The employment gap between whites and blacks was growing. Housing stock in the cities had deteriorated, and slums had spread. Linking these developments to the urban disorders of the summer before, Rustin said that the riots "were not race riots, they were outbursts of class aggression in a society where class and color definitions are converging disastrously." Civil rights was not the issue; social and economic conditions were. A struggle that began as protest now had to "translate itself into a political movement."

One obstacle to building this political movement came from "whites of good will" who believed that legal equality was enough. With civil rights laws in place, their argument went, African Americans, like the Irish and Italians and Jews, could now climb the economic ladder. Rustin dismissed this claim as specious. Its proponents ignored the his-

torical legacy of slavery and failed to acknowledge the changing economy. "The lower rungs of the economic ladder" that once provided
mobility "are being lopped off" as automation eliminated unskilled
jobs. Calls by liberals for "self-help" were misguided. Like the self-help
advocated by the Black Muslims, it would only preserve a ghetto that
needed dismantling. Real self-help, Rustin declared, involved "mobilizing people into power units capable of effecting social change."

Rather than dwell on those who denied the problem, Rustin concerned
himself with those who recognized the obstacles but saw no solutions.
He identified two "contradictory lines of thought" that, paradoxically,
"simultaneously nourish and antagonize each other." One he described
as the *New York Times* moderate," who thought the problems were so
enormous that militant activism was futile. These moderates saw the
economic and social context as so intractable that only modest changes
were possible. Their failure to imagine radical solutions amounted to
"admonitions to the Negro to adjust to the status quo," a stance Rustin
described as immoral. Because the moderate position left blacks isolated and without hope, it helped spawn a group he defined as "no-win"
activists. These activists saw no mainstream forces ready to advocate
radical programs, and so they concluded that the only strategy was to
shock white America and expose the hypocrisy of the establishment.
"They seek to change white hearts," Rustin wrote, "by traumatizing
them." But hearts were not the issue. "Neither racial affinities nor
racial hostilities are rooted there," he said. "It is institutions—social,
political, and economic institutions—which are the ultimate molders of
collective sentiments." Remake these institutions, and "the ineluctable
gradualism of history" will form new attitudes on race. Meanwhile, the
no-win militants continued with their sound and fury to no avail, since
"militancy is a matter of posture and volume and not of effect." All the
shouting in the world would not reconstruct a single core institution of
American life.

Rustin called the black struggle "essentially revolutionary." By revolutionary he meant "the qualitative transformation of fundamental institutions, more or less rapidly, to the point where the social and
economic structure . . . can no longer be said to be the same." To be

victorious—that is, to achieve the fact of equality—the civil rights movement needed bold programs for full employment, the abolition of slums, and the building of quality schools. The movement had to go beyond advocacy of civil rights and put forward an agenda whose goal was the "refashioning of our political economy."

Radical objectives like these could be achieved only through political power, but the black community could not win power alone. "We need allies," Rustin declared. "The future of the Negro struggle depends on whether . . . a coalition of progressive forces . . . becomes the *effective* political majority." As a model, he pointed to the array of forces behind the March on Washington and the Civil Rights Act. Aware that the movement often cast its objectives in a moral framework and mindful of Atlantic City, Rustin warned that coalition required compromise. "The difference between expediency and morality," he wrote, "is the difference between selling out a principle and making smaller concessions to win larger ones."

Rustin had no illusions about the difficulty of building a winning coalition, but he saw no alternatives. He rejected the claim circulating in SNCC and the New Left that liberals were "the main enemy." No, he wrote, "the objective fact is that Eastland and Goldwater are the main enemies—they and the opponents of civil rights, of the war on poverty, of medicare." The movement for racial justice would advance only when social and economic security came to be "inextricably entangled" with civil rights. Support for such an agenda was most likely to come from trade unions, the socially conscious religious community, and Democratic Party liberals.

The need to switch from protest to politics, the need for allies, his belief in the strength of the civil rights coalition, and his sense of the historical moment all led Rustin to his conclusion. There was nothing inevitable about the future. The Johnson majority was not permanent but unstable. "Here is where the cutting edge of the civil rights movement can be applied," he wrote. "We must see to it that the reorganization of the 'consensus party' proceeds along lines which will make it an effective vehicle for social reconstruction." Drive the Southern racists out. Shift the balance of forces in the party. "If the mandate is seized upon to set fundamental changes in motion, then the basis can be laid for a new mandate, a new coalition." The Mississippi Freedom Democrats, he declared, were showing the way. "They launched a political revolution whose logic is the displacement of Dixiecrat power. They launched that revolution within a major political institution and as part of a coalitional effort." Now the challenge was "to broaden our social vision" and put forward a radical program inside a mainstream institution. The movement had to contest the notion "that our integration into American life, so long delayed, must now proceed in an atmosphere of competitive scarcity instead of in the . . . abundance which technology makes possible. We cannot claim to have answers to all the complex problems of modern society. . . . But we can agitate the right questions by probing at the contradictions which still stand in the way of the Great Society."

At this distance in time, it is not easy to grasp the novelty of Rustin's argument. Several decades later, it is hard to imagine the Democratic Party as a vehicle for anything of consequence. Since Rustin wrote, it has grown weaker, become increasingly ineffectual, and lost the reforming zeal it once had. Moreover, as market values have extended their sway in American culture, as the infrastructure of public life crumbles and suspicion of government deepens, a programmatic agenda like the one put forward by Rustin seems anachronistic, an artifact of a past era.

But the strategy articulated in "From Protest to Politics" is most surprising because it came from Bayard Rustin. Nothing in his history might have led anyone to expect him to argue that the cutting edge of progressive change involved transforming the Democratic Party. Rustin had impeccable radical credentials. His long record of arrests stood as striking evidence of his antimajoritarian beliefs. His importation to the United States of Gandhi's philosophy and methods added to his radical profile. So did his determination to take wildly unpopular stands around issues of war, peace, and the global conflict against communism and to devote his adult life to building movements outside the structures of American politics. Radicals with this kind of history simply did not make the Democratic Party the staging ground for their work.

Paradoxically, Rustin's willingness to espouse the ideas in "From Protest to Politics" was another version of a distrust of orthodoxy—this time of the left—so characteristic of his public life.

Meant for broad public consumption, the *Commentary* article did not expose the whole of Rustin's thinking. In private gatherings, he tempered the optimistic rendering of "From Protest to Politics" with a more candid assessment of the dangers of the moment. Rustin believed that, despite the Johnson landslide, "the racist political appeal is greater than appears at first glance." He feared that the rising winds of nationalism in the black community foretold a spreading "abstention from the struggle." And he especially worried that the youthful militancy of what he called "the spontaneous left" was heading toward "intransigence and refusal of all compromise." But whichever prognosis he offered, whether public optimism or private alarm, Rustin still came down in the same place. "We cannot talk about the democratic road to freedom unless we are talking about building a majority movement," he told one grouping of activists. He urged them to make "the program for racial equality . . . so intertwined with progressive economic and social policies as to make it impossible to choose one without the other."[13]

THE HOPEFUL PROGNOSIS of "From Protest to Politics" seemed confirmed by what was happening in Alabama. The struggle for voting rights in the town of Selma that winter served as the symbolic center of a movement conducting demonstrations in scores of communities across the country. The Selma operation was the project of King and the SCLC. Invited by local people dissatisfied with the assistance they were receiving from SNCC, King saw the voter registration work there as equivalent to the battle for civil rights in Birmingham two years before. He meant it to be a dramatic campaign that would provoke retaliation from the local white power structure and, in response, rouse the national conscience. On January 2, 1965, not long after his return from Europe, King issued a public call for a sustained voter registration drive throughout Alabama. If the state government stood in the way, he told supporters, "we must be willing to go to jail by the thousands."[14]

At first glance, the scenario that unfolded in Selma looked depressingly familiar. Civil rights organizers faced registrars who used a maze of technicalities to turn blacks away; a judge who prohibited public assemblies by as few as three African Americans; a sheriff, Jim Clark, every bit as vicious as Bull Connor; the demagoguery of George Wallace, who demonized civil rights organizers as "professional agitators with pro-Communist affiliations"; and white supremacists whose violence left two dead and many more beaten. When protests began in January, Clark and his deputies responded by assaulting demonstrators and arresting them en masse; television cameras captured Clark beating a black woman. King himself was physically attacked and jailed. By early February, local students were marching to the county courthouse and being arrested by the hundreds, and demonstrations in support of voting rights were erupting elsewhere in Alabama. One protester, Jimmy Lee Jackson, died from gunshot wounds inflicted by a state trooper after Jackson tried to protect his mother from assault. Wallace ordered state troopers to help contain the unrest. The next month, SCLC attempted to organize a several-day march from Selma to Montgomery, the state capital. State police and county deputies brutally attacked the peaceful crowd before they had left town; a week later, sympathy marchers in Montgomery faced clubs and cattle prods.[15]

Yet Selma also revealed the distance the nation had traveled since the Birmingham demonstrations two years earlier. In Birmingham, the African American community had, at least publicly, fought alone. Black organizations planned the demonstrations; black leaders negotiated; black bodies marched in the streets. Intervention from Washington came in the form of efforts to negotiate peace rather than bring justice, and Kennedy officials often acted as if the extremism of Negro demonstrators was comparable to the extremism of the Klan. Selma revealed a different configuration of forces. Early on, the Justice Department filed voting bias suits. A delegation from the House of Representatives came to Selma to investigate. President Johnson promised to invoke provisions of the 1964 Civil Rights Act as a tool to extend voting rights. The escalating violence provoked numbers of Northern whites, particularly clergy, to journey to Alabama to express their solidarity. Nicholas Katzenbach, the attorney general, promised to prosecute state police for using "totally unreasonable force." Later in March, when civil rights forces finally made their trek from Selma to Montgomery, thousands of whites joined them, including prominent church, labor, and political figures. All of this seemed to verify Rustin's estimation that the conditions for a moral coalition in favor of racial justice were present and that the postelection political climate was pregnant with opportunities.

Most remarkable of all perhaps was the role played by President Johnson. Well into February, key administration officials were telling civil rights leaders that the moment was not auspicious for voting rights legislation. Yet once the crisis deepened, Johnson moved decisively. He called Wallace to the White House for a private meeting and gave him a dressing down, telling him that "the brutality in Selma . . . must not be repeated." Two days later, on March 15, Johnson spoke to a joint session of Congress and promised to send the legislature a tough new voting rights bill. He used stirring rhetoric to endorse not only the goals but also the methods of the civil rights movement. "We seek order, we seek unity, but we will not accept the peace of stifled rights or the order imposed by fear or the unity that stifles protest—for peace cannot be purchased at the price of liberty," he told Congress. "The real hero of this struggle is the American Negro. His actions and protests, his courage to risk safety, and even to risk his life, have awakened the conscience of this nation." Embracing one of the anthems of the freedom struggle, Johnson said that "it's all of us who must overcome the crippling legacy of bigotry and injustice. And we shall overcome." King wept as he watched the speech on television. Rustin called it "the most forthright ever made by a President" on the theme of racial justice.[16]

If the response to Selma indicated how much the mainstream had shifted in just two years, it also marked the vast distance Rustin had traveled in the same time. Early in 1963, he was still, in a sense, on probation from the movement. He watched it from afar as he busied himself with a pacifism at the margins of American life. Now, as the Selma crisis deepened, Rustin found himself close to the center of discussions about strategy. Early in February, he accompanied King and Andrew Young, the SCLC executive director, to Washington, where they pressed Vice President Humphrey, Attorney General Katzenbach, and con-

gressional leaders to take bold action to protect voting rights. Throughout the weeks of demonstrations in Selma, Rustin stayed in regular
contact with King by phone and met with him when King came to New
York. He consulted even more frequently with Young, who was closer
to the day-to-day operations of the campaign than was King. When
Ralph Abernathy communicated to Rustin that an exhausted and emotionally depressed King needed time away but was "completely broke,"
Rustin raised money so that King could take a few days of vacation. As
King agonized about whether to violate a federal injunction against
marching, Rustin unequivocally urged him to move forward. "Not to do
so would cause incalculable harm" to his credibility as a leader, Rustin
told him. Defying the injunction was vital "for the sake of people who
believe in nonviolence." A few days later, when King turned back in the
face of a phalanx of Southern law enforcement officers, Rustin told his
friend, Robert Gilmore, that, as he had expected, King was now "under
heavy attack from people who feel that he sold out by retreating from
his announced march." On Sunday, March 14, Rustin was at the head
of a massive demonstration in Harlem in support of civil rights workers
in Alabama. He rallied the crowd with a fiery speech, saying that "we
will stay in these damn streets until every Negro in the country can
vote." Late in the month, when the mass march to Montgomery finally
took place, Rustin sat on the speakers' platform at the rally outside the
Alabama state capitol.[17]

Rustin saw Selma as a testing time for both the vitality of nonviolence and the ability of the civil rights movement to translate its power
in the streets into an effective political force. He thought that the
demonstrations and the ensuing violence had roused such outrage that
"the battle has shifted from Selma, Alabama to Washington, D.C." Not
only voting rights, but other proposals for economic and social justice
could be placed on the national political agenda with reasonable expectations of success. At a meeting of the SCLC board in April, he stressed
the importance of an economic foundation for black progress. Not just
voting rights but a higher minimum wage and appropriations for public works projects mattered too.[18] Rustin particularly emphasized the
link between voting rights and economic justice. To remake the Demo-

cratic Party, as he was advocating, depended on black enfranchisement in the South, but for what purposes would the vote be used? During the spring, when the Senate broke the filibuster against voting rights legislation, it became apparent that the long struggle for enfranchisement was nearing its end. SCLC began planning the next stage of its work in the South. Rustin counseled King and the SCLC staff to "make every church in the South a precinct headquarters on the right to vote—voter education and the issues must be stressed." In June, when SCLC launched a summer-long voter registration and political education program in the South, Rustin shaped the training and spent most of a week in Atlanta working with the volunteers.[19]

Early in August, Rustin traveled to Washington to witness Johnson's signing of the Voting Rights Act. He stood in the room where a century earlier, Lincoln had signed into law a bill freeing some of the South's slaves. Rustin received one of the pens Johnson used in the ceremony. By the time he arrived home, federal registrars were already heading South to enter African Americans on the voting rolls. The Justice Department suspended literacy tests across the region and filed suit in court to challenge the constitutionality of state poll taxes.

As RUSTIN WATCHED Johnson sign the Voting Rights Act, some of his former colleagues in the peace movement stood mutely outside the White House. Muste, David Dellinger, and Staughton Lynd, along with Bob Moses of SNCC, had gathered in Washington on the twentieth anniversary of the bombing of Hiroshima. Several hundred others joined them in a silent vigil in front of the White House as a protest against the president's policies in Southeast Asia: over the preceding month, Johnson had ordered the deployment of almost 200,000 military personnel to fight in the war that was raging in Vietnam. To the pacifists outside the White House, Rustin's presence inside symbolized a parting of the ways.

The juxtaposition of events was the latest moment in an uncanny parallel chronology in the history of the civil rights movement and the Vietnamese struggle for independence. In 1954, the same month as *Brown*, French colonial rule in Southeast Asia had collapsed. As protests erupted in Birmingham in the spring of 1963, they exploded across South Vietnam as well. As the civil rights supporters converged on Washington for a historic march, Kennedy and his advisers initiated plans for a coup in Saigon. The same month as the confrontation in Atlantic City over the MFDP, Congress passed the Gulf of Tonkin resolution, giving Johnson a free hand to launch military strikes in Vietnam. Now the federal government was finally taking meaningful action to ensure black voting rights at the same time that the president was dispatching masses of Americans to fight a ground war in Southeast Asia.

Although the United States had maintained a military presence in South Vietnam for a decade, in the months after the 1964 election Johnson escalated American military involvement in Southeast Asia alarmingly. In February and March 1965, he authorized massive bombing raids of North Vietnam; he also approved sending battalions of marines to protect U.S. airfields in South Vietnam. Although the administration had secretly debated actions like these for months, Johnson explicitly campaigned for reelection in the fall as a peace candidate. He drew a sharp distinction between himself and a trigger-happy Goldwater, and he promised that if elected, he would not have American soldiers fighting an Asian war. Instead, over the succeeding months, Johnson followed the winter bombing campaign against North Vietnam with a huge commitment of ground troops to fight a land war in Asia. Especially within progressive political circles, Johnson's actions that year felt like a great betrayal. Dissent surfaced almost immediately, especially on college campuses, where spring teach-ins against the war sometimes drew audiences in the thousands.

While Rustin was still at the WRL, he participated in early pacifist initiatives against American militarism in Vietnam. Early in the summer of 1964, Turn Toward Peace, on whose board Rustin served, initiated wide-ranging discussions of U.S. policy in Southeast Asia. It advised its constituent organizations that "every opportunity be taken to demonstrate that there is actually much unrest here over the U.S. Southeast Asia policy" and said that the American penchant for a military solution "must be deemed a failure." As editors of *Liberation*, Muste, Rustin, and Dellinger composed and circulated a "Declaration of Conscience" against the war. In August, along with Norman Thomas and the journalist I. F. Stone, Rustin addressed an antiwar rally in Greenwich Village. The U.S. "should withdraw [its] forces from South Vietnam," he told the crowd. He called the conflict a "civil war" and compared the situation of the Vietnamese to that of African Americans in Harlem and Bedford-Stuyvesant. "The people will no longer tolerate being without dignity and being poor," he said, as he linked the war to police brutality in New York, the bombing of Hiroshima in World War II, and his own decision a generation earlier to go to jail as a conscientious objector.[20]

Shortly after the 1964 election, Students for a Democratic Society (SDS), the main voice of white student activism in the early 1960s, decided to call for a rally in Washington the following spring to protest administration policy in Vietnam. Among pacifist organizations, there was some resentment at SDS for announcing an action of this magnitude without consultation. SDS also provoked concern because it had opened the demonstration to participants across the political spectrum. Throughout the cold war years, the American peace movement had taken pains to draw a line that separated it from Communist-inspired initiatives. It prided itself not only on its nonalignment in cold war politics but also on its criticism of both sides for their actions. As the date of the SDS rally approached, a group of pacifists centering around Turn Toward Peace—Robert Pickus and Bob Gilmore of the AFSC; Muste and Norman Thomas; and Rustin who at this point was no longer at the WRL—circulated a comradely statement that both supported the call to demonstrate and raised the issue of Communist involvement. The statement created a flurry of misunderstanding between those associated with the burgeoning New Left and an older generation. The younger radicals saw themselves being pulled unwillingly into the coils of anti-Communist fervor. Their elders, whose memories stretched back to the 1930s, saw the exclusion of Communists as articles of political faith and matters of common sense. A few weeks later, Turn Toward Peace tried to mend fences by inviting New Left representatives to a joint forum. Although the gathering generated "a fair amount of heat," according to the minutes, it "frequently emitted flashes of light as well," enough so that participants wanted to move ahead with discussions among a larger group. [21]

Rustin was notably absent from the meeting. He knew that not everyone who planned to attend was inclined to call a truce and that he, in particular, had become a target of intense ire. In May 1965, *Liberation* published a broadside against him by David Dellinger, who surveyed the first wave of antiwar activity. Dellinger chided "the equivocations and divided loyalties of some peace leaders tragically compromised by their devotion to a liberal-labor-Negro coalition within the Democratic Party." He praised effusively the SDS's antiwar rally, juxtaposing the spirit of the 25,000 who attended it with that of the 1963 March on Washington. The earlier march, he claimed, had muted its criticism of the Kennedy administration. Its leadership had funneled protest into "an unhealthy (if uneasy) alliance" with labor and the Democrats that "has troubled and confused the movement ever since." Although Dellinger avoided singling out Rustin, his reference to the leadership of the March made the primary object of his animus unmistakably clear.[22]

In June, *Liberation* targeted Rustin even more pointedly when Staughton Lynd ripped into Rustin's *Commentary* article. Titling his own essay "Coalition Politics or Nonviolent Revolution" as counterpoint to Rustin's views, he spun out of Rustin's recent actions a tale of political betrayal. Lynd saw in Rustin's behavior over the previous year a series of maneuvers designed to cripple the black insurgency and contain a spreading radical impulse. He dismissed Rustin's strategy as "a kind of elitism" intended to disempower ordinary people, branded him "a labor lieutenant of capitalism," and accused him of advocating "coalition with the marines."[23]

Lynd's rhetoric displayed all the characteristics of a slash-and-burn, take-no-prisoners style of leftist debate. He meant his language to spark outrage in his readers and mark his antagonist as outside the circle of comrades. As Dave McReynolds described it, the polemic sounded "as if [Lynd] had just emerged from a Communist Party meeting in the 1930s with the news that social democrats are the true class enemy." It conspicuously departed from the tone that Muste and Rustin—and Dellinger too—had established when they founded *Liber-*

ation a decade earlier as a voice for revolutionary nonviolence, distinct from Old Left styles of political agitation. Dellinger, who had become the chief editor as Muste aged and Rustin focused on civil rights, had invited Lynd onto the editorial board. The tone of both pieces was intentional, not inadvertent, since they rejected suggestions before publication to temper their language.[24] Lynd in particular anticipated a style of rhetorical excess soon to become commonplace among radicals.

Lynd's charges referred to particular actions taken by Rustin over the preceding year. The accusation of elitism, for instance, grew out of the Atlantic City experience. Lynd had spent much of the summer of 1964 in Mississippi. He shared with SNCC workers the emotional intensity of working in a war zone surrounded by white terrorists. He shared, too, the outrage toward the Democratic Party for its compromise proposal and toward the civil rights leaders who urged acceptance. Lynd felt a particular sting of betrayal in Rustin's stance. He told readers of *Liberation* that "men like Rustin will become the national spokesmen who sell the line agreed on behind doors to the faithful followers waiting in the streets." In answer to the question, "Are plain people from Mississippi competent to decide?" Lynd asserted that Rustin's answer was "no."[25]

The phrase "coalition with the marines" packed a particularly sharp punch. Lynd tied together Rustin's call for engagement with the Democratic Party and his signature on the statement criticizing the antiwar rally of SDS. The latter became evidence that the former required acquiescence to America's cold war imperial designs. Rustin, a pacifist jailed while Lynd was still in high school, stood indicted as little better than a jingoist.

But Rustin's willingness to sign on to the criticism of the April antiwar rally did not imply approval of American fighting in Vietnam. A hallmark of his pacifism had always been the censure of both sides in a conflict. His actions against the nuclear arms race criticized the United States and the Soviet Union; his work in Africa had countenanced neither guerrilla warfare nor armed insurrection. Rustin's pacifism stood outside conventional political frameworks of left and right. His condemnations of Western imperialism, which were many, never carried endorsement of violent opposition to it. Rustin had also taken, for more than two decades, repeated stands against cooperative ventures with the Communist Party. He had never forgotten how quickly the party changed its positions on race and foreign policy a generation earlier, and he had tangled too often with members in succeeding years. His experience had taught him that Communists came with hidden agendas that heralded disruption and betrayal. Thus, there was nothing surprising, novel, or inconsistent about his endorsement of a statement that both applauded SDS efforts to organize against the war and cautioned against a willingness to include all political persuasions in the mobilization.

Lynd's criticism was especially odd because, as debate over Johnson's policies intensified that spring and summer, Rustin remained firmly aligned with dissent against the war. In June, just as Lynd's charges appeared in print, SANE organized a major antiwar rally in New York. It drew 17,000 people to Madison Square Garden. Senator Wayne Morse, one of a very few outspoken congressional critics, was the headline speaker. Rustin also addressed the crowd and advised them to "take their crusade to the streets." Near midnight, Dr. Benjamin Spock, the famed pediatrician who took an early stand against the war, asked the throng to follow Rustin's advice. He, Norman Thomas, Coretta King, and Rustin led thousands through the streets to the United Nations, where Rustin spoke once again. His presentation that night was compelling. It induced words of praise even from participants who were harboring new misgivings about his politics. One of them wrote afterward that "your speech was by far the most inspired, principled denunciation of our foreign policy. . . . It brought sharply into focus the connections between the struggle for civil rights and the need for an end to militarist actions abroad." The next week, Marie Runyon, one of the chief organizers of the event, sent him an appreciative letter. "I said it before, and I say it again—MAGNIFICENT!" she praised. "You contributed so greatly to the success of our Rally last Tuesday, and both we and the cause are in your debt."[26]

Rustin's relationship to antiwar politics in these months was framed by his focus on issues of racial justice. The escalating war placed many civil rights organizations in a quandary. To many, the links between racial injustice at home and military adventures abroad were compelling. Andrew Young described how one of his youngsters, watching the evening news, asked, "Why are the marines shooting at the colored people?" But a movement already straining to meet the needs of its own freedom struggle felt constrained to act. That summer, at CORE's national convention, James Farmer forced the repeal of a resolution opposing the war. To Farmer, demonstrating against the Vietnam War was "a cop-out," an easy way for the organization to avoid increasingly complicated issues in the fight for racial equality. To no one's surprise, Roy Wilkins was especially adamant that civil rights organizations should stay away from foreign policy matters. "We have enough Vietnams in Alabama," he said.[27]

Rustin was clear that the issues were linked but troubled as to how best to express the connections. In a memo to King early in the fall, he wrote that the war "obscures the needs of people domestically. . . . The extreme right in this country gets more and more power as war continues." In a public response to reproaches that Wilkins directed at King, Rustin described himself as "a strong critic" of the Johnson administration's war policies. "The Negro's experience ought to make him particularly sensitive to the fate of social justice anywhere," he wrote. But "a member of the NAACP has not delegated anyone to speak for him on Viet Nam; a member, however, of the Fellowship of Reconcilation has." The point had merit, though Rustin's reasoning glossed over his insistence, two decades earlier, that a peace organization like the FOR had to take a stand against racism.[28]

While some of Rustin's public comments bespoke caution, privately he looked for ways to bind the causes together. Throughout the spring and summer, Rustin talked frequently with King and pushed him to use his prestige in ways that might hasten an end to the conflict. He encouraged King to sign the declaration of conscience that he, Muste, and Dellinger had prepared, and he discussed with King the idea of a national vigil of religious leaders to protest the war. With Harry Wachtel, another King confidant, Rustin debated ways to "creatively inject [King] into the Vietnam crisis." Rustin felt that the "civil rights movement was not ready to speak to the world on Viet Nam, but that King could speak as an individual, thereby getting the impact of the civil rights movement behind him." In August, Rustin helped prepare the resolution on Vietnam that came before SCLC's convention. Although the delegates affirmed that "the primary function of our organization is to secure full rights for the Negro citizens of this country," they also authorized King, if circumstances changed, "to alter this course and turn the full resources of our organization to the cessation of bloodshed and war."[29]

OF ALL THE BARBS Lynd directed at Rustin, "labor lieutenant of capitalism" would have sounded most arcane to anyone not initiated into the historical traditions of the left. It suggested the basest sort of class betrayal, conjuring images of corrupt union leaders who marched their workers away from the barricades into the arms of their robber baron bosses. Coming within a few months of Rustin's founding of the Randolph Institute with AFL-CIO money, Lynd's comment suggested the consternation that organized labor provoked among radical pacifists.

Rustin had elected to build APRI not because it was his ideal option but because of the limitations under which he had worked for so long. For years, he had tried to juggle the competing demands of a pacifist organization that needed the full attention of its leader and a civil rights movement that he yearned to shape. Especially after Montgomery, Rustin rebelled, often inwardly and sometimes openly, at the perfectionist outlook of a peace movement whose moral absolutism kept it pure but marginal. He chafed against the constraints that his sexual identity and his early leftist history threw around him. So often in the past, either pacifists or civil rights leaders had shunted him to the side rather than defend his past political choices or accept his sexual difference. Only Randolph had proved unswervingly accepting of him. And so when Randolph offered to lend his stature so that Rustin could build an institutional vehicle for himself, Rustin accepted. It squared with his wish to inject economic issues into the body of the civil rights movement, and it seemed to promise that he would enjoy some autonomy at last.

The Randolph Institute remained Rustin's home for the rest of his life. In some ways, it did give him a secure base from which to pursue his own political program and argue for his own strategic vision within the precincts of the civil rights movement. He no longer was pulled be-

tween a pacifist organization and a burgeoning struggle for racial justice. Nor did his place at the table depend on the sufferance of others
who might jettison him because of his sex life or his radical politics. But
the notion that APRI made him a free agent able to operate however he
wished was illusory. The AFL-CIO paid the bills. It was amenable to
the theme Rustin was sounding in these years—that progress in the
quest for racial justice required an economic program. To someone like
George Meany, Rustin's call for an alliance promised an expansion of
the political power of labor and, perhaps, a respite from criticisms of
racial discrimination in the AFL-CIO.

But labor backing also meant that Rustin now carried all the political
burdens that came with its history. Many in the civil rights movement
viewed unions as just one more institution of white America that barred
the door to blacks; labor's history of discrimination was long and ugly.
To Rustin's old colleagues in the peace movement, the AFL-CIO—and
Meany in particular—was a mainstay of cold war militarism. When
Lynd called Rustin a labor lieutenant of capitalism, he was judging
Rustin in the light of a trade union movement that no longer occupied
an oppositional role in American life but that, instead, was wrapped
within the framework of a cold war corporate state. Labor's absorption
into the liberal postwar consensus cast suspicion on those who argued,
as Rustin now did, that an alliance with labor would bring radical
change closer.

Even so, the criticisms that Lynd and Dellinger leveled at Rustin in
the spring of 1965 could best be described as anticipatory, as predictive
of a political turn that had not yet happened. At worst, their attacks
were unprincipled, ironically so since they came from peace activists
who cloaked their censure of Rustin in a higher political morality. It
was an odd logic that allowed Dellinger to invest the SDS antiwar rally
with value in part by deflating the significance of the 1963 March on
Washington. Nor was Lynd's characterization of Rustin any more bal-
anced. A mild criticism of an antiwar rally that a group of pacifists
signed became for Lynd a maneuver concocted by an apostate pacifist
to disable antiwar sentiment.

Publicly, Rustin acted as if the accusations pointed at him just rolled off his back. He never addressed them head on, never responded in kind. In November 1965, after a suitable amount of time had elapsed, he wrote to Muste rather than Dellinger. Rustin told Muste that he was "distressed and concerned" at the direction the magazine was taking, but that he was too deeply involved in the civil rights movement to attend meetings and debate the politics of the journal. "I reluctantly feel that the only responsible thing for me to do now is to resign from the editorial board," he wrote.[30]

Even as Rustin appeared to move on, the charges of Dellinger and Lynd continued to reverberate long after they were made. Dave McReynolds characterized their pieces as "a virtual declaration of war" and asked whether *Liberation* meant to announce to the left that it was now "open season" for attacks on Rustin.[31] The articles put into print questions about his politics and his integrity. Their location in a magazine respected among radicals gave those doubts more substance, investing them with the mantle of truth and allowing them to circulate and recirculate among radical networks just as these networks were expanding. Lynd and Dellinger had spun an interpretation of Rustin's actions that thrust Rustin outside the worlds that had shaped his career for decades. Among radicals, the double-barreled attack served to narrow rather than widen debate about strategies at a moment when the broadest range of possibilities was needed. In the volatile climate of radical protest and political upheaval soon to characterize America, the ground on which Rustin stood began to shift until the claims made against him came to seem credible.

CHAPTER EIGHTEEN

"In the Shadow of War"
1965–1967

IN JUNE 1965, the same month that Lynd's polemic appeared in *Liberation*, Lyndon Johnson delivered the commencement address at Howard University. He paid tribute to the courage of civil rights activists and invested the movement with great historic significance. "Nothing is more freighted with meaning for our own destiny than the revolution of the Negro American," he told the assembly. Anticipating passage of the Voting Rights Act, he appropriated Winston Churchill's comments after the Battle of Britain in World War II. Its enactment, he said, "is not the end. It is not even the beginning of the end. But it is, perhaps, the end of the beginning." He asked his audience to look toward a future where the objective was "not just freedom but opportunity . . . not just equality as a right and a theory but equality as a fact and equality as a result." Johnson read off a spate of statistics to show the widening economic gap between whites and blacks in America. He promised that "we will increase, and we will accelerate, and we will broaden this attack" until the country had vanquished the "inherited gateless poverty" that trapped much of black America.[1]

Johnson's speech was extraordinary. It framed civil rights in terms that Rustin himself might have crafted, linking racial justice to a more expansive agenda. It validated the general thrust of Rustin's strategic thinking and allowed him to wave aside the attacks coming from the radical wing of the peace movement as distractions from the main event. It encouraged him in the belief that this was a propitious time for shifting the American political system to the left and that the movement for civil rights was indeed the leading edge of a much broader push for economic and social change.

JOHNSON HIMSELF SEEMED TO suggest the next locus of Rustin's attention. At the end of his Howard address, the president announced his intention of convening a major White House conference on race. Set in the context of so bold a speech, the conference promised to shift the civil rights struggle from matters of legal equality toward issues of jobs and income. Assigning key staff to the project, the White House let it be known that it would hold an initial planning conference in the fall, followed by a much larger event sometime in 1966.

Johnson's call for the conference reflected what Ramsey Clark, soon to be the attorney general, remembered as "a buoyant atmosphere" in the administration in those months. The voting rights bill was almost law and, "as soon as we got through with that bill, we were beginning to look for something next . . . we felt a sweep and we felt a power for more action." The idea of being encouraged to devise solutions to undo the legacy of centuries of oppression injected a crusading spirit into White House circles. The staff saw its work as an effort to arouse "the Great White Whale," the majority of white Americans who were neither militantly for nor rabidly against the goals of the civil rights movement. "The White House Conference would stimulate a dialogue which is not taking place to any significant extent," said the staff of the Civil Rights Commission.[2]

Within the administration, the earliest thinking about the conference was shaped by a report on the black family prepared by Daniel Patrick Moynihan, an assistant secretary of labor. Drafts of it had circulated within the administration since the spring. A reference to "the breakdown of the Negro family structure" had made its way into Johnson's Howard speech, and Moynihan's ideas were influencing how some officials in the executive branch conceptualized the conference. Lee White, Johnson's aide in charge of civil rights, advised the president that "the focus on family structure in the Negro community, on the

psychology of instilling strong desires to secure education and training . . . should prove useful subjects for exploration."[3]

As the content of the report became known, however, it ignited a
firestorm of controversy within both civil rights and academic circles.
Moynihan described the contemporary black family as a "tangle of
pathology"; he singled out the high rate of female-headed households
as a primary symptom of its weakness and argued that no amount of
civil rights legislation would bring equality unless this social problem
was addressed. Moynihan placed the blame on centuries of oppression,
from the institution of slavery, which broke up families, to discrimination in employment, which denied jobs to black men. But the inflammatory language of the report outraged the civil rights community. The
suggestion that families needed to be fixed as a prelude to meaningful
progress raised the fear that the federal government was shifting responsibility for inequality from white institutions to black households.[4]

Rustin was the first, in the recollections of Harry McPherson, Johnson's chief counsel, to dampen the enthusiasm in the White House. At
a meeting early in August 1965, he told McPherson and other staff that
"the direction in which we were heading was wrong." The idea that the
family was "a point of cure for the Negro American . . . was a bum place
to go," he continued. "There was trouble about this, a lot of trouble,"
Rustin warned. McPherson came away from the encounter appreciative
of what he characterized as Rustin's "extremely sensitive antenna"; he
later placed Rustin "in my pantheon of, say, the five smartest men in
America." McPherson sent Clifford Alexander and Berl Bernhardt, two
other figures in the planning process, to New York to meet with Rustin
and "negotiate" the shape of the conference. "We gave up the idea of
having the family as the focus, and we just treated the family as one
other problem."[5]

Soon after Rustin's first meeting at the White House and just a few
days after he attended the signing of the Voting Rights Act, the direction of the White House Conference suddenly came to seem even more
urgent. In Watts, a large black section of Los Angeles, serious rioting
broke out after police arrested a young man for drunken driving. The

civil warfare lasted for six days. Mayor Sam Yorty and Police Chief William Parker dispatched much of the Los Angeles police force to the area, and Governor Pat Brown sent 14,000 National Guard troops to pacify the population. When it was all over, thirty-four persons were dead, more than a thousand injured, and almost four thousand arrested. Most of the dead and injured, as well as virtually everyone arrested, were black.

Rustin was in Birmingham for SCLC's annual conference when the rioting began, and King asked Rustin what he thought about the wisdom of flying to Los Angeles. Rustin discouraged the idea. It would only create the appearance that King was coming to quiet the rioters. Rustin suggested instead that King issue a statement that condemned both the violence and the social conditions that produced it. As the seriousness of the outbreak became obvious, King reconsidered and asked Rustin to join him. Touring the devastated neighborhood, they passed block after block that had burned to the ground and row after row of looted businesses. On street corners in Watts, Rustin engaged residents in conversation. When one youth told him "we won," Rustin challenged him. "How have you won?" he countered. "Homes have been destroyed, Negroes are lying dead in the streets, the stores [where] you buy food and clothes are destroyed, and people are bringing you relief." But the young man was adamant. "We won because we made the whole world pay attention to us. The police chief never came here before; the mayor always stayed uptown. We made them come." Although Rustin had spent his entire adult life advocating nonviolence as the route to social justice, he refused to condemn what had happened. The turmoil in Watts had "brought out in the open," in his words, "the despair and hatred that continue to brew in the Northern ghettos. . . . It marked the first major rebellion of Negroes against their own masochism and was carried on with the express purpose of asserting they would no longer quietly submit to the deprivation of slum life."[6] The situation in Watts far exceeded anything Rustin had encountered in Harlem the summer before. And it disturbed King immensely. "Martin was absolutely shaken by it," Rustin recalled. "He was absolutely undone." In Rustin's view, Watts was the moment when

King "really understood" the centrality of economics to the movement for racial equality.[7]

Rustin accompanied King to meetings with Mayor Yorty and Chief Parker, both of whom were unshakable in their conviction that the residents of Watts had no legitimate grievances and that all the force used to suppress the disorders was necessary. Parker described the rioters as "monkeys" and "the criminal element." Any attempt to challenge the mayor and police chief, to argue that a closed political system and grindingly harsh economic conditions might push a community to take desperate measures, met with a firm rebuff. There was no racial prejudice in Los Angeles, they told Rustin and King. As Rustin described it afterward, even though he and King "had considerable experience in talking with public officials who do not understand the Negro community, our discussions with Chief Parker and Mayor Yorty left us completely nonplused."[8]

Watts dramatized for Rustin the potential importance of the White House Conference, and so he spent much of the fall working to shape the planning and mobilize civil rights groups to take the event seriously. Johnson had named Randolph the honorary chairman of the event and provided him with a Washington office. Delegated by Randolph to act as his representative, Rustin had ready access to the White House staff and a place to work during his frequent trips to Washington. Norman Hill was also on the planning staff, and he gave Rustin a picture of the debates within the administration. Through Hill and his own observations on the scene, he knew that the conference was more or less rudderless, without a firm sense of direction. Nor was the civil rights community of one mind and one voice in its response to the presidential initiative. Within the NAACP, the very premises of Johnson's Howard speech threw into question the organization's entire approach to racial inequality. Henry Moon, the staff member in charge of national public relations, quickly understood the problem. "If the NAACP is to be in a position to offer concrete proposals at the White House Conference," Moon wrote in a memo to Wilkins, "we must first divest ourselves of the idea that equality of opportunity is all that is needed. We must do some hard, clear rethinking."[9]

Rustin pushed hard to mobilize the resources of civil rights organizations around the project. "I am thoroughly convinced," he wrote to many of them in mid-October, "that the success or failure of the conference will depend on the attention and work expended by the major civil rights organizations." To the White House staff, he penned memos pressing for an expansive agenda that subordinated the family issue to more substantial matters. He insisted that the conference address "economic instability" as "the fundamental problem" facing black Americans. "What Congress and the courts give," he wrote, "the market place could take away." At a key meeting in late October between representatives of the Big Six and the planning staff, civil rights leaders expressed "virtually unanimous agreement . . . with the position taken by Bayard Rustin on the subject matter of the Planning Session." A few days later, civil rights leaders learned that the president's advisers were in "full agreement" that "economic security" would receive the "major attention" at the planning session.[10]

The November meeting proved almost nightmarish for the Johnson administration. It brought to Washington a varied group of 250 participants that reached beyond an established civil rights leadership long accustomed to working together. Most of them had not been consulted beforehand, and they arrived in Washington unclear about the purpose of the gathering. They expected to be debating concrete proposals for future government action and instead found a collection of White House aides who had come to listen to them. McPherson described the scene in this way: "a predictable amount of sulfurous language, a good deal of bickering back and forth. . . . A crowd of people on the outside of power, many of whom had never met each other, blew off steam." Moynihan, whose report was now public, attended the meetings and was "thoroughly trashed." It looked as if the Johnson administration had run out of ideas and was passing the buck to them, at a time when many of the attendees harbored deep dissatisfaction over the slow enforcement of federal civil rights legislation. The meetings revealed unmistakable signs of a spreading militancy, a shift away from appreciation of Johnson and toward heightened expectations about government's responsibility to correct racial wrongs.[11]

Rustin was pleased by the contentious tone and the absence of concrete proposals. It provided an opening for him to float the idea of a "Freedom Budget." A still developing project of the Randolph Institute, the Freedom Budget was "something like a Marshall Plan" for the United States. It called for federal expenditures of $100 billion over the course of a decade. The proposal dwarfed the Johnson administration's antipoverty efforts. Rustin's move confirmed the worry among some White House officials that he "might take [the meetings] in a different direction than they wanted to." Morris Abram, one of the cochairs of the planning session, recalled that Rustin "came out of a socialist model . . . he sees human rights as also embracing economic and social rights." Reflecting afterward on Rustin's efforts to upstage Johnson's Great Society agenda, Abram commented: "You can imagine how the President felt."[12]

The planning session served as a wake-up call to Johnson's staff. Clifford Alexander, the highest-placed black aide in the White House, used the experience to press for a spring event that was both more inclusive and more structured. He proposed that the event be placed in the hands of a high-powered executive council whose stature would signal that racial justice was "not solely the concern of a handful of civil rights leaders and the government." His goal was to "stir the imagination of the nation" and unleash initiative throughout civil society. Alexander's concept won approval. Johnson appointed Ben Heineman, a Chicago railroad executive and Democratic party loyalist, as chair of the White House Conference. Council members included major corporate executives; presidents of foundations, labor unions, and universities; and the heads of the national civil rights organizations. Its mandate was to shape a comprehensive set of recommendations for action and present these to the conference as a whole in early June.[13]

Attending the council meetings as Randolph's representative, Rustin "contributed substantially" to the discussions, Heineman wrote. He pushed hard for proposals that extended beyond Johnson's Great Society legislative agenda. He maintained a critical stance and attempted to bring pressure from the outside so that the planning group would have to reach beyond centrist solutions. At one point, in response to public statements that Rustin was making, Heineman found himself answering tough questions from the press. Would the White House Conference be "totally irrelevant," one reporter wanted to know, unless it endorsed the guaranteed income that the Randolph-Rustin "Freedom Budget" called for?[14]

The report that the executive council finally produced exceeded Rustin's expectations. The family focus was discarded. Instead, issues of economic security dominated the agenda, along with attention to education, housing, and the administration of justice. The recommendations reflected the administration's hope that the conference, in framing solutions, would "direct the attention of the participants . . . to places outside of the Federal Government." The proposals were meant to draw in "persons and groups not involved in civil rights" and to have participants "return to their communities with a sense of urgency and involve the great mass of citizens in further efforts." Yet at the same time, the report charted an expanded role for government. It laid out a responsibility to provide jobs when the private sector failed. It declared that the construction of federally subsidized housing must expand significantly. The council's recommendations would have set an economic floor beneath which no American, black or white, could fall. "Awfully goddamned good," Alexander reflected afterward. Taken together, the proposals pointed toward a Scandinavian-style social democratic welfare state.[15]

Well over 2,000 people assembled for the conference in Washington on June 1. There was healthy attendance by civil rights groups and federal officials. But the guest list also extended deeply into business and industry, higher education, labor, local and state govenment, the foundation world, and religious organizations. It reached beyond the civil rights establishment to include a large collection of representatives from "community and grassroots organizations." During one of the plenary sessions, Johnson made an unscheduled appearance. It was "absolutely convulsive," according to McPherson. "People were on their feet yelling 'LBJ! LBJ!' " Although there was some grumbling, by and large enthusiasm remained high and the conferees overwhelmingly endorsed the council's work. A few days afterward, McPherson penned a memo to Johnson urging actions to demonstrate that "we have taken the recommendations seriously. . . . What is vital," he went on, "is that the work of this conference not become a dead letter—a stone dropped into the still waters of government. . . . We must consider its recommendations in a vigorous, virile, and aggressive way."[16]

THE JOHNSON ADMINISTRATION had named the conference "To Fulfill These Rights." The title played off the report, "To Secure These Rights," issued in 1947 by Truman's civil rights commission. In the intervening decades, pressure from the civil rights community had forced the desegregation of the military. Supreme Court decisions had toppled segregation's claims to constitutionality. And Congress had passed historic legislation. "To Fulfill These Rights" nodded toward Johnson's belief that an era in American race relations was ending and that it was leading smoothly into another.

But there was to be nothing smooth or easy about the coming politics of race in America. More and more signals were appearing of deep dissatisfaction with the pace and direction of change. The reaction of SNCC and other radicals to the events at the Atlantic City convention, the rioting in Harlem in 1964 and the massive uprising in Watts in 1965, the tensions between SNCC and the rest of the civil rights establishment over tactics, strategy, and goals—all these and any number of other local events pointed to an emerging shift in the mid-1960s away from the rhetoric of nonviolence and the platform of civil rights.

The preparations for the White House Conference revealed the fissures that were cracking open. SNCC almost completely absented itself. In January 1966, it released a strongly worded statement against the war in Vietnam. It drew links between the federal government's toleration of lawlessness in the South and the Johnson administration's disregard for international conventions in Southeast Asia. It openly urged black men to avoid military service. Although John Lewis, SNCC's chairman, attended a planning session for the conference in March, as far as he could tell it looked like a ploy by Johnson to build a consensus around his administration's policies. To Lewis, "there was no consensus anymore," and he stopped going to the planning sessions.

Yet Lewis remained very much wedded to a philosophy of nonviolence and racial reconciliation. In May, he was ousted as chairman in an election that left much bitterness and came to symbolize the end of an era in SNCC's brief history. Stokely Carmichael, his successor, had always been skeptical of nonviolence as anything but a tactic. Impressed with the militant anticolonial writings of Frantz Fanon, he began to move SNCC in new directions. Carmichael quickly dissociated it from the White House conference and announced that it would not attend. It labeled the White House initiative an effort to "shift responsibility . . . from the oppressors to the oppressed."[17]

CORE, too, had experienced a changing of the guard. James Farmer, who along with Rustin had been an architect of its Gandhian approach, resigned as executive director in January. The election to replace him also left feelings raw. Floyd McKissick, who succeeded Farmer, was fond of rhetorical extravagance and, under his leadership, CORE became outspokenly critical of Johnson. Although McKissick brought a CORE contingent to the conference, he used it as a platform to launch a pointed attack on the Vietnam War. The administration's effort neatly to separate domestic issues and foreign policy was not working.[18]

Just days after the conference ended, an episode unfolded in Mississippi with as much significance for the course of the black freedom movement as the Montgomery bus boycott or the lunch counter sit-ins of 1960. James Meredith, an iconoclastic black activist whose efforts to integrate the University of Mississippi provoked massive violence in 1962, announced that he was making a solitary march from Memphis to Jackson. He wanted to demonstrate the right of black Mississippians to have safe access to public space in the Deep South. On June 6, the day after he set out from Memphis, gunmen ambushed and seriously wounded him. SNCC and CORE activists issued a call to civil rights organizations to continue the march. King, Wilkins, and Whitney Young all responded favorably.

In a telephone call with several of his advisers, King urged Rustin to join him and help coordinate the event. He told Rustin that as many as 2,000 were expected to make the march and that ten times that number would attend the rally in Jackson. Rustin was disinclined to go. He said that "it might degenerate into a black nationalist thing" and that "Carmichael and McKissick and other left-wingers would take advantage" of his presence to associate him with their brand of racial politics. Stanley Levison, who was also on the call, pressed him to reconsider. Levison said that "the best way to bury their doctrine" was for people like him to be there. In years past, Rustin undoubtedly would have seized the opportunity. He would have fought to shape the message, the tone, and the style of the event. Now he decided to stay away.[19]

Perhaps because Rustin had known Carmichael for almost a decade, his intuition about the Mississippi march proved correct. Carmichael used it as an opportunity to assert on a grand stage his evolving nationalist politics. In a meeting with Wilkins and Young to plan the march, he started "acting crazy, cursing real bad." Wilkins had wanted the march to focus on enforcement of civil rights legislation. As Carmichael recollected, "I said, 'You sellin' out the people, and don't think we don't know it. We gonna getcha.'" The NAACP and Urban League angrily withdrew, leaving King with the choice of appearing to align with SNCC if he stayed or with the most moderate wing of the movement if he left. He opted to remain. Over the next several days, the marchers faced the menacing antagonism of local police and state troopers who, at various points, used tear gas to disperse rallies and arrested many. The brutality of Southern law enforcement kept emotions roiling. At a rally in Greenwood, Carmichael decided to use a slogan that another SNCC activist had been trying out along the way. He called for "Black Power!" The effect on the crowd was electrifying, and he repeated it many times in the next several days. Though King refused to identify with the phrase, the media quickly fixed on it as the defining feature of the Meredith March and played up the obvious disunity among civil rights forces that the slogan had revealed.[20]

The rifts became even more evident as the summer wore on. In July, at its national convention, CORE publicly affirmed its allegiance to "black power." Carmichael applauded the shift in direction, telling them, "We don't need white liberals." The convention went on to reject nonviolence, a central feature of CORE since its founding. McKissick called it "a dying philosophy." That same month, at the

NAACP national meeting, Wilkins condemned black power unequivocally: "It is a reverse Mississippi, a reverse Hitler, a reverse Ku Klux Klan."[21] Within SNCC, important veterans began an exodus. Julian Bond resigned, as did Lewis. "I felt in a sense like it was the end," Lewis said soon after. "It was not the movement that I knew. . . . I had no other choice but to resign from SNCC in order to live with myself." Even Carmichael, who rode black power to national notoriety, acknowledged that its effects on SNCC were disastrous. "Black Power killed SNCC," he commented later.[22]

Rustin's reaction to the rhetoric of black power was reflexively negative. "Black Power is not a radical, but a conservative slogan," he wrote to a correspondent who inquired that summer about his views. "There can be no 'black socialism' or 'white socialism.'" In the wake of "the great fight" that Carmichael's move provoked, Rustin tried his usual gambit of having Randolph issue a call to "get the leaders together so they can fight, if they must, behind closed doors—but present a picture of unity to the opposition." But unlike in the past, when Randolph's stature as elder statesman could at least bring squabbling organizations to the table, this time the chasm that had opened was too wide to jump. Rustin's efforts failed completely. "It is not always easy," he wrote with obvious understatement.[23]

But Rustin was unwilling to let the matter end there. He composed a sharp critique of black power, one of the first to appear, that *Commentary* published in September. Unlike "From Protest to Politics," in which Rustin's "no-win" activists remained nameless and in which he wrote respectfully about SNCC, this piece named names and drew clear lines. He took Carmichael and McKissick—and, by implication, SNCC and CORE—to task for "shouting a slogan . . . that is calculated to destroy them and their movement." He called the black power debate "the most bitter the community has experienced since the days of Booker T. Washington and W.E.B. Du Bois" and said that it "threatens to ravage the entire civil rights movement."[24]

Rustin found the promise of black power chimerical. In one way, he wrote, there was "nothing wrong" with the idea because, "in its simplest and most innocent guise," it merely called for the election of blacks to office. Such a move hardly warranted Carmichael's "extravagant rhetoric" since few areas had a black population large enough to win elections based on racial solidarity alone. Rustin also challenged the value of black representation in itself. "The relevant question," he argued, "is not whether a politician is black or white, but what forces he represents." Offering the example of Adam Clayton Powell, he said that the best black power might offer would be the election of a few machine-style black politicians.

But black power already connoted much more than this, and in its larger meanings, Rustin found much to worry about. He termed it "simultaneously utopian and reactionary." He saw efforts to create a Black Panther Party as doomed, since African Americans did not have the numbers for a viable independent political force. Rustin thought the move toward black power would leave SNCC and CORE more isolated than ever before. "Southern Negroes," Rustin wrote, "are going to stay in the Democratic party—to them it is the party of progress, the New Deal, the New Frontier, and the Great Society—and they are right to stay." By embracing black power, SNCC and CORE "have diverted the entire civil rights movement from the hard task of developing strategies to realign the major parties of this country, and embroiled it in a debate that can only lead more and more to politics by frustration."

Rustin used his *Commentary* piece not only as a broadside against black power but also as a platform to lecture whites whose support for racial justice was wavering. Whatever the current rhetoric, Rustin said, "The issue was injustice before black power became popular, and the issue is still injustice. . . . We must see to it that in rejecting black power we do not also reject the principle of Negro equality." Rustin reminded his readers that black power emerged among those who once considered white liberals the closest friends of the civil rights struggle. It was a cry of disappointment over the failure of liberalism to move beyond legal equality. "It is up to the liberal movement," Rustin concluded, "to prove that coalition and integration are better alternatives."

EVEN AS BLACK POWER came to dominate racial politics, Rustin remained wedded to building a progressive coalition. He was more committed than ever before to linking the goals of racial and economic equality. Throughout 1966 and 1967, he devoted himself to the "Freedom Budget." Intended as a left critique of Johnson's War on Poverty, the Freedom Budget was ambitious. It would, Rustin claimed, raise income levels, put the jobless to work, expand the housing stock, improve the quality of education, provide health care services to everyone, and, in ten years' time, eliminate poverty in America.

In November 1965, when Rustin and Randolph first floated the notion of a Freedom Budget at the planning session for the White House Conference, it was both concrete and bold enough that the press latched on to it and gave the idea currency.[25] Over the next months, as Rustin worked on the conference, he kept putting the concept forward as a way to keep economic issues front and center in the minds of committee members. Meanwhile, he assembled a team of economists and social scientists to craft the idea into a plan around which a political movement might coalesce. Rustin's brain trust on the budget included Vivian Henderson, the president of Clark University; Herbert Gans, an urban sociologist; Michael Harrington; and a number of labor economists working for the AFL-CIO. The key figure was Leon Keyserling, a progressive Keynesian economist who had helped shape the Employment Act of 1946 and had served as chair of the Council of Economic Advisers under Truman. He had the impeccable professional credentials that a proposal of this sort needed in order to have credibility. Keyserling's task was not only to provide the economic analysis undergirding the project but also to draft the document, which Rustin hoped to launch at the White House Conference. But Keyserling was slow to produce it, and Rustin reluctantly concluded that "it would be premature" to announce the budget there.[26]

As the black power controversy intensified that summer, Rustin began approaching first the civil rights leadership and then liberal, church, and labor organizations to secure their endorsements. Whitney Young was enthusiastic. "We not only heartily endorse the plan, but stand ready to assist in any way in its implementation," he wrote. The NAACP also came on board, a sign of how far it had traveled from a single-minded civil rights focus. The SCLC readily supported it. King that summer had begun talking about the need for the domestic equivalent of a Marshall Plan, and he promised to write a foreword to Rustin's popular edition. But Stokely Carmichael wondered whether there was not "a possible contradiction" in seeking their support when Rustin and Randolph had said that "SNCC is dying," and SNCC never came around to backing the project.[27]

By the end of the summer, Rustin had accumulated more than 600 endorsements. The support of labor leaders was the easiest to obtain, and most of the major union heads signed on. So too did activist liberal organizations like Americans for Democratic Action, the American Jewish Congress, and the social action lobbies of many Protestant denominations. Celebrity endorsements came through the initiative of Harry Belafonte, whose help Rustin solicited. Early approaches to journalists also gave him reason to feel encouraged. Tom Wicker, a *New York Times* columnist who had written in favor of a more expansive antipoverty effort, believed that "there may be a good deal of support for such a program as this."[28]

Rustin finally unveiled the Freedom Budget at a press conference in Harlem late in October 1966. Besides himself, Randolph spoke, as did Keyserling, Wilkins, Don Slaiman of the AFL-CIO, and representatives of several religious organizations. Randolph described the budget as an effort to move from "haphazard piecemeal efforts" toward "an overall plan of attack, a coordinated mobilization . . . a real *war* on poverty." He invoked the spirit of the March on Washington, as he commented on the broad sponsorship that the budget enjoyed. Rustin then outlined the scope of the project. He described plans to "work with grass-roots leaders as well as with liberals, Congressmen, students, the labor movement and the religious community." He and several economists planned to tour major cities to drum up interest in the campaign; tens of thousands of copies of the budget were already in distribution; and the brief edition would have even wider circulation. The institute was hiring organizers to work with community groups around the country and help them connect the Freedom Budget to local problems and needs.[29]

Rustin and Keyserling were each pleased by the launch. The budget received major notice in the *New York Times* and the *Washington Post* as well as front-page coverage and editorial commentary in many other papers. "I trust that we can follow through on all fronts to maximize the results," Keyserling wrote to Rustin. "The send off in New York on Wednesday was excellent." Rustin was similarly excited. "You were even the hit of the press conference," he responded. "An amazing number of people stopped me on 125th Street to say that 'Keyserling really gave it to them the other day.' And 'that's an intellectual who can talk sense.' . . . You simultaneously created a realistic, complex and highly developed Freedom Budget and at the same time made it comprehensible to the people in the ghetto."[30]

For the next year, Rustin made the Freedom Budget his main enterprise. It embodied the thinking in "From Protest to Politics." By obliterating poverty, it would do much to eliminate the worst effects of racism. It depended on the ability to build a majority coalition across race and class lines. The campaign required that mainstream liberalism and the Democratic Party commit to much more than the rhetorically inspiring but programmatically modest initiatives of the Great Society. It also required enthusiastic backing from the growing numbers of "movement" people who were both the conscience and the foot soldiers propelling Rustin's political vision forward. The Freedom Budget was Rustin's test case for determining whether the energy of the black freedom struggle and student activism could combine with the institutional strength of liberals to change the distribution of wealth and political power in America.

A key element in the campaign was the popular version of the budget, produced in pamphlet-sized form. Rustin had it composed in a style aimed at the ordinary citizen without complex knowledge about economic theory and fiscal policy. In simple language, it described how the elimination of poverty would be achieved and why this would be good for the country. It appealed to the moral sensibilities of middle- and working-class Americans and tried to calm fears that a campaign against poverty would take from them. It made the elimination of poverty seem not only desirable but also attainable if only a majority of Americans applied their hard-headed practicality to the task.[31]

"The Freedom Budget," it began, is a "step-by-step plan for wiping out poverty in America during the next 10 years." It will mean higher incomes, better schools and homes, and adequate medical care for everyone. It will accomplish this "at no increased cost, with no radical change in our economic system, and at no cost to our present national goals." It will do this with "no doles. No skimping on national defense. No tampering with private supply and demand. Just an enlightening self interest." The Freedom Budget would strengthen the private sector since working families lifted out of poverty would sustain corporate growth by their spending.

The Freedom Budget promised this not through new taxes but through something Keyserling described as "the growth dividend." Estimates of economic growth projected additions to the gross national product of $2.4 trillion over the next decade. Without touching the tax rate, this growth would generate at least $400 billion more in federal revenues. By earmarking $185 billion of this toward critical social needs, the poor would become employed, and everyone would be better off. This was not, Rustin's pamphlet emphasized, a form of welfare. "The key is jobs," it declared. Employing people to meet basic human needs would lift the poor out of destitution. The whole society would benefit from their labor and skills.

Rustin planned a two-pronged campaign that simultaneously targeted the influential and built a grass-roots mobilization. He and Randolph approached New York's liberal senators, Jacob Javits and Robert Kennedy, to arrange bipartisan briefings in Congress. Building on connections he had made through the White House Conference, he went to Clifford Alexander in search of administration endorsement. He sent the Freedom Budget to every member of Congress, all the governors, the mayors of large cities, the heads of foundations, the presidents of colleges, and the chairs of economics departments. Everyone who attended the White House Conference received a copy, as did the heads of unions, their research and education directors, and the presidents of state labor federations. Rustin contacted all of the organizations affiliated with the Leadership Conference on Civil Rights and many newspaper editors as well.[32]

At the same time, Rustin expected to build a populist campaign to pressure both Congress and the White House. In many quarters, the launch had provoked great excitement. Leon Shull, the director of Americans for Democratic Action, wrote Rustin that "chapters everywhere have been enthusiastic, and I would like ADA to put a major part of its effort into working for the Freedom Budget. I am sure that will come about." Women's chapters of the American Jewish Congress made the budget a focus of study. Emanuel Tabachnick of the UAW encouraged Rustin to set the objective of "establishing Freedom Budget chapters in local communities throughout the country." The UAW could provide "some of the organizational sinews." Matthew Ahmann, who had been the Catholic representative to the March on Washington, believed that the religious community could rally around an "extensive national campaign." Most of all, Rustin expected the Freedom Budget to be taken up by the young. He worked closely with Charlotte Roe, the director of the U.S. Youth Council, an umbrella agency that brought together national organizations in a cooperating network. Roe promised to convene regional youth conferences around the budget.[33]

Rustin expected these two streams of activity to converge in legislative activity. In December 1966, soon after the launch, he testified at hearings that Senator Abraham Ribicoff conducted on the social and economic conditions that were producing so much unrest in American cities. Rustin spoke about the need for a federal commitment to provide jobs and physical reconstruction that reached beyond what the Johnson administration was doing. Keyserling was especially keen that Rustin take the initiative in drafting legislation to implement the Freedom Budget, and Rustin pushed the Leadership Conference on Civil Rights (LCRR), on whose board he served, to take the lead in the legislative arena. Discussions on the budget began just before Christmas and, early in 1967, LCCR set up a special committee to prepare a legislative package. Looking ahead, Rustin expected that all the local activities in 1967 "should eventually culminate in massive lobbying for the Budget. We hope by 1968 at the major party conventions to be ready to demand that the Budget be a major plank in both party platforms and to march around the convention floors for those demands."[34]

At first, Rustin had reason to be hopeful. He and Keyserling set out across the country on multicity tours, sometimes appearing together and sometimes separately. They often spoke to audiences of several hundred, and in a number of cities chapters formed to continue the work. Yet the campaign never took off. A year after the press conference that presented the Freedom Budget, it was obviously an utter failure. Increasingly frustrated, Keyserling told Rustin, "I marvel that you do as much as you do," but nonetheless "the army of supporters" who had initially gathered around the project "seems to be vanishing in thin air." As far as Keyserling could tell, the project had become "dormant."[35]

The Freedom Budget failed so abysmally because, even as Rustin was giving birth to it, the opportunities for a progressive coalition were evaporating. Two weeks after his successful Harlem press conference, Americans voted in midterm elections. The results shook any hope Rustin entertained about an American electorate shifting to the left. Republicans made significant gains in the House of Representatives. They won extra seats in the Senate and defeated some key liberals, like Paul Douglas of Illinois. Republicans seized governorships in eight states. In California, a wave of anger over student protests at Berkeley and the riots in Watts carried Ronald Reagan into the state house. A party that the electorate had devastatingly rejected just two years earlier now found itself reinvigorated, ready to do battle in Congress and looking with hope toward 1968. Although the Democratic majority in Congress was still large, the Republican minority and conservative Democrats together were again in a position to shape legislative debates. Resentment over Johnson's Great Society juggernaut in the previous Congress, reaction to black militancy and urban violence, and the mounting demands of the Vietnam War combined to make the new Congress more conservative. The impact on key elements in Rustin's imagined coalition was immediate. Rather than push new initiatives, like the Freedom Budget, member organizations of the LCCR spent most of 1967 "bogged down in holding actions," as Rustin wrote to one associate.[36]

But it was not only the civil rights establishment and Democratic Party liberals who had something other than the Freedom Budget on

their mind. The people whom Rustin saw as so vital to movements for
social justice—those whom he had described two years earlier as "the
spontaneous left"—were also working with a new political calculus. By
late 1966, when the Freedom Budget was born, the war in Vietnam
dominated their concerns. In just two years, Johnson and his advisers
had turned a modest overseas commitment into a major conflagration
involving almost 400,000 American troops and massive aerial bombing
of North and South Vietnam. Draft calls and casualties were climbing
disturbingly. Within his own party, Johnson faced opposition from
both those who felt that the war required pulling back from domestic
spending programs and those who expressed reservations about the
policy of military escalation. Agitation against the war was growing
steadily on college campuses, and the discontent was reviving the peace
movement to a degree not seen since the 1930s. For white activists especially, opposition to the war was becoming their top political priority.

In preparing the Freedom Budget, Rustin and Keyserling had made
the deliberate decision to sidestep the issue of "guns versus butter."
They constructed an economic plan for eliminating poverty that was
not dependent on choosing between a war in Vietnam and a war to end
poverty. In their projections about economic growth, tax revenues, and
government spending, they assumed that over the course of their ten-
year plan, defense appropriations would rise by almost a third. "In making this estimate," they wrote, "the Freedom Budget neither endorses
nor condemns present military policies. . . . Even if military spending
increases faster than now envisioned, the Freedom Budget proves that
we can afford to carry out the necessary programs. But the abolition of
poverty is too precious a goal to be made *contingent* on such a reduc-
tion." In other words, unlike those on both the right and the left who
were demanding that Johnson pick one or the other, Rustin was claiming that the nation could fight its wars abroad, if that was what it chose
to do, but that it did not have to fight them on the backs of the poor.[37]

Criticism of this aspect of the budget surfaced early. Norman
Thomas flagged it for Rustin even before the final draft was done when
he pointed to the cutbacks in domestic programs that were already
forecast by the summer of 1966. McKissick of CORE remarked that

this feature of the budget put into Rustin's mouth the same argument that the Johnson administration was making. "We [in CORE] cannot accept the current premise of the administration that we can afford both guns and butter, particularly in the light of the massive requirements for social reconstruction outlined in the Freedom Budget." Even Herbert Gans, part of Rustin's advisory team on the project, reacted strongly to the "casual acceptance of the war effort" that the framing of the budget implied.[38]

The loudest, and most troublesome, attack came from Seymour Melman, an academic economist whose work centered on a critique of the military-industrial complex. During the 1960s, Melman wrote widely about the damaging effects of military spending on American society. He said it distorted capital investment priorities, poured public money into programs that employed relatively few people for the amount spent, and produced billions of dollars of socially useless goods while basic human needs went unmet. Just a few days after the press conference in which Rustin premiered the Freedom Budget, Melman sent a "Dear Friends" letter to many of the figures who had endorsed it. Outraged that the budget seemed to countenance a rise in military spending, Melman told the signers, "I read with disbelief and dismay that you have fixed your name to this proposal." He ripped into it as "a war budget" that was "written in the White House." Before long, Rustin and Keyserling found themselves responding to calls and letters from concerned supporters.[39]

Rustin repeatedly had to answer his critics. Sometimes he spoke the language of strategy and tactics. "The most effective method of redirecting our economic energies away from the war in Viet Nam," he wrote in a memo that outlined an action plan on the budget, "is to mobilize people around the needs of the poor and the priorities of the Freedom Budget. The slogan to get out of the war has fewer possibilities for political organization than a determination to mount a counteroffensive against poverty." Rustin said that it was unreasonable to demand agreement on all issues as a condition for cooperation on a particular issue. "We decided from the outset not to exclude those people who supported the war," he replied to one correspondent. "We have

steadfastly kept our endorsement of the Budget separate from our foreign policy positions." At other times Rustin framed his stance as a matter of principle. "I cannot accept the notion that because the political
and psychological impact of the war curtails domestic reform we must
abandon calling for those reforms. . . . We have a moral responsibility
to continue to fight for freedom even in the shadow of war—in fact, it
is particularly important to fight for freedom under such circumstances."
He lashed out against his left critics. Rustin claimed that opponents of
the war were effectively saying that the poor, in the meantime, would
have to bear the cost. "At some point," he wrote, "the Vietnam war will
be over, and unless the concepts expressed in the Freedom Budget are
accepted, then the funds which will become available will be diverted
to . . . sending rockets to Venus rather than to alleviate the social condition of the poor."[40]

Rustin's arguments had little impact on an activist world in which the
war loomed ever larger and in which almost every initiative was judged
according to where it stood on the war. Among many church-based activists, the absence of a critique of the war was, by 1967, a fatal flaw. A
staff member at the National Council of Churches lambasted the
budget. He saw it as a crass scheme "to provide 'responsible' positions
from which to attack 'militants' and 'radicals' who link foreign and domestic policy" and as a way to bring radicals into "a consensus coalition
that will 'get them off the streets.'" Nor was the budget faring well
among students activists. Charlotte Roe of the U.S. Youth Council told
Rustin that efforts to mobilize the council's constituent organizations
were coming up against deep skepticism. The president of the NAACP
Youth Council in New York told her that "you couldn't call for guns
and butter." The National Student Association was taking a "wait and
see" attitude. Roe described them as "more susceptible" to the views of
campus radicals in the New Left and black power movements for whom
opposition to the war had become normative and working with the
Johnson administration anathema. Commenting on the budget, the
Harvard Crimson expressed disbelief that there was "a total disregard"
for the war. "It would seem almost impossible to bring a major coalition
which does not take that war into account." Michael Kazin, an under-

graduate active in the Harvard SDS chapter, called the budget "welfarism at home and imperialism abroad. . . . They're willing to keep all the defense money intact just so they can get George Meany on their side."[41]

The irony in these arguments was immense. Rustin had shaped his public career by steadfastly advocating Gandhian nonviolence and had worked in pacifist organizations for more than two decades. He had chosen jail rather than fight in a war against fascism and had dissented from American militarism at the height of the cold war, when the voices of dissent were few and far between. Now, as a popular mass movement was building against American military action abroad, Rustin was choosing to avoid the issue. Having stood apart from his society as a radical pacifist, he was now standing apart from pacifism just when a cry for peace was reaching millions.

CHAPTER NINETEEN

"A Strategist Without a Movement"
1966–1968

IN JANUARY 1969, in the waning days of the Johnson administration, Bill Moyers, the president's former press secretary, wrote to Harry McPherson, another of Johnson's aides. "How do you judge a President's performance when you cannot begin to understand the currents of change and upheaval that engulfed his era?" Moyers asked. "I cannot help but think as the end draws near that he was in office at what must have been the most turbulent conjunction of elemental forces since the collisions of the 1850s."[1]

Unlike Johnson, Rustin did not hold public office. In his hands did not rest the fate of the nation or, indeed, much of the rest of the world. Yet he had fashioned a life for himself that aspired to have just that sort of impact. Like others in these years, Rustin found himself suddenly moving, as Moyers phrased it, amid "currents of change and upheaval" too tumultuous for him to shape or control.

IN 1960, FEW could have predicted, and least of all Rustin, that foreign policy issues would soon divide Americans more bitterly than any issue since slavery. The cold war had created a deep consensus about the need to contain communism. It justified an American military presence around the world. Rustin had felt the isolation that dissent from this consensus brought. But the Vietnam War—or "the American War," as it was called in Southeast Asia—shattered any semblance of unity in foreign policy. It brought to the United States a level of domestic contentiousness not seen previously in the twentieth century. Starting first among knots of college students, intellectuals, and militant civil rights activists, antiwar forces swelled steadily. Dissent surfaced in every segment of American life, eventually reaching into the armed forces and Johnson's circle of trusted advisers.

Many things contributed to the discontent. Johnson never asked Congress for a declaration of war, as the Constitution specifies, yet in less than three years he had committed more than half a million troops to fight in Vietnam. There was never a full and open debate about the reasons for war or a persuasive articulation of the national interests that were at stake beyond a litany of platitudes about honoring commitments and defending freedom. Skeptics answered the administration's rhetoric with a recitation of the recent history of Vietnam: America supported first France, the colonial power, and then a series of autocratic governments; the United States and South Vietnam were acting in violation of international agreements; the division of the country was never meant to be permanent; the fighting could reasonably be construed as a civil war, which made the United States the aggressive foreign power in the region. It was hard to sustain the claim that the security of the United States depended on the outcome of a civil conflict more than 8,000 miles away. Yet against a nation of peasants, the greatest military power in the history of the world was unleashing an aerial firepower that exceeded the force used in World War II. American soldiers burned villages to the ground and employed chemical weapons like napalm, which seared the skin off its victims. At the same time, evidence accumulated that the administration dissembled about decisions it made behind closed doors. A credibility gap opened between the government and its critics, and it yawned wider as the war dragged on.

Until 1968, a majority of Americans supported Johnson's policies; if anything, many Americans wanted an even more vigorous prosecution of the war. Nonetheless, public manifestations of dissent kept spreading and grew more militant as the war escalated. College students went from attending peaceful "teach-ins" to blocking military recruiters from campus and occupying university buildings. The size of peace marches expanded geometrically until they included hundreds of thousands. Borrowing some of the methods of the antinuclear movement that Rustin had helped shape in the 1950s, antiwar activists obstructed the movement of troop trains and the functioning of army induction centers. Dissenting senators held televised hearings and subjected officials in the State Department and the Pentagon to tough scrutiny. Peace candidates ran for elective office. Imitating the tactics of SNCC in Mississippi in 1964, students organized Vietnam Summer in 1967. They went door to door in communities across the country to build a grass-roots antiwar movement. Young men facing military service burned their draft cards and urged their fellows to resist conscription, much as Rustin had done in the 1940s.

A few years earlier, without any question, Rustin would have been at the front of many of these demonstrations. He would have plotted and planned the course of the antiwar movement, debating strategy, developing tactics, shaping the message that opponents of the war projected to the public. But despite his early statements against the war and his decades as a pacifist, Rustin was nowhere to be found in the largest antiwar movement in the history of the United States. By 1966, he had disappeared from the precincts of peace activism. He remained mostly silent on the issue and detached from the struggle. When he did make statements about the building opposition to the war, he tended toward criticism of the movement. Search the antiwar movement's greatest moments, its signature protests, and Rustin's absence is glaring. Scan the roster of speakers who addressed rallies against the war, and Rustin will not be on the list.

Rustin's refusal to align himself unambiguously with the antiwar movement allowed many to view him as a supporter of Johnson's war policies. In the polarized environment of the late 1960s, the war quickly became a litmus test of an individual's entire political worldview. To partisans on either side, one was either a hawk or a dove; there was no middle ground. But Rustin was never an apologist for the war. He remained a pacifist, as he explained to correspondents who reproached him for his failure to lead the antiwar crusade. "I must tell you," he wrote one of them, "that if I were drafted I would refuse to fight on the same basis that I refused to fight in an earlier period, and that is that as a pacifist, I consider all wars evil." He publicly expressed his distaste for the war on a number of occasions. Addressing the fiftieth anniversary convention of the Women's International League for Peace and Freedom, Rustin unequivocally declared, "I am opposed to escalating the war in Vietnam. It will help no living soul who believes in freedom. . . . I stand in the United States and I condemn that policy." In a column in the *Amsterdam News* in the spring of 1967, he described the Vietnam War as "a tragic conflict" and said "it must be brought to a speedy end." He denounced the "over representation of black people on the casualty lists" and the right wing's deployment of the war "as an excuse to cut back on the war on poverty and the struggle against racism." Rustin supported the liberal antiwar position that called for a negotiated settlement, and he wanted to include at the negotiating table representatives of the National Liberation Front, or Vietcong, a position the Johnson administration adamantly rejected. Yet at a time when many radical antiwar activists were framing the issue in stark moral terms, Rustin's arguments sometimes sounded opportunistic and his proposed solutions weak and compromising.[2]

To the dismay of many in the peace movement, Rustin seemed far more willing to criticize antiwar activists than he was to throw himself into the struggle. As Muste, Dellinger, and McReynolds helped craft an inclusive antiwar coalition open to liberals, independent progressives, and members of sectarian Communist organizations, Rustin decried the WRL's "dangerous flirtation with the old line Communists." He accused WILPF members from outside the United States of "the highest immorality" for attacking U.S. military actions in Asia. "The nations of the world have aided and abetted and encouraged America to do precisely what she is now doing," he told them. He instructed them to go home and pressure their own governments to reject the protection of America's nuclear shield. At a conference of independent leftists that Irving Howe, the editor of *Dissent*, convened in May 1967, Rustin lashed into the pediatrician Benjamin Spock, who had put himself in the front ranks of the antiwar movement. He accused Spock of "political naïveté" in working alongside Maoists and Trotskyites to end the war in Vietnam." Concerned about the calls for a Vietcong victory that were increasingly heard at antiwar demonstrations, Rustin charged that "no effective and enduring peace movement can be built, or win influence, with the American people, which becomes publicly identified with groups that want, not peace, but a Vietcong victory." He was keenly skeptical of the white male college students whose antiwar activities were rocking the nation's campuses. To Michael Randle, with whom Rustin had organized antinuclear protests in Africa, Rustin prophesied that "as soon as the Vietnam War was over, and with it the threat of conscription, the students would go quietly back to their studies and from there to their comfortable middle class lives."[3]

Rustin's detachment from the antiwar cause seemed like apostasy to many pacifists. It stunned, puzzled, and even angered his former colleagues. One night near the end of the 1960s, when Rustin arrived late to a WRL party, Jim Peck, who had known him since their days of resistance against conscription during World War II, walked over and jabbed his finger accusingly into Rustin's chest. "How can you live with yourself?" Peck spat out. His comment took everyone aback until Rustin graciously smoothed things over by saying, "Jim has paid his dues. He has a right to ask that question." Around the same time, the easygoing and always affable Ralph DiGia wistfully wrote Rustin after seeing a picture of him in the *Village Voice:* "I wish somehow you were with the hell raisers where you belong." George Willoughby, who headed the Committee for Nonviolent Action, recalled that during these years, "there was a feeling among some people that you couldn't trust Bayard."[4]

Pacifists who knew Rustin tried to explain his stance. DiGia thought that, for Rustin, the pacifist movement was no longer "wide enough. . . . He had to get out beyond it. . . . He was just tired of working on a shoestring . . . he did sort of change . . . he started working within the system." Homer Jack, who had worked with CORE in the 1940s and became national chairman of SANE, thought "this rightward trend of Bayard . . . a lot of that has to do with Bayard's increasing involvement in the AFL-CIO." His dependence on Meany and the labor movement made it impossible, in Jack's view, to maintain a high-profile stance as a critic of American foreign policy. Dave McReynolds, who never lost his affection for Rustin, thought that "power was what seduced Bayard." Ever since the Atlantic City convention, when the effort to negotiate a compromise brought him into close contact with Hubert Humphrey and Walter Reuther, Rustin had seemed to McReynolds tempted by the allure of political power. Dave Dellinger felt that from 1965, when Rustin first began to distance himself from his pacifist friends, "it was all downhill for Bayard." Dellinger never forgave Rustin for not joining him outside the White House to protest the war after being inside the mansion for the signing of the Voting Rights Act. It proved to him that Rustin was in the pocket of the Johnson administration, pursuing the strategy of "coalition with the marines," as Staughton Lynd had charged. In later years, Dellinger circulated rumors that Rustin was on the payroll of the CIA.[5]

Some of these pacifist critiques were not without substance. Just as many on the left made one's position on the war a litmus test for belonging, so too did many on the other side of the issue. As dissent spread and threatened to disrupt Johnson's liberal mandate in Congress, allies such as George Meany, always a cold warrior, made support for the president an undebatable proposition within the AFL-CIO. Had Rustin become too strongly identified with antiwar forces, there was a risk he might have lost funding for the Randolph Institute. Johnson himself reacted strongly to criticisms of the war. In private comments, Rustin seemed conscious of this as he tied expressions of antiwar sentiment by civil rights leaders to concern about relations with the administration. In April 1966, in the midst of preparations for the White House Conference, Rustin reportedly was "very sore" when SCLC issued a strong statement urging consideration of "prompt withdrawal" from Vietnam. The following year, at a closed gathering of leaders of the major civil rights organizations, including Wilkins, Whitney Young, King, and McKissick, Rustin asserted that "the civil rights movement could gain nothing without President Johnson's support. . . . The President's support might be diluted if civil rights leaders took strong stands against the Administration's policy in Vietnam."[6]

These interpretations of Rustin's motivation are not entirely convincing since Rustin could also be scathingly critical of the Johnson administration. Late in 1966, at a Senate hearing on urban problems, Rustin accused the White House of "putting the price of the Vietnam War on the backs of the poor" and condemned the budget cutting that was destroying the War on Poverty. Speaking at Hunter College around the same time, he declared that "Johnson himself is to blame" for the violent disorders that threatened peace in America's cities. "He has cut away the little carrot we had," Rustin said, referring to the lack of spending on domestic needs. His censure of Johnson's policies became so sharp that in early 1968, Johnson scribbled on a document that bore Rustin's name a brusque note that read, "Tell them to cut this stuff out."[7]

Neither Rustin's financial dependence on organized labor nor his desire to work with the Democratic Party can explain his distance from the growing antiwar movement. Vietnam had injected such contention among liberals that it made Democratic politics extraordinarily fluid. Coalitions were shifting, and new alliances were forming. Party stalwarts were breaking with the president. During these years, Rustin sat on the national board of Americans for Democratic Action, a pressure group founded in the 1940s in part to make anticommunism an integral component of the liberal agenda. By 1967, antiwar sentiment was sweeping through the organization. Had he elected to do so, Rustin might have participated in the construction of a progressive coalition that linked racial and economic justice at home to a critique of militarism abroad.

Rustin's defenders explained his decision as a choice to put race first. Rachelle Horowitz, who worked at the Randolph Institute during some of these years, remembered Rustin asserting something along the lines of, "I'm in the black movement now, I'm not a peacenik anymore."[8] But this segmenting of issues makes little sense in either the context of the times or Rustin's career. Many black leaders, King especially, were searching for ways to integrate the fight for racial justice and the call for peace, much as Rustin had done in the 1940s when he helped make fighting racism a key part of the FOR's mission.

Moreover, Rustin did devote time during these years to some foreign policy issues. In 1966, he accompanied Norman Thomas on fact-finding missions to the Dominican Republic, where Johnson had sent the marines the preceding year. He was part of a team that observed elections on the island. Rustin also associated himself with campaigns launched by the American Jewish community to train international attention on the persecution of Jews in the Soviet Union. He lent his name to petitions, wrote to Soviet diplomats, and spoke at major rallies called by coalitions of Jewish organizations.[9]

No simple explanation or neat political logic deciphers the mystery of Rustin's detachment from the war and the vigorous dissent it spawned. The best that can be said, perhaps, is that a trait that had brought him such distinction decades earlier now served him badly. As a younger man, Rustin had won admirers because of his penchant for articulating a stand forcefully, unambiguously, and without compromise. In the 1940s, his espousal of an absolutist pacifism had raised his moral stature among the tightly knit band of religious pacifists. Two decades later, he had formulated a political strategy just as forcefully and with as much conviction. He had staked his reputation as an activist on the move from protest to politics and on building a progressive coalition within the Democratic Party. Now, as the war reconfigured everything, Rustin was not willing to question his premises. If he had once held fast to war resistance in the face of all the evidence about Hitler, he was unlikely to reconsider his call to build a new political majority at home through an alliance with labor and liberal Democrats.

Or maybe the mystery is not so complex at all. George Houser, who had worked closely with Rustin at the FOR, thought he "just made a practical decision that, 'if I'm going to be able to survive in this world, then I have got to play a different game, because there's no place for me in just maintaining contact with a small radical group. How do I manage to secure myself?' I think he made a conscious decision about that." As if to confirm Houser's surmise, around this time, Shizu Asahi Proctor, a former FOR secretary whom Rustin had thoroughly captivated in the 1940s, ran into him on a subway platform in Manhattan. She hadn't seen him in many years but had followed his career. Talking about old times and commenting on his current circumstances, Rustin made a comment that, almost three decades later, remained engraved in her memory. "You get tired after a while," he told her, "and you have to come home to something comfortable and something you can count on."[10] Well into his fifties at the time of this encounter, Rustin had experienced a lifetime on the margins. The Randolph Institute provided a secure political home, allowed a considerable measure of autonomy, and gave him the opportunity to express his prodigious energies. As America began to spin out of control because of the passions unleashed by the war, Rustin chose to set himself firmly on particular ground, and he never reconsidered.

IN CONTRAST TO his disengagement from issues of war and peace, Rustin remained in the thick of the black freedom struggle. He threw himself fully into the conflicts that were bursting out among activists and organizations. These years were not the best for someone with Rustin's views. The framework for understanding racial issues was changing, and a militancy different from Rustin's coursed through segments of the African American community. Fueled by the rhetoric of black power, nationalist sentiment was pushing aside an earlier emphasis on nonviolence and integration. Rather than love and compassion, rage was the emotion most in evidence, expressed through the urban rebellions that erupted each summer around the country, but heard also in the everyday comments of community activists. The new militancy accented culture and consciousness more than it did politics and formal legal rights. It self-consciously nurtured pride in the heritage of Africa. It fostered a sense of distinctiveness from white America as a counterpoint to the deep, almost reflexive assumption of European superiority.

This reorientation was neither distant from Rustin's immediate political world nor restricted to small cadres of young activists. Whatever the magnitude of its appeal within the black community, this outlook extended its reach broadly as a white-controlled news media exhibited a fascination with the new militants and projected images of black pride and the rhetoric of black power widely through America. As often as not, Rustin found himself invited to speak not as a sole presenter on civil rights or racial justice but as a member of a panel, squaring off with a proponent of a black-centered politics. In the past, he had competed for influence with Wilkins and the NAACP; now he found himself locked in combat with those who questioned the premises not only of the old-line civil rights movement but also of Rustin's own call for coalition and engagement with mainstream institutions. Early in 1967, in a debate at Miami University where, just three years earlier, he had helped train volunteers for Mississippi Freedom Summer, Rustin squared off against George Weir, a SNCC representative. "I say to white people and Western civilization," Weir declaimed, "we have found you out. . . . If you try to stop us, we will help wreck your Western civilization." Closer to home, Jesse Gray, a Harlem activist with whom Rustin had tangled during the summer riots in 1964, was building a following through his attacks on white liberals. "The quicker we get the white liberals out of the black community, the better off we'll be," he told an interviewer in 1967. "White liberals are the slimiest snakes on earth." In a debate in New York City, Stokely Carmichael, who had once venerated Rustin as a political mentor, heaped scorn on the notion of coalition. "What is good for this country is not good for black people," he said. "This country is racist from top to bottom, from right to left, and for black people to become a part of that is for them to become in fact anti-black."[11]

Rustin found the style and content of the new black militancy viscerally repellent. He saw in it a repudiation of his whole life experience, of values that resided at the core of who he was. Rustin moved comfortably in white worlds. He had, in a sense, taken possession of Western culture. Even in his most militant days, he always believed the other person could be reached and won over. Courage was an inner quality, displayed through deliberate action rather than combative poses. He had no use for the exaggerated masculinity of the new black radicalism, the equation of revolution with the fatigues of the guerrilla warrior.

As Rustin dove into battle with the new black militants, he held back nothing. "To talk about blackness is silly," he said at one point. "As soon as you move into the economic struggle you're in a totally new universal ball game with universal objectives. . . . Anybody who talks about a black agenda is a reactionary." Despite the rhetoric of revolution emanating from nationalist circles, Rustin described it as an evasion of the hard-nosed political mobilization that was needed. "The alternative to politics," he told a writer for the *New York Times*, "is to cop out and talk about hair, about what name you wanted to be called, and about soul food." Barely concealing his contempt, he told the reporter that "wearing my hair Afro style, calling myself an Afro-American, and eating all the chitterlings I can find are not going to affect Congress." To one of his correspondents, Rustin expressed his frustration at what was passing for politics. "The need today is for less sloganeering and gimmicks and more thought," he wrote. To others he complained of "the ideological deterioration of the 'militant wing' of the civil rights movement."[12]

Some of Rustin's consternation came from his assessment of the work ahead. It was not that his ideas about coalition politics forced him to moderate his message. Even as his antagonists castigated him for growing conservative, Rustin continued to speak about revolution. In a public debate with Carmichael, he told the audience that "basic in the demands of the Negro people today is a fundamental challenge to this society. We are asking first of all for what this society does not want to hear: a redistribution of wealth. . . . This society must dig deep and be prepared to make revolutionary change in its economic and social life. And nothing short of that." These were not the words of someone who had scrapped his allegiance to a radical vision of economic democracy in exchange for proximity to the politically powerful.[13]

Rustin's resistance to the new militancy reflected his continuing allegiance to what might be called a moral economy of nonviolence. Rustin's espousal of nonviolence had always rested on the melding together of means and ends. Violence in word or deed generated more of the same; respect for an opponent left open the door for reconciliation. The discipline of nonviolence required that its advocates put aside the spontaneity of raging emotions in the interest of measured ethical reflection. Rustin listened to the rhetoric emanating from black power advocates and saw instead a movement grounded in frustration. Black power, he said, "is nothing but an emotional reaction to 300 years of second-class citizenship." This was the last thing that the movement for racial justice needed. "The minute you had black anger, rage," he told an interviewer in the 1970s, "you automatically had to have white fear, because we're always enumerator to their denominator. . . . These two things have to move with each other."[14]

For Rustin the tragedy of these years was encapsulated in the way that "futile extremist cries of 'black power'" and "a vicious white backlash" fed one another. At times it provoked comments from him that seemed almost apocalyptic. In the midst of the Detroit riots in July 1967, Rustin predicted a wave of repression if the disorders continued unabated. "They will be a threat to all civil liberties," he declared. "There will be a fantastic backlash." Likening the situation to when "the North withdrew the Union armies from the South" in the 1870s, Rustin said that black violence would be the excuse the nation needed to back away from its newly legislated commitment to equality. His assessment led him to reiterate the need for carefully nuanced strategy and finely honed tactics. "It's not that we don't need militance," he told one reporter, "but that we need militants who can tread that thin line, and not go over to where militance causes reaction."[15]

In the polarized climate of the late 1960s, Rustin's adversarial stance toward the new radicalism inevitably meant that he turned toward the moderate wing of the civil rights movement for support and alliances. He found himself in steady dialogue with his former adversary Roy Wilkins. Rustin served on the board of the Leadership Council on Civil Rights, a coalition long dominated by the NAACP. He won its endorsement of measures like minimum wage legislation, as he successfully persuaded the LCCR's constituent groups that economic measures were the cutting edge of the struggle for racial equality. He pushed Wilkins to take a stand on labor-related issues and brought him to Memphis early in 1968 to address a rally of striking sanitation workers.

As these examples suggest, Rustin in these years approached issues of race from the vantage point of economics. When George Wiley, a CORE stalwart in the 1960s, left the organization to build a mass movement among welfare recipients, Rustin backed the effort. He addressed demonstrations outside the headquarters of New York's welfare department as women were occupying offices inside. At a rally of 18,000 municipal workers in Madison Square Garden in May 1967,

Rustin championed their right to strike in the face of a new state law that forbade government workers from walking off the job. With a large grant from the Labor Department, he hired Ernest Green, one of the students who had desegregated Little Rock's Central High School a decade before, to develop a project designed to challenge racial barriers in the crafts. The institute recruited young blacks and Hispanics to take the entrance tests for various apprenticeship programs and tutored them so that they were positioned to pass the exams. It successfully maneuvered applicants around the obstacles that kept them out of unions representing plumbers, bricklayers, electricians, steam fitters, roofers, boilermakers, and others.

In certain ways, Rustin was resoundingly successful. The mainstream civil rights movement did come to see its core mission as including more than a commitment to legal equality. Minimum wage legislation, protecting the right of workers to bargain collectively and to strike when necessary, expanding access to welfare for those who could not work, and campaigning for full employment through proposals like the Freedom Budget were all elements of Rustin's strategic orientation, and they came to be the agenda of organizations like the NAACP, the National Urban League, and the Leadership Council on Civil Rights.

But the strategy articulated in "From Protest to Politics" crucially depended on the cooperation of the radical forces from which Rustin was now estranged. His hope that the Democrats might be remade needed the progressive elements in American political life to coalesce within the party in order to pull it toward the left. Instead, many of these groupings were moving in another direction. Militant activists who once gathered in SNCC and CORE were rushing away from mainstream institutions and electoral politics. Many in the white religious community who had signed on to the civil rights movement's coalition of conscience in the mid-1960s now marched and organized against the war. Even the crusading liberals in the Democratic Party, whom Rustin had assumed could be turned in a more progressive direction, were enmeshed in the politics of the war. By 1967, liberal activists in the party were organizing a "dump Johnson" movement, and even when other liberals resisted it, the controversy drained attention from the domestic issues Rustin cared about. So Rustin kept moving toward the Democratic Party, but almost no one from his earlier political worlds followed. His allies became figures like Wilkins, whose vision of racial justice extended just a few paces beyond the ground of formal legal equality, or union leaders for whom liberal reform, not the restructuring of the political economy, was the outer limit of what they could imagine.

RUSTIN'S RELATIONSHIP WITH King offers one way of measuring the shift in his political posture. Despite the periods of estrangement and distance provoked by reactions to Rustin's sexuality, Rustin's influence on King had remained fairly consistent over the years. He pointed King toward militant nonviolence, organizational strength, and engagement with politics. From early on, he had pushed King to think beyond civil rights and the demise of Jim Crow toward a more capacious platform that linked social justice for black Americans to economic justice for all Americans.

While King's adherence toward nonviolence came quickly and instinctively, it took him longer to adopt the rest of Rustin's package. Rustin, of course, was never the only influence on King. Other voices offered advice and, especially in the 1960s, many enjoyed closer access to him. King learned through experience as well. Yet it is notable that by the mid-1960s, SCLC's platform and King's articulation of his politics often sounded as if Rustin still worked as his ghostwriter. SCLC called on blacks "to enter alliances." It described programs for domestic reconstruction that echoed the Freedom Budget. It stressed the need to move beyond protest and amass "organized power," and it called for "joint organized activities" with labor.[16] At a retreat for SCLC staff late in 1966, King made remarks that were as close to a complete political manifesto as he ever gave. The phrasing and the style were very much his own, but the structure and content bore an uncanny resemblance to "From Protest to Politics." King assessed the achievements since the *Brown* decision as "surface changes . . . not really substantive changes." The movement, he told his staff, "did not defeat the monster of racism." Just as Rustin had criticized "no-win" militants,

King found "despair and disappointment" among the self-declared radicals who espoused black power. Defining the work ahead, he said, "We are now dealing with class issues." The movement had to "address itself to the restructuring of the whole of American society."[17]

Yet a huge gulf was opening between Rustin and King over matters of strategy and tactics, the very areas where Rustin had once offered such astute guidance. The SCLC campaign in Chicago in 1966 was the first major instance in which this pattern emerged. The year before, King had come away from Watts wanting to grapple with the problems of the urban ghettos outside the South. Some of his associates were already arguing for him to move his campaigns north, and community activists in Chicago were specifically pressing SCLC to come there to help them. In what Andrew Young described as a two-day "marathon" meeting a few weeks after Watts, SCLC staff and King's "kitchen cabinet" of advisers, including Rustin, gathered in Atlanta to debate the idea.[18]

Rustin was perhaps the most outspoken voice against setting up shop in Chicago. "You don't know what Chicago is like," Rustin kept saying. "It's not a clean slate that you can move into. There are powerful political figures. You've got the Daley machine to deal with, you've got the powerful black ministers who are going to be jealous of you coming in here. You've got problems . . . which you don't have in the little southern communities that you are accustomed to." After Chicago, Rustin queried, What next? New York and Adam Clayton Powell? Instead, he argued, the new voting rights legislation made it all the more important that SCLC stay focused on the South. He urged King to go "from city to city, and from county to county, leading people into voter registration centers." He conjured an image of King as a "pied piper" inducing Southern blacks into political activity. But "there was no political vacuum" in Chicago. "You are going to kill yourself in Chicago," he told King. "You're going to be wiped out."[19]

Despite Rustin's reasoning, King decided to make Chicago the site of SCLC's next major campaign, and early in 1966, he launched an organizing drive there. Almost immediately, as Andrew Young remembered, they came up against just the kind of problems Rustin warned them about. In the South Side neighborhoods where they worked, tenants lived in dilapidated buildings in unheated apartments suffering from the bitter cold. Young realized there was a "plethora of bad housing" in the city and countless individual landlords exploiting tenants. Unlike in Birmingham, Chicago meant slow, plodding work without either the intervention of the federal government or media coverage to tip the scales of public opinion. There could be no court decision or overarching legislative solution to work toward or claim as a victory. And there was not a single overarching enemy to symbolize injustice. Chicago's Mayor Richard Daley "was no Bull Connor."[20]

King and his staff were in and out of Chicago for much of 1966. As the weather warmed, they held large rallies in black neighborhoods, at Soldiers Field, and in Grant Park in downtown Chicago. In July, serious rioting broke out in Chicago as it had in other Northern cities. Instead of being seen as a beacon of nonviolence, King found his campaign blamed for the disorders. Later in the summer, SCLC shifted its focus to open housing marches in white neighborhoods. King and his aides faced a "lynch mob howling for blood," according to Young, who thought the white hatred as bad as anything he had faced in the South. The disturbances eventually led to conferences with Mayor Daley and some agreements around housing issues, but as Young acknowledged, "there were no guarantees on implementation." Altogether, the campaign was a disappointing intervention.[21]

Despite Rustin's dissent from the decision to go north, he continued to work with King and offered support on the campaign. In April, he took time off from planning for the White House conference to fly to Chicago for a few days, where he helped negotiate a unity agreement among competing community groups. In July, as he pushed to complete the Freedom Budget, he traveled there again, this time to accompany King at a string of rallies across the city. But his willingness to aid in the effort did not signify a shift in his point of view. "I knew he had to fall on his face," he recalled. "Daley cut Martin Luther King's ass off."[22]

The difficulties notwithstanding, the Chicago work cemented King's new understanding of what racial justice required. "We knew that poverty . . . equaled powerlessness," Young claimed, and SCLC's work "increasingly concentrate[d] on ways to attack it at its root." This was Rustin's program. As Rustin prepared to unveil the Freedom Budget in October, King in his public statements drew attention to it, urging "all elements of the civil rights movement to unite" behind the budget. Echoing Rustin's strategic formulations, he called for "a coalition that would include churches, labor unions, civil rights groups, and colleges.[23] The two seemed to be moving toward the same goals.

Yet the next few months did not see them grow closer but instead aggravated the strains between them. One provoking agent was the way the cry of black power reverberated through the movement that summer and fall and reconfigured alliances. Soon after Rustin's critique of black power appeared in *Commentary*, he began to engineer a collective response to the new black militancy, as well as to the gathering reaction among some white liberals against the civil rights agenda. He brought together Wilkins, Whitney Young, Dorothy Height, who was president of the National Council of Negro Women, and Randolph to endorse a long statement, "Crisis and Commitment," that appeared as a three-quarter page ad in the *New York Times* in October 1966. As the title suggested, the statement both described the deepening crisis in race relations in America and affirmed a commitment to core principles of the civil rights movement. The signatories, which included Rustin, reiterated their allegiance to democratic processes and peaceful protest, to integration and the removal of all barriers to full participation in American life, and to the responsibility of the whole society for achieving racial justice. They repudiated calls for violence. They condemned urban rioting and the rhetoric that encouraged it. Their text made no reference to the phrase *black power* and did not censure anyone by name. In fact, most of the statement focused on mainstream institutions and called them to task for their fading commitment to racial equality. Yet the press, and particularly the *New York Times*, treated the ad not only as a repudiation of the concept of black power but of SNCC and CORE as well.[24]

Two days before the ad appeared, Rustin met with King in Atlanta for a wide-ranging discussion about the emerging black power ideology. Saying that King could not continue to occupy a noncommittal middle ground, Rustin pushed—without success—for him to sign "Crisis and Commitment." Then, after the ad appeared, King found himself bombarded by reporters pressing him to explain why he had not signed it and where he stood in relation to black power. At least as the *Times* reported it, King seemed to waffle, claiming he supported the statement one day but then dissenting from it the next. He tried to draw a distinction between the sentiments, which he endorsed, and the divisiveness that the ad fanned, which he did not. Following the uproar closely, Rustin told Levison that King "had to make up his mind publicly and state whether he endorses the statement." Later, Levison talked with King, who was upset at how the press had gotten him "into a bind." Levison replied that he was "convinced that Rustin did that . . . Rustin wanted to box King in."[25]

While black power stoked tensions in Rustin's relationship to King, they remained fundamentally in agreement on the issue itself. Neither saw it as productive. Both considered it a dangerous departure from core principles that had guided the black struggle. By contrast, the Vietnam War exposed a chasm between their outlooks that was impossible to paper over. As the war intensified and Rustin resisted engaging the politics or morality of the war, King found himself inexorably pulled toward an outspoken antiwar stance.

In the early stages of the conflict, Rustin had prodded King to use his stature to speak out against the war but in ways that did not claim to represent the civil rights movement. After 1965, his emphasis shifted, and he became a voice of caution, discouraging King from venturing near the war. Rustin was not alone in this. Many of King's close advisers, Andrew Young among them, were nervous about the war and about too close an alignment between the peace movement and civil rights. For much of 1966, King repeatedly raised the issue of the war in consultations with those around him, but then, in the words of one FBI memo, "acceded to their advice" to speak and act circumspectly.[26]

By 1967, King concluded that he could no longer sit on the fence. Bernard Lee, his personal assistant, recalled King reading an article in *Ramparts*, a radical magazine, with a picture of a Vietnamese infant killed by American military action. "That's when the decision was made," Lee claimed.[27] The editors of *The Nation* had invited King to give an address in late February at a forum in Los Angeles. He elected to use it as an opportunity to speak forthrightly about the war. Still struggling over how to do it and not drag the civil rights movement into the maelstrom of antiwar politics, he wanted Rustin to draft the speech. But Levison, himself leery of King's ventures in this direction, advised against it, calling Rustin "very weak on the subject of Vietnam." King's speech became a front-page news item. According to the *Times*, an "overflow audience of 1,500" heard King castigate the American government for "supporting a new form of colonialism." King told the crowd that "the promises of the Great Society have been shot down on the battlefield of Vietnam," and he exhorted them to do something about it: "Those of us who love peace must organize as effectively as the war hawks."[28]

Once King declared himself unambiguously against the war, the demands on him to draw even closer to the antiwar movement became persistent. A coalition of peace groups was sponsoring a rally in New York's Central Park in April 1967, followed by a march to the United Nations. James Bevel, a member of King's staff, had taken a leave of absence to direct the spring mobilization, and he pressed King to lead the crowd and speak at the rally. King convened his committee of advisers, including Rustin, to ask for their counsel. Except for Bevel, everyone opposed his participation. As he often did at moments that called for a contentious decision, King waited before committing himself, but then resolved to go ahead.[29]

Trying to lay the groundwork for this very public stand against the war, he granted an interview with a *New York Times* reporter and scheduled an address at Riverside Church a few days before the big march. To the *Times* he stressed that in opposing the war, he was speaking as an individual, not as head of the SCLC or for the civil rights movement. In fact, much of the interview spoke about the hard work still ahead to achieve racial equality and how it would continue to occupy the bulk of his attention. Yet he also spoke of the connections between the two concerns. "You can't really have freedom without justice," King said. "You can't have peace without justice, and you can't have justice without peace, so it is more of a realization of the interrelatedness of racism and militarism and the need to attack both problems." A few days later, before more than 3,000 listeners at Riverside Church in Manhattan, King delivered his most passionate and politically explosive statement about the war. He spoke of his need to "break the betrayal of my own silences and to speak from the burnings of my own heart." He described the United States as the "greatest purveyor of violence in the world today." Its priorities were so misguided that the country was "approaching spiritual death." He said the nation had placed itself in the way of revolutionary aspirations around the globe and that American leaders had been "wrong from the beginning" about Vietnam. He urged young men to boycott the war by becoming conscientious objectors. The next week, King marched from Central Park to the United Nations at the head of a crowd that, by some estimates, exceeded the numbers that had gathered in Washington in 1963.[30]

In one sense, Rustin assessed accurately the political repercussions from too bold a stance against the war. While antiwar activists cheered King's stand, it engendered hostility almost everywhere else—from much of the press, both white and black; from the mainstream civil rights leadership; and from the Johnson administration and Democratic Party officials. Yet at the same time, the sentiments King expressed that winter and spring perfectly embodied the essence of Rustin's public life in the 1940s and 1950s. Two decades earlier, when Rustin had delivered the William Penn lecture to American Quakers, he proclaimed that the violence of the cold war was leading to "moral suicide" in America, that "the spark of God in each of us is . . . all but completely smothered." He held out a moral challenge: "We cannot remain honest unless we are opposed to injustice wherever it occurs."[31] These were the kind of sentiments he had brought to King early on. Now the pupil had surpassed the teacher. King was reaching audiences larger than any that had ever heard Rustin's old antiwar message, but Rustin neither listened nor approved. While King was now declaring, "We must stop this war," Rustin seemed to be saying, "I will not let this war stop me."

Yet the war was stopping him. All through 1967, Rustin struggled to

build a political movement around his Freedom Budget. His every effort seemed stymied by the war. The allies he expected to line up were
either absorbed by antiwar activities or suspicious of Rustin for not taking the war into account. He faced a White House and a Congress preoccupied by the conflict and unwilling to appropriate significant
monies to domestic reconstruction while the war was going on. Now,
King too seemed about to drown in the storm of antiwar politics.

Not completely, however. While Rustin's Freedom Budget was going nowhere, King and his advisers were formulating their own antipoverty effort. Late in 1967, they began conceiving a "poor people's
campaign" for the following spring. Intending to bring thousands of
the nation's poor to Washington for an extended stay, they projected a
sustained exercise in civil disobedience. "We are going to Washington,"
the prospectus explained, "not for a single dramatic event, but to dislo-
cate the city's functioning if necessary. . . . It is there that policy is determined, and it is there that the power to reform resides." In the past,
Rustin had often spoken of "social dislocation." When he had first conceived the March on Washington, he imagined sit-ins and other acts of
civil disobedience to stop the business of government. Now, according
to Levison, he "showed his true colors" by opposing the disruptive tactics that King was proposing. Several summers of urban disorders,
Rustin argued, had made the public too nervous and the government
too jittery for such a campaign to be effective. Instead, it would only
raise the threat of repression and the likelihood of backlash. With views
such as these, it is small wonder that Rustin described his relationship
to King and his circle as "essentially non grata." By early 1968, he recalled, "We were continuously invited, but nobody paid any attention
to us."[32]

IN A TUMULTUOUS DECADE, 1968 was the most turbulent year of
all. It brought battlefield reversals and rising casualties in Vietnam; the
crumbling of a presidency; assassinations of charismatic figures; urban
uprisings and a national capital in flames; rebellions on scores of campuses; and pitched battles between police and citizens outside a national

political convention. There had not been a time in living memory when the country was so bitterly fractured.

Late in January, the North Vietnamese and the Vietcong launched a major offensive throughout South Vietnam during the Tet holiday. American forces eventually beat back the attacks after weeks of heavy fighting, but the intensity of the onslaught disturbed a public accepting of Johnson's claims that the war was nearing an end. Editorial commentary from the *Wall Street Journal* to Walter Cronkite, the CBS evening news anchor, expressed skepticism about the possibility of a military victory. When William Westmoreland, the U.S. commander in Vietnam, asked for another 200,000 troops, Johnson's own advisers wavered. At the end of March, the president announced on national television a halt in the American bombing campaign and expressed a willingness to enter negotiations to end the war.

To the surprise of virtually everyone, including some of his closest advisers, Johnson ended his speech by revealing that he would not seek reelection that year. Just three weeks earlier, Senator Eugene McCarthy had run as a peace candidate in the New Hampshire primary and mounted a credible challenge against Johnson. Robert Kennedy, the president's nemesis in politics, had also declared his intention to campaign for the nomination. The war had evaporated the support that swept Johnson to victory in 1964, and it was dramatically rewriting the script for the coming national elections.

By this point, Rustin had no ties with the peace movement. He had so completely disengaged from the issue of the war that the Tet offensive and the upheaval it was causing in American politics played only in the background for him. As the opposition to Johnson's whole presidency grew, Rustin was unwilling to plot a course correction and reconsider his political strategy. A stance of critical support for Johnson remained the pivot around which his views revolved. Yet everywhere he looked, once likely allies in his dream of a new coalition politics were themselves reconsidering their loyalties. Within the United Auto Workers, important officials began working on McCarthy's campaign. In the middle of the Tet offensive, a vigorous debate broke out within Americans for Democratic Action about whether to break with Johnson and endorse McCarthy. A majority voted to support the challenger, but Rustin, who sat on the board, balked. Even when Walter Reuther, the head of the UAW, finally took a dovish position in the summer of 1968, Rustin still shied away from a stand that might have placed him in the camp pressing for an antiwar Democratic Party. Johnson was no longer running for reelection, yet Rustin continued to act as if the war was an issue that he could sweep into the corners of his consciousness, away from the main business of political engagement.

On April 4, just a few days after Johnson announced he would not seek reelection, James Earl Ray shot and killed Martin Luther King, Jr., in Memphis, Tennessee. King was there to support a strike of black sanitation workers that had polarized the city and drawn national attention. That evening, even before the news had been broadcast widely, Rustin received a call from James Lawson, who was in Memphis, telling him what had happened and asking him to come immediately. Rustin booked himself an early morning flight, but then found his plane diverted to Washington's Dulles Airport. Johnson's aides were tracking down key figures in the civil rights movement and shepherding them to the White House for an emergency meeting. Johnson told the group that he was proclaiming Sunday a national day of mourning and that he intended to address a joint session of Congress. Now he was seeking their counsel. Thurgood Marshall, whom Johnson had appointed to the Supreme Court, emphasized the need for the president to break the "mood of depression" that was overtaking the country. Rustin said that King's legacy could best be honored by actions that gave the poor in America "a reasonable hope that their condition would be relieved." Later, after he had finally arrived in Memphis, Rustin reiterated this theme. "Dr. King understood that political and social justice cannot exist without economic justice," he said at a public meeting in support of the sanitation workers. Rustin described the strike, which bound issues of race and class tightly together, as a "totally new stage" in the civil rights struggle, "the entry into economic justice" for all Americans.[33]

King's murder was a tragedy of immense proportions. It inevitably drew comparisons with the assassination of President Kennedy four years earlier. But whereas the days after Kennedy's death witnessed an orderly transfer of authority that emphasized the strength of American institutions, the killing of King seemed to snap social bonds weakened by years of racial conflict, war, and civil disorder. The next few days saw explosions of anger across the country. Riots erupted in over a hundred cities. The states and the federal government deployed over 60,000 troops to restore order. Thousands were arrested, dozens killed, and many more injured. Large portions of black neighborhoods in Chicago and Washington were engulfed by flames. Responding to the tragedy, Congress rapidly passed a fair housing bill that had long been stalled in committee, but its action could do little to quiet the fury or soften the grief that consumed the many Americans, black and white, whom King had touched.

King's assassination changed every calculation about the Poor People's Campaign that SCLC was sponsoring later in the spring. The plans called for the convergence on Washington of poor people from around the country. They would set up camp on the Mall, present themselves and their demands to official Washington, and stay until they received a response that satisfied them. King had also envisioned a larger march to punctuate the campaign, when allies of the poor would come to Washington just as supporters of racial justice had assembled there five years earlier. But now the national capital had lived through days of rioting. Almost 10,000 troops were guarding the District of Columbia, protecting the seat of government from its own citizens. Entire blocks in black neighborhoods smoldered from hundreds of fires, and many residents were now homeless. The prospect of tens of thousands of the poor setting up a vast tent city in sight of the White House, the Capitol, and other federal buildings disturbed a government already badly shaken by civil strife.

A dozen years earlier, Rustin had helped create the Southern Christian Leadership Conference. As he told Levison after King's assassination, he had seen it "as an extension" of the man he described in his grief as "the most dynamic personality of the century."[34] To stem any perception of drift and any competition for power within the organization, Coretta Scott King quickly anointed Ralph Abernathy as her husband's successor. Although he was a loyal lieutenant and friend, Abernathy lacked King's charisma. Rustin described him as "not the brightest person in the world." He remained "mostly asleep" through countless meetings about strategy. "Never in any discussion that I was in did I feel that [he] made any intellectual contribution whatever."[35] Now Abernathy was taking the helm in a national climate more volatile than any King had confronted.

The Poor People's Campaign sorely needed a skilled hand to save it from disaster. Caravans from around the country had departed for Washington at the end of April and by mid-May were converging on "Resurrection City," a makeshift encampment in the heart of the District. By every account, it was a fiasco. The weather was terrible. SCLC staff put little attention on the complex logistics of the operation. Residents lacked heaters, hot food and drinks, and dry clothes. They tramped around in the mud as they looked for any relief from their miserable shanties, many of which were damaged by the rains. Roger Wilkins, the nephew of Roy Wilkins and an official in the Johnson administration, described the morale as "very low" and the people as "cold, damp, and angry." Many of them, he noted, were "depressed, demoralized, and anxious to return to their rural southern homes." The dream of an interracial nonviolent army of the poor never materialized. Instead, racial tensions erupted as Mexican Americans and Native Americans confronted an SCLC leadership that spoke about a multiracial movement but made few efforts to include them.[36] Meanwhile, residents of Resurrection City visited various government offices, staged demonstrations, and conducted some sit-ins, but with little focus or sense that their efforts were contributing to a carefully designed campaign.

Rustin offered his services to Abernathy even before the caravans began arriving in Washington. He expressed a willingness to organize the large demonstration that was to bring supporters to the capital on June 19. Rustin wanted to enlist participants in lobbying around a concrete list of achievable demands. He thought the work of the campaign should be coordinated with the efforts of other civil rights organizations through the Leadership Council on Civil Rights, whose executive committee he chaired. Abernathy brought Rustin into the campaign, but his involvement was no more successful than the campaign itself. Taking on to himself the task of drawing up demands for the march, Rustin antagonized much of the staff of SCLC. The controversy spilled into the press, with one staffer calling Rustin "out of order" in his attempts to set policy for the campaign. Rustin tendered, and Abernathy accepted, his resignation. When the march did finally take place, it drew only 50,000 people, and a few days later federal authorities dispersed the last remaining campers from the Mall. Rustin's association with the fiasco only deepened the disdain in which many in SCLC were coming to hold him. It pushed him further away from important circles of black activism.[37]

AND STILL THE TURMOIL in the country continued. Late in April, as Rustin was starting work on the Poor People's Campaign, radical students at Columbia University seized buildings and shut down the campus in protests that drew together concerns about institutionalized racism and the university's support of the war. The actions at Columbia dominated the headlines of New York's dailies for days. They led to hundreds of arrests and triggered demonstrations at many other campuses. In June, just as Rustin was offering his resignation to Abernathy, Robert Kennedy fell victim to an assassin hours after a victory in the California primary made his campaign for the Democratic nomination seem credible. Later in the summer, when the Democrats convened in Chicago for their convention, Mayor Daley sent his police force into the city's parks and downtown areas where protesters had gathered. National television captured the police clubbing demonstrators and bystanders indiscriminately, bringing anarchy to the city and mayhem to the deliberations inside the convention.

Four years earlier, in Atlantic City, a few civil rights activists and some Southern segregationists left the Democratic National Convention feeling angry and betrayed but, overall, the party emerged ebulliently confident, ready for a triumphant national referendum. Chicago, by contrast, was a disaster. The convention nominated Hubert Humphrey, Johnson's vice president and approved successor, and adopted a platform that dutifully endorsed the president's war policies. More

white Southerners were bolting, some supporting the independent candidacy of George Wallace and others permanently shifting their alle-
giances to the Republicans. Many in the party's Northern white liberal
wing were enraged by how Humphrey, Daley, and the party regulars
had treated the peace forces at Chicago. Others were still disoriented
by the assassination of Robert Kennedy and demoralized at the way the
party leadership brushed aside internal dissent. Young activists who had
campaigned for McCarthy and Kennedy felt repudiated by the outcome, their enthusiasm for political participation dampened. Democrats returned home from Chicago in disarray. They were poorly
prepared for a national election as important as any since the one that
brought Franklin Roosevelt to the White House in 1932 and made the
Democrats the majority party for a whole generation.

In 1960, when John Kennedy and Richard Nixon faced each other in
a campaign for the presidency, Rustin had looked on the election with
disdain. Neither party unambiguously aligned itself with the goals of
the civil rights movement, and both candidates spoke the militarist language of the cold war. By 1968, the world had changed and he saw national politics through different eyes. However inadequate he judged
Johnson's Great Society programs and whatever misgivings he held
about the war, he still believed Johnson "will go down in history as having done more for civil rights than any single President who ever lived."
The gulf between the liberalism that Hubert Humphrey represented
and the politics of racial resentment that both Nixon and Wallace projected was huge. Tom Kahn, Rustin's close friend and associate, remembered thinking in those months that "I was seeing the face of
fascism. I thought it was the scariest thing I ever saw, this confrontation, this polarization, the violence." To Rustin, a Humphrey victory in
November was vital.[38]

Rustin threw himself into electoral politics in a way that he never had
before. He campaigned actively for Humphrey, riding with him in mo-
torcades, appearing with him at rallies, and signing on to fund-raising
efforts. Most of all, he tried to cut through the disenchantment, even
disgust, that existed among antiwar liberals, black militants, and white
leftists, and shake them out of their refusal to support Humphrey. Black

Americans especially, he argued, had "a life-and-death stake" in the election. The victor would appoint new justices to the Supreme Court, name the attorney general charged with enforcing civil rights legislation, and shape the staff of the federal agencies that implemented social and economic welfare policies. A Nixon victory, he wrote, will produce "a new era of social neglect at best, and repression at worst." Wallace was "openly pursuing the racist Bourbon strategy that succeeded so grotesquely well nearly a century ago." The next president, Rustin claimed, "will have the power to turn back the clock" in the way that the election of 1876 had ended Reconstruction and opened the way for the reassertion of white supremacy.[39]

By this time, Rustin had little expectation that radicals of any race who were espousing a rhetoric of revolution would rouse themselves to participate in an electoral campaign. But it distressed him that the antiwar forces in the Democratic Party would hold back their support from Humphrey. It bespoke, he thought, a disinterest among many white liberals in racial matters, a willingness to jettison progress toward racial justice because of anger about the war. To figures like Eugene McCarthy and his supporters, Rustin described the election as "a moral test for American democracy." On its results depended "the destiny of millions of black Americans" over the next generation or longer. "The threat of an American apartheid *must* repel you," Rustin wrote in an open letter that he circulated widely that October.[40]

LOCAL EVENTS IN New York City that fall mirrored the polarization in national politics. There, school issues sounded the death knell for a multiracial cross-class coalition. Between the opening of the fall term and mid-November, the city suffered through three teacher strikes that shut down the public school system and left antagonisms that lingered for a generation. It poisoned race relations, exposing deep fault lines between blacks and Jews, the labor movement and black community organizations. It left Rustin standing apart from most of the city's black leadership, both the new generation of militants and the older mainstream ones.

In the time since Rustin had organized the massive school boycott in the winter of 1964, African American and Hispanic parents had met repeated rebuffs from the New York City Board of Education. The schools became steadily more segregated, and community activists despaired of any movement toward quality integrated schooling. Many accordingly shifted ground. They campaigned instead to diminish the power of the central bureaucracy and transfer the authority to run the schools to local community boards. By 1967, Mayor John Lindsay and the Board of Education were supporting experiments in decentralization and, with funding from the Ford Foundation and state legislative approval, set up three demonstration projects.

In May 1968, Rhody McCoy, the administrator of one of the experimental districts, Ocean Hill–Brownsville in Brooklyn, informed thirteen white teachers that he was transferring them out of the district. Bernard Donovan, New York's school superintendent, called McCoy's action illegal. Albert Shanker, the president of the United Federation of Teachers, the union that represented public school teachers, attacked the action as a violation of due process guaranteed teachers under the terms of their contract. The summer saw maneuvers by all the parties to the dispute, including intense lobbying of the state legislature, court cases to return the teachers to their classrooms, and demonstrations by angry supporters of McCoy. When the school year began and the thirteen teachers were not reinstated, the UFT struck. Over the next three months, Shanker led his union in three work stoppages, disrupting the education of New York's children and the lives of almost 1 million families.

With so much racial strife engulfing the nation, it was virtually inevitable that the conflict in New York would be framed in racial terms. Membership of the UFT was almost entirely white and heavily Jewish; the families in Ocean Hill–Brownsville and the other experimental districts were overwhelmingly black and Hispanic. The move toward community control evolved out of long-standing efforts to counter the de facto segregation of schools in New York and the inferior education that the system provided children of color. The teachers' union had fought in recent years for special funding supplements for schools where student performance was below the system's average; it was also on record as supporting decentralization in principle. But its strikes threatened to sabotage the experiment before it had a chance to prove itself, and Shanker's hard-line stance antagonized not only community residents and militant activists but also much of the mainstream civil rights leadership. Whitney Young declared that a "historic intuitive sense" about prejudice shaped the strong reaction of black parents toward white teachers and that the urgency of the experiment outweighed the legal provisions of a collective bargaining agreement. Black and Puerto Rican labor leaders in the city threatened to lead a revolt in their unions if other union heads did not bring pressure to bear on Shanker.[41]

Rustin had conceived the Randolph Institute as an organization that would address controversial issues like educational policy. Early in 1968, as the first experiments began, Rustin staked out a position on the issue. Cautiously supportive in principle, he also sounded clear warnings. "Decentralization," he wrote, "must not be permitted to institutional-ize segregation." Conceived as an innovation to strengthen democratic structures, community control was to be applauded. But framed as "ethnic separation for the purpose of achieving 'self-determination,'" it appeared to Rustin as acquiescence to a stratified society that would never bring equality for African Americans. It became a new way of "in-stitutionalizing one of the worst evils in the history of this society— segregration" by hiding it in the guise of transferring power to the black community. "After all the years of our struggle," he commented, "we are now being asked to accept the idea that segregated education is in fact a perfectly respectable, perfectly desirable and perfectly viable way of life in a democratic society."[42]

When the teachers' strike began, Rustin positioned himself on the side of the UFT. Echoing the union's position, he described "the central issue" as "due process . . . the right of every worker to be judged on his merits—not his color or creed . . . [and] the right of every worker to job security." He called the Board of Education's experiment in decentralization "a giant hoax . . . perpetrated on black people by conservative and 'establishment' figures." The Board of Education, the mayor, and the elites who ran the Ford Foundation, not the teachers who worked in the schools, were the real obstacles to educational change. "I am not fooled into thinking that giving a local board control of a system will by itself substantially affect the educational system," he wrote one of his critics. "Local control is a hoax when it does not include real power, democracy and the funds to carry out new programs." Assessing the real distribution of power in New York and the rest of the country, Rustin asked, "What will prevent white community groups in Queens from firing black teachers—or white teachers with liberal views? What will prevent local Birchites and Wallaceites from taking over *their* schools and using them for *their* purposes?" Wallace, Rustin pointed out, had already "taken over the cry for local control" as he ran on a third-party ticket in the presidential campaign.[43]

As the strike dragged on and the political rhetoric of antagonists became ever more inflammatory, Rustin strove behind the scenes to exert a moderating influence on Shanker and the union. But, publicly, he never wavered in his support for the teachers, holding fast to a view of the dispute as one of due process and collective bargaining rights. He organized black trade union activists to come out in support of the teachers. When the union sponsored a rally outside City Hall, Rustin addressed the crowd and backed the strike. The reactions he received— "insulting telephone calls, vulgar letters, and general denunciation in the press," he told one reporter—suggested that there was not much appreciation in New York's black communities for his stance. From the scolding reminder that "you were black . . . before you were a trade unionist" to the more charged epithet of "house nigger," Rustin's correspondence displayed the heat and passion that the strike engendered and that partisans of community control directed at him.[44]

THE YEAR FINISHED badly. Nixon was elected president in a campaign that in its final days had grown so close that many pollsters believed just a little more time might have given Humphrey a victory. Nixon and Wallace together had received a clear majority of the popular vote. The outcome suggested a shift in the electorate away from the generous, expansive, and optimistic mood that had carried Johnson and the Democrats to power four years earlier. In New York, the teacher strikes finally ended in ways intended to be face-saving for both sides:

the move toward decentralization was affirmed, but so too were the rights of teachers to due process according to the provisions of their labor contract. The strikes and the settlement locked into place a hard core of bitterness between activists concerned about racial inequities in education and a teachers union that seemed hostile to community needs. Nationally and locally, Rustin's hopes for a progressive majority lay in tatters. Rather than work together, it seemed that everywhere the potential elements of Rustin's political coalition were squaring off against each other. The tensions between cold war foreign policies and the reform impulse at home, between the hard-won rights of a white labor movement and the not-yet-realized aspirations of African Americans, between demands for order and cries for justice, proved more potent than the strategic arguments of an independent black radical.

As the 1960s hurtled to a close, Rustin had a higher public profile than he had ever enjoyed but little shaping influence over the issues and events that mattered to him. He was now prominent enough to warrant a profile in the *New York Times Magazine*. Yet the central message of the article was the alienation of Rustin from the main currents of the black movement. It quoted Jim Farmer to the effect that "Bayard has no credibility in the black community. . . . Bayard's commitment is to labor, not to the black man." By 1969, when the article was written, Rustin's politics seemed so different from what he had formerly espoused that it became difficult for some even to remember what Rustin had once stood for. For instance, Andrew Young had become so accustomed to Rustin "advis[ing] us against things" that he told an interviewer in 1969, "He advised against the March on Washington." Summing up the central dilemma of Rustin's situation, the *Times* titled its profile "A Strategist Without a Movement."[45]

CHAPTER TWENTY

"Freedom Is Never a Final Act"
1969–1987

To RADICALS AND LIBERALS alike, the full import of Nixon's election was not immediately apparent. In the first years of his presidency, waves of protest continued to engulf the country. Black communities remained afire as local groups picketed school board meetings, targeted negligent landlords, occupied welfare offices, and rallied outside police precincts. Inspired by the example of African Americans, Puerto Ricans in the Northeast, Mexican Americans in California and the Southwest, and Native Americans throughout the West were organizing movements of their own. Deep discontent among women was spawning a revival of militant feminism. Soon women's liberation groups were campaigning against abortion laws, workplace discrimination, and sexually objectifying media images. The antiwar movement especially seemed to mushroom under Nixon's watch. In 1969, it mounted demonstrations that made the March on Washington look modest by comparison. The following year, when Nixon extended U.S. military operations into Cambodia, unrest exploded on campuses as never before, with students at several hundred schools boycotting classes. With a Republican in the White House, many congressional Democrats felt a new freedom to attack the war, which contributed to a surge in sentiment to end the conflict. When Nixon had to resign from office in 1974 because of the far-reaching Watergate scandal, it almost seemed as if his years in office were but a brief interregnum in a longer period of liberal rule.

Yet in retrospect, the 1968 election marked a major turning point in

American politics. It closed an era that began with the election of Franklin Roosevelt in 1932. For more than a generation, a cluster of liberal ideas had shaped the overall political environment. The federal government came into its own as a major force in the country's life. In the 1930s, the national state embarked on an activist role at home as it established programs designed to mitigate some of the harshest effects of capitalism's inequalities. By the 1960s, it took up the cause of civil rights and became a defender of basic constitutional freedoms across the color line. Abroad, liberalism shaped an internationalist outlook that found expression in the war against German and Japanese fascism and, later, opposition to Soviet expansionism.

This long liberal ascendancy had shaped the trajectory of Rustin's public life. It allowed him to be the gadfly, the critic on the outside who pointed to the contradictions and hypocrisies in government policy and pushed beyond liberalism's limitations. He pressed against its most glaring failure, its willingness to tolerate white supremacy and racial apartheid for so long. He challenged its confidence that military force, an arms race, and a burgeoning defense establishment would ever succeed in permanently bringing peace or justice to the world. In a sense, liberalism enabled Rustin's career and outlook. It created an environment in which he was able to agitate. As liberalism's star grew steadily weaker in the 1970s and 1980s, the opportunities for Rustin to build popular movements of resistance dimmed too.

Nixon's election marked a turning point for Rustin in another more immediate way: it instantly reshaped the political context. It closed the strategic opening that had elicited Rustin's most provocative challenge to the civil rights movement and the left. No longer could one plausibly claim that a progressive coalition might seize the initiative and construct a new majority. Instead, the Nixon White House played to the polarization that was fracturing American society and did all it could to cripple progressive political mobilizations.

From the beginning, Rustin knew that Richard Nixon in the White House spelled bad news for everything he cared about. "We're in a period like the Red Queen described to Alice in Wonderland," he told a gathering of young socialists in 1969. "It takes a great deal of running to stand still." Summarizing the political outlook, he reported to the Randolph Institute's directors that "white fear and black rage smolder— and sometimes explode—as a result of a do-nothingism, conservatism, empty rhetoric, and strategies that are often deliberately divisive." Nixon was ushering in "a period in which the Federal Government can no longer be depended upon as an ally in the struggle for racial justice, but is rather an enemy." At an AFL-CIO convention, he decried the steps the White House had taken to build "a new conservative coalition to keep the Republican Party in power for the next twenty years." The administration, said Rustin, was "paying off Strom Thurmond" for his shift to the Republican Party. Nixon's "Southern strategy" was deliberately wooing the white South into the Republican fold by temporizing on racial equality, pulling back from enforcement of civil rights legislation, and making appointments to the federal judiciary designed to appeal to conservatives.[1]

The adverse political environment initially spurred Rustin forward. He used the concern in liberal circles about Nixon's election to step up his fund-raising for the Randolph Institute, and its budget more than doubled in 1969. He put Norman Hill in charge of an initiative to expand voter registration and increase political participation among African Americans, the very kind of work he had repeatedly urged on King and the SCLC. Tapping into networks of black trade unionists, the Randolph Institute quickly built a chain of affiliates spread across the country: from 24 groups in 1970, to 150 by 1974, to almost 200 by the end of the decade, with a presence in almost every state that had a significant black population. Although the effort was technically nonpartisan, more than 90 percent of the voters whom APRI turned out each November cast ballots for Democratic candidates. As more and more blacks in the North and the South ran for office in the 1970s, the Randolph Institute helped provide the political base that elected them.[2]

Rustin also wrote prolifically during this period. In 1971, he published a collection of his political essays, *Down the Line*. He turned out a regular column that dozens of newspapers picked up. Major pieces appeared in mainstream publications like *Harper's*, and he received invitations to contribute to mass circulation magazines like *Newsweek*. Rustin sounded a consistent message. He called liberals to task for abandoning any serious hope of achieving social justice, and he pressed them to keep crusading instead of accommodating to the new conservatism. He praised labor for its loyalty to a legislative agenda that, if enacted, would raise the economic floor for working Americans and reduce the ranks of the poor. And he held fast to his belief in coalition, which now served for him as a path out of the morass of the Nixon era.

Rustin reserved some of his most cutting prose for the penchant toward black separatism that still held sway among many community activists in the early 1970s. He was merciless in his criticism of its proponents. Many of them, he said, had become "household names through the notoriety [black power] generated." But where were they now? Stokely Carmichael had left the United States for Africa. H. Rap Brown, who had succeeded Carmichael as chairman of SNCC, was in jail, and Eldridge Cleaver, another high-profile militant, was under house arrest in Algeria. Floyd McKissick, who had led CORE away from its allegiance to nonviolence, had become a real estate entrepreneur and a Republican. Rustin lashed into nationalist politics as a "new tribalism" that promoted "a fantasy view of society." He described it as "a politics of escape" that vindicated "a withdrawal from social struggle into a kind of hermetic racial world." He attacked it for promoting conservative self-help strategies. With their own words, he exposed militants like Hosea Williams, a fiery SCLC staff member who had often attacked Rustin's politics. "I'm now at the position Booker T. Washington was about sixty or seventy years ago," he quoted Williams as saying. "Passionate self-assertion," Rustin wrote in response, "can be a mask for accommodation."[3]

Rustin openly criticized not only the rhetoric of black nationalists but also key goals that animated activists in the early 1970s. He saw the continuing focus on community control of the schools as a disaster and described the concept as "incompatible with a political program committed to social and racial justice." With political power shifting toward conservatives, community control would inevitably degenerate into "a refuge for bigotry" deployed by whites to avoid both integration and a commitment to quality education for everyone.[4] For decades, local control had been part of the rhetoric of Southern whites resisting any interference in racial matters; now Northern white suburbanites could wield the concept to keep their schools free from blacks in neighboring communities. The growing emphasis on affirmative action similarly struck Rustin as misplaced. The poor turn that the economy took after Nixon became president and the continuing hard economic times of the 1970s made affirmative action an ineffective strategy. It could not work "if it must function within the context of scarcity," he testified at a congressional hearing. Only the creation of new jobs, coupled with compensatory education and training, would lift the economic standing of the African American poor.[5]

For all his activity, however, Rustin felt himself swimming against a political tide far more powerful than his exhortations. Invited to give the 1970 commencement address at Tuskegee Institute, he used the historic setting to place the moment within the broad sweep of African American experience. "What is happening today is not very different from what happened in the 1870s," he told the overwhelmingly black assemblage. A century ago, an interracial movement of Southern blacks and Northern whites was collapsing as the federal government withdrew its support for the freed population and the Republican Party made common cause with white supremacists in the South. The end of Reconstruction "initiated the darkest period in the history of American Negroes," he reminded them. "The system of Jim Crow was constructed, and lynchings and terrorism became commonplace." Like then, the nation was now "at a crossroads." Nixon's strategy for building a Republican Party was ushering in a new period of racist politics. "I can think of no President who has more blatantly sacrificed the ideals of equality and racial justice for his own political ends. . . . Nixon is not simply riding the wave of reaction. He is encouraging that reaction." A century earlier at Tuskegee, Booker T. Washington had constructed a self-help philosophy that had acquiesced to segregation. To Rustin, contemporary radicals were making the same mistake. Separatist approaches "can only aid and abet Nixon's Southern Strategy. . . . Separatism is the opposite of self-determination . . . it can only lead to the continued subjection of blacks."

Rustin cautioned the graduates against the growing tendency to "indulge in any way in the feeble decadence of [an] end-of-the-world school of thought." The situation was not hopeless, he told them, yet his own words belied his hopes. "History is a dialectical process," Rustin lectured. "It consists of alternating periods of movement and stagnation, of action and reaction, of tremendous hope and enthusiasm . . . followed by a descent into cynicism and exhaustion." He meant these words as preface to the point that understanding the rhythms of history was a first step toward the power to shape the future. But his own pessimistic pronouncement—"the pendulum of history has *already* begun to swing downward"—could not have offered much encouragement to his young audience.[6]

Rustin had lived through periods far bleaker than the Nixon years. In the early 1950s, he confronted not only cold war hysteria, when almost any form of dissent elicited the charge of "Communist," but also the stigma of Pasadena. Now, at least, many others were out in the streets, aroused and engaged. But with each passing month, Rustin sensed that the capacious opportunities of a few years earlier, when the potential of the black freedom struggle seemed unlimited, were fast receding into history. His own frenzied pace had little impact on events, and frustration bred a deep gloom. The new mood showed. After Rustin visited his Aunt Bessie early in May 1971, she expressed her worry directly. "You are so busy and so much in demand," she wrote. "I am much concerned about you. You seem depressed, not as jolly or as happy as you used to be."[7] That fall, the pressure he worked under exacted its toll. While visiting Bob and Joyce Gilmore at their country estate in upstate New York, Rustin suffered a massive heart attack and was rushed to a nearby hospital.

This was not Rustin's first health scare. He had checked himself into the hospital a couple of times in the 1960s when he feared he might be experiencing a heart attack. But these panics had proven groundless and, except for some failed attempts to stop smoking, he continued life as before. This time, he had a close brush with death. He spent three weeks in the hospital and then, still convalescing, moved to the Gilmore house in Greenwich Village, where he could more easily receive the kind of attention he needed. An extra phone line was installed so that Rustin could make and receive calls. But his doctors ordered him to "stay out of the office for several months" since too quick a return to his usual pace of work could be fatal.[8]

The enforced break proved to be something more than a temporary respite. After it, he never again quite threw himself into campaigns for racial justice and economic reforms in the same way. He still made efforts to mobilize black voters during election years. When Andrew Young ran for a seat in the House of Representatives in 1972, Rustin was "glad to do all I can to help."[9] He supported Jimmy Carter's campaigns for the presidency in 1976 and 1980. He testified at numerous congressional hearings, and he remained in close touch with organizational leaders like Vernon Jordan of the Urban League and Roy Wilkins, who still headed the NAACP. He raised money to keep the Randolph Institute growing. But he turned more and more of its daily work over to Norman Hill. The institute became his pulpit, allowing him to speak out on issues as he saw fit. When he did address domestic policy, he stressed the need for "a nonracial strategy" to achieve equality. But all these were words lost in the vast pool of public debate. By the time Nixon left office in disgrace in 1974, Rustin already was no longer the organizer attempting to build the next phase of a black freedom movement. Domestic matters elicited his opinions but rarely his actions.

As Rustin retreated from the role of movement builder and strategist at home, he turned once again to international affairs. In the last fifteen years of his life, he devoted more of his time to events abroad than in any other stretch of his career, yet his focus was very different from the years when he worked for pacifist organizations. No longer did he walk picket lines in front of the French embassy or the Pentagon, bring peace caravans to American communities, or lead marches against nuclear weaponry. Rustin now traveled in very different circles. He was on a first-name basis with individuals such as Donald Rumsfeld, President Ford's secretary of defense, and Cyrus Vance, the secretary of state during the Carter administration. He attended international conferences where he rubbed shoulders with heads of major corporations and key officials in foreign governments. The photographic record shows Rustin in conversation with, among others, Golda Meir, the Israeli prime minister, and Lech Walesa, the leader of the Solidarity movement in Poland.

Though it would be an exaggeration to claim that Rustin had become part of a policy-making elite, he did circulate among a network of influential public figures who devoted themselves to human rights and global humanitarianism. According to one of his closest associates in these years, "Bayard never gave up his personal pacifism, he just didn't. . . . He always believed that nonviolent tactics were ultimately the best way to go [and] you weren't going to create a peaceful society by conducting war." But pacifism had come to seem "politically irrelevant" to him. Nations were not going to relinquish arms because someone exhorted them to do so, but warfare might become less commonplace if democratic rights were the global norm and the wealthier states extended humanitarian assistance more freely.[10]

Rustin's turn toward foreign affairs came just as the United States as a whole was experiencing what became known as the Vietnam syndrome. In the wake of the calamitous war in Southeast Asia, neither Congress nor the electorate was much inclined to support the interventionism that had defined policy for much of the cold war. The constraints on the use of American military power in the 1970s and early 1980s reverberated around the world. Anti-Communist dictatorships that the United States supported, like the Somoza regime in Nicaragua, the shah in Iran, and the Marcos government in the Philippines, succumbed to revolutionary upheavals. In the Middle East, oil-producing states demonstrated a new assertiveness about control of their natural resources. They provoked an economic crisis in the United States when they imposed an embargo on oil exports and substantially raised prices. Reflecting this changed environment, President Jimmy Carter made support for human rights rather than containment of communism the rhetorical centerpiece of his foreign policy.

Positioning himself as an advocate of democracy and human rights, Rustin worked primarily through two organizations, Freedom House and the International Rescue Committee (IRC). The two groups had similar histories. Each was established in the 1940s in response to the spread of Nazi power in Europe. Eleanor Roosevelt and Wendell Willkie, the Republican nominee for president in 1940, were among the founders of Freedom House, which took pride in a bipartisan internationalism that supported democratic institutions around the globe. After World War II, it easily reconstituted itself as an element in the anti-Communist consensus that shaped American foreign policy, though it emphasized support for human rights and the exposure of totalitarian abuses rather than military intervention. IRC had a more focused mission. Initially created to spirit Jews out of Nazi-occupied Europe, it converted itself in the postwar era into an agency devoted to refugee problems around the globe. Leo Cherne, who led the organization from the early 1950s into the 1990s, built it into a major force. Assessing his own career, Cherne once said, "I hope I'll be remembered as a cold warrior," and, consistent with this self-assessment, the IRC especially publicized refugee problems that stemmed from Russian rule.[11] In 1980, Cherne abandoned a lifelong allegiance to the Democratic Party and supported Reagan for president because of his hard-line cold war views. Thus, Rustin's work with Freedom House and the IRC inevitably strengthened the anti-Communist inflection in his outlook even if he expressed it through support for human rights.

In the 1970s and 1980s, Rustin circled the globe many times on missions for Freedom House. The organization enlisted him as one of its election observers, a role that he had first undertaken in the mid-1960s when he traveled to the Dominican Republic with Norman Thomas. He toured Zimbabwe in 1979 and again in 1980 as it made its transition from a white-settler-dominated regime to black majority rule. He drove through towns and villages in El Salvador in 1982, as its people attempted to vote in the middle of a civil war. He made trips to Lebanon, South Africa, and Barbados as well. In most cases, his evaluations were sharply qualified, combining modest optimism with an acknowledgment of the constraints that many nations faced. He described the Zimbabwe elections as "free but not entirely fair." About El Salvador he said that while the election was a "forward step," the country would face for years to come "serious problems of human rights, security, law-lessness, and economic decline."[12]

In these years, the agony of refugees seemed to release Rustin's passions in the way that advocacy of an absolutist pacifism once did. In the last decade of his life, he became one of the chief emissaries of the IRC, as he participated in numerous international missions and advocated for a more humane policy to admit refugees into the United States. He spoke out about the suffering of Ugandans who fled the brutality of Idi Amin's rule. He visited camps overflowing with refugees in Somalia and Sudan, where more than a million had escaped fighting in Ethiopia and Eritrea. He toured sites in Pakistan filled with Afghans who left after the Soviet Union invaded. He witnessed the impact of civil conflict in Guatemala and El Salvador as residents escaped to Mexico to avoid the violence of both right-wing death squads and left-wing guerrillas. He glimpsed apartheid through the eyes of refugees in Lesotho and Botswana. Rustin's travels served as an itinerary marking the world's most intense trouble spots.

Most of all, Rustin agitated on behalf of refugees displaced by war and revolution in Southeast Asia. In the wake of the final American departure from Vietnam in 1975 and the collapse of the South Vietnamese government, hundreds of thousands tried to escape the country. In neighboring Cambodia, a flood of humanity crossed into Thailand in flight from the mass slaughter perpetrated by the Khmer Rouge. Perhaps because American policy had contributed so directly to the chaos in the region and he had done so little about it, Rustin seemed especially intent on exposing the suffering in the region. He made four trips to the camps in Thailand. After the first one in February 1978, Rustin returned home ready to lobby for expanding the number of refugees that the United States admitted each year. He and other members of the IRC delegation met with Vice President Walter Mondale and Zbigniew Brzezinski, Carter's national security adviser, as well as officials in the State Department. Rustin secured endorsement from the executive committee of the AFL-CIO, a not insignificant achievement since immigration of any kind was a volatile issue among union members. He collected signatures from a who's who of black leadership for an ad in the *New York Times* backing admission of refugees. "If our government lacks compassion for these dispossessed human beings," Rustin wrote, "it is difficult to believe that the same government can have much compassion for America's black minority, or for America's poor." He expressed similar sentiments in testimony before the House Judiciary Committee.[13]

While Rustin's work on behalf of refugees certainly was consistent with the spirit of his earlier pacifist activity, his stance on Middle East issues troubled many of his old associates in the peace movement. Ever since the 1967 Six-Day War, when Israeli military forces launched a preemptive attack and occupied parts of Syria, Jordan, and Egypt, segments of the American New Left and antiwar movement came to interpret the conflict in the Middle East through the lens of anticolonialism. In this view, Israel was perceived as the region's surrogate for the Western powers. Like Ho Chi Minh and the National Liberation Front in Vietnam, Yasir Arafat and the Palestinian Liberation Organization were viewed as freedom fighters resisting imperialist power. While support for Israel grew stronger among American liberals and conservatives after 1967, it waned steadily among radicals on the left.

In 1970, Rustin plunged into the politics of the Middle East when he rallied a group of civil rights leaders and black public officials behind an appeal to Washington to supply Israel with jets and guarantee its right to exist. He was forthright in his defense of Israel. "It is by far the most democratic country in the Middle East," he wrote in response to criticism. "Countries like Iraq, Syria, and Egypt are dictatorial one-party states." He bemoaned the fact that Palestinian guerrillas had became "culture heroes" to many young American radicals. Recalling Marx's statement that religion was the opiate of the people, he said that Israel had become "the opiate of the Arabs." Hatred of Israel was deliberately wielded by "proto-fascist dictatorships" in the region. Their "prolonged and inflammatory calls for the destruction of Israel can only divert precious attention, energy, and resources away from an attack on the pressing social and economic problems of the Arab people." Revolution was needed in the Middle East, Rustin declared. "But it is not a revolution that will involve the destruction of Israel, but rather one that would require the overthrow of conservative and oil-rich Arab governments who have done little or nothing to liberate their people from poverty and misery."[14]

Rustin never wavered in his support for Israel even as he acknowledged that it "created a tension" with his personal pacifism. In 1975, after the General Assembly of the United Nations passed a resolution describing Zionism as a form of racism, Rustin formed the Black Americans to Support Israel Committee to counter the claim. He was particularly appalled by the willingness of some civil rights leaders to express sympathy for the PLO. In a series of op-ed pieces written in 1979, after Andrew Young and Jesse Jackson made highly publicized contacts with the PLO, Rustin characterized it as "an organization committed to racism, terrorism and authoritarianism." To embrace Arafat was to repudiate the legacy of Martin Luther King, Jr., and the civil rights movement, he asserted. Instead, he argued for recognition of the historic affinity of blacks and Jews—"the only groups in American society systematically targeted by the Ku Klux Klan, the Nazis, and other extremist sects." Speaking to the Anti-Defamation League in 1980, Rustin declared that blacks and Jews were "inextricably linked in a world often hostile to their interests. They are linked by their common suffering and they are linked by their commitment to human rights and freedom." He described his work for human rights, the black freedom struggle in the United States, and the efforts of Jews to preserve a homeland as planks in the platform of what he called "the international party of human rights."[15]

AS THE COUNTRY GREW more conservative in these years, Rustin never retreated into private concerns. Yet his personal life took a direction that he had little reason to anticipate. On a sunny afternoon in April 1977, a month after he turned sixty-five, love finally arrived in his life. Waiting for the light to change on a corner of Times Square and 42nd Street, Rustin glanced over at the pedestrian standing beside him.

It was an unseasonably warm day for early spring, and he noticed that the younger man was wearing shorts. Their eyes locked, and as they crossed the street, they began chatting, the spark of desire obvious to each of them. The object of Rustin's interest introduced himself as Walter and explained that he was on his way to Hotaling, a vendor of out-of-town newspapers a few doors down the block. Rustin said he would wait and, when his new acquaintance returned with a San Francisco newspaper, the two walked together to Rustin's apartment a mile away in Chelsea.

Walter Naegle had grown up in a suburban town in northern New Jersey. Trained as a musician in his childhood, he was strongly attracted to the folk scene of the early 1960s and its socially conscious lyrics. Black protest was at its height during his high school years, and he remembered Rustin as a frequently quoted figure in the New York press. By the time Naegle was in college, the rising draft calls of the Vietnam era forced him to scrutinize his beliefs about war, and he wrote to organizations like the AFSC and the FOR for information about conscientious objection. He eventually dropped out of college to become a volunteer in VISTA, a Great Society program that was the domestic equivalent of the Peace Corps. Initially assigned to a senior citizens program on the South Side of Chicago, he returned east early in 1970 to work at a psychiatric hospital in Manhattan.

Naegle was twenty-seven when he met Rustin. He had come to Times Square that afternoon because he had just decided that he wanted to move to San Francisco and was seeking a local newspaper to scout out the job and housing market. For someone like Naegle, San Francisco's allure was almost irresistible. Seedbed of the hippie counterculture and a center of progressive politics, it had become in the 1970s a mecca for gay men from around the country. His chance encounter with Rustin changed his plans abruptly.

The relationship posed challenges for each of them. "I hadn't had a long-term relationship at that point," Naegle reminisced. "I saw myself pinching myself a little bit, wondering if this could be happening to me, being involved with this magnificent person who was somewhat of a hero to me, whom I had known about when I was growing up." On Rustin's side, a certain wariness tempered his enthusiasm. According to Naegle, Rustin "was scared, I know, especially during the first few months because I had this [plan], I was going to San Francisco. So you're developing a relationship with someone, you're developing feeling for someone, but there's this sword of Damocles hanging over you. How far do you want to go?" Yet before long, they were seeing each other almost every evening. "We were both fairly comfortable immediately," Naegle claimed. By summer, the relationship had deepened enough that "I pretty much made up my mind that I was going to stay here and pursue this."[16]

Rustin was notoriously tight-lipped about his personal life. He virtually never spoke for the record about his earlier relationships with Davis Platt, Tom Kahn, or any of the other men with whom he had briefer connections; he preserved to the end his generation's habits of discretion. Neither did he talk publicly about Naegle, except once. In the last year of his life he described to an interviewer what the relationship meant to him and how he had changed:[17]

The most important thing is that after many years of seeking, I've finally found a solid, ongoing relationship with one individual with whom I have everything in common, everything. . . . I spent years looking for exciting sex instead of looking for a person who was compatible. I really did. I overemphasized sex and underemphasized relationships. I'm not talking for anyone but myself. That was the basis of my problem. I had three other early experiences. One lasted for four years and one for three, but they were never really real. I was trying to make something of them, but they were not real. It seems unbelievable at my age, particularly. Let me tell you what my final answer is in this regard. . . . It's a matter of being lucky enough to run into someone with whom one is just completely *simpatico*. I don't think that we do it. I think it is, somehow, done unto us. It's like being born. We haven't anything to do with it.

By the first anniversary of their meeting, the two were already living to-gether. They settled into a comfortable domesticity that lasted for the rest of Rustin's life.

It was a good time for Rustin to build a relationship. He had just handed over the reins of the Randolph Institute to Norman Hill. Rustin remained its titular head, and he still wrote a regular column that ap-peared in papers around the country. But he no longer had to attend to the day-to-day operations of an organization. The urgency that had of-ten driven him in the past had subsided. "He was more easy going" is how Naegle described him. "You know, you're not going to solve all the world's problems, the world's been around for a hell of a lot longer than you have. You do what you can . . . he was more relaxed, more philo-sophical in his attitude . . . he was really able to enjoy the time that he had with friends and people."

During his years with Naegle, Rustin was finally able fully to indulge his love of the city. These were difficult times for New York. It teetered on the verge of bankruptcy, was placed in receivership, suffered through a major power blackout and a major strike of garbage collectors, and became a national symbol of urban decay. In Rustin's words, it was "dirty, congested, crime ridden." When the city ran a major advertising campaign promoting itself as "the Big Apple," Rustin joked to an old friend that it was more like "the mellow peach—that stage between ripe and rotten." Yet "somehow I love this place because, in spite of all its faults, it still has a busyness, a vitality, a dynamism, a stench, a joy."[18] On weekends, he and Naegle often wandered the streets of Lower Man-hattan. They browsed a large flea market on Sixth Avenue and stopped in many of the antique shops, chatting with the dealers whom Rustin knew from long years of buying. At the end of the day, they wound their way to Greenwich Village, where Bob Gilmore and his wife, Elizabeth, lived, as did Charley Bloomstein, an old friend from the 1930s who had returned to New York and kept the accounts for the Randolph In-stitute.

With more time on his hands, Rustin's passion for collecting, espe-cially antique furniture and religious objects, burst all bounds. He at-tended auctions frequently and often came away with yet another purchase. Bloomstein, who sometimes accompanied Rustin, described him as "insatiable. . . . [He] never sold anything, only acquired." Naegle described it as "a frenzy . . . this frenzied pace of acquiring things. Nice things, beautiful things, but nevertheless they had to be dusted, they had to be paid for, they had to be [cared for]." Their apartment resembled a museum. "The rooms are alive with a multiformity of free-standing sculpture, architectural ornaments, Chinese porcelain, ceremonial objects and furniture," one visitor wrote. African wood sculpture and ivories mingled promiscuously with European religious artifacts.[19]

Naegle helped Rustin heal some of the old wounds from the 1960s. Though Naegle had not crafted an activist life of his own, he did have pacifist inclinations and encouraged Rustin to renew his ties to at least some of his former comrades. "He never harbored any personal dislike" toward those with whom he had broken politically, Naegle recalled, and "he had great affection for David [McReynolds] and for Ralph [Di-Gia] and for Igal [Roodenko]" at the War Resisters League. In the 1980s, they began going to WRL events. Rustin helped raise money for the War Resisters International Triennial Conference in India in 1985 and, accompanied by Naegle, attended it. McReynolds was there, and Michael Randle too, along with others who had participated in the antinuclear mobilizations and African independence activities of the 1950s and 1960s. Randle remembered that "in the evening he would 'hold court'—I can't think of any other description for it—in the canopied area in one corner of the Ashram." To McReynolds, Rustin appeared "exciting, alive" and he wondered if, perhaps, Rustin was not "edging his way back to us at the end."[20]

Naegle exerted another kind of influence as well. Through him, Rustin tentatively inched toward the new gay world that was forming in New York and other large American cities. The upheavals of the 1960s had extended beyond matters of racial justice and American foreign policy. In the words of Charles Kaiser, a historian of urban gay life, "Because everything was being questioned, for a moment anything could be imagined—even a world in which homosexuals would finally win a measure of equality."[21] In June 1969, Greenwich Village had been the scene of several nights of rioting after police raided the Stonewall Inn, a popular gay bar. Within a matter of months, "gay liberation" groups were forming in cities and university towns around the country. Many of the young gay men and lesbians who had been radicalized by the events of the sixties were now choosing to march "out of the closets and into the streets," as a popular slogan of the times phrased it, for their own freedom. Their new organizations mobilized against police harassment, challenged the erasures and distortions of media coverage of gay life, and fought the widespread discriminatory practices typical in almost every sphere of American society. In the course of the seventies and eighties, a quasi-fugitive subculture reconfigured itself as an urban community. Gays and lesbians created an impressive array of institutions—community centers, health clinics, churches, synagogues, newspapers, magazines, recreational organizations, and professional associations.

Although Naegle himself had not been actively involved in gay liberation groups, he was of that age cohort and shared its ethos. "Bayard came from a generation that really didn't talk about these things," he recalled. "I was more open than he was." At first, this openness simply translated into new patterns of socializing—for instance, going dancing on a Saturday night at one of the many discos that gay men now patronized, confident that police would leave them alone. Greenwich Village in these years was a neighborhood transformed as gay men lounged on street corners openly expressing affection and congregated outside popular meeting places.

By the 1980s, Naegle was pushing Rustin to take a next step. There were still relatively few homosexuals of stature who had come out, whereas Rustin's sexual identity was a matter of public record. He was wanted as a role model, or spokesperson, by a movement that claimed allegiance to ideals of justice and equality to which Rustin had devoted his life. As invitations from gay organizations arrived in the mail, Naegle "encouraged him to go speak at these things. I think if I hadn't been working in the office at the time, when these invitations came in he probably wouldn't have done them. . . . Something else would have taken priority." Gay black men especially sought him out. In the early 1980s, he addressed the national conference of Black and White Men Together, an organization explicitly focused on supporting interracialism and fighting manifestations of racism inside and outside the gay community. Soon he began receiving requests regularly—from local chapters in eastern cities, from religious organizations like Integrity, which represented gay and lesbian Episcopalians, and increasingly from groups that were more directly engaging the political process.

Meanwhile, the appearance of AIDS was adding a life-and-death urgency to the fight against gay oppression. From the beginning, the epidemic had disproportionately hit gay and bisexual men of color. Moreover, New York was one of the epicenters of this terrifying new public health crisis, and the metropolitan area was the site of more than half the recorded cases of AIDS in the first years of the epidemic. AIDS also brought to the surface deeply rooted antagonisms toward homosexuality, and incidences of violence and discrimination grew alarmingly. Gay organizations multiplied their efforts to have the New York City Council add sexual orientation to the list of protected categories in its human rights code. First proposed by gay activists in 1971, the measure had remained bottled up in committee for years.

A citywide Coalition for Lesbian and Gay Rights enlisted Rustin in its effort to break the legislative logjam. In 1985 and 1986, he exerted his not inconsiderable influence by lobbying Mayor Ed Koch and the city council. After meeting with gay activists, Rustin sent a letter to Koch, with whom he was on a first-name basis, offering to help "in any way that I can" to pass the "long overdue lesbian and gay rights bill." To African American members of the city council, many of whom were opponents of the bill, he described the refusal to vote the bill out of committee as "tantamount to the filibustering that succeeded in blocking the Civil Rights Legislation in the U.S. from 1876 until 1964." He described the "false assumptions and unfounded fears" preventing passage as "similar to those which were cited in the attempts to block previous civil rights legislation." After the city council finally approved the bill in March 1986, a move emerged among opponents to introduce amendments that would scuttle the new law. Rustin testified at city council hearings against any revisions. Describing himself as chairman of the executive committee of the national Leadership Conference on Civil

Rights and laying claim to two dozen arrests for human rights, he told members of the city council that "history demonstrates that no group is ultimately safe from prejudice, bigotry, and harassment so long as any group is subject to special negative treatment."[22]

Rustin's lobbying for the gay rights bill led to additional involvements. After the Supreme Court sustained the constitutionality of sodomy laws in *Bowers v. Hardwick* in June 1986, he spoke at a rally held by gay groups outside the federal courthouse at Foley Square, where he had addressed civil rights issues in the past.[23] He gave a series of interviews to gay activists, journalists, and scholars.[24] The interviews touched many of the high points of his career. But unlike interviews he did for the Johnson Presidential Library or the Columbia University Oral History Project, these discussed the ways that homophobia curtailed his influence in the civil rights movement, and they provide the only recorded reflections of his gay experience.

In all of these interviews, the final message that Rustin offered to his contemporary audience was the same: "prejudice is of a single bit." In the 1960s, he said, "The barometer of people's thinking was the black community. Today, the barometer of where one is on human rights questions is no longer the black, it's the gay community." Discussing the role of churches in struggles for justice, Rustin declared that "there are very few liberal Christians today who would dare say anything other than blacks are our brothers and they should be treated so, but they will make all kinds of hideous distinctions when it comes to our gay brothers. . . . There are great numbers of people who will accept all kinds of people: blacks, Hispanics, and Jews, but who won't accept fags. That is what makes the homosexual central to the whole political apparatus as to how far we can go in human rights."

Even with his forays into this new gay world and politics, Rustin remained not quite of it. Early in 1986, Joseph Beam invited Rustin to contribute to an anthology of writings by black gay men. "After much thought," Rustin wrote, "I have decided that I must decline. . . . I did not 'come out of the closet' voluntarily—circumstances forced me out. While I have no problem with being publicly identified as homosexual, it would be dishonest of me to present myself as one who was in the forefront of the struggle for gay rights. The credit for that belongs to others. They are the ones who should be in your book. While I support full equality, under law, for homosexuals, I fundamentally consider sexual orientation to be a private matter. As such, it has not been a factor which has greatly influenced my role as an activist."[25]

Though Rustin might have wished for a world in which sexuality remained sequestered in the private realm, he could not avoid the workings of gay oppression. Settling into a committed relationship in his older age, he had to confront the lack of formal recognition for his connection to Naegle. Same-sex marriage and domestic partnership had not yet become contested public issues, and the question of how to secure Naegle's standing as his next of kin was a vexing one. Rustin's death could leave Naegle homeless, since New York's rent control laws did not recognize same-sex partners as family; it would also leave matters of inheritance open to challenge from family members in West Chester. A few years into the relationship, when Rustin learned that his dear friend, Bob Gilmore, had been diagnosed with Alzheimer's disease, he resolved to act. Scribbling a note to his lawyer, he commented that the news about Gilmore has "led me to some reflection. I do not know how to state it, but I should like a codicil to my will to give Walter Naegle complete authority to handle my affairs including personal property, real and unreal, including stocks, bonds, or anything else I possess." The difference in their ages allowed his attorney to devise a way to evade the inability to marry. In order to strengthen Naegle's claim as heir and closest relative, Rustin adopted him as his son.[26]

Rustin was able to share with Naegle the honors and recognition that came his way in his final decade. President Carter named him to the Holocaust Memorial Commission. Harvard, Yale, and a number of other institutions awarded him honorary degrees. Though no longer in the thick of political struggles, he had the ear of many in government and public life who sought his advice. Vernon Jordan of the Urban League described Rustin in these years as the "chairman of the ideas committee" for the nation's black leadership, "an intellectual bank where we all had unlimited accounts and were never told that we were overdrawn." Sometimes the celebrity would get to him. "There were moments when he was full of himself," Naegle recalled, but there was also, always, "this little boyish quality" about him. About Rustin's sense of self-importance, Naegle said "he just didn't *believe* it."[27]

RUSTIN TURNED SEVENTY-FIVE on March 17, 1987, with a party of some 600 guests and a formal dinner at the New York Hilton. He was showing no signs of slowing down. The previous year he had traveled to three continents to observe elections, met with opposition groups in various countries, and reviewed the progress of the Helsinki Accords. In the months after his birthday, he journeyed to Thailand to visit once again the camps for Cambodian refugees; to Chile and Paraguay to make contact with individuals working to restore democracy in the two countries; and to Haiti to assess whether the elections proposed for the fall had much chance of taking place without violence and intimidation.[28]

Naegle accompanied Rustin on the trip to Haiti and, after they returned in late July, both fell ill. Their doctor said they were suffering from intestinal parasites and prescribed medication. Naegle was soon better, but Rustin continued to complain of abdominal pains and was running a mild fever. A second doctor put him on another treatment regimen, but it was no more effective than the first. Naegle recalled that Rustin "was getting worse. He didn't have any energy, he was spending a lot of time in bed, he wouldn't get up, he'd sort of plod his way through a day." On Friday, August 21, with the pain steadily worsening, Naegle took him to the emergency room at Lenox Hill hospital on Manhattan's East Side. The medical staff diagnosed a burst appendix and peritonitis, and a team of physicians performed emergency surgery.

Naegle spent much of the weekend at the hospital. On Sunday, he recalled, Rustin began "acting strange. He was saying things that weren't rational. He had this vision of himself being in London, and he was talking about people he knew from the old days and singing London-based British hymns, conducting the orchestra with his hands, lying in bed with this *lovely* smile on his face. There was nothing hostile or unhappy about it." The doctors thought it was probably a reaction to one of the painkillers since all the medical indicators suggested he was recovering according to expectations. Naegle went home at the end of the day and spent the evening calling friends and close associates of Rustin to report on his condition. As he got ready for bed, he received a call from one of their private-duty nurses telling him that "Mr. Rustin is having some trouble and he's asking for you. Could you possibly come up?" Naegle raced to the hospital, but the staff would not let him see Rustin even though he was listed as next of kin. Naegle frantically telephoned his sister, who had been president of the state nurses' association, in the hope that she could pull some weight. Once she arrived, they finally received permission to go upstairs. They waited in the hall as doctors worked on Rustin. Just after midnight, the attending physician told Naegle that Rustin had died of a heart attack.

Rustin's body was cremated according to his wishes and, later, his ashes were buried in upstate New York, at the Gilmore estate where he had spent much time over the previous two decades. In October, a memorial service was held at the Community Church in Manhattan. Rustin had spoken there many times in the past—debating Malcolm X, memorializing the slain children of Birmingham, explaining the progress of the freedom struggle in the South to a New York audience. Now it was the turn of others to talk about him. Most of the speakers were from the last period of Rustin's life: Norman Hill, who had run the Randolph Institute for the last ten years; Rabbi Marc Tanenbaum of the American Jewish Committee and Liv Ullmann, the Swedish film actress, both of whom had traveled with Rustin to refugee camps in Thailand; Vernon Jordan; Lane Kirkland, the president of the AFL-CIO. But the Reverend Thomas Kilgore, who had worked with him on the Prayer Pilgrimage, and John Lewis, now a member of Congress, were there to pay tribute to the glory years of the civil rights movement. Charles Bloomstein, who had known Rustin the longest, made passing reference to the pacifism that informed his early life.[29]

Despite the tributes and the many front-page obituaries, Rustin remained as elusive in death as he had in life. The accounts of his life were rife with inaccuracies. He was said to have met Gandhi; his diction was attributed to West Indian roots or a London education. Even the attempts to characterize his politics stumbled. The *New York Times* attempted to trace a career trajectory that moved from radical to conservative, but

Rustin's own words spoke out defiantly. "I know that I have changed," the obituary recorded him as saying. "But the changes have been in response to the objective conditions." As if finally to acknowledge the rebelliousness that had characterized his life, the editor chose this as the featured quote: "I believe in social dislocation and creative trouble."[30]

In the last years of his life, Rustin was fond of repeating a statement that he attributed to A. Philip Randolph: "The struggle must be continuous, for freedom is never a final act." A few months before Rustin died, a young admirer asked how he kept hopeful in dismally conservative times. "I have learned a very significant message from the Jewish prophets," Rustin replied. "They taught that God does not require us to achieve any of the good tasks that humanity must pursue. What the gods require of us is that we not stop trying."[31]

ACKNOWLEDGMENTS

ONE OF THE GREAT pleasures of finishing a book is the opportunity
it provides to acknowledge the support and assistance of others. In this
case, I feel especially fortunate to have received so much help at every
stage along the way.

Bert Hansen first pointed me in the direction of Rustin's life. Jed
Mattes, my agent, negotiated for me a contract generous enough to
provide a first block of free time to do concentrated research. He has
maintained his interest in the book through the long years it has taken
me to complete it, and has offered not only sage counsel but friendship
as well. Joyce Seltzer acquired the project for Free Press, and after she
left, Bruce Nichols remained committed to it through the many dead-
lines that I failed to meet. He also provided astute and constructive editorial advice that has made the final book better than the manuscript
he originally read. Over the years, Walter Naegle, Rustin's surviving
life partner, has responded to repeated requests for assistance, helped
me find individuals I wanted to interview, sat through an interview himself, made boxes of his photographs available to me, and, most of all,
never impinged on my freedom to write Rustin's biography in the way
that made sense to me.

Many institutions have provided grants and fellowships that have
seen me to the finish line. I began my initial exploration of Rustin while
a fellow at the Center for Advanced Study in the Behavioral Sciences in
Stanford, California, with funding provided by the National Endowment
for the Humanities, Grant RA-20037–88, and the Andrew W. Mellon
Foundation. Over the years, additional support has come from fellowships for individual research provided by the John Simon Guggenheim
Memorial Foundation; the Humanities Research Centre of Australian
National University; the National Endowment for the Humanities; and
the Institute for the Humanities of the University of Illinois at Chicago.

The University of North Carolina at Greensboro gave me a year-long research leave, and the Office of the Vice-Chancellor for Research at the University of Illinois at Chicago provided me with funds for a research assistant in the last stages of the book. The John F. Kennedy Presidential Library, the Lyndon B. Johnson Presidential Library, and the American Philosophical Society provided travel-to-collection grants.

Librarians and archivists make historical research and writing possible. I have benefited enormously from the helpful competence of staff at the following institutions: John F. Kennedy Presidential Library; Boston University; Schlesinger Library of Radcliffe College; Columbia University; New York Public Library; Schomburg Library; Tamiment Library of New York University; Swarthmore College Peace Collection; American Friends Service Committee Archives; National Archives; the Moorland-Spingarn Research Center of Howard University; Library of Congress; George Meany Memorial Archives; Martin Luther King, Jr. Center; University of Georgia; Wayne State University; and Lyndon B. Johnson Presidential Library. I especially want to mention Wendy Chmielewski of the Swarthmore College Peace Collection. Her devoted labors make it possible to reconstruct the history of pacifist agitation in the United States.

Research and writing is a collaborative process, even when only one name appears as author. The prior work of many historians and journalists has facilitated my own, and I owe a debt to everyone whose books and articles are listed in the bibliography. Three historians deserve special mention because their scholarship has been indispensable for understanding the context of Rustin's life: David Garrow on Martin Luther King, Jr.; Maurice Isserman on the American left; and Lawrence Wittner on the peace movement. In addition, a number of scholars have generously shared with me documents that they found and that I might otherwise have missed: Scott Bennett, John Howard, Maurice Isserman, Nancy Kates, Bennett Singer, R. Allen Smith, and Marc Stein. Milton Viorst kindly made available to me interviews he did with Rustin and others for his fine book, *Fire in the Streets*, and I found them invaluable.

Over the years, I have been blessed with a succession of able student research assistants. All of them contributed mightily to the final product: Katie Batza, Laurinda Debeck, Day Irmiter, Nina Schichor, Heather Shields, Todd Shuman, Neil Soiseth, Tim Stewart-Winter, and Judith Whyte. Pippa Holloway and Amy Schneidhorst each worked with me on the project over an extended period, and responded quickly, efficiently, and creatively to my requests for yet more information on one subject or another. I could not have asked for more.

Along the way, many schools have invited me to give talks on Rustin. Comments and questions from the audience have helped me to clarify as well as modify my understanding of Rustin's life. The enthusiasm of those who listened to my lectures kept me remembering that Rustin's story was worth telling. The audience members (and there always was at least one) who came up to me afterward and shared their own reminiscences of encounters with Rustin have helped to enrich the final version of the biography. Special thanks go to John Ballard and Jill Mathews for organizing the "Regimes of Sexuality" Conference at Australian National University in 1993, and to William McFeely for inviting me to deliver a paper at the Harvard Conference on Biography that same year. These were the first venues in which I lectured on Rustin's life and were particularly important to me. I am also deeply indebted to Jill Dolan, Alisa Solomon, and the Board of Directors of the Center for Lesbian and Gay Studies of the City University of New York. Their invitation to deliver the David Kessler Lecture in 1999 gave me the chance to grapple with some of the thornier issues I faced as I struggled through my first draft. And special thanks of another sort go to Mary Beth Rose and Linda Vavra, the director and associate director, respectively, of the UIC Institute for the Humanities. My final year of writing took place there, a wonderful environment in which concentrated intellectual activity and lively exchanges of ideas regularly occur. My lecture at the institute helped me sort through some of the complexities of Rustin's politics in the mid-1960s, and the other fellows responded to my seminar with great and genuine interest. Sue Levine and Katrin Schultheiss constituted a dependable biweekly writing support group that year, made all the more pleasurable by the fact that we met over food each time.

A number of individuals took large chunks of time out of their own lives in order to read drafts of this manuscript and provide me with subtle and searching responses. I owe a great debt to Martin Duberman, Nan Enstad, Estelle Freedman, Gary Gerstle, Steven Lawson, Diane Middlebrook, Jim Oleson, Peter Skutches, and Nancy Stoller. I haven't always taken their advice—and I will probably live to regret it—but I have listened closely and their comments have made it easier for me to get it the way I wanted. Some of them—Nan Enstad, Estelle Freedman, Jim Oleson, and Peter Skutches—were generous enough to read more than one draft. There is no way to calculate what I owe them.

Finally, there are some forms of thanks that words—even for a writer—can't quite express. Diana de Vegh opened her home to me during long research trips in Washington, D.C., through a brutally cold winter. Estelle Freedman has been a friend and support for so long that I can't remember a time before. Ruth Eisenberg always seemed to be near a phone when I needed propping up. My time each week with Nancy Robertson in the last two years of work on the book has kept me grounded. First, last, and always is Jim Oleson. He has put up with a lot. He's the only person happier than I am that the book is done and that Bayard has finally taken leave of our premises so that now we can get on with the rest of our life together.

NOTES

ABBREVIATIONS USED IN NOTES

AFSC	American Friends Service Committee
AFSCA	American Friends Service Committee Archives, Philadelphia, PA
AMP	August Meier Papers, Schomburg Library, New York, NY
APR	A. Philip Randolph
APRP	A. Philip Randolph Papers, Library of Congress, Washington, D.C.
BPNA	Bureau of Prison Records, National Archives, Washington, D.C.
BR	Bayard Rustin
BR-FBI	Rustin FBI File, Copy in Author's Possession
BRP	Bayard Rustin Papers, Microfilm Edition, University Publications of America
CCHS	Chester County Historical Society, West Chester, PA
CDG	Collected Document Group
CIRM	Communist Influence in Racial Matters
CNVAP	Committee for Nonviolent Action Papers, Swarthmore College, Swarthmore, PA
CPUSA	Communist Party, United States
CRDP	Civil Rights Documentation Project, Moorland-Spingarn Research Center, Howard University, Washington, D.C.
CUOHC	Columbia University Oral History Collection, New York, NY
DG	Document Group
DLN	West Chester *Daily Local News*
DPL	Davis Platt Letters, in possession of Davis Platt, New York, NY
FOR	Fellowship of Reconciliation
FORP	Fellowship of Reconciliation Papers, Swarthmore College, Swarthmore, PA
GMA	George Meany Memorial Archives, Silver Spring, MD

JDI   Interviews conducted by John D'Emilio

JFKL   John F. Kennedy Presidential Library, Boston, MA

LBJL   Lyndon Baines Johnson Presidential Library, Austin, TX

LC   Library of Congress

MLK   Martin Luther King, Jr.

MLKBU   King Papers, Boston University, Boston, MA

MLKC   Martin Luther King, Jr., Center, Atlanta, GA

MLKP   King Papers, King Center, Atlanta, GA

MVI   Milton Viorst Interviews, Moorland-Spingarn Research Center, Howard University, Washington, D.C.

NQ   Negro Question

NTP   Norman Thomas Papers, New York Public Library, New York, NY

NUL   National Urban League Papers, Library of Congress

NYPL   New York Public Library, New York, NY

SAC   Special Agent in Charge

SCPC   Swarthmore College Peace Collection, Swarthmore, PA

SHSW   State Historical Society of Wisconsin, Madison, WI

WRL   War Resisters League

WRLP   War Resisters League Papers, Swarthmore College Peace Collection, Swarthmore, PA

WSU   Labor and Urban Affairs Archives, Wayne State University, Detroit, MI

1: "Any Road Will Take You There"

1. Quoted in Jonathan Gottlieb, unpublished manuscript, AMP, Box 58. The Gottlieb manuscript is based in part on interviews he conducted with Rustin, dated 2/6/76, 4/18/78, and 6/19/78.
2. *Ibid.*; Doris Grotewohl to BR, 6/25/44, BRP, Reel 20; BR to Davis Platt, 4/20/45, DPL.
3. On Janifer's origins see his obituary, DLN, 4/20/45, in Rustin clipping files, CCHS.
4. Information on Julia Davis comes from DLN, 6/17/41 and 4/29/57, in Rustin clipping files, CCHS; and Rustin Interview, CUOHC.
5. DLN, 6/17/41 and 4/20/45, in Rustin clipping files, CCHS; Rustin Interview, CUOHC; A. J. Muste to BR, 4/24/45, BRP, Reel 20; "List of Ap-

proved Visitors," 4/7/44, BPNA; Gottlieb manuscript, AMP, Box 58; and BR to Platt, 4/20/45, DPL.

6. DLN, 5/29/14 and 5/27/15, in Rustin clipping files, CCHS; Julia Rustin to James Bennett, 11/3/45, BPNA.

7. Gottlieb manuscript, AMP, Box 58; Rustin interview, CUOHC.

8. *Ibid.*

9. *Ibid.*

10. Bruno Interview, JDI; Rustin Interview, CUOHC.

11. Rustin Interview, CUOHC, and Rustin Interview, MVI. For other accounts of discrimination, see the obituary and related article in the Philadelphia *Inquirer*, 8/25–26/87, in Rustin clipping files, CCHS. My interviews with contemporaries of Rustin from West Chester—Nick Bruno, Joseph Derry, and Mary Frances Boyd Thomas—all offered examples.

12. Thomas Interview, JDI; Rustin Interview, CUOHC; Philadelphia *Inquirer*, 8/26/87, Rustin clipping files, CCHS; *Lives of Some Negroes Who Made Their Contributions to the History of West Chester, Pennsylvania*, n.d., compiled by Warren H. Burton, CCHS.

13. Thomas Interview, JDI.

14. Rustin Interview, CUOHC.

15. Thomas Interview, JDI.

16. *The Garnet and White*, 1928–1932, copies in CCHS; Julia Rustin, letter to editor, DLN, 3/1/44, Rustin clipping files, CCHS.

17. *The Garnet and White*, April 1931, pp. 13–14; January 1932, p. 5; April 1932, p. 8; June 1932 (Commencement Issue), all in CCHS.

18. Philadelphia *Inquirer*, 8/26/87, Rustin clipping files, CCHS; DLN, 10/19/31 and 11/16/31.

19. Bruno Interview, JDI.

20. See Bruno, Thomas, and Rodgers Interviews, JDI; Rustin Interview, CUOHC; Philadelphia *Inquirer*, 8/26/87, and DLN, 8/25/87, Rustin clipping files, CCHS. The quotation is from John Rodgers.

21. Rustin Interview, CUOHC.

22. Gordon Roehrs to BR, 2/22/64, BRP, Reel 20; *The Garnet and White* (Commencement Issue, 1932), p. 51; Philadelphia *Inquirer*, 8/26/87, Rustin clipping files, CCHS.

23. Gottlieb manuscript, AMP, Box 58. For "The Creation," see Johnson, *God's Trombones*.

24. DLN, 6/16/32, p. 1, and 6/17/32, p. 1.

25. Rustin Interviews, CUOHC and MVI.

26. Information on the history of Wilberforce comes from Frederick A. McGinnis, *A History and Interpretation of Wilberforce University* (Wilberforce, OH, 1941); Wilberforce University Bulletin, April 1933; and *The Forcean* (Wilberforce yearbook), 1933.

27. Quoted in Gottlieb manuscript, AMP, Box 58.
28. DLN, 3/6/34, Rustin clipping files, CCHS; Rustin Interview, CUOHC; Gottlieb manuscript, AMP, Box 58; and letter to draft board, 1943, summarized in FBI report, 12/18/43, BR-FBI.
29. Gottlieb manuscript, AMP, Box 58.

2: "A Young Radical"

1. BR to Platt, 3/16/45 and 9/1/44, DPL.
2. On the student peace movement see Eagan, *Class, Culture, and the Classroom.*
3. See "Cheyney Institute of International Relations, 1937," in Peace Section Institute, 1929–1937, AFSCA.
4. Information in this paragraph comes from an FBI report on Rustin, dated 12/18/43 and based on an examination of his Selective Service file and letters he wrote to his draft board in 1940 and 1941, BR-FBI.
5. *Ibid.*; and BR to Platt, 7/28/44 and 7/14/44, DPL.
6. On Whitney see Adele Rickett, ed., *Norman Whitney: Spectator Papers* (Philadelphia: AFSC, 1971), and R. Allen Smith, "Mass Society and the Bomb: The Discourse of Pacifism in the 1950s," *Peace and Change* 18 (1993), pp. 347–72. I am indebted to Smith for calling my attention to materials on Whitney and sharing with me his research.
7. Steve Cary Interview, JDI.
8. Rustin Interview, MVI; Rustin Interview, 5/29/74, AMP, Box 58.
9. Rustin Interview, 2/2/87, by Mark Bowman, copy of tape in author's possession.
10. Davis Platt Interview, 7/17/92, JDI.
11. See Greenberg, *"Or Does It Explode?"* and Naison, *Communists in Harlem,* for discussions of Harlem in the 1930s.
12. FBI Reports, 12/18/43 and 2/28/44; AND Larkin to WPA, 3/11/44, BPNA.
13. Rustin Interview, Bowman.
14. Quoted in Duberman, *Paul Robeson,* p. 238.
15. *New York Times,* 1/11/40, p. 18.
16. Siegel, *The Glory Road,* p. 63
17. Charles Bloomstein Interview, JDI.
18. See Rustin Interviews, CUOHC and MVI.
19. Carl Rachlin Interview, AMP, Box 57.
20. Rustin Interview, CUOHC. Interview with Dorothy Height in Hill, ed., *The Black Women Oral History Project,* vol. 5, p. 59. See also the interview with Maida Springer Kemp, in *ibid.,* vol. 7, pp. 57, 60.
21. BR to Muste, 8/5/41, FORP, Series D, Box 21, Puerto Rico Folder.

3: "A WAY OF LIFE"

1. Jack and Smiley Interviews, JDI.
2. Hentoff, ed., *The Essays of A. J. Muste*, pp. 87, 225, 181.
3. *Ibid.*, pp. 129, 131.
4. *Ibid.*, pp. 134–35.
5. *Ibid.*, p. 209.
6. *Ibid.*, pp. 201, 220, 230.
7. *Ibid.*, p. 223.
8. Bromley Interview, JDI.
9. Foote Interview, JDI.
10. Most of the biographical information in this paragraph comes from my interviews with the individuals in question. For more extensive information about Farmer, see *Lay Bare the Heart*. The "lean and hungry" comment comes from Muste's autobiography, in Hentoff, *The Essays of A. J. Muste*, p. 79.
11. "Report of Youth Secretary—Bayard Rustin," 9/12/42, and "Field Worker—Bayard Rustin," 12/11/42, FORP, Box 3, Reports 1942.
12. Meier and Rudwick, *CORE*, p. 12, and *Adventures in Reconciliation*, International Fellowship of Reconciliation Leaflet No. 8, FORP, Series D, Box 1, Folder 2.
13. Rustin Interview, MVI. Bayard Rustin, "Non-Violence vs. Jim Crow," reprint from *Fellowship*, July 1942, FORP, Series D, Box 1, Writings and Speeches.
14. Cary and Bromley Interviews, JDI.
15. Paul Hayes to John Swomley, 9/25/42, FORP, Series D, Box 1, Folder 2, and FOR Executive Committee Minutes, 11/10/42, FORP, Box 3; and Bromley, Margaret Rohrer Swomley, Cary, and Caleb and Hope Foote Interviews, JDI.
16. Gara, Asahi, Jack, Winnemore, and Smiley Interviews, JDI.
17. Doris Grotewohl Baker Interview, JDI; Emily Morgan to author, 3/11/94.
18. BR to Dear Friend, 8/15/42, FORP, Series D, Box 1, Folder 6.
19. Finch Interview, JDI; "Report of Youth Secretary—Bayard Rustin," 9/12/42, FORP, Box 3, Reports 1942.
20. See Muste to BR, 5/4/42, and Muste to Arthur Swift, 4/18/42, FORP, Box 10, Rustin Folder.
21. "Field Worker—Bayard Rustin," 12/11/42, and "Youth Field Worker—James Farmer," n.d., FORP, Box 3, Reports 1942.
22. "What the Negro Thinks," in "Report of Youth Secretary—Bayard Rustin," 9/12/42, FORP, Box 3, Reports 1942.
23. Du Bois quoted in Kapur, *Raising Up a Prophet*, p. 11. The information in this and the following paragraphs on the relation of African Americans to Gandhi is drawn from Kapur.
24. Quoted in Farmer, *Lay Bare the Heart*, p. 110.

25. James Farmer, "Provisional Plans for Brotherhood Mobilization," 2/19/42, and "Supplemental Memorandum to Brotherhood Mobilization," n.d., reprinted in Farmer, *Lay Bare the Heart*, pp. 355–60.

26. Bayard Rustin, "The March on Washington Movement and the Detroit and Harlem Riots," FORP, Series D, Box 1, Writings and Speeches.

27. Houser Interview, CRDP; Foote Interview, JDI.

28. Foote letter quoted by him in his interview, JDI; Hope Foote and Margaret Rohrer Swomley Interviews, JDI.

29. "The March on Washington Movement and the Detroit and Harlem Riots," FORP, Series D, Box 1, Writings and Speeches; Morgan to D'Emilio, 3/11/94.

30. Pauli Murray Interview, CRDP.

31. E. Pauline Myers, "The March on Washington Movement and Non-Violent Civil Disobedience," APRP, Box 26.

32. FOR Executive Committee Minutes, 1/12/43 and 1/26/43, FORP, Box 3.

33. Quoted in Anderson, *A. Philip Randolph*, p. 77.

34. Quoted in Garfinkel, *When Negroes March*, p. 63.

35. "Keynote Address," *March on Washington Movement: Proceedings of Conference Held in Detroit*, 9/26–27/42, FORP, Box 21; and "Remarks of A. Philip Randolph at Carnegie Hall," 5/2/44, NAACP Papers, Group II, Series A, Box 507, LC.

36. J. Holmes Smith, "Report of the Secretary of the Committee on Non-Violent Action," 9/12/42, FORP, Box 3, Reports 1942.

37. Muste to APR, 1/11/43, and APR to Muste, 5/25/43, FORP, Box 21; FOR Executive Committee Minutes, 1/12/43 and 2/23/43, FORP, Box 3; and BR to Muste, 2/22/43, FORP, Box 10.

38. Rustin Interview, CUOHC; Muste to E. A. Schaal, 5/21/43, FORP, Box 10, Rustin File.

39. Smith to Muste, 7/8/43, FORP, Box 21. See also the Baltimore *Afro-American*, 7/10/43, which reported extensively on the conference, including mention of Rustin's presentations.

40. *Ibid.*

41. *Ibid.*

42. FOR Executive Committee and National Council Minutes, 9/14/43, and 9/24–26/43, FORP, Box 3.

43. Farmer, *Lay Bare the Heart*, pp. 85, 111, 115, 151.

44. FOR Executive Committee Minutes, 9/24/43; Swomley and Houser Interviews, JDI; FOR Executive Committee Minutes, 5/8/45, FORP, Box 3.

45. Jack, Swomley, Asahi, and Smiley Interviews, JDI.

46. Marion Bromley Interview, JDI.

47. Marion Bromley, Grotewohl, and Asahi Interviews, JDI.

48. Houser Interview, JDI; Muste to BR, 9/29/43, FORP, Box 10, Rustin File.

49. Grotewohl, Asahi, Margaret Rohrer Swomley, and Hassler Interviews, JDI.
50. Hassler and Asahi Interviews, JDI.
51. Finch Interview, JDI.
52. Grotewohl, Joseph Felmet, Smiley, and Swomley Interviews, JDI.
53. Margaret Swomley, Asahi, Houser, Hassler, Grotewohl, and Platt Interviews, JDI.
54. Unless otherwise specified, quotes from Platt in this and the following paragraphs come from Platt Interview, JDI.
55. Margaret Swomley and John Swomley Interviews, JDI.

4: "An Extremely Capable Agitator"

1. Rustin letter, 4/18/41, quoted in FBI report on Rustin, 12/18/43, BR-FBI.
2. Quoted in Tracy, *Direct Action*, p. 12; Muste, "Memorandum on COs in Prison," tentative draft, 11/10/43, BRP, Reel 20.
3. Sutherland to BR, 8/28/43, BRP, Reel 20.
4. Mecartney to BR, 11/17/43, and Price to his mother, 10/30/43, BRP, Reel 20.
5. Bromley Interview, JDI.
6. FBI Report, 12/18/43, BR-FBI.
7. Vogel to BR, 2/21/44, Norman Whitney Papers, DG 61, Box 5, SCPC; APR to BR, 4/17/44, APRP, Box 1; Houser to BR, 1/25/44, FORP, Series D, Box 1; Dixon to BR, 12/6/43, BRP, Reel 20.
8. DLN, 11/27/43, 2/26/44, and 3/1/44, Rustin clipping files CCHS; Rustin Interview, CRDP.
9. Sayre to Julia Rustin, 3/9/44, FORP, Series D, Box 1.
10. Central File Chronological Record, 3/2/44, BPNA.
11. Frank Loveland to Mylton Kennedy, 2/25/44, BPNA.
12. Transcript of Interview with BR, 3/6/44, BPNA.
13. Loveland to Mylton Kennedy, 3/16/44, and Loveland to Hagerman, 3/16/44, BPNA.
14. See "List of Authorized Correspondents," and "Authorization for Disposition of Mail and Property," 3/9/44, and the series of inquiries from R. M. Larkin to various police departments, dated 3/11/44, all in BPNA.
15. Julia Rustin to Sayre, 3/15/44, FORP, Series D, Box 1.
16. Officer W. E. Storm to Associate Warden, 3/27/44, BPNA. Information about how the COs communicated with one another comes from my interviews with Joseph Felmet and Larry Gara, and from Charles Butcher in letters to me dated 3/14/94 and 3/30/94. All three men were in Ashland when Rustin arrived.
17. BR to Hagerman, 3/30/44, BPNA.

18. Hagerman to Bennett, 3/27/44, BPNA.
19. Hagerman to Bennett, 3/31/44 and 4/3/44, BPNA.
20. Howard Gill to Hagerman, 4/10/44, BPNA.
21. E. J. Weale to Associate Warden, 4/8/44; E. W. Yates to Captain, 4/10/44; Conduct Record, 4/11/44; Benjamin Frank to Hagerman, 4/12/44; BR to Captain Huntington, 4/15/44; R. M. Larkin, memos dated 4/17/44 and 4/18/44; all in BPNA. Eleanor Clark to Doris Grotewohl, 5/3/44, BRP, FOR Folder, Reel 1.
22. Rustin to Platt, 5/5/44, DPL.
23. Eleanor Clark to Doris Grotewohl, 5/3/44, BRP, FOR Folder, Reel 1; Gara Interview, JDI.
24. Grotewohl to BR, 5/5/44, BRP, Reel 20; Bronson Clark to Grotewohl, 5/28/44, and BR to Grotewohl, 5/5/44, BRP, Reel 1.
25. Rustin Interview, CUOHC; and Rustin Interview, MVI.
26. *Ibid.*
27. Grotewohl to Rustin, 3/31/44 and 4/25/44, BRP, Reel 20.
28. Grotewohl to Rustin, 5/2/44, 6/8/44 and 5/19/44, BRP, Reel 20.
29. Grotewohl to Rustin, 4/11/44, 5/2/44, and 4/18/44, BRP, Reel 20.
30. BR to Platt, 5/5/44, DPL.
31. BR to Platt, 6/16/44, DPL.
32. BR to Platt, 5/12/44, DPL.
33. BR to Platt, 8/7/44 and 6/9/44, DPL.
34. BR to Platt, 6/2/44 and 6/9/44, DPL.
35. BR to Platt, 7/4/44 and 8/7/44, DPL.
36. BR to Hagerman, 7/15/44, BPNA.
37. BR to Hagerman, 7/15/44, BPNA.
38. BR to Platt, 7/28/44, DPL.
39. Muste to Hagerman, 7/31/44, BPNA; "Memo on Visit to Ashland," 7/27/44, NAACP Papers, Group II, Series A, Box 374, LC.
40. BR to Carl Johnson, 8/7/44, and BR to Hagerman, 8/21/44, BPNA; Gara Interview, JDI.
41. BR's Handwritten Notes, 8/22/44–9/8/44, BPNA.
42. *Ibid.*, and BR to Friends, Hall D, 9/8/44, BPNA.

5: "Hard and Bitter Experience"

1. BR to Platt, 2/1/45, DPL.
2. Bennett, *I Chose Prison*, p. 28; BR to Platt, 2/1/45, DPL.
3. Loveland to Mylton Kennedy, 2/25/44; "Post-Sentence Report," by Harold Dean and Leon DeKalb, 3/8/44; "Central File Chronological Record," 3/2/44; all in BPNA.
4. Wetzel, *Pacifist*, pp. 173–4.

5. Butcher to author, 3/14/94. Junior Officer Brown to Warden, 9/24/44, and Junior Officer Green to Warden, 9/24/44, BPNA.

6. Mulhall to Hagerman, 8/21/44, and Storm to Hagerman, 8/23/44, BPNA.

7. Canby, *Walt Whitman*, pp. 199–200.

8. Transcripts of interviews conducted by A. C. Huntington, 8/18/44, BPNA.

9. "Memo," 9/12/44, and "Signed Statement," 9/13/44, BPNA.

10. Unless otherwise noted, the information and quotations in this and the following paragraphs come from "Disciplinary Board Hearing," 9/13/44, BPNA.

11. *Ibid.*; "Committee Action," 9/15/44, BPNA.

12. Gara Interview, JDI.

13. Grotewohl to BR, 9/19/44, BRP, Reel 20.

14. Unless otherwise noted, the information and quotations in this and the following paragraphs are taken from Clemmer to Bennett and Loveland, 9/25/44, BPNA.

15. Muste to BR, 9/29/44 and 10/22/44, BPNA.

16. BR to Platt, 10/2/44, DPL.

17. Muste to BR, 10/22/44, BPNA.

18. Dr. H. M. Janney, Neuropsychiatric Report, 10/25/44, BPNA.

19. BR to Muste, 10/26/44, BNPA.

20. Hagerman to Bennett, 10/27/44, BPNA; Muste to BR, 11/7/44, BRP, Reel 20; BR to Platt, 11/3/44, DPL.

21. William Measaw, Supplementary Report, 11/14/44, BPNA. See also Conduct Record, Report #1, 11/13/44, and #2, 11/14/44; Lieutenant Weale to Associate Warden, 11/14/44; G. R. Shalter to Hagerman, 11/14/44; Mulhall to Huntingon, 11/14/44; all in BPNA.

22. Hagerman to Bennett, 11/15/44; Bennett to Hagerman, 1/9/45; "Parole Progress Report," 1/45; and Hagerman to Bennett, 5/9/45; all in BPNA.

23. BR to Platt, 4/20/45, DPL.

24. BR to Platt, 12/2/44, DPL.

25. BR to Platt, 1/18/45, DPL.

26. Lee to BR, 11/25/44, BPNA.

27. Lee to BR, 11/25/44, BPNA.

28. Unless otherwise noted, the information and quotations in this and the following paragraphs are taken from two letters: BR to Platt, 4/5/45 and 4/20/45, DPL.

29. Julia Rustin to Warden, 3/27/45, BPNA.

30. Platt Interview, JDI; BR to Platt, 4/5/45, DPL.

31. Winnemore to Breland, 8/6/44, and Hagerman to Bennett, 5/4/45, BPNA.

32. Muste's comments are referred to by Rustin in his letter to Platt, 4/20/45, DPL.

33. Muste to BR, 4/24/45, BRP, Reel 20.
34. Muste to BR, 6/18/45, BRP, Reel 20.
35. Muste to BR, 7/4/45, BRP, Reel 20.
36. Muste to BR (n.d., but in response to a July 6 letter he received from Rustin), BRP, Reel 20; and BR to Platt, 7/20/45, DPL.
37. BR memo, 6/4/45, BPNA.
38. Bennett to Hagerman, 6/15/45; Special Progress Report, 6/21/45; Dr. H. M. Janney, Special Progress Report, 6/19/45; Hagerman to Bennett, 6/22/45; all in BPNA.
39. DiGia Interview, JDI.
40. Gara Interview, JDI.
41. Templin Interview, JDI.
42. T. J. Fitzpatrick to W. H. Hiatt, 11/11/45, and Julia Rustin to Hiatt, 1/31/46, both in BPNA.
43. Grotewohl to BR, 5/23/45, and Houser to BR, 12/5/45, both in BRP, Reel 20.
44. Muste to Bennett, 3/24/46, and BR to Bennett, 3/24/46, BPNA.
45. Hiatt to Muste, 3/25/46; Bennett to Muste, 4/2/46; and Hiatt to Bennett, 5/1/46; all in BPNA.

6: "The Gadfly Which Has Stirred Men into Action"

1. Quoted in Bennett, "'Pacifism Not Passivism,'" p. 379; Miller Interview, JDI; Sanders to Urich, 6/19/46 and 10/31/46; Urich to U.S. Board of Parole, 3/3/47; and Bennett to Fraser, 4/21/47: all in BPNA.
2. Muste, "Prospectus for Study Conference on Philosophy and Strategy of Revolutionary Pacifism," n.d., 1944, and Muste to Rustin, 3/1/45, both in Reel 20, BRP.
3. Muste, "Memorandum on Some Aspects of the F.O.R. Post War Program," 10/15/45, FORP, Box 3, Reports 1944–45.
4. National Council Meeting Minutes, 5/29–31/47, FORP, Box 3.
5. Excerpts from Alfred Anderson Letter, 2/17/48, BRP, Reel 20.
6. Cary, McReynolds, and Houser Interviews, JDI.
7. National Council Meeting Minutes, 10/24–26/46, FORP, Box 3; and Fellowship 12, No. 10 (October 1946), p. 168.
8. National Council Meeting Minutes, 11/20–22/47, FORP, Box 3.
9. National Council Meeting Minutes, 5/20–22/48, FORP, Box 3; FBI Memo, NY Office, 12/17/63, CPUSA, NQ, CIRM, BR-FBI.
10. See discussions in Tracy, Direct Action, pp. 50–52, and Bennett, "'Pacifism, Not Passivism,'" pp. 357–61.

11. Peacemakers, Draft Manifesto, 4/28/48, FORP, Box 3, Reports, 1946–49; BR to Platt, 9/3/48, BRP, Reel 20.

12. *Ibid.*

13. For more extended discussions of Peacemakers see Tracy, *Direct Action*, pp. 60–7, and Bennett, "'Pacifism, Not Passivism,'" pp. 361–72.

14. BR to Platt, 9/3/48, BRP, Reel 20.

15. National Council Meeting Minutes, 11/20–22/47, FORP, Box 3; Platt to BR, 9/3/48, BRP, Reel 20.

16. Houser to BR, 12/5/45, BRP, Reel 20.

17. Muste to Sayre, 8/13/46, FORP, Series D, Box 1, Folder 2.

18. Background information on Houser comes from Houser Interview, JDI.

19. *Morgan v. Virginia*, 328 U.S. 373 (1946); George Houser and Bayard Rustin, "Memo on Bus Travel in the South," n.d., NAACP Papers, Group II, Series A, Box 374, LC.

20. Rustin Interview, CRDP; Houser Interview, JDI.

21. Houser Interview, JDI.

22. George Houser, "A Personal Retrospective on the 1947 Journey of Reconciliation," typescript in possession of author.

23. Key sources for reconstructing the Journey are George Houser and Bayard Rustin, "Journey of Reconciliation: A Report," 1947, and "Log on Journey of Reconciliation," FORP, Series D, Box 1; Houser and Rustin Interviews, CRDP; Rustin Interview, CUOHC.

24. Bromley and Houser Interviews, JDI.

25. "Log"; Pittsburgh *Courier*, 4/5/47, p. 1; "Report."

26. Felmet Interview, JDI; *Report.*

27. Stewart, quoted in Houser, "A Personal Retrospective on the 1947 Journey of Reconciliation," typescript in Houser's possession.

28. Pittsburgh *Courier*, 4/19/47, p. 1.

29. Houser and Rustin, "Report."

30. Rustin Interview, CUOHC; Houser Interview, JDI.

31. Houser Interview, JDI.

32. Stewart, quoted in Houser, "A Personal Retrospective on the 1947 Journey of Reconciliation," typescript in Houser's possession.

33. Houser Interview, JDI.

7: "Mad Enough to Do Something Desperate"

1. On Reading and Buffalo, see Mills to BR, 11/16/46, and BR to Livermore, FORP, Series D, Box 1; on St. Paul, see *Fellowship* 13 No. 3 (March 1947), p. 48.

2. *Fellowship* 13 No. 11 (November 1947), p. 180.

3. Houser Interview, JDI.

4. "The Interracial Workshop," FORP, Series D, Box 1.
5. Houser Interview, CRDP; Rustin Interview, CUOHC.
6. Memorandum to Mr. White from Mr. Wilkins, 4/9/48, NAACP Papers, Group II, Series A, Box 370, LC.
7. Worthy to APR, 8/14/47, APRP, Box 16.
8. *Ibid.* See also APR to Worthy, 8/15/47, and Worthy to APR, 8/20/47, APRP, Box 16.
9. BR to APR, 11/11/47, APRP, Box 16, Committee to End Jim Crow in Military Service and Training; Press Release, 11/23/47, APRP, Box 15, Committee to End Jim Crow in Military Service and Training.
10. Staff Minutes, 12/18/47, FORP, Box 5; Worthy to APR, 2/5/48, APRP, Box 16, Committee to End Jim Crow in Military Service and Training.
11. Houser to APR, 2/14/48, APRP, Box 16; Houser, "A Proposal for a Civil Disobedience Campaign Against Military Jim Crow," APRP, Box 16.
12. Testimony of A. Philip Randolph Prepared for Delivery before the Senate Armed Service Committee, 3/31/48, in APRP, Box 15.
13. Morse to White, 4/6/48 and 4/20/48, NAACP Papers, Group II, Series A, Box 370, LC; Reynolds to APR, 4/17/48, APRP, Box 16.
14. White to Morse, 4/14/48; "Civil Rights Retreat Denounced by White," Press Release, 4/22/48; Wilkins to White, 4/9/48, all in NAACP Papers, Group II, Series A, Box 370, LC; and White to APR, 4/21/48, APRP, Box 16.
15. For accounts of the military desegregation campaign see the biographies of Randolph by Anderson and Pfeffer, and Dalfiume, *Desegregation of the U.S. Armed Forces.*
16. "Negro Youth Leader Pledges Support to Randolph Civil Disobedience Program," FOR Press Release, 4/11/48, NAACP Papers, Group II, Series A, Box 370, LC.
17. Statement on Refusal to Continue the Payment of Taxes, 4/14/48, and Bulletin #1, Action Committee of Committee Against Jim Crow in Military Training and Service, 6/4/48, APRP, Box 15; National Council Meeting Minutes, 5/20–22/48, FORP, Box 3; Pfeffer, *A. Philip Randolph*, p. 140.
18. "Randolph to Urge Negroes in Army to Drop Guns if Russell Segregation Amendment Passes," Press Release, 5/14/48; Bulletin #1, Action Committee of Committee Against Jim Crow in Military Training and Service, 6/4/48; and Lem Graves to APR, 5/15/48, all in APRP, Box 15.
19. "Questions on Civil Disobedience," Bulletin #2, Action Committee of Committee Against Jim Crow in Military Training and Service, 6/17/48, APRP, Box 15.
20. *Ibid.*
21. "The Strength of the Movement for Civil Disobedience Against Military Segregation," League for Non-Violent Civil Disobedience, APRP, Box 15; Muste to APR, 6/9/48, APRP, Box 16.

22. Pittsburgh *Courier*, 7/17/48, "Randolph Will Invite Arrest for Treason Saturday," clipping in FORP, Series D, Box 1.

23. Rustin Interview, MVI; Schoenebaum, ed., *Political Profiles*, p. 242.

24. Theodore Stanford, in the Pittsburgh *Courier*, 7/24/48, clipping in FORP, Series D, Box 1.

25. BR to Staff, Officers, Volunteers, 7/16/48, APRP, Box 15.

26. Reynolds to APR, 7/24/48 and 7/25/48, APRP, Box 16.

27. Muste to APR, n.d., APRP, Box 16.

28. Muste, "Memorandum on Executive and Administrative Arrangements Involving the Committee Against Jim Crow and the League for Non-Violent Civil Disobedience," n.d., APRP, Box 16.

29. Quoted in Dalfiume, *Desegregation of the U.S. Armed Forces*, p. 171.

30. New York *Times*, 7/27/48, p. 1

31. "A. Philip Randolph's Statement Following Issuance of President Truman's Executive Order," and St. Clair Drake to APR, APRP, Box 16.

32. Reynolds to APR, 8/10/48, APRP, Box 16.

33. APR to Reynolds, 8/13/48; APR to Raymond Henderson, 8/24/48; APR to Mabel Spearman, 9/30/48, all in APRP, Box 16.

34. Campaign to Resist Military Segregation, "We Have a New Look," APRP, Box 16.

35. BR to Platt, 9/3/48, BRP, Reel 20.

36. Statement by Grant Reynolds and A. Philip Randolph, 10/11/48, NAACP Papers, Group II, Series A, Box 370, LC.

37. Rustin Interview, CUOHC.

8: "An Iron Lung of Militarism"

1. Pittsburgh *Courier*, 5/10/47, p. 6.

2. Newton to Muste, 11/2/48, BRP, Reel 2, India File.

3. Newton to BR, 7/1/48, FORP, Series D, Box 1.

4. Holmes to BR, 9/14/48, BRP, Reel 2, India File.

5. Trocme to Sayre, 11/8/48, Sayre Papers, DG 117, Series A, Box 14, SCPC.

6. Sayre to Muste, 10/15/48, and Sayre to BR, 11/4/48, BRP, Reel 2, India File.

7. BR to Sayre, n.d., BRP, Reel 2, India File.

8. BR to George Paine, 10/27/49, FORP, Series D, Box 1; interview with Dorothy Height in Hill, ed., *The Black Women Oral History Project*, vol 5, p. 125.

9. BR to Sayre, Muste, Newton, and Bartlett, n.d., Sayre Papers, DG 117, Series A, Box 14, SCPC; and Dick [Koithahin?] to Sayre, 12/26/48, BRP, Reel 2, India File.

10. Lester to Muste, 12/26/48, FORP, Series D, Box 1; Selma Platt to BR, 1/27/49, BRP, Reel 20; Consul and Embassy reports contained in FBI reports on Rustin, 8/12/63 and 8/16/63, BR-FBI.

11. Notes of Sayre about BR's India visit, and BR to Ewbank, 3/28/49, in FORP, Series D, Box 1.

12. National Council Meeting Minutes, 5/19–21/49, Rustin report on India, copy in FORP, Series D, Box 1.

13. Koithahin to Sayre, 12/26/48, BRP, Reel 2, India File, Rustin Papers, and Lester to Muste, 12/26/48, FORP, Series D, Box 1.

14. Muste to Lester, 1/4/49, Sayre Papers, DG 117, Series A, Box 14, SCPC.

15. Hefner to BR, 3/14/49, FORP, Series D, Box 1.

16. Felmet Interview, JDI.

17. "A Report on Twenty-Two Days on the Chain Gang at Roxboro, North Carolina," typescript, 1949, in CDG-A, Rustin File, SCPC.

18. Edgar Jones to BR, 5/31/49, FORP, Series D, Box 1, "Roxboro."

19. See clippings in FORP, Series D, Box 1, "Roxboro."

20. BR to Connie et al., handwritten memo, n.d., in *ibid.*

21. Platt Interview, JDI.

22. Vogel to author, 5/24/94; Houser Interview, JDI.

23. FBI Report on Rustin, 8/12/63 and 8/16/63, BR-FBI; BR to Judge Lanzetta, 10/28/47, and Rustin to Dear Friend, 10/10/47, both in FORP, Series D, Box 1, Folder 4; James Peck, "Underdogs and Upperdogs," typescript memoir, SHSW; Smiley Interview, JDI.

24. Swomley Interview, JDI. Hoskins to Clark, 2/6/53, and Hoskins to Jones, 2/9/53, General Administration, Individuals: Bayard Rustin, 1953, AFSCA.

25. McReynolds Interview, JDI.

26. Davison to BR, 10/8/64, BRP, Reel 21, and Hassler to Dear Friends, 1/15/52, BRP, Reel 20.

27. See, for instance, *Fellowship*, September 1950, pp. 9–15; "Peace Training Unit: Log 1951," BRP, Reel 4.

28. Rustin Memo, "Re: Robert Montgomery Broadcast," 4/6/51, Sayre Papers, DG 117, Series A, Box 14, SCPC.

29. BR to Perry, 7/29/47, BRP, Reel 20.

30. "Statement on the Communist Issue," June 1948, CORE, Subgroup C, Series I, Box 27, National Advisory Committee Meetings and Convention, MLKP; "The Peace Movement and the United States," FOR Statement, July 1950, in American Section, 1951, National Division: FOR, AFSCA.

31. BR to Perry, 7/29/47, BRP, Reel 20; on the Civil Rights Congress see BR to Thomas Emerson, 8/18/49, FORP, Series D, Box 1, Folder 3.

32. National Council Meeting Minutes, 1/13/50 and 12/1–2/50, and Report on FOR Retreat, 4/12–14/51, all in FORP, Box 4.

33. Rustin Memo, 11/9/50, Sayre Papers, DG 117, Series A, Box 14, SCPC, and BR to Muste et al., 2/2/50, BRP, Reel 20.

34. *Ibid.*

35. Finch Interview, JDI.
36. BR to Marian Neuman, 2/6/52, BRP, Reel 20.
37. BR to Beverly White, 5/3/50, FORP, Series D, Box 1, Folder 5.
38. *Ibid.*
39. FOR Executive Committee Minutes, 9/15/52, FORP, Box 4.

9: "Bayard's Trouble"

1. Quoted in Goldman, *The Death and Life of Malcolm X*, p. 173; Rustin, "Negro America: Inspiration to Africa," WRLP, Series B, Box 18.
2. Rustin Memo, October 20, 1952, FORP, Series D, Box 1, "Writings and Speeches."
3. Unless otherwise noted, the quotations in this and the following paragraphs come from a series of essays by Rustin, typescript in WRLP, Series B, Box 18, "Rustin: 1962" Folder. The titles are "Non-Violent Revolution in the Gold Coast"; "Revolution Reaches Africa"; "Nkrumah, Man of Ghana and God"; "Negro America: Inspiration to Africa"; and "Nnamdi Azikiwe: Nehru of Nigeria."
4. BR to Jim Bristol, 10/7/52, "American Section, 1952. Peace Education," AFSCA; BR to Carl Murphy, 9/26/52, FORP, Series D, Box 1, Folder 4.
5. FOR Executive Committee Meeting Minutes, 10/6/52, FORP, Box 4, Minutes and Reports, 1950–1960.
6. BR to Bristol, 10/7/52, "American Section, 1952: Peace Education," AFSCA.
7. Lawrence Hantz to BR, 12/6/52, FORP, Series D, Box 1, Folder 3; William Fuson to Friends, 12/4/52, "American Section, 1952: Peace Education," AFSCA.
8. BR to Smiley, Vogel, et al., 12/10/52, "American Section, 1952: Peace Education," AFSCA.
9. BR to Muste, 11/30/52, WRLP, Series B, Box 18, "Rustin: 1962" Folder.
10. *Ibid.*
11. FOR Executive Committee Meeting Minutes, 1/5/53, FORP, Box 4, Minutes and Reports, 1950–1960.
12. *Ibid.*
13. *Ibid.*
14. *Ibid.* Sayre to Percy Bartlett, 1/15/53, Sayre Papers, DG 117, Series A, Box 14, Rustin File, SCPC.
15. KECA Broadcast, 1/21/53, AFSCA, Pasadena Regional Office, Peace Section, 1953.
16. Los Angeles *Mirror*, 1/23/53, clipping in AFSCA, Pasadena Regional Office, Peace Section, 1953.
17. The account is drawn from Felony Report Case 66360; Statement of Wayne Marvin Long; and Booking Sheets of Long, Louie Buono, and

Bayard Rustin; all in Mississippi Sovereignty Commission Files, Mississippi Department of Archives and History, Jackson, Miss. I am indebted to John Howard for calling these documents to my attention.

18. Los Angeles *Times*, 1/22/53 and 1/23/53, as placed in *Congressional Record*, U.S. Senate, 8/13/63, p. 14837; Smiley Interview, JDI.

19. Smiley and Houser Interviews, JDI; Swomley to BR, 1/27/53, FORP, Swomley Box 2, Rustin Folder.

20. FORP, Series D, Box 1, Folder 2.

21. For a more extended discussion, see D'Emilio, *Sexual Politics, Sexual Communities*, pp. 40–53, and "The Homosexual Menace: The Politics of Sexuality in Cold War America," in Peiss and Simmons, eds., *Passion and Power*, pp. 226–40.

22. See discussions of gay life in Chauncey, *Gay New York*, and Beemyn, *Creating a Place for Ourselves*.

23. Powell quoted in Philadelphia *Tribune*, 10/9/51, p. 13. I am indebted to Marc Stein for calling my attention to this material. On the fears about male sex crimes in this era see Estelle B. Freedman, "'Uncontrolled Desires': The Response to the Sexual Psychopath, 1920–1960," in Peiss and Simmons, eds., *Passion and Power*; and Miller, *Sex-Crime Panic*.

24. Berube, *Coming Out Under Fire*.

25. D'Emilio, "The Homosexual Menace" in Peiss and Simmons, eds., *Passion and Power*.

26. Hassler and Smiley Interviews, JDI.

27. Brissette to Mattachine Foundation, 2/15/53, James Kepner Papers, One Institute Archives, Los Angeles; Cory, *The Homosexual in America*.

28. Hassler and Margaret Swomley Interviews, JDI.

29. Cary to Clarke, 2/16/53, and Jamison to Hoskins, 2/3/53, AFSCA, General Administration, Individuals, Bayard Rustin, 1953.

30. Clarke to Hoskins, 2/2/53, Jones to Hoskins, 2/16/53, and Hoskins to Clarke, 2/6/53, all in AFSCA, General Administration, Individuals, Bayard Rustin, 1953.

31. McReynolds Interview, JDI. BR to Sayre, 2/27/53, Sayre Papers, DG 117, Box 14, Rustin Folder, SCPC. BR to Swomley, 3/8/53, FORP, Swomley Files, Box 2.

32. McReynolds to BR, 2/3/53, McReynolds Papers, DG 134, Series I, Box 1, 1953 File, SCPC; McReynolds Interview, JDI. I am indebted to Maurice Isserman for calling my attention to this and other relevant letters in the McReynolds Papers.

33. Whitney to Rustin, 2/2/53, Whitney Papers, Box 3, "Correspondence Unidentified" File, Syracuse University; and Rustin Interview, conducted by Ruth Geller, c. 1985, copy provided by R. Allen Smith. I am indebted to Smith for calling my attention to both of these sources and to alerting me to the significance of Rustin's relationship with Whitney.

34. Ascher Interview, JDI. The quotations in this and the succeeding paragraphs are from this interview unless otherwise noted.

35. FOR Executive Committee Meeting Minutes, 4/6/53, FORP, Box 4, Minutes and Reports, 1950–60.

36. Sayre to Nelson, 1/30/53, and Sayre to Trocme and Bartlett, 1/30/53, FORP, Swomley Files, Box 2; Houser Interview, JDI.

37. Helen Siegrist, Director of Social Service, Social Service Sheet, 7/14/53, Robert Ascher Papers, New York City.

10: "I Can Again Be Useful"

1. DiGia and Finch Interviews, JDI.

2. DiGia Interview, JDI.

3. Executive Committee Meeting Minutes, 4/27/53, and Roy Finch, Memo to the Executive Committee and National Advisory Council, 8/25/53, WRLP, Series B, Box 1; Finch to Hughan, 8/24/53, WRLP, Series B, Box 12.

4. Muste to Finch, 8/29/53, WRLP, Series B, Box 12.

5. Finch to Hughan, 8/24/53, and Finch to Tatum, 8/29/53, WRLP, Series B, Box 12.

6. Dellinger to Finch, 9/6/53, WRLP, Series B, Box 12.

7. Roy Finch, Confidential Memo to Executive Committee and National Advisory Council, n.d., WRLP, Series B, Box 1; Finch to EC and NAC members, 10/1/53, WRLP, Series B, Box 12.

8. Finch Interview, JDI.

9. *Ibid.*

10. DiGia Interview, JDI.

11. Rustin, CUOHC. Figures on the size of the WRL come from Executive Committee Meeting Minutes, 1953–54, WRLP, Series B, Box 1.

12. Information on Rustin's early work at the WRL can be gleaned from the Executive Committee Meeting Minutes, 1953–1956, WRLP, Series B, Box 1.

13. DiGia and Finch Interviews, JDI.

14. Executive Committee Meeting Minutes, 1/23/56, 6/11/56, and 10/26/54, WRLP, Series B, Box 1.

15. Discussions of the civil defense protests can be found in Isserman, *If I Had a Hammer;* Tracy, *Direct Action;* Wittner, *Rebels Against War* and *Resisting the Bomb;* and Garrison, "'Our Skirts Gave Them Courage,'" in Meyerowitz, ed., *Not June Cleaver.*

16. *Commonweal* and *Post-Gazette* clippings in BRP, PDC 1955 File, Reel 5.

17. Muste, "Proposal for a Bi-Monthly Magazine," 2/21/55, WRLP, Series B, Box 12, Liberation—Formation.

18. Muste, Subcommittee on Magazine, "Monthly Magazine Prospectus," n.d., WRLP, Series B, Box 12, Liberation—Formation.

19. McReynolds Interview, JDI.

20. DiGia Interview, JDI.

21. McReynolds Interview, JDI.

22. McReynolds to Ben, 10/9/53, McReynolds Papers, DG 134, Series II, Box 1, SCPC. I am indebted to Maurice Isserman for calling my attention to this letter.

23. Finch Interview, JDI.

24. Cary to Ed Sanders, 11/10/54, AFSCA, General Administration—Information Service, Publications, 1954.

25. *Speak Truth to Power: A Quaker Search for an Alternative to Violence* (Philadelphia: AFSC, 1955), p. 10.

26. *Ibid.*, pp. 35, 39, 40.

27. Sanders to Cary, 11/5/54, and Rustin to Cary, 12/17/54, AFSCA, General Administration—Information Service, Publications, 1954.

28. Bristol to Ascher, 10/28/55; Poinsard to Ascher, 11/28/55; and Ascher to Poinsard, 11/30/55; all from the files of Robert Ascher, copies provided by Walter Naegle.

11: "No Force on Earth Can Stop This Movement"

1. Rustin, "New South, Old Politics," *Liberation*, 10/56, pp. 23–26.

2. APR to Dear Friend, 2/17/56, and Thomas to APR, 3/8/56, NTP, Reel 30, Series I.

3. Levison Interview, CRDP, and Rustin Interview, CUOHC. Grant mentions Baker's acquaintance with Parks in her biography of Baker, p. 102.

4. Quoted in Burns, *Daybreak of Freedom*, p. 17.

5. Rustin Interview, CUOHC.

6. Smith to MLK, 3/10/56, Lillian Smith Papers, Box 15, File 40, University of Georgia; and Rustin, "Montgomery Diary," *Liberation*, 4/56, pp. 7–10.

7. Farmer Interview, CUOHC; WRL Executive Committee Minutes, 2/20/56, WRLP, Series B, Box 1.

8. Rustin, "Montgomery Diary."

9. *Ibid.*

10. *Ibid*; BR to Arthur Brown, 2/23/56, CDG-A, Rustin File, SCPC.

11. *Ibid.*

12. BR to Brown and DiGia, 2/25/56, CDG-A, Rustin File, SCPC.

13. Rustin, "Montgomery Diary."

14. Rustin Interview, CUOHC.

15. *Ibid*; Smiley Interview, JDI.

16. Rustin Interview, CUOHC.

17. Montgomery *Advertiser*, 3/7/56, p. 1.

18. BR to Brown and DiGia, 2/25/56, CDG-A, Rustin File, SCPC. Information on Worthy comes from Smiley to Swomley and Hassler, 2/29/56, FORP, Swomley Files, Box 2.
19. Swomley to Wilson Riles, 2/21/56, FORP, Swomley Files, Box 2.
20. Swomley to Smiley, 2/29/56 and 3/1/56, FORP, Swomley Files, Box 2; Thomas to Jack, 3/12/56, NTP, Reel 30, Series I.
21. Swomley to Smiley, 2/29/56 and 3/1/56, FORP, Swomley Files, Box 2; Swomley to Walker, n.d., BRP, Reel 4, MIA Folder.
22. Smiley to Swomley, n.d., FORP, Swomley Files, Box 2.
23. Smiley to Swomley, 2/29/56, FORP, Swomley Files, Box 2; Smiley Interview, JDI.
24. McReynolds Interview, JDI.
25. Martin Luther King, Jr., *Stride Toward Freedom*. See also, as examples of Rustin's neglect, Wilkins, *Standing Fast*, and Abernathy, *And the Walls Came Tumbling Down*.
26. Rustin Interview, CUOHC; Jack Interview, JDI; Jack Memo, 3/9/56, BRP, Reel 4, MIA Folder.
27. "Our Struggle," *Liberation*, 4/56, pp. 3–6; BR to MLK, 3/8/56, MLKBU, Box 5, Folder 79.
28. Wilkins to Norman Thomas, 6/22/56, NTP, Reel 31, Series I, Correspondence 1956.
29. Rustin, "Terror in the Delta," *Liberation*, 12/56, pp. 17–19.
30. See, for instance, MLK to BR, 7/10/56, and BR to MLK, 10/18/56, MLKBU, Box 64A, Folder 22; BR to MLK, 9/12/56, MLKBU, Box 67, Folder 34; MLK to BR, 9/20/56, BRP, Reel 3, MLK File.
31. Rustin, "The Revolution in the South," 12/56, AFSCA, General Administration, American Section, Community Relations Program, 1956; untitled draft, BRP, Reel 4, MIA Folder.
32. Rustin, "The Revolution in the South."
33. Rustin, "New South, Old Politics." Unless otherwise noted, analysis and quotations contained in this and the following paragraphs come from this article and from Rustin, "The Revolution in the South."
34. Burns, *Daybreak of Freedom*, p. 307.
35. New York *Times*, 11/14/56, p. 1.
36. Smiley, Report from the South #2, 8/15/56, MLKP, Series I, Box 10, FOR File.
37. Baker Interview, CRDP.
38. BR to MLK, 12/23/56, and "The Negroes' Struggle for Freedom," and "Memo," all in BRP, Reel 3, MLK File.
39. "Memo," BRP, Reel 3, MLK File.
40. The Baltimore conversation is discussed in Levison Interview, CRDP.
41. Working Papers, BRP, Reel 5, SCLC File.
42. "A Statement to the South and Nation," BRP, Reel 5, SCLC File.

12: "MORE GOING ON THAN MOST PEOPLE WOULD GATHER"

1. Muste, Draft Proposal, 10/31/56, NTP, Reel 31, Series I.
2. BR to Muste, 5/20/57, MLKBU, Box 64A, Folder 22.
3. Harrington, *Fragments of the Century*, pp. 63, 97, 103.
4. "Nonviolence and the New Year," *Liberation*, 1/57.
5. For accounts of the founding of SANE, CNVA, and the late-1950s revival of pacifist agitation in the United States, see Isserman, *If I Had a Hammer*; Wittner, *Rebels Against War* and *Resisting the Bomb*; Tracy, *Direct Action*; and Katz, "Radical Pacifism and the Contemporary American Peace Movement."
6. The group, which originally called itself Non-Violent Action Against Nuclear Weapons, did not change its name to CNVA until fall 1958.
7. Executive Committee Meeting Minutes, 5/6/57, WRLP, Series B, Box 1; *WRL News*, September–October 1957.
8. Peck quoted in Isserman, *If I Had a Hammer*, p. 150.
9. Executive Committee Meeting Minutes, 9/10/57 and 10/22/57, WRLP, Series B, Box 1.
10. "Remarks by Bayard Rustin at Trafalgar Square," BRP, Reel 20.
11. Belmont to Boardman, 4/8/58, BR-FBI.
12. "To the Finland Station," *Liberation*, 6/58, 9-10.
13. *Ibid.*, and Executive Committee Meeting Minutes, 4/25/58, WRLP, Series B, Box 1.
14. Scott Memo, 7/28/58, "Where have we been and what should be our next step toward peace," CNVAP, Box 3; "To the Finland Station."
15. Executive Committee Meeting Minutes, 6/10/58, WRLP, Series B, Box 1.
16. "To the Finland Station."
17. For accounts, see Isserman, *If I Had a Hammer*; Katz, "Radical Pacifism"; and Scott Memo, 7/28/58, CNVAP, Box 3.
18. Quoted in Isserman, *If I Had a Hammer*, p. 128.
19. Scott Memos, 7/28/58 and 2/2/59, CNVAP, Box 3.
20. Quoted in Katz, "Radical Pacifism," p. 76.
21. Scott Memo, 7/26/58, CNVAP, Box 3.
22. Draft of Telegram, 2/14/57, BRP, Reel 20; and Rustin Memo, "Prayer Pilgrimage," n.d., WRLP, Series B, Box 1.
23. Rustin Interview, MVI; Digest of In Friendship Activities, 3/6/57, APRP, Box 23; Baker, Rustin, and Levison, "Memo Regarding Prayer Pilgrimage," NAACP Papers, Group III, Series A, Box 245, LC.
24. Rustin Memo, "Prayer Pilgrimage," n.d., WRLP, Series B, Box 1.
25. Memo on Opening Remarks, 4/18/57, APRP, Box 30; Press Release, n.d., BRP, Reel 4.

26. Program, 5/17/57, BRP, Reel 4; Clark to Randolph, 5/21/57, APRP, Box 30.

27. New York *Amsterdam News*, 6/1/57, clipping in NAACP Papers, Group III, Series A, Box 245, LC.

28. Wilkins to MLK, 6/4/57, MLKBU, Box 62, Folder 12; Wilkins to C. B. Powell, Publisher, 6/4/57, NAACP Papers, Group III, Series A, Box 245, LC.

29. BR and Levison to MLK, n.d., MLKBU, Box 5, Folder 29; Memo for Conference with Vice President Nixon, 6/13/57, BRP, Reel 3, MLK File.

30. Baker and Levison Interviews, CRDP; Horowitz Interview, JDI.

31. BR to MLK, 5/10/57, BRP, Reel 4, Prayer Pilgrimage Folder.

32. See especially the letters in MLKBU, Box 5, Folder 29, and in BRP, Reel 3, MLK Folder.

33. MLK to BR, 11/5/58, MLKBU, Box 5, Folder 29; Levison to MLK, 6/10/58, 1/24/58, and 9/1/59, MLKBU, Box 2, Folder 10.

34. DiGia Interview, JDI.

35. Bowles to MLK, 1/28/59, copy in BRP, Reel 3, MLK Folder.

36. Bristol to Dee _____, 2/25/59; Bristol to Corinne Johnson, 3/10/59; Johnson to Bristol, 3/26/59, all in AFSCA, "Foreign Service 1959, International Centers Program."

37. "Position on the Civil Rights Legislation; Relation of 'Crusade for Citizenship' to Southern Struggle and Civil Rights Legislation," handwritten memo, n.d., MLKBU, Box 5, Folder 29.

38. "Crusade for Citizenship Project #1: Workshop on Registration and Voting" and "Proposed Plans for Kick-Off Meetings," BRP, Reel 5; BR to MLK, 11/18/57, BRP, Reel 3.

39. Baker Interview, CRDP.

40. "Report of Activities in Local Communities since February 12 Meetings," 4/3/58, MLKBU, Box 48, File 154; Levison to APR, 4/22/58, APRP, Box 30, Prayer Pilgrimage File.

41. Baker to BR and Levison, 7/16/58, and Baker to MLK, 7/16/58, BRP, Reel 3, MLK File; Baker Interview, CRDP.

42. Telegram, 9/3/58, APRP, Box 34.

43. Press Release, 10/25/58, BRP, Reel 6, Youth March Folder.

44. Levison to MLK, 11/3/58, MLKBU, Box 2, Folder 10; "Interim Report: Youth March of 1958," 12/30/58, APRP, Box 34; Wilkins to APR, 11/20/58, APRP, Box 34.

45. APR to Bates, 3/14/59; APR to Wilkins, 4/8/59; BR to Randolph, 1/26/59, all in APRP, Box 33; Notice of Meeting on 4/3/59, APRP, Box 34.

46. Wilkins to APR, 5/26/59, and APR to Wilkins, 6/5/59, APRP, Box 33.

47. Horowitz Interview, JDI; Lerner, *Fireweed*, p. 354; Carmichael Interview, MVI.

48. Davis to BR, 8/10/59, BRP, Reel 20. On the hospital workers strike see Fink and Greenberg, *Upheaval in the Quiet Zone*.

49. McReynolds and Horowitz Interviews, JDI; Harrington, *Fragments of the Century*, pp. 68, 71, 97.
50. Horowitz and McReynolds Interviews, JDI.

13: "AN EMPLOYEE OF OTHERS"

1. Carter to Willoughby, 7/15/59, CNVAP, Box 13, Sahara Project.
2. Willoughby to CNVA Committee Members, 7/30/59, and Hassler to Willoughby, 9/14/59, CNVAP, Box 13, Sahara Project.
3. Carter to Willoughby, 8/5/59 and 9/9/59, and Randle to Willoughby, 8/20/59, CNVAP, Box 13, Sahara Project.
4. "Sahara Protest," Direct Action Committee Against Nuclear War, 8/15/59, CNVAP, Box 13, Sahara Project.
5. DiGia to BR, 10/31/59, and Kahn to BR, 10/29/59, BRP, Reel 20; BR to Willoughby, 10/18/59, CNVAP, Box 13.
6. BR to Willoughby, 10/18/59, CNVAP, Box 13.
7. Randle to Jervis Anderson, 7/3/89, copy in author's possession.
8. BR to Peck, 11/10/59, CNVAP, Box 13.
9. BR to Willoughby et al., 11/5/59, and BR to DiGia, 11/22/59, CNVAP, Box 13.
10. BR to Willoughby et al., 11/5/59, and "Progress Report on Sahara Project, n.d., CNVAP, Box 13.
11. BR to Willoughby et al., 11/5/59, CNVAP, Box 13.
12. Kahn to BR, 11/23/59, BRP, Reel 20; MLK to Levison, 11/19/59, MLKBU, Box 2, Folder 10; King's statement quoted in Garrow, *Bearing the Cross*, p. 124; Levison to BR, 11/1/59, BRP, Reel 20.
13. Levison to BR, n.d., BRP, Reel 3; Kahn to BR, 10/29/59, BRP, Reel 20.
14. BR to Willoughby et al., 11/5/59, CNVAP, Box 13.
15. Muste and Levison to BR, 11/14/59, BRP, Reel 20.
16. Muste to BR, 11/15/59, BRP, Reel 20.
17. "Report #3," 11/16/59, CNVAP, Box 13, Sahara Project; Muste to Norman Thomas, 11/20/59, NTP, Reel 37, Series I.
18. Muste to Willoughby, 11/26/59, CNVAP, Box 13.
19. Muste to *Liberation*, 12/6/59, CNVAP, Box 13.
20. Muste, "Memo for Liberation," 12/12/59, CNVAP, Box 13.
21. Randle Cables, 1/14/60 and 2/1/60, CNVAP, Box 13; New York *Times*, 1/30/60, p. 3; 1/31/60, p. 13; 2/22/60, p. 3; 2/13/60, p. 1; and 4/1/60, p. 1.
22. Levison to BR, 11/1/59, BRP, Reel 20.
23. Kahn to BR, 11/25/59, and Levison to BR, 11/1/59, BRP, Reel 20.
24. Executive Committee Meeting Minutes, 1/11/60 and 2/2/60, WRLP, Series B, Box 1.
25. Chafe, *Civilities and Civil Rights*, p. 71; Wilkins to State Conferences et al., 3/16/60, NAACP Papers, Group III, Series A, Box 289, LC; Alexan-

der J. Allen, "Sit-in Demonstrations," 4/13/60, NUL, Part I, Series I, Box 47; "The Student Protest Movement, Winter 1960," 4/1/60, prepared by Southern Regional Council, in MLKBU, Box 6, Folder 34.

26. BR to Ballou, 3/4/60, MLKBU, Box 64A, Folder 22.

27. *Ibid.*; BR to MLK, 3/3/60, MLKBU, Box 4, Folder 22; BR to MLK, 6/16/60, MLKBU, Box 5, Folder 29.

28. New York *Times*, 3/29/60, p. 25.

29. Levison to MLK, n.d., MLKBU, Box 2, Folder 10.

30. *Ibid.*, and BR to MLK, 5/19/60, MLKBU, Box 71A, Folder 9B.

31. Current to Wilkins, 4/8/60, NAACP Papers, Group III, Series A, Box 289, LC, and Current to Wilkins, 5/16/60, NAACP Papers, Group III, Series A, Box 201, LC.

32. Quoted in Carson, *In Struggle*, p. 23.

33. Farmer to Wilkins, 6/10/60, NAACP Papers, Group III, Series A, Box 214, LC.

34. Wilkins to MLK, 4/27/60, NAACP Papers, Group III, Series A, Box 289, LC.

35. EMB to [?], 6/29/60, NAACP Papers, Group III, Series A, Box 177, LC.

36. Wilkins to APR, 6/14/60, NAACP Papers, Group III, Series A, Box 246, LC.

37. Pittsburgh *Courier*, 6/25/60, p. 3.

38. Rustin Interview, CUOHC; Press Release, 6/23/60, NAACP Papers, Group III, Series A, Box 244, LC.

39. Rustin Interview, MVI; George Chauncey, Jr., and Lisa Kennedy, "Time on Two Crosses: An Interview with Bayard Rustin," *Village Voice*, 6/30/87, pp. 27–29.

40. Rustin Interview, MVI; Pittsburgh *Courier*, 7/9/60, p. 2.

41. See, for example, Gloster Current to Ike Adams, 7/6/60, and Current to Dempsey Travis, 7/6/60, NAACP Papers, Group III, Series A, Box 246, LC.

42. McReynolds Interview, JDI; Hentoff column, 7/14/60, copy in AMP, Box 59, Folder 10; James Baldwin, "The Dangerous Road before Martin Luther King," *Harper's Magazine*, February 1961, pp. 33–42.

43. BR to MLK, 2/6/61, and MLK to BR, 3/6/61, MLKBU, Box 56A, Folder 39; Horowitz Interview, JDI.

44. Farmer Interview, CUOHC.

45. Barry to Stembridge, 7/13/60, SNCC Papers, MLKC, Box 9, Subgroup A, Series IV; Stembridge to McReynolds, 8/9/60, SNCC Papers, MLKC, Box 23, Subgroup A, Series IV; Barry to Meany, 9/16/60, SNCC Papers, MLKC, Box 1, Subgroup A, Series I; and Stembridge to John, 9/26/60, SNCC Papers, MLKC, Box 25, Subgroup A, Series V; Baker to APR, 6/5/61, APRP, Box 2.

14: "Ours Is Not a World-Shaking Project"

1. Gottlieb to APR, 3/2/60, BRP, Reel 6, WRL Folder; McReynolds Interview, JDI.
2. DiGia Interview, JDI.
3. BR to Norman Thomas, 10/6/60, NTP, Series I, Reel 38.
4. Quoted in Burner, *John F. Kennedy and a New Generation*, p. 58; and Parmet, *JFK*, p. 87.
5. CNVA Executive Committee Meeting Minutes, 10/21/60, CNVAP, Box 1.
6. *The War Resister*, First Quarter, 1961, "Tenth Triennial Conference Report."
7. *WRL News*, No. 106 (March/April 1961), pp. 2–3.
8. Rustin, "Non-Violent Direct Action for Racial Integration," *Bhoodan*, December 23, 1961.
9. *The War Resister*, First Quarter, 1961; Rustin, "Non-Violent Direct Action for Racial Integration," *WRL News*, No. 106 (March/April 1961), pp. 2–3.
10. Willoughby Interview, JDI.
11. Carter Interview, JDI; CNVA Executive Committee Meeting Minutes, 1/6/61, CNVAP, Series 1, Box 1.
12. BR to Muste et al., 3/23/61, and Carter and BR to Muste et al., 4/7/61, CNVAP, Box 14.
13. "Report to CNVA on Matters Arising out of Weekend Conference," 3/13/61, and "Confidential Memo," 4/22–23/61, both in CNVAP, Box 14.
14. Memo from Carter and BR to Muste et al., 4/6/61, CNVAP, Box 14.
15. Carter and BR to European Contacts, 4/28/61, CNVAP, Box 14.
16. Memo from Carter and BR to Lyttle et al., 5/24/61, CNVAP, Box 14.
17. BR to Muste, 5/17/61, and BR to Muste et al., 5/23/61, CNVAP, Box 14.
18. Carter Interview, JDI.
19. *Ibid.*
20. Muste, "Organizational and Political Note," 6/22/61, CNVAP, Box 14.
21. Randle to Jervis Anderson, 7/3/89, copy in author's possession.
22. "Tenth Triennial Conference Report," *The War Resister*, First Quarter, 1961.
23. *Ibid.*, and Rustin, "Report from India," *WRL News*, No. 106 (March/April 1961), pp. 2–3.
24. Siddharaj Dhadda, "World Peace Brigade: The Task Before the Beirut Conference"; Bill Sutherland, "Comments on World Peace Brigade," 10/18/61; April Carter and Michael Randle, "Memo on World Peace Brigade and Suggested Action," all in Randle Papers, copies in author's possession.
25. Sutherland, "World Peace Brigade—Further Comments," n.d., and Lyttle, Memo to Peace Brigade Conference, n.d., Randle Papers, copies in author's possession.
26. Barbara Deming, "International Peace Brigade," *The Nation*, 4/7/62, pp. 303–306.

27. Rustin, Scott, and Randle, "Memorandum on Positive Action in Southern Africa," n.d., Randle Papers, copy in author's possession.

28. BR to Muste, 2/22/62, World Peace Brigade Papers, Box 1, Folder 3, SHSW.

29. "Crisis in Northern Rhodesia," *Peace News*, 3/2/62, and "First Peace Brigade Project," *WRL News*, March–April 1962.

30. Rustin Memo, 3/8/62, World Peace Brigade Papers, Box 2, Folder 1, SHSW; "Dar—the Invasion Springboard," *Sunday Nation*, 3/4/62, clipping in APRP, Box 2.

31. See the report, "Brigade in Africa," Randle Papers, copy in author's possession.

32. BR to Muste, 5/10/61, CNVAP, Box 15.

33. Thomas to Dear Friend, 9/11/61, and Thomas to James Carey, 9/25/61, NTP, Reel 64, Turn Toward Peace material.

34. CNVA Executive Committee Meeting Minutes, 1/26/62, 11/1/62, and 3/9/63, CNVAP, Box 1.

35. Farmer, King, and White Interviews, JFKL.

36. Transcript of Rustin / Malcolm X Debate, video copy in author's possession.

37. BR to Charley, 10/17/61, SNCC Papers, Subgroup A, Series IV, Box 23, MLKC.

38. Ed Brown Interview, CRDP.

39. Momeyer to author, 4/18/2001.

15: "ONE OF THE GREAT DAYS IN AMERICAN HISTORY"

1. "The March Remembered," 7/27–28/83, transcript in BRP, Reel 4.

2. Hill Interview, CRDP.

3. First Draft, BRP, Reel 7, Folder 4.

4. Rustin Interview, MVI.

5. BR to Friends, 2/17/63, BRP, Reel 20; BR to Muste, 2/14/63 and 2/17/63, World Peace Brigade Papers, Box 1, Folder 4, SHSW, and North American Regional Council Minutes, 2/27/63, World Peace Brigade Papers, Box 3, Folder 7, SHSW.

6. Bond to APR, 4/1/63, Farmer to APR, 4/1/63, and Jones to APR, 5/6/63, BRP, Reel 7, "General Correspondence March–June 1963"; Hill Interview, MVI; Horowitz Interview, JDI.

7. Young to APR, 4/2/63 and 4/30/63, NUL, Part II, Series I, Box 25.

8. APR to Wilkins, 3/25/63, and "Press Release," Negro American Labor Council, 5/22/63, BRP, Reel 7, Folder 6.

9. Muste to APR, 4/5/63, and APR to Muste, 4/15/63, BRP, Reel 7, Folder 6.

10. Young, *An Easy Burden*, p. 185.

11. Quoted in Garrow, *Bearing the Cross*, p. 247.

12. Lee White Interview, JFKL.

13. Marshall, "Memorandum for the Attorney General," 4/23/63, Burke Marshall Papers, Box 16, JFKL, and "Press Release," 5/12/63, copy in Lee White Papers, Box 19, JFKL.

14. Burke Marshall Interview, JFKL.

15. Burke Marshall Interview, JFKL, and Oberdorfer to Robert Kennedy, 7/9/63, President's Office Files, Box 97, JFKL.

16. Speech to U.S. Conference of Mayors, 6/9/63, Lee White Papers, Box 21, JFKL; televised speech quoted in Parmet, *JFK*, p. 271.

17. New York Field Office File 100-36585, BUF 100-106670, 7/22/63, King and Levison FBI File, MLKC, Box 1, Section 4; Young, *An Easy Burden*, p. 269.

18. Rustin Interview, in "1963 March on Washington: the March Remembered," 7/27–28/83, unidentified transcript in BRP, Reel 7; "The Meaning of Birmingham," reprinted in Rustin, *Down the Line*, pp. 107–108; "The Great Lessons of Birmingham," reprinted in Broderick and Meier, eds., *Negro Protest Thought*, pp. 304–313; Hefner to Muste, 6/17/63, BRP, Reel 20.

19. "Proposed Plans for March," 7/2/63, BRP, Reel 7, Folder 2.

20. *Ibid.*, and Rustin Interview, MVI.

21. Marshall and White Interviews, JFKL; Diggs to King, 6/27/63, NUL, Part II, Series I, Box 25; Lewis Interview, CRDP.

22. Lewis and Rustin Interviews, MVI; Rustin Interview, CUOHC.

23. Thomas Hanlon to Whitney Young, 8/1/63, NAACP Papers, Group III, Series A, Box 228.

24. Lewis, *Walking with the Wind*, p. 217.

25. Rustin Interview, CUOHC.

26. *Ibid.*

27. National Convention Minutes, 6/27–30/63, CORE Papers, Subgroup C, Series I, Box 28, MLKC; Allen to Young, 7/17/63, NUL, Part II, Series I, Box 25. On the SCLC see Jones to MLK, 7/11/63, and Kahn to MLK, 8/6/63, MLKP, Series I, Box 25; Rustin Interview, CUOHC.

28. Hanlon to Young, 8/1/63 and 8/13/63, NAACP Papers, Group III, Series A, Box 228, LC; "1st Plan of Operations," 7/8/63, BRP, Reel 7, Folder 3; "Organizing Manual #2," BRP, Reel 7, Folder 1.

29. Horowitz Interview, JDI; Hill Interview, CRDP; Hill Interview, JDI; Bill Mahoney, "Report: March to Washington Committee Meeting," 7/19/63, SNCC Papers, Subgroup C, Box 163, MLKC; tape of Rustin Interview, WINS Radio, 8/21/63, MLKBU, Box 122.

30. Guthman to Robert Kennedy, 8/15/63, "Weekly Report on Civil Rights Demonstrations," Burke Marshall Papers, Box 31, JFKL; New York *Amsterdam News*, 7/27/63, p. 1; Robert F. Kennedy Interview, JFKL.

31. Rustin Interview, CUOHC.

32. Transcript of Conference with Civil Rights Leaders, 7/11/63, George Reedy Office Files, Box 8, LBJL.

33. Hoover quoted in Congressional *Record*—Senate, 8/2/63, p. 13968; O'Reilly, *Racial Matters*, p. 129.

34. O'Reilly, *Racial Matters*, p. 94; Congressional *Record*—Senate, 8/2/63, pp. 13968–13975, and 8/7/63, pp. 14454–14463. The quotations can be found on p. 13968.

35. Congressional *Record*—Senate, 8/13/63, p. 14840.

36. Washington *Post*, 8/11/63.

37. Donald Roney to NY Office, 8/12/64, Bureau File #100-158790, BR-FBI.

38. Congressional *Record*—Senate, 8/13/63, p. 14837ff.

39. "Statement by A. Philip Randolph, 8/12/63, *Bayard Rustin*," NAACP Papers, Group III, Series A, Box 229, LC.

40. Philadelphia *Inquirer*, 8/27/83, in Rustin clipping file, CCHS; Rustin Interview, CUOHC; BR to Current, 8/24/63, NAACP Papers, Group III, Series A, Box 228, LC; Kahn Interview, MVI; Kahn to Stembridge, 8/19/63, BRP, Reel 7, March on Washington Correspondence.

41. Sisson Memo, 8/7/63, President's Office Files, Box 97, JFKL; BR to Bill Becker, 8/7/63, BRP, Reel 7, March on Washington Correspondence; Jones to King, 8/2/63, MLKP, Series I, Box 11, "Gandhi Society" Folder; New York *Herald Tribune*, 8/25/63, p. 24.

42. Rustin Interview, CUOHC.

43. Horowitz Interview, JDI; New York *Amsterdam News*, 8/10/63, p. 1; New York *Herald Tribune*, 8/27/63, p. 1. Information on travel also comes from Burke Marshall Papers, Box 32, JFKL, and NAACP Papers, Group III, Series A, Box 228, LC.

44. Hedgeman to APR, 8/16/63, NUL, Part II, Series I, Box 25; Murray to APR, 8/21/63, BRP, Reel 7.

45. New York *Times*, 8/26/63, p. 1.

46. New York *Times*, 8/27/63, p. 23; New York *Herald Tribune*, 8/27/63, p. 1.

47. Lewis Speech, copy in NAACP Papers, Group III, Series A, Box 229, LC.

48. Rustin Interview, MVI; Lewis, *Walking with the Wind*, p. 226.

49. Hill Interview, JDI.

50. *Newsweek*, 9/9/63, p. 20.

51. New York *Times*, 8/29/63, p. 17.

52. "Speeches by the Leaders: The March on Washington for Jobs and Freedom," NAACP Papers, Group III, Series A, Box 229, LC.

53. *Time*, 9/6/63, p. 15; New York *Times*, 8/29/63, p. 1; "Speeches by the Leaders."

54. New York *Times*, 8/29/63, p. 16.

55. BR to Sherwood, 9/9/63, BRP, Reel 7, March on Washington Correspondence.

56. Hill and Horowitz Interview, JDI; Rustin, "A Sense That All Was Possible," clipping in BRP, Reel 4; Rustin Interview, CUOHC.

16: "ON THE THRESHOLD OF A NEW POLITICAL MOVEMENT"

1. Thomas to BR, 9/16/63; Knoke to BR, 11/1/63; Lee to BR, 9/23/63; all in BRP, Reel 20; DLN, 9/21/63, letter to editor.
2. Rustin Interview, MVI; BR to Sherwood, 9/9/63, and BR to Dorothy Hassler, 9/9/63, BRP, Reel 7, March on Washington Correspondence.
3. Rustin Interview, CUOHC; BR to Chairmen, 9/27/63, NAACP Papers, Group III, Series A, Box 228, LC; and BR to Hassler, 9/9/63, BRP, Reel 7.
4. BR to Ten Chairmen, 9/5/63, NAACP Papers, Group III, Series A, Box 229, LC; BR to Chairmen, 9/27/63, NAACP Papers, Group III, Series A, Box 228, LC.
5. "Memo on Strategy of the Integration Movement," 11/5/63, MLKP, Series I, Box 20; "Local Hearings on Terror in the South," n.d., NAACP Papers, Group III, Series A, Box 229, LC.
6. BR to Local Committees and Contacts, 9/16/63, SNCC Papers, Subgroup A, Series IV, Box 16, MLKC; Rustin Statement, Press Conference, 9/18/63, and Rittenberg to BR, 9/29/63, BRP, Reel 20; New York *Herald Tribune*, 9/24/63; Nat Hentoff, "Socrates of the Civil Rights Movement," New York *Herald Tribune*, Sunday Magazine, 6/28/64, pp. 6ff.
7. See the series of undated memos from Rustin, along with a memo of 9/5/63, NAACP Papers, Group III, Series A, Box 229, LC.
8. BR to Chairmen, 9/27/63, NAACP Papers, Group III, Series A, Box 228, LC.
9. Whaley to Young, 9/27/63, NUL, Part 2, Series I, Box 25; Notes on Conversation with Norman Hill, 11/30/63, AMP, Box 56; Moon to John Johnson, 11/6/63, NAACP Papers, Group III, Series A, Box 229, LC; Notes on Conversation with Tom Kahn, 1/14/64, AMP, Box 58.
10. Notes on Conversation with Norman Hill, 12/6/63, AMP, Box 56; FBI Memo, NY Office, 12/6/63, CPUSA, NQ, CIRM, BR-FBI; and Notes on Conversation with Kahn, 1/14/64, AMP, Box 58.
11. BR to Ed Nash, 11/1/63, BRP, Reel 20; FBI Memo, 11/29/63, BR-FBI; "Protesters Warned of Using Gimmicks," Washington *Post*, 8/30/63, clipping in AMP, Box 58; undated tape recording of Rustin talk, George Wiley Papers, SHSW.
12. New York *Times*, 12/2/63, p. 1.
13. Recollections of Conversation with Norman Hill at Howard University SNCC Conference, 11/30/63, AMP, Box 56; BR to Frankel, 12/5/63, BRP, Reel 20.

14. *Peace News*, 1/10/64, clipping in AMP, Box 59; Duff to Muste, 1/16/64, and Duff to BR, 2/7/64, BRP, Reel 20.

15. Kullos to BR, 1/17/64; [?] to BR, 1/18/64; and Pierre to BR, 2/1/64, all in BRP, Reel 20.

16. FBI Memo, NY Office, 1/21/64, CPUSA, NQ, CIRM, BR-FBI; King-Levison File, Box 1, Section 6, 11/4/63, NY Office, MLKC.

17. FBI Memo, NY Office, 1/28/64 and 2/5/64, CPUSA, NQ, CIRM, BR-FBI.

18. Unless otherwise noted, the account in this and the following paragraphs draws heavily from Taylor, *Knocking at Our Own Door*.

19. Morsell Interview, 1/31/64, AMP, Box 56.

20. New York *Journal American*, 2/2/64, p. 1; New York *Times*, 1/31/64, pp. 1, 25.

21. New York *Times*, 2/3/64, pp. 1, 18, and 2/4/64, pp. 1, 20.

22. New York *Journal-American*, 2/3/64, p. 1, and New York *Times*, 2/4/64, pp. 1, 20.

23. New York *Times*, 2/4/64, pp. 1, 20.

24. *Daily News*, 2/5/64, p. 1, and *Journal-American*, 2/5/64, p. 7. Editorial quoted in SAC/NY to FBI Director, 2/6/64, BR-FBI.

25. FBI Director to NY Office, 10/4/63, CPUSA, NQ, CIRM, BR-FBI.

26. SAC/NY to FBI Director, 11/18/63 and 11/29/63, CPUSA, NQ, CIRM, BR-FBI.

27. Donald Roney to SAC/NY, 2/4/64, CPUSA, NY File 100-129802, BR-FBI.

28. SAC/NY to FBI Director, 2/12/64 and 3/4/64, and FBI Director to SAC/NY, 3/19/64, BR-FBI.

29. New York *Times*, 2/5/64, p. 21; FBI Memo, NY Office, 2/12/64, CPUSA, CIRM, and FBI Memo, NY Office, 2/26/64, CPUSA, NQ, CIRM, BR-FBI.

30. FBI Memo, NY Office, 2/5/64, CPUSA, NQ, CIRM, File 100-3-116, BR-FBI.

31. Hoover to Robert Kennedy, 3/9/64, King-Levison FBI File, Box 8, Section 11, and FBI Memo, NY Office, 3/2/64, File 100-3-116, Box 1, Section 10, both in MLKC; SAC/NY to FBI Director, 3/25/64, File 100-3-104-34, BR-FBI.

32. FBI Memo, NY Office, 9/11/63, File 100-106670, BR-FBI.

33. *Ibid.*; SAC/NY to FBI Director, 9/23/63, Box 8, Section 10, King-Levison File, MLKC; SAC/NY to FBI Director, 9/23/63, and SAC/NY to FBI Director, 10/1/63, BR-FBI.

34. Rustin Interview, CUOHC.

35. FBI Memo, NY Office, 3/25/64 and 4/15/64, BR-FBI.

36. Nat Hentoff, "Socrates of the Civil Rights Movement," New York *Herald Tribune*, Sunday Magazine section, 6/28/64, pp. 6 ff.

37. New York *Times*, 3/3/64, p. 2; 3/10/64, p. 19; 3/11/64, pp. 1, 25; and 4/23/64, p. 28; Strickland to BR, 4/22/64 and 5/5/64, BRP, Reel 20.

38. FBI Memo, NY Office, "Racial Situation, New York Division," 4/1/64, BR-FBI; Farmer Interview, 10/14/70, AMP, Box 58.
39. FBI Memo, NY Office, 2/10/64, CPUSA, NQ, CIRM, BR-FBI; FBI Memo, 2/11/64, File 100-3-116, King-Levison FBI File, Box 1, Section 9, MLKC.
40. New York *Times*, 3/3/64, p. 22, and 3/17/64, pp. 1, 25.
41. New York *Times*, 5/18/64, p. 23, and 5/19/64, pp. 1, 29.
42. Hassler to Duff, 3/3/64; Muste to Duff, 3/13/64; and BR to Keith Robins, 3/23/64, BRP, Reel 20.
43. Lyndon B. Johnson, "Address Before a Joint Session of the Congress," 11/27/63, reprinted in Schulman, *Lyndon B. Johnson and American Liberalism*, pp. 169–73.
44. Clarence Mitchell Interview, LBJL.
45. Rustin, "From Protest to Politics," in *Down the Line*, p. 111.
46. Quoted in Patterson, *Grand Expectations*, p. 533.
47. "Remarks at the University of Michigan," 5/22/64, in Schulman, *Lyndon B. Johnson and American Liberalism*, pp. 174–77.
48. Quoted in Matusow, *The Unraveling of America*, p. 137.
49. William Higgs to James Farmer, 3/13/64, CORE Papers, Subgroup A, Series I, Box 2, "Democratic Convention 1964," MLKC.
50. Lawson to BR, 3/10/64, Workers Defense League Papers, Box 30, Folder 2, WSU; FBI Memo, NY Office, 6/9/64 and 7/1/64, CPUSA, NQ, CIRM, BR-FBI; *The New Yorker*, 4/11/64, pp. 33–35.
51. Belfrage, *Freedom Summer*, pp. 8, 19–20.
52. Interview with Ed King, in Anne Cooke Romaine, "The Mississippi Freedom Democratic Party through August 1964," M.A. Thesis, University of Virginia, 1969, MLKC; see also interview with Walter Tillow in Romaine.
53. New York *Times*, 7/20/64, p. 1. The account of the events in New York is drawn from *Times* coverage of July 18–22, 1964.
54. FBI Memo, NY Office, 9/4/64, CIRM, "Demonstration and Violence in NYC Following Shooting of James Powell," BR-FBI.
55. BR to Podhoretz, 2/21/67, and BR to Young, n.d., BRP, Reel 21.
56. FBI Memo, NY Office, 7/28/64, CPUSA, NQ, CIRM, BR-FBI.
57. Malcolm X to MLK, 6/30/64, MLKP, Series I, Box 15; BR to Jane Relin, 6/9/64, Workers Defense League Papers, Box 30, Folder 5, WSU; Rustin, "Nonviolence on Trial," *Fellowship*, July 1964, pp. 5–8.
58. Telegram, Wilkins to King, Farmer, Young, Randolph, and Lewis, n.d., NAACP Papers, Group III, Series A, Box 247, LC.
59. BR to Priscilla Berry, 7/14/64, BRP, Reel 21.
60. Statement of Civil Rights Organization Leaders, 7/29/64, NAACP Papers, Group III, Series A, Box 247, LC.
61. Valenti to Lee White, 8/4/64, White House Central Files, HU2/ST24, Box 27, LBJL; "Why We Continue to Demonstrate," NAC Steering Committee

Minutes, 8/8–9/64, CORE Papers, Subgroup C, Series I, Box 28, MLKC; and Hill to Farmer, 8/14/64, CORE Papers, Series I, Box 6, MLKC.

62. FBI Memo, NY Office, 8/3/64, CPUSA, NQ, CIRM, BR-FBI; and Rustin Interview, CUOHC.

63. Moses to Field Staff, 7/19/64, MLKP, Series I, Box 16, MFDP materials; and King/Levison FBI File, Box 1, Section 14, 7/26/64, MLKC; FBI Memo, NY Office, 7/28/64, CPUSA, NQ, CIRM, BR-FBI.

64. FBI Memo, NY Office, 8/14/64, CPUSA, NQ, CIRM, BR-FBI; New York *Times*, 7/20/64, p. 1.

65. Lewis to LBJ, 8/19/64, HU 2 / ST 24, Box 27; White to LBJ, 8/11/64, EX / GEN, PL 1 / ST 24, Box 52; and Moyers to LBJ, 8/19/64, White House Central Files, HU 2 / ST 24, Box 27; all in LBJL.

66. On Rustin's conversations with King, see FBI Memos, NY Office, 8/6/64, 8/10/64, 8/14/64, 8/20/64, BR-FBI. On the White House discussions about contact with Rustin and King, see White to Valenti, 8/11/64; White to LBJ, 8/12/64, 8/13/64, and 8/19/64; all in White House Central File, EX / GEN, PL 1 / ST 24, Box 81, LBJL.

67. Washington *Post*, 8/20/64, pp. A4, A5; New York *Times*, 8/16/64, p. 36, and 8/20/64, p. 1.

68. New York *Times*, 8/23/64, p. 1.

69. Rauh Interview, LBJL.

70. Ed King Interview in Romaine, "The Mississippi Freedom Democratic Party," MLKC; Rauh Interview, CRDP.

71. Lewis, *Walking with the Wind*, p. 291–292, and Lewis Interview, CRDP; Gitlin, *The Sixties*, pp. 161–162; Ed Brown Interview, CRDP; Staughton Lynd, "The New Radicals and 'Participatory Democracy,'" *Dissent* 12, No. 3 (Summer 1965): pp. 324–326.

72. Beschloss, *Taking Charge*, p. 526; Political News Summary, DNC, in Moyers Office Files, Box 19, LBJL; New York *Times*, 8/26/64, p. 28, and 8/27/64, p. 23; clippings in DNC Records, Series I, Boxes 77 and 78, LBJL.

73. Annie Devine Interview, CRDP; Theresa Del Pozzo to BR, 9/19/64, BRP, Reel 21.

74. BR to Del Pozzo, 9/29/64, BRP, Reel 21; Rustin Interviews, MVI and CUOHC.

17: "From Protest to Politics"

1. Lewis Interview, CRDP.

2. Ernest Calloway to BR, 9/29/64, and Bill Sanborn to BR, 11/17/64, BRP, Reel 21.

3. BR to Jack Heyman, 10/13/64, BRP, Reel 21; BR to Karl Bernhard, 8/28/64, Workers Defense League Papers, Box 30, Folder 7, WSU.

4. Rustin Interview, MVI; Hill to Farmer, 8/14/64, MLKP, Series I, Box 6.

5. "Annual Report to SCLC Eighth Annual Convention, 9/28–10/2/64," APRP, Box 2; Resolutions Adopted at 8th Annual Convention, MLKP, Series I, Box 31; FBI Memo, NY Office, 10/6/64, CIRM, BR-FBI.

6. FBI Memo, NY Office, 10/20/64, CIRM, BR-FBI, and Hoover to Bill Moyers, 11/6/64, BR-FBI.

7. See FBI Memos, NY Office, 11/10/64 and 11/17/64, CIRM, and FBI Memo, NY Office, "Martin Luther King," 12/7/64, BR-FBI; Randle to Jervis Anderson, 7/3/89, in author's possession.

8. FBI Memo, NY Office, 10/16/64, CIRM, and FBI Memo, "Martin Luther King, Jr.," 2/4/65, BR-FBI.

9. Baumgardner to Sullivan, 12/17/64 and 11/16/64; Jones to Deloach [date blacked out]; San Francisco Office to Director, 1/12/65, BR-FBI.

10. FBI Memo, NY Office, 9/29/64, CIRM, BR-FBI; "Statement of Income and Expenses, 5/65–8/65," APR Institute File, SCLC Papers, Subgroup B, Series IV, Box 42, MLKC; Reuther to BR, 4/8/65, Walter Reuther Papers, Box 518, Folder 1, WSU; Slaiman Interview, GMA.

11. BR to Reuther, 3/22/65, and APRI Prospectus, both in Walter Reuther Papers, Box 518, Folder 1, WSU.

12. "From Protest to Politics: The Future of the Civil Rights Movement," *Commentary*, February 1965, reprinted in Rustin, *Down the Line*, pp. 111–122. The quotations in the following paragraphs are all drawn from this article.

13. Rustin, "The Influence of the Right and Left in the Civil Rights Movement," APRP, Box 17.

14. "Alabama Chronology," MLKP, Series I, Box 22.

15. *Ibid.*

16. *Ibid.*; FBI Memo, NY Office, 3/18/65, CIRM, BR-FBI.

17. FBI Memos, NY Office, 2/16/65, CIRM; Martin Luther King, Jr., 2/18/65; Registrars of voters, Dallas County, Alabama, 3/11/65; and CIRM, 3/16/65, all in BR-FBI. New York *Times*, 3/15/65, pp. 1, 23, and 3/26/65, pp. 1, 22.

18. FBI Memos, NY Office, 4/2/65 and 3/18/65, CIRM, File 100-442529, BR-FBI; SCLC Board Meeting Minutes, 4/1–2/65, MLKP, Series I, Box 29.

19. SCLC Board Meeting Minutes, 4/1–2/65, MLKP, Series I, Box 29; Agenda—Orientation Session, 6/13–18/65, Workers Defense League Papers, Box 103, Folder 28, WSU.

20. "Report of the Special Open Meeting of the TTP Issues Committee," 6/29/64, CDG-A, Turn Toward Peace, Box 1, SCPC; FBI Memo, NY Office, 8/7/64, BR-FBI.

21. National Executive Committee Minutes, 5/20/65, and National Council Minutes, 6/9/65, CDG-A, Turn Toward Peace, Box 1, SCPC.

22. Dellinger, "The March on Washington and Its Critics," *Liberation*, 5/65, pp. 6–7.
23. Lynd, "Coalition Politics or Nonviolent Revolution?," *Liberation*, 6/65, pp. 18–21.
24. David McReynolds, "Transition: Personal and Political Notes," *Liberation*, 8/65, pp. 5–10.
25. Lynd, "Coalition Politics or Nonviolent Revolution?," p. 19.
26. New York *Times*, 6/9/65, p. 4; Tobin to BR, 6/10/65, and Runyon to BR, 6/14/65, BRP, Reel 21.
27. New York *Times*, 7/5/65, p. 4; Farmer Interview, JFKL.
28. "Bayard Rustin, 9/28/65," typescript, SCLC Papers, Subgroup A, Series I, Box 4, Rustin File, MLKC; Rustin, letter to editor of New York *Post* [date indistinct], copy in FBI Memo, NY Office, 7/26/65, BR-FBI.
29. FBI Memos, NY Office, 5/4/65, CIRM, File 100-442529; Martin Luther King, Jr., 8/5/65; and Communist Infiltration of SCLC, File 100-438794, 8/10/65, all in BR-FBI; New York *Times*, 8/14/65, p. 3; Muste to King, 7/11/65, SCLC Papers, Subgroup A, Series I, Box 4, Muste File, MLKC.
30. BR to Muste, 11/16/65, BRP, Reel 21.
31. McReynolds, "Transition: Personal and Political Notes," pp. 5–10.

18: "In the Shadow of War"

1. "To Fulfill These Rights: Commencement Address at Howard University," 6/4/65, text reprinted in Schulman, *Lyndon B. Johnson and American Liberalism*, pp. 201–208.
2. Ramsey Clark interviews, 1968–69, LBJL; Rowland Evans and Robert Novak, "Inside Report," Washington *Post*, 4/20/66, copy in Bill Moyers Office Files, Box 115, LBJL; William Taylor to Lee White, 7/15/65, Lee White Office Files, Box 5, LBJL.
3. White to LBJ, 8/3/65, White House Central Files—EX HU2/MC, GEN HU2/MC, Box 23, LBJL; McPherson Interviews, LBJL.
4. U.S. Department of Labor, *The Negro Family: The Case for National Action* (Washington: Government Printing Office, 1965). For an overview of the controversy, see Rainwater and Yancey, *The Moynihan Report and the Politics of Controversy*.
5. McPherson Interviews, LBJL.
6. Rustin, "The Watts 'Manifesto' and the McCone Report," in Rustin, *Down the Line*, pp. 140–153.
7. Rustin Interviews, MVI and CUOHC; Garrow, *Bearing the Cross*, p. 439.
8. Rustin, "The Watts 'Manifesto' and the McCone Report."
9. Moon to Wilkins, 7/21/65, NAACP Papers, Group III, Series A, Box 66, White House Conference File, LC.

10. BR to Morsell, Randolph, Height et al., 10/18/65, NAACP Papers, Group III, Series A, Box 66, LC; BR, "Background Paper," White House Planning Conference, November 1965, APRP, Box 32; BR to Lee White, 10/7/65, APRP, Box 2; Memo, "Confidential," n.d., Box 5, Lee White Office Files, LBJL; Abrams and Coleman to CUCRL, 10/25/65, White House Central Files, EX HU2/MC, 11/22/63–11/15/65, Box 22, LBJL.

11. McPherson and Abram Interviews, LBJL.

12. Abram Interview, LBJL.

13. Alexander Memo, n.d., Spring Conference, White House Central Files, Human Rights, EX HU2/MC, 11/16/65–1/4/66, Box 22, LBJL; White House Conference, "To Fulfill These Rights," *Council's Report and Recommendations to the Conference*, June 1–2, 1966 (Washington: Government Printing Office, 1966).

14. Heineman to APR, 3/9/66, APRP, Box 32; Transcript of Press Conference, 5/24/66, White House Central Files, EX HU2/MC, 1/5/66–4/13/66, Box 22, LBJL.

15. Alexander to LBJ, 1/22/66, White House Central Files, EX HU2/MC, 1/5/66–4/13/66, Box 22, LBJL; Cabinet Meeting Minutes, 6/1/66, Cabinet Papers, Box 5, LBJL; White House Conference, *Council's Report and Recommendations*; Alexander Interview, LBJL.

16. "Outline for Attorney General's Cabinet Presentation on White House Conference," Cabinet Meeting, 6/1/66, Cabinet Papers, Box 5, LBJL; Alexander and McPherson Interviews, LBJL; McPherson to LBJ, 6/10/66, White House Confidential Files [CF], HU2, 1964–66, Box 56, LBJL.

17. Lewis, *Walking with the Wind*, p. 379; SNCC statement quoted in Carson, *In Struggle*, p. 204.

18. CORE, "Statement of Position," White House Conference, June 1966, MLKP, Series I, Box 26, White House Conference.

19. FBI Memo, NY Office, 6/14/66, Bureau File 100-442529, BR-FBI.

20. Carmichael Interview, MVI.

21. McKissick quoted in Meier and Rudwick, *CORE*, p. 414; Wilkins quoted in Randall Kennedy, "Reflections on Black Power," in Macedo, ed., *Reassessing the Sixties*, p. 238.

22. Lewis Interview, CRDP; Carmichael Interview, MVI.

23. BR to Kulikowski, 8/8/66, and BR to Bob Hill, 7/12/66, BRP, Reel 21.

24. Quotations in this and the following paragraph are from " 'Black Power' and Coalition Politics," *Commentary*, 9/66, reprinted in Rustin, *Down the Line*, pp. 154–165.

25. See, for example, the column by Rowland Evans and Robert Novak in the Washington *Post*, 11/24/65, A17.

26. For the planning group, see Rustin Memo, 12/9/65, BRP, "Freedom Budget Files," Reel 12. See also the extended correspondence between Rustin and Keyserling in Reel 13, and Rustin Memo, 5/24/66, Reel 12.

27. Young to APR, 8/26/66; Morsell to APR, 9/16/66; Carmichael to APR, 8/16/66, BRP, Reel 13.

28. Wicker to BR, 8/12/66, and BR to Belafonte, 9/8/66, BRP, Reel 14. An abundance of material on the Freedom Budget campaign can be found in BRP, Reels 12, 13, and 14.

29. Press Conference Agenda, 10/26/66, and Statements by APR and BR, BRP, Reel 12.

30. Keyserling to BR, 10/31/66, and BR to Keyserling, 11/4/66, BRP, Reel 12.

31. The description and quotes in this and the following paragraphs come from "A Freedom Budget for All Americans: A Summary," January 1967, copy in BRP, Reel 12.

32. Rustin Memo to community leaders, "What you can do about the 'Freedom Budget,'" n.d., and BR to Keyserling, 11/11/66, BRP, Reel 12.

33. Shull to BR, 1/17/67, BRP, Reel 14; Naomi Levine to AJC Chapters, 11/18/66, BRP, Reel 13; Tabachnick to BR, 1/16/67, BRP, Reel 14; Ahmann to BR, 1/5/67, BRP, Reel 14; Roe to BR, 10/28/66, BRP, Reel 13.

34. Keyserling to BR, 1/6/67, BRP, Reel 13; BR to Al Mellman, 12/7/66, BRP, Reel 14; BR Memo to community leaders, n.d., BRP, Reel 12.

35. Keyserling to BR, 10/19/67, BRP, Reel 12.

36. BR to John Cort, 11/27/67, BRP, Reel 13.

37. "A Freedom Budget for All Americans: A Summary," BRP, Reel 12.

38. Thomas to BR, 8/31/66, BRP, Reel 13; McKissick to Randolph, 10/10/66, BRP, Reel 13; Gans to BR, 12/12/66, BRP, Reel 14.

39. Melman to Dear Friends, 11/1/66, and Penn Kemble to Rachelle Horowitz, n.d., BRP, Reel 13; Shull to BR, 11/18/66, BRP, Reel 14. For an example of Melman's writings, see "Great Society Priorities: War, Peace, and the Managerial Bent," *Commonweal*, 8/5/66, 494–497.

40. BR Memo to community leaders, "What you can do about the 'Freedom Budget,'" and BR to Robert Paehlke, 3/15/67, BRP, Reel 13.

41. James Breeden, "Memorandum on a Freedom Budget for All Americans," 2/67, BRP, Reel 12; Roe to BR, 1/10/67, BRP, Reel 13; Harvard *Crimson*, 11/15/67, copy in BRP, Reel 13.

19: "A Strategist Without a Movement"

1. Moyers to McPherson, quoted by McPherson in his oral history, 1/16/69, LBJL.

2. BR to Hunter and Rudolph, 5/23/67, BRP, Reel 21; *Proceedings of 16th International Congress of WILPF, 1965*, pp. 98–100, SCPC; "Vietnam: Where I Stand," *Amsterdam News*, 5/20/67.

3. FBI Memo, NY Office, War Resistors [*sic*] League, 11/17/65, BR-FBI; *Proceedings of the 16th International Congress of WILPF, 1965*, pp. 98–100;

New York *Times*, 5/8/67, p. 33; BR to New York *Times*, 5/10/67, BRP, Reel 21; and Randle to Anderson, 7/3/89, copy in author's possession.

4. McReynolds and Willoughby Interviews, JDI; DiGia to Rustin, 10/19/66, BRP, Reel 21.

5. DiGia, Jack, and McReynolds Interviews, JDI; Dellinger, *From Yale to Jail*, pp. 219–220.

6. See Boyle, *The UAW and the Heyday of American Liberalism*, and Levy, *The New Left and Labor in the 1960s*; FBI Memo, NY Office, 4/26/66, CIRM, File 100-442529, BR-FBI; "Viet Nam," SCLC Board Resolution, 4/12/66, MLKP, Series, I, Box 29; New York *Times*, 6/15/67, p. 31.

7. New York *Times*, 12/7/66, p. 32, and 12/15/66, p. 34; Watson to LBJ, 2/27/68, Rustin Name File, LBJL.

8. Horowitz Interview, JDI.

9. BR to Committee Members, 6/20/66, NTP, Reel 67; BR to Lumer, 3/14/67, BR to Bubnov, 2/1/67, and Prinz to BR, 6/12/67, BRP, Reel 21.

10. Houser and Asahi Proctor Interviews, JDI.

11. FBI Memo, Cincinnati Office, "Re: Voices of Dissent, Miami University," 3/8/67, BR-FBI; Jesse Gray Interview, CRDP; transcript of debate, videotape provided by Bennett Singer.

12. Rustin Interview, MVI; Thomas Brooks, "A Strategist Without a Movement," New York *Times Magazine*, 2/16/69, pp. 24–25ff; BR to Richard Boone, 1/16/67, BRP, Reel 21; Executive Director's Report, APR Institute, 9/66–8/67, in SCLC Papers, Subgroup B, Series IV, Box 42, MLKC.

13. Transcript of debate, videotape provided by Bennett Singer.

14. New York *Times*, 8/27/66, p. 15; Rustin Interview, MVI.

15. BR to NT, 8/24/66, NTP, Reel 51, Series I.

16. Summary of 9th Annual Convention, 8/9–13/65; Keynote Address of Walter Fauntroy, 10th Annual Convention, 8/9/66; "SCLC-Labor Cooperation," SCLC Board Resolution, 8/11/66, MLKP, Series I, Box 31, SCLC Conventions.

17. Transcript of Frogmore Speech, 11/14/66, SCLC Papers, Subgroup II, Series IV, Box 49, Staff Retreats, MLKC.

18. Young, *An Easy Burden*, pp. 381–382.

19. Kahn Interview, MVI; Rustin Interview, 2/1/66, AMP, Box 58.

20. Young, *An Easy Burden*, pp. 390, 406.

21. *Ibid.*, pp. 413, 415.

22. Rustin Interview, MVI.

23. Young, *An Easy Burden*, p. 421; New York *Times*, 10/15/66, p. 14.

24. "Crisis and Commitment," New York *Times*, 10/14/66, p. 35. See also 10/14/66, p. 27; 10/15/66, p. 14; 10/16/66, Section IV, p. 2; and 10/17/66, p. 42.

25. FBI Memo, NY Office, 10/17/66, CIRM, File 100-442529, BR-FBI.

26. FBI Memo, NY Office, 2/2/66, Files 100-438794 and 100-106670, BR-FBI.

27. Garrow, *Bearing the Cross*, p. 543.
28. FBI Memo, NY Office, 2/14/67, Files 100-438794 and 100-149194, BR-FBI; New York *Times*, 2/26/67, pp. 1, 10.
29. FBI Memo, NY Office, 3/9/67, Files 100-438794 and 100-149194, BR-FBI.
30. New York *Times*, 4/2/67, p. 1, and 4/5/67, p. 1; Young, *An Easy Burden*, p. 428.
31. "In Apprehension How Like a God!," 1948 William Penn Lecture, BRP, Reel 17.
32. "Statement of Purpose: Washington, D.C. Poor People's Campaign," SCLC Papers, Subgroup II, Series IV, Box 49, MLKC; FBI Memo, NY Office, "Washington Spring Project," 2/2/68, BR-FBI; Rustin Interview, LBJL.
33. New York *Times*, 4/6/68, pp. 1 and 23, and 4/7/68, p. 65.
34. FBI Memo, NY Office, SCLC—RM, 7/24/68, BR-FBI.
35. Rustin Interview, LBJL.
36. Poor People's Campaign—Community Relations Service Daily Log, Ramsey Clark Papers, Box 73, LBJL.
37. New York *Times*, 6/5/68, p. 22; King and Levison FBI File, Box 8, Section 13, New York Office Memo, 6/5/68, MLKC.
38. Rustin Interview, LBJL; Kahn Interview, MVI.
39. BR to Aaron Henry, 10/14/68, Henry Papers, Series II, Box 9, WSU.
40. *Ibid.*
41. New York *Times*, 10/6/68, p. 40, and 11/14/68, p. 39.
42. "Decentralization," n.d., BRP, Reel 18; New York *Times*, 4/7/68, p. 60.
43. "An Appeal to the Community from Black Trade Unionists," New York *Times*, 9/19/68, p. 39, copy in BRP, Reel 6; BR to Curvin, 10/9/68, BRP, Reel 6. Rustin drafted the copy for the New York *Times* and organized the campaign to amass signatories.
44. Thelma Griffith to BR, 9/20/68, and John Hunter to BR, 9/25/68, BRP, Reel 6; Thomas Brooks, "A Strategist Without a Movement," New York *Times Magazine*, 2/16/69, pp. 24–25ff.
45. Brooks, "A Strategist Without a Movement," and Andrew Young Interview, LBJL.

20: "Freedom Is Never a Final Act"

1. New York *Times*, 9/8/69, p. 45; Executive Director's Report, 11/30/68–11/1/69, SCLC Papers, Subgroup B, Series IV, Box 42, APR Institute File, MLKC; "Coalition or Conflict," Address to AFL-CIO, 10/3/69, reprinted by APR Institute, 11/69.
2. Executive Director's Report, 11/30/68–11/1/69, SCLC Papers, Subgroup B, Series IV, Box 42, APR Institute File, MLKC; "The History of

the A. Philip Randolph Institute," 1976, BRP, Reel 19; BR to Louis Martin, 3/30/79, BRP, Reel 23.

3. "Black Power's Legacy," *Newsweek*, 11/13/72; "The Failure of Black Separatism," *Harper's Magazine*, 1/70; "The Blacks and the Unions," *Harper's Magazine*, 5/71.

4. *Newsweek*, 8/29/83, p. 11; BR to Editor of *Newsweek*, 8/28/73, BRP, Reel 23; BR, "Separatism Repackaged," *The New Leader*, 6/12/72, pp. 10–11.

5. BR, Letter to Editor, *The Wall Street Journal*, 3/25/74, and "Affirmative Action in an Economy of Scarcity," Testimony to the Special Subcommittee on Education, U.S. House of Representatives, 9/17/74, copies of each in BRP, Reel 17.

6. "Black America at the Crossroads," Commencement Address, Tuskegee Institute, 5/31/70, BRP, Reel 18.

7. Bessie to BR, 5/9/71, BRP, Reel 22.

8. APR to Scruggs, 11/19/71, BRP, Reel 22.

9. BR to Hurst, 11/28/72, and BR to Young, 9/6/72, BRP, Reel 22.

10. Walter Naegle Interview, JDI.

11. See the obituary of Cherne in the New York *Times*, 1/14/99.

12. Press Release, 3/1/80, BRP, Reel 17; "Rhodesia–Zimbabwe Elections"; "The Election in El Salvador," *Freedom at Issue*, No. 66, 5–6/82, p. 19.

13. "Black Americans Urge Admission of the Indochinese Refugees," New York *Times*, 3/19/78, copy in BRP, Reel 5; Aaron Levenstein, *Escape to Freedom: The Story of the International Rescue Committee* (Westport, CT: Greenwood Press, 1983), pp. 263–269.

14. New York *Times*, 6/28/70, p. 11, and Section IV, p. 5; "Israel: A Beleaguered Bastion of Democracy and Socialism," 1970, BRP, Reel 18.

15. Rustin, "The Israeli Incursion into Lebanon," 1982, BRP, Reel 18; Rustin's opinion pieces in the Washington *Post*, 10/7/79; New York *Times*, 8/30/79; *Newsday*, 10/7/79; *The New Leader*, 9/10/79; "Human Rights in the World," Speech to the Anti-Defamation League, 10/25/80, BRP, Reel 18.

16. Unless otherwise noted, information and quotations about the relationship come from Naegle Interview, JDI.

17. Redvers JeanMarie, "An Interview with Bayard Rustin," *Other Countries: Black Gay Voices* 1 (Spring 1988), p. 15.

18. BR to Virginia Patterson, 6/24/75, BRP, Reel 23.

19. Bloomstein, comments from the memorial service held at the Community Church in Manhattan, October 1987, videotape in possession of Walter Naegle; Naegle Interview, JDI; Susan Ginsburg, "Bayard Rustin: Portrait of a Collector," *Auction* 5/70, pp. 39–41.

20. Naegle and McReynolds Interview, JDI; Randle to Anderson, 7/3/89, copy provided by Randle.

21. Charles Kaiser, *The Gay Metropolis, 1940–1996* (Boston: Houghton Mifflin, 1997), p. 138.
22. BR to Koch, 2/25/85; BR to Pinkett and Foster, 3/22/85; BR to Wooten, Spigner, Samuel, and Williams, 3/22/85; BR, "Statement on Proposed Amendments," 4/17/86; all in BRP, "Gay Rights" Folder, Reel 2.
23. Allen Ellenzweig to BR, 10/7/86, BRP, "Gay Rights" Folder, Reel 2.
24. Bowman Interview, 2/2/87, copy in author's possession; JeanMarie, "An Interview with Bayard Rustin"; George Chauncey, Jr., and Lisa Kennedy, "Time on Two Crosses: An Interview with Bayard Rustin," *Village Voice,* 6/30/87, pp. 27–29. An interview with Beam is referred to in a letter from Rustin to Beam, 4/21/86, in Beam Papers, Schomburg Center, New York Public Library. I am indebted to Tracy Morgan for providing me with a copy of this letter.
25. BR to Beam, 4/21/86, Beam Papers, SL.
26. Handwritten note, 3/15/82, BRP, Reel 23.
27. Jordan comments, Rustin Memorial Service, 10/87, NYC, videotape in possession of Walter Naegle; Naegle Interview, JDI.
28. "Bayard Rustin: A Biographical Sketch," Vertical File—BR, GMA.
29. Videotape of memorial service, in possession of Walter Naegle.
30. See obituaries of Rustin in the New York *Times,* Washington *Post,* Los Angeles *Times,* and Chicago *Defender,* all 8/25/87. See also New York *Amsterdam News,* 8/29/87; *New Republic,* 9/28/87; *Guardian,* 9/9/87; and *New Leader,* 9/7/87.
31. "Human Rights in the World: Speech to the Anti-Defamation League," 10/25/80, BRP, Reel 18; Rustin Interview, Bowman.

BIBLIOGRAPHY

Abernathy, Ralph David. *And the Walls Came Tumbling Down: An Autobiography.* New York: Harper & Row, 1989.

Anderson, Jervis. *A. Philip Randolph: A Biographical Portrait.* New York: Harcourt Brace Jovanovich, 1973.

———. *Bayard Rustin: Troubles I've Seen: A Biography.* New York: HarperCollins, 1997.

Anderson, Terry H. *The Movement and the Sixties.* New York: Oxford University Press, 1995.

Baldwin, James A. *The Fire Next Time.* New York: Dial Press, 1963.

Bates, Beth Tompkins. *Pullman Porters and the Rise of Protest Politics in Black America, 1925–1945.* Chapel Hill: University of North Carolina Press, 2001.

Beemyn, Brett, ed. *Creating a Place for Ourselves.* New York: Routledge, 1997.

Belfrage, Sally. *Freedom Summer.* New York: Viking Compass, 1968.

Bennett, James V. *I Chose Prison.* New York: Alfred A. Knopf, 1970.

Bennett, Scott. "'Pacifism Not Passivism': The War Resisters League and Radical Pacifism, Nonviolent Direct Action, and the Americanization of Gandhi, 1915–1963," Ph.D. dissertation, Rutgers University, 1998.

Berube, Allan. *Coming Out Under Fire.* New York: Free Press, 1990.

Beschloss, Michael R., ed. *Taking Charge: The Johnson White House Tapes, 1963–1964.* New York: Simon & Schuster, 1997.

Boyle, Kevin. *The UAW and the Heyday of American Liberalism 1945–1968.* Ithaca: Cornell University Press, 1995.

Branch, Taylor. *Parting the Waters: America in the King Years, 1954–63.* New York: Touchstone Books, 1989.

———. *Pillar of Fire: America in the King Years, 1963–65.* New York: Simon & Schuster, 1998.

Broderick, Francis, and August Meier, eds. *Negro Protest Thought in the Twentieth Century.* Indianapolis: Bobbs-Merrill, 1965.

Burner, Eric R. *And Gently He Shall Lead Them: Robert Parris Moses and Civil Rights in Mississippi.* New York: New York University Press, 1994.

Burner, David. *John F. Kennedy and a New Generation.* Glenview, IL: Scott Foresman & Company, 1988.

Burns, Stewart. *Daybreak of Freedom: the Montgomery Bus Boycott.* Chapel Hill: University of North Carolina Press, 1997.

Canby, Henry Seidel. *Walt Whitman, An American: A Study in Biography*. Boston: Greenwood Publishing, 1943.

Carmichael, Stokely, and Charles V. Hamilton. *Black Power: The Politics of Liberation in America*. New York: Vintage, 1967.

Carson, Clayborne. *In Struggle: SNCC and the Black Awakening of the 1960s*. Cambridge, MA: Harvard University Press, 1981.

Caute, David. *The Year of the Barricades: A Journey Through 1968*. New York: HarperCollins, 1988.

Chafe, William H. *Civilities and Civil Rights*. New York: Oxford University Press, 1980.

———. *Never Stop Running: Allard Lowenstein and the Struggle to Save American Liberalism*. New York: Basic Books, 1993.

Chauncey, George. *Gay New York*. New York: Basic Books, 1994.

Cleaver, Eldridge. *Soul on Ice*. New York: McGraw-Hill, 1968.

Conot, Robert E. *Rivers of Blood, Years of Darkness*. New York: Bantam, 1967.

Cory, Donald Webster. *The Homosexual in America*. New York: Greenberg Publishers, 1951.

Curry, Constance, et al. *Deep in Our Hearts: Nine White Women in the Freedom Movement*. Athens: University of Georgia Press, 2002.

Dalfiume, Richard. *Desegregation of the U.S. Armed Forces: Fighting on Two Fronts, 1939–1953*. Columbia: University of Missouri Press, 1969.

Dallek, Robert. *Flawed Giant: Lyndon B. Johnson, 1960–1973*. New York: Oxford University Press, 1998.

DeBenedetti, Charles. *An American Ordeal: The Antiwar Movement of the Vietnam War*. Syracuse: Syracuse University Press, 1990.

Dellinger, David. *From Yale to Jail: The Life Story of a Moral Dissenter*. New York: Pantheon Books, 1993.

D'Emilio, John. *Sexual Politics, Sexual Communities: The Making of a Homosexual Minority in the United States, 1940–1970*. Chicago: University of Chicago Press, 1983.

Dittmer, John. *Local People: The Struggle for Civil Rights in Mississippi*. Urbana: University of Illinois Press, 1995.

Duberman, Martin Baumi. *Paul Robeson*. New York: Ballantine Books, 1990.

Eagan, Eileen. *Class, Culture, and the Classroom: The Student Peace Movement of the 1930s*. Philadelphia: Temple University Press, 1981.

Egerton, John. *Speak Now Against the Day: The Generation Before the Civil Rights Movement in the South*. Chapel Hill: University of North Carolina Press, 1995.

Erenberg, Lewis A. *Swingin' the Dream: Big Band Jazz and the Rebirth of American Culture*. Chicago: University of Chicago Press, 1998.

Eskew, Glenn T. *But for Birmingham: The Local and National Movements in the Civil Rights Struggle*. Chapel Hill: University of North Carolina Press, 1997.

Fanon, Frantz. *Black Skin, White Masks.* New York: Grove Press, 1967.

———. *The Wretched of the Earth.* New York: Grove Press, 1963.

Farmer, James. *Lay Bare the Heart: An Autobiography of the Civil Rights Movement.* New York: Plume, 1985.

Fink, Leon, and Brian Greenberg, *Upheaval in the Quiet Zone: A History of Hospital Workers' Union, Local 1199.* Urbana: University of Illinois Press, 1989.

Fischer, Louis. *Life of Mahatma Gandhi.* New York: Collier Books, 1962.

Fraser, Ronald. *1968: A Student Generation in Revolt.* New York: Pantheon Books, 1988.

Fraser, Steve, and Gary Gerstle, eds. *The Rise and Fall of the New Deal Order, 1930–1980.* Princeton: Princeton University Press, 1990.

Fried, Richard M. *Nightmare in Red: The McCarthy Era in Perspective.* New York: Oxford University Press, 1991.

Gaines, Kevin Kelly. *Uplifting the Race: Black Leadership, Politics, and Culture Since the Turn of the Century.* Chapel Hill: University of North Carolina Press, 1996.

Garfinkel, Herbert. *When Negroes March: The March on Washington Movement in the Organizational Politics for FEPC.* New York: Free Press, 1959; Athenaeum edition, 1973.

Garrow, David J. *Bearing the Cross: Martin Luther King, Jr., and the Southern Christian Leadership Conference.* New York: Vintage, 1988.

———. *The FBI and Martin Luther King, Jr.* New York: Viking Press, 1983.

Gitlin, Todd. *The Sixties: Years of Hope, Days of Rage.* New York: Bantam Books, 1987.

Goldman, Peter Louis. *The Death and Life of Malcolm X.* Urbana: University of Illinois Press, 1979.

Goodwin, Doris Kearns. *Lyndon Johnson and the American Dream.* New York: Harper & Row, 1976.

Goodwin, Richard N. *Remembering America: A Voice from the Sixties.* Boston: Little, Brown, 1988.

Graham, Hugh Davis. *The Civil Rights Era: Origins and Development of National Policy, 1960–1972.* New York: Oxford University Press, 1990.

Grant, Joanne. *Ella Baker: Freedom Bound.* Indianapolis: John Wiley & Sons, 1999.

Greenberg, Cheryl Lynn. *A Circle of Trust: Remembering SNCC.* New Brunswick, NJ: Rutgers University Press, 1998.

———. *"Or Does It Explode?": Black Harlem in the Great Depression.* New York: Oxford University Press, 1991.

Gregg, Richard B. *The Power of Non-Violence.* Philadelphia: J. B. Lippincott Company, 1934.

Hallie, Philip. *Lest Innocent Blood Be Shed: The Story of the Village of Le Chambon and How Goodness Happened There.* New York: HarperPerennial, 1994.

Hampton, Henry, and Steve Fayer. *Voices of Freedom: An Oral History of the Civil Rights Movement from the 1950s Through the 1980s.* New York: Bantam Books, 1991.

Harrington, Michael. *Fragments of the Century: A Personal and Social Retrospective of the 50s and the 60s.* New York: Saturday Review Press, 1973.

Harris, William H. *Keeping the Faith: A. Philip Randolph, Milton P. Webster, and the Brotherhood of Sleeping Car Porters, 1925–37.* Urbana: University of Illinois Press, 1977.

Hayden, Tom. *Reunion: A Memoir.* New York: Collier, 1989.

Hentoff, Nat, ed. *The Essays of A. J. Muste.* Indianapolis: Bobbs-Merrill, 1967.

Herring, George. *America's Longest War: The United States and Vietnam 1950–1975,* 2nd ed. New York: Alfred A. Knopf, 1986.

Hill, Ruth Edmonds, ed. *The Black Women Oral History Project.* Westport, CT: Meckler, 1991.

Hirsch, Arnold R. *Making the Second Ghetto: Race and Housing in Chicago, 1940–1960.* Chicago: University of Chicago Press, 1998.

Hodgson, Godfrey. *America in Our Time.* New York: Doubleday, 1977.

Howe, Irving. *A Margin of Hope: An Intellectual Autobiography.* New York: Harcourt Brace Jovanovich, 1984.

Isserman, Maurice. *If I Had a Hammer: The Death of the Old Left and the Birth of the New Left.* Urbana: University of Illinois Press, 1993.

———. *The Other American: The Untold Life of Michael Harrington.* New York: Public Affairs, 2000.

Isserman, Maurice, and Michael Kazin. *America Divided: The Civil War of the 1960s.* New York: Oxford University Press, 2000.

Johnson, James Weldon. *God's Trombones: Seven Negro Sermons in Verse.* New York: Viking Penguin, 1927.

Kapur, Sudarshan. *Raising Up a Prophet: The African-American Encounter with Gandhi.* Boston: Beacon Press, 1992.

Katz, Neil H. "Radical Pacifism and the Contemporary American Peace Movement: The Committee for Nonviolent Direct Action, 1957–1967," Ph.D. dissertation, University of Maryland, 1974.

King, Coretta Scott. *My Life with Martin Luther King, Jr.* New York: Holt, Rinehart, and Wilson, 1969.

King, Martin Luther, Jr., *Stride Toward Freedom: The Montgomery Story.* New York: Harper and Brothers, 1958.

———. *Where Do We Go from Here.* New York: HarperCollins, 1967.

———. *Why We Can't Wait.* New York: Signet, 1964.

Lawson, Steven. *Black Ballots: Voting Rights in the South, 1944–1969.* New York: Columbia University Press, 1977.

———. *In Pursuit of Power: Southern Blacks and Electoral Politics, 1965–1982.* New York: Columbia University Press, 1985.

Lee, Chana Kai. *For Freedom's Sake: The Life of Fannie Lou Hamer.* Urbana: University of Illinois Press, 2000.

Lerner, Gerda. *Fireweed: A Political Autobiography.* Philadelphia: Temple University Press, 2002.

Lessing, Doris. *Walking in the Shade: 1949–1962.* New York: HarperPerennial, 1998.

Levine, Daniel. *Bayard Rustin and the Civil Rights Movement.* New Brunswick, NJ: Rutgers University Press, 1999.

Levy, Peter B. *The New Left and Labor in the 1960s.* Urbana: University of Illinois Press, 1994.

Lewis, David L. *King: A Biography,* 2nd ed. Urbana: University of Illinois Press, 1978.

Lewis, John, with Michael D'Orso. *Walking with the Wind: A Memoir of the Movement.* New York: Harvest Books, 1999.

Lewy, Guenter. *The Cause That Failed: Communism in American Political Life.* New York: Oxford University Press, 1997.

———. *Peace and Revolution: The Moral Crisis of American Pacifism.* Grand Rapids, MI: Eerdmans Publishing Co., 1988.

Lichtenstein, Nelson. *Walter Reuther: The Most Dangerous Man in Detroit.* Urbana: University of Illinois Press, 1997.

Macedo, Stephen, ed. *Reassessing the Sixties: Debating the Political and Cultural Legacy.* New York: W. W. Norton & Co., 1997.

MacPherson, Fergus. *Kenneth Kaunda of Zambia: The Times and the Man.* London: Oxford University Press, 1976.

Matusow, Allen J. *The Unraveling of America: A History of Liberalism in the 1960s.* New York: Harper & Row, 1984.

Mayer, Martin. *The Teachers Strike.* New York: Harper & Row, 1969.

Meier, August, and Elliott Rudwick. *CORE: A Study in the Civil Rights Movement, 1942–1968.* Urbana: University of Illinois Press, 1975.

Meyerowitz, Joanne, ed. *Not June Cleaver.* Philadelphia: Temple University Press, 1994.

Miller, James. *"Democracy Is in the Streets": From Port Huron to the Siege of Chicago.* New York: Simon & Schuster, 1987.

Miller, Neil. *Sex-Crime Panic.* Boston: Alyson Books, 2002.

Mills, Kay. *This Little Light of Mine: The Life of Fannie Lou Hamer.* New York: Plume, 1994.

Myrdal, Gunnar. *An American Dilemma: The Negro Problem and Modern Democracy.* 2 volumes. New York: Harper & Row, 1969.

Naison, Mark. *Communists in Harlem During the Depression.* Urbana: University of Illinois Press, 1983.

Oates, Stephen B. *Let the Trumpet Sound.* New York: HarperCollins, 1982.

O'Reilly, Kenneth. *Racial Matters: The FBI's Secret File on Black America, 1960–1972.* New York: Free Press, 1991.

Palermo, Joseph A. *In His Own Right.* New York: Columbia University Press, 2001.

Parmet, Herbert S. *JFK: The Presidency of John F. Kennedy.* New York: Penguin Books, 1984.

Patterson, James T. *Grand Expectations: The United States, 1945–1974.* New York: Oxford University Press, 1996.

Payne, Charles M. *I've Got the Light of Freedom: The Organizing Tradition and the Mississippi Freedom Struggle.* Berkeley: University of California Press, 1996.

Peiss, Kathy, and Christina Simmons, eds. *Passion and Power: Sexuality in History.* Philadelphia: Temple University Press, 1989.

Perlstein, Daniel. "The Case Against Community: Bayard Rustin and the 1968 New York School Crisis." *Educational Foundations* 7, No. 2 (Spring 1993): 45–67.

Pfeffer, Paula F. *A. Philip Randolph, Pioneer of the Civil Rights Movement.* Baton Rouge: Louisiana State University Press, 1990.

Plummer, Brenda Gayle. *Rising Wind: Black Americans and U.S. Foreign Affairs, 1935–1960.* Chapel Hill: University of North Carolina Press, 1996.

Podair, Jerald E. "'White' Values, 'Black' Values: The Ocean Hill–Brownsville Controversy and New York City Culture, 1965–1975." *Radical History Review*, No. 59 (Spring 1994): 36–59.

Powledge, Fred. *Free at Last?: The Civil Rights Movement and the People Who Made It.* New York: HarperPerennial, 1992.

Raines, Howell. *My Soul Is Rested: Movement Days in the Deep South Remembered.* New York: Viking Press, 1983.

Rainwater, Lee, and William Yancey. *The Moynihan Report and the Politics of Controversy.* Cambridge, MA: MIT Press, 1967.

Read, Anthony, and David Fisher. *The Proudest Day: India's Long Road to Independence.* New York: W.W. Norton & Company, 1999.

Rossinow, Doug. *The Politics of Authenticity.* New York: Columbia University Press, 1998.

Rustin, Bayard. *Down the Line: The Collected Writings of Bayard Rustin.* Chicago: Quadrangle Books, 1971.

———. *Strategies for Freedom: The Changing Patterns of Black Protest.* New York: Columbia University Press, 1976.

Sale, Kirkpatrick. *SDS.* New York: Vintage, 1974.

Schoenebaum, Eleanora, ed. *Political Profiles: The Truman Years.* New York: Facts-on-File, 1978.

Schulman, Bruce J. *Lyndon B. Johnson and American Liberalism: A Brief Biography with Documents.* New York: Bedford/St. Martin's, 1995.

Shridharani, Krishnalal. *War Without Violence.* New York: Harcourt, Brace & Company, 1939.

Siegel, Dorothy Schainman. *The Glory Road: The Story of Josh White.* Boston: Shoe Tree Press, 1991.

Small, Melvin, and William D. Hoover. *Give Peace a Chance: Exploring the Vietnam Antiwar Movement: Essays from the Charles DeBenedetti Memorial Conference.* Syracuse: Syracuse University Press, 1992.

Sullivan, Gerald, and Nancy Zaroulis. *Who Spoke Up?* New York: Holt, Rinehart & Winston, 1985.

Swerdlow, Amy. *Women Strike for Peace: Traditional Motherhood and the Radical Politics of the 1960s.* Chicago: University of Chicago Press, 1993.

Taylor, Clarence. *Knocking at Our Own Door: Milton A. Galamison and the Struggle to Integrate New York City Schools.* New York: Columbia University Press, 1997.

Taylor, R., and C. Pritchard. *The Protest-Makers.* Oxford, Eng.: Pergamon Press, 1980.

Taylor, Richard K. S. *Against the Bomb: The British Peace Movement, 1958–1965.* Cambridge, Eng.: Oxford University Press, 1995.

Tracy, James. *Direct Action: Radical Pacifism from the Union Eight to the Chicago Seven.* Chicago: University of Chicago Press, 1996.

Tyson, Timothy B. *Radio Free Dixie: Robert F. Williams and the Roots of Black Power.* Chapel Hill: University of North Carolina Press, 2001.

Van Deburg, William L. *Black Camelot: African-American Culture Heroes in Their Times, 1960–1980.* Chicago: University of Chicago Press, 1999.

———. *New Day in Babylon: The Black Power Movement and American Culture, 1965–1975.* Chicago: University of Chicago Press, 1993.

Viorst, Milton. *Fire in the Streets.* New York: Simon & Schuster, 1979.

Wald, Alan M. *The New York Intellectuals: The Rise and Decline of the Anti-Stalinist Left from the 1930s to the 1980s.* Chapel Hill: University of North Carolina Press, 1987.

Ward, Brian, and Tony Badger, eds. *The Making of Martin Luther King and the Civil Rights Movement.* New York: New York University Press, 1996.

Weisbrot, Robert. *Freedom Bound: A History of America's Civil Rights Movement.* Boston: E.P. Dutton, 1991.

Wells, Tom. *The War Within: America's Battle over Vietnam.* Berkeley: University of California Press, 1994.

Wetzel, Donald. *Pacifist.* Sag Harbor, NY: The Permanent Press, 1986.

Wilkins, Roy. *Standing Fast: The Autobiography of Roy Wilkins.* New York: Viking Press, 1982.

Witcover, Jules. *The Year the Dream Died: Revisiting 1968 in America.* New York: Warner Books, 1998.

Wittner, Lawrence S. *One World or None: A History of the World Nuclear Disarmament Movement Through 1953.* Palo Alto, CA: Stanford University Press, 1993.

———. *Rebels Against War: The American Peace Movement, 1933–1983.* Philadelphia: Temple University Press, 1984.

———. *Resisting the Bomb—A History of the World Nuclear Disarmament Movement, 1954–1970.* Palo Alto, CA: Stanford University Press, 1998.

Wolpert, Stanley A. *Gandhi's Passion: The Life and Legacy of Mahatma Gandhi.* New York: Oxford University Press, 2001.

X, Malcolm, and Alex Haley. *The Autobiography of Malcolm X.* New York: Grove Press, 1965.

Young, Andrew. *An Easy Burden: The Civil Rights Movement and the Transformation of America.* New York: HarperCollins, 1998.

Young, Marilyn B. *The Vietnam Wars, 1945–1990.* New York: HarperPerennial, 1991.

INDEX

ABOUT THE AUTHOR

JOHN D'EMILIO is professor of history and of gender and women's studies at the University of Illinois at Chicago. A Guggenheim and National Endowment for the Humanities fellow, from 1995 to 1997 he served as the Founding Director of the Policy Institute at the National Gay and Lesbian Task Force. He earned his Ph.D. from Columbia University in 1982.

ILLUSTRATION CREDITS

31: Courtesy of Bayard Rustin Estate

32: Photo by Jerry Soalt, ILGWU / Courtesy of Bayard Rustin Estate

33: Courtesy of Bayard Rustin Estate

34: Courtesy of Bayard Rustin Estate

35: Courtesy of Bayard Rustin Estate

36: Courtesy of Bayard Rustin Estate

37: Photo by Jerry Goldman / Courtesy of Bayard Rustin Estate

DATE DUE

NOV 1 7 2003	
JAN 3 1 2004	
MMAY 1 8 2004	
MAY 4 2004	
MAY 1 8 2004	
OCT 1 5 2004	
JUN 7 2005	
OCT 2 6 2007	
FEB 2 7 2008	
JUN 1 1 2011	
JUL 0 5 2011	

DEMCO, INC. 38-2931